The Making of
New World Slavery

From the Baroque to the Modern
1492–1800

◆

ROBIN BLACKBURN

VERSO

London · New York

For Barbara Webber

First published by Verso 1997
© Robin Blackburn 1997
Paperback edition first published by Verso 1998
All rights reserved

Verso
UK: 6 Meard Street, London W1V 3HR
USA: 180 Varick Street, New York NY 10014-4606

Verso is the imprint of New Left Books

ISBN 1-85984-195-3

British Library Cataloguing in Publication Data
A catalogue record for this book is available from the British Library

Library of Congress Cataloging-in-Publication Data
Blackburn, Robin
    The making of New World slavery : from the Baroque to the Creole /
Robin Blackburn.
        p.   cm.
    Includes index.
    ISBN 1-85984-890-7
    1. Slavery—America—History.   I. Title.
HT1048.B56   1996
306.3'62'097–dc21   96–45603
                                                                    CIP

Typeset by CentraCet, Cambridge
Printed by Biddles Ltd, Guildford and King's Lynn

Contents

Acknowledgements

I would like to thank Perry Anderson for valuable comments on a draft of this book; at an earlier stage Mike Davis also offered helpful advice, emboldening me to separate the present study from its companion, *The Overthrow of Colonial Slavery, 1776–1848.*

Chapter I is based on a paper given at a conference in Williamsburg organized by the *William and Mary Quarterly* in April 1996 and I am grateful to all the participants in that event, and in particular to Michael McGiffert, for comments; Emory Evans, Benjamin Braude and William Evans generously shared with me the benefit of their research on topics dealt with in this chapter. (The papers delivered at this conference are published, with revisions, in a special issue of the *William and Mary Quarterly*, January 1997.) I would also like to thank Michael Bush for his comments on Chapter I. James Sweet and Ivan Nunes kindly read Chapters II, III, IV, V, X and XI, offering helpful advice and saving me from several mistakes. Seymour Drescher kindly read Chapters V, X and XII. I am grateful to Joyce Chaplin for reading and commenting on Chapters VI, VIII and XI. David Geggus commented on a draft of Chapter X and offered helpful advice on French colonial history. David Eltis, Richard Saville and R.C. Nash all furnished most helpful comments on drafts of Chapter XII and Sebastian Budgen commented helpfully on the Introduction and the Epilogue. Guillermo Bustos, Madalena Santos, Guillermo Sosa, Marcus Rediker, Renato Mazollini, Peter Hulme, Gareth Stedman Jones and Miri Rubin helpfully pointed me in the direction of research literature. Of course none of the foregoing are responsible for mistakes or problems that remain, and their generosity is the more evident since several have reached different conclusions from those found here.

I am grateful to the Woodrow Wilson International Center for Scholars, Washington D.C., for a Fellowship in 1993–94 which enabled me to write Part One. Likewise I wish to thank Heraclio Bonilla, who invited me to give a course at FLACSO (Facultad Latinamericano de Ciencias Sociales), Quito, Ecuador, in the first quarter of 1995, enabling me to redraft Part Two.

I would like to thank Robert Conrad for permission to quote his trans-lations of several documents relating to Brazilian slavery which were first published in *Children of God's Fire*, and both Cambridge University Press and the author for permission to quote on several occasions from *Natural Rights Theories: Their Origins and Development* by Richard Tuck.

I would particularly like to thank my colleagues at New Left Review and Verso for their patience and support, and I am grateful to Gillian Beaumont, Jane Hindle, Benedikt Hüttel and Sophie Arditti for their work in preparing the MSS for the press. Ian Weber and Helen Simpson kindly read the proofs and suggested a number of improvements. Many of the approaches adopted in the book benefited from conversations with Tariq Ali. Finally I must thank Margrit Fauland Blackburn; her encouragement and scepticism were both equally necessary and productive.

RB, August 1996

Introduction
Slavery and Modernity

... [the] plantation is a little world of its own, having its own language, its own
rules, regulations and customs. The troubles arising here are not settled by the civil
power of the state.

Frederick Douglass

The twentieth-century Western mind is frozen by the horror of men selling and
buying others as slaves and even more stunned at the irony of black men serving as
agents for the enslavement of blacks by whites. Shocking though it is, this human
barter was truly the most stark representation of what modernism and Western
capitalist expansion meant to traditional peoples. In the New World, people
became items of commerce, their talents, their labors, and their produce thrown
into the market place, where their best hope was to bring a decent price. The racial
wrong was lost on African merchants, who saw themselves as selling people other
than their own. The distinctions of tribe were more real to them than race, a
concept that was yet to be refined by nineteenth- and twentieth-century Western
rationalists.

Nathan Huggins, *Black Odyssey* (1977)

Counterfeit is the dominant scheme of the 'classical' period, from the Renaissance
to the industrial revolution. . . . The way lies open to unheard of combinations, to
all the games, all the counterfeits – the Promethean verve of the bourgeoisie first
plunged into the *imitation of nature* before throwing itself into production . . .
There is a strict correlation between the mental obedience of the Jesuits ('perinde
ac cadaver') and the demiurgic ambition to exorcise the natural substance of a
thing in order to substitute a synthetic one. Just like a man submitting his will to
an organization, things take on an ideal functionality of the cadaver. All
technology, all technocracy are incipiently there . . . That architectural sauce of
stucco and baroque is a great apparatus of the same kind. All of the above precedes
the productive rationality of capital, but everything testifies already – not in
production, but in counterfeit – to the same project of control and universal
hegemony.

Jean Baudrillard, *Simulations* (1983)

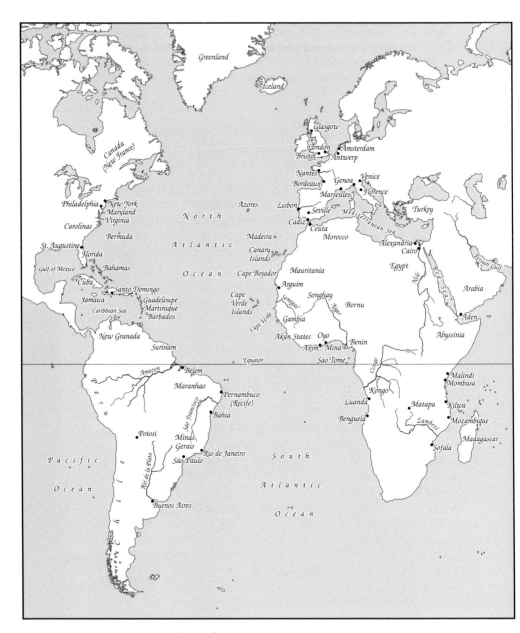

The Atlantic in the early colonial period

This book furnishes an account of the making of the European systems of colonial slavery in the Americas, and seeks to illuminate their role in the advent of modernity. These slave systems were themselves radically new in character compared with prior forms of slavery, yet they were assembled from apparently traditional ingredients. They became intensely commercial, making Atlantic trade the pacemaker of global exchanges from the sixteenth century to the nineteenth, yet within the plantations money played an apparently modest – even negligible – role. Slave-grown tobacco, sugar and cotton facilitated the birth of an expansive new world of consumption – one that was antithetical to slave rations and self-provision. The enterprises which battened on slave labour and produce embodied, as I will try to show, apparently advanced forms of technical and economic organization.

The acquisition of some twelve million captives on the coast of Africa between 1500 and 1870 helped to make possible the construction of one of the largest systems of slavery in human history. The Atlantic slave trade itself was to become remarkable for its businesslike methods as well as its scale and destructiveness. Over a million and a half captives died during the 'Middle Passage' between Africa and the New World; an unknown, but large, number died prior to embarkation; and once in the New World, between a tenth and a fifth of the slaves died within a year. Those who survived found their life drastically organized to secure from them as much labour as possible. The slaves met their own subsistence needs in one or two days' work a week, working the remainder of the time for their owners – a rate of exploitation or surplus extraction with few parallels even among other slave systems. In most parts of the Americas overwork, malnutrition and disease took a grim toll, and the slave labour force had to be replenished by further slave purchases. During the eighteenth century the slaves of British North America, unusually for any enslaved population, registered a positive natural growth rate, for reasons to be explored in Chapter XI. The total slave population in the Americas reached around 330,000 in 1700, nearly three million by 1800, and finally peaked at over six million in the 1850s, probably exceeding the numbers of slaves in Roman Italy, who were most numerous in the first century BC.

African slaves were brought to the Americas in the first place at a time when the indigenous population was suffering a terrible catastrophe. Thousands of Africans helped to strengthen the colonial apparatus and perform both menial and supervisory tasks. Once plantation development was under way, the slavery of the New World battened principally on those of African descent, with Indians being dispossessed and thrust to the margins, and Africans becoming highly concentrated in the most arduous employments. The slavery of the Ancient World had been far more diversified, both in the pattern of employment and in its ethnic composition, with Greek slave tutors, Egyptian slave administrators, English slave servants, German slave labourers and many more (though very few black

Africans). And while slave status was transmitted by inheritance in the Ancient World, and in other slave societies, there were two constraints on this as a source of reproduction of the slave labour force. First, slaves had few children; secondly, where they did have offspring there was usually a gradual improvement in the status of their descendants: later generations acquired some rights, or even benefited from manumission. Manumission did occur in the New World colonies, though it was most unusual where plantation development was strongest. So far as the overwhelming majority was concerned, New World slavery was a curse that even the grandchildren of the grandchildren of the original African captive found it exceedingly difficult to escape. This was a strong, even unprecedented, species of enslavement.

But the slavery of the Americas not only presented many novel features. Its development was associated with several of those processes which have been held to define modernity: the growth of instrumental rationality, the rise of national sentiment and the nation-state, racialized perceptions of identity, the spread of market relations and wage labour, the development of administrative bureaucracies and modern tax systems, the growing sophistication of commerce and communication, the birth of consumer societies, the publication of newspapers and the beginnings of press advertising, 'action at a distance' and an individualist sensibility. The Atlantic world of this epoch was subject to rapid, uneven but combined development. People separated by an ocean were brought into vital relationship with one another. The demand for sugar in London or Amsterdam helped to bring into being plantations in the Caribbean, which in turn were supplied with provisions from North America and slaves from Africa. The dynamic of the Atlantic economy was sustained by new webs of social trust, and gave birth to new social identities. It required business planning and methods for discounting risk; it was associated with distinctive modern traditions of reflexive self-consciousness.

Exploring the many ways in which American slavery proved compatible with elements of modernity will help to dispel the tendency of classical social science – from Adam Smith to Ludwig von Mises, Auguste Comte to Max Weber – to identify slavery with traditionalism, patrimonialism and backwardness. Weber raised interesting questions, but supplied the wrong answers: he did not realize that the slave population of North America became naturally self-reproducing, while he believed that the slave colonies had made a negligible contribution to European economic advance (these errors are tackled in Chapters XI and XII).[1] The colonial slave systems were closely associated with the mercantilist epoch, and this helped to nourish the view that they were inherently rigid and dependent on state patronage. Of course slavery is indeed a very ancient human institution, but it has also been highly flexible, and a great facilitator of social mobility and adjustment or transition. The role it played in the transition to modernity was not, therefore, out of character.

Anthony Giddens has written that modernity characteristically effects a 'disembedding' of individuals and institutions, which tears them away from their traditional contexts. He sees money, as well as power or ideology, as a potent lever in this disembedding. Paul Gilroy has urged that some of the most distinctive structures and mentalities of modernity are already evident in New World slavery.[2] The Atlantic slave trade effected a protracted 'disembedding' process, plunging the African slave into a new and unexpected system of social relations. Slavery existed in Africa prior to the Atlantic trade, and long continued to have a social meaning there which was very different to that prevailing in the Americas. In Africa slaves were often soldiers, for example, or recognized concubines. But the 'new' slave could be sold, a circumstance which permitted a transformation in slavery, both in the Americas and, eventually, in many parts of Africa too, as the transatlantic traffic grew in volume. Thus both institution and individual were disembedded, as they were inserted into a new set of social relations. The slave trade itself employed a battery of economic devices ranging from sophisticated patterns of credit and insurance to complex forms of barter. The New World slave was caught up in systems of social identification and surveillance which marked him or her as a black, and closely regulated their every action. The slave's kinship identity was wiped out, and new ties to 'shipmates', partners and relatives were vulnerable, since the slave could be sold at any time.

While the slaves were subordinated to a rigid new role, the vortex of Atlantic economy threw up disruptive new patterns of wealth and power. Control of the commodities produced by the slaves conferred great economic power – a power distributed between, and disputed by, states, merchants, bankers and slaveholders. The slaves were driven to work long hours and an intense rhythm; the appropriation of the fruits of their labour required the construction of an elaborate apparatus of supply, supervision, transport, processing and distribution, much of this engaging free labour. There was ample scope here for conflicts between different would-be appropriators, and between exploiters and exploited.

Civil Slavery and the Colonial State

The link between modernity and slavery gives us good reason to be attentive to the dark side of progress. Modern social powers, as we now have many reasons to know, can conduce to highly destructive and inhuman ends. Given the history of the twentieth century, it might seem that this lesson needs no further elaboration. After the slaughter of the First World War, the grim record of colonial repression, the horrors of Stalinism and the genocidal projects of Nazism, there can be few who believe that history is a simple forward march. From several points of view the history of the slavery of the Americas nevertheless merits our attention. We have yet to slough off all the ideologies and institutions produced in the era of racial slavery. Then again, the history of New World slavery, as I will try to demonstrate, shows that civil society, in a modern sense of the term, can itself powerfully – and, as it were, 'spontaneously' – contribute to highly destructive patterns of human conduct. Writers of quite varied allegiance have identified the disasters of modernity with a disorder of the state. Such phenomena as totalitarian violence and colonial war can be traced to the alienation of the state from civil society, to a fatal conjunction of bureaucratic rationality and fantasies of total power. In different ways this has been argued by the sociologist Zygmunt Bauman and the then Sartrean–Marxist Ronald Aronson, in analyses of Nazism and Stalinism (Bauman) or Nazism, Stalinism and imperialism (Aronson) seen as forms of pure state power. It can even be shown that the most destructive modern famines have resulted as much – if not more – from state negligence as from the working out of market forces.[3]

The tradition of writing about slavery in the Americas, from Adam Smith to Eric Williams, which associates it with the policies of 'colonial mercantilism' can also encourage a view that it was essentially a product of state voluntarism. These mercantilist policies owed much to the commercial principles of the Absolutist states and to the mimetic response of their commercial rivals. So it could be concluded that the slave systems of the Americas show, in an early form, the perils of state alienation from civil society. But the impressive scholarship on American slavery which has accumulated over the last half-century shows that this would be a quite misconceived conclusion. The message of this history is, I will argue, that the spontaneous dynamic of civil society is also pregnant with disaster and mayhem.

For a considerable time the conjunction of slavery, colonialism, and maritime power permitted the more advanced European states to skew the world market to their own advantage. What has been called the 'European miracle'[4] in fact depended not only on the control of intercontinental exchanges but on the profits of slavery. The latter also helped to furnish some of the conditions for a global industrial monopoly. The enormous gains achieved were based on the opportunities opened up by transferring forced labourers to parts of the globe under European control, and favourably situated for supplying European markets with exotic produce. But monopolies decreed from European capitals were of limited efficacy unless they were backed up by a host of independent merchants and planters, displaying entrepreneurial qualities.

In the account which follows, it will be shown that the early modern states bore their share of responsibility for the cruelties of the Atlantic slave traffic and for the subsequent merciless and inhuman operation of the slave systems. The Portuguese monarchs promoted and licensed slave trading in Africa from the mid fifteenth century. The Spanish authorities formally regulated the slave traffic via the *asiento* from the sixteenth century to the eighteenth. The Dutch, the British and the French all set up state-sponsored slave trading concerns, with forts and trading posts in Africa, in the seventeenth century. Once the captives arrived in the Americas their conditions of life were – supposedly – regulated by public legislation. Rather more effectively, governments sought to regulate, and profit from, the commerce in slave produce.

But this state sponsorship of slavery was closely linked to the dynamic of civil society – and as slavery flourished, so the state was confined to a more restricted role. It was not based on the abstraction or alienation of the colonial state from the dominant forces in colonial society. Quite the contrary. The public authorities were responding, in ways I will explore, to the insistent and specific prompting of powerful social actors. In Chapter II the royal regulation of Portugal's spice trade with the East is contrasted to the incipiently autonomous plantation and slave trade of the Atlantic. A recent account argues that the first Atlantic sugar colony achieved takeoff in the late fifteenth century because of commercial and settler initiative: 'The plantations of Madeira ... developed independently of Portuguese national authority.'[5] If we turn to Spanish America, the introduction of some thousands of African slaves each year from the middle of the sixteenth century was a response to the eagerness of colonial planters, manufacturers and mine concessionaries to employ them – a process explored in Chapter III. Referring to the use of African slaves, as well as other forms of labour not controlled by the colonial state in sixteenth-century Spanish America, Steve Stern writes:

> These relationships had emerged in 'civil society', as expressions of 'private' relations and coercions relatively free of direct sponsorship by the formal political structure of the state. . . . Slavery, personal lordship and contracted labor . . . bound exploiter and exploited directly to one another. The colonial state, at various times and in different degrees, legally sanctioned, encouraged, and even purported to regulate such relationships. But the initiation, internal dynamics and socioeconomic significance of these relationships reflected private or extra-official initiative more than state edict.[6]

In Spanish America the colonial state was to play a large and intrusive role, but – as we will see in Chapter III – this was greatly to cramp the development of plantation slavery. Matters turned out differently in Portuguese Brazil, but here – as I seek to explain in Chapter IV – the state was less active in ordering colonial society – especially when it came to slavery. As Stuart Schwartz writes: 'in the matter of slavery, the state and its officers are notably absent'.[7]

The process of colonization itself was to a greater or lesser extent state-sponsored, and so were some ancillary varieties of enslavement. The Castilian state acquired a mandate from the Pope to validate its conquest of the New World. The Papacy sponsored the Treaty of Tordesillas (1494), which divided the world beyond Europe into separate spheres of Castilian (Spanish) and Portuguese colonization. Tordesillas ratified the Portuguese monopoly of the African slave trade and endorsed Spain's claim to the lion's share of the as yet still barely 'discovered' Indies (North East Brazil was to fall just inside the Portuguese sphere). While the Papacy allowed the Portuguese to sell African slaves to the Christian kingdoms of Spain, it did not countenance their sale to Muslims, since enslavement was meant to lead to conversion. The Spanish doctrine of conquest affirmed that native peoples who resisted Castile's divinely appointed role could be condemned to slavery. However, the scope of enslavement practised by Spanish colonists was to become the subject of a famous controversy; as we will see, the monarch and his officials distrusted the greed and rapacity of their own colonists. Eventually (as is described in Chapter III), the Spanish monarch forbade the enslavement of the native inhabitants (though loopholes were left, since rebellious Indians could still be reduced to bondage). The imperial state also issued licences permitting the introduction and sale of African captives. If the slave plantation systems of the New World had been constructed on the basis of a Spanish model, as some have wrongly supposed, then it would be necessary to acknowledge a much larger degree of state sponsorship than there actually was. In fact the slave plantations of Spanish America made only a very modest contribution to Atlantic commerce in the sixteenth and seventeenth centuries. It is true that Brazilian plantations became major producers in the last decades of the sixteenth century, and that the Portuguese Crown was at this time united with that of Spain. But (as is explained in Chapter IV) Brazilian growth was tolerated rather than promoted by Madrid, and was anyway soon interrupted by a Dutch invasion which the Spanish connection helped to provoke – circumstances recounted and analysed in Chapter V.

The real takeoff of the plantation economies, it will be argued, took place in the seventeenth century. The New World ambitions of France, the Netherlands and England challenged the Iberian monopolies, and the Papal rulings on which they were based, with Protestant captains and colonists often playing a leading role. Neither France nor Britain could accept the Papal demarcation made at Tordesillas. Under the terms of the Treaty of Cateau-Cambrésis in 1559 France, Spain and England made peace in Europe while leaving open the precise status of territories 'beyond the line' – that is, beyond the prime meridian passing through the Azores or South of the Tropic of Cancer.[8] While Spain continued to assert its claims, French and English privateers, many of them Protestant, disputed its commercial monopoly. By this time a swarm of French adventurers and would-be colonists were staking their claim to trade or territory in the New World. The English soon followed. By the 1580s and 1590s the Flemish and Dutch 'sea beggars' joined them without even respecting the line. Down to the Treaty of Ryswick in 1697 the territory 'beyond the line' – the whole of the

Americas and most of the African coast – was to continue to be excluded from the terms of European peace treaties. The inability of the European states to come to terms concerning these crucial areas meant that they remained a battleground, a sort of 'wild West' in which traders and colonists founded a new order, eventually being obliged to defer to one or other of the colonial sheriffs. Without the tenacity and resources of these colonial entrepreneurs, little or nothing could be achieved.

The theory of empire which the Portuguese, Spanish, French, Dutch and English came to expound appealed to God-given rights, but with interesting differences of emphasis. The Portuguese emphasized their rights as 'discoverers' not so much of the land as of the sea routes between Europe and the newly discovered coast; Portuguese captains were required to register navigational details of their discoveries as well as marking them with a stone cross. The Spanish monarch claimed to rule the Americas by a God-given right of conquest, so long as the ceremony of the 'Requirement' demanding peaceful submission had been observed. Supposedly the Aztec and Inca rulers, having failed to respond and having obstructed the Spaniards' free movement, had been conquered in a 'just war'. The French believed the Spanish 'Requirement' and conquest were a mockery of Christian behaviour and violated the God-given natural rights of the indigenous peoples. The French, therefore, appeared in the New World as the friends and allies of the natives, and supposedly established colonies only with their unforced consent. The Dutch asserted their right not simply as navigators but principally as traders; in contrast to the Iberian powers, they believed that there was a God-given natural right of all to sail the high seas in pursuit of trade, and to the better life that commerce brought with it. Finally, the English laid stress on the fact that their colonists, as cultivators or 'planters', were making better use of the land than native hunters-and-gatherers or colonial rivals, and thus enjoyed Divine sanction.

This bare summary simply picks out the most salient feature in each imperial ideology; in practice the various powers constantly sought to imitate one another's successes and learn from their mistakes.[9] But their competitive success naturally depended upon the resources and institutions each could dispose of. While the Spanish approach, at one extreme, was highly dependent on state initiative and control, the English formula, at the other, critically depended upon the initiative and competence of the colonists themselves, albeit within the terms of some royal charter or bequest. In the various chapters of Part One it will be shown that African slaves could be introduced to boost each and every one of these colonial projects, though by far the most rewarding was to be the use of slaves in plantation agriculture.

The workings of the slave systems were terribly destructive and oppressive, but they came to display the routines of regular business. The slave traders and their crews, and the slave masters and their overseers, worked in the expectation of earning a salary or making a profit. They proved capable of sadistic ferocity, and sought to crush slave resistance with displays of exemplary cruelty. But research into the impressively detailed records which the planters and merchants left behind reveals a convergence on average rates of profit and standard methods of procedure. The pressures of commercial competition helped to diffuse new techniques and to discipline the wayward or self-indulgent planter. While most of the free employees implicitly consented to the degradation of black people, they did not have to be motivated by racial hostility. Episodes of gratuitous violence were far from unknown, because of the vulnerability of the slaves, but the successful slave systems harnessed coercion to production and the maintenance of order in a systematic way. Handbooks of plantation management generally stressed that punishment should be meted out in a methodical and predictable way. The overpacking of the ships in the Atlantic slave trade, and the inadequate food and water provisions for the captives, produced much higher mortality rates than were found among free migrants. But such methods were more profitable, since larger numbers of slaves could be delivered on each voyage. The average workings of the slave systems displayed something of the impersonality and functional logic of modern organization. Yet the slave plantations themselves were based on the distinctive face-to-face relationship between overseer, driver and slave crew.

The thoroughly commercial character of most New World slavery differentiates it from earlier practices of slavery. At the high point of slavery in the Ancient World – roughly 200 BC to AD 200 – very large numbers of slaves were captured by Roman armies, then distributed or sold in ways that reflected the policy of the state or a particular general rather than the play of economic forces. One might say that many Roman slaves were sold because they had been captured, while many African slaves entering the Atlantic trade had been captured so that they might be sold. Likewise, the estates of the Roman Empire generally marketed less of their output and relied less on purchasing inputs than was the case for the plantations of the Americas. Consequently, accounting methods and financial instruments were less elaborate. The slaves of Rome also had a much better chance of ending up in some non-menial job. Roman slavery was highly geared to the capacities of the imperial state, a point to which we return in the next chapter; in the New World the colonial states strove to batten upon a 'civil slavery' geared to commercial networks spread across and beyond the Atlantic – and eventually this civil slavery was emancipated from metropolitan tutelage. Despite all this the slavery of Ancient Rome came closer to the New World experience, for which it furnished important legal formulas and justification, than did other slave systems outside Europe.[10]

That the real dynamic of the Atlantic slave trade was not statist or mercantilist was to be shown in the course of the seventeenth and eighteenth centuries, when the instruments of mercantilist regulation were dismantled or suppressed. The volume of the Atlantic traffic vastly increased as more concerns entered it and the official slave trading companies were forced to the margins. John Thornton writes of the early period: 'although the states of the Atlantic persistently sought to direct and control the trade, their purpose was really more to enhance their revenue by marginally distorting the market'.[11] Thornton's judgement is intended to apply to both European and African states which, despite their different capacities, ultimately shared an inability to dominate the slave traffic in a monopolistic fashion. It was the private initiative of merchants and planters that led to the successively larger-scale employment of slaves on the plantations on the Atlantic islands, in Brazil and in the Caribbean. The formula of American plantation slavery achieved its most potent expression on the islands of the Eastern Caribbean in the mid seventeenth century, at a time when none of them was effectively regulated by the metropolis, as we will see in Chapters VI and VII. At this time Dutch mercantile skills, Portuguese and Brazilian knowledge of sugar-making, and the enterprise of English and French planters and settlers created and multiplied large-scale plantations, relying on African slave labour and harnessing the latest advances of commerce and manufacture. Karl Polanyi ascribed the 'explosion of the slave trade' to this 'epochal event as specific as the invention of the steam engine by James Watt some 130 years later'.[12]

Recent research shows that even the large chartered slave trading companies, such as England's Royal African Company, found that they had to respect market principles, and learn the precise wants and needs of hundreds of suppliers on the African coast and thousands of purchasers in the American colonies. After scrutinizing details of some eighty thousand transactions recorded in the archives of the African Company, David Galenson concludes:

> This study has provided strong evidence of diligent and systematic behaviour aimed at profit maximisation by English slave traders and West Indian sugar planters in the late seventeenth and early eighteenth centuries. These traders and planters were hindered by severe handicaps, yet the evidence shows they responded to these energetically and intelligently. The evidence of rational responses to market stimuli comes from both quantitative evidence on aggregate outcomes in the slave trade and qualitative evidence that affords a rare glimpse into the internal operation of a large company operating in the late seventeenth century. What emerges overall is a picture of a series of closely connected competitive economic markets, in Africa and America, in which large numbers of traders and planters responded promptly and shrewdly to economic incentives.[13]

The trade in plantation goods was somewhat more amenable to regulation, since the route between colony and metropolis was easier to invigilate. There was probably more smuggling between the colonies of different powers than between the different metropolitan markets, since most European states had an apparatus for controlling the latter. Nevertheless, the trade in tobacco, sugar, rum, cotton and other plantation products had a spontaneous momentum that could take the authorities by surprise. Tobacco smoking became widespread without any official support – and despite fitful attempts to suppress it.

Once flourishing slave colonies existed, rival colonial states certainly saw the advantage of controlling them. And since other colonial states constituted a lively threat, they were able to offer military protection. The colonial state could also offer to protect the slaveowners against their own slaves. But American slaveowners, from an early period, aspired to control their own means of defence, in the form of militia and patrols. Metropolitan garrisons were sometimes remote and often under strength; their role was as much to control the wayward impulses of the colonists as to protect them. The planters' need to recruit support from free persons without slaves was to shape the racial structure, as we will see.

The racial character of New World slavery was invented by European traders and settlers with little prompting from state functionaries. The early Spanish and Portuguese authorities justified slavery as a means to the conversion of Africans. European traders and colonists of the early modern period had few qualms about the enslavement of heathens, whether Native Americans or Africans or – if they could get away with it – Asians, while they rarely displayed any eagerness to convert them. But some slaves converted none the less, putting a strain on both official and popular conceptions. In the English colonies specific legislation was to be enacted by the local assemblies stipulating that conversion did not confer freedom on the slave. A religious sanction for enslavement was available. As we will see in Chapter I, early modern Europeans found in the Bible sanctions for the enslavement of strangers, with some believing that Africans, as 'sons of Ham', had been singled out for this fate, even if they became Christians. In subsequent chapters examples are given of the use of this myth to justify a system of enslavement that had come increasingly to focus exclusively upon those of African descent. This doctrine represented one expression of a burgeoning Christian, European or 'white' racial consciousness which both protected fellow Europeans from the rigours of full slavery and designated Africans or blacks as its proper victims. The need for such an ideology became acute in the wake of the plantation revolution, since there were many more hugely exacting and unpleasant tasks to be carried out.

Shifting Identity and Racial Slavery

In practice, slaves were conceived of as an inferior species, and treated as beasts of burden to be driven and inventoried like cattle. Yet like all racist ideologies, this one was riddled with bad faith. The slaves were useful to the planters precisely because they were men and women capable of understanding and executing complex orders, and of intricate co-operative techniques. The most disturbing thing about the slaves from the slaveholder's point of view was not cultural difference but the basic similarity between himself and his property. Africans could procreate with Europeans, and occupied the same ecological niche. As Benjamin Franklin was to observe, slaves, unlike sheep, could rise in rebellion. The great world religions all registered the anthropological fact of common humanity. And while they might aspire to the brotherhood of man and comity of nations, their attitude to infidels often revealed an awareness of humanity's greatest enemy. As Jean-Paul Sartre pointed out:

> Nothing – not even wild beasts or microbes – could be more terrifying for man than a species which is intelligent, carnivorous and cruel, which can understand and outwit human intelligence, and whose aim is precisely the destruction of man. This, however, is obviously our own species as perceived by each of its members in the context of scarcity.[14]

The American planter who treated his slaves like subhumans would typically reveal a fear and surplus aggression towards them which stemmed from a belief that they could take over his plantation and his womenfolk if they were given the slightest real opportunity to do so. Sartre's insight links up with Foucault's thesis that racism is an expression of permanent social war. In his 1976 lectures at the Collège de France, Foucault actually identified the origins of racial consciousness in the sixteenth and seventeenth centuries with popular antagonism to the aristocratic element in the pre-modern state, itself based on racial conceits (Saxons against aristocratic Normans in England, Franks against aristocratic Goths in France, and so forth). In this conception, however, the racial feeling which could challenge the aristocracy could also be deployed against outsiders.[15]

Oceanic migration, both voluntary and forced, bringing previously distant human groups into intimate contact with one another, created the need to work out new systems of ascribed identity. In the world of Atlantic exchange and confrontation, the given and fixed quality of all traditional social identity was threatened by flux and intermixture. Jack Forbes has shown that even such apparently clear terms as 'Negro' were remarkably labile in the sixteenth century, often referring to those later called 'Indians' or to a variety of ethnic mixtures.[16] The world opened up by the 'Discoveries', as Vitorino Magalhães Godinho has observed, plunged Europeans into a vertiginous sense of novelty wherever they looked, with new plants, new fruits, new animals, new customs, new peoples and a new sky at night.[17] In North America in the 1530s the would-be *conquistador* Nuñez Cabeza de Vaca, together with his African slave Estevanico and two companions, were captured by Indian peoples following the foundering of an expedition of which he was treasurer. His fascinating account of their subsequent fate – of the Indians' insistence that they were possessed of the power of healing, of their travels among a succession of Indian peoples, and of their disillusioning return to the rapacious and brutal world of Christian slave hunters – conveyed to a wider public the strange moral reversals which could take place at the borderlands of empire and beyond.[18] The *Peregri-nation* of the late-sixteenth-century Portuguese seafarer Fernão Mendes Pinto furnished further astonishing and unsettling stories of this type.

Michael Pietz gives an example of shifting identities in an anecdote relating to a time and place where they were, perhaps, at their most fluid. It is told by a Portuguese, and relates to an encounter with the slave of a friend of his in the Gambia river in 1624:

> I met a black Mandinga youth, by name Gaspar Vaz. The black was a good tailor and button maker. As soon as he knew that I was in port he came to see me and paid a call on me with great enthusiasm. He embraced me, saying he could not believe it was me he saw, and that God had brought me there so that he could do me some service. For this I gave him thanks, saying that I was very pleased to see him too, so that I could give him news of his master and mistress and acquaintances, but that I was distressed to see him dressed in a Mandinga smock, with amulets of his fetiches (Gods) around his neck [*com nominas dos seus feitiços ão pescoço*[, to which he replied: 'Sir, I wear this dress because I am nephew of Sandeguil, Lord of this town, whom the tangomaos call Duke, since he is the person who commands after the King. On the death of Sandeguil, my uncle, I will be inheritor of all his goods, and for this reason I dress in the clothes that your honour sees but I do not believe the Law of Mohammed, rather I abhor it. I believe in the Law of Christ Jesus, and so that your honour may know that what I say is true' – he took off his smock, beneath which he wore a doublet and a shirt in our fashion, and from around his neck he drew out a rosary of Our Lady – 'every day I commend myself to God and the Virgin Our Lady by means of this rosary. And if I do not die, but come to inherit the estate of my uncle I will see to it that some slaves are sent to Santiago and when I have found a ship to take me I will go to live in that island and die among Christians.' It was no small advantage to me to meet him in the Gambia, because he was of service to me in everything, and what I bought was at the price current among the people themselves, very different from the price they charge the tangamaos. And he served me as interpreter and linguist.[19]

While this was evidently a happy accident, the ambivalent identities it revealed were not those to be required by slaveowning planters who needed labourers fixed to one spot and one role. Skin colour came to serve as an excellent and readily identified marker which everyone carried around on their face and limbs, ruling out any hope of imposture or dissimulation. If necessary, some systems of racial classification could give importance to different shades or phenotypes; in other cases skin could be 'lightened' by paying fees to the authorities. But the baseline of this system of racial classification was simply pigmentation. New World slavery was peculiarly associated with darker pigmentation or 'black' skin. Not every black was a slave, but most blacks were, and on this assumption every black could be treated like a slave unless they could prove free status – and even then, they would still be treated worse than white colonists. In the colonies of the Catholic and Latin powers the racial hierarchy was a little more complex and baroque, in ways to be mentioned below. But skin colour remained a vital social marker, one highly correlated with enslavement.

Thus, in the racial theory which became peculiarly associated with plantation slavery, the abstracted physiological characteristics of skin colour and phenotype come to be seen as the decisive criteria of race, a term which had hitherto had a more ample sense of family or kind, nature or culture. The reduction at work met practical tests. It furnished an identity document in an epoch when many were illiterate. It also corresponded to a fetishistic logic which Pietz's essay seeks to unravel. The European traders and travellers believed that Africans were victims of a strange category mistake and an inability to grasp general concepts; instead they had their 'fetishes', assortments of strange objects which were imbued with supernatural powers. The word fetish was not taken from any African language but simply derived from the Portuguese *feitiço* – from the verb to make, but in this form usually referring to witchcraft.

Just as skin colour and phenotype helped to fix race, so the complex systems of trade and barter helped to produce a schedule of equivalents, reducible to gold or silver, or shells or currency, or – as was often to be the case by the eighteenth century – by notional iron bars used as a *numéraire*. Such currencies were general equivalents in terms of which anything, most especially slaves, could be valued. But slaves themselves were increasingly, and then exclusively, acquired as a means to the production of other commodities. To begin with, the Portuguese were mainly interested in gold dust, spices and modest consignments of sugar; the Spanish were obsessed with specie, and only tiny quantities of dyestuffs, sugar and chocolate. The Dutch, the French and the English merchants or planters eventually took the lead with larger quantities of sugar, rum, molasses, tobacco, indigo, cotton, and coffee. And in a new Atlantic – indeed, global – dance of commodities, European and Eastern manufactures moved in a reverse direction: to the colonies and the African coast.

The elaborate and competitive processes of exchange which led to these diverse goods being presented in the marketplace helped to obscure their conditions of production and minimize the sense of social or moral responsibility of all those involved. Thus the planter or merchant could say to himself: if I refuse to buy the slave, then someone else will. This logic of atomization and serialization, in which each feels obliged to mimic the other in himself, has also been theorized by Sartre.[20] Given the manifold uncertainties and frequent obscurity of the new market society, and the novel encounters on which it was based, it is not surprising that it bred new anxieties and truncated perceptions. Thus early modern Europeans, encountering Native Americans or Africans, believed them to be living outside culture and morality in some 'wild' and 'natural' state. This aroused both phobic fears and fantasies, and utopian longings and projections.[21] The ideologies of enslavement found ways to mobilize the former – though, as will be argued below, it was by no means clear that it was either prudent or profitable to acquire and rely on wild savages, depraved cannibals, murderous devils, and the like. In fact the identity of the slave had to be domesticated, normalized or naturalized. Their reduction to the status of a chattel was a decisive element in this process.

The social relations of unsupervised economic exchange have sometimes been thought to promote a rough-and-ready equality between buyer and seller. In fact this was to be the case both on the African coast and in the Americas, though pointedly excluded from its scope were to be those captives who were themselves to be traded. In an influential essay on the origins of eighteenth- and nineteenth-century abolitionism Thomas Haskell has argued that the new world of long-distance trade promoted a sense of human interconnectedness, and of the efficacy of long-distance action, which spontaneously undermined the legitimacy of slavery. On the other hand Ellen Meiksins Wood argues that the formal equality implied by the new salience of capitalist relations in the early modern period was more likely to have exactly the opposite consequences, fostering new doctrines of race, ethnicity and gender to explain and justify substantive inequality and exclusion. While the slavery of the Ancient World had not denied the basic humanity of the slave, the emergent capitalist societies of seventeenth-century Europe could only recognize the humanity of those who had something to sell – of the African merchant or monarch, but not the African captive.[22]

Thomas Holt has argued that American slavery had its roots in a new configuration of the everyday, so that the decision of a consumer to buy a pound of sugar refers us to the global social relations which made this possible:

> A woman buying a pound of sugar ... has a doubled aspect: hers is at once a simple gesture but one within which are inscribed complex social relations. Her action not only expresses but makes possible a global structure of imperialist politics and labor relations which racialize consumption as well as production.[23]

It is part of the purpose of this book to explore how these structures were established, and to locate the role of the everyday in their elaboration and reproduction. At a certain level the consumer did indeed have a critical part to play. Early modern Europe witnessed the emergence of a cash demand for popular luxuries, fuelled by the larger numbers of people who now received rents, salaries and wages. Those with money – who included new poor as well as new or old rich – had recourse to the market to add sugar and spice to their existence. Carole Shammas observes:

> The changeover made by so many people [to foreign groceries] completely reorganized trade and promoted colonization and slavery.... Since Keynes it has been customary to ask about the impact of the state on consumer demand. But in the seventeenth and eighteenth centuries the causal order was the reverse; consumer demand's effects on the state.[24]

But Shammas's consumers are not all sovereigns, since she also identifies new proletarianized populations separated from traditional sources of food – the family cow or garden plot – finding in the new sweetened beverages and confections solace and badly needed calories. The dynamics of civil society were, in fact, shot through with class as well as racial hierarchies. It is also clear that the new exotic products could be produced in a variety of ways. For over half a century tobacco was cultivated mainly by free farmers and European indentured servants. Most of what became the typical slave plantation crops – cotton, indigo, coffee and even sugar – could be grown and/or processed using free or indentured labour. It was merchants and planters above all who decided how the demand for plantation produce would be met, and in contexts they had helped to shape. In Chapter VIII I ask whether they could have chosen any differently. Independent small producers, native communities, free or indentured migrants generally lacked much influence on governments or the sort of help or protection that might have given them leverage against the merchant and planter elite.

One way of securing social inclusion and fixing identity in early modern Europe was national allegiance. But national sentiment does not fully explain why some could be enslaved and others not. The traders and the New World colonists felt their way towards new systems of racial classification, inventing not one but several racisms, as we will see, successively refining the identity of the colonial and slaveholding community as 'Christian', 'European', and 'white'. While national identities came to mobilize one European people against another, they were not thought to justify the enslavement of the subjects of another monarch or the citizens of another state; and under normal conditions the same consideration was even extended to the subjects of a Muslim monarch. By contrast the new racisms furnished critical principles of domestic subordination within the civil society of the colonies. African captives were deemed stateless and acquired as chattels; they then became part of the slaveholding household. Once a slave was acquired by a new owner then they also acquired their owner's national belonging, becoming, in common parlance, 'an English Negro' or 'a French Negro'. In the early modern period many suffered degrees of social and political exclusion and only a minority of adult males, together with a few widows, could exercise the rights of a head of household. The status of the slave was thus a limiting case of a species of exclusion to which women, minors, and those with little or no property were subject. And the racial sentiment animating it can be linked, as Benedict Anderson suggests in a similar case, to class rather than nation.[25]

The conjunction of modernity and slavery is awkward and challenging since the most attractive element in modernity was always the promise it held out of greater personal freedom and self-realization. The late medieval communes produced an aspiration to citizenship which gave early expression to this notion of civic freedom; it was often claimed that the 'free air' of the municipality dissolved the bonds of servitude. The Reformation yielded a religious version of this promise with its notion of the role of individual conscience. The rise of distinctive 'nations', first among students and merchants and then among wider layers in the population, gave birth to the idea that the people realized their freedom in the creation of a national community. National sentiment, promising a notional liberty, or even share in sovereignty, to each member of the nation, was to be part of the structure of modernity as it emerged in the sixteenth and seventeenth centuries. But property and patriarchy qualified this promise and effectively excluded slaves from it altogether. Free blacks were inclined to claim civic rights but when they did so had to contend with white colonists; the colonial state sometimes deemed it apppropriate or convenient to accord at least some rights to free people of colour as a way of stimulating their loyalty. But the slave was effectively beyond the reach of the colonial state.

Within the new secular space opened up by modernity, slavery was thrown into dramatic and negative relief. From some time in the seventeenth century this word became among the most frequently used in the vocabulary of social or political agitation. It is therefore all the more puzzling that slavery was developed to its greatest extent in the New World precisely by the peoples of North Western Europe who most detested it at home. They saw in slavery a notion of intense and comprehensive domination that was the antithesis of citizenship and self-respect. Of course, the notion of the free wage labourer was at an early stage of development, with many aspiring to the role of independent small producer or artisan. The labourer who was able to depend on regular wages to meet all his or her subsistence costs, and hence able to live without independent means of existence or other claims to support, represented a particular outcome of a lengthy and contested social development. In the sixteenth century the hired servant might have some land or instruments of a trade; on the other hand, they might owe service for years at a time. The master often had the right to administer physical punishment; on the other hand, the labourer could appeal to a variety of customary rights *vis-à-vis* an employer. The popular notion of the condition of the slave was one in which he or she was stripped bare of all customary rights and independent means of existence, and thus subordinated to the naked, perpetual and comprehensive domination of the master. In the course of this book it will be shown that this was indeed the formal statute of enslavement in the Americas, but that other opposed or different tendencies were also at work, many of them difficult to identify with the aid of the formal juridical concepts of European chattel slavery. The African captives brought with them skills and expectations that helped them to survive, adapt and ultimately challenge or undermine the modern European notion of enslavement. The innovation of colonial slavery was launched by European merchants and planters, then ratified by jurists or statesmen; ultimately, it created new identities and new solidarities which different jurists and political leaders saw advantages in recognizing.

The social relations of colonial slavery borrowed from an ancient stock of legal formulas, used contemporary techniques of violence, developed manufacture and maritime transport on a grand scale, and anticipated modern modes of co-ordination and consumption. Slavery in the New World was above all a hybrid mixing ancient and modern, European business and African husbandry, American and Eastern plants and processes, elements of traditional patrimonialism with up-to-date bookkeeping and individual ownership. The key crops – maize and manioc as well as tobacco, sugar, coffee, indigo, and so forth – had been unknown in Europe, and the means of producing, processing and consuming them had to be learned from others. These borrowings necessarily involved innovation and adaptation, as new social institutions and practices, as well as new crops and techniques of cultivation, were arranged in new ensembles. The tests of war and market survival brought about a 'historical selection' of social institutions and practices – one which, for a considerable time, favoured plantation slavery.[26] The institution of colonial slavery furnished a potent if unstable momentum to the whole complex – for a while.

The intricate and enforced co-ordination of labour required by the production of the new plantation staples – the art of sugar-boiling, with its seven different copper basins – had about it a baroque complexity and art. The versatility and luxury of white-sugar confections became a staple of aristocratic display; as plantation production brought down the price, the consumption of sugar spread to broader layers of the population while continuing to supply the icing to ceremonial cakes on special occasions. Polite rituals such as the taking of sweetened coffee, tea or 'baroque chocolate' (a brew made with spices) also spread down the social scale.

Nevertheless, because the new exotic products were associated with the advent of new popular pleasures, there was also movement in the other direction. The particular drugs and stimulants that flourished were not necessarily those approved by the authorities – most of whom disapproved of tobacco until they tumbled to its revenue-raising possibilities. The taste for smoking, chewing or snuffing tobacco was brought back to Europe by seamen and adventurers. It was the first exotic luxury to become an article of mass consumption. At the same time, the pleasure principle was seemingly disciplined by a need for self-control. Tobacco, like tea or coffee, was stimulating without befuddling or numbing the senses. In Chapter VI it will be suggested that such stimulants were eventually selected because they were compatible with alertness and control, and allayed the appetite.[27] The plantations also produced cotton and dyestuffs that soon influenced middle-class and even popular apparel – especially in the Netherlands and Britain, which were the pacesetters in the new bourgeois world of consumption. Although the new civility often aped the Court, its dynamic spread the consumption of plantation produce into every crevice of the new money economy. The growth of capitalism in Europe thus sucked in a stream of exotic commodities, which themselves helped to sugar the often bitter pill of wage dependence.

From the Baroque to the Creole

One term for evoking the ethos and aspirations of early European coloni- alism is 'the baroque'. This word, originally referring to a misshapen pearl and then applied to tortuously elaborate demonstrations in scholastic logic, became attached to the discrepant, bizarre and exotic features of post- Renaissance culture. It was finally adopted to evoke those principles of power and harmony which could reconcile such discordant elements. The baroque appears in a Europe confronting Ottoman might and discovering the material culture of Asia, Africa and America. It is first sponsored by the Jesuits, the Counter-Reformation and the Catholic monarchs and courts in an attempt to meet the challenge of Puritans, though subsequently some Protestant monarchs also adopted aspects of the baroque. Xavier Rubert de Ventos, writing of the consequences of the colonization of the Americas, observes:

> The baroque generally – and more singularly in Spain – seems to be an attempt to retain the classical ideals in a world in which everything seems to overwhelm them: a portentous effort to contain elements from overflowing any figurative perimeter. Against all the odds, baroque artists try to offer a tangible translation of a world torn apart by Christianity, aggrandised by the Church and disjointed by the State, disqualified by monetary economy, and thrown off centre by cosmological and geographical discoveries.[28]

In a similar way, Carl Friedrich links the baroque to the world of colonial slavery:

> Looking back upon this period of colonial expansion, it is not difficult to perceive that the spreading of the Gospel, the lure of gold and silver, strategic considerations, the need for outlets for surplus population, the search for raw materials and markets, the effort to increase governmental revenue and naval training, together with the psychology of adventure and escape, all played their roles, in fact and in propaganda. The lust for power, the basic motif of the baroque age, was involved in all of them. But not only the lust *for*, but even more perhaps the revelling *in*, the gorgeous feeling *of*, power were most wonderfully at work in this field. If one confronts the slave trader and the Puritan, the 'get-rich-quick' speculator and the Quaker mystic and pacifist as they sailed the seven seas and expanded Europe until it circled the globe, one beholds once more the basic polarities of the baroque. Both the search for inward and outward power propelled the colonial expansion of Europe . . .[29]

Expanding the concept of the baroque to embrace also the Puritans and Quakers gives an undue latitude to the term, since – José Maravall has argued – the baroque really represented an alternative modernity to that associated with the Puritan ethic, and exulted in species of display that the Puritans detested.

Since the baroque had a special link to the Counter-Reformation, it loomed larger in Catholic than in Protestant countries, and everywhere it was associated with royal and aristocratic display, focusing on a utopia of harmony, a cornucopia of abundance and a diorama of elegance. It is in baroque painting that the figure of the black page is often found, gazing gratefully at the master or mistress, or placidly at the viewer. The baroque favoured a sanitized and controlled vision of civil society. While Louis XIV's *Code Noir* sought to instantiate a species of justice within the world of slavery, the Portuguese Jesuit – and sometime royal chaplain – António Vieira delivered a masterpiece of baroque prose denouncing the cruel slaveowners and exalting their victims. Ultimately the courtly baroque wished to tame the wilful slaveowner rather than yield him all the power he craved. While the baroque as spectacle retained a link to the world of colonial slavery, it exhibited a public entrepreneurship, the positive face of mercantilism, which contrasted with the private enterprise that was the driving force behind the New World's civil slavery. Vieira was also the architect of the Brazil Company, a chartered body which helped to save the colony for Portugal.

The planters of the English Caribbean and North America, where slavery proved most dynamic, were plunged in a workaday world and made fewer concessions to their subject peoples than the kings of Spain and Portugal. But they saw themselves as sovereigns of all they surveyed, and occasionally patronized the diversions of their people. The Great Houses of the planters received African adornments, while echoing the Palladian mansions of the English or French aristocracy, the latter in their turn being influenced by Versailles. Since plantation cultivation destroyed the forests, the planters had little difficulty finding sites with commanding views. They built not fortresses or castles but theatres of gracious living. The religion and culture of the Protestant and Anglo-Saxon slave colonies were resistant to cultural admixture – though, as we will argue in Chapter XI, this was by no means absent, even in Virginia. While the planters supplied the necessary ingredients of the new bourgeois lifestyles, they themselves cultivated the dignity of gentlemen. There were not a few learned colonial planters, connoisseurs of Indian customs and artifacts, whose explorations can be seen as projects of a cultural mastery or, more sympathetically, as efforts to transcend European models and to discover an American identity.

Tzvetan Todorov has argued that the Spanish *conquistadores* combined an ability to enter the world of the pre-Colombian societies, playing ruthlessly and skilfully on their internal fault lines, with a lust for gold and cultural arrogance which repressed the basic humanity of the conquered. [30] Typically, the European colonists portrayed themselves as engaged in a mission of civilization, saving the 'good' natives from the 'bad' natives who preyed upon them. In this splitting of the 'Other' the bad native was inherently vicious, given to cannibalism (a word derived from the name of the Carib people) and other unspeakable practices; the 'good' native, on the other hand, still required the tutelage as well as the protection of the Conqueror. The subsequent process of building colonial systems retained many of the characteristics identified by Todorov, but involved a proliferation – a baroque proliferation – of identities built up by polyphonic counterpoint.

The African slave was different from the conquered Indian, and within both categories many distinctions were made. The Spanish permitted – or even encouraged – the Indians and Africans of different *naciones* to parade in distinctive dress, sometimes an adaptation of Spanish peasant costumes with Indo-American or Afro-American folkloric elaboration, on royal feast days. Within the plantation system the planters liked to distinguish different African peoples, to whom real or imagined skills and temperaments were attributed. Thus English planters favoured 'Coromantins' – their term for the Akan peoples of West Africa – for their initiative, hardiness and bravery, but also feared their propensity to revolt. At least twenty different African peoples were regularly distinguished by French planters in Saint Domingue, and there were significant differences in the kinds of work assigned to them.[31] These African 'nations' were conceived of roughly on the model of European nations, without registering the complex of kinship relations, thus actually bringing about the reduction of a complex identity to a simple one. The mixed or mulatto populations were elaborately classified: the French planter-*philosophe* Moreau de St-Méry produced a table of separate terms distinguishing 128 different categories of mixed blood. The Portuguese authorities organized the following separate companies of free persons of colour in eighteenth-century Minas Gerais: *pardos e bastardos forros* (free mulattoes and half-castes), *pretos e pardos forros* (free blacks and mulattoes), *pretos e mestiços forros* (free blacks and free mixed-bloods), *indios e bastardos* (Indians and half-castes). Colonial slavery was thus typically accompanied by a complex hierarchy of Others, and the stance towards the enslaved Other was that of instrumentalization rather than simple suppression or exclusion, fates which were reserved for the incorrigible 'bad native'.

The category of the baroque illuminates the transitional character of colonial slavery, allowing it to be seen as an ancient and traditional form of domination transformed and thrown forward. It helped to propel the forward movement, while those who contributed the motor energy were confined to a narrower space than ever before. The slave plantations were enormously productive, but some of the methods of cultivation were needlessly laborious. If the planter wished to remain in control, and to appropriate a prodigious surplus, then everything had to be adapted to the slave gang or to a labour process that could be easily overseen. On the other hand, the planters continually relied on the slaves' craft and skill, their ability to build with local materials and live on local flora and fauna.

The baroque sought to address the impact of other cultures upon Europe, a feature that was particularly pronounced in the Americas. The colonial baroque generally acquired a syncretistic and popular character by comparison with the metropolitan baroque of Versailles or a royal procession on the Thames, though the public display of power was common to both.[32] In the Andes, Mexico and Brazil, indigenous or African themes were incorporated in objects of religious devotion; gold and silver were plentifully applied, asserting a primacy of symbolic value over exchange value. The baroque even promised an aestheticized and transfigured world beyond that of an oppressive mundane reality.

Those elements of the baroque which implied any restraint on the commercial dynamic of plantation slavery were gradually whittled away by the relentless pressure of military and economic competition between rival slave systems. The slave systems of the late eighteenth and nineteenth centuries became attuned to more industrial rhythms, losing first their baroque and then their colonial features. But these processes also brought into view the informal work of cultural and productive synthesis underlying the productivity of the slave systems. The colonial version of the baroque anticipated elements of the creole. The creole mixtures thrown up by plantation development became increasingly confident and coherent, escaping beyond European forms and models. The African coastal depots, the Atlantic island reprovisioning points, the American ports, plantations, marketplaces and backlands were new spaces, and they gave rise to new languages, new musics, new religions and new laws. They gave birth to the creole, to mixtures of European, African and Amerindian elements. While the colonial baroque articulated and qualified slavery 'from above', the creole sometimes did so 'from below'. The term creole was used of the American-born, whether white or black or every shade between, though the emphasis was to shift according to place and period. The word itself was thus close in meaning to that of 'American' as used in England's North American colonies. It originated, however, from the Spanish *criada*, or nurse, thus implying that the *criollo* was suckled as well as born in the Americas, very possibly by an Indian or African nurse. It seems appropriate that the new forms of life born in the colonies are often called creole, with the more or less conscious realization that they represented a new synthesis or mixture, arrived at through the struggles within and between the various components of the colonial population. Within narrow limits creolization could qualify slavery. But without some more or less revolutionary emancipation, the creole impulse was caged.

The servitude of the slaves, imprisoned on a tiny patch of soil and forced to devote nearly all their waking time to furnishing the conveniences and luxuries of a diverse metropolitan population, was the transatlantic complement of European economic advance. Captive Africans and their descendants paid with their blood and sweat and incarceration for the phenomenal expansion of human possibilities in the Atlantic world. This is how it happened. But was it the inescapable and 'necessary' price of economic advance? If it was a necessary price, then it might even appear, at this distance in time, a price worth paying.

The problem with such a view is that the human costs of slavery continue to be paid in the poisonous legacies it bequeathed. The slavery of the colonial epoch was associated with a new species of racialization, a predatory and destructive mode of production and an oblivious and irresponsible mode of consumption. I believe we must scrutinize all the various causal links in the chains of American slavery. Their complexity and counterpoint could have yielded a variety of outcomes. At each moment in the construction of the slave systems there were forms of resistance, queries and objections, even proposals that matters be arranged differently. Because of the fact that these systems of slavery had to provide for the reproduction of some human resources, as well as wastefully consuming them, new social subjects were produced in the Atlantic zone, with their own proposals and forms of life. New sources of productivity were being tapped, new needs met, and new motivations discovered. Would it not have been possible to combine these in ways which avoided the systematic, onerous and destructive coercion of American slavery and the Atlantic slave trade? The history reconstructed below will on occasion seek to identify signs and possibilities that other paths of development were considered, and might have been chosen. Even if some such clues can be detected, we are left with what happened. Yet some daylight is admitted to the modernity–slavery couplet by acknowledging the possibility that there might have been a path to modernity that avoided the enormity of enslavement and its contemporary legacy.

In pursuing this idea, I will critically refine the work of those classical and Marxist economists who always stressed the inherent limitations of slave labour and the projects of 'merchant capital'. Ultimately merchant capital, with its reliance on tied labour, was conservative and rigid, and the slave plantations it sponsored raised output mainly by multiplying units of production, not by raising labour productivity. In *Karl Marx's Theory of History*, G.A. Cohen urged that unfree labour could not, in the long run, be compatible with cumulative improvements in the forces of production.[33] Marx fully acknowledged that New World plantation slavery had played a critical role in exploiting natural monopolies, imposing a new scale of co-operation and furthering an extended process of 'primitive accumulation'. But he saw nothing 'premature' in the defeat of the Confederate South at a time when its planters were still producing the cotton needed by capitalist industry. The work of such distinguished historians of slavery as Eugene Genovese, Elizabeth Fox Genovese, Jacob Gorender and Manuel Moreno Fraginals, influenced by classical political economy and Marxism, has sought to view the spectacular advances of the plantations from the standpoint of the *longue durée* of the modern epoch taken as a whole. From this perspective the blockages and costs of the slave systems appear more clearly than they do in the New Economic History.[34] In Chapter VIII and Part Two I will show that it is possible to reconcile the classical critique of the slave plantations with a recognition of their modernity. While I seek to outline new patterns and perspectives it will, I hope, be clear that the work of synthesis attempted here owes everything to the multitude of scholars, and smaller number of witnesses, upon whom it draws.

This book is divided into two parts. In Part One I confront the paradox that slavery had become marginal or non-existent in Western Europe at the time of the Discoveries. I then trace, country by country, the emergence of forms of colonization and enslavement in the course of which a new slave trade from Africa was developed, the institutions and ideologies of a racial slavery were established, forms of commercial organization were tested, and the slave plantation itself was perfected as a productive enterprise. The period 1492 to 1713 can be seen as one of a ruthless struggle for survival between early modern states which tested their capacity to tap new sources of economic and military strength. Britain's precarious lead in colonial development in 1713 was the prize of challenges to Spain and the Netherlands, alliance with Portugal and an arduous and unfinished struggle with France.

By 1713 plantation slavery had been established on a racial basis in Brazil, the Caribbean and North America. Statesmen who had always been preoccupied with gold and silver gradually realized that the plantation trades could be vastly more valuable. Part Two of the book explores the prodigious growth of the various slave systems, set in the context of the eighteenth-century commercial boom and the onset of the Industrial Revolution. Then, country by country and colony by colony, it explores how such a destructive system made a vital contribution to industrial and military success, and accumulated many of the social and political antagonisms which were to engulf the Americas and Europe in an age of revolution.

Notes

1. Adam Smith, *An Inquiry into the Nature and Causes of the Wealth of Nations*, Oxford 1976, p. 96; Max Weber, *General Economic History*, London 1927, pp. 300–01. But see also pp. 80–84, 298–9.
2. Anthony Giddens, *The Consequences of Modernity*, Stanford, CA 1990, pp. 21–9, 55–78; Anthony Giddens, *Modernity and Self-Identity: Self and Society in the Late Modern Age*, Stanford, CA 1991, pp. 14–15; Paul Gilroy, *The Black Atlantic: Modernity and Double Consciousness*, London 1993, especially pp. 41–71.
3. Zygmunt Bauman, *Modernity and the Holocaust*, London and Ithaca, NY 1989, p. xiii; Ronald Aronson, *The Dialectics of Disaster*, London 1983; Jean Drèze and Amartya Sen,

Hunger and Public Action, Oxford 1989. But see also Gilroy, *The Black Atlantic*, pp. 187–224 (especially pp. 213–14).

4. E.L. Jones, *The European Miracle: Environments, Economics and Geo-Politics in the History of Europe and Asia*, 2nd edn, Cambridge 1987, pp. 75–85.

5. Sidney Greenfield, 'Plantations, Sugar Cane and Slavery', in Michael Craton, ed., *Historical Reflections/Réflexions Historiques*, vol. 6, no. 1, Summer 1979, pp. 85–120 (p. 86).

6. Steve Stern, *Peru's Indian Peoples and the Challenge of Spanish Conquest*, Madison, WI 1982, p. 141.

7. Stuart Schwartz, *Sugar Plantations in the Formation of Brazilian Society: Bahia, 1550–1835*, Cambridge 1985, p. 261.

8. Arthur P. Newton, *The European Nations in the West Indies, 1493–1688*, London 1933, p. 122.

9. My account here draws mainly upon Patricia Seed, *Ceremonies of Possession in Europe's Conquest of the New World, 1492–1640*, Cambridge 1995, though I have altered her sequence and necessarily omitted nearly all the fascinating detail. For a further helpful and relevant discussion, see Anthony Pagden, *Lords of All the World: Ideologies of Empire in Spain, Britain and France, c1500-c1800*, New Haven, CT 1996, especially pp. 63–102. Subsequent chapters will, I hope, fill out and justify the interpretation offered.

10. A question further explored in Chapter I; but see also Robin Blackburn, 'The Elementary Structures of Slavery', in Michael Bush, ed., *Slavery and Serfdom in Comparative Perspective*, London 1996.

11. John Thornton, *Africa and Africans in the Making of the Atlantic World, 1400–1680*, Cambridge 1992, p. 71.

12. Karl Polanyi, *Dahomey and the Slave Trade*, Seattle, WA and London 1964, p. 17.

13. David Galenson, *Traders, Planters, and Slaves: Market Behaviour in Early English America*, Cambridge 1986, p. 143. This study is based on the records of the sale of more than 74,000 slaves in the West Indies between 1673 and 1725.

14. Jean-Paul Sartre, *Critique of Dialectical Reason*, vol. 1, London 1976, p. 132.

15. Michel Foucault, *Genealogía del Poder, Genealogía del Racismo*, Madrid 1992. Ann Stoler criticizes Foucault for not attending sufficiently to the colonial state as a source of racism; one might add that the slaveowner, even prior to the colonial state, actually claimed most of its regulatory powers. See Ann Laura Stoler, *Race and the Education of Desire: Foucault's* History of Sexuality *and the Colonial Order of Things*, Durham, NC and London 1995, pp. 55–94.

16. Jack Forbes, *Africans and Native Americans: The Language of Race and the Evolution of Red-Black Peoples*, Urbana and Chicago 1993.

17. Vitorino Magalhães Godinho, *Mito e Mercadoria: Utopia e Prática de Navigar, séculos XIII–XVIII*, Lisbon 1990, pp. 57–152.

18. Here is Cabeza de Vaca's description of an incident following their first contact with their fellow countrymen:

> They [the Indians accompanying them] were willing to do nothing until they had delivered us into the hands of other Indians, as had been their custom. . . . Our countrymen became jealous at this, and caused their interpreter to tell the Indians that we were of them, and for a long time we had been lost; that they were the lords of the land who must be obeyed and served, while we were persons of mean condition and small force. The Indians cared little or nothing for what was told them; and conversing amongst themselves said the Christians lied: that we had come whence the sun rises, and they whence it goes down: we healed the sick, they killed the sound; that we had come naked and barefooted, while they had arrived in clothing on horses with lances; that we were not covetous of anything, but that all we were given, we directly turned to give, remaining with nothing; that the others had the only purpose to rob whomsoever they found, bestowing nothing on anyone.

Alvar Nuñez Cabeza de Vaca, *Relation of Nuñez Cabeza de Vaca*, Ann Arbor, MI 1966, pp. 186–7. Alvar Nuñez Cabeza de Vaca, *Naufragios y Comentarios*, ed. R. Ferrando, Madrid 1985, pp. 131–2. The first edition of this work was published in 1542.

19. Quoted in William Pietz, 'The Problem of the Fetish, II', *Res*, no. 13, 1987.

20. Sartre, *Critique of Dialectical Reason*, pp. 65–7, 256–69.

21. Many examples of the former will be found in Winthrop Jordan, *White Over Black: American Attitudes toward the Negro, 1550–1812*, Chapel Hill, NC 1968. Precursors of the

idealization of the 'noble savage' include Las Casas and Jean de Léry; but see also Anthony Pagden, *European Encounters with the New World*, New Haven, CT 1993, pp. 42–7, 121–6 and Sergio Buarque de Holanda, *Visão do Paraiso*, fifth edn, São Paulo 1996.

22. Thomas Haskell, 'Capitalism and the Origins of the Humanitarian Sensibility', Part I, *American Historical Review*, vol. 90, no. 2, April 1985, and Part II, *American Historical Review*, vol. 90, no. 3, June 1985; Ellen Meiksins Wood, 'Capitalism and Human Emancipation', *New Left Review*, no. 167, January–February 1988, pp. 1–21 (p. 7).

23. Thomas Holt, 'Marking: Race, Race-Making, and the Writing of History', *American Historical Review*, February 1995, pp. 1–20 (p. 10). Here Holt is using the approach of Henri Lefebvre, *Critique of Everyday Life*, London 1994.

24. Carole Shammas, *The Pre-industrial Consumer in England and America*, Oxford 1990, pp. 297–8.

25. See Benedict Anderson, *Imagined Communities*, London 1991, pp. 149–52.

26. See W.G. Runciman, 'The "Triumph" of Capitalism as a Topic in the Theory of Social Selection', *New Left Review*, no. 210, March–April 1995, pp. 33–47, and the same author's *A Treatise on Social Theory*, vol. II, *Substantive Social Theory*, Cambridge 1989. The distinctiveness of this author's use of the Darwinian notion of 'historical selection' is that it applies to particular social practices rather than to whole social formations; for an interesting example of the latter approach see Christopher Bertram, 'International Competition in Historical Materialism', *New Left Review*, no. 183, September–October 1990, pp. 116–28. While Runciman's focus on particular practices boosts the explanatory power of such an approach, his own theory is less attuned to questions of directionality in social development: see the essay on Runciman in Perry Anderson, *Zones of Engagement*, London 1992.

27. For valuable studies of the new culture of consumption see Sidney Mintz, *Sweetness and Power: The Place of Sugar in Modern History*, London 1986; Jordan Goodman, *Tobacco in History: The Culture of Dependence*, London 1993; and Wolfgang Schivelbusch, *Tastes of Paradise: A Social History of Spices, Stimulants, and Intoxicants*, New York 1992.

28. Xavier Rubert de Ventos, *The Hispanic Labyrinth: Tradition and Modernity in the Colonisation of the Americas*, New Brunswick 1991, p. 116. But for an influential Spanish interpretation, which undoubtedly influenced the above formulation, see José Antonio Maravall, *La Cultura del Barroco*, fourth edn, Barcelona 1986.

29. Carl Friedrich, *The Age of the Baroque, 1610–1660*, New York 1952.

30. Tzvetan Todorov, *The Spanish Conquest of the New World: The Problem of the Other*, New York 1988.

31. David Geggus, 'Sugar and Coffee Cultivation in Saint Domingue and the Shaping of the Slave Labor Force', in Ira Berlin and Philip Morgan, eds, *Cultivation and Culture: Labor and the Shaping of Slave Life in the Americas*, Charlottesville, VA and London 1993, pp. 73–100.

32. A point made by Bolívar Echeverría in Horst Kurnitsky and Bolívar Echeverría, *Conversaciones sobre el Barroco*, Mexico D.F. 1993, p. 15. See also Carlos E. Fernández de Córdoba, 'El Método de la pasión: Max Weber y la racionalidad religiosa', *Nariz del Diablo*, no. 21, n.d., FLACSO, Quito, Ecuador.

33. G.A. Cohen, *Karl Marx's Theory of History: A Defence*, Oxford 1978.

34. See Eugene Genovese, *The Political Economy of Slavery*, New York 1968; Eugene Genovese and Elizabeth Fox Genovese, *The Fruits of Merchant Capital: Slavery and Bourgeois Property in the Rise and Expansion of Capitalism*, Oxford 1983; Jacob Gorender, *O Escravismo Colonial*, São Paulo 1982; Manuel Moreno Fraginals, *El Ingenio*, 3 vols, Havana 1977.

Part One

The Selection of New World Slavery

I

The Old World Background to New World Slavery

Si fault de faim périr les innocens
Dont les grands loups font chacun jour ventrée,
Qui amassent à milliers et à cens
Les faux trésors; c'est le grain, c'est le blée,
Le sang, les os qui on la terre arré
Des pauvres gens, dont leur esperit crie
Vengeance à Dieu, vé à la seignorie.

(The innocents must starve With which the wolves fill their belly every day, Who by thousands, and hundreds hoard Ill-gotten treasures; it is the grain, it is the corn, The blood, the bones of the poor people, which have ploughed the earth And their souls cry out to God for vengeance and woe to lordship.)

Anon, France, fifteenth century

I refer you to the Grand Pantagruelian Chronicle for the Knowledge of the Genealogy and Antiquity whence Gargantua is descended unto us. . . . Would to God that every one had as certain Knowledge of his genealogy from Noah's Ark up to the present age.

Rabelais, *Gargantua*, Book I, Chapter I

About the end of the fifth Year, Grandgousier returning from the conquest of the Canarians paid a visit to his son Gargantua.

Rabelais, *Gargantua*, Book I, Chapter XIII

Gargantua was not merely large; he was everywhere. His insatiable appetites threatened to drain the resources of the kingdom. . . . When Gargantua went to war he was invincible; his numerous enemies were slaughtered in the most various manner, and barely managed to inflict losses on the giant's army. Although Gargantua took up his military career only after education had transformed him from an ignorant boor into a temperate sophisticate, we might take the two sides of his character as simultaneous aspects of the same personality, for he displays as much excess in massacre as in feasting.

Julian Stallabrass, *Gargantua*

Jacob Jordaens, *Moses and Zipporah* (Rubenshuis, Antwerp)

There are many features of medieval Europe which appear to anticipate the colonial slavery of the New World; they deserve to be registered, but with care taken that we are not seduced by a fully fledged myth of origins into belittling the latter's novelty.[1]

The powers which successfully colonized the Americas had their roots in medieval kingdoms, each of which displayed a propensity for ethno-religious intolerance and persecution, territorial expansion, colonial settlement, arrogant impositions on subject peoples, and the theological justification of slavery, racial exclusion and sordid enterprise. More generally, late medieval Europeans were prone to stigmatize the infidel and the pagan, and entertained fanciful notions of 'wild' or 'monstrous' peoples. Arab techniques of sugar production were adopted in the Levant, Sicily and Andalusia, with servile labourers cultivating and processing cane. In much of Latin Europe there was a theory and practice of slavery itself which descended from the Roman Empire. Latin Christendom was a vigorously expansionist force, doubling in land area between the tenth and fourteenth centuries. Robert Bartlett concludes a powerful account of this expansion by observing: 'The mental habits and institutions of European racism and colonialism were born out of the medieval world, the conquerors of Mexico knew the problem of the Mudéjars; the planters of Virginia had already been planters in Ireland.'[2] In the same vein Charles Verlinden has dubbed the medieval or early modern sugar estates of the Levant the laboratories of the New World slave plantations, and asserted, in a formula cited by David Brion Davis, that 'The slave economy of the modern period is purely and simply the continuation of that of the medieval colonies.'[3]

Yet such observations do not identify what was new and distinctive about New World slavery. Thus the English seized land in Ireland for their 'plantations', and subjected the natives to many harsh impositions; but they did not, or could not, enslave the Irish. Likewise the Mudéjars and Moriscos of Spain were sometimes temporarily enslaved, but their eventual fate was to be either assimilation or expulsion. So far as the sugar estates of the Levant are concerned, they represent a rather different impulse from that of either feudal expansion or cultural conquest. They were set up with the help of merchants from Venice or Genoa to supply Europe's craving for sugar, but their scale of operations was limited by the relative shallowness of demand in late medieval Europe, and by the militarily precarious position of the Christian outposts in the Levant. The sugar output of Cyprus or Candia (Crete) or Sicily was to be overtaken by that of the Atlantic islands in the sixteenth century, then entirely eclipsed by that of the Brazilian and Caribbean estates in the seventeenth.[4] Levantine slaves were ethnically diverse, and evidence for the use of field slaves on the Levantine estates is anyway very weak, as we will see. It was not until the seventeenth century that the plantation as an integrated unit was perfected; the rise of this new type of enterprise itself transformed slavery. Each stage of development was sponsored by new commercial forces – first Italian, then Dutch, then

English – since they commanded the necessary resources for constructing plantations and ensuring access to broader markets. Although the Dutch republic was ultimately unsuccessful as a colonial power in the New World, it played a key role in fostering a dynamic Atlantic trade in slaves and slave products. Yet the Dutch polity and social formation set a new standard of tolerance and pluralism in its domestic arrangements, rejecting much of the medieval legacy which might be thought to have paved the way for colonial slavery. Indeed, the Dutch provinces banned the entry of slaves to the metropolis, and the great Dutch painters portrayed Africans as individuals, not stereotypes.

The rise of medieval Christendom coincided with a secular decline of slavery in most parts of the continent. By the time the New World slave plantations took off, slavery was extinct in England, the Netherlands and France, the powers most associated with this takeoff. Slavery had declined throughout late medieval Europe, despite those elements in medieval expansionism which did indeed contribute to the later practice of colonial slavery, as the authors I have quoted rightly maintain. Slavery in the New World was not based on an Old World prototype. Its bonds were woven from a variety of materials – ethnic identities, legal codifications, technical resources, economic impulses, and so forth – and all these together comprised something quite new.

Rome and the Christian Embrace of Slavery

While the evidence for slavery in the later Middle Ages is scanty and controversial, this certainly cannot be said for Antiquity, which left behind – as Frederick Engels once put it – a 'poisonous sting', as encapsulated in what Greek philosophy, Roman law and Christian doctrine had to say about the legitimacy of enslavement. In Ancient Rome slavery was concentrated at the centre, in Italy and Sicily. While slaves certainly discharged many roles, the bulk of them toiled in the fields, often driven in gangs and housed in barracks. The slaves themselves were captured from many outlying regions, and comprised a multitude of ethnicities. Their status was that of chattels who could be disposed of at the will of their owner, who in theory had the power of life and death over them. Roman slavery had been nourished and held in place by the military exploits of Republic and Empire, the source of large slave hauls. The impressive network of roads widened the markets available to the slave estates, and allowed military help to arrive in case of difficulty. The legion's special discipline and combination of military and economic capacity furnished elements of a model for the slave estate.

It was a tenet of Roman law that all human beings were free according to the law of nature, but the unrestrained exercise of this freedom would be destructive; the status of the slave, like the concept of property, belonged to the *jus gentium* or law of nations, the basis of all civilized living. Safeguarding private property, including chattel slavery, and furnishing the principles which could adjudicate rival claims, was a central task for the legislator. The Emperor Justinian drew up a late Roman legal code which was to have enduring authority. It summarily announced: 'Slaves are in the power of their masters; for we find that among all nations slaveowners have the power of life and death over their slaves, and whatever a slave earns belongs to his master.'[5] If it was true – or nearly true – that 'all nations' had a conception of slavery, the specificity of Roman law was, on the one hand, the thoroughness with which it codified slaves as private property or chattels and, on the other, its formal lack of interest in the slave's ethnic or racial provenance. The Roman slave became part of the household of the owner; while slaves might be thought of as Greeks, Syrians, Britons or Germans, the institutions of slavery and manumission produced such a mingling of nations that after a generation or two, and sometimes less, the resulting population was comprised of Roman slaves and Roman freedmen or women. The combination of slavery and imperial rule fostered a distinctive Roman cosmopolitanism.[6]

Greek thought and law had been animated by a stronger sense of the gulf between Greeks and barbarians; the metic, or resident alien, needed a citizen sponsor, paid special taxes, and could never become a citizen (as could *peregrini* in Rome). Aristotle had developed a doctrine of 'natural slavery' which wrapped together class-like and ethnic features. The 'natural slave', according to Aristotle, was a barbarian whose inclination was to defer and who was distinguished by brawn, not brain; the 'natural slaves' needed the direction of those who were gifted with independence of character as well as intelligence and civilization. There was something flexible – not to say circular – about this 'theory', since it was admitted that some captives might display a nobility and intelligence which showed that they were not natural slaves; but in such a case their fortitude and character would enable them to bear their condition. Like women and domestic animals, slaves belong within the household of their owner, and are a species of property. Referring to animals and slaves, Aristotle observes:

> If nature makes nothing without some end in view, nothing to no purpose, it must be that nature had made all of them for the sake of man. This means that it is according to nature that even the art of war, since hunting is a part of it, should in a sense be a means for acquiring property: and that it must be used both against wild beasts and against such men as are by nature intended to be ruled over but refuse; for that is the kind of warfare which is just.[7]

Aristotle's doctrine of the 'natural slave' was long to remain a reference point of learned discussion, but Geoffrey de Ste Croix argues that many later Roman writers preferred the Stoic view that enslavement stemmed from Fortune, and that it could not harm the person of noble character – a view that was easier to reconcile with Roman cosmopolitanism.[8]

The early Christian Church accepted slavery and, by substituting Divine providence for the dispensation of nature or Fortune, saw spiritual advantages in the slave condition, such that the true Christian was a slave of Christ, seen as the realization of Christian freedom. In I Corinthians 7: 21 St Paul not only urges believers to accept slavery, if that is their condition, but writes: 'Even supposing you could go free, you would be better off making the most of your slavery.'[9] So far as St Augustine was concerned, the doctrine of 'original sin' meant that all deserved to be slaves. The slave was fortunate that his or her sinfulness, shared with all humankind, was receiving earthly punishment; at least the slave of a temporal master was relieved of part of the burden of enslavement to their own base lusts. Gervase Corcoran explains St Augustine's view as follows:

> Everyone who is a slave, is justly a slave. From this one cannot conclude that every master is unjustly a master because he is a sinner too. According to St Augustine to be a master is a condemnation too, because he is exposed to the *libido dominandi*, and the more he acts as a master (i.e. disposes of his inferiors for his own use), the more he is a slave.[10]

The early Christian communities were recruited to a disproportionate extent from freedmen and women. They saw no inherent taint or degradation in either slave origins or the slave condition.

The Christian Empire upheld and continued the Roman legal doctrine that the slave was entirely the property of the master in this world – even if, in the life to come, he or she might be shown to be the master's equal or superior. The dominant view within the Church came to be that the Empire and its secular arrangements themselves had a providential character, since they facilitated the spread of the Gospel of salvation. It was perfectly licit for a Christian master to hold Christian slaves, and the Church itself became a large-scale slaveowner. The period of persecution did not lead Christians to condemn slavery, and the advent of Christian emperors confirmed the basic Christian stance of urging the virtues of obedience on citizen and slave. Believers were described as 'slaves of Christ'. While masters were urged not to abuse their slaves, slaves themselves were advised to see their unhappy lot in this world as a spiritual advantage in preparation for the next.[11]

In the later Empire and the Dark Ages, the numbers and condition of slaves reflected the waning effectiveness of imperial structures and the incursion of new warrior aristocracies. The decline in the vigour of the Empire from about the third century onwards was associated with a gradual mutation in the slave system. The imperial authorities co-opted semi-Romanized Germanic armies to defend the social order against both internal threats – such as the Bacaudae slave rebellions of the third and fourth centuries – and incursions from 'barbarian' forces not under their control. The Germanic military reinforcements helped to maintain the subjection of slaves and to prolong the life of the Empire, but at the cost of increasing warlordism and fragmentation. The disruption of commerce in the late Roman world restricted the scope for large, commercialized estates. The Roman state itself had a declining ability to purchase wheat and supplies from such estates, while the rulers of each province had to be more self-reliant. From late Roman times the lords often found it more advantageous to cultivate their estates not with slave gangs housed in barracks, but by means of the *colonus*, or 'hutted slave', given the use of a parcel of land and expected to furnish tribute in kind or labour. With continuing – but uninvited – barbarian incursions, this decentralized pattern of power also proved more secure.[12]

In the earlier phases of the development of serfdom and a feudal order slavery survived as a juridical form and name, while its content was gradually redefined. In Roman law, as indicated by Justinian, the bundle of powers claimed by masters could be broken down, allowing slaves to ply a trade, or be hired out, or work on plots by themselves, but with the master claiming the resulting earnings. The master's ability fully to control the 'hutted slave' could not be sustained by legal formulas alone. With the decline of the effective power of the imperial centre in much of Western and central Europe, the leverage of the *servi* could be boosted by overlapping jurisdictions or the emerging strength of a village community. The settled population of serfs gradually became more homogeneous than had been a slave population replenished by slave hauls. But moderating pressure from below was not reinforced by the Church, which sought to ingratiate itself with the barbarian warrior aristocracies, reckoning that their conversion was critical to its survival. When the barbarians of Germany or the Balkans converted to Christianity, they saw no reason to renounce the lucrative practice of slave-raiding, which gave them the resources they needed to buy equipment and luxuries from the merchants.[13]

The bishops of the Church, ensconced in their Roman towns, believed that the barbarian chiefs, not the benighted country folk, should be the chief target for conversion. Pragmatically adjusting to barbarian military strength, they could often be indulgent to barbarian pillage and ethnic conceit. In this context St Patrick's ministry in Ireland, and his famous letter to Coroticus and his followers, were quite exceptional. St Patrick attacked the soldiers of the British or Scottish ruler Coroticus as 'ravening wolves' [*lupi rapaces*] who carried off God's people, including monks and nuns, and sold them as slaves to such as the 'apostate Picts'. Evidently Coroticus, or at least his followers, regarded themselves as Christians, or it would make little sense to pronounce them excommunicated. St Patrick's fine denunciation is directed also at Christians who condone the enslavement of fellow believers:

> I make this earnest appeal to all you men of piety and humble heart, it is not right to curry favour with such as these nor to take food and drink with them, nor ought one to take their alms until they make amends to God by gruelling

penance, with shedding of tears, and free God's servants and the baptized handmaidens of Christ.[14]

St Patrick also points out that in Gaul the more respectful Franks are willing to accept ransom for Christian captives rather than sell them into slavery.

Between the sixth and the eighth centuries or later, outright slavery, including the enslavement of Christian by Christian, persisted, and was even seen as an instrument for the spiritual education of the peasant mass. But the Church's accommodation to the barbarian warrior aristocracies was challenged by the advent of Muslim conquerors in the eighth century and afterwards. The slow consolidation of a feudal order in the core areas of Christendom led to a modification of the practice and theory of enslavement.[15]

The Visigoths are a good example of a barbarian warrior aristocracy who combined a species of Christian piety with rapacious slave-raiding or, once they settled down, oppressive slaveholding. In Spain the Visigoths sought to maintain slave-worked estates, and for a time they succeeded. St Isidore of Seville was a ferocious defender of slave subordination, seeing it as a necessary part of the mundane order, a chastisement for sin which was ubiquitous. He also believed that ancestral sin had perverted entire races of humankind: 'Just as among individual races there are certain members who are monsters, so also among mankind as a whole, certain races are monsters, like the giants, the Cynocephali, the Cyclops and others.'[16] For Isidore, monsters were not 'against nature', as they had been for some classical writers, but in their very strangeness revealed the divine purpose; thus a physical flaw could well be the sign of a moral flaw. Pierre Bonnassie summarizes St Isidore's position as embracing '[t]he divine origin of slavery, the genetic perversity of slaves and the necessity of servitude as a means for the redemption of humanity through penitence – these were all ideas which became commonplace.'[17] Isidore prescribed stern discipline and punishments for recalcitrant slaves, yet his very insistence on this point shows that those who were enslaved contested their role. However, it was unwise for relatively small groups of invaders to attempt to maintain in complete slavery a large settled population with some traditions of communal self-organization and control over means of production. St Isidore's highly selective history of the Visigothic Kingdom omits all mention of the Bacaudae rebellions.[18] Subsequently, the swift Muslim advance in the Iberian Peninsula in 711 was facilitated by the tensions of a oppressive social order where the servile classes had some history of resistance. The advance of Tariq, the freedman commander of the Muslim forces, turned into 'an unexampled triumphal procession'.[19]

Slavery became progressively less important within the Christian kingdoms which held out against the Muslims in the North of Spain until, by the eleventh century, it may have virtually disappeared. The struggle with

Islam prompted the beginnings of a new doctrine, partly because there was no prospect of converting the new invaders and partly because the *élan* of the Muslim foe itself owed something to a ban on the enslavement of fellow believers. But the emergence of a new doctrine concerning the proper scope of enslavement, later ascribed to Charlemagne, was to be adopted very unevenly and slowly, and was only one element tending to reduce the incidence of slavery. The conjunctural pressure of confrontation with Islam – to be considered below – helped to generate a new approach to slavery because of the structural possibilities of the emergent feudal order. A diminishing significance of outright slavery was evident throughout Christendom as lords established their dominion over settled communities of serfs – slavery was then left as an institution which had a localized or temporary importance in frontier zones and in enclaves. Slaves could sometimes be used to strengthen lordly power, but such slaves or their descendants would, in time, themselves become retainers or serfs. The social formula of Latin Christendom began to reproduce serfdom, not outright slavery; villagers owed tribute in labour or kind or cash to their lord, and were forbidden to move without his permission. Such serfs could not be sold separately from the estate. They worked the land in their own way, and could look to the village community for a degree of protection from the serflord.

Within the system of feudal social relations, however, pockets of slavery persisted, for a host of particular reasons. Greater stability and a more coherent structure of lordly power enhanced the social formation's capacity to turn captives into slaves, and – at least for a time – keep them that way. Holding a few slaves could boost the autonomy of decentred feudal power and wealth. In the towns rich merchants favoured slave servants, since they were beholden to neither lords nor guilds. In the countryside the lords might retain some slaves as permanent labourers on the demesne, the land reserved for their own direct use. The possession of such slaves available for work throughout the year may have boosted the lord's ability to impose himself on the wider peasantry, where this was still necessary, but this was not a slave system or 'mode of production'. The lord's main source of agricultural surplus was in the form of produce or labour services or rent. While the possession of slaves for work on the demesne was still common in Carolingian France, Saxon and early Norman England, or early medieval Italy, slavery waned thereafter, and many even of those still called *servi* enjoyed rights of possession and usufruct.[20]

At the time of the Domesday Book (1086) slaves were still reported to comprise as much as one-tenth of England's population, with the figure rising to a fifth in the West Country. From this point on, evidence for true slaves in England declines sharply. William the Conqueror himself declared: 'We forbid anyone [to] sell a man out of the country.'[21] From the standpoint of the new monarch the export trade in English slaves might enrich the merchants of Bristol or Dublin, but could only impoverish his kingdom.

The Norman feudal system also led to an attenuation of the numbers of English slaves. Those employed as servants or as specialist workers on the demesne were not reproduced across generations in a fully servile condition. In England in the eleventh century the slave ploughman was being replaced by, or converted into, the smallholding *bovarius*.[22] When lords were absent from their estates, as was increasingly the case in the epoch of the Crusades, it probably made sense to diminish the size of their demesnes and to settle any slaves they possessed on land as serfs, and concede some improved status to their children.

While residual slaveholding could give the lord some leverage over peasants, other more effective means underpinned the developed feudal social order of the Middle Ages. In the heartland of Western Europe the stabilization of lordly power was based on advances in military and agricultural technique, at a time when wider imperial structures were ineffective. The lords came to control not only superior means of violence, underpinned by castle construction, but also horses, ploughs, grain mills and trade routes. The mounted warrior, allied to the large-scale introduction of the heavy plough and the water mill or windmill, permitted a more effective exploitation of the direct producers. The lords in their castles could offer villagers protection – from one another as well as invaders. Feudal warfare was directed at the acquisition of land rather than of captives, though every effort would be made, of course, to attach the labourers to the land. The castle and 'banal' mill gave support to the power of the lord, enabling him to assert control at a crucial stage of the production process and to claim a sizeable surplus. While the slave latifundist had to ensure detailed invigilation of the producer, this was no longer the case for the feudal lord, whose bailiffs had the more limited task of ensuring that peasant grain was taken to the lord's mill. This was one reason why, as serfdom was consolidated, field slavery declined and even disappeared. It also explains why the withering away of agricultural slavery coincided with a loss of rights for some free villagers.[23]

Slavery's eclipse in South West Europe is explained by Pierre Bonnassie as a result of growing solidarity within the rural population in a context of technical and economic relations of production incorporating grain mills and horse-drawn ploughs, such that 'all factors tending to its [slavery's] disappearance operated simultaneously'. He writes:

Adherence to Christian beliefs, for long formal and hesitant, became general amongst the rural population; this carried the seeds of the first 'popular religious movements', and promoted, above all, the spiritual unification of the peasantry in all its component elements. The technical progress which lightened human labour became more widely diffused. The expansion of the agrarian economy, increasingly apparent, necessitated an ever greater mobility on the part of the rural workers, which required enfranchisement. The state structures broke down in the wake of new invasions, and with them the whole repressive apparatus which depended upon them. There developed everywhere what Giovanni Tabacco has called for Italy 'a spontaneous movement of liberation'.[24]

Bonnassie attributes many of the technical advances incorporated in, and underpinning, the new social mix to peasant smallholders, but this did not prevent 'banal' lords, claiming a territorial jurisdiction, from battening upon them. Christianity did not pose any direct challenge to enslavement, and it was still permissible to hold fellow Christians in bondage, but to the extent that the whole rural population became incorporated within the Church, it could furnish an ideal medium within which solidarity could develop between the free and the enslaved. Both free and servile had cause to rue the power of the lords, and wish to set some limit upon it by making slaveholding difficult. If there was a moment of true 'liberation' for the peasantry, it must have been short-lived, as they were soon labouring under a new regime of power and property. Feudal social arrangements had no need for outright enslavement to obtain tribute or rent from the direct producers, since the lords controlled more effective instruments of production and violence.

Thus the windmill or water mill potentially raised productivity; if it was controlled by the lord, it also increased his leverage over the peasants. Of course, once in possession of such leverage lords might insist on deliveries to their mill even if the cost to the peasant of hauling grain reduced the real productivity advantage of the wind- or water-assisted mill to zero, as Pierre Dockès suggests it often did.[25] The spread of mills or of horse-drawn ploughs was uneven, and did not raise productivity everywhere to the same extent. But where they occurred, technical advances allowed the resistance of peasant communities to have a ratchet effect. As the direct domination of the serflords was pressed back by peasant resistance, the lords discovered that they could live with – and even contrive to benefit from – the elements of greater freedom claimed by the peasants, such as communal or private possession of land in return for labour services. The substitution of money rents for labour services or tribute in kind could operate in the same way.

Throughout much of Western Europe the villagers gradually established rights against their lords. In England there were still many unfree peasants or villeins in the thirteenth century. But while they were formally subject to the will of the lord, their condition was also regulated by 'the custom of the manor'. They were *de facto* owners of goods; they could buy and sell land and make wills. They might owe their lord as much as half of the output of the main arable crop, but if other sources of non-arable output are taken into account, he received not much more than a quarter of the value of their gross output.[26] The field slave in Roman Sicily, or later in the New World, received much less of the product and was made to work only by direct physical coercion.

Christian Resurgence and the Challenge of Islam

I have suggested that the gradual change in attitudes towards slavery in Western Europe was, like the notion of Christendom itself, deeply marked by confrontation with Islam. It was only after the Muslim advance to the heart of Europe that Christian doctrine began cautiously to modify its acceptance of the enslavement of believers. Charles Verlinden writes:

> From the Old Testament came the idea that if the master and the slave were of the same race and religion, slavery should be barred, but it took centuries for this concept to penetrate the West. Only in the Carolingian age did it appear in the idea of Christian society as one in which no member should be reduced to slavery.[27]

This new doctrine became effective only gradually, in a process of competitive selection of social practices. Its spread reflected both social pressures within Christendom of the sort noted above, and Western Christendom's need to transform itself to meet the Muslim threat. Islam was from the outset a faith which formally barred its adherents from enslaving co-religionists – indeed, Islamic law went further and prohibited the enslavement of Christians and Jews so long as they were living peaceably under Islamic rule, and paying a special tribute.

Bernard Lewis points out:

> The Qur'an, like the Old and New Testaments, assumes the existence of slavery. It regulates the practice of the institution and thus implicitly accepts it. . . . But Qur'anic legislation, subsequently confirmed and elaborated in the Holy Law, brought two major changes to ancient slavery which were to have far-reaching effects. One of these was the presumption of freedom; the other, the ban on the enslavement of free persons except in strictly defined circumstances.[28]

The Holy Law held that only infidels could be reduced to slavery. This doctrine could help to create a more intense sense of religious community and attract persons vulnerable to enslavement. And for infidels who were enslaved, the institution was meant to serve as a 'means for converting outsiders into insiders'.[29] Infidel slaves who converted could not, of course, expect manumission, but with time it was likely that the situation of some, generally those given responsible positions, would improve, while that of menials would remain degraded and lowly, but not wholly bereft of rights. Those who converted as free persons gained an important immunity. Charlemagne, whose grandfather had repulsed a Muslim army at Poitiers and who himself unsuccessfully sought to extend the Christian bridgehead in Spain, was certainly keenly aware of the military threat posed by the warrior religion. But the challenge of Islam was ideological as well as military: it concerned core beliefs and practices of Christianity, disputing its claim to be monotheistic or to realize the prophecies of the Old

Testament, or to create a true community of believers. The notion of Christendom itself was born out of this clash, and was marked in many ways by it.[30]

The possibility that Christians should reduce one another to slavery, or even sell Christian slaves to Muslim buyers, became the subject of bitter controversy. In the eighth, ninth and tenth centuries Western Europe had little to offer foreign traders except slaves, yet its privileged classes craved the luxuries and exotic goods which could be bought in the East. Muslim or Jewish traders established in Marseilles and Garde Freinet offered good prices for slaves. Young, healthy Celts or Anglo-Saxons, captured by Vikings or purchased by Frisian merchants, were sent to Paris or to Verdun; also arriving at Verdun for onward transshipment to Spain or North Africa were Slavs taken prisoner in the East. There was a lively Muslim demand for castrated slaves, but both Muslim purchasers and Jewish slave traders had religious scruples about performing the act of castration – at Verdun Christians, who had no such scruples, were engaged to emasculate the wretched pagans (if that is what they were). Venice, Lombardy, and even Rome itself also supplied slaves for Eastern markets.

The Church Councils at Estinnes in 743 and at Meaux in 845 denounced the sale of Christian slaves to pagans, in the latter case urging that they should be sold to Christians instead. Charlemagne urged that it was blasphemous to allow Christians to be sold to Muslims or heretics. In 776 Pope Adrian I was obliged to write to Charlemagne denying that he had condoned the sale of Christian slaves to 'the unspeakable race of Saracens' or to the 'unspeakable Greeks'. His defence was revealing: 'We did our utmost, and call God to witness that we strove mightily to prevent this scandal. . . . But as we have said many families were sold by the Lombards at a time when famine was pressing them hard.'[31] Although the traffic in Christian slaves became a source of controversy in the Carolingian epoch, it was not effectively suppressed because the Empire itself broke up amid conflict and turmoil. Paradoxically, the absence of a strong central power both discouraged rural slavery and ruled out regulation of the slave trade. It also permitted new Saracen incursions into Southern France and Italy, accompanied by deliberate attempts to incite slaves against their masters. Reflecting on Saracen conquests abetted by emancipated slaves, the sixteenth-century political philosopher Jean Bodin observed: 'Little by little this forced the Christians to relax servitude and to free slaves, excepting only certain *corvées* . . .'.[32]

The vulnerability and fragmentation of Christendom was reflected in the slave trade which battened upon it. In the early medieval period the Vikings had conducted a wide-ranging slave trade reaching along the Russian rivers to the Black Sea, the Adriatic and the Levant, or via the Baltic and the North Sea to England, Ireland, Iceland and the Atlantic. The Vikings practised long-distance slave-raiding and slave-trading from the eighth century to the eleventh. Although they were initially pagan they often found

Christian purchasers for their slaves, irrespective of the latter's religion. The Viking mastery of long-distance maritime and riverine transport was a vital ingredient in their ability to 'produce' and sell slaves. They established far-flung colonies, sustained by a captive labour force, in the North Atlantic, and set up the Varangian state in Russia, which allowed them to supply Byzantium with slaves captured in Eastern and Northern Europe. The Viking longboat, whose shallow draught allowed it to navigate rivers as well as oceans, was adapted to a trade in quite small numbers of expensive slaves; it could not carry more than about twenty or thirty captives at a time. Within Scandinavia itself slave labour was pendant to a free peasantry organized in clan communities, with a weak development of private property. According to one account a typical farm at this period might have attached to it three slaves, twelve cows and two horses. The presence of as many as ten or eighteen slaves on one farm would be the upper limit, and probably unusual. The absolute numbers of slaves absorbed by the Viking colonies in Iceland and elsewhere were quite modest; in tenth-century Iceland there were probably around two or three thousand slaves, comprising a third or a half of the population.

Slaves were stigmatized by humiliating stereotypes; swarthy English or Irish thralls were regarded as unreliable and lazy, and appear with such names as 'Lump', 'Coarse', 'Thickard', 'Noisy' and 'Torrent-talker'. The scale of slavery in these Scandinavian societies was reduced first by military setbacks which cut off the supply of new slaves and then by the emergence of more hierarchy and differentiation within the ranks of the free population, as the descendants of slaves, if any, were absorbed in the wider community as tied labourers or tenants. The eclipse of slavery was accompanied by a diminution in the independence of free peasant villages and the rise of a local nobility, with more extensive landholdings. These developments coincided with the completion of a slow process of conversion to Christianity. In the marchlands of Russia and Eastern Europe, however, slavery remained important.[33]

The strengthening of the feudal order in Latin Christendom and renewed clashes with Islam in Spain and the Levant favoured the resuscitation of the Carolingian ban on any traffic in Christian slaves, the establishment of religious orders dedicated to the redemption of Christians held in captivity by Muslims, and the elaboration of new formulas of colonization. The strengthening of the privileges associated with being an insider was linked to an intensified stigmatization of outsiders.

Feudal Expansion and Ideologies of Persecution

Robert Bartlett describes the expansionary formula of European feudalism from the tenth century to the thirteenth as comprising both a reinforced aristocracy, deploying an enhanced military technology, and communities of free peasants, offered land to cultivate in return for rents or services. Newly conquered areas would be secured by introducing colonies of free peasants, accompanied by the forced cultural assimilation of the indigenous population. The colonists were often attracted by being offered some years of exemption, or rents rather than labour services. The feudal formula of consolidation and expansion also critically embraced the establishment of churches, monasteries, chartered towns and universities. These institutions were all necessary to the replication of feudal social relations in new settings. The cultural dimensions of conquest were as important as the mounted knights, pikemen or archers. They helped to maintain the conquerors' identity, and to impose a subject identity on the conquered. As Bartlett writes: 'Conquest, colonization, Christianization: the techniques of settling in a new land, the ability to maintain cultural identity through legal forms and nurtured attitudes, the institutions and outlook required to confront the strange and the abhorrent, to repress it and to live with it, the law and religion' were all indispensable to the formula of expansion, enabling the new communities to become 'autonomous replicas not dependencies'.[34]

The imposition of Latin liturgy and laws regulated and defined the social order. The *gens latina* and those within the *ecclesia* had access to rights that were not available to pagans like the Lithuanians, or to 'wild peoples' or 'primitive Slavs'. Any people which failed to conform to settled agriculture and to the cultural and religious norms of Latin Christendom was relegated to a rigorously subordinate status; at the limit to slavery. The greater stress on religious mobilization and solidarity displayed by Latin Christendom in its period of resurgence and expansion was accompanied by greater stress on principles of exclusion and correction.

The Christian Europe of the eleventh and twelfth centuries witnessed, Robert Moore claims, a far more vigilant and ferocious policing of those who did not partake of the dominant religious, ethnic, corporeal and sexual regime. Jews, homosexuals ('sodomites'), lepers, Manichees and other heretics were deemed to be carriers of a perilous contagion that demanded a sterilizing punishment and persecution if they were not to contaminate the social order. Thus the whitened skin and deformity of the leper was deemed an outward sign of mortal sin. The stigmatized groups were those which were thought to challenge the spiritual underpinnings and pretensions of the new order; standing behind them was the spectre of persons without a lord, such as itinerant preachers, pedlars, mendicants or lepers, and of women without a man to answer for them. Thus the followers of Robert of Arbissel were described in alarm as 'men of every condition, women both servile [*pauperes*] and noble, widows and virgins, old and young, whores and spurners of men . . . turning away neither the poor nor the weak, the incestuous nor the depraved, lepers nor the helpless'.[35] The persecution of every type of deviant perfected a will to comprehensive ideological subordination that did indeed have ominous implications for those who came into the path of European expansion. It helped to forge the identity of Europe. The campaigns against the various types of deviancy were orchestrated on a continent-wide basis by decisions of the Third and Fourth Lateran Councils in 1179 and 1215. But while the persecutory apparatus was designed to exclude and suppress, it also sought to recuperate and include, if possible. Robert of Arbissel was eventually beatified, long after the ideological threat he had been thought to present had passed.

Following the Lateran Councils, it was more common for the formal status of the Jews to be defined as one of slavery. They were deemed to be chattels of the King – a designation with great advantages for the monarch, since it enabled the Jewish community to be subject to arbitrary royal tallage. The Jews were held collectively responsible for the death of Christ. While attempts would be made to convert Jews, the presence of Jewish communities was thought to furnish a living symbol of the Scriptures, and some held that it would not be until Judgement Day that the Jews would convert *en masse*. Jews themselves were formally forbidden to own Christian slaves, though various loopholes might allow this rule to be circumvented. The status of being the monarch's chattel allowed the Jews to be in, but not of, medieval Christendom. It permitted monarchs to tax Jews at will, and gave them an interest in protecting them. Jews were usually required to wear special markings and to live in designated areas. Although only a minority of Jews were moneylenders, the Lateran decisions strengthening the Christian prohibition of usury offered them more openings for this activity than ever before.

St Thomas Aquinas did not favour harsh treatment of Jews, but he wrote in a letter to the Duchess of Brabant in 1270 that 'the guilt of the Jews caused them to be condemned to perpetual slavery'.[36] Rulers should protect their Jews, but the latter owed everything to their sovereign. Thus, as slavery was being eclipsed in much of Europe, a notion of enslavement still survived as a part of the social imaginary. Robert Grosseteste, the influential thirteenth-century Bishop of Lincoln who was to be esteemed by Wyclif and later Protestant divines as an upholder of the distinctive virtues of the English Church, urged a radicalization of the notion of Jewish enslavement, aimed at denying them also all profit from usury – even if the state was to suffer thereby. Southern summarizes a letter written by Grosseteste to the Countess of Winchester in 1231 in the following passage:

> God condemned Jews to be wanderers and the slaves of all nations, and this state of affairs would last until the end of history when their redemption would come. Meanwhile the rulers of the world had the duty to keep them captive – not killing them but allowing them to live by the sweat of their brow. They were like the descendants of Cain, cursed by God, given over to slavery.... Rulers who receive any benefit from the usuries of Jews are drinking the blood of victims whom they ought to protect.

He adds: 'In this summary I have softened rather than exaggerated the virulence of Grosseteste's words.'[37] Grosseteste's more extreme approach reflected a strong impulse to doctrinal purity, and drew on popular hostility to moneylenders. Repeated royal tallage of the Jewish community forced up the rates of interest charged by Jewish moneylenders and pawnbrokers, and stimulated debtors' desire to be rid of them. The advice tendered by Grosseteste led to the expulsion of the Jews from various towns. In 1290 England became the first European kingdom to expel the Jews; by this time overtaxation had so reduced the financial resources of the Jewish community in England that the royal exchequer was no longer receiving significant sums from it.[38]

The persecuting impulse could be stimulated by feudal expansion as well as internal tensions, since expansion posed new problems for the maintenance of identity. The Anglo-Norman and English conquerors of Ireland argued that the Irish were a species of wild people because of their pastoralism, distinctive kinship practices and supposed religious irregularities or laxities. The twelfth-century historian Gerald de Barri observed:

> The Irish are a rude people, subsisting on the produce of their cattle only – a people that has not yet departed from the primitive habits of pastoral life. In the common course of things, progress is made from the forest to the field, from the field to the town, and to the social condition of citizens; but this nation, holding agricultural labour in contempt, and little coveting the wealth of towns, as well as being exceedingly averse to civil institutions – lead the same life their fathers did in the woods and open pastures, neither willing to abandon old habits or learn anything new.[39]

Of course the 'new' habits indicated here were the essential basis for construction of a feudal order. In 1155 Henry II of England persuaded Pope Adrian IV to issue the Bull Laudabiliter, encouraging him to go to Ireland 'to enlarge the boundaries of the Church, to reveal the truth of the Christian faith to the unlearned and savage peoples, and to root out from the Lord's field the vices that have grown in it'.[40]

In the initial phases of feudal conquest and colonization there was commonly a rigorous 'judicial dualism' such that colonists, and those who had accepted assimilation, would be tried by different courts according to different laws from those which applied to the newly conquered population. In Ireland this was known as 'exception of Irishry', and meant that there would be a different, lighter penalty for killing an Irishman than for killing an Englishman – in one such case the penalty, a fine of 70 shillings, was payable to the lord of the victim. The Irish could be described as 'not being of free blood', though their condition was meant to be that of a degraded serf, not a true slave. Such procedures would be defended as rights and privileges by the colonizers and the assimilated and, if comprehensively enforced, served as an incentive to assimilation. But the practices of legal dualism could also be temporarily relaxed as another method of securing the social and political integration of a still heterogeneous population. There were conjunctures when blatantly discriminatory practices could come to seem inconvenient to the royal power as it sought to consolidate or extend its authority. Some of the colonizers or conquerors could also wish to reach a compromise with the conquered. In Ireland some of the Anglo-Norman lords themselves adjusted to Irish customs, and were to become the target of later interventions by English monarchs. Sometimes judicial dualism itself constituted a concession to conquered populations who, on certain limited matters, were permitted to be tried according to their own laws and customs.

Over time the consolidation and extension of the social order required a more even treatment of subjects. In Spain the Laws of Santa Maria de Cortes in 1182 declared that 'nobles, knights and Jews and Muslims who come to settle shall be liable to the same fines and the same judicial regime as the other settlers'. The Darocca municipality of Aragon likewise promised that 'Christians, Jews and Muslims shall have one and the same law regarding blows and accusations'.[41] These were concessions offered to consolidate a new power, and they could be withdrawn once it was secure. And anyway the non-Christian populations would normally be required to pay a special tribute – labour for the Muslims, cash for the Jews.

Following widespread anti-Jewish riots in Castile and Aragon in 1381, there was great pressure on Jews to convert to Christianity. In fifteenth- and sixteenth-century Spain there was to be a growing wave of intolerant homogenization afflicting the status not only of Jews or Muslims but also of those who converted to Christianity or were the descendants of converts. Those who openly professed the Jewish religion were eventually expelled in 1492. The ethnically Jewish *conversos* became the target of persecution in the fifteenth century, on the usually spurious grounds that they were continuing the clandestine practice of their former religion. The *converso* success in gaining royal and professional appointments aroused the envy and hostility of Old Christians. In Toledo in 1449 the city council promulgated laws stipulating that *limpieza de sangre* was a precondition for office-holders. The category 'tainted blood' undoubtedly had a mainly racial and national content, though bastards of Christian Spanish descent were also barred from holding office. The pressure to establish the principle of *limpieza de sangre* came mainly from plebeian Spaniards who employed it against what they saw as an aristocratic/*converso* alliance.

From 1480 the problem of the *conversos* was dealt with by the Holy Office or Inquisition. Out of a *converso* population of around 100,000, some 2,000 were handed to the secular arm to be burnt at the stake; others suffered imprisonment and fines; and large numbers were driven into exile; on the other hand, the persecution of the remaining descendants of *conversos* abated after the 1520s. The Inquisition still vetted aspirants to preferment, but did not organize regular *autos-da-fé*.

The racial-religious stigmatization of New Christians led to terrible results, but not to enslavement. It was designed to exclude them from advantageous employments; so far as the authorities were concerned, it permitted special fiscal exactions. While a very few might end up as convicts (or exceptionally as slaves), it would have been unseemly to subject most New Christians, many of whom had the manners of gentlemen [*hidalgos*], to menial employment. Jews and New Christians were eventually expelled, killed – or absorbed without trace. The principle of *limpieza de sangre* as a condition for obtaining royal or clerical-professional appointment was also subsequently used to exclude Moriscos and those of Native American or African descent. While the royal authority simply sought to exploit racial jealousy, it was pressed to the limit by insecure Hispanic clerics, avid for professional office and inspired by an ethnically warped religious integralism.[42]

Slavery in Iberia's Christian Kingdoms

Spain and Portugal, the two powers responsible for the initial European discovery, conquest and settlement of the Americas, were, of course, heirs to Christian kingdoms which were prime exponents of the territorial aggrandizement of Western Christendom. Enslavement, albeit of fluctuating importance, remained part of the institutional repertoire of the Iberian powers. The Roman, Byzantine and Visigothic practice of slavery influenced the legal precepts of Christian Iberia, but so did the centuries of front-line confrontation with Islam. Following that moment in the eleventh century when – according to Bonnassie – slavery was extinct in Northern Spain, it reappeared in the interstices of the Christian kingdoms as they undertook the Reconquest and participated in the revived Levantine trade of the fourteenth and fifteenth centuries. As the free populations were mobilized for conquest and colonization, they found inspiration in the teachings of St Isidore of Seville,[43] but now considered it natural to abstain from enslaving fellow Christians. In the Reconquest itself slavery played a role, as an occasional instrument of Christian power and means of forced accultura-tion. Of course the Christian kingdoms of Spain in the thirteenth and fourteenth centuries were by no means single-mindedly bent upon Recon-quest. They pursued quarrels with one another, engaged in pacific exchanges with the Muslims, and participated in the growth of Mediterra-nean trade. These latter activities were as much responsible for the presence of some slaves in Christian Spain as the crusade against Islam, since the numbers of permanent slaves acquired by purchase from Levantine mer-chants could have been as great as those seized in slave-raiding *razzias* carried out in the Muslim areas. Those seized in a *razzia* were usually offered back to their family or community through the practice of *rescate*, the ransoming of prisoners for cash, which seems often to have been more advantageous than slaveholding or slave trading. Only captives who were already slaves would be likely to be kept in that condition. Slaves did not constitute the fundamental labouring population in any part of Spain. They were used in domestic and artisanal roles, or for particularly unpleasant and hard labour.[44]

The religious justification for holding some Muslim slaves was that slavery would encourage conversion as well as ensure a proper subordination of the infidel. The effective ban on Christians enslaving one another was calculated to raise morale. The 'Carolingian' ideal of the Christian community had suffered setbacks, like the Empire itself, and had only patchy consequences; Charlemagne's canonization in the twelfth century marked a revival. There were Papal Bulls denouncing the lack of religious scruple in the slave trafficking of the Venetians. In 1206 Innocent III expressed concern that masters in Spain were becoming alarmed at the prospect of conversion among their slaves: 'When a public baptismal ceremony is celebrated in your Church, and many Saracens gather for it eagerly seeking baptism, their owners, whether Jews or even Christians, fearing to lose a profit, presume to forbid it.'[45]

The new doctrine did not, as we have pointed out, argue that a slave would became free upon conversion or at any definite future date; nevertheless, it did formally increase the slave's rights. In the Peninsula as elsewhere there were socioeconomic developments which, albeit unevenly, diminished the significance of slavery and furnished a more favourable context for observance of some restraint in slaveholding. Likewise, respect for a Christian monarch would prevent enslavement of his subjects. But it is likely that such factors – to be considered in more detail below – were still assisted by Latin Christendom's mixed experience of taking the offensive against Islam. The vicissitudes of both the Crusades and the Iberian *Reconquista* had been calculated to bring home to Latin Christians the need for greater religious solidarity. The Crusader kingdom of *Outre Mer* came to grief in part because of the Crusaders' harshness towards the local Christians. The Christian kingdoms of Spain gradually evolved a new socioreligious ethic, influenced by that prevailing among their Muslim neighbours. For one Christian to hold another as a slave became less common and enslavement of fellow believers was excluded.

The celebrated codification of Alfonso the Wise in the thirteenth century, the *Siete Partidas*, can be seen as a transitional document, moving towards a milder slave doctrine than St Isidore had allowed. Where the *Partidas* did allow Christians to be slaves, it sought to alleviate the harshness of their condition and protect their ability to lead Christian lives. The code permitted individuals, municipal corporations and religious bodies to own slaves and envisaged several routes to manumission, providing that the slaves gave good service and displayed religious conformity. Those who were rightly enslaved comprised (1) those captured in war who were enemies of the faith; (2) children of a slave mother; (3) those who had voluntarily sold themselves into slavery. Two further categories were added to this basic list: children of priests, who were to become slaves of the religious institution to which their father belonged; and bad Christians who sold war matériel to the Moors. Masters were forbidden to treat slaves cruelly, to starve them or to interfere sexually with their wives or daughters; a master breaching these rules could be brought before a court (by whom is not stated), and if the offence was proved, then the slaves would be sold to another master. A virgin who was proved to have been raped by her master or hired out as a prostitute would be manumitted by the court.

No infidel could hold a Christian slave, and any slaveholder indicted as a counterfeiter would lose his slaves. Slaves who were Christians could marry one another, with their master's permission, and he could not withhold this unless he could prove that his interests were damaged thereby. Masters could let their slaves ply a trade, turning over a part of their earnings and eventually buying their freedom. While lack of religious conformity enhanced vulnerability to enslavement, race was not mentioned. Notwithstanding the attempts to restrain masters, it was still baldly stated in the *Partidas* that slavery was 'the basest and most wretched condition into which anyone could fall because man, who is the most free and noble of all God's creatures, becomes thereby in the power of another, who can do with him what he wishes as with any property, whether living or dead'. A slave's duty to his master had precedence over his duty to his wife. The slave's ability to invoke the protection of the *Partidas* would be very limited on a rural estate, slightly greater in towns, if the slave had free relations or protectors. The stipulations of the *Partidas* are described clearly as laws, yet many of them were little more than exhortations – for example, it is laid down that kings should take great care of their people's welfare, be faithful to their wives, and rigorously abstain from bad language.[46]

The *Siete Partidas* were the product of a society where slavery was now mainly domestic and temporary in character, and where the slaves were usually drawn from some religious outgroup. Yet they did uphold the lawfulness of slavery, concede wide powers to the master and, under some conditions, permit the holding of fellow Christians as slaves. In areas conquered from the Muslims, those who continued to offer armed resistance were indeed to be liable to enslavement. The secular leaders usually negotiated terms of capitulation, so that the incorporation of the Muslim *ta'ifas*, or small kingdoms, involved promises of good treatment to the mass of Moorish subjects. While most became a subject caste, or left for Muslim areas, few remained as slaves for long. The Muslim cultivators in the countryside were often *exaricos* or sharecroppers: sometimes they owed tribute to a new lord; their rights contracted and attempts at their forcible conversion were subsequently made. The essential formula of feudal colonization was to combine the repopulation of conquered land – that is, its settlement by free Christians offered land on attractive terms – with the forced assimilation of subject peoples, who could retain some reduced access to land or employment only by conversion. Cultural discrimination and coercion aimed to prevent the Christian immigrants from going native, and to promote eventual assimilation. Raids on the Muslim areas continued to yield a harvest of captives, who were put to menial labour pending payment of a ransom or a swap for Christian prisoners. The redemption of captives was organized by *alfaqueques* who specialized in this work. In cases where a prisoner raid violated an agreed truce, the royal authorities might order release without payment.[47]

The trading empire of the Catalans and Aragonese in the thirteenth and fourteenth centuries brought them into contact with the Levantine commerce in slaves and sugar. There were reported to be 2,800 slaves in the countryside in Majorca in 1328, while by 1400 the slave population of Catalonia was estimated at 4,375. The Christian kingdoms exported some slaves to Granada, and imported cotton, sugar, indigo and wood in return. In Granada, as in Muslim Spain more generally, slaves were found among administrators and soldiers as well as servants and craftsmen. The first African slaves in Spain were probably sold by North African merchants to the Muslim *ta'ifas*. In the course of the Reconquest some were seized by the Christian forces. An elite corps of 3,000 African slave soldiers put up a stiff resistance to forces personally commanded by King Ferdinand at the Siege of Malaga in 1487; following rendition of the city, a hundred of them were sent as a gift to the Pope. Other Africans and last-ditch defenders were distributed as slaves to those who had conducted the siege, or sold to defray expenses. However, the surrounding Muslim towns and villages swore allegiance as Mudéjars, Muslim subjects of the Catholic monarchs, in the hope of conserving their property and status. For the time being this was accepted. The Capitulations at Granada in 1492 stipulated that captive slaves in Moorish hands who managed to escape to the territory covered by the Christian rulers would be free – but specifically excluded from this clause Canary Islanders or black slaves from 'the [Atlantic] islands'. Following resistance or rebellion, those alleged to be involved would be killed, or could be enslaved, but the remaining Muslims were pressured either to leave or to convert to Christianity. The aim of the Catholic monarchs was to disperse the Muslims, not to conserve them as an enslaved and hostile mass.[48]

From the 1440s onwards Portuguese voyages down the coast of Africa led to the arrival of a stream of African captives, sold as slaves in the Peninsula. By 1500 about a tenth of the population of Lisbon and Seville were African slaves. They were owned in ones, twos and threes, generally working as servants, craftworkers or menials. They occupied the social roles which for some time had been filled elsewhere in Europe by the so-called 'esclavos' or 'escravos'. Thus by the sixteenth century Castile's slave population was swelled by the purchase of African and Berber captives from the Portuguese; like those purchased or captured in North Africa, they mainly became urban servants. A study of slave inventories in Malaga in the 1570s reveals a wide ethno-religious gamut, including 'berberisco negro cristiano', 'berberisco moro', 'negro de la nacion de moros', 'berberisco mulatta', 'negro de nacion portuguesa', 'cristiana de casta de moros', 'negro de guinea', 'negro de la India de Portugal'. Out of a total of 493 slaves, 185 were described as Moros and 78 as Christians; one was described as a Jew and one as a Turk. However, a 'black of the Portuguese nation' meant a black owned by a Portuguese, or speaking Portuguese, or born in Portugal.[49]

In sixteenth-century Spain there was still a large population of Christian Moriscos, most of them peasants in Valencia and Granada subject to harsh exploitation, despite their supposed conversion. The Morisco New Christians rose in revolt on a number of occasions, and were eventually expelled in 1608–12. This final episode in the eradication of religious and racial difference affirmed Spain's national identity and was accompanied by a new spirit of civic egalitarianism, with a softening of the fierce social distinctions which had characterized feudal Iberia. Slavery was an institution which allowed for subordinate or correctional inclusion, not the total exclusion or suppression that was the eventual fate of the Jews and Moors. Those Moors who were enslaved were generally not expelled, since they were regarded as part of their owner's household. The expulsion of the Moriscos was undertaken at a time when the royal authorities wished to compensate for the humiliation involved in agreeing a truce with the Dutch rebels. The expelled Moriscos themselves were generally not welcome in North Africa, and many were killed.[50]

The expulsion of the Moriscos, following that of the *conversos* and the Jews, highlighted in a striking and terrible fashion ethno-cultural assumptions that appear to have been indissolubly wedded to the religious faith of the epoch. The proceedings against both *conversos* and Moriscos were accompanied by repeated and obsessive attempts on the part of the religious and secular authorities to prove that the accused were guilty of heresy and deception. It need not, of course, be doubted that pressurized or forcible conversions were often insincere. On the other hand, before about 1480, it does seem that many *conversos*, or their children, genuinely practised as Christians; this was also the case for at least some Moriscos, or their children, in the early decades of the sixteenth century. But once the course was set for persecution and expulsion, the authorities' approach was not to build on and encourage signs of conversion but, rather, to seize on any and every real or supposed proof of heresy and apostasy. If a *converso* or Morisco refused to eat pork, this was regarded as *prima facie* evidence that they were not a real Christian. Failure to speak Castilian was itself taken as a sign of religious deviancy or treachery. If a *converso* or Morisco woman wore coloured clothes, this again would be suspect. Family get-togethers coinciding with Jewish or Muslim festivals, or even regular washing, were also regarded with deep suspicion. To satisfy their religious or secular critics the *conversos* and Moriscos were required, in effect, to adopt the culture as well as the religion of the Christian Spaniards – and sometimes even that would not be enough.[51]

The expulsion of the Moriscos seems to exemplify the sorts of racial exclusion which produced slavery in the Americas. But in that case, why were the Moriscos not enslaved and sent to the New World? At the very time of the expulsions, Spanish Americans were buying tens of thousands of captive Africans. One reason why Moriscos were not sold in the Americas was that they were deemed a security threat; the expulsion itself was partly motivated by the argument that 'the Moorish nation of Valencia' had conspired with the King's enemies, and was likely to assist Muslim or Protestant invaders. Moriscos had long been excluded from the New World on the grounds that they might assist enemies of the Crown. This, however, was not necessarily a decisive consideration, since African slaves had not only often rebelled but had also collaborated with English marauders in the Isthmus. Perhaps the possibility of enslaving the Moriscos and selling them, if necessary to Muslim purchasers, was also unacceptable to the Spanish royal authorities, on the grounds that it would have been dishonourable. Muslims would have purchased the Moriscos only if they were thoroughly convinced that they were infidels; on the whole, Muslims did regard the Moriscos as renegades, but the Spanish authorities were the last who could afford to acknowledge this. The Spanish did not themselves directly undertake the enslavement of Africans, as they would have to have done in the case of the Moriscos. Instead they purchased them from Portuguese traders, who in turn purchased them from traders or chiefs on the coast of Africa. These commercial processes had a distancing effect – one which was even, as we will see below, reflected in dominant theological discourse.

Slavery and the Slavs

The term 'slave' in all West European languages refers simply to Slavs, who were seen as congenitally heretic or pagan. Between the tenth and sixteenth centuries the Slav lands furnished the Vikings and the Italian traders with their main source of slaves. The Eastern Adriatic and the Black Sea were major sources of supply. Eventually the Eastern Adriatic became Europe's main 'slave coast'. Evans has explained this in terms of a 'crisis slavery', that 'brutal means whereby a region, torn by violence and reduced to misery, converts surplus population into a resource'.[52] The feuding peoples of the Caucasus or Bosnia, where Latin Catholics were pitted against Bogomil heretics or those who followed the Greek liturgy, furnished a steady supply of supposedly heretical captives. On one occasion a Hungarian girl was able to bring a case against enslavement in an Italian court on the grounds that she was a Latin Christian; the court ruled that she was not a full slave, but owed to her purchaser the price he had paid to 'ransom' her from her captors, and must serve him until the obligation had been fully discharged.[53] This convenient formula, which applied primarily to Latin Christians who lacked a protector, was sometimes also used to 'redeem' many held captive by the Moors in the Peninsula, and reduce them to a new servitude.

The expansion and prosperity of medieval Europe helped to generate some marginal slavery in the Mediterranean world, in contrast to the North West. Slaves still nowhere constituted the fundamental labour force, and were drawn mainly from Eastern Europe and the Levant. The rise of commerce and of medieval towns stimulated the trade in slaves as house servants: Venice and Ragusa were entrepôts for slave servants purchased by the wealthy merchants and landowners of North Italy. Urban artisans occasionally acquired a slave helper, though some municipalities banned this. The slave trade from the Caucasus and Black Sea regions was greatly diminished by the rise of Ottoman power; the Ottomans had their own need for slaves from these regions as recruits to the corps of Janissaries. But there was still some supply of slaves from Europe's 'slave coast' on the Adriatic. Mediterranean pirates would also sell slaves of diverse origins. Occasionally a 'Turkish' slave might be found in Italy or one of the Italian colonies, but in general captured Turks would be ransomed or exchanged. The religion of such captives might not be respected, but their sovereign or their wealth would be.[54]

If slavery had largely disappeared from Western and Northern Europe, the same could not be said of Muscovy, where slaves comprised as much as a tenth of the population in the late Middle Ages and early modern period. In Russia slaves were not often used for large-scale agricultural work but, rather, engaged as menial domestic servants, general labourers, or even, in a few cases, as stewards, treasurers or bailiffs. Some soldiers were technically slaves.[55] The precarious conditions prevailing in the steppes could make the slave condition attractive, with individuals selling themselves, or being sold by their parents, into slavery.

The most remarkable feature of Russian slavery is that both slaveowners and enslaved were of the same ethnicity – though it appears that the sense of a common ethnicity was weak, with aristocrats cultivating the myth that they were really Italian, French or German. A weak ethnic identity was combined with a strong religious identity, so that individuals defined themselves as *pravoslavnye*, or Orthodox, rather than as Russians – a description that would anyway have been inaccurate for many.[56] The Orthodox Church supported slavery, owned slaves and upheld Justinian's slave code. Its Christianity was indeed Orthodox, in the sense that it remained somewhat closer in its practices to those prevailing under the Christian empire.

The Eclipse of Serfdom and the Rise of Agrarian Capitalism

The last remnants of slavery in England did not survive the impact of the Black Death, the Peasants' Revolt and the Wars of the Roses. These events also set the scene for a weakening of other forms of servitude, combined with a strengthening of the role of the market and the effective claims of the state.

Robert Brenner has pointed out that the severe depopulation in the wake of the Black Death had quite different results in Eastern and Western Europe, depending on the outcome of peasant resistance and revolt in the two areas.[57] East of the Elbe peasant resistance was completely crushed, and the so-called 'second serfdom' was imposed. In many parts of Europe West of the Elbe landlords, facing the same labour shortage as those in the East, attempted to impose a return to the harsher forms of servitude, but failed. While peasant revolts were put down, these should be seen as only the most visible and dramatic expressions of peasant aspirations which also found outlet in a myriad of local tests of strength, and in the varying ability of serfs to escape beyond the control of their lord.

The extent and forms of peasant success in checking the serflord offensive were different in France and in England. In France the peasants not only won their freedom, but significant numbers acquired control of land. An independent landholding peasantry established itself, allowing for the emergence of some rich *laboreurs*, and a mass of smallholders, side by side with the seigneurial aristocracy: the figure of Gargantua suggests the fantasies and frustrations unleashed by this half liberation. In England, matters were quite different. The peasants were able to assert their freedom, but the lords retained control of the greater part of the land. The English serflords became landlords, engaging tenant farmers to work their estates with the aid of free wage labour. This new social formula led to a market not only in consumption goods but in means of production. Competition between different producers encouraged them to look for improved methods of cultivation, either economizing on labour, which was now an identifiable cost, or raising yields. The result was the emergence of a precocious agrarian capitalism which, by the fifteenth and sixteenth centuries, raised rent rolls and widened the internal market. There were increasingly unimportant residues of villeinage, which was never suppressed as a legal form.

Looking back on this waning of villeinage and slavery, the Tudor statesman Thomas Smith wrote in 1565:

Neither of the one sort nor of the other do we have any number of in England. And of the first I never knewe any in the realme in my time; of the second so fewe there be, that it is almost not worth the speaking. But our law doth acknowledge them in both these sorts ... I think in France and England the chaunge of religion to a more humane and equall sort ... caused this old kinde of servitude and slaverie to be brought into that moderation ... and little by little extinguished it finding more civil and gentle means and more equall to have done that which in times of gentility (heathenesse) [i.e.pagan Antiquity] servitude or bondage did.[58]

Thus the eclipse of slavery by more moderate religious precepts had been accompanied, in Smith's view, by new and more effective social arrangements for inducing labourers to work – the latter, presumably, referring to enclosures, frequently far from 'civil and gentle', but leading to a new regime of exclusive private property and hence to conditions in which free landless labourers were obliged to sell their labour-power in order to feed themselves and their families.

In Ireland the same social arrangements were not to be found, and proved extremely difficult to introduce. English would-be landlords displayed great violence and ferocity in their efforts to dispossess the Irish. The land was in the possession of Gaelic tribes who, under their chiefs, whether Irish or Old English, clung tenaciously to their lands and way of life. Smith himself was to be the architect of a colonization plan in Ulster which aimed to reduce the Irish to servitude, denying them land or rights, the better to 'reform so barbarous a nation'.[59] Smith's project of colonizing the Ards in 1572 ended, like most Tudor attempts to uproot or enslave the Irish, in a bloody fiasco, and the leader of the expedition, Smith's bastard son Thomas, was killed by his own frustrated followers.

As former counsellor to Protector Somerset, Smith had been in a good position to assess the significance of 'slavery' in Tudor England. During his brief period of power, Somerset sought to address the problems of poverty, unemployment and vagrancy in what could be seen as the first attempt to deal with social questions aggravated by the rise of capitalism. Somerset's measures have sometimes been applauded, since they seemed to acknowledge that private charity was not enough, and that the state itself had responsibilities for the poor. However, as part of this novel concept of social legislation, Somerset also introduced the penalty of 'slavery' into his Vagrancy Act of 1547. Vagrants who rejected offers of gainful employment would be sentenced to some years of 'slavery', during which time they would be forced to work, deprived of freedom of movement, and obliged to wear distinctive dress. This measure proved impossible to implement, being opposed not only by those at whom it was directed but also by labourers who did not wish to be undercut by convict labour and magistrates who thought it provocative. There were few takers for the proposed slave labourers. After two years the Act was abandoned.[60]

It is quite possible that the Vagrancy Act had been inspired, in part, by

Thomas More's *Utopia* (1516), where slaves were used for several unpleasant and morally dubious tasks, such as the slaughtering of animals. More refers in his preface to the deplorable condition of England and the need to combat poverty, idleness and discontent. It is as if the very growth of social freedom itself prompted those in authority to thoughts of a corrective discipline. More's supposed informant remarks:

> By the way, the slaves that I've occasionally referred to are not, as you might imagine, non-combatant prisoners-of-war, slaves by birth, or purchases from foreign slave markets. They're either Utopian convicts or, much more often, condemned criminals from other countries, who are acquired in large numbers, sometimes for a small payment, but usually for nothing. Both types of slave are kept hard at work in chain gangs, though Utopians are treated worse than foreigners. The idea is that it's all the more deplorable if a person who has had the advantage of a first rate education and a thoroughly moral education still insists on becoming a criminal – so the punishment should be all the more severe. Another type of slave is the working class foreigner who, rather than live in wretched poverty at home, volunteers for slavery in Utopia. Such people are treated with respect, and with almost as much kindness as Utopian citizens, except that they're made to work harder, because they're used to it.[61]

The offences carrying the penalty of servitude included adultery, failure to perform labour, or unauthorized travel. In the preliminary discussion of non-Utopian societies, a species of slavery is also prescribed as the punishment for theft; such slaves are to wear the same-colour clothing, and to be available for hire from the public authorities. The severity of the servitude recommended in *Utopia* was tempered both by the fact that it was milder than the death penalty of Tudor legislation and because it was not necessarily permanent – good behaviour could lead to emancipation:

> The normal penalty for any major crime is slavery. They say it's just as unpleasant for the criminals as capital punishment, and more useful to society. . . . But the prospects of those who accept the situation aren't absolutely hopeless. If after being tamed by years of hardship, they show signs of feeling really sorry, not merely for themselves, but for what they've done, their sentence is either reduced or cancelled altogether, sometimes at the discretion of the Mayor and sometimes by general plebiscite.[62]

More's utilitarian conception of servitude is complemented by the justification offered for the colonial expansion of the Utopians:

> If the whole island becomes overpopulated, they tell off a certain number of people from each town to go off and start a colony at the nearest point on the mainland where there's a large area that hasn't been cultivated by the local inhabitants. Such colonies are governed by the Utopians, but the natives are allowed to join in if they want to. When this happens, natives and colonists soon combine to form a single community with a single way of life, to the great advantage of both parties – for, under Utopian management, land which used to be thought incapable of producing anything for one lot of people produces

plenty for two. If the natives won't do what they're told, they're expelled from the area marked out for annexation. If they try to resist the Utopians declare war – for they consider war perfectly justifiable, when one country denies another its natural right to derive nourishment from any soil which the original owners are not using themselves, but are simply holding on to as a piece of worthless property.[63]

The supposed justification of English colonization in the Americas was thus clearly anticipated, with those who cause the soil to be worked or planted having precedence. No doubt More's 'utopia' reflected claims already made for the attempted Tudor colonization of Ireland, which aimed to replace transhumance with permanent cultivation. So far as the Americas are concerned, More's ideas, and arguments similar to them, were to shape and justify the colonizing project.[64] The first English translation of his Latin text appeared in 1551, and went through many editions. More challenges some features of Tudor social relations while endorsing others, displaying an experimental approach to social arrangements in which servitude or colonialism would be perfectly justifiable if they promoted the more intensive use of natural and human resources.

Perhaps aware of the huge problems English power confronted there, More did not imagine his Utopia in Ireland but precisely 'nowhere', in a just-discovered New World. The attempts of the Tudor gentry to establish plantations in Ireland failed to achieve the hoped-for cultural and economic results. Gaelic culture, Irish religious deviancy, the Brehon legal system, the tribal way of life, and the Irish or Old English aristocracy fought a long rearguard action. English gentlemen adventurers visited a pitiless repression upon the recalcitrant Irish, but failed to make their plantations solidly productive or profitable. Because of these failures the English Crown, for a while, compromised with Catholic Irish aristocrats and clan leaders who still owned most of the land. The only half-successful plantation in Ireland – that in Ulster – was sustained by the Scots, and even there Catholic Irish tenants yielded better rents than the settlers.

Men like Thomas Smith had hoped that England could repeat in Ireland the exploits of Spain's *conquistadores*, but the results were very different. There was no swift conquest, there was no gold or silver, and Irish armed resistance, coalescing around the idea of a Catholic King of Ireland, continued to flare until 1690–91. Many of the English fortune-hunting gentry who sought to subjugate Ireland later embarked on privateering expeditions to the Caribbean and Spanish Main. But they did not export to the New World a successful model of colonial plantation – partly because there was no such model, and partly because the privateers lacked the stamina and economic sinew for the setting up of successful colonies.

The English experience in Ireland certainly influenced those who were to be successful in colonizing the Americas, and establishing slave plantations, but as much by negative as by positive example. The English state was to assert itself in the New World in Protestant and national terms, just as it

did in Ireland, and its colonists also had recourse to terror and extermination; in the New World they were largely successful in displacing the
natives, and then introduced captives from another continent. In both cases
race and religion were used as principles of exclusion, but within quite
different structures of oppression. The eventual English colonial regime in
Ireland was made possible by victories in 1649–53 and 1690–91, by which
time Barbados and Virginia were already flourishing. English rule was to
embody the principle of religious and political exclusion (the 'Protestant
ascendancy') and economic dispossession, with the mass of the Irish
remaining or becoming propertyless peasants or labourers. In the plantation
colonies the emphasis was increasingly to be placed on race and slavery, a
more intimate, physical and absolute species of bondage, as we will see.
(For a time Irish prisoners were deported to the plantations, but the
experiment was not pursued because of its risks, in circumstances to be
discussed in Chapter VI.) The traits which led to the exclusion and
exploitation of the Irish were their religion and their national identity –
qualities which they had accepted for themselves, and were embodied in
deeply rooted collective institutions, notably the Church. The captive
Africans were held as Negroes and slaves – identities which they often did
not accept and which, to begin with, offered few collective resources. Yet,
different as they were in these and other ways, the Protestant ascendancy
and black slavery were both to be yoked to a capitalist accumulation
process. While the slave plantations would never have come into existence
unless they had been profitable, the English regime in Ireland was to be
gradually adapted until it, too, finally became a paying proposition.[65]

Both Thomas More and Protector Somerset envisaged slavery as a correctional device wielded by the state rather than a resource commanded by the
subject, and in this their conception was to be in contrast to the plantation
slavery that was to appear in the Atlantic islands and the New World. The
withering away of slavery in Western Europe reflected political as well as
socioeconomic developments. Medieval towns had long been wont to boast
that serfs or slaves could not breathe their 'free air'; simply to live for a
year and a day in a town such as Toulouse, after 1226, conferred freedom.
Hilton writes:

> When the Commune of Bologna emancipated the serfs of its contado in 1256,
> the book called Paradisus, in which the names of masters and serfs were entered,
> had a preamble that serfdom was due to the fall of man, freedom being man's
> natural condition, and Bologna the home of freedom.[66]

City-states and nascent kingdoms found that such declarations attracted
the support of the common people – who, even if they were free themselves,
preferred to live in a polity with other free people, not with masters and
slaves. Sovereigns themselves could easily find irksome the absolute power

over his chattel claimed by the slaveholder; there was the suspicion that the slave magnate would make a poor subject.

The sixteenth century witnessed the consolidation of a process of state formation in England, Spain, France and the Netherlands which appealed to concepts of nationhood and the liberty of the subject. Monarchs had not infrequently competed with municipalities and parliaments to present themselves as champions of their subjects' true rights. The Valois and Bourbons in France, the British Tudors, the Spanish Habsburgs, and the House of Orange in the Low Countries sought, in different ways, to associate themselves with national values and declare themselves the champions of true liberty. In conjunction with the withering away of servitude, and in a context of sharp international rivalry, appeals to national sentiment naturally chimed in with celebration of a notion of civil liberty which, while still distant from the concepts of modern liberalism, held that the national soil should not be sullied with slavery. The new type of state, whether absolutist or bourgeois, found slaveholder claims in Europe derogatory to its own power.

Jean Bodin, advocate of an absolute sovereignty, attacked slaveholding in *Les Six Livres de la République* in the 1570s. The decision of an English court in 1567 to prevent the entry of a Russian slave, the declaration of the Parlement of Guyenne in 1571 that France, 'the mother of liberty', could not tolerate slavery, and the decision of Middelburg to free a boatload of Africans in 1597, all reflected versions of this new 'free air' doctrine.[67] There were signs of a popular anti-slavery reflex; Bodin, whose conclusions were so much at variance with those of other learned men, acknowledged as much: 'Lawyers, who measure the law not by the discourses and decrees of philosophers, but according to the common sense and capacity of the people, hold servitude to be directly contrary to nature.'[68] Bodin also expressed a certain 'common sense' of 'slave-free' areas of Western Europe that they should remain that way:

> ... seeing it is proved by the example of so many worlds of years, so many inconveniences of rebellions, servile warres, conspiracies eversions and chaunges to have happened to Commonweales by slaves; so many murders, cruelties and detestable villanies to have been committed upon persons of slaves by their lords and masters: who can doubt to affirm it to be a thing most pernicious and dangerous to have them brought into a commonweale; or having cast them off to receive them again?[69]

Popular anti-slavery did not necessarily involve a rejection of ethnic conceit or xenophobia, as such sentiments did not themselves recommend the introduction of enslaved aliens. But independent citizens or subjects, like monarchs, looked with distrust and foreboding on the slaveholder. Even in Spain, where domestic slavery remained legal, the introduction of new

African slaves had virtually ceased by the beginning of the seventeenth century, discouraged both by royal regulations and by more attractive slave prices in the Americas. Of course even in England, France and the Netherlands the outlawing of the slave condition was an *ad hoc* affair, unsupported by clear general legislation; and it was to have no force outside the metropolis, where nationals of these states were soon vying to participate in the Atlantic slave trade. Nevertheless, it is significant that beyond a scattering of servants in Spain and Portugal, there were very few true slaves left in Western Europe by the end of the sixteenth century.

Yet in the realm of philosophy, the Renaissance did little to weaken ideas supportive of the legitimacy of slavery in some universal, non-ethnocentric, sense. The rediscovery of classical authorities did nothing to undermine belief in the lawfulness of slavery. Indeed, by diffusing a greater awareness of the cultural achievement of Antiquity and contributing to a sense that Christendom was its legitimate heir, the Renaissance could lead to a sense of shared cultural superiority which dovetailed with the classical Aristotelian doctrine that barbarians were natural slaves. There was also a belief that any system of order and subordination had a value of its own, even if this was heathen, since it would furnish a better basis on which to establish the Christian message. Likewise, the absence of anything resembling Christian civilization meant that it would be appropriate for a Christian power to introduce it, if possible. So far as slavery was concerned, there was a fork here: if the non-Christian order was thought comparable in some way to classical Antiquity, as some were to claim was the case with the Aztec and Inca civilizations, then it would be legitimate to adopt the forms of servitude it had produced; on the other hand, those peoples thought to be lacking civilized institutions could legitimately be colonized, and if they resisted they could be punished with enslavement.[70]

When the Castilians and Portuguese sought to conquer and colonize the Canary Islands in the fifteenth century, they claimed that this was to promote Christianity, and sought Papal blessing for the enterprise. King Duarte of Portugal observed in 1436 that the inhabitants needed governance: 'The nearly wild men who inhabit the forests are not united by a common religion, nor are they bound by the chains of law, they are lacking social intercourse, living in the country like animals.'[71] The Papacy accepted that colonial expansion was justified by reference to a civilizing and Christianizing mission, but believed that the slave-hunting of rival Iberian colonizers would damage the work of conversion. The Castilians gained the upper hand, and in 1579 Portugal and Castile agreed that the islands should belong to the latter as part of a more general settlement. Now it was the turn of the Castilian royal authorities to mitigate the ferocity of their colonists. The latter claimed that native conversions were a sham, and that only the rigorous tutelage of slavery could bring home to the colonized the value of a settled life, hard work, Christian marriage, fidelity and the renunciation of superstition. There was a series of revolts by the natives which were suppressed with much bloodshed, with rebels being shipped as slaves to the Peninsula.

Eventually, however, the cycle of colonization was completed. The Canarians had been decimated, by unfamiliar diseases as well as slave-raiding, repression and overwork. But those who collaborated with the colonial project were eventually absorbed, with women being taken in marriage by Castilians.[72] The representations of the Church probably helped to protect some converts from the greed of the colonists; if the Papacy had been able somewhat to arbitrate the colonial process, this was because of the rivalry between the two Iberian powers. Once their respective spheres of colonization were demarcated by the Treaty of Tordesillas in 1494, allotting the Canaries once again to Castile, this leverage was greatly reduced. By the beginning of the sixteenth century the remnants of the indigenous peoples comprised about a quarter of the population; the enslavement of natives of the islands was replaced, for a while, by the introduction of Africans.

If the Canarians had been initially condemned for living 'like animals', without law or proper social intercourse, the African slaves introduced to work the sugar estates were held to be justifiably enslaved for the opposite reason. They were found living in societies organized in states, with their own laws, and participating in commerce. The captive purchased on the African coast was legitimately a slave, some argued, because he or she had been produced as such by the coastal slave trading or slave-raiding complex.

The continued currency of ideas supportive of slavery was to combine the notion that particular traits – seen as flaws of origin or defects of civilization – justified enslavement and the idea that developed chattel slavery was itself a sign of civilization. Richard Tuck has drawn attention to the paradox that the theories of natural rights which emerged in the late medieval period, and enjoyed widespread influence down to the end of the seventeenth century, acknowledged the validity of slavery. Thomas Aquinas had given a certain impulse to rights theory when he launched his critique of the practice of apostolic poverty by the Franciscan order. He pointed out that 'possessions and slavery were not the product of nature, but were made by human reason for the advantage of human life'.[73] The Franciscan claim not to be holding property was considered to be at odds with their recourse to personal consumption. As it happened, the medieval philosopher most sceptical about the validity of slavery was Duns Scotus, a Franciscan.[74] Jean Gerson, chancellor of the University of Paris, developed Aquinas's critique in a direction which led to acceptance of the view that a person was capable of bartering away his natural liberty and, in certain circumstances, might be presumed to have done so. This Gersonian approach was developed and radicalized in the course of the sixteenth century, with results that had a direct bearing on the Atlantic slave trade. As Tuck observes:

For a Gersonian, liberty was property and could therefore be exchanged in the same way and under the same terms as any other property. . . . Once again (and this is a recurrent, perhaps *the* recurrent theme in the history of rights theories) a theory of rights permitted practices which an anti-subjectivist theory prohibited. This theoretical difficulty was important given the murky character of the events in their own countries which led to the Africans being enslaved. The white men generally found them already traded as slaves at the coast, and had merely to be confident that a fairly wide variety of slaveries was in principle permissible in order to be able to trade in them themselves with a clear conscience.[75]

The justifications of slavery to which Tuck refers had a general political logic of recognition of African judicial and commercial processes; they did not rely upon a stigmatization of particular ethnicities or descent groups. In Tuck's view the influence of Gersonian rights theory is clearly present in the writings of Luis de Molina, Hugo Grotius, John Selden and Thomas Hobbes, explaining why they all 'openly endorsed such institutions as slavery'.[76]

The Bible, Slavery and the Nations of Man

The Reformation was no less broadly supportive of the validity of slavery than the Renaissance or Catholic theology. Luther and Calvin both emphasized the necessity of respecting secular subordination and private property. Luther even urged Christian slaves in Turkish hands not to seek to steal themselves away from their masters.[77] Nevertheless seventeenth-century Protestants were sometimes to betray unease at the implications of slavery. While Catholics wished to reassure themselves that captives offered for sale were really slaves, Protestants had most trouble with the relationship between the slave and the community of believers. At the time of the Synod of Dordt in 1618, the last united gathering of the Reformed Churches, there was a discussion of whether slaves born in Reformed households should be baptized and of whether baptism would free them – with the difficulty that if baptism did free the slave, it would discourage slaveowners from allowing it. The Synod took no formal position on this matter, preferring to leave it to be settled by the individual churches. Though there was disagreement on the consequences of baptism, all those who recorded an opinion favoured leaving the discretion on whether to baptize to the head of household: 'Baptism, a public imperative for the Catholic church, became a *household* choice for the Reformed Christian.'[78] Protestantism, associated with the emergence of a more independent civil society, failed to produce a critique of the Atlantic slave trade or of colonial slavery despite the fact that there was, as yet, no significant Protestant stake in either.

That heathens or pagans would benefit from becoming slaves to Christians was an argument with appeal to both Catholics and Protestants. Some of the European adventurers and colonists of the sixteenth and seventeenth centuries were not particularly God-fearing men. But the privateers and settlers still considered themselves, whether Catholic or Protestant, bearers of a new civilized order and representatives of true religion. Notwithstanding religious strife, Christianity still furnished what Michel Certeau has called 'the totalising framework of reference' for early modern Europeans.[79] Even those with no pretension to piety would describe themselves as Christians and non-Europeans as heathens. Both Protestantism and Counter-Reformation Catholicism laid a new stress on individual conscience, to be stimulated by regular Bible reading for Protestants, confession for Catholics, and prayer for both. These spiritual techniques helped to reinforce an identity which anyway they carried around with them, whatever their mundane or profane objective. The encounter with different kinds and conditions of men in foreign climes reminded them of a Christian identity which was implicitly based on European models. Thus those from Spain, Portugal and France thought their languages, because of their link to Latin, to be inherently Christian, whereas other non-biblical tongues were corrupted and twisted. German, Dutch and English Protestants believed their own vernaculars capable of expressing the Gospel message, but did not readily extend similar recognition to other languages, seen as gibberish and gobbledegook, or at any rate lacking in the capacity to express spiritual truth. Any characteristic which seemed unchristian in this special sense rendered a people more vulnerable to colonization or even enslavement, unless, like Turks or Chinese, they had the means to command respect. While it was often urged that heathens might benefit from subjugation, it was not the case that compulsion was ever seen as the only, or even the most desirable, route to conversion; many Protestants argued that baptism should be voluntary and conscious. If the acquisition of heathen slaves was justified on religious grounds then this obliged the slaveholder to furnish the slave with religious instruction. Since Protestants inclined to assert the equal condition of believers within the Church, the slave convert, or even more the slave born into a Christian household, was often thought to be entitled to manumission. Since slaveholders rarely welcomed such conclusions they were motivated to find other justifications.

Both Catholics and Protestants were to find in the Bible and in traditions of biblical interpretation ideas which justified enslavement, ideas which could reassure the slaveholder or slave trader if they were pious – and perhaps even if they were not. The Bible could also be read as furnishing a genealogy for the peoples comprising the whole of humanity, and, or so some authors claimed, hints as to which peoples were destined to slavery.

Genesis dramatically asserts the common descent of humanity from Adam and Eve. But the universalist implications of this belief were undermined when non-European peoples were blamed for having rejected the principles of their forefathers. Genesis contains a vivid story which shows Noah, the primordial 'good man', condemning one of his grandchildren to slavery. Taken together with other passages it seems that

Genesis sanctions not simply slavery in the abstract, as St Paul did in I Corinthians, but the enslavement of particular descent groups.

Genesis 9 furnishes a list of the immediate descendants of Noah's three sons – Shem, Japheth and Ham – concluding: 'These are the families of the sons of Noah, after their generations, in their nations: and by these were the nations divided in the earth after the flood' (Genesis 10: 32, Authorized King James Version). This sketch follows closely upon the incident that led Noah to curse one of Ham's sons to perpetual servitude:

> And the sons of Noah that went forth from the ark, were Shem, Ham, and Japheth: and Ham is the father of Canaan. These are the three sons of Noah: and of them was the whole earth overspread. And Noah began to be an husbandman, and he planted a vineyard. And he drank of the wine, and was drunken; and he was uncovered in his tent. And Ham, the father of Canaan, saw the nakedness of his father, and told his two brethren without. And Shem and Japheth took a garment, and laid it upon both their shoulders, and went backward, and covered the nakedness of their father; and their faces were backward, and they saw not their father's nakedness. And Noah awoke from his wine, and knew what his younger son had done unto him. And he said, Cursed be Canaan; and a servant of servants shall he be unto his brethren. And he said blessed be the Lord God of Shem; and Canaan shall be his servant. God shall enlarge Japheth, and he shall dwell in the tents of Shem; and Canaan shall be his servant. (Genesis 9: 18–27)[80]

Ham had committed an offence against his father's manhood; according to patriarchal logic, Ham is punished by the servile degradation of his issue. The King James version renders Canaan's fate as that of 'a servant of servants', whereas it would have been more accurate to write 'a slave', as did some earlier translations. The resort to euphemism was perhaps prompted by unease at slaveholding in a society which no longer knew slavery; however, the original sense was there to those who might wish to insist upon it. Many early modern Christians thought that this passage justified slavery, and even furnished the basis of a taint of hereditary inferiority. This message was reinforced by Leviticus, where it is said that the people of Israel should practise two different sorts of enslavement according to the origin of the slave, with the more severe to be strictly reserved for those who are not themselves children of Israel:

> I am the Lord your God, which brought you forth out of the land of Egypt, to give you the land of Canaan, and to be your God. . . . Both thy bondmen, and thy bondmaids, which thou shalt have, shall be of the heathen that are round about you; of them shall ye buy bondmen and bondmaids. Moreover of the children of the strangers that do sojourn among you, of them shall ye buy, and of their families that are with you, which they begat in your land: and they shall be your possession. And ye shall take them as an inheritance for your children after you, to inherit them for a possession; they shall be your bondmen for ever: but over your brethren the children of Israel, ye shall not rule one over another with rigour. (Leviticus 25: 38, 44–6)[81]

The Old Testament was not unusual in prescribing different regimes of servitude for insiders and for outsiders. As Moses Finley observes, in the Ancient World and in most societies slavery has been a fate reserved for vulnerable aliens.[82] But most slave systems have had difficulty perpetuating slavery down through successive generations; usually the children or grandchildren of slaves, if any, would begin to acquire the characteristics of insiders and achieve a partial improvement of their condition. The conjunction of Noah's curse and the prescriptions of Leviticus could help to convert slavery into a hereditary condition; the strangers it referred to were usually 'Canaanites', the previous inhabitants of Israel. Genesis itself identifies Canaan's issue with the inhabitants of Sodom and Gomorrah, whose offences, whatever they were, also recommended them for captivity. The biblical account of the conquest of the land of Canaan, given in Joshua and in Deuteronomy 20, makes it clear that the original inhabitants were deserving only of extermination, subjugation or expulsion.

The biblical genealogies indicate that the sons of Ham peopled the area we know as North Africa and the Horn, notably Egypt, Libya, the land of Cush – as Ethiopia was called by biblical writers – and parts of Arabia and Palestine. 'Cush' means black in Hebrew; 'Ham' is close to the word for hot. Many of the Canaanites subsequently expelled from Israel settled in North Africa at Carthage.[83] But did all sons of Ham share in the curse placed upon Canaan? This was not stated in the Bible, though the reference simply to Canaan is certainly a case of metonymy – Ham's son stands in for all Canaanites, if not all sons of Ham. The descendants of Ham include many of those who oppress or obstruct the children of Israel – not only the Egyptians and Canaanites but also the rulers of Egypt and Babylon. It seems that all those who are black descend from Ham – though some of these are positive figures, as we will see below. Like many such stories there was a built-in flexibility, allowing for a broader or narrower interpretation as convenience might dictate. Ham's original offence and punishment is later echoed in the terms of a prophecy, Isaiah 20: 4–5, concerning the Egyptians and Ethiopians, who will, it is said, be taken prisoner and captive by the Assyrians, with the 'Ethiopians' being dragged away in captivity 'young and old, naked and barefoot, even with their buttocks uncovered, to the shame of Egypt'.[84]

While the biblical account of Noah's curse clearly justified a species of ethnic enslavement, possible links to colour or 'Africa' remained to be developed. When sixteenth- or seventeenth-century Europeans made one or another of these claims they thought they were explaining the meaning of Holy Scripture, aided by new translations, or by stories from the Talmud, or the reported beliefs of Islamic merchants who offered them African slaves. Titbits found in the Talmud or picked up from Muslims helped them embroider the biblical story. Rabbinical speculations first set down in the sixth century AD sought to explain how some of Ham's progeny had acquired a black skin, postulating another, prior 'curse', but not linking it explicitly to slavery. Thus Sanhedrin 108B of the Babylonian Talmud refers to a story that Ham was 'smitten in the skin' because, like the raven and the dog, he copulated on the Ark, thus violating the injunction of abstinence laid down by Noah; this story could link Ham, and his line, to skin colour, but other interpretations are possible and the story does not mention enslavement. The Jerusalem Talmud contains speculations that Ham, when he emerged from the Ark, was 'charcoal coloured', and the Genesis Rabbah refers to Ham's seed becoming dark.[85] The Talmud and Mishnah contain a vast number of illustrations, conundrums, anecdotes and arguments, usually presented in dialectical fashion. While ritual purity is an ever-present concern, and the presence of slaves, including 'Canaanite slaves', is taken for granted, no prominence attaches to the few sparse paragraphs referring to maledictions pronounced against Ham. In any case, the presence of anecdotes connecting Africa to the sons of Ham only enlarges upon the hints which are already present in Genesis itself.

In the early Christian era the Jewish populations of Israel held slaves who, by this time, would have been 'Canaanite' only in a loose or metaphorical sense.[86] The precise ethnic character of slaves held by the Jews at this time is not clear. The Jews of Israel, or of Mesopotamia, might have acquired African slaves from Arab or Berber merchants, but there is no direct evidence for this. It seems likely that the scope of permissible enslavement came into dispute within the Jewish milieu early in the Christian epoch, either because Jews were enslaving other Jews or because Roman legal concepts of chattel slavery jarred with their ethical sensitivities; the sect of Essenes, according to the Alexandrian philosopher Philo Judeus, denounced all slaveholding as both impious and contrary to natural equality. The speculations reported in the Talmud could thus have been prompted by controversies over enslavement and the contemporary meaning of 'Canaanite slave'. Bernard Lewis discounts the possibility of a Judaic origin for the link between blackness and any curse placed on Ham or Canaan, and suggests instead that the fourth-century Syrian Christian Saint Ephrem of Nisibis could have been the first to propose it, though he warns that the only surviving version of St Ephrem's text is not contemporary, and could have been embellished.[87] At all events, between roughly the fourth and the eleventh centuries the notion that the curse of Noah applied to all Ham's progeny, and that black people descended from Ham, was to be reported or adopted by a number of Judaic, Christian and Muslim writers and teachers, many of them based in parts of North Africa or the Middle East where African slaves were to be found.

Among the early Christian Fathers Origen adopted and spread a version of the curse of Ham, though he somewhat softened it by contrasting the virtue of many blacks with the inward blackness (sinfulness) of so many whites.[88] St Augustine had declared: 'The state of slavery is rightly regarded as a penalty upon the sinner, thus the word slave does not occur in the Scriptures until the just man Noe branded with it the sin of his son.'[89] St

Augustine saw the Donatists, with their subversive social message, as the most dangerous heretics facing the Church; many of the most militant Donatist agitators, the 'circumcellions', were Numidians or Mauretanians and thus 'sons of Ham', though not dark in complexion. St Augustine found significant the fact that the name of Ham, the 'wicked brother', meant that he was the ancestor of those hot with the spirit of impatience, the 'tribe of heretics'.[90] However, St Augustine, as noted above, did not single out sons of Ham as uniquely deserving of enslavement; in his view, all men were miserable sinners and deserving of slavery. The Christians of the late Empire and Dark Ages continued to hold mainly white slaves but some entertained the notion, unknown in pagan times, that there was an affinity between blackness and slavery.[91] The Qur'an did not repeat the story of the curse on Ham's son, and in the time of Muhammad faith was held to erase all distinctions of race. Subsequently, however, a number of Muslim commentators adopted the myth of the curse, citing and embellishing Judaic and Christian sources.[92] The version which became current, though not unchallenged, in the Muslim world was to have a more consistent stress on the link between Ham, black skin and menial slavery than was to be the case with medieval Christian writers. Undoubtedly this was because there were significant numbers of black slaves in North Africa and the Middle East, while there were few or none in medieval Europe (on which more below).

Medieval Christians were looking for allies against Islam, not justifications of black slavery. There were biblical images of black Africans which associated them with exalted and non-servile roles. Living in the shadow of Egypt, biblical writers or redactors sometimes had a benign view of the black Africans to the South, and this had some influence on the Christian tradition. The Bible describes Moses' wife, Zipporah, as a Cushite or black African; when Moses' sister Miriam objected to the union, Yahweh punished her: 'Behold Miriam became leprous, white as snow' (Numbers 12: 10). The Queen of Sheba, ruler of a kingdom friendly to Israel, was held to be black as well as beautiful. The Christian belief that one of the three wise kings, or Magi, paying homage to the infant Jesus was a black African was a symbol of universalism.

The colour black was often linked to sin by theology, but this did not rule out the occasional valorization of black Africans. In the fourteenth century the religious centres of the Holy Roman Empire, such as Magdeburg, encouraged the study of the sacred texts of the Ethiopian Church and supported the Emperor's claim to sovereignty over the Levant and beyond. During the time of the Emperor Frederick II it came to be believed that St Maurice, a Theban soldier of legendary stoicism and fidelity, had been a black African; the cult of the black St Maurice was patronized by the Hohenzollerns in Brandenburg, and enjoyed support throughout the Empire.[93] Medieval Christians were led to positive evaluations of Africans by the consideration that they could be strategic allies against Islam, whether they were already Christian or simply ripe for conversion. This notion also played a significant part in the policy of Portugal and the Papacy in the fifteenth and sixteenth centuries, as we will see in the next chapter.

Nevertheless, Latin Christians still often equated the colour black with the Devil, sin and sexual licence, and subscribed to the notion that the heat of the tropics degraded the inhabitants. The Devil was invariably seen as inspiring heathen customs, since the latter had been adopted in preference to the pure Noachidian code; those under the Devil's influence were also often depicted with dark hues. Influential medieval mappamundi designated the known parts of Africa as the land of Ham's descendants; St Isidore of Seville drew up a map with this designation. The mappamundi were configured in the so-called T–O format, enclosed by a circular sea perimeter, with Jerusalem at the centre and the letter T formed by a stylized Mediterranean as the stem, crossed by the Nile and the Don. They subordinated geographical features, which were anyway only very approximately known, to a moral mapping of mankind.[94]

Isidore and many later medieval writers were inclined to draw on classical authorities, such as Pliny, and their own speculative fancy, in further defining the characteristics of the world's peoples. Isidore himself, following the ancient historian Polybius, attributed differences in skin colour to climate, not sin; but he also believed that very hot climates weakened moral fibre, and encouraged the view that Ethiopia was inhabited by perverse races. The Ebbsdorf mappamundi of 1240 and the Hereford mappamundi of 1290 depicted the monstrous races as mainly inhabiting the hot South, though a few were to be found in the cold North East – where the unclean peoples of Gog and Magog, descendants of Japheth, are placed by the Ebbsdorf map.[95] It was often held that the excessive heat of the Sahel and sub-Sahara regions had a deleterious effect on all organisms. While there was agreement that many strange beasts were to be found in the equinoctial zone, there was disagreement concerning its effect on humans. Vincent of Beauvais was convinced that the heat produced premature aging, and others alleged that Ethiopians (from the Greek for burnt skin) were ugly and lazy. However, Albert Magnus argued that heat stimulated the mental faculties; this explained why Africans were philosophical and inventive. Roger Bacon's *Opus Majus* abstained from the wilder anthropological speculations concerning the 'torrid' zone. Following his mentor, Robert Grosseteste, he believed it likely that there was a temperate area at the equator, since the hours of sunlight were fewer, but also described Ethiopians as sons of Ham.[96]

As for the story of Noah's curse, in medieval Europe this was often mobilized to justify servitude and to lend religious sanction to aristocratic beliefs in the right to rule of Normans, or Goths – who consequently supplied themselves with genealogies, often via Troy, to Japheth or Shem.[97] Biblical genealogies, which were both complex and vague, could be adapted for this purpose. Thus Rigby points out: 'The estate of labourers was denounced by the early fourteenth century *Cursor Mundi* as the descendants of Ham.'[98] Friedman and Davis also cite similar attempts at this period to justify serfdom with reference to Noah's curse: a thirteenth-century Cambridge bestiary and Andrew Horn's *Mirror of Justices*.[99] But in the Holy Roman Empire the link to Ham could have a quite different significance. In biblical genealogies Ham was the ancestor of great rulers, leading a late-fifteenth-century Nuremberg genealogist to claim that no less a personage than the Emperor Maximilian was of Hamitic descent; however, Maximilian's own vigorous ethno-social animosities are suggested in a reference he made to Swiss rebels in a public proclamation describing the Helvetic peoples, heroes of some of the first victories to be won by the commons in Europe, as 'an ill-conditioned, rough and bad peasant-folk, in whom there is to be found no virtue, no noble blood, and no moderation, but only hatred and disloyalty towards the German nation'.[100] Some of the uncouth or menacing habits portrayed as being those of the wild and monstrous peoples – such as ugliness and the waving of sticks and clubs[101] – were reminiscent also of representations of Saracens, devils and the rebellious peasant (a word with the same Latin root as pagan). Those who laboured in the open were seen as crude, menacing, and of a dark and weathered complexion. The evocation of threat itself justified the idea of restraint. In early modern Europe flogging and the stocks, burning and dismembering, were punishments visited on many thousands of witches and heretics, mutineers and peasant rebels. Those in receipt of poor relief were sometimes obliged to wear badges, while deviants and offenders could be branded. Servants would be known by diminutives and nicknames, like pets.

Subsequent stereotypes of black slaves were to recycle the social and gender prejudices of early modern Europe, portraying them as dangerous if they were not under control, as incorrigibly wayward, childlike, irrational, and prone to resentment, as a source of sexual danger, and so forth. And the argument could also be reversed. In Elizabeth Cary's play *The Tragedy of Mariam* (1613) a male character explains to a woman: 'Cham's servile curse to all your sex was given, / Because in Paradise you did offend',[102] though perhaps the author hoped that the spectator would recoil from the sentiment. The slave plantations and racial stigmatization were to constitute a highly distinctive version of the modes of power and discipline which were gathering force throughout early modern Europe.

The slave was someone entirely in the household of the master, like the *feme couverte*, yet like the unprotected or loose woman, the slave was a source of sexual anxiety. William McKee Evans argues that the myth of Noah's curse was particularly congenial to 'legitimist' members of the slaveholder's family – notably wives and sons alarmed that the impregnation of slave women by the master would produce rival favourites and successors.[103] The notion that the slave was of some congenitally degraded descent would, from such a standpoint, both discourage the wayward slaveholder and furnish a guarantee if lasciviousness triumphed none the less. As with later racial discourses, the legend of the curse of Noah, as constructed or reconstructed during the early modern period, was to be replete with signs that it was linked to sexual anxiety and notions of purity and danger. As we have seen, one version claimed that Ham had breached his father's command that there should be no sexual congress on the Ark, calculating that an extra son would enable him to claim more land.[104]

Towards the middle of the fifteenth century the Portuguese began to acquire slaves on the coast of Africa for sale in the Peninsula or Atlantic islands. At this time there were probably already a few black African slaves in Castile and Aragon, acquired from Muslims. Following the arrival of many tens of thousands of enslaved Africans in the years 1450–1500, Christian Europeans began to make a stronger link between slavery and black Africans, especially since the number of white slaves was diminishing. It began to occur to some that the new and perhaps disturbing practice of trafficking in, or holding, African slaves could be explained by reference to Genesis, perhaps garnished with supposed scraps of scriptural exegesis taken from Judaic or Muslim sources. However, neither the Papacy nor the Portuguese Crown chose to dwell on Noah's curse since they aimed to win the friendship of African kingdoms, with the aim of fostering trade and making converts. As will be recounted in the next chapter, the Portuguese established contact with the Ethiopian Empire and conducted a joint campaign with it against the Ottomans in the 1530s. Paradoxically Portugal's pioneering role in the slave traffic, involving as it did the cultivation of good relations with African royal houses, led to a downplaying of racial themes. As late as 1607–08 the Portuguese *Mesa da Conscencia e Ordens*, a body charged with both colonial strategy and court matters, recommended that the Christian son of the monarch of the African kingdom of Warri be accorded the status of 'Old Christian of noble blood' and permitted to marry a Portuguese noblewoman of the House of Bragança.[105]

Those who challenged Portugal's African monopoly in the early seventeenth century had a quite different approach; relations with African rulers were to be short-term and commercial. The story of the curse of Noah had the advantage that it could be offered in explanation of a slave trade and slavery which some found disturbing. It could serve as a meeting-point between prejudice and respectable learning. Many of those who were to lead the colonizing movement had acquired a smattering of biblical learning as part of their education at Oxford, Cambridge, Paris or Leiden.

Nevertheless David Brion Davis argues that Noah's curse was not yet of much significance: 'I am convinced that the "Hamitic myth" played a relatively minor role in justifying black slavery until the late eighteenth and the nineteenth centuries. . . . Before then, for Jews, Christians and Muslims alike, it was sufficient that blacks were Gentiles, pagans, or infidels, and the Noachidian curse served as an occasional, if forceful, obiter dictum.'[106] The evident flexibility with which the so-called curse has been interpreted should certainly induce caution and it is absurd to suppose that traders or planters ever acquired slaves because they believed that Holy Scripture obliged them to do so. However, the legend of the curse did play a part, especially in the Protestant and Anglophone world, in justifying slavery in cultures that had become allergic to it and in justifying racializing practices in a milieu formally committed to the common descent of humankind from Adam and Eve. Moreover, the curse was, if anything, more significant in the period 1550–1750 than in the subsequent period. If our focus is on the formative period, the 'forceful obiter dictum' added vital reinforcement to the argument from heathenism. The curse of Noah was more specific than a justificatory theory which limited itself to such an inherently impermanent and non-hereditary characteristic as paganism; the new type of slave system which was to develop in the late seventeenth century had a voracious demand for labour and proved inimical to traditional conceptions which allowed several routes to manumission of slaves.[107]

For those who believed in the literal truth of the Bible – as did nearly everyone in sixteenth- and seventeenth-century Europe – the Noah story furnished an approach to slavery and genealogy which at least had to be seriously considered. Even men as rational as Hugo Grotius and Isaac Newton believed that all mankind was descended from Noah and his sons, despite the difficulty of fitting the peoples of the New World into the Noachid formula. In 1646 Sir Thomas Browne described the notion that black skin was linked to the curse of Ham as a 'common error': 'There is another opinion concerning the complexion of negroes that is not only embraced by many of the more Vulgar Writers but likewise by that ingenious Traveller Mr Sandys . . . and these would have the Blackness of Negroes an effect of Noah's curse ratify'd by God, upon Cham.'[108] George Sandys, an official of the Virginia Company, wrote a travel account, drawn upon by Samuel Purchas, in which he observed that Africans sold by Cairo merchants as slaves were 'descended of Chus, the sonne of cursed Cham; as are all of that complexion'.[109] (The Chus referred to was the Cush of the King James version, just as Cham was a variant of Ham.) Purchas's compilation echoed the influential collection *Principall Navigations*, edited by Richard Hakluyt, containing George Best's *A True discourse of the late voyage of discoverie* (1578), in which the author disputes the climatic theory of skin colour and proposes instead that the most probable cause of black skin is a 'natural infection' which is passed from parent to child; the original cause of this 'natural infection' is, he writes, the 'curse of Ham'.[110] Even those authors who use a less loaded language than Best still believe that the ancestors of the newly encountered peoples must have renounced God, the state of being a pagan representing an abandonment of Noah's knowledge of the true God. Samuel Purchas concluded: 'so by Noah's curse it may appear, and by the nations descended from him, that Cham was the first Author, after the Flood, of irreligion.' However, while he mentions in a marginal note that some believe that black skin is a sign of the curse, he gives more emphasis to a view at odds with crude white supremacism, namely that the 'Great Sheepheard' 'hath pleased in this varietie to diversify his works, all serving one human nature'.[111]

Reference to one or another version of the curse was in fact made by many of those who wrote about a trade in slaves on the African coast – its earliest appearance is a garbled reference by the fifteenth-century Portuguese royal chronicler Gomes Eannes de Zurara. In the late sixteenth and early seventeenth centuries references begin to multiply, especially among English writers. It appears in different versions in the works edited by Hakluyt and Purchas, and in the 1620s report of Richard Jobson to the Guinea Company. Reference to the curse of Ham (but not black skin) as justifying slavery is made by Sir Edward Coke in his authoritative *Institutes of the Laws of England* (1628). John Selden clearly indicates Africa as the abode of 'Cham and his posterity' in his work on *The Right and Dominion of the Sea* of 1662, while a Leiden professor, Georgius Hornius, urged that African Negroes were Hamites in his *Arca Noae* (1666).[112] Some Spanish and English writers, such as Buenaventura de Salinas and William Strachey in *The Historie of Travel into Virginia Britannia* (1612), urged that the curse might properly be applied to the natives of America, but this demonstration of the elasticity of the myth afforded no protection to Africans and argued the acceptance of a proto-racial notion that the peoples of the world belonged to distinct, and biblically rooted, descent groups. The works of the first-century Jewish General and historian Flavius Josephus were drawn upon by some to embellish the biblical account of what befell the sons of Noah.[113]

In fact no other doctrine of enslavement could be made so clearly to single out Africans; as noted above, the Bible itself, while not mentioning colour, makes it clear that Ham's descendants peopled the lands Europeans have known as Africa. The notion that matters to do with slavery were related to Noah's curse was probably to be more widely diffused in the sixteenth and seventeenth centuries than ever before because of the Bible's greater availability. The idea that the curse was linked to blackness was encouraged or confirmed by intercourse with Islam. As contacts with Africa extended southwards then its population grew blacker, while to Northern Europeans even North Africans were fairly dark. Several of the references I have cited are the more forceful as an indication of learned and popular mentalities precisely because they are relatively casual observations, made by those with little stake in the matter; thus Sandys was not particularly concerned to justify the actions of Cairo slave traders, but did think that he could explain them. Belief in the curse was to be entertained even by clerics who denounced the inhumane treatment of African slaves, such as the Spaniard Alonso de Sandoval, who ministered to the slave arrivals at Cartagena, and the Portuguese António Vieira, who preached against the abuse of slaves in Brazil. Without endorsing it, the English cleric Morgan Godwyn, author of the *Negro's and Indians Advocate* (1680), took the legend of the curse very seriously. A 1703 document of the Dutch Church in South Africa referred positively to the baptism of one of Ham's unfortunate African progeny. Reference to the 'sons of Ham' sometimes served to acknowledge the humanity of Africans, to affirm the need for humane enslavement, and to deny the ultra-racist notion that black slaves were simply beasts of the field – a notion that was to gain ground, as we will see, in the plantation colonies.[114]

Richard Jobson, who disdained the slave trade, nevertheless seems to have been influenced by the legend of Noah's curse. In the 1620s he was sent by the Guinea Company to a part of West Africa where Islam was a presence, to report on commercial possibilities. He writes of the West Africans: 'these people sprang from the race of Canaan, the sonne of Ham, who discovered his father Noah's secrets'. This does not lead Jobson to favour slave trading himself. He writes that when offered slaves to buy by a local chief: 'I made answer, We were a people, who did not deale in any such commodities, neither did wee buy or sell one another, or any that had our own shape.' But he does note what he sees as a resemblance between the Irish and the Fulbies, since 'their manner of lives had great resemblance in following of their cattle, and as they were out of heart in one ground, to move whole Townes together'. After this it is not so surprising when we learn: 'among themselves a prophecy remains, that they shall be subdued, and remain subject to a white people: and what know we but that determinate time of God is at hand, and that it shall be His Almighty's pleasure, to make our nation his instrument'.[115] Variable as were the conclusions that could be extracted from the legend of the curse, none of them favoured those of African descent and most of them boosted the legitimacy of ethnic oppression.

The Noachid legend was only one strand in Latin Christendom's approach to slavery, and – but for the European 'discoveries' of the fifteenth century and subsequent colonial rivalry – might have remained of little importance. It never bore the sole brunt of explaining or justifying enslavement. Europeans also often believed that slavery could be the best fate for heathens, cannibals, the descendants of Cain (sometimes carelessly conflated with the sons of Ham or Cham), those punished with slavery for some grave offence by the laws of their own sovereign, and the various categories mentioned in the *Siete Partidas*. Once Africans were encountered they were often condemned under several rubrics, but the reworked Noachid doctrine directly targeted black Africans, distinguishing them from other heathens and cannibals whose enslavement proved less satisfactory, and allowing their descendants to be kept as slaves even if born Christian. Those who engaged slaves as servants or artisans did not wish to think of them as cannibals and savages, and the Noachid myth did not require them to. The linking of slavery and skin colour also proved to be highly functional, marking the slave population and its intercourse with the free. This link was already available – latent, as it were – at the time of the rise of the plantations. While the first plantations, as we will see, had a mixed labour force, including free and unfree whites or non-African natives, the vigorous demand for plantation produce caused a labour shortage which traders and planters found could most conveniently and profitably be met by purchasing slaves from Africa. In this context the legend of Noah's curse usefully allayed qualms which might be felt by those Christians who found this disturbing or distasteful.

While ideological justifications are often highly flexible, some are better adapted to their purpose than others. Irrespective of the details, the slavery-justifying notions in the Bible helped to keep alive the idea of slavery as a sort of 'floating signifier'. There were other aspects of the Bible which could lend themselves to benign interpretations, such as the notion of humanity's common descent, or the rainbow as a sign of Yahweh's pact with humanity and other creatures; or the idea of Jubilee, to be celebrated by the cancelling of the milder species of bondage. Even the story of the curse could have been recuperated if it was insisted that only descent in the female line counted, or that the different descent groups had thoroughly mingled at some point. The sacred roles of the indisputably black Ethiopians – credited with speaking one of the Ur-languages of Paradise rather than one of the common corrupted tongues – could have been dwelt upon. If some powerful universal injunction *against* any type of slave trading or slaveholding had been subscribed to by Christians in sixteenth- and seventeenth-century Europe, then perhaps other means would have had to be found to recruit labour for the plantations. At the very least there would have had to be more of a struggle over the development of racial slavery.[116] In Western Europe itself, the powerful generally felt obliged to respect the limited anti-slavery aspirations of the early modern 'free air' doctrine; in the colonies they were to be far less constrained, partly because authoritative religious ideas were congruent with racial slavery and with the practice of holding Africans in bondage even when they were born Christians.

The Mediterranean, the Atlantic and Black Bondage

It is not true that sugar can be grown and processed only by slaves. It now seems that the Mediterranean sugar industry of the fourteenth and fifteenth centuries did not engage many slaves. The type of slavery found in the Eastern Mediterranean in the twelfth to fifteenth centuries had been mainly artisanal and domestic. Some specialist slaves may have been used in the development of sugar plantations in the Levant in the wake of the Crusades, but most of the 'honey cane' was probably grown by serfs. The Crusaders, and the merchants who accompanied them, learned the new Arab – originally Indian – methods of extracting sugar from cane by means of a simple mill and the boiling of the cane juice. The prosperity of feudal Europe stimulated demand for this much-prized luxury. The Crusader kingdom of *Outre Mer* had helped to introduce sugar to Europe in the twelfth and thirteenth centuries. The Crusaders were always on the lookout for sources of wealth, whether to sustain their enterprise or to make their own fortunes. They would have had no scruples about either purchasing or using slaves on their estates. However, they would have found it more advantageous to use the labour of conquered serfs so far as the cultivation of sugar cane was concerned. Organizing gangs of Muslim slaves would anyway have been a dangerous undertaking.[117]

With the sponsorship of Venice and Genoa, sugar cultivation was encouraged in Crete (Candia), Cyprus and Sicily when the Crusaders were evicted from Syria and Jordan. Control of sugar supplies became a critical factor in the rivalry between Italian merchants; those who owned sugar estates, such as the Cornaros of Venice and Cyprus, were people of great power.[118] The processing of the cane required exceptionally skilled, intense and continuous labour. The Levantine peasantry could grow sugar cane but may have resisted, or been unsuited to, the labour of the sugar works. The owners of the sugar factories needed a core of workers trained in the secrets of sugar processing and able to perform long hours of work. Peasant farmers offering labour services might perform some tasks, but could not supply the skilled core or the handful of toilers who kept the mill going in a long harvest season. There are scraps of evidence indicating that recourse was made to slave labour for these purposes, including the labour of Syrian or 'Saracen' captives who could occasionally be purchased from the Levantine pirates. But sugar commanded very high prices, and one document referring to those who worked on the Episcopi estate in Cyprus speaks of labourers being paid wages. In any case, the extraction of sugar from cane was highly skilled, as we observed above; the artisans engaged in it, whether free or servile, would have ranked with silversmiths or weavers of fine textiles. The most probable division of labour would have been a core group of salaried specialists, plus a few general labourers or slaves, with the growing and transport of the sugar cane carried out by an enserfed peasantry.

William Phillips's study of late medieval and early modern slavery concludes that the labour force in the Mediterranean sugar industry, whether Christian or Muslim, included very few slaves: 'Although here and there some slaves may have been used, they were unusual. The close identification of sugar cane and slave labor came later. . . .'[119] This conclusion is echoed by Marie Louise von Wartburg, after thorough archaeological and documentary research. She finds only one unequivocal reference to the employment of a slave, a Muslim said to be working as a sugar-maker in 1426. She concludes:

> It is without doubt that, in certain cases, slaves were employed in Cyprus to produce sugar. The sources are nevertheless much too sparse to sustain the hypothesis that slaves constituted the bulk of the work force. The social structure

of Cyprus in the middle ages rather suggests that recourse was made to the large number of serfs (paroikoi) present in the island.[120]

Nevertheless, there are other reasons for at least half-endorsing the claim that these Levantine sugar estates were laboratories for the development of the plantation. They were usually established through the initiative of merchants, bankers and ship owners who displayed a new type of entrepreneurialism and practised advanced methods of accounting. Double-entry bookkeeping, commercial partnership and insurance all helped to promote this early feat of mercantile capitalism.[121] But the precarious conditions prevailing in the Levant meant that these entrepreneurs were intimately linked to the political and military order. Furnishing their own means of coercion, they were also able to exercise monopolistic controls. The transport of sugar from Cyprus had to be entrusted to a tightly organized fleet system.[122] The space afforded for the flourishing of free enterprise was to be even more narrow than that which was later permitted in the Portuguese, English or French colonial empires. The relatively modest levels of output reflected not only shallow demand but also the monopolist's instinct that small quantities meant high prices and higher profits. This began to change in the last decades of the fifteenth century and the early sixteenth century with the spread of sugar cultivation to the Atlantic islands – a development encouraged by Italian and Flemish merchants, we will see in Chapter II. African slaves came to comprise about half of the labour force on the islands, but many more were brought as servants and menials to Portugal or Spain, where they were bought by nobles, clergy and some craftsmen.

The overwhelming majority of Africans in Iberia in the sixteenth century were slaves, though some would have been trusted and responsible servants. There were a few freedmen or free children of partly African parentage. Just occasionally African nobles would be brought to Lisbon as part of the monarch's diplomatic, commercial and religious projects. Portugal's sudden prosperity in the aftermath of the Discoveries allowed it to set a fashion for Renaissance courts, where the presence of a few African retainers was thought to lend distinction. African musical skills were particularly esteemed. Thus a small group of Africans were attached to the Court of King James IV of Scotland, including a drummer ('taubonar') and a choreographer who devised a dance for twelve performers. In 1507 the King took the part of the black knight championing the cause of a black lady, played by an African woman, in a Court spectacle. These Africans received various payments, and at least one of them, a 'more las', was christened. Quite possibly they were not slaves. Henry VII of England also had a black musician at his Court.[123] So far as Northern Europe was concerned, the link between Africans and slavery was, as yet, somewhat notional, but white Europeans took themselves as the norm and supposed that deviations, especially in something so obvious as skin colour, must be a sign of a defect and God's displeasure. Moreover, it was known that in the Mediterranean and North Africa the blacks were often slaves. By the Elizabethan and early Stuart period the arrival of sugar from the islands, and gold and spices from Africa, was beginning to set up its own chain of associations. A taste for the exotic was whetted. References to blacks or Africans in Elizabethan England combine repugnance, ambivalence and curiosity. There would be no tragedy in Shakespeare's *Othello* if there was not nobility in the Moor, yet this construction was itself portrayed as a reversal of a received stereotype. As the baroque epoch dawned, representations of African slaves or servants increasingly came to adorn precious objects, and black pages act as a foil in portraits of aristocratic ladies or gentlemen: the black has become an object of value, an adornment and an exotic pet.[124] In these pictures everything is under control, most particularly the black pageboys, while the resplendently domineering manner of the military man or merchant is itself emphasized by dark hues. Thus blackness is subject to dialectical inversion. It is the colour not only of sin but of power, seriousness and sobriety; melancholy itself – the darkest of the four humours in Galen's theory – was now revalued by Burton and others. But positive though some of these re-evaluations were, they gradually replaced the notion of a proper alliance of equals against Islam, such as had nourished the search for Prester John.

Africans and the Islamic Slave Trade

Before 1440 Christendom had no direct access to an African slave trade. For some centuries, however, Islam had acquired slaves from black Africa, and such slaves were common in the provinces of the Ottoman Empire and in the North African kingdoms. While the Prophet himself had prominent black aides, and asserted that his message could be received by all conditions of men, Muslims were permitted to own, buy and sell slaves – with the important proviso, as we have seen, that they were infidels, or had been when they were first enslaved. By the tenth century an association between blackness and menial slavery had developed in the Muslim and Arab world: the word *'abd*, or black, became synonymous with slave. As early as the seventh century black Africans were regarded as desirable slaves in Arabia and its dependencies; a treaty or capitulation entered into by the Christian kingdom of the Nubians as early as the year 31 (AD 652 of the Christian calendar) stipulated that the latter would supply three hundred slaves annually to the Caliphate. Although it was subject to reinterpretation, this *baqt* was observed for some six centuries.[125] Slaves were also acquired from East Africa in the eighth and ninth centuries to work in the salt marshes, and on sugar, cotton and indigo estates, in Lower Iraq. However, this precocious slave system was shaken by the great revolts of the Zanj led by Mahommed Ali in 255–69 (AD 869–83).[126] This sustained revolt helped to precipitate a crisis of the Abbasid Kaliphate, and discouraged subsequent attempts to resort to large-scale gang slavery. Popovic writes that henceforth 'the normal and preferred labour system in Islamic sugar production was the compulsory labour of indigenous peasants – a sort of corvée'.[127]

Subsequently, African slaves continued to be selected, on a prudently smaller scale, for employment in North Africa and Syria. In the eighth century the Ibadi Berber traders of North Africa also secured trans-Saharan sources of supply for black slaves. From the tenth century to the fifteenth it has been estimated that an annual average of some five thousand slaves a year were dispatched across the Sahara from West Africa. They were destined to become gold or copper miners in West Sudan, porters or sugar workers in Egypt, or domestic servants and menials throughout the Arab world. In the Maghreb African slaves sometimes became soldiers, while in the Middle East this was less common.[128] Islamic societies were quite prepared to enslave anyone, of any colour or race, so long as they were initially infidel. The extensive use of enslavement to recruit soldiers had no West European counterpart – Spain and France used galley slaves in their naval forces, but they never enjoyed positions of command. The religious and racial code of the Ottoman Empire, the major Islamic formation of the time, was distinctly more tolerant and pluralist than that of Europe's new Absolutist regimes.

The trade in African slaves nevertheless contributed a racial element to Islamic slavery, with the curse of Noah being widely invoked to justify it. The spread of Islam in and beyond the African Sahel and savannah furnished more secure conditions for a steady flow of black slaves. Individual African peoples may have adopted Islam in part as a way of insulating themselves from the slave traffic, but often without success. A fourteenth-century King of Bornu – today part of Northern Nigeria – wrote to the sultan of Egypt complaining that Arab raiders had 'devastated all our land . . . they took free people among us captive, of our kin among Muslims . . . they have taken our people as merchandise'.[129]

There can be little doubt that this was a general pattern. It aroused the concern of some Muslim clerics in the afflicted lands, notably Ahmed Baba of Timbuktu (1556–1627), who produced a legal treatise, or Mi'raj, aimed at this indiscriminate slave-raiding. Ahmed Baba's work cited earlier Muslim writings on wrongful enslavement of Africans, including a critique of the curse of Noah by Ibn Khaldun. In his general writings the great historian praised the redemptive function of Islamic slavery, and speculated on why black Africans were suited to the condition. But – perhaps because as a Berber he was himself a 'son of Ham' – Khaldun objected to any extension of the curse of Noah:

Because they were unaware of the nature of creatures, some of the genealogists believed that the Sudan (that is the children of Ham, son of Noah) were distinguished by black colour due to a curse against Ham from his father, and that the effect of the curse appeared both through colour and through slavery which befell his descendants. Now the pronouncement of Nuh [Noah] is in the Torah and in it there is no mention of black colour. It only mentions that his children will be slaves to the children of his brothers and nothing else.[130]

Baba himself urged:

> The origin of slavery is unbelief, and the black kafirs are like the Christians, except that they are majus, pagans. The Muslims among them, like the people of Kano, Katsina, Bornu, Gobir, and all of Songhai, are Muslims, who are not to be owned. Yet some of them transgress on the others unjustly by invasion as do the Arabs, Bedouins, who transgress on free Muslims and sell them unjustly, and thus it is not lawful to own any of them. . . . If anybody is known to have come from these countries, he should be set free directly, and his freedom acknowledged.[131]

Such representations, which strangely parallel some arguments made by a few Portuguese and Spanish clerics (see Chapters II and III), had little effect on the activities of the slave-raiders and traders. Portuguese merchants in fifteenth- and sixteenth-century West Africa began by tapping into already established trade routes at the mouths of the larger rivers. Slavery was probably at least as widespread in West Africa at this time as it had been in Domesday England or in medieval and early modern Muscovy. Metalworking appears to have developed in West Africa between the third century BC and the third century AD. The more intensive forms of agricultural cultivation this made possible would have increased the numbers of potential slaves with agricultural skills; the European traders were well aware that hunter-gathering peoples made poor field slaves and were, additionally, more prone to run away and live in the wild.

West Africa shared with other regions where slave trading was common – the Caucasus, the Balkans, the Russian steppe of medieval times, and pre-Norman England – a relatively high degree of political fragmentation. Internecine warfare generated captives and destroyed those forms of regional solidarity that might inhibit slave exports. The European traders on the African coast generally treated the authorities with whom they dealt with respect. Indeed, they usually cultivated a special relationship with one or another of the rulers of the African coastal states. But the bulk of the captives they purchased had been subjects of some other ruler, often unknown to the traders; anyway, the latter supposed that the captive's former sovereign was incapable of – and uninterested in – extending the sort of protection which, say, even an Anatolian peasant could expect from the Sublime Porte.

John Thornton has urged that the West African states of the early modern period were by no means wholly at a disadvantage in their dealings with European traders.[132] The forts established by the Europeans simply offered a measure of protection to the trading posts, with their warehouses and provision grounds. Such posts flourished only when they were on good terms with the local rulers. On the other hand, the Europeans did enjoy an effective monopoly of sea transport, and this must have given them more leverage than Thornton allows. The willingness of European traders to buy large numbers of captives eventually stimulated slave-raiding in the interior and encouraged African chiefs to distort judicial sanctions which led to enslavement. But the traders usually found it most advantageous to leave their suppliers to obtain slaves in whatever way they thought best. The purchase of slaves was anyway easier than their capture; this practice entailed fewer risks and seemed to many early modern Europeans to come with its own commercial justification.

Thornton advances, as a further general reason for the prevalence of slavery in West Africa, the view that the social relations of the region were marked by the objective of controlling labour rather than the landholding that was becoming typical of much of Europe.[133] Slaves in West Africa were the major form of wealth; as potential soldiers they were a factor of power; and female slaves could bear children as well as till the field. Land, by contrast, was relatively plentiful, and could be worked and secured by those with enough slaves at their command. Thornton himself stresses the potential for diversity among the several hundred states and kingdoms in West and Central Africa, so there was evidently much scope for variations on this theme – and, no doubt, beyond it. At various times – some to be noted in subsequent chapters – particular African states withdrew from the slave traffic, but in so doing they diminished their ability to acquire the bars of iron, horses, cutlasses, firearms, and so forth offered by the slave traders, thus weakening their position in conflicts with other states.

The ability of the European traders to offer an impressive range of trade goods for slaves was also a fundamental circumstance permitting the rise of the trade; it reflected slave prices in the New World, and the productivity advantage of mining and agriculture in the Americas compared with West Africa.[134] In any event, traditional African slavery was something quite distinct from the plantation slavery that was to be constructed in the New World, though it was itself to be transformed by the pressures of the Atlantic slave trade, especially once the plantation boom got under way. The diversity of the slave condition in Africa was to be replaced in the New World by an overwhelming concentration of slaves on field work and cash crop production. While slaves in Africa were often of alien origin, they were not destined to become part of an inflexible racial hierarchy such that they and their descendants through many generations would remain outsiders and slaves, as was to happen in the New World.

Conclusion

I have argued that slavery underwent a secular, though not uninterrupted or uniform, decline in Western Europe between the eighth and fifteenth centuries. Neither high feudalism nor early agrarian capitalism required or reproduced slavery, though both proved compatible with pockets of slaveholding. The clash with Islam eventually encouraged Christians to follow the Muslim lead in barring the enslavement of fellow believers, while retaining it for those who were, or had been, non-believers. The expansion of Latin Christendom was accompanied by a battery of persecutions which sought to impose ever greater religious and ethno-cultural homogeneity. The decline of serfdom in Western Europe did little or nothing to weaken the vitality of doctrines supportive of enslavement. Jurists throughout the continent repeated the endorsement of slavery by the Roman *jus gentium*, or law of nations. Neither the Renaissance nor the Reformation attacked the legitimacy of slavery. Nevertheless, a marked popular prejudice against slavery, even the slavery of others, encouraged rulers to pose as the champions of their subjects' civil liberty. However, piecemeal limitations on the proper scope of slavery were accompanied by a continuing, even increased, willingness to enslave religious and racial outsiders.

The printing of the Bible in the vernacular put in wider circulation the myths of Noah's curse or curses. Judaism, Christianity and Islam have each, in their different ways, made a huge contribution to the moral advance of humanity, but in the early modern period these systems of belief were tolerant of slaveholding. Their universalism was shadowed by ethno-religious notions which riveted together descent and servile status.

All these developments took on a more ominous significance with the growth of an increasingly independent realm of commercial consumption and with related notions of capitalist private property. The demand for sugar and spices reflected the growing purchasing power of those who were drawing larger rents from the countryside, and of an urban milieu headed by master manufacturers and merchants. By the sixteenth and seventeenth centuries the spread of capitalist social relations in the towns and country-side of North West Europe began to create elements of mass demand. The plantation revolution of the seventeenth century, traced in subsequent chapters, was intimately linked to this development. The notion of a moral economy that rejected slave trading was to be overwhelmed by the rising tide of commerce and *raison d'état*. And the notion of private property was to gain greater independence and wider scope.

Notes

1. The classic critique of the idol of origins is, appropriately enough, furnished by a scholar who devoted himself to the study of medieval slavery and serfdom. See Marc Bloch, *The Historian's Craft*, Manchester 1992, pp. 24–9. Bloch points out that the notion of 'origins' commonly confuses *first appearance* with *causes*, and that the whole problematic has a religious aura. In what follows, I argue that the type of slavery which came to dominate the New World was not already seen in medieval and early modern Europe, but that certainly *some* of its causes are to be found at work there.

2. Robert Bartlett, *The Making of Europe: Conquest, Colonization and Cultural Change 950–1350*, Princeton, NJ 1993, p. 313.

3. Charles Verlinden, *The Beginnings of Modern Colonisation*, Ithaca, NY 1970; Verlinden is cited by Davis as follows: 'L'économie esclavagiste des économies modernes est purement et simplement la continuation de celle des colonies médiévales.' David Brion Davis, *The Problem of Slavery in Western Culture*, Harmondsworth 1970, pp. 57–8, apparently from Verlinden, 'Le Problème de la continuité en histoire coloniale: de la colonisation médiévale à la colonisation moderne', *Revista de Indias*, Madrid 1951, XI, pp. 219–36. See also David Brion Davis, *Slavery and Human Progress*, London 1984, pp. 54–7. That Verlinden's judgements have been widely influential stems from the fact that he is the author of a massive study of slavery in the Middle Ages, *L'Esclavage dans l'Europe médiévale*, 2 vols, I, Bruges 1955, II, Ghent 1977. Material on Crete and Cyprus found in the second volume, pp. 876–93 and 970–74, is more cautious about the extent of slave employment in these islands.

4. See, for example, Fernand Braudel, *Civilization and Capitalism*, vol. I, *The Structure of Everyday Life*, London 1985, pp. 224–7. While he is noncommittal about the significance of slavery on the Mediterranean estates, Braudel also links them very directly to the New World plantations.

5. Quoted in W.R. Brownlow, *Lectures on Slavery and Serfdom in Europe*, New York 1969 (originally Plymouth 1892), p. xxx. See also W.W. Buckland, *The Roman Law of Slavery: The Condition of the Slave from Augustus to Justinian*, New York 1969 (originally Cambridge 1908).

6. That this was the case emerges clearly from the work of a historian uncomfortable with racial mixture, since he sees it as introducing to the Roman West the corrupting and enervating influence of Eastern peoples and Eastern religions. R.H. Barrow, *Slavery and the Roman Empire*, New York 1996 (first edn 1928), pp. 208–29.

7. Aristotle, *The Politics*, Harmondsworth 1981, p. 79; see also pp. 65–79, 397. For an elucidation of Aristotle's notion of 'natural slavery', see Patricia Springborg, *Western Republicanism and the Oriental Prince*, Austin, TX 1992, pp. 23–40.

8. Geoffrey de Ste Croix, *The Class Struggle in the Ancient Greek World*, London 1981, pp. 418–25. Of course Roman cosmopolitanism, as Ste Croix makes clear, was perfectly compatible with yawning class differences; it is just that these were not strongly racialized.

9. 'Servus vocatus es, non sit tibi curae, sed potes liber fieri, magis utere', cited by Duns Scotus, 'Peccatus Servitutis', in *Duns Scotus on the Will and Morality*, ed. and trans. by Allan B. Wolter, O.F.M., Washington, DC 1986, p. 527. Duns Scotus was sceptical about justifications for enslavement, but finds this a clinching argument.

10. Gervase Corcoran, *St Augustine on Slavery*, Rome 1985, p. 71.

11. Dmitri Kyrtatas, *The Social Structure of Early Christian Communities*, London 1987, pp. 29 ff. For the imbrication of Empire and Church, see Michael Mann, *Sources of Social Power*, vol. 1, *A History of Power from the Beginning to AD 1760*, Cambridge 1986, pp. 301–40.

12. E.A. Thompson, *Romans and Barbarians: The Decline of the Western Empire*, Madison, WI 1982, pp. 17–38; Geoffrey de Ste Croix, *The Class Struggle in the Ancient Greek World*, pp. 497–503; Marc Bloch, *Slavery and Serfdom in the Middle Ages*, Berkeley, CA 1975, pp. 1–31.

13. E.A. Thompson, *The Visigoths in the Time of Ulfila*, Oxford 1966, pp. 40–43.

14. David N. Dumville *et al.*, *Saint Patrick AD 493–1993*, Woodbridge, VA 1994, pp. 119–20; see also pp. 207–31 and E.A. Thompson, *Romans and Barbarians*, pp. 246–8.

15. William D. Phillips, *Slavery from Roman Times to the Early Transatlantic Trade*, Manchester 1985, pp. 43–65. For the feudal 'synthesis' and its variations, see also Perry Anderson, *Passages from Antiquity to Feudalism*, London 1974, pp. 128–72.

16. John Block Friedman, *The Monstrous Races in Medieval Art and Thought*, Cambridge 1981, p. 116.

17. Pierre Bonnassie, *From Slavery to Feudalism in South-West Europe*, Cambridge 1991, pp. 26–7. For the Visigoths' extensive practice of slavery, see P.D. King, *Law and Society in the Visigothic Kingdom*, Cambridge 1972, pp. 159–81. And for the slave-raiding proclivities of the Visigoths in an earlier epoch, see E.A. Thompson, *The Visigoths in the Time of Ulfila*, pp. 40–43.

18. E.A. Thompson, *Romans and Barbarians*, pp. 217–21.

19. C.H. Becker, 'The Expansion of the Saracens', in *The Cambridge Medieval History*, Cambridge 1913, pp. 329–90, 371–3.

20. Pierre Riché, *Daily Life in the World of Charlemagne*, Liverpool 1978, pp. 102–4; Sally P.J. Harvey, 'The Extent and Profitability of Demesne Agriculture in England in the Later Eleventh Century', in T.H. Aston et al., eds, *Social Relations and Ideas*, Cambridge 1983, pp. 45–72, especially pp. 60–61; Chris Wickham, 'From the Ancient World to Feudalism', *Past and Present* 103 (1984), p. 32, n.34.

21. Quoted in W.R. Brownlow, *Lectures on Slavery and Serfdom in Europe*, p. 112.

22. Reginald Lennard, *Rural England, 1086–1135*, Oxford 1959, pp. 82, 91, 98, 241, 389; Rodney Hilton, *Bond Men Made Free*, London 1963, pp. 56–7, 86; Sally Harvey, 'The Extent and Profitability of Demesne Agriculture', pp. 69–70.

23. Bonnassie, *From Slavery to Feudalism in South-West Europe*, pp. 104–31. See also T. Bisson, 'The "Feudal Revolution"', *Past and Present* 142 (1994), pp. 6–42. See also Georges Duby, *The Early Growth of the European Economy*, Ithaca, NY 1974, pp. 172–5, 187–97; Anderson, *Passages from Antiquity to Feudalism*, pp. 182–5; Pierre Dockès, *Medieval Slavery and Liberation*, London 1982, pp. 183–97; and the contributions by Chris Wickham and others in Wendy Davies and Paul Fouracre, eds, *Property and Power in the Early Middle Ages*, Cambridge 1995, pp. 221–6, 245–51, 260–71.

24. Bonnassie, *From Slavery to Feudalism in South-West Europe*, p. 55.

25. Dockès, *Medieval Slavery and Liberation*, pp. 182–3.

26. S.H. Rigby, *English Society in the Later Middle Ages: Class, Status and Gender*, London 1995, pp. 29–33. See also Rodney Hilton, *The Decline of Serfdom in Medieval England. Second Edition*, London 1983, pp. 9–19; and Werner Rösener, *Peasants in the Middle Ages*, Oxford 1985, pp. 224–53.

27. Charles Verlinden, 'Slavery, Slave Trade', *Dictionary of the Middle Ages*, New York 1988, pp. 334–40.

28. Bernard Lewis, *Race and Slavery in the Middle East*, Oxford 1990, p. 5.

29. Shaun Marmon, 'Slavery, Islamic World', *Dictionary of the Middle Ages*, pp. 330–33.

30. The classic statement of this case dwelt mainly on economic arguments: see Henri Pirenne, *Mohammad and Charlemagne*, London 1939. For subsequent re-evaluations, see Alfred Havighurst, ed., *The Pirenne Thesis: Analysis, Criticism and Revision*, London 1976; and Richard Hodges and David Whitehouse, *Mohammed, Charlemagne and the Origins of Europe*, London 1983. While such work is also relevant, my concern here is with the ideological challenge of Islam. See Judith Herrin, *The Formation of Christendom*, Oxford 1987, pp. 6, 8–9.

31. Quoted in Phillips, *Slavery from Roman Times to the Early Atlantic Trade*, pp. 62–3. For the early medieval slave trades, see pp. 43–65 of this work; also Verlinden, *L'Esclavage dans l'Europe médiévale*, I, pp. 213, 706; and Cecil Roth and I.H. Levine, eds, *The World History of the Jewish People*, Second series, *Medieval Period*, vol. 2, *The Dark Ages: Jews in Christian Europe 711–1096*, Rutgers, NJ 1966, pp. 29–32, 386.

32. Jean Bodin, *Les Six Livres de la République*, 4th edn, Paris 1579, pp. 57–8, quoted in Dockès, *Medieval Slavery and Liberation*, p. 237.

33. Peter Foote and David Wilson, *The Viking Achievement*, London 1970, pp. 65–78; Ruth Mazo Karras, *Slavery and Society in Medieval Scandinavia*, New Haven, CT 1988, pp. 122–66; Anderson, *Passages from Antiquity to Feudalism*, pp. 173–8.

34. Bartlett, *The Making of Europe*, pp. 309, 313.

35. Quoted in R.I. Moore, *The Formation of a Persecuting Society: Power and Deviance in Western Europe, 950–1250*, Oxford 1987, p. 102.

36. Quoted in R.W. Southern, *Robert Grosseteste: The Growth of the English Mind in Medieval Europe*, London 1986, pp. 248–9.

37. Ibid., pp. 246–7.

38. Rigby, *English Society in the Later Middle Ages*, pp. 284–302. The exclusion of Jews from England was not to be lifted until the advent of the Commonwealth in the mid seventeenth century, and even then by executive order rather than formal legislation. Léon Poliakov, *The History of Anti-Semitism*, London 1966, pp. 203–9.

39. Quoted in A. Simms, 'Core and Periphery in Medieval Europe: The Irish Experience in a Wider Context', in W.J. Smyth and K. Whelan, eds, *Common Ground*, Cork 1988, p. 24. See also Gerald of Wales, *The History and Topography of Ireland*, London 1995, pp. 101–12.

40. Quoted in Seymour Phillips, 'The Outer World of the European Middle Ages', in Stuart Schwartz, ed., *Implicit Understandings: Observing, Reporting and Reflecting on the Encounters Between Europeans and Other Peoples in the Early Modern Era*, Cambridge 1994, pp. 23–63 (p. 51). There are some doubts about the text of *Laudabiliter*, but even if it is a contemporary forgery it reveals the mindset of early English imperialism. See John Gillingham, 'The Beginnings of English Imperialism', *Journal of Historical Sociology*, vol. 4, no. 4, December 1992, pp. 379–91.

41. Quoted in Bartlett, *The Making of Europe*, pp. 132, 206.

42. J.H. Elliott, *Imperial Spain: 1469–1716*, Harmondsworth 1970, pp. 106–10, 220–28, 305–8. Henry Kamen, 'The Secret of the Inquisition', *New York Review of Books*, 1 February 1996. When *converso* office-seekers sought to prove honourable descent, they naturally pointed to their Jewish lineage and the special role of the Jewish people. B. Netanyahu explains: 'It was only the constant harping of their foes on their racial perversion and inferiority that forced them [the *conversos*] to come up with the opposite idea – namely that of their *original racial excellence*, with which they defended not only their own but also their ancestors' honor. . . . Actually, however, the conversos were interested not in superiority but in equal opportunity. Accordingly, they had little regard for racial differentiation between social classes as well. They believed that differences between social classes should be based on individual talents, merits and achievements, rather than on lineages.' B. Netanyahu, *The Origins of the Inquisition in Fifteenth Century Spain*, London 1996, pp. 979–80. This is anachronistic. For a critique of this study see David Abulafia, *London Review of Books*, 31 October 1996. See also Israel Shahak, *Jewish History, Jewish Religion: The Weight of Three Thousand Years*, London 1994, pp. 59–61; and Ivan Hannaford, *Race: The History of an Idea in the West*, Washington, DC 1996, pp. 100–124.

43. Bonnassie, *From Slavery to Feudalism in South-West Europe*, pp. 55, 74, 93, 102.

44. Manuel González Jiménez, 'Frontier and Settlement in the Kingdom of Castile (1082–1350)', in Robert Bartlett and Angus MacKay, eds, *Medieval Frontier Societies*, Oxford 1992, pp. 49–74.

45. Richard Fletcher, *Moorish Spain*, London 1992, p. 140.

46. Gregório López, ed., *Las Siete Partidas del Rey Don Alfonso el Sabio*, 4 vols, Paris 1850(?), especially Partida Quarta, Titulo II, Ley 11; Titulo V, Ley 1; Titulo XXI on Slavery and Titulo XXII on Liberty. The King's duties are set out in the Segunda Partida.

47. José Enrique López de Coca Castañer, 'Institutions on the Castilian–Granadan Frontier', in Bartlett and MacKay, *Medieval Frontier Societies*, pp. 126–51, especially pp. 135–41, 147–8.

48. J.N. Hillgarth, *The Spanish Kingdoms, 1250–1516*, 2 vols, Oxford 1976 and 1978, I, pp. 86–9, 160, II, pp. 24–7, 83–7; Jacques Heers, *Esclavos y servientes en las sociedades mediterraneas durante la Edad Media*, Valencia 1989; L.P. Harvey, *Islamic Spain, 1250–1500*, Chicago and London 1990, pp. 294–301, 317–18.

49. Bernard Vincent, *Minorias y marginados en la España del Siglo XVI*, Granada 1987, pp. 239–60, especially pp. 243–4.

50. Elliott, *Imperial Spain*, pp. 305–8.

51. See the documents contained in Rodrigo de Zayas, *Les Morisques et le racisme d'Etat*, Paris 1992.

52. Daniel Evans, 'Slave Coast of Europe', *Slavery and Abolition*, vol. 6, no. 1, May 1985, pp. 41–58 (p. 42).

53. Ibid. (p. 52).

54. *Shorter Oxford English Dictionary*, 3rd edn, Oxford 1968, p. 1912. John Julius Norwich, *A History of Venice*, London 1983, pp. 270–71; Francis Carter, *Dubrovnik (Ragusa), A Classic City State*, London 1972, pp. 239–42.

55. David Hellie, *Slavery in Russia, 1450–1720*, Chicago 1982.

56. Ibid., p. 392.

57. Robert Brenner, 'Agrarian Class Structure and Economic Development', *Past and Present* 70, 1976. See also T.H. Aston and C.H.E. Philpin, *The Brenner Debate*, Cambridge 1985.

58. Sir Thomas Smith, *De Republica Anglorum*, ed. Mary Dewar, Cambridge 1982, pp. 135–6.

59. Angus Calder, *Revolutionary Empire: The Rise of the English-Speaking Empires from the Fifteenth Century to the 1780s*, London 1981, p. 61. Steven G. Ellis argues that Tudor attempts to conquer and colonize Ireland were undermined by the failure of the state to concentrate the resources and commitment that such an arduous undertaking required. Steven G. Ellis, *Tudor Ireland: Crown, Community and the Conflict of Cultures*, London 1985, pp. 314–20.

60. See C.S.L. Davies, 'Slavery and Protector Somerset: The Vagrancy Act of 1547', *Economic History Review*, 2nd series, vol. XIX, no. 3, 1966, pp. 533–49.See also C.S.L. Davies, *Peace, Print and Protestantism, 1450–1558*, London 1977, pp. 261, 266–87, for the context.

61. Thomas More, *Utopia*, trans. Paul Turner, London 1961, pp. 101–2. See also pp. 51–3, 70, 81, 84, 95. In the sixteenth-century translation of More's work *servitus* was often translated as 'bondman'; however, it also explained that 'all vile service, all slavery and drudgery, is done by bondmen.' *More's Utopia*, introduced by John Warrington, New York 1970, p. 73.

62. Ibid., pp. 104–5.

63. Ibid., pp. 79–80. The discussion on p. 93 makes it clear that utilitarian principles, a public-spirited conception of 'pleasure', reign in Utopia.

64. Pagden, *Lords of All the World*, pp. 76–7.

65. A striking account of the parallels involved is found in Theodore Allen, *The Invention of the White Race*, vol. I, *Racial Oppression and Social Control*, London 1994. See especially pp. 52–90 for the construction of the Protestant ascendancy in Ireland.

66. Hilton, *The Decline of Serfdom in Medieval England*, p. 28.

67. Jean Bodin, *Les Six Livres de la République*, pp. 45–66. Davis points out that Bodin was present in Toulouse when the 1571 case had inspired the declaration of the Guyenne parlement, and points out that the Latin edition of the *Six Livres* was more uncompromisingly anti-slavery than the French edition. Davis, *The Problem of Slavery in Western Culture*, p. 130. The Guyenne declaration is cited in Charles Verlinden, *L'Esclavage dans l'Europe médiévale*, I, p. 851; for the action of the Middelburg authorities, see Seymour Drescher, *Capitalism and Anti-Slavery*, London 1987, pp. 14, 172.

68. Jean Bodin, *The Six Bookes of the Commonweale*, done into English by Richard Knolles, London 1606, p. 33. For celebrations of France as a 'free monarchy' in the early seventeenth century, see Blandine Barret-Kriegel, *L'Etat et les esclaves*, Paris 1979, pp. 51, 75–6.

69. Bodin, *The Six Bookes of the Commonweale*, p. 44.

70. The former line of argument was to be taken by José de Acosta in his *Historia natural y moral de las Indias* (1570), the latter by Juan Ginés de Sepúlveda; see D.A. Brading, *The First Americans: The Spanish Monarchy, Creole Patriots, and the Liberal State, 1492–1867*, Cambridge 1991, pp. 88, 184–5. The position of the Spanish authorities is explored in Chapter III below.

71. Quoted in Peter Hulme, 'Tales of Distinction: European Ethnography and the Caribbean,' in Stuart B. Schwartz, ed., *Implicit Understandings*, p. 187.

72. Eduardo Aznar Vallejo, 'The Conquests of the Canary Islands', in Schwartz, *Implicit Understandings*, pp. 134–56.

73. Aquinas, *Summa Theologiae*, quoted in Richard Tuck, *Natural Rights Theories: Their Origin and Development*, Cambridge 1979, p. 19.

74. See John Duns Scotus, 'Peccatum Servituti', in *Duns Scotus on the Will and Morality*, selected and trans. with an Introduction by Allan B. Wolter, Washington, DC 1986, pp. 522–33.

75. Tuck, *Natural Rights Theories*, p. 49.

76. Ibid., p. 3.

77. Davis, *The Problem of Slavery in Western Culture*, pp. 124, 128; Herbert Marcuse, 'A Study on Authority', in *Studies in Critical Philosophy*, London 1972, pp. 56–78.

78. Robert C.H. Shell, *Children of Bondage: A Social History of the Slave Society at the Cape of Good Hope, 1652–1838*, Hannover, NH 1994, p. 334. Shell quotes from the

published Latin proceedings as follows: 'Baptized slaves should enjoy equal right of liberty with other Christians and ought never to be handed over again to the powers of the heathens (*potestati ethnicorum*) by their Christian masters either by sale or by any other transfer of possession.' *De Ethnicorum Pueris Baptizandis*, quoted p. 335. The most radical representation, made by the Swiss theologian Giovanni Deodatus, urged that baptized slaves be treated as 'hired servants clearly according to the customs of other Christians'. Quoted p. 335.

79. Michel Certeau, *The Writing of History*, New York 1988, p. 227.

80. *The Holy Bible*, Authorized King James Version, Cambridge University Press. As noted in the introduction, the English cited a different verse – Genesis 1: 28 – in support of their colonial claims, arguing that since they could make better use of the land than others, it belonged to them. This religious version of the utilitarian argument already cited from More above had wide currency in English-speaking areas but not elsewhere, no doubt because it relied on reading rather a lot into the biblical text (cf. Seed, *Ceremonies of Possession*, pp. 34–5). By contrast, it would take some very elaborate exegesis to argue away the link between Noah's curse and slavery.

81. The use of 'bondman' and 'bondmaid' for *avaday*, *eved* and *amay* instead of 'slave' again suggests uneasiness. For an interpretation of this passage and parallels in the legal codes of Solon and Hamurabi, see Bernard S. Jackson, 'Biblical Laws of Slavery: A Comparative Approach', in Léonie Archer, ed., *Slavery and Other Forms of Unfree Labour*, London 1988, pp. 86–101.

82. M.I. Finley, 'Slavery', in *International Encyclopedia of the Social Sciences*, vol. 14, New York 1968, pp. 307–13; G. Chirichigno, *Debt-Slavery in Israel*, Sheffield 1993, pp. 145–85.

83. For the interweaving of geographical and patriarchal notions in the so-called 'Table of Nations' in Genesis, see John Skinner, *A Critical and Exegetical Commentary on Genesis*, London 1910, pp. 181–223. While firmly rejecting the biblical notion that 'nations are formed through the expansion and genealogical division of families' (p. 194), Skinner also refused to assimilate ancient ethnic conceits to modern racist ideas. In this he was very different from another eminent biblical scholar, William Allbright, who celebrated the destruction and expulsion of the Canaanites. Writing in the 1930s, Allbright furnished an example of the bivalency of racial stigmatization which, in Orientalist mode, condemns not the primitive but the sophisticated and decadent:

It was fortunate for the future of monotheism that the Israelites of the Conquest were a wild folk, endowed with primitive energy and a ruthless will to exist, since the resulting decimation of Canaanites, with their orgiastic nature worship, their cult of fertility in the form of serpent symbols and sensuous nudity, and their gross mythology, were replaced by Israel, with its pastoral simplicity and purity of life, its lofty monotheism, and its severe code of ethics. In a not altogether dissimilar way, a millennium later, the African Canaanites, as they still called themselves, or the Carthaginians, as we call them, with the gross Phoenician mythology which we know from Ugarit and Philo Byblius, with human sacrifices and the cult of sex, were crushed by the immensely superior Romans. . . . (W.F. Allbright, *From the Stone Age to Christianity*, New York 1957, pp. 280–81)

For a critique see Keith Whitelam, *The Invention of Ancient Israel*, London 1996, pp. 79–101. However, it would, of course, be anachronistic to attribute Allbright's absurd prejudice to early modern Europeans.

84. David Aaron, a critic of attempts to lend decisive significance to later Talmudic or midrashic elaborations of Noah's curse, which supposedly linked it to blackness, writes: 'There is enough of a textual handle in Genesis itself to make the Talmud irrelevant to the justification of black servitude. That is to say, Christians who claimed the Old Testament as their own, were not in need of midrashic parables on the descendants of Noah to find a theological justification for slavery.' David H. Aaron, 'Early Rabbinic Exegesis on Noah's Son Ham and the So-Called Hamitic Myth', *Journal of the American Academy of Religion*, vol. LXIII, no. 4, 1996, pp. 721–57 (p. 752). Strictly speaking the first statement says too much and the second too little. It was a type of ethnic or descent-group slavery that Genesis justified, neither 'black slavery' nor 'just' slavery. But Aaron is right to point to the shared legacy of Christianity and Judaism in this area. For the significance of Isaiah 3–4 see p. 742 of this informative article. For the use of genealogy to buttress social hierarchy see the title essay in Edmund Leach, *Genesis as Myth and Other Essays*, London 1969, pp. 7–23 (p. 21).

85. 'Our Rabbis taught: three copulated on the ark, and they were all punished – the dog,

the raven and Ham. The dog was doomed to be tied, the raven expectorates (his seed into his mate's mouth) and Ham was smitten in his skin.' *Sanhedrin* 208B, Rabbi Dr I. Epstein, ed., *The Babylonian Talmud. Seder Nezikin*, vol. II, *Sanhedrin*, chs VIII–XI, trans. by H. Freedman, London 1935, p. 745. The other examples are cited by Aaron, 'Early Rabbinic Exegesis', p. 741. Englishmen involved in colonization were to refer to such stories to explain why Ham's descendants were black, as was pointed out by Winthrop Jordan in a major study of English sixteenth- and seventeenth-century racial attitudes, *White Over Black: American Attitudes Toward the Negro, 1550–1812*, Chapel Hill, NC 1968, pp. 18, 35–7, 41–3. See also William McKee Evans, 'From the Land of Canaan to the Land of Guinea: The Strange Odyssey of the Sons of Ham', *American Historical Review*, vol. 85, no. 1, February 1980, pp. 14–43, especially pp. 25–6 and Edith Sanders, 'The Hamitic Hypothesis', *Journal of African History*, vol. X, no. 4, 1969, pp. 521–32. So far as the rabbinical contribution is concerned, Jordan and Sanders cited a literary work that was not well-adapted to the task, since it was a poetic compilation from several sources and given an independent editorial gloss: Robert Graves and Raphael Patai, *Hebrew Myths*, London 1964, pp. 120–24. These accounts registered a developing myth of Noah's curse, with some errors or imprecisions which have been challenged by Ephraim Isaac, David Lewis, David Goldenberg and David Aaron. Isaac and Aaron furnish translations of rabbinical texts which are either more precise, or more attuned to variant readings. Yet these authors do not convince when they seek to deny or minimize the Judaic contribution to Christian and Muslim doctrines of ethnic slavery. Clearly Genesis and Leviticus derive from Judaic sources and justify slavery of a descent group; they even furnish some hints which could be mapped on to later notions of 'Africa' and 'blackness'. All these authors rightly insist that a few incidental comments in the Talmud and Mishnah should not be accorded obligatory status within the corpus of Judaism; indeed, most lay believers will have been unaware of their existence. Nevertheless, the accounts supplied by these authors, whatever their intentions, actually confirm that a few rabbinical commentaries did elaborate on the curse of Noah, and on the link between blackness and Ham, in ways that left only a little further work to be done by Muslim or Christian writers. Unfortunately, the latter rummaged through Judaic texts, ignoring everything but the scraps convenient to their purpose; Muslims and Christians certainly bear full responsibility for their sometimes fanciful appropriations. But the record shows that all three of the 'religions of the book' admitted notions supportive of ethnic enslavement – notions that eventually came to be challenged, of course, by enlightened believers as well as non-believers. See Ephraim Isaac, 'Genesis, Judaism, and the Sons of Ham', in J.R. Willis, ed., *Slaves and Slavery in Muslim Africa*, vol. 1, London 1985, pp. 75–91; Bernard Lewis, *Race and Slavery in the Middle East*, pp. 123–5, n.9, and David H. Aaron, 'Early Rabbinic Exegesis on Noah's Son Ham and the So-called "Hamitic Myth"', *Journal of the American Academy of Religion*, vol. LXII, no. 4, 1995, pp. 721–55; David M. Goldenberg, 'The Curse of Ham: A Case of Rabbinic Racism?', forthcoming in a book to be edited by Cornel West. While these texts sometimes opt for apologetics, read in conjunction they correct one another, somewhat in the dialectical spirit of the Talmud itself. Thus Isaac's claim that the Judaism of ancient times entailed uniform respect for all non-Israelites, including Canaanites, with 'no explicit or implicit denial of their human dignity and their equality with the Israelites as human beings' (p. 79) would qualify as 'grossly anachronistic' in Aaron's terms (p. 748), since the latter recognizes that 'ethnocentric' and 'xenophobic' attitudes are often to be found in these Judaic texts. Likewise, Aaron offers a reading of the expression 'black but beautiful' in the Song of Songs (p. 745, n. 37) directly at odds with Lewis's claim that this should read 'black and beautiful'; on the other hand Goldenberg grants that 'red eyes' was a trope used about blacks, while Aaron contests it (p. 737). And so forth. See also the account in Hannaford, *Race*, especially pp. 90–95, 133–4.

86. Thus Martin Goodman shows that Roman Galilee in the second and third centuries was well connected to long-distance trade routes, exported olive oil and practised small-scale slavery, so that a household 'might have between one and four slaves to help in the fields and serve in the house'. Martin Goodman, *State and Society in Roman Galilee, A.D. 132–212*, Totowa, NJ 1983, p. 37–8; also pp. 17–24. However, this study has no specific mention of black slaves. Alien slaves were still referred to as Canaanite slaves: see Paul V. McC. Flesher, *Oxen, Women, or Citizens? Slaves in the System of the Mishnah*, Atlanta, GA 1988, pp. 54–9.

87. Lewis, *Race and Slavery in the Middle East*, p. 5 for the Essenes and p. 124 for St Ephrem. See also David Brion Davis, *Slavery and Human Progress*, pp. 21–2, 42–3, 86–7, and 337. Aaron expresses some scepticism as to St Ephrem's priority and states that anyway

the rabbis developed their own conclusions. Talmudic interpretations had authority for Christians and Muslims but the reverse did not apply.

88. Frank M. Snowden, *Before Color Prejudice: The Ancient View of Blacks*, Cambridge 1983, pp. 99–108.

89. St Augustine, *De Civitate Dei*, lib. xix, c. 15. Quoted in 'Letter of Pope Leo XIII', Brownlow, *Slavery and Serfdom in Europe*, pp. xxvii–xlviii (p. xxix). See St Augustine, *The City of God*, London 1984, p. 874. See also Book XVL pp. 648–53.

90. St Augustine declared in one of his epistles: 'What master is there who is not compelled to live in dread of his own slave, if the slave puts himself under the protection of the Donatists.' Quoted in Gervase Corcoran, O.S.A., *Saint Augustine on Slavery*, Rome 1985, p. 21.

91. See Jean Vercoutter *et al.*, *The Image of the Black in Western Art*, vol. 1, *From the Pharaohs to the Fall of the Roman Empire*, Cambridge 1976; and Jean Devisse, *The Image of the Black in Western Art*, vol. 2, *From the Early Christian Era to the 'Age of Discovery'*, Part 1, *From the Demonic Threat to the Incarnation of Sainthood*, Cambridge 1979, especially pp. 55–80 for Christian understandings of Noah's descent. All these books are furnished with appropriate and splendid illustrations.

92. Thus the ninth-century Persian chronicler al-Tabari cites Muslim writings that appear to echo the Babylonian Talmud; *The History of al-Tabari*, vol. 1, *General Introduction* and *From the Creation to the Flood*, trans. and annotated by Franz Rosenthal, Albany, NY 1989, pp. 365, 368. Several examples of the Muslim adoption of the legend of the curse are cited in J.R. Willis, ed., *Slaves and Slavery in Muslim Africa*, vol. 1, London 1985, and the entry in *The Encyclopedia of Islam*, ed. Bernard Lewis, V.L. Ménage *et al.*, London 1986, vol. 3, pp. 104–5.

93. Devisse, *The Image of the Black in Western Art*, II, Part 1, *From the Demonic Threat to the Incarnation of Sainthood*, pp. 149–208.

94. See John B. Friedman, 'Cultural Conflicts in Medieval World Maps', in Stuart Schwartz, ed., *Implicit Understandings*, pp. 64–96; John B. Friedman, *The Monstrous Races in Medieval Art and Thought*, pp. 100–03. Friedman reproduces a tenth-century map based on Isidore with the clearly visible designation Africa – Cham. Benjamin Braude has pointed out the haziness of much medieval ethno-cosmography but his information qualifies rather than contradicts Friedman's account. Cf. Benjamin Braude, 'The Sons of Noah and the Construction of Racial Identity in the Medieval and Early Modern Periods', *William and Mary Quarterly*, scheduled to appear in January 1997.

95. Friedman, *Monstrous Races*, pp. 45–6.

96. The views of Vincent of Beauvais, Albert le Grand and Roger Bacon are discussed and documented in François de Medeiros, *L'Occident et l'Afrique (XIIIᵉ-XVᵉ siècle)*, Paris 1985, pp. 122–56, 273–86.

97. Many of these claims are cited in Poliakov, *The Aryan Myth*, New York 1996. This work probably influenced the claim made in Foucault's 1976 Collège de France lectures that early modern class struggle was often couched in racial terms (e.g. English Saxons throwing off the 'Norman yoke' in the seventeenth century). Michel Foucault, *Genealogía del Poder, Genealogía del Racismo*, Madrid 1992.

98. Rigby, *English Society in the Later Middle Ages*, p. 312.

99. The views advocated by Andrew Horn in *The Mirror of Justices* are cited by Davis, *The Problem of Slavery in Western Civilization*, p. 115, and the reference to a thirteenth-century Cambridge bestiary deriving an element of the social order from the servi de Cham. Friedman, *Monstrous Races*, p. 236, n. 60.

100. Quoted in H.A.L. Fisher, *A History of Europe*, London 1936, p. 342.

101. Friedman, *Monstrous Races*, pp. 34–5.

102. Quoted in Kim Hall, *Things of Darkness: Economies of Race and Gender in Early Modern England*, Ithaca, NY and London 1995, p. 177. For the general treatment of the poor or deviant see Robert Jutte, *Poverty and Deviance in Early Modern Europe*, Cambridge 1994, pp. 158–62. The 'disorder of women' in the early modern period was held to require complete female subordination in the household and salutary punishment for those, such as female witches, who stepped outside it. Over the period 1560–1760 as many as 50,000 witches, four-fifths of them women, were burnt in Germany, several thousand were burnt in France and the British Isles – some 3,687 were accused in Spain, but in this case the Inquisition's role actually moderated the frenzy so that many fewer of the accused ended up going to the stake. Anne Llewellyn Barstow, *Witchcraze: A New History of the European Witch Hunts*, London 1995,

pp. 21–2, 179–81. See also Susan Dwyer Amussen, *An Ordered Society: Gender and Class in Early Modern England*, Oxford 1995.

103. Evans, 'From the Land of Canaan to the Land of Guinea', pp. 16–21. David Aaron also argues that the legend of the curse 'must be understood in part as a strategy against the breakdown of endogamy'. 'Early Rabbinic Exegesis', p. 741.

104. This story was invoked by George Best, 'A True discourse of the late voyage of discoverie', in Richard Hakluyt, ed., *The Principall Navigations, Voyages, Traffiques and Discoveries of the English Nation*, 2nd edn, London 1598, vol. 1, pp. 47–96 (p. 52). The Talmudic version is roughly given in Graves and Patai, *Hebrew Myths*, pp. 120–24 – but Isaac points out some inaccuracies in the translation. One version has it that Ham himself was physically changed as a consequence of his abuse of his father:

> (Canaan was cursed) but as for Ham because he saw with his eyes the nakedness of his father, his eyes became red; and because he spoke with his mouth, his lips became crooked and because he turned his face the hair of his head and his beard became singed and because he did not cover the nakedness (of his father) he went naked and his prepuce became stretched. (*Tanhuma, Noah* 13, cited by Isaac, 'Genesis, Judaism and Noah's Curse', in Willis, *Slaves and Slavery in Muslim Africa*, p. 86)

This and similar speculations were drawn upon to explain, or construct, racial difference by some early modern European commentators. Isaac also cites a passage describing the sons of Canaan which evokes stereotypical slave-like qualities: 'Canaan commanded his sons to do five things: Love one another, love robbery, love fornication, hate your masters and do not tell the truth.' *Pesahim*, 113, cited in Isaac, 'Genesis, Judaism and Noah's Curse', p. 85. See also Ronald Sanders, *Lost Tribes and Promised Lands: The Origins of American Racism*, Boston, MA 1978, pp. 62, 223–4.

105. John Thornton, Communication to the Conference on 'Constructing Race: Differentiating Peoples in the Early Modern World, 1400–1700', Institute of Early American History, Williamsburg, VA, April 1996.

106. Davis, *Slavery and Human Progress*, p. 337, n.144.

107. Davis also believes that Jews, Christians and Muslims all had to wrestle with the 'extraordinary anomaly of Genesis 9: 22–7: Noah's curse fell not against his offending son Ham but against one of Ham's four sons, Canaan.' Ibid., p. 337, n.144. But to many premodern or early modern peoples the individual existed only in and through the kin group and lineage. As in other biblical curses Ham is punished in his posterity and Canaan could be seen as simply standing in for the notion of 'son of Ham', just as Eve, with her tempting ways, stands in for womankind, and earns for them the pains of childbirth and servitude to men. As its name implies, Genesis is preoccupied with stories describing the origins of key relationships. But for an analogous problem see Avi Sagi, 'The Punishment of Amalek in Jewish Tradition', *Harvard Theological Review*, vol. 87, no. 3, 1994, pp. 323–46.

108. Sir Thomas Browne's *Pseudoxia Epidemica* (1646), ed. Robin Robbins, vol. 1, Oxford 1981, p. 159. Browne's objections are discussed in Chapter 6. Newton argued in his theological and historical writings that Ham's Egyptian descendants had been responsible for the corruption of Noachid wisdom. See John Gascoigne, '"The Wisdom of the Egyptians" and the Secularisation of History in the Age of Newton', in Stephen Gaukroger, ed., *The Uses of Antiquity*, Amsterdam 1991, pp. 171–212 (pp. 190–92).

109. George Sandys, *A Relation of a Journey Begun An: Dom: 1610*, 2nd edn, London 1621, p. 136. See *Purchas His Pilgrimes, or Hakluytus Posthumous*, London 1625–6, p. 913.

110. George Best, *A True Discourse*, in Hakluyt, *The Principall Navigations*, vol. 1, p. 52.

111. Samuel Purchas, *Purchas his Pilgrimage or Relations of the World and the Religions observed in all ages*, 3rd edn, vol. I, London 1617, pp. 51, 821, 822. Purchas's invocation of the essential unity of humankind in the Lord echoes a classic Christian belief. But when he writes (p. 822) of 'variety being swallowed up in an ineffable unity', 'without any distinction of Colour, Nation, Language, Sexe, Condition' he does not mean to challenge the this-worldly significance of such distinctions, any more than did St Paul. Cf. Ste Croix, *Class Struggle in the Ancient Greek World*, pp. 419–20.

112. See Gomes Eannes de Azurara, *The Chronicle of the Discovery and Conquest of Guinea*, Hakluyt Publications, 1st series, no. 95, London 1895, pp. 54–5; Richard Jobson, *The Golden Trade or a Discovery of the River Gambia, and the Golden Trade of the Ethiopians*, London 1623, pp. 65–6; George Best, *A True Discourse*, in Hakluyt, *Principall*

Navigations, VII, p. 236; Ronald Sanders, *Lost Tribes and Promised Lands: The Origins of American Racism*, pp. 62, 223–4; John Selden, *The Right and Dominion of the Sea*, London 1662, p. 21; Poliakov, *The Aryan Myth*, pp. 142–3. Further examples are given in several of the following chapters and in Alden T. Vaughan, *Roots of American Racism*, New York 1995. See also Hannaford, *Race*, pp. 89–91, 112, 137, 143, 170–71 for the pervasive influence of the Hamitic myth. Its invocation to justify African slavery in seventeenth- and early-eighteenth-century Brazil is noted by Ronaldo Vainfas, *Ideologia e Escravidão*, Petrópolis 1986, pp. 95–7. Vainfas points out that one source of the Hamitic legend cited by Portuguese writers was a work by the convert Leo Africanus published in 1550, *In Descriptiones Africa*.

113. David Brading, *The First Americans: The Spanish Monarchy, Creole Patriots, and the Liberal State, 1492–1867*, Cambridge 1991, pp. 278–9, 319; Giuliano Gliozzi, *Adamo e il Nuovo Mondo*, Florence 1977, pp. 444–513. For Josephus see Hannaford, *Race*, pp. 89–94, 180, 182; William Byrd, one of Virginia's leading colonists in its early years as a slave colony, used to read Josephus in Hebrew on a daily basis – see the entries for May, June and July 1709 in Louis B. Wright and Marion Tinling, eds, *The Secret Diary of William Byrd of Westover*, Richmond, VA 1941.

114. Alonso de Sandoval, *Un Tratado sobre esclavitud*, Madrid 1977 (a translation of *De Instauranda Aethiopum Salute*, Madrid 1647), pp. 74–5; *Obras completas do Padre António Vieira, Sermões*, vol. xii, Porto 1909, pp. 301–34; Morgan Godwyn, *The Negro's and Indians Advocate*, London 1680, p. 19; C. Spoelstra, ed., *Bouwstoffen voor der Nederduitsch-Gereformeerde Kerken in Zuid-Afrika*, vol. 1, Amsterdam 1906, pp. 33–4.

115. Richard Jobson, *The Golden Trade*, London 1623, reprinted with a new introduction by Walter Rodney, London 1968, pp. 46, 70, 65–6, 93.

116. Christian abolitionism was to play a significant role, together with radical democratic movements and slave resistance, in the suppression of New World slavery in the eighteenth and nineteenth centuries; of course, supposedly Christian and abolitionist colonial powers themselves practised racial oppression and forced labour. Nevertheless, abolitionist legislation did play a part in rallying anti-slavery forces and suppressing enslavement, as I try to show in *The Overthrow of Colonial Slavery*. In succeeding chapters some early critics of New World slavery will be noted, and in Chapter VIII the implications of an early ban on the slave trade are explored.

117. Hugh Trevor Roper, *The Rise of Christian Europe*, London 1965, pp. 101–30.

118. Norwich, *A History of Venice*, pp. 236, 271, 364; Charles Verlinden, *The Beginnings of Modern Colonization*, Ithaca, NY 1970.

119. Phillips, *Slavery from Roman Times to the Early Transatlantic Trade*, p. 97.

120. See Marie Louise von Wartburg, 'Production de sucre de canne à Chypre', in Michel Balard and Alain Ducellier, *Coloniser au Moyen Age*, Paris 1995, pp. 126–31. The account of the sugar factories in Cyprus given by William Deerr in *A History of Sugar* (London 1949–50, 2 vols) vol. 1, p. 84, cites a report that 'all the people are paid every Saturday' at the Cornaro estate of Episcopia. Wartburg's conclusion is reached notwithstanding the claims of Verlinden, *L'Esclavage dans l'Europe médiévale*, pp. 76–80, 883–93, 970–74. However, Verlinden also concedes that landlords preferred serfs to slaves.

121. An impressive recent account brings out the relative modernity of Venetian and Genoese enterprise. See Giovanni Arrighi, *The Long Twentieth Century*, London 1994. For their role in the Levantine sugar industry, see Jean Meyer, *Histoire du Sucre*, Paris 1989, pp. 66–71.

122. Bernard Doumerc, 'Les flottes d'état, moyen de domination coloniale pour le Venise (XVᵉ siècle)', in Balard and Ducellier, eds, *Coloniser au Moyen Age*, pp. 115–24.

123. Peter Fryer, *Staying Power: The History of Black People in Britain*, London 1984, pp. 2–4.

124. Kim Hall, *Things of Darkness*.

125. François Renault, *La Traité des Noirs au Proche-Orient médiéval, VII–XIVᵉ siècles*, Paris 1989. See also Bernard Lewis, 'The African Diaspora and the Civilization of Islam', in Martin L. Kilson and Robert I. Rotberg, eds, *The African Diaspora: Interpretive Essays*, Cambridge, MA 1976, pp. 37–56.

126. See *The Revolt of the Zanj*, vol. XXXVI of *The History of al-Tabari*, trans. and ed. by David Waines, Albany, NY 1992; and A. Popovic, *La Révolte des Esclaves en Iraq au III/IXᵉ siècle*, Paris 1976.

127. Popovic, *La Révolte des Esclaves*, p. 195.

128. E. Savage, 'Berbers and Blacks: Ibado Slave Traffic in Eighth Century North Africa', *The Journal of African History*, vol. 33, no 3, 1992, pp. 351–68.

129. Quoted in Lewis, *Race and Slavery in the Middle East*, p. 53.

130. Quoted in Willis, 'Islamic Africa: Reflections on the Servile Estate', *Studia Islamica*, p. 196.

131. Bernard Barbour and Michelle Jacobs, 'The Mi'raj: A Legal Treatise on Slavery by Ahmad Baba', in Willis, *Slaves and Slavery in Muslim Africa*, pp. 125–59 (pp. 130–31).

132. John Thornton, *Africa and Africans in the Making of the Modern World, 1400–1680*, Cambridge 1992, pp. xii–xxxvii, 43–71.

133. Ibid., pp. 72–97. For varieties of slavery in West Africa, see Claude Meillassoux, ed., *L'Esclavage en Afrique précoloniale*, Paris 1975.

134. Patrick Manning, *Slavery and African Life: Occidental, Oriental and African Slave Trades*, Cambridge 1990, pp. 27–37.

II

The First Phase:
Portugal and Africa

Vasco da Gama on the Coast of Angola

. . . it was no less demonstrably a miracle to all of us, a thing to strike terror in our hearts, to see the clouds drinking up, as though through a long spout, the waters of the ocean. First a thin smoky vapour formed in the air and began to swirl in the breeze; then out of it there took shape a kind of tube stretching right up to the sky, but so slender that one had to strain one's eyes to see it – made, as it were, of the very stuff of clouds. Gradually it grew and swelled until it was thicker than a masthead, bulging here, narrowing there as it sucked up the water in mighty gulps, and swaying with the ocean swell. At its summit a thick cloud formed, that bellied heavier and heavier with the mass of water it absorbed. Sometimes a beast, drinking rashly from an inviting spring, will pick up a leech that fastens on its lip and then slakes its thirst with the animal's blood: it sucks and sucks, and swells and swells. In the same way this mighty column waxed ever mightier and with it the black cloud that crowned it.

. . . looking up I saw my men returning with a black-skinned stranger in their midst, whom they had taken by force as he was gathering honey-combs on the mountain-side. His face betrayed his alarm in such a predicament. A savage more uncouth than Polyphemus, he could not understand us, nor we him. I showed him samples of gold, silver, of spices: they made no impression on him whatever. Then I bade the men produce baubles of no value, glass beads, tiny tinkling bells, a bright red cap; and it was at once clear from his signs and gestures that these delighted him greatly.

Luís Vaz de Camões (Camoens), *The Lusiads*, Canto V

The Portuguese initiated the Atlantic trade in African slaves in the mid fifteenth century, and for the next century and a half they virtually monopolized it. Portuguese princes obtained a species of Papal sanction for the trade, and the monarch established a *Casa dos Escravos* to tax and regulate it. They drew on the most advanced astronomical and mathematical thinking, ignoring the religious animosities of fellow Christians, in order to facilitate and replicate the voyages of discovery. They established colonies of settlers and imported slaves on a string of Atlantic islands; with help from Italian and Flemish merchants they turned these islands into producers of sugar, cotton and dyestuffs as well as wheat and cattle products. These institutional innovations were to have a major influence on the European colonization of the New World. They were the work of a kingdom and people at the cutting edge of Christendom, linked to commercial centres and possessed of a culture whose Latin matrix incorporated Muslim–Arab and Jewish components.

The Portuguese Reconquest was earlier and swifter than that of Spain; Lisbon was captured in 1147, and the last Muslim stronghold fell in 1249. The kingdom of Portugal had its origins in an earldom established around Oporto by Burgundian knights; the capture of Lisbon was accomplished with the help of English Crusaders, and in the years leading to the capture of the Algarve Italian ecclesiastics and French knights wielded influence. Merchants from all these lands accompanied the Crusaders; for all concerned, Portugal seemed a far more promising project than the Crusader kingdoms of the Levant, which it otherwise somewhat resembled.

The new kingdom of Portugal corresponded roughly to the old Roman province of Lusitania, conquered by Julius Caesar and thereafter colonized by Roman soldiery. Five centuries of Roman rule left the country with a strongly Latinate vernacular language, with only a few Celtic survivals. During some four centuries of Muslim rule the language remained Latin-based, but Arabic words were adopted for a range of technical terms relating to agriculture, irrigation and navigation. The late Roman period and subsequent Visigothic interlude had Christianized much of the population; a few Christian chiefs held out in the Northern hills following the Muslim conquest in the eighth century. The Muslim rulers tolerated a significant Christian minority in the towns, and a smaller Jewish community. When the knights of Portugal undertook the Reconquest of Lisbon and the Algarve, it was blessed as a Crusade and received decisive backing from the military religious orders as well as foreign Crusaders. The South was colonized, and slowly Christianized, in the thirteenth and fourteenth centuries, with small pockets of urban Jews and rural Muslims resisting conversion. Having drawn on support from several parts of Christendom to accomplish the Reconquest, Portugal's rulers kept alive these links as a guarantee of independence *vis-à-vis* the formidable kingdom of Castile. Indeed, there were times when their relations with Granada were better than those with their Christian neighbour. But as Castile also thrust southwards, Portugal shared with it an ethos which combined crusading pillage with feudal expansion, religious zealotry with pragmatic borrowings from the material culture of the Muslims, and Latin languages with Arabic accretions. Slavery was an accepted but marginal institution; Muslim agriculturists were generally reduced to serfdom, not slavery. However, Muslims who refused to yield could be enslaved. Sometimes Christian knights would raid the areas still controlled by the Muslims and seize hostages, in the hope that they would then be ransomed. Muslims captured on such raids would be subject to a kind of temporary slavery. Finally, the rich and powerful could buy slave domestics – usually heretics from the Black Sea or Bosnia. But although there was a labour shortage in the South, there was no recourse to large-scale slavery but, rather, an attempt to replicate the familiar formula of feudal expansion, with free Christian colonization and forced assimilation of the newly conquered population.

In the thirteenth and fourteenth centuries neither Portugal nor Castile had a strong mercantile class or navy of their own. Italian and Flemish merchants took a lively interest in helping them to digest the rich new lands that had fallen to them, and in marketing the salt of Setúbal and the wool of Castile, two crucial commodities in medieval and early modern commerce. The monarchs of Portugal and Castile were perennially short of cash. They had conferred tax exemption and generous land grants to those prepared to take the field against the Muslims. Special military–religious orders of monks and knights – of Avis, Santiago and Christ in Portugal; of Santiago, Calatrava and Alcantara in Spain – played an outstanding part in the Reconquest, and could also claim exemptions and land. Thus the fruits of the Reconquest in both kingdoms were garnered by a military aristocracy and the Church, leaving a comparatively modest portion for the royal domain. These circumstances help to explain the characteristic thirst for specie of the Iberian monarchs, and their willingness to consider money-making projects of exploration and colonization.

In 1382–83 a succession crisis in Portugal led to a clash between Castilian and Portuguese pretenders in which the latter prevailed, with backing from the Cortes of Coimbra and the guilds of Oporto and Lisbon. The new King, João I, master of the military order of Avis, defeated the Castilian forces in 1395; his line subsequently helped to foster a precociously national mystique based on military and mercantile exploits, undertaken as a crusade for the true faith. English bowmen played a role in the victory over Castile; João I was married to the granddaughter of England's Edward III, and concluded a 'perpetual alliance' with the English in 1396. When the English were distracted by their own conflicts, Portugal's rulers looked to Italy or France for help.[1] When Jews were driven from Aragon or Castile they were admitted to Portugal, where they contributed scientific and commercial skills.

The crusading goals of the Reconquest recommended projects of invasion of North Africa, where Muslim power was seen as vulnerable. In

1415 the town of Ceuta on the North African coast was captured by a Portuguese expedition, and turned into a fortified strong point. This event was hailed throughout Christian Europe. Over the next century or more the Portuguese seized, held, or sometimes lost a string of forts and small enclaves on the North African coast, including Algericas and Tangiers. Not all the Portuguese raids were successful, but booty and captives could be seized, the latter often exchanged for ransom. Portugal was variously encouraged and abetted in these raids by Castile, Aragon, Genoa and Venice, which all wished to see Muslim power challenged and the activities of the North African corsairs curbed. The Portuguese enclaves in North Africa also served as convenient conduits for trade, a circumstance of special interest to Genoa and Venice.

Portugal was not strong enough to make substantial inroads into North Africa, despite the instability of the Marinid rulers of Morocco and the gaps in their control of the North West of the continent. Whereas Portugal had a population of only a million, Morocco had a population of around six million, who could be mobilized in a jihad against Christian invasion, or any too-accommodating policy towards the Christians by local rulers. The trans-Saharan gold trade was controlled by the Sharifa of Morocco, or his vassals, in the North, and by the Muslim empires of Mali or Songhai in the South. The Portuguese found defending North African outposts an arduous and costly business. However, it brought prestige, kept alive the hope of eventual advance into North Africa, and furnished some possibilities for trade and commercial intelligence.

Exploring the African Coast

Portugal's ruling house remained critically short of financial resources, despite the glory it had won in North Africa. In Ceuta the Portuguese learnt details of the gold routes of the Sahara, of the wealth of Timbuktu and of the great river which flowed through it. One of João's sons, the Infante Henrique, sponsored a succession of Atlantic expeditions to the South and West from 1419 until his death in 1460. The primary aim of these expeditions was to outflank the Muslim power and find maritime access to the gold routes. But the prevailing winds and currents on the West African coast were a major obstacle – several who sailed down the coast never returned. The Infante Henrique, dubbed 'Henry the Navigator' by an English nineteenth-century historian, did little or no navigation himself, visiting North Africa only briefly three times in the course of a long life. However, the expeditions sponsored by Henrique led to impressive results: the setting up of trading posts and connections far down the African coast and the settlement of a series of islands, some of them well out into the Atlantic. Henrique contrived to be on the winning side of family conflicts, so that he always received backing from the King or Regent. However, he based himself at Sagres in the Algarve, and gave opportunities to the merchants and corsair captains of the local port of Lagos. The spirit he at first adopted has recently been described as 'The chivalrous ideology of "honourable robbery" and the superiority of armed force over the spirit of enrichment through pacific commerce.'[2] Nevertheless, as a royal prince he was perfectly prepared to combine raids on the African coast with the systematic work of island colonization.

Prince Henry encouraged his mariners to draw on the most advanced mathematical thinking and map-making of the time. The son of the Jewish map-maker Abraham Crespes found sanctuary in Portugal when he was driven out of Aragon. Iberian Jewish astronomers and mathematicians were conversant with the achievements of Muslim scientists, and extended the application of trigonometry to navigation. The Portuguese royal authorities shrouded the work of exploration in secrecy. Other Europeans might know that the Portuguese had discovered some new source of gold or spices down the African coast, but without the necessary charts and instruments they could not replicate their voyages.[3] While trigonometry and the astrolabe had been used to establish the direction of Mecca by Muslim savants, and celestial calculations used by Jewish savants to confirm the date of the Passover, the Portuguese princes encouraged the application of these techniques to celestial navigation and map-making. The settlement of a string of islands gave the Portuguese experience and staging posts for exploration.

Madeira was settled from 1419, the Azores in the years 1427–50, the Cape Verde Islands in 1450–60. These islands were previously uninhabited, unlike the somewhat closer Canary Islands. The costs of settling the new, uninhabited islands could be met by the introduction and culling of livestock, which multiplied rapidly in semi-wild conditions; by harvesting honey, by felling trees for wood – hence the name Madeira, which means 'wood' in Portuguese – and by fishing. Subsequently the islands proved suitable for the production of wheat, olive oil and wine. Early wheat yields were high, but the colonists were keen to find other cash crops. With varying success attempts were made on every island to cultivate sugar cane, Italian and Aragonese merchants supplying both the incentive and an element of expertise. Urzela and other dyestuffs were also produced. Enough of what was produced could be marketed to sustain a growing commerce with the metropolis. As more knowledge was gained of the complex wind systems and currents of the Atlantic, the islands also served as bases for trading and raiding further down the coast of Africa, with gold and spices acting as the lure.

The Portuguese and Aragonese were beginning to use a new vessel, the three-masted caravel, which, by using a lateen rig, could sail closer to the wind than other European ships of the time. This vessel represented a fusion of the nautical traditions of the Mediterranean, with its Arabic influences, and that of the Atlantic and Northern seas. It was an 'artisanal' craft, smaller and cheaper to build than the merchant ships of Genoa or Venice. The caravel made possible reliable round trips to the Atlantic islands to the West and South. Although Henrique undoubtedly sponsored persistent attempts to reach down the African coast, some voyages may have been undertaken by freelance traders. At Henrique's initiative a school of navigation was set up in Lisbon. While they preserved as much secrecy as possible, mariners and scientists sought to adapt celestial navigation to the skies of the southern hemisphere, and to improve the daytime readings of the astrolabe. Each voyage of discovery was registered with portolans, or navigation routes enabling it to be reproduced, backed up by mathematical formulas relating to latitude and distance.[4]

After Henrique's death in 1460, the royal authorities opted to license nautical expeditions to contractors who received commercial rights to exploit their discoveries in return for paying a fee and bearing the costs of exploration. The results of Portuguese expansion were to be dramatic, but in the mid fifteenth century its rhythms were gradual and experimental, advancing a few hundred leagues each decade. Portuguese rulers hoped to find a route to the East, to outflank the Muslim world, to find Christian allies, to acquire land and glory; but expeditions that paid dividends were best of all, and easiest to repeat. Early Portuguese accounts – like those of Zurara, to be considered below – played down the fact that trade with Muslims proved one of the most profitable activities. As they reached further down the Atlantic and African coast, the Portuguese captains found that they could exchange European or North African textiles or metalware for gold, malaguette pepper or ivory. They also discovered that the large 'Barbary horses' from North Africa were much prized, as they did not reproduce naturally in the West African savannah region.

So far as the royal authorities were concerned, the overriding preoccupation was to secure a supply of gold on advantageous terms. The Portuguese currency had been repeatedly devalued in the first part of the century, reflecting the monarchy's inadequate sources of revenue. To begin with the voyages netted modest amounts of gold dust, but at prices which dropped as the Portuguese advanced down the coast. Cape Bojador was turned in 1434, Senegal reached in 1444, the Cape Verde Islands in 1461–62. Finally the 'Gold Coast' was reached in 1470–71. In the 1480s and 1490s a string of forts, the best known of which were El Mina and Axim, were established on the Gold Coast. Remittances of gold to Lisbon rose dramatically. João II, who ascended the throne in 1481, was attentive to the message of gold receipts and sponsored exploration further down the coast of Africa. Diogo Cão reached the Kongo, and Bartolomeu Dias the Cape of Good Hope, planting stone crosses claiming their landing points for their monarch. Finally, in 1497–99, Vasco da Gama sailed beyond the Cape to India with an impressive expedition of 2,500 men, its costs underwritten by the profits of the Africa trade.

The Beginnings of a Slave Trade

In 1441 a Portuguese expedition on the West African coast captured two nobles; some gold was acquired by handing them back, as in the traditional Iberian practice of *rescate* or ransom. In 1444 a cargo of 235 captives, comprising both 'whites' (Berbers) and 'blacks', were seized in another Portuguese raid on the African coast, and taken for division and disposal to Lagos in the Algarve. However, the Portuguese captains soon discovered that they could, with less trouble and expense, also buy slaves and sell them to those involved in settling the islands, or to Portuguese or Spanish purchasers who wished to acquire an African servant or labourer.

West Africa was already a well-established source of slaves for the trans-Sahara slave trade at the time of the first Portuguese expeditions. The caravan traffic across the Sahara had developed strongly from about the ninth century with the exploitation of the gold mines of Western Sudan and the growing demand in the Mediterranean and Levant for African products; the slaves were a doubly convenient form of merchandise, since they walked and could carry other goods. The peoples of West Africa had practised settled agriculture and metalworking for well over a millennium before this; such skills, of course, made them more desirable as slaves. The expansion of Islam in the whole circum-Sahara region had helped to regularize the Saharan trade networks.

On the other hand, West Africa was still afflicted by fragmentation and endemic warfare, conditions that favoured enslavement and were exacerbated by the rise of the Islamic empires in the medieval period. The armies of Mali, Great Fulo, Kokoli, Mane, and Songhai undertook wars and expeditions in which large numbers of captives were taken. The empires of the savannah could have a devastating effect on the smaller communities of the forest zone, but were less effective against Moroccan troops. The marauding empires supplied captives and other merchandise to the Muslim merchants who organized long-distance trade. The smaller states of the coastal region were able to resist incorporation into the inland empires, and gradually to acquire the means to strengthen themselves through the sale of gold, pepper, provisions and captives.[5]

The first Portuguese *feitorias*, like that established by the Infante Henrique at Arguim, on the Mauretanian coast, were sited to divert gold, spices and slaves from the Saharan trade. The missions of Diogo Gomes in 1446–62 led to trade agreements with the African rulers of the coast, covering both gold and slaves. The Portuguese would offer the ruler regular presents or tribute in return for the right to trade. The merchants in their turn would pay Infante Henrique – or, after 1460, the Portuguese monarch – a fee for the licence to trade on these coasts, or risk being seized if they failed to do so. Occasional Castilian or Italian interlopers notwithstanding, such arrangements helped to establish Portuguese hegemony on the coast.

The Portuguese trading posts had provisioning and storing facilities, and could supply some protection.[6]

Along the Mauretanian coast opposite their island base at Arguim, the Portuguese found slaves easier to acquire than gold, though this usually meant dealing with Muslim traders. Slaves could be bought on good terms for Flemish or English cloth, copper, brass utensils, glass beads from Italy, salt, and horses.

The Portuguese were to be less secretive about their slave trading than about their search for gold, since they gave it a religious gloss. Bringing African or Berber captives to the Atlantic islands or to the Peninsula could be represented as entirely consonant with the objective of winning souls for Christ. In the 1440s and 1450s the Infante Henrique sought the Pope's approval for the colonization of Madeira and the Azores, and for the trading activities undertaken on the African coast. Since these islands, unlike the Canaries, were uninhabited and there were no rival claimants, and since the requests were made by a Portuguese princely Crusader, approval was forthcoming in a series of Papal Bulls issued between 1442 and 1456, the most comprehensive of which were *Romanus Pontifex* and *Inter Cetera*. The Bulls conferred on Henrique the task of spreading the faith by colonizing the islands and establishing trading and missionary posts on the African coast. He was appointed commander of the Order of Christ, a body which was to receive institutional privileges; on Henrique's death this title was to be assumed by the kings of Portugal. The Infante could claim a monopoly on the African trade, and offer spiritual as well as material incentives to those involved in his ventures. From 1442 onwards Henrique's expeditions were deemed a crusade, which covered raiding infidels and making captives. *Romanus Pontifex* (1455) declared that captives could be purchased so long as arrangements were made to win them for Christ; they could even be bought from Muslims, since the profits could be contributed to crusading activities and because pagans could be saved from the infidel and introduced to the Gospel message. However, Portuguese traders were not to offer firearms or war matériel for captives, since this would strengthen Muslim or pagan power. Those whom it was permissible to acquire were described as 'nigri' and inhabitants of Guinea.[7]

These Papal Bulls undoubtedly influenced official Portuguese accounts of what they were doing on the African coast. Writing in around 1453–54, when the slave trade was thriving but not yet endorsed by *Romanus Pontifex*, the royal chronicler Zurara compiled an account of the events of 1444 which stresses the overall religious justification for acquiring pagan or Muslim captives, while implying reservations about slave-hunting.

The capture:

> [T]hese two captains made preparations, and they took five boats manned by thirty men, six in each boat, and set out at about sunset. Rowing the entire night, they arrived about daybreak at the island they were looking for. And

when they recognised it by signs the Moors had mentioned they rowed for a while close to the shore, until, as it was getting light, they reached a Moorish village near the beach where all the island's inhabitants were gathered together. Seeing this our men stopped for a time to discuss what they should do. . . . And after giving their opinions, they looked toward the village where they saw that the Moors, with their women and children, were leaving their houses as fast as they could, for they had seen their enemies. The latter, crying the names of St James, St George, and Portugal, attacked them, killing and seizing as many as they could. There you could have seen mothers forsaking their children, husbands abandoning their wives, each person trying to escape as best they could. And some drowned themselves in the water; others tried to hide in their huts; others, hoping they would escape, hid their children among the sea grasses where later they were discovered. And in the end our Lord God, who rewards every good deed, decided that, for their labours undertaken in His Service, they should gain a victory over their enemies on that day, and a reward and payment for all their efforts and expenses.

Reporting to the Prince:

The caravels arrived at Lagos . . . and the next day, Lançarote, as the man who had the main responsibility said to the Prince: 'Sir! Your grace knows full well that he must accept a fifth of these Moors, and of everything we took in that land, where you sent us in the service of God and yourself. And now these Moors, because of the long time we have been at sea, and because of the obvious sorrow in their hearts at finding themselves far from their birthplace and held in captivity, without possessing any knowledge of what their future will be; as well as because they are not used to sailing in ships; for all these reasons they are in a rather poor condition and sickly; and so it seems to me useful that you will order them removed from the caravels in the morning and taken to that field that lies outside the city gate, and there divided up into five parts according to custom, and that Your Grace go there and select one of the parts which best suits you.' The Prince said that he was well pleased . . . but before doing anything else, they took the best of the Moors as an offering to the Church of that place, and another little one who later became a friar of St Francis they sent to São Vicente, where he always lived as a Catholic Christian.

The division of spoils:

On the next day . . . those captives, placed together in that field were a marvellous thing to behold, because among them there were some who were reasonably white, handsome and genteel; others, not so white, who were like mulattoes; others as black as Ethiopians, so deformed both of face and body that it seemed to those who guarded them that they were gazing upon images of the lowest hemisphere. But what human heart, no matter how hard, would not be stabbed by pious feelings when gazing upon such a company of people? For some had their heads held low and their faces bathed in tears, as they looked upon one another. Others were moaning most bitterly, gazing towards heaven, fixing their eyes upon it, as if they were asking for help from the father of nature. Others struck their faces with the palms of their hands, throwing themselves prostrate on the ground; others performed their lamentation in the form of a chant, according to the custom of their country, and, although our people could not understand the words of their language, they were fully appropriate to the level of their sorrow. But to increase their suffering even more, those responsible for dividing them up arrived on the scene and began to separate one from another, in order to make an equal division of the fifths; from which arose the need to separate children from their parents, wives from their husbands, and brothers from their brothers. Neither friendship nor kinship was respected, but instead each one fell where fortune placed him! Oh powerful destiny doing and undoing with your turning wheels, arranging the things of this world as you please! Do you even disclose to these miserable people some knowledge of what is to become of them, so that they may receive some consolation in the midst of their tremendous sorrow? And you who labour so hard to divide them up, look with pity upon so much misery, and see how they cling to each other, so that you can hardly separate them!. . . . And so with great effort they finished the dividing up, because, aside from the trouble they had with the captives, the field was quite full of people, both from the town and from the surrounding villages and districts, who for that day were taking time off from their work, which was the source of their earnings, for the sole purpose of observing this novelty. And seeing these things, while some wept, others took part in the separating, and they made such a commotion that they greatly confused those who were in charge of dividing them up. The Prince was there mounted upon a powerful horse, accompanied by his retinue, distributing his favours, like a man who wished to derive little material advantage from his share; for of the forty-six souls who belonged to his fifth, he quickly divided them up among the rest, since his main source of wealth lay in his own purpose; for he reflected with great pleasure upon the salvation of those souls that before were lost. And his thoughts were certainly not in vain. . . . I who have brought this history together in this volume saw boys and girls in the town of Lagos, the children and grandchildren of those people, born in this land, Christians as good and true as though they were descended from the beginnings of Christ's law, through the generation of those who were first baptised.[8]

At some points the vividness of these accounts belies the martial and religious comforts offered by the chronicler. Contrary to the portrayal of blacks in Italian and German paintings of the time, he insists here that they are essentially ugly – as he points out when he first mentions blacks, this is a sign of the curse of Noah.[9] But the account of enslavement remains disturbing, and the conclusion could be drawn that the objective of winning souls for Christ could be better accomplished by purchasing those already captive and in the hands of infidels or pagans. But at the same time the episode Zurara recounts protects the Prince from any charge of mercenary motives. Lançarote, a ruthless colonial entrepreneur, appears in the noble guise of a crusading captain. The figure of the wheel of destiny concedes the mutability of all human affairs. Zurara also urges further reflections on enslavement, arguing that it benefits body as well as soul, since many Africans live 'like beasts', not only unilluminated by the holy faith but also 'not knowing what bread is, or wine, or decent clothing or housing; and what is worse, an ignorance of who they are, having no knowledge of what is right, and living in beastly idleness'.[10] African captives could thus, through enslavement, be introduced to a useful life. It was to take Portugal and Christian Europe time and effort to construct for itself a justification of the Atlantic slave trade, but Zurara was already making headway, and doing so in terms that could be reconciled with the Papal Bulls. The chronicle's description of the reaction of the common people – some of whom wept and others, perhaps, protested the division of the captives – combines with the abruptly pious ending to mark the fact that the Portuguese were not yet fully inured to their new role as slave traders.

One of the more important branches of the early Portuguese slave traffic scarcely lent itself to religious justification, since it involved selling the slaves back to African traders or princes. This trade helped to boost gold receipts from the *feitoria* at El Mina. The goods which had been acceptable on the upper parts of the coast needed to be supplemented if the most was to be made of gold trading on the Mina coast. The traders found that to acquire gold at Mina on favourable terms, they also needed to be able to offer slaves as well. There were, in fact, no mines at El Mina, which was instead an outlet for the gold produced in the Akan forest region to the North. If slaves could be offered at El Mina, the African traders there could use them to carry other goods to the interior, where the gold was actually mined; some of these slaves were probably then employed mining gold. The result was swelling gold receipts at El Mina.

In fact, the Portuguese discovered for themselves that slaves were a flexible resource, serving some of the functions of money and making possible the holding of convenient patches of territory. Slave labour was used to fortify Arguim in 1455 and El Mina in 1480–82, and to maintain a supply of provisions for visiting ships. The slaves needed for trade at El Mina could be acquired on the Benin coast, which the Portuguese reached in the 1470s. The islands of São Tomé and Fernando Pó were settled by the Portuguese in the 1470s and 1480s, for use as a trading and slaving base; the labour of slaves was itself used to build fortifications, warehouses and churches. The Portuguese were able to control the coastal trade in slaves because of the efficiency of their caravels, and because maritime transport was far easier and more secure than land transport. While sailing ships, with their guns and raised decks, could usually defend themselves against African canoes, their dependence on the wind could expose them to danger. The Portuguese sent galleys to the Gold Coast, manned partly by local allies and slaves, to give them a flexible defence capability. These galleys were particularly useful for dealing with French or English interlopers.

Portuguese monarchs played down their trade in gold as much as possible, to discourage interlopers, but found this increasingly difficult once large and regular shipments began arriving. The surge in Lisbon's gold receipts reflected the success of a trading complex which drew on the profits of trading between the islands and the coast, as well as a gain on the exchange of Portuguese or European goods for the precious metal. The growing traffic in slaves not only contributed to these profits but also helped to meet the labour demands of the entrepreneurs of island settlement.

As the trade grew, the monarch raised the price of trading licences and introduced special taxes. In 1469 Fernão Gomes had leased the trade of all Guinea south of Sierra Leone for the modest sum of 200,000 reis a year – no more than 1,000 ducats – by promising to explore the coast to the South. He had developed the Gold Coast trade and established the first trading post at El Mina in 1572. In 1490 Bartolomeo Marchionni paid 1,100,000 reis – or about 5,000 ducats – for the trade of just the Rios dos Escravos region. The post of El Mina sent back about 58,000 ducats a year to Lisbon during this decade. In the 1480s a *Casa dos Escravos* was set up in Lisbon under the royal authority to organize the slave traffic to the islands and Peninsula, and to levy two taxes which comprised 30 per cent of the value of the slaves. Merchants purchased a contract to buy and sell slaves on a given coast or island, for a stipulated period; slave numbers were reckoned in terms of *peças*, or pieces, with each 'piece' being equivalent to an adult male slave, aged approximately fifteen to thirty and in good health; children or older slaves would be reckoned at a proportion of a *peça*, with taxes adjusted accordingly. On the islands female slaves were usually worth less than male slaves.

The *Casa da Mina* in Lisbon, chartered by the King and with its office in his palace, supervised the Mina trade, receiving the royal fifth on all gold transactions. By about 1500 a caravel would leave El Mina every month with gold worth more than 10,000 ducats. The Portuguese cruzado or ducat, once plagued by devaluation, was now acceptable throughout Europe. As we have seen, the gold sent to the *Casa da Mina*, or otherwise smuggled to Lisbon by sailors, had often not been directly acquired with Portuguese goods but represented the profits of Portuguese traders on the African coast, whether officially sponsored or not. Once Portuguese traders had a licence, they engaged in quite diverse trading activities. They employed local pilots and interpreters, and established local agents who often married into African trading families. The remittances of gold from El Mina and Arguim also reflected the profits of these activities.

Contracts for the slave trade with West Africa, excluding Mina and Arguim, remitted 4.2 million reis, or over 10,000 ducats, in the years 1511 and 1513. The King's total income from contractors in the slave trade and from the sale of the 'King's slaves' in around 1511 to 1513 is assessed by Saunders at 7 million reis a year, or some 18,000 ducats, a useful addition to the larger profits made on the Mina trade. The spice trade to the Indian ocean was worth 400,000 ducats at this time – however, the heavy expenses of the India trade reduced net receipts to 35,000–40,000 ducats in 1506; in that year the Mina traffic yielded 120,000 ducats, or 48 million reis, before expenses, the latter running at some 30,000 ducats, so that net receipts, at 80,000 ducats, were actually twice as large as those yielded by the fabulous trade of the East.[11]

The *Casa dos Escravos* organized a steady slave trade to the Peninsula – Spain as well as Portugal – since in both there was a demand for African captives. The captives were brought to Lisbon, where they were publicly auctioned. African slaves were thought to be more reliable than Moriscos, and more open to conversion to Christianity. They were, therefore, acquired as servants as well as labourers. There were already a few thousand African slaves in Seville in the 1470s; their well-being and control were entrusted to a city steward, the *Juez de los esclavos*, in 1475. There were repeated complaints at the Africans' turbulent behaviour, including those festive occasions when they drank, gambled or danced. But in the context of Spanish hostility towards and fear of the Muslims and Moriscos, the Africans were seen as a providential aid. While many were to be brought to the Peninsula, their numbers did not become so large as to be themselves threatening. They did not object to Christianity, and some even formed small religious brotherhoods. And with no hope of escape, they could be made to work hard. The cultivation of sugar cane spread in Valencia, conditions there being more secure than in the Eastern Mediterranean. The relatively brief prominence of Valencia in sugar-making is not well documented, but sugar-making skills were probably acquired from Sicily, and it is possible that some of the 2,500 African slaves who entered the port of Valencia between the years 1482 and 1516 were purchased for the demanding toil of the sugar works – though others will have been purchased as servants.[12] By this time, however, the lead in sugar production, and its attendant slave trade, was being taken by the Atlantic islands.

The Atlantic Islands

The Infante Henrique sponsored sugar production in Madeira, an island whose colonization had been granted to him and to the Order of Christ, of which he was governor. Keen to find a way of paying for his explorations and for further acts of conquest, he saw the sugar industry as a key to profitable colonization. Cane and processing equipment were brought from Sicily in 1446, and sugar masters from Valencia were engaged. The making of sugar was a complex and expensive business, and the growth of capacity was slow. As a dedicated monopolist Henry may have aimed at marketing a small, highly priced crop, using his contacts with Italian merchants. As the 'donatory' Henry granted large tracts of land to a few 'captains' who were charged with attracting settlers; this in turn could be done only by offering land on good terms to those willing to undertake the arduous tasks of preparing it for cultivation. The Portuguese settlers [*moradores*], while they were content to cultivate food crops and cane, were averse to the appalling toil of tending the sugar-boilers and mill, unless in some well-paid supervisory capacity. In 1456 there were said to be only 800 people on Madeira, of whom 150 were *moradores* or householders. The Order of Christ set up a sugar mill and produced 6,000 *arrobas* of sugar in the same year, equivalent to about eighty tons or a tenth of the sugar output of Cyprus. This was a modest beginning, but financially more advantageous than constructing another fort on the Moroccan coast. Enslaved Africans contributed to the labour force on the island, together with the Portuguese and Valencian specialists. *Romanus Pontifex* singled out for eulogy Prince Henry's successes in the work of colonization on this island.[13]

After Henry's death in 1460 sugar output developed rapidly in Madeira and the other islands, helped by a growing slave trade and a relaxation of Henry's privileges. Commercial prompting, with Genoese and Flemish merchants anxious to encroach on the Venetian near-monopoly of Levantine sugar production, played the crucial part in this development. Clearing, irrigating and planting land with cane was laborious. Equipping a sugar mill and staffing it with salaried sugar masters and slaves was costly. Both foreign merchants and Portuguese slave traders figured among those who owned mills. In 1480 Madeira's sugar trade attracted 20 large ships and 40 smaller ones to the island. Output rose to 80,000 *arrobas*, or over 1,000 tons, in 1494; four years later a decree sought to limit production to 120,000 *arrobas*, presumably in the interests of maintaining prices, but it was flouted by the producers. The island had now overtaken Cyprus as a supplier of sugar, and conducted a direct trade with Northern Europe and the Mediterranean. In around 1500 there were 2,000 slaves in Madeira, mostly engaged in sugar-making (though probably some servants as well), out of a total population of 15,000–18,000, including a large number of foreigners.[14]

The initial process of colonization had employed land grants to religious orders and feudal donatories, but there was no native peasantry to divide up. The expansion of sugar production was sponsored by merchant capital, and engaged a mixed labour force – Portuguese or foreign paid workers, African or Canarian slaves – with smallholding *moradores* supplying some of the cane for the mills. Around 1500–10 Madeira had 211 producers, but four-fifths of the crop of 120,000–220,000 *arrobas* was produced by 84 medium-sized producers, with an output of between 251 and 2,000 *arrobas*, the great majority of whom had their own sugar mill. About 130 smaller producers had to negotiate the milling of their cane with the owners of the mill. Two-thirds of the sugar estates were owned either by foreigners, especially Genoese and Florentines, or by New Christians. After 1521 Madeiran production dropped below 100,000 *arrobas* and never regained its former level. Undoubtedly it was hit by competition from São Tomé and the Canary Islands. Madeira's proximity to the Peninsula was a major advantage, facilitating both the arrival of settlers and the dispatch of crops, but cane did not thrive on the upper slopes of this volcanic island.[15]

*

The Canary Islands had been fought over by rival conquerors – Norman French, Aragonese, Castilian and Portuguese – since the mid fourteenth century. The native inhabitants successfully defended several of the principal islands down to the latter half of the fifteenth century. The Portuguese engaged in piecemeal trading and settlement of the Canaries wherever it proved possible, but did not undertake a comprehensive plan of conquest. Following a war between the kings of Portugal and Castile in 1476–79, the peace treaty allotted the Canary Islands to the latter. This marked the beginning of a protracted Castilian conquest and 'pacification' of the archipelago, to which reference was made in Chapter I. Doña Beatriz de Bobadilla, seignorial tenant of the island of Gomera, argued that the Gomerans required enslavement because they refused baptism, used non-Christian names, did not wear clothes and practised polygamy.

Those responsible for colonizing the Canary Islands were granted *encomiendas* by the Castilian Crown – these grants entrusted stretches of land to the leading colonists. The labour of the Canarian peoples was divided up among the estates by the parallel institution of *repartimiento*. Disease, enslavement, overwork and forced assimilation drastically reduced the native population. The Crown interceded in 1485, seeking to protect the Canarians from abuse and decreeing emancipation of those who had been taken in slavery to Castile. But controlling the settlers was difficult, especially since the Canarian peoples stubbornly continued resistance, though doomed by Castilian power and their own divisions. The numbers of native Canarians dropped from more than 10,000 in the middle of the fifteenth century to barely a thousand in 1500, but by this time the proprietors of estates in the Canary Islands were also producing sugar, and had the resources to attract free settlers and to purchase some slaves from Portuguese traders.[16]

By the early sixteenth century there were about thirty sugar *ingenios* on the Canaries, and output rose to about 70,000 *arrobas*. As on Madeira, mercantile sponsorship assisted this growth. The Welsers, the German banking family, at one point owned four sugar estates in the Canaries. One of the merchants of Tenerife is recorded in 1508 as having advanced 4.5 million maravedis (about 12,000 ducats) to enable landowners to build sugar mills. The owner of a sugar mill would engage sugar masters at high salaries, and often purchase the cane from other cultivators. Slaves were sometimes acquired for the skilled and unremitting labour in the boilers and mill of the *ingenio*. One large mill in the Canaries employed 23 slaves, of whom 20 were Africans. Smaller cane cultivators, who owned few or no slaves themselves, evidently disliked the terms offered by the mill owners and induced the municipality to set up its own communal mill on Tenerife; although this project failed, it suggests the commercialized and competitive milieu associated with sugar cultivation and processing.

Altogether about a thousand African slaves laboured at this time in the Canaries, but the labour force was quite heterogeneous, including free workers, native tied labourers, those of mixed Spanish and native descent (sometimes called *mamelucos*), immigrants from the Peninsula, and Berber or black African slaves. For a short time even Native American slaves were brought to work in the Canaries. Many of the smaller producers were Portuguese. Comparing the Canarian system with the later slave plantations of the Americas, Fernández-Armesto writes: 'The Canarian system evokes far more the methods of the Old World, and the equal sharing of produce between owners and workers is most akin to the farming *a mezzadria*, which developed in late medieval northern Italy and in some parts is still practised today.'[17]

The Azores had too temperate a climate for sugar cultivation, and no more than about 20,000 *arrobas* annually were ever produced, but slaves were engaged in the production of cotton and urzela, a purple dye. The westerly location of the Azores made them particularly useful as a way-station on the return trip to Lisbon and a staging post for North Atlantic fishing; these functions gave employment to some slaves and freedmen. The Cape Verde islands, lying in the tropics close to the African coast, were also used as a stopping point, and developed some slave-based agriculture. Too dry for successful sugar cultivation, they could nevertheless raise provisions and grow cotton; by the mid sixteenth century the latter was worked into cloth, most of which was traded for slaves on the coast.[18]

The southerly islands of São Tomé and Príncipe, lying close to the equator in the Gulf of Guinea, were to develop into major suppliers of sugar in the sixteenth century, their plantations readily stocked with slaves from the mainland. There were sixty sugar mills on São Tomé in 1522, and the large planters were said to own up to 300 slaves each, probably employed in cultivation as well as processing. By 1552 output had grown to 150,000 *arrobas*, or 2,150 tons, by which time it had long overtaken that of Madeira.[19] While slaves were part of the labour force on the other sugar islands, they were certainly not the only – and perhaps not the main – element. Here at last we find slave plantations that really are precursors to the pattern which subsequently developed in the Caribbean. However, the composition of the slaveowning elite was very different. Some 2,000 Jewish New Christian children had been deported to colonize the island in the 1490s. These involuntary settlers later intermarried with Portuguese traders, *tangomãos*, and aristocratic women from the kingdom of the Kongo.[20]

São Tomé's Afro-Jewish, Luso-Catholic planter class was not able to sustain its commanding position in the supply of sugar for long. The well-watered volcanic soil of São Tomé was well suited to cane cultivation, and slaves could be cheaply purchased, but other circumstances were to inhibit its sugar industry. It took three to six months for ships to make their way back to the Peninsula. The island's role as a way-station in the transatlantic slave trade created a demand for provisions which was a rival claim on its agriculture. Another inhibiting factor was the presence of large numbers of 'raw' slaves in transit; the revolt and flight to which they were prone proved disruptive. For a combination of these reasons São Tomé's role as a sugar producer was eventually to be eclipsed by the rise of Brazilian plantations – but the cultivation and processing of sugar in Brazil began slowly and hesitantly in the 1540s and, because of organizational and labour problems of its own, remained modest until it effected a takeoff after 1570 (discussed in Chapter IV below).[21]

The commercial style of the Portuguese monarchs still reflected the typical mentality of feudal business, with its preference for smallish quantities, high prices and a commerce that was visible and taxable. The traffic in Asian spices fitted-well with such an approach. The Portuguese Crown deployed its special agents, *feitores*, fortified trading posts and monopoly system to engross the maritime spice trade until, in the last decades of the sixteenth century, Dutch and English interlopers broke into it. In Asia as in Africa inter-local freelance trading activities – cabotage – constituted a wide basis which helped to finance the more restricted intercontinental trade. But the critical profit was reaped by the dispatch to Europe of a handful of galleons laden with spices – often no more than two or three a year. The Atlantic sugar trade was bulkier, and in some ways less easy to supervise. Royal officials could, of course, monitor the expensive equipment of the *engenhos de açúcar*, and the numbers of slaves engaged. But the trade in sugar, slaves and other ancillary goods involved a relatively large number of quasi-autonomous commercial agents and undertakings; it had developed a scale and momentum that pressed against the limits of feudal business. Northern merchants were permitted to visit Madeira or the Canary Islands to purchase wine, and were eager to acquire sugar as well. And while gold or silver was needed to purchase Asian spices, the entrepreneurs of the islands needed to buy European clothing, tools and provisions, so trade with them had a reciprocal dynamic. There can be no doubt that this was the beginning of the Atlantic slave complex.

African Slaves in the Peninsula

The overall slave population of the Atlantic sugar islands must have ranged around 10,000 during most of the sixteenth century. Philip Curtin has estimated that the trade in slaves from the African coast to Europe and the Atlantic islands totalled 175,000 in the century-and-a-half between 1450 and 1600. Of this total, he thinks, about 50,000 went to the Peninsula and other parts of Europe, which seems low in the light of the build-up of the slave population in Portugal alone. José Ramos Tinhorão estimates that between 136,000 and 151,000 slaves were brought to Portugal and its islands in the shorter period 1441 to 1505.[22] By 1550 there were 9,500

African slaves in Lisbon, comprising nearly 10 per cent of the total population, and – according to Saunders's careful and conservative count – 32,370 slaves and 2,580 freedmen in Portugal as a whole. These African slaves were clustered in Lisbon, Évora and the Algarve, but employed in ones, twos and threes by a wide range of corporations and individuals, including hospitals and government offices, nobles, priests, the servants of nobles, lawyers, shoemakers, goldsmiths, *lavradores* (rich farmers), shepherds, locksmiths, barbers, and in a wide range of other professions and trades – including the service of prostitutes, who were not allowed to hire free servants. Female slaves were nearly as numerous as male, a very different pattern from the norm on the islands.

Portugal had experienced commercial prosperity and otherwise retained a Mediterranean type of economy, based on wine, oil, some wheat, some fruits and vegetables, and certain special products, such as cork. Saunders suggests that an economy of this type, if an exception is made of those enriched by commerce and government, could absorb only a limited number of slaves, rising at most to 10 per cent of the labour force. Slave prices rose steadily in the sixteenth century – from an average around 12.5 cruzados in 1500 to 20 in 1520, 37.5 in 1540 and over a hundred in 1552, falling back to the range 37.5–75 cruzados in later decades. This rise reflected both general economic conditions and demand from the Americas. While small numbers of slaves could be worked hard in Portugal as artisanal helpers, there was little or no gang slavery. Before 1530 slaves destined for the Americas were meant to be brought to Lisbon or Seville, but from that year the Portuguese King permitted a direct slave trade with America.[23]

Notarial records for Seville, Granada and Córdoba for the years 1500–15 give details of 623 slaves owned by 443 owners. Nineteen nobles owned a total of 71 slaves, forty-five merchants a total of 66 slaves, and one hundred and seventy-eight artisans a total of 149 slaves, with others held by a scattering of professions and institutions.[24] By 1565 there were 14,500 African slaves in the bishropric of Seville, where they constituted 3.5 per cent of the population; in the city of Seville, where the proportion of African slaves rose to 7 per cent, they still worked as servants to the wealthy, as assistants to artisans or in the harsh environment of the soap works. While some of the domestics were female, the artisans and menial labourers were mostly male. Slaves were generally denied the opportunity to find partners or have children; to the extent that some few did, their descendants were probably thought of as servants or dependants. The numbers of African slaves declined rapidly in the last quarter of the sixteenth century. The demand for slaves in the Americas had raised prices on the African coast. In 1570 an African slave could be bought for around 22 ducats in Africa and sold for 64 ducats in Spain; by 1595 the cost of a slave in Africa had risen to 60 ducats, while the selling price in Spain was only 80 ducats – around this time such a slave could be sold in the New World for 150 ducats.[25]

In 1556 Castile's director-general of mines requested permission to acquire a hundred African slaves for employment in the silver mines at Guadalcanal. He argued that with an annual mortality rate of 5–6 per cent, such slaves would cost 17,676 maravedis compared with 19,264 maravedis for a free worker; the latter, rather well-paid German workers, had responded to an attempt to lower their wages by going on strike. The Africans had to work long hours in atrocious conditions; to make this possible, those put to the hardest work received a daily ration of over two pounds of bread, one pound of meat and a litre of wine, plus vegetables and other items. Through one contract in 1560, 88 African men and 12 women aged between eighteen and thirty were purchased for 72 ducats each; other slave purchases brought the total to 125. Four years later only 73 slaves were still alive, despite the fact that two more had been bought. Slave numbers dropped to 26 – 21 men and 5 women – in 1570, and to just 5 when the mines were closed in 1576: American silver production had rendered exploitation of the Spanish mines uneconomic. Five children born to the female slaves had been sold off. The employment of slaves had been more expensive than planned, but in this special branch of economic activity the investment had been recouped; moreover, in such mining there were some tasks that were so unpleasant and risky that free workers would shun them whatever the pay.[26]

The Atlantic islands absorbed an average of just under a thousand slaves a year, in Curtin's view. São Tomé would have been the largest purchaser, and was to remain a slave society. Because few female slaves had been bought, and because of the hard toil in the mills, the slave populations of the Atlantic islands did not reproduce themselves. São Tomé's estates, whether they produced sugar or provisions, could be built up by further purchases, or worked by slaves awaiting shipment to the Americas.[27] But on the other, northerly, Atlantic islands slavery was on the wane by the close of the sixteenth century, if not before.

Imperial Portugal, Africa, and Atlantic Civilization

The monarchs of Portugal had discovered the potential of commercial colonialism long before they were able to make good their claim to Brazil. As early as the beginning of the sixteenth century, royal revenue deriving from overseas commerce (African gold, slaves and spices; Asian spices brought by the Cape route; and Atlantic island sugar, dyes and cotton) comprised no less than two-thirds of the Crown's total income. In 1515, when the Asian spice trade was still young, Crown revenues from these sources comprised 68 per cent of the total.[28] About a third of all voyages in the latter half of the fifteenth century and the early part of the sixteenth were directly sponsored by a member of the Royal Family, Dom Manuel I (1495–1521). Manuel maintained the outposts in North Africa, but gave primacy to organizing the new trade of the islands and of Sub-Saharan Africa, and to establishing a direct trade with the East.

The monarch could use commercial profits to turn members of the *nobreza militar* and the military orders into royal employees and pensioners. In principle, however, the noble-born retained fiscal privileges and exercised a monopoly over positions of command. Thus the captain of a Portuguese galleon would have to be a *fidalgo*, whether or not he had any skill as a seaman; in fact all matters relating to navigation were reserved to commoner pilots. Likewise those to whom land was granted for colonization were also expected to be *fidalgos*, though the latter might subcontract to commoners. Flemish, Italian and German merchants made some investment in the effort to develop the islands and long-distance trade, but they were not averse to letting the Portuguese King and his gentleman adventurers take much of the risk. When sugar mills were established some owners enjoyed special privileges, thanks to their relationship to a donatory or their rights as a religious order. This was still a regulated form of feudal business but the royal authorities, their subjects and their foreign partners found that it had a generally expansive character because of the buoyant, European-wide markets to which they catered.

Portugal's role in the trade of the Atlantic and Asia helped to increase the size of its mercantile community, but this community retained a decidedly cosmopolitan composition. Portugal itself was too small to furnish a major market. Italian and Flemish merchants supplied the outset capital and could market the return cargo. In 1492 Portugal's trading community had been strengthened and enlarged when the King agreed to admit many of the Jews who had been expelled from Castile. Only those who agreed to Christian conversion were permitted to remain, but – at least as far as the wealthy and well-connected were concerned – this requirement was weakened by an understanding that the genuineness or otherwise of conversions would not be investigated. Portugal's so-called 'New Christians' were a vital force within a maritime empire that was on the brink of an extraordinary expansion, working as savants in Portugal or as *feitores* and independent traders in Asia, Africa or the sugar colonies. In the 1480s the Jewish astronomer Abraham Zacuto had drawn up a *Regimento do Astrolábio* which enabled latitude to be determined from any part of the globe. Jewish learning continued to inform the work of navigation, and Jewish commercial networks went on funding voyages even though Jews were subject to intermittent persecution. In Bruges or Antwerp most members of the 'Portuguese nation' – as Portugal's mercantile contingent was known – were New Christians.

The monarchs of Portugal were not keen to see the development of a strong, and hence self-assertive, Portuguese mercantile community. Such an entity would have threatened their monopolistic commercial practices, and might well have challenged the moves towards royal Absolutism which were a feature of the reigns of João II and Manuel I in particular. These monarchs were to find it convenient that Portugal's mercantile wealth was largely in the hands of a vulnerable community of New Christians, whose special status was never erased and which depended on royal protection. While Jewish commercial success derived from superior know-how, and far-flung networks of trust, it attracted the envy and resentment of some Portuguese. The kings of Portugal appeased this sentiment by restrictions which, echoing the categories of the Spanish Inquisition, reserved official posts to those who could prove their 'purity of blood'. The main beneficiaries of employment in posts of potential gain in the colonies were *fidalgos*, usually members of the quite numerous petty nobility. But the vicious notion of 'purity of blood' potentially offered some prospect to any Christian Portuguese who could prove he had no Jewish – or Morisco – ancestors.[29]

In the 1530s the eminent historian and royal counsellor João de Barros wrote that the Africa trade was the Crown's most dependable source of revenue:

> I do not know in this kingdom any yoke of land, toll, tithe, excise or any other royal tax which is more certain in each yearly return than is the revenue of the commerce of Guinea. It is, besides, so peaceful a property, quiet and obedient, that without our having to stand at the touch-hole of the bombard with lighted match in one hand, and lance in the other – it yields us gold, ivory, wax, hides, sugar, pepper, and it would produce other returns if we sought to explore it further.[30]

Barros neglected to mention the slave traffic, about which he may have been uneasy, yet he was otherwise right to stress the diversity of the Guinea trade – a category that included receipts from São Tomé, Príncipe and the Cape Verde islands. As it happened, the gold trade was to enter a decline from about this time, and Portugal's enjoyment of its colonies was to be increasingly challenged. Yet the sugar and slave trades compensated for the decline in gold, and gave Portugal every reason to defend itself against the interlopers.

In the second half of the sixteenth century, Africa-related and island-related trade came to loom even larger in Portuguese exchanges because of problems in Asia and the Ottoman success in serving as a participant in, and conduit for, East–West trade. By this time Portugal's African gold trade suffered from a revived trans-Saharan traffic, from New World production, and from foreign interlopers. In around 1560 the Mina trade was worth 14.1–18.7 million reis, or about 40,000 ducats, annually; while the slave trade, and other West Africa trade, reached a value of 34.7 million reis, or nearly 90,000 ducats. The buoyancy of this commerce reflected the success of sugar cultivation, the continuing trade in pepper and, most significantly, the growing trade to America.[31]

Slavery and the slave trade had turned out to be crucial to the whole enterprise of colonization in the Atlantic world. Quite apart from the direct trade in African slaves there was their critical contribution to gold trading, the maintenance of the coastal *feitorias* and the success of sugar-making. Then, from around 1520, Portugal supplied growing numbers of slaves for Spanish America, initially delivered to Seville. The fact that large numbers of slaves were brought to Lisbon for exhibition and sale suggests a brazen approach. Nevertheless, Manuel and his successors sought to protect themselves from charges of religious neglect in the conduct of the trade. In 1513 he obtained permission from the Pope to allow captains of ships sailing for Lisbon to administer baptism to mortally ill captives, and to erect a font in Lisbon exclusively for the baptism of slaves. Between 1514 and 1521 the so-called *Ordenações Manuelinos* comprehensively regulated the lives of the slaves and the conduct of the slave trade. Thus a royal edict of 1519 made provision for the baptism of slaves in the islands and coastal factories. Rules were laid down for their accommodation and feeding on board the ships (though no effective sanction ensured that they were obeyed). There were also regulations for the baptism of slaves prior to embarkation, though the provision of religious instruction was seen as a problem. While the spiritual and material welfare of the captives was the ostensible object of royal concern, so was control: the decree stipulated that slaves arriving in São Tomé should be branded with a cross (later changed to a G, the *marca de Guiné*), and a tax was payable on each slave. Manuel's laws were to constitute a slave code, systematizing previous legislation and reconciling it with Portugal's religious and military duties, and diplomatic objectives.[32]

The Manueline legislation on slavery was part of an attempt to construct a coherent stance towards the Portuguese role in Africa and the Atlantic. Portuguese embassies to African rulers were instructed to sound out the possibility of converting them to Christianity. If such rulers, as sometimes happened, expressed an interest in acquiring firearms, it was explained that such a supply could be arranged only for firmly Christian allies. The ruler of the Kongo accepted baptism in 1491 as João I, but was inclined to reserve the powerful mysteries of Christianity for his own exclusive use; his son Afonso I (1506–43) was eventually persuaded to declare Christianity the official religion of his realm. Young Kongolese princes were sent for education to Portugal, and one of them was consecrated as a bishop in 1518, with the Pope graciously waiving his reservations at this elevation of a twenty-four-year-old. The religious bond strengthened military and commercial ties: a letter from Afonso I to Manuel of 5 October 1514 spoke of military assistance received, of slaves sold to the Portuguese, and of other commercial possibilities.

In 1514 the ruler of Benin sent an envoy to the Portuguese King requesting a Christian mission and the dispatch of firearms, and complaining at the slave trading activities of the Portuguese on Principe and São Tomé. He died before these negotiations could get anywhere. Subsequently the ruler of the small neighbouring kingdom of Warri accepted conversion, and offered facilities for Portuguese slave traders, but the recalcitrance of the Beninois was to remain a problem. The Portuguese authorities and clergy expended much effort in following up conversions, seeking to ensure that they were genuine and permanent. This in turn put some pressure on Portugal to enhance the theological justification for such actions.[33]

In 1513 Manuel received an embassy from the Empress of Ethiopia promising 'mountains of provisions and men like unto the sands of the sea' for the common fight against the infidel. The Portuguese monarch responded warmly. Protracted and difficult negotiations ensued, including an unsuccessful attempt to arrange a dynastic alliance. Eventually, in the 1540s, the Ethiopian Emperor Geladewos again asked for Portuguese assistance in repelling an Ottoman-backed occupation of much of his lands; a Portuguese expedition of 400 musketeers commanded by Cristovão da Gama, son of Vasco, helped the Christian ruler to confront the invaders. After an initial reverse, in which da Gama was killed, the Christian forces, skilfully commanded by Geladewos, emerged victorious at the Battle of Woina-Dega in 1543. The Ottoman move had been blocked, and the Christian position in the Horn retrieved. Until the early seventeenth century, when the Jesuits secured a brief and disastrous conversion to Catholicism of a later member of the Solomonic dynasty, Portuguese hopes continued to be invested in securing some sort of alliance with the Empire, but the problems of communication were considerable.[34]

Portugal's only real success with religious colonialism was the kingdom of the Kongo, and here serious tensions were to develop, stemming from the pressure of the slave trade and a Portuguese refusal to allow their Kongolese acolytes more than a token margin of autonomy. The rulers of the Kongo repeatedly complained at what they saw as the disruptive activities of Portuguese merchants, breaching their royal monopoly and failing to respect the Kongolese conception of the legitimate scope of the slave trade. Afonso wrote to João III in 1526 complaining that the Portuguese traders who swarmed over his country were robbers and men of bad conscience: 'They bring ruin to the country. Every day people are enslaved and kidnapped, even nobles, and even royal kinsmen.'[35]

The Portuguese authorities themselves disapproved of freelance traders who escaped their own fiscal exactions, many of whom operated from Luanda, to the south of the Kongo, but in the end the monarchs of both Portugal and the Kongo found it convenient to tolerate the traders, however undisciplined or disreputable. The Portuguese found the *Pombeiros* essential for the supply of slaves for São Tomé or the Atlantic trade, and Afonso found that the freelance traders slightly reduced his stifling dependence on the Portuguese authorities in his relations with the wider world. Thus the Kongolese King sought to acquire a ship, but was continually fobbed off with one excuse or another as to why this was impossible or inappropriate. Likewise Afonso and his successors wanted the power to appoint their own bishops, and to have direct relations with the Holy See, but the Portuguese authorities frustrated and delayed this. Evidently African conversion was really welcome only if it was subservient to Portuguese temporal interests and power. In the 1560s the Kongo kingdom was invaded by the Jagas, a predatory military formation whose war culture, David Birmingham suggests, may have been shaped by the slave trade. The Portuguese successfully mounted an expedition to restore the kingdom, leaving it, for a time, more dependent on Portugal, its traders and clerics than ever.[36]

From the patriotic piety of Camões's *Lusíades* to the picaresque saga of Fernão Mendes Pinto's *The Peregrination*, it is clear that in this era the Portuguese felt that their country's destiny, its mission to spread the faith, rendered permissible many a bloody or sordid undertaking. While both authors, despite their many differences, were impressed by the nobility of China's celestial kingdom, in a world menaced by Muslim intrigue they thought Portugal was justified in resorting to what, in another context, would be simple piracy. And from Mendes Pinto there is the further implicit defence that life was a lottery in which the captain must be prepared to become a slave, just as the slave may hope to become a captain. Despite their impressive literary qualities, neither the adventurer's philosophy of Mendes Pinto, nor Camões's more elevated celebration of Lusitanian courage and virtue, straightforwardly addresses the mundane realities of the slave trade. Near Angola Camões's heroes witness the awesome spectacle of a gigantic whirlwind sucking up the ocean, but at São Tomé they simply note with satisfaction the worthy name it bears; during a brief landing on the African coast the only person kidnapped is a member of the Portuguese crew, taken by a crowd of Africans.

   The Peregrination does address enslavement and abuse, but through the device of reversal. Mendes Pinto himself is twice enslaved in the opening chapters. On the first occasion French pirates seize his ship and propose to sell him to the Moors in North Africa; they are deflected from this only by the capture of a ship from São Tomé, laden with sugar and African slaves, which they judge will be most advantageously disposed of in France. On the second occasion the author is captured by Muslims and auctioned in a public slave mart in Mocha, later to be sold back to the Portuguese at Ormuz by a Jewish trader. A popular compilation of accounts of shipwreck, many on the African coast involving treks back to a Portuguese trading post – the *História Trágico-Marítima* (1535) – showed that Mendes

Pinto's notion of enslavement as simply another turn of fortune's wheel was no singular conceit. In Portugal's precocious national drama, snatches of dialogue allude to the offence of racial stigmatization, but most pieces simply relayed patronizing stereotypes of blacks.

Yet sixteeenth-century Portugal also produced a trenchant denunciation of the slave trade in Fernão Oliveira's *Arte da Guerra do Mar* (1555). Oliveira damned his countrymen for being 'the inventors of an evil trade' which involved 'buying and selling peaceable free men, as one buys and sells animals', subjecting captives to every species of indignity. He insisted: 'And in this connection it is no excuse to say that they sell one another, because he who buys what is wrongly sold is still guilty, and because the laws of this land and others condemn him. If there were no buyers there would be no wrongful sellers.' While Oliveira's treatise was mainly concerned to instruct the Portuguese in better methods of naval warfare, he considered it necessary to preface this with a denunciation not only of the slave trade but also of any unprovoked aggression against 'Moors, Jews or gentiles who wish to be at peace with us. . . . To seize lands, to prevent their cultivation, to capture their people . . . is manifest tyranny.'[37]

It is not, perhaps, surprising that the man responsible for this indictment was soon in trouble with the Inquisition. More puzzling is the publication of the book in the first place. At this time Oliveira was the newly appointed director of the University Press at Coimbra. A curious mixture of scholar and adventurer, he had already been in trouble with the Inquisition for making remarks critical of the Church and favourable to England's Protestant monarchs.[38] His knowledge of English, French and Algerian naval methods seems to have recommended him to Portuguese patrons who found his unconventional views disturbing. The *Arte da Guerra do Mar*, the first published work on the topic, argued for a thoroughgoing professionalization of Portuguese warships, warning against aristocratic dilettantism and stressing the exacting skills and commitment required of the naval captain. In this work, and in a later treatise on naval construction, Oliveira argued that the training, morale and initiative of the crew was also a vital consideration, and denounced the French galleys, manned by slaves, as monstrous and ineffective.

At the time when Oliveira wrote, as we have noted, ships of the Portuguese royal squadron had to be commanded by members of the nobility, with questions of seamanship delegated to a subordinate professional seaman.[39] By the 1550s there was good reason to re-examine the principles governing Portugal's vital maritime communications, because of heavy losses at sea. In the years 1541 to 1549 the Portuguese had lost an annual average of 18 ships to French pirates, a figure which rose to 28 ships annually in 1550 and 1551. During a period when the Crown's maritime revenues averaged 500,000 cruzados a year, losses at sea averaged 213,000 cruzados: from piracy, shipwreck, and regular naval engagements. It is likely that Oliveira won a hearing, despite his unconventional views, because he had the knowledge and experience needed to address this situation. His books served to instruct the Portuguese in the naval techniques of some of their most dangerous foes – the English, French and Algerians.[40] Oliveira's arguments against the slave trade were to be taken up by a Spanish cleric, Martin de Ledesma, in his *Secunda Quartae* (1560), also published by the University of Coimbra.[41] The writings of these two men feed into a minority tradition of Dominican – and later Jesuit – questioning of the slave traffic, as subsequent chapters will show.

In the Age of Discoveries Portugal had circumnavigated the globe and brought its continents into regular communication for the first time. The Africa and island trade was only a small part of this but, quite unintentionally, it began to create elements of a new culture which overflowed the colonial project. There are increasing references to *Fala de Guiné* which, at first, seems to be no more than pidgin Portuguese. This is the language of many Portuguese seamen, who include black freedmen, of the descendants of the Portuguese *lançados* on the African coast, of many inhabitants of the islands and of the black population of the metropolis. There is already evidence in the sixteenth century for creole languages on the islands, representing a fusion of elements of Portuguese, Bini, and Kongo, with other Bantu lexical contributions. In this new cultural world a diffuse Christianity mingles with African beliefs, and new dances are referred to – the *mangana*, the *guinéo*, the *ye ye*, the *zarambeque*, and so forth. A well-known slave trader was noted for his rendition of the *mangana*, a slow, sad dance. Portuguese municipal legislation begins to regulate or sanction the *festas de negros*, seeing in them disorderly possibilities. Workmen and slaves are prohibited from playing ball games during the working day – slaves risk a whipping, and whites a double fine if they are caught playing with blacks. As might be expected, there is black or Afro-Lusitanian song and music, and the absorption of African words into Portuguese.[42]

In architecture and the plastic arts the Manueline period was notable for a clarity and strength, with a new openness towards Asian or African motifs, and the depiction of exotic flora and fauna (pineapples, elephants, and the like), with a profusion of gold leaf – the resulting decorative discordance has been called Manueline pre-baroque. The early-sixteenth-century Jeronymite monastery in Lisbon is a striking and sublime monument to this style.[43]

The Portuguese imperial project, kingdom and dynasty were plunged into crisis in 1578 when the childless young King Sebastião led his forces to a stunning defeat in North Africa at Alcácer-Quibir, resulting in the death or capture of a good proportion of the military nobility. The succession passed to the elderly and childless Cardinal Henrique, and immense sums had to be raised to redeem the woebegone crusaders in Muslim hands. The Portuguese House of Avis and the Spanish Habsburgs had long practised a

courtly species of matrimonial roulette, marrying one another in the hope
that their descendants would inherit the other's realm. When news arrived
of Sebastião's death, it seemed that the Habsburgs had won. On the death
of the Cardinal King in 1580 the main claimant to the throne was Philip II
of Spain, a grandson of Manuel, posing a profound threat to Portugal's
independent existence.

There were mobilizations in Portugal and its possessions against Philip's
succession and in favour of Don António of Crato. Don António was the
recognized son of Prince Luis de Beja, a brother of João III, and Violante
Gomes, a New Christian, though their union had never been publicly
celebrated. Don António was a Knight of Malta who had fought at the
Battle of Alcácer-Quibir; managing to make an early escape from his
captors, he had returned to Lisbon to popular acclaim in October 1578.
His candidature was backed by a number of urban, mercantile and colonial
interests, but his followers could not prevent Philip's forces entering the
Portuguese capital, though António did not leave Portugal until eight
months after the entry of a Spanish army commanded by the Duke of Alba.

In both Portugal and the islands, blacks were noted as taking part in
resistance to the succession of the Spanish King, some of them slaves who
were offered their freedom; some accounts say that Fernão Oliveira rallied
to Don António. Support for Don António was strong in the Atlantic
islands, and forces loyal to him held out in the Azores until July of 1583.
However, although Don António also received the backing of England and
France, he could not prevent Philip consolidating his hold on the kingdom.
Portugal's ruling powers, including the religious and military orders with
their investments in the islands, secured guarantees at the Cortes of Tomar
in 1581 that their interests and institutions would be protected by Philip.
With this endorsement armed expeditions were mounted to secure the
loyalty of the Azores, São Tomé, Príncipe and El Mina, where support for
Don António persisted.[44]

The Duke of Alba's troops and the Spanish fleet were convincing
arguments for a Spanish succession – not only because of their preponderant
force, but because Portugal's dominant class was suffering from a peculiar
crisis of confidence. This blow fell at a time when Portugal was struggling
to retain its hegemony in the East, and faced an interloper problem in the
Atlantic. The King of Spain, with his armadas, his silver, and his Counter-
Reformation zeal, appeared a providential protector to the conservative
sections of the Portuguese possessing classes. Many members of the Atlantic
colonial trading complex had cordial relations with the Dutch and the
English; those who were New Christians, as many were, must have seen a
Spanish succession as ominous. But Spain's royal authorities soon helped
to cement the loyalty of many Portuguese African traders by greatly
escalating the traffic in slaves.

*

From the standpoint of the history of New World slavery, the Portuguese had developed a source of slave supply unmatched in the New World itself. The African captives were generally inured to the disciplines of working the land, and some had useful knowledge of placer mining. They had resistance to a number of tropical diseases. Drawn from many different peoples and lacking common ties, they were inclined to adopt at least some of the language and culture of their owners. The distinctive colour they did share allowed them to be readily distinguished from Native American and settler alike. Unlike servants from other parts of Europe, their introduction was thought to pose only a modest political or religious risk. And while the ethics of enslaving Indians was soon in question, responsibility for reducing the Africans to slavery could be pushed back along the chain of purchase until it was invisible. For these and other reasons, as we will see in the next chapter, there was a keen demand for African slaves in Spanish America.

Notes

1. A.H. Oliveira Marques, *History of Portugal*, 2 vols, vol. 1, New York 1972; Flausino Torres, *Portugal, uma Perspectiva da sua História*, Porto 1974, pp. 87–94; Raymundo Faoro, *Os Donos do Poder*, São Paulo 1975, pp. 33–72.

2. See the entry for Escravatura in *Dicionário de História dos Descobrimentos Portugueses*, ed. Luis de Albuquerque, vol. 1, Lisbon 1994, pp. 367–84 (p. 377); and the entry for Henrique, pp. 485–90.

3. Seed, *Ceremonies of Possession in Europe's Conquest of the New World*, pp. 118–20.

4. De Oliveira Marques, *History of Portugal*, vol. II, New York 1976, pp. 133–64; Vitorino Magalhães Godinho, *L'Economie de l'empire portugais au XVᵉ et XVIᵉ siècles*, Paris 1969, pp. 40–41; Jacques Heers, *Société et économie à Gênes (XIVᵉ–XVᵉ siècle)*, London 1979, articles III, IV, X; Pierre Chaunu, *L'Expansion européenne du XIIIᵉ au XVᵉ siècle*, Paris 1969, pp. 120–66; Seed, *Ceremonies of Possession*, pp. 107–15.

5. Claude Meillassoux, 'The Role of Slavery in the Economic and Social History of Sahelo-Sudanic Africa', in J.E. Inikori, ed., *Forced Migration: The Impact of the Export Slave Trade on African Societies*, London 1982, pp. 74–99, especially pp. 76–80. The dimensions of the trans-Sahara slave trade are surveyed in Ralph A. Austen, 'The Trans-Sahara Slave Trade: A Tentative Census', in Henry A. Gemery and Jan S. Hogendorn, eds, *The Uncommon Market: Essays in the Economic History of the Atlantic Slave Trade*, New York 1979, pp. 23–76, especially pp. 65–6. For Islam and black slavery, see Bernard Lewis, 'The African Diaspora and the Civilization of Islam', in Martin L. Kitson and Robert I. Rotberg, eds, *The African Diaspora: Interpretive Essays*, Cambridge, MA 1976, pp. 37–56.

6. Pierre Vilar, *A History of Gold and Money*, London 1976, pp. 46–61; Bailey W. Diffie and George D. Winius, *Foundations of the Portuguese Empire, 1415–1580*, Minneapolis, MN 1977, pp. 76–88; John Thornton, *Africa and Africans in the Making of the Atlantic World, 1400–1680*, Cambridge 1992, pp. 43–72.

7. Levy Maria Jordão, ed., *Bullarium Patronatus Portugalliae Regum*, vol. 1, Lisbon 1868, pp. 31–4; James Muldoon, ed., *The Expansion of Empire: The First Phase*, Philadelphia, PA 1977, p. 54; François de Medeiros, *L'Occident et l'Afrique (XIIIᵉ–XVᵉ siècle)*, Paris 1985, pp. 265–6; C.R. Boxer, *The Portuguese Seaborne Empire*, London 1969, pp. 20–24; José Ramos Tinhorão, *Os Negros em Portugal: uma presença silenciosa*, Lisbon 1988, pp. 56–7.

8. I have used the modern English translation in Robert Edgar Conrad, ed., *Children of God's Fire: A Documentary History of Black Slavery in Brazil*, Princeton, NJ 1983, pp. 6, 9–10. See also Gomes Eanes de Zurara, *Crónica dos Feitos da Guiné*, Lisbon 1949, cap xxv; and Gomes Eannes de Azurara, *The Chronicle of the Discovery and Conquest of Guinea*, 2 vols, London 1886–87, vol. 1, pp. 63–83. The context is illuminated by A.C. de C.M.

Saunders, *A Social History of Black Slaves and Freedmen in Portugal, 1441–1555,* Cambridge 1982, pp. 5, 35; and Saunders's comments on p. 189; see also the entry for Zurara in Albuquerque, *Dicionário de História dos Descobrimentos Portugueses,* pp. 1096–7.

9. Gomes Eannes de Zurara, *Crónica da Guiné,* ed. José de Bragança, Lisbon 1973, p. 73; Azurara, *Chronicle of the Discovery and Conquest of Guineau,* pp. 54–5. The curse is said to fall on Cã, suggesting a confusion between Cain and Cham or Ham.

10. Zurara, *Crónica de Guiné,* p. 126.

11. Saunders, *A Social History of Black Slaves and Freedmen in Portugal,* p. 32. John Vogt argues that Mina made a clear profit, even after clearing annual expenses of over 30,000 cruzados a year during the years 1480–1540, John Vogt, *Portuguese Rule on the Gold Coast, 1469–1682,* Athens, GA 1979, pp. 90–92, 218–19.

12. W.D. Phillips, *Slavery from Roman Times,* pp. 160–64; Jean Meyer, *Histoire du Sucre,* Paris 1989, p. 71.

13. C.R. Boxer, *The Portuguese Seaborne Empire,* pp. 20–22; François de Medeiros, *L'Occident et l'Afrique (XIIIᵉ–XVᵉ siècle),* Paris 1985, pp. 257–64.

14. Diffie and Winius, *Foundations of the Portuguese Empire,* pp. 306–7; Noel Deerr, *A History of Sugar,* 2 vols, London 1949–50, I, pp. 100–01. (The output given by Diffie and Winius for the 1450s seems more soundly based than that of Deerr.)

15. Entry for Açúcar, *Dicionário de História dos Descobrimentos Portugueses,* pp. 15–19.

16. Anthony M. Stevens-Arroyo, 'The Inter-Atlantic Paradigm: The Failure of Spanish Medieval Colonization of the Canary and Caribbean Islands', *Comparative Studies in Society and History,* vol. 35, no. 3, July 1993, pp. 515–43; Eduardo Aznar Vallejo, 'The Conquests of the Canary Islands', in Stuart B. Schwartz, *Implicit Understandings: Observing, Reporting and Reflecting on the Encounters Between Europeans and Other Peoples in the Early Modern Era,* Cambridge 1994, pp. 134–56.

17. Felipe Fernández-Armesto, *The Canary Islands after the Conquest,* Oxford 1982, pp. 76–92 (p. 85). William Phillips, 'The Old World Background of Slavery', in Barbara L. Solow, ed., *Slavery and the Rise of the Atlantic System,* Cambridge 1991, pp. 43–61 (pp. 51–6).

18. Sidney M. Greenfield, 'Plantations, Sugar Cane and Slavery', in Michael Craton, ed., *Roots and Branches: Current Directions in Slave Studies,* vol./tome 6, no. 1, Summer 1979, of *Historical Reflections/Réflexions Historiques,* pp. 85–120 (p. 113).

19. Frédéric Mauro, *Le Portugal et l'Atlantique au XVIIᵉ siècle, 1570–1670,* Paris 1960, pp. 186–91; *Dicionário de História dos Descobrimentos Portugueses,* p. 18.

20. Stuart Schwartz, *Sugar Plantations in the Formation of Brazilian Society: Bahia, 1550–1835,* Cambridge 1985, has a good discussion of São Tomé's sugar industry on pp. 13–14, 506–7;. Joseph Miller, 'A Marginal Institution on the Margins of the Atlantic System', in Solow, ed., *Slavery and the Rise of the Atlantic System,* pp. 120–50 (p. 125); Greenfield, 'Plantations, Sugar Cane and Slavery', *Historical Reflections/Réflexions Historiques,* pp. 115–16.

21. Schwartz, *Sugar Plantations in the Formation of Brazilian Society,* pp. 14–15, 507.

22. Philip D. Curtin, *The Atlantic Slave Trade: A Census,* Madison, WI 1969, pp. 17–20; Tinhorão, *Os Negros em Portugal,* p. 80. For an informative discussion see Ivana Elbl, 'The Volume of the Early Atlantic Slave Trade, 1450–1521', *Journal of African History,* vol. 38, no. 1, 1997, pp. 31–75.

23. Saunders, *Black Slaves and Freedmen in Portugal,* pp. 27, 59–88.

24. José Luis Cortes López, *La Esclavitud Negra en la española peninsular del Siglo XVI,* Salamanca 1989, pp. 35–6.

25. Ibid., p. 178.

26. Allesandro Stella, 'L'esclavage en Andalousie', *Annales,* vol. 47, no. 1, Jan.–Feb. 1992, pp. 36–63. For slavery in sixteenth-century Spain, see Antonio Domínguez Ortiz, *The Golden Age of Spain: 1516–1659,* London 1971, pp. 161–5.

27. For the population of Lisbon see Mauro, *Le Portugal et l'Atlantique,* p. 147; but note the warning given by Oliveira Marques about the tendency to exaggerate the size of the slave population in Portugal and in Lisbon – the latter nearer to 5,000 in the mid sixteenth century in his view (*History of Portugal,* pp. 167, 294–5).

28. Vitorino Magalhães Godinho, 'Finanças públicas e estrutura do estado', *Ensaios,* II, *Sobre História de Portugal,* Lisbon 1968, pp. 25–64; for an account of the Portuguese social formation at this time, see also Vitorino Magalhães Godinho, *A estrutura na antiga sociedade portuguesa,* Lisbon 1971, pp. 68–94.

29. Boxer, *The Portuguese Seaborne Empire*, pp. 266–7.

30. João de Barros, *Décadas de Ásia*, vol. 1, Lisbon 1777, p. 264. Quoted in Vogt, *Portuguese Rule on the Gold Coast*, p. 93.

31. Saunders, *Black Slaves and Freedmen in Portugal*, p. 33.

32. Ibid., pp. 13–14, 40–42, 114.

33. The correspondence of the kings of Portugal with African rulers and with the Pope is reproduced in António Brásio, ed., *Monumenta Missionaria Africana: Africa Occidental (1471–1531)*, Lisbon 1952, pp. 291–358. See also J.D. Fage, 'Upper and Lower Guinea', in Roland Oliver, ed., *The Cambridge History of Africa*, vol. 3, Cambridge 1977, pp. 463–518, especially pp. 516–18; John K. Thornton, *The Kingdom of the Kongo: Civil War and Transition 1641–1718*, Madison, WI 1983, pp. xiv–xv, 133.

34. Taddesse Tamrat, 'Ethiopia, the Red Sea and the Horn', in Oliver, ed., *The Cambridge History of Africa*, 3, pp. 98–182, especially pp. 181–2; M. Abir, *Ethiopia and the Red Sea: The Rise and Decline of the Solomonic Dynasty and Muslim–European Rivalry in the Region*, London 1980, pp. 98–100. While Portuguese help for the Ethiopians was encouraged by sentiments of religious solidarity, the decisive factor may well have been Portugal's struggle to control the Red Sea, which it was blockading in defence of its monopoly of the Eastern spice trade.

35. Brásio, *Monumenta Missionaria Africana*, pp. 468–51, 470. After several more such letters João eventually responded, three years later but more positively than was subsequently to be the case (pp. 521–39); see also David Birmingham, *Trade and Conflict in Angola*, London 1966.

36. David Birmingham, 'Central Africa from Cameroun to the Zambezi', in Oliver, *The Cambridge History of Africa*, 3, pp. 519–66, especially pp. 550–53.

37. Padre Fernão Oliveira, *A Arte da Guerra do Mar*, Lisbon 1983, an extended reprint of a 1937 edn also comprising a fascimile of the original of 1555, published at Coimbra. The passages on the slave trade are at pp. 23–5 of the modern transcription.

38. Oliveira, born in 1507, entered the Dominican Monastery at Évora, where he had been taught by the humanist scholar and literary compiler André de Resende, and been accepted as a member of the order. In the 1530s he acted as tutor to the children of João de Barros, also an outstanding humanist scholar, counsellor of the kings of Portugal and philosopher of the Empire. In 1536 Oliveira published the first grammar of the Portuguese language. In the 1540s he had renounced Holy Orders and sailed as pilot to a French admiral, in which capacity he was captured by the English. His talents brought him to the attention of Henry VIII and Protector Somerset; the latter sent him as an emissary to João III of Portugal. See the entry for Oliveira in the *Dicionário de História dos Descobrimentos Portugueses*, pp. 815–16; and the editorial preamble to Padre Fernão Oliveira, *A Arte da Guerra do Mar*.

39. Vicente de Moura C. Almeida, *Lições de História Marítima Geral*, Lisbon 1973, p. 39.

40. For Portuguese losses, see Vitorino Magalhães Godinho, 'As Incidencias da pirataria, no sistema português do século XVI', in *Mito e Mercadoria*, especially pp. 463 and 475.

41. Doctoris Fratris Martini Ledesmii, *Secundae Quartae*, Coimbra 1560, pp. 225, 472 (Biblioteca Nacional, Madrid).

42. Tinhorão, *Os Negros em Portugal*, pp. 169–358.

43. Torres, *Portugal: Uma Perspectiva da sua História*, pp. 176–80; Saunders, *Black Slaves and Freedmen in Portugal*, pp. 105–7; William Washabaugh and Sidney M. Greenfield, 'The Portuguese Expansion and the Development of the Atlantic Creole Languages', *Luso-Brazilian Review*, vol. 18, no. 2, Winter 1981, pp. 225–38.

44. Entry for António, D., Prior do Crato, in *Dicionário de História de Portugal*, supervised by Joel Serrão, Lisbon 1971, pp. 157–9; Vogt, *Portuguese Rule on the Gold Coast*, pp. 127–49; Walter Rodney, 'Africa in Europe and the Americas', in Richard Gray, ed., *The Cambridge History of Africa*, 4, Cambridge 1975, pp. 578–611 (p. 583); Mary Elizabeth Brooks, *A King for Portugal: The Madrigal Conspiracy, 1594–95*, Madison, WI 1964, pp. 24–33.

III

Slavery and Spanish America

> Ver en un día . . .
> sombre y luz como planeta
> pena y dicha como imperio
> gente y brutas como selva
> paz y quietud como mar
> triunfo y ruina como guerra
> vida y muerte como dueño
> de sentidas potencias
>
> Calderón

With what right and with what justice do you keep these poor Indians in such cruel and horrible servitude? By what authority have you made such detestable wars against these people who lived peacefully and gently on their own land? Are these not men? Do they not have rational souls? Are you not obliged to love them as yourselves?

Fr. Antonio de Montesinos, Santo Domingo, 1511

Portugal owed its sixteenth-century Empire to oceanic navigation and naval gunnery. In the New World it was Spain's ability to conquer the indigenous Empires that enabled it to play the major role. So far as mainland Asia was concerned the military balance of power was such as to rule out European conquest on any but the most modest scale. The same was true of West Africa, where the Portuguese factories depended on agreement with local rulers. But in the New World Spain conquered, ruled and defended huge tracts of territory, while Portugal secured strips of land along a lengthy coast. Spain acquired by far the greater extent of land in the Americas, much of it densely populated, while commercial and maritime enterprise were more important to Portugal. Spain's *Carrera de las Indias* and Manila galleon were instruments of commerce, it is true, but they were to be subjected to, and constrained by, considerations of imperial strategy; Portugal's trading activities required a network of fortified islands and coastal enclaves, but many of these were not true colonies. Brazil was to be different, but until 1549 it was settled and run as a string of island-like coastal enclaves, with populations of a few thousand each and poor communications with one another (about which more in Chapter IV).

Pierre Vilar has called Spanish imperialism in the New World the 'highest stage of feudalism', while for Patricia Seed the ritual of the 'Requirement', invoking biblical history to justify conquest and inviting the native peoples to submit, was an echo of the Muslim practice of jihad.[1] Spain's monarchs aimed to turn conquered peoples into subjects and exact tribute from them. Whatever the original ideas of Columbus and his sponsors, the objective was not trade but mines and land, together with labour that could make them profitable. This was a different *modus operandi* from that of the Portuguese in Asia, who certainly practised forced trade, but found commerce generally more advantageous than conquest. There was a Caribbean trade in gold objects, cacao, feather garments, obsidian, and the like but the Spanish made no attempt to foster it. Instead they captured Indians for forced labour and planned expeditions to the mainland. Sometimes these raids represented simply a hunt for more captive labourers. On other occasions, as with several murderous meanderings through Florida and Tierra Firme, the Spanish unsuccessfully sought peasants to lord it over. Formal expeditions of conquest were meant to include, according to the stipulations of the Requirement, a call to the Indians peaceably to submit, in which case they would only owe tribute; if they failed to submit they faced enslavement. The royal authorities soon discovered that tribute, where it could be exacted from settled populations, was easier to keep track of than the profits of enslavement, which tended to accrue to individual colonists.

Cortés and Pizarro succeeded in defeating, demoralizing and taking over the empires of the Mexica and the Incas. Their expeditions were to take a dire toll, but succeeded in conquering people and land together. The conquests pitched small numbers of mounted and armoured soldiers, with steel swords and firearms, against warriors armed with stone axes, wooden shields and cloth armour. Horses and mastiffs contributed to worsting the defenders while large numbers of native auxiliaries were mobilized by the invaders. The empires of both the Mexica and the Inca contained large numbers of subject peoples who rallied to the outsiders. Barely more than 2,000 *conquistadores* were responsible for these conquests; their *caudillos* displayed great boldness, skill and ruthlessness, playing on the tensions within the Aztec or Inca order. The royal administration subsequently rose to the challenge of consolidating these gains, developing a formidable royal bureaucracy to impose a tribute system and bring wayward *conquistadores* to heel. The discovery of vast deposits of precious metal furnished both motive and resources for building an effective central administration.

From the outset the Catholic monarchs were jealous of their providential new acquisition; Cardinal Ximénez Cisneros, before as well as during his brief regency, ensured that the Church would be a resource of royal power – not only a watchdog of orthodoxy, but also the supplier of educated servants of the Crown, lay as well as clerical. The elements of the system of empire were elaborated by Charles V, now Charles I of Spain, (1516–56), and perfected by his bureaucratically minded son Philip II (1556–98). Huge advances from the Fuggers and Welsers helped Charles of Ghent to secure his election as Holy Roman Emperor, and make good his claim to be monarch of Castile and the Indies; the Welsers subsequently obtained the concession to exploit the pearls and salt of Tierre Firme (Venezuela), while both German banking houses were to make large advances on American silver. In 1520–21 the royal power confronted and suppressed the revolt of the *comuneros* and of the *germanias*, which gave expression to the urban, middle-class and popular forces who felt threatened or neglected by the new imperial settlement. The great nobles and merchants who controlled the wool trade, as well as those looking to benefit from the Indies, came to the aid of the royal power; a timely subsidy was even received from the Portuguese king.

Once they were firmly back in control, Charles and his ministers asserted a royal power which respected the particular privileges of aristocrats and *hidalgos*, merchants and historic corporations, but reserved for itself the central levers of power and the mission to impose a general design on monarchy and empire. The construction of a monarchy of a new and more universalistic type was briefly associated (roughly 1523–33) with royal encouragement of the humanist philosophy of Erasmus, prior to wholesale commitment to militant Counter-Reformation. Charles's option to become a truly Spanish king must have been encouraged by news of his expanding dominions in the Indies. His marriage to a Portuguese princess in 1526 acknowledged the need to take account of new worlds. He sought to use the resources and prestige of the Spanish Indies to further Habsburg and Christian goals in the Old World; in 1540 he dragged Hernán Cortés, the conqueror of Mexico, with him on his expedition to seize Algiers. Whatever the subseqent fortunes of the monarchy, the Americas loomed increasingly large as the ultimate proof of Spanish power.[2]

The most dignified and senior posts in the service of the Crown, the viceroys and provincial governors, came to be reserved to members of the nobility, usually cadet members of the leading families or holders of titles of the second rank. Some of the early, important viceroys – Mendoza in New Spain (Mexico) and Toledo in Peru – remained for more than a decade in their posts, but shorter terms then became more usual. When they had concluded their term there was an obligatory investigation of their perform- ance, often conducted with great thoroughness. Below them were various officials also answerable to the Crown, including the salaried *corregidor*, often a lawyer, who had important powers and responsibilities of his own. Both fiscal administration, *hacienda*, and justice, dispensed through the *audencias* (High Courts), had a parallel apparatus. Each of these instances employed *escribanos* to note all decisions and file reports. Towards the close of the sixteenth century a collection of royal legislation was published containing 3,500 decrees. While the bureaucracy of the *monarquía española* was hampered in Europe by traditional interests and exemptions, in the New World it proved able to impose itself successfully on both colonists and colonized. All commercial exchanges between the Old World and the New were channelled through the Casa de Contratación established in Seville in 1503, a historic capital commanding the resources and situation necessary for the task. The revenues obtained from this trade and from the sale of concessions and offices related to the Indies, boosted the credit of the monarchy and enabled it to manipulate the Cortes and other institutions.

From about 1519 the Council of the Indies met weekly, sometimes with the King in attendance, to consider the mass of petitions and memoranda submitted to the royal authority. The great majority of the 249 members of the Council appointed between 1519 and 1700 were university-educated *letrados*, very few of whom had ever visited the Americas; most Presidents of the Council were members of the nobility. The King could use the Church, the religious orders and the Holy Office to check the power of nobles and colonists, or to monitor the performance of officials. The Spanish Inquisition had two or three thousand people burnt at the stake as heretics between 1481 and 1530; the great majority supposedly Judaizing New Christians, but also others accused of adulterating the true religion with blasphemy, witchcraft or Islam, or with practising sodomy or bigamy. Between 1560 and 1700, 50,000 cases were investigated for a wide range of supposed religious offences, resulting in five hundred burnt at the stake, including some Protestant sympathizers, and many other sanctions, such as seizure of property. The Inquisition also issued certificates of *pureza de sangre* – that is, proofs of Castilian and Christian descent, free from the taint of Moorish or Jewish blood. The *patronato real* gave the monarch the right to present candidates for all religious posts, to authorize the passage of clerics to the Americas and, from 1568, to revise all correspondence between the Vatican and the Indies.

The religious orders were given extensive responsibilities for the spiritual conquest of the Indians, the invigilation of the colonists and the training of clerical and lay officials in seminaries, colleges and universities. A militant new order, the Company of Jesus or Jesuits, founded by a Spaniard, was entrusted with governance of Indian communities in a string of strategic areas. While American-born whites gained some representation, very few Indian or mestizo clerics were recruited, despite a shortage of priests who could speak the Indian languages. By 1630 Spanish America had 10 High Courts (*audiencias*), several hundred municipalities, 5 archdioceses, 29 dioceses, 10 universities, 334 monasteries, 74 convents, 94 hospitals and 23 *colegios*. Spain's feudal order had reproduced itself without a crucial ingredient: a Hispanicized peasantry. Instead, it confronted a majority Indian subject population, with only a relatively small intermediary layer of *castas*.[3]

African slavery and the Atlantic slave trade eventually made a significant contribution to the Spanish imperial formula. The introduction of African slaves to the New World had two aspects from the standpoint of the metropolitan authorities. First – and always a lively concern – the sale of licences to introduce Africans raised money for the royal treasury. Secondly, it helped the colonizing power to supply the urban centres and new enterprises with a labour force at a time when the indigenous population had been decimated.

The Conquest led to a catastrophic decline among the indigenous peoples of the continent. The population of the Americas was perhaps 50 million in 1500, with some estimates much higher, but barely 8 million in 1600. In the Caribbean the original population of the larger islands resisted enslavement, suffered from disease and overwork, and was either destroyed or driven to seek refuge out of reach of the conquerors. The populations of the islands of the Lesser Antilles, mainly peoples known as *Caribes*, resisted effectively enough to dissuade the Spanish from bothering to colonize them. The population of Mexico and Central America fell from 8–15 million in 1520 to a low point of 1.5 million by the middle of the next century. In the Andes, the other area of intensive cultivation and high density, the population fell from 9 million or more in the 1540s to under a million by the next century. The immediate cause of these terrible losses – among the worst known to history – was the unfamiliar plagues brought by the conquerors. Within a few decades the microbes that had been incubated for millennia by the dense populations of Europe, Asia and Africa were unleashed on the isolated American peoples; smallpox, measles and other ailments had a devastating impact on those with no resistance to them. The ravages of disease must have been gravely aggravated by the destruction of Indian communities, the disruption of established patterns of agriculture and the conscription of Indian labourers for deadly toil in the gold workings, mercury and silver mines, and sugar or cacao plantations. The administrative vigour of the conquerors contributed to the disaster, since they sought to concentrate the Amerindian populations in townships they could control; in doing so they helped to maximize exposure to disease.[4]

During the first three or four decades of the Conquest Indians were divided up by *encomienda* or *repartimiento*, and set to work cultivating food for the conquerors and washing for gold in the rivers and streams. This latter work is likely to have been particularly destructive because it meant prolonged immersion in water, increasing vulnerability to many diseases, and because there was no harvest cycle, with its periods of less intensive work. The peoples who inhabited the Antilles at the time of the discovery were hunter-gatherers, unused to the rigours of systematic cultivation, and now subjected to gold-panning or the notoriously implacable demands of the sugar mill. The first expeditions sent to the American mainland by the colonists of the Antilles had slave-raiding as their primary objective; in the period 1515–42 as many as 200,000 Indians were seized in Nicaragua alone and brought as slaves to the Antilles.[5] Yet the death rate was so high that Santo Domingo and Cuba lacked the labourers needed to maintain agriculture or support public works programmes. The reckless ferocity of the colonists was only accentuated by the resistance of Indian peoples. By the end of the 1530s the settlers' control of the larger islands of Santo Domingo and Cuba was menaced by large bands of rebels, some of whom had been brought to the islands as slaves.

On the mainland itself, Indians who resisted Spanish rule could be taken into outright slavery. Those Indian communities that submitted were required to supply foodstuffs, or labour for the roads or mines. Despite the inroads of disease, this latter method of labour recruitment proved more reliable, and enabled the conquerors to share the burden of procurement and invigilation with leaders from within the Indian communities. The indigenous peoples of the Americas had developed exceptionally high-yielding crops – maize, manioc, potatoes – which, if intensively cultivated, permitted a considerable agricultural surplus. The Mexica and their prede-cessors had intensified cultivation by means of an impressive irrigation programme; they had also established hegemony over a number of subject peoples throughout Meso-America. The Inca Empire drew together a patchwork of peoples in a highly organized and productive system. The social regime that formed in Spanish Central America and the Andes fused Pre-Columbian and Hispanic modes of domination and exploitation. Much of the Mexica ruling class willingly converted to Christianity and offered its services to the conquerors.[6] In the Andes many of the local *karaka* (lords) of the non-Inca peoples were willing to work with the *encomenderos*, and the more astute of the latter gave them an interest in the partnership by securing an *encomienda* for them too. Following the crisis and resistance provoked by the rapacity and clumsiness of the first conquest settlement, Francisco Toledo's tenure as Viceroy of Peru (1569–81) led to the reconstruction of a communal tribute system based on a detailed census and an appeal to Inca precedent. The massive resettlement programme he ordered had a devastating impact on the Indian population, but it did furnish the labour levies required by the mines and the tribute goods needed to maintain the imperial establishment.[7]

Some representatives of Crown and Church were alarmed at the decimation of the Indian peoples and the rapacity of many of the *conquistadores*. The Dominican friar Bartolomé de Las Casas, himself a colonist and an *encomendero*, campaigned against the mistreatment of Indians and managed to reach the Court with his representations. The royal authorities became alarmed at the prospect that the greed and recklessness of the colonists would stimulate further resistance and revolt. The 'New Laws' of 1542 and after abolished Indian slavery and the *encomienda* system by which Indians were bound to Spanish masters. (Significantly, the three mendicant orders rallied to the defence of *encomienda* in an effort to ingratiate themselves with the Spanish colonists.)

The Crown promulgated the 'New Laws' to curb the pretensions of the new lords of the Americas and to protect their patrimony from the most obvious source of devastation. The ending of *encomienda* was widely resented by mainland colonists, but the provisions suppressing slavery were more acceptable, since slave-raiding expeditions from the Caribbean depleted their available labour force. Once the main centre of gravity of Spanish America shifted from the islands, reliance on enslavement was bound to decline. Even the reduced Indian populations of the mainland still outnumbered their conquerors a hundred to one, while individual Indian slaves found escape even easier than did those of Hispaniola or Cuba. Despite official concern, enslavement of Indians did not entirely cease, especially at the periphery of the region of Spanish control. Those who revolted, or could be claimed to have done so, remained in danger of enslavement – but to fix their slave condition they usually had to be taken far from their place of origin, as were the *pueblo* Indians brought to the Isthmus. By 1550, however, slaves were not to be found any more among the Nahua peoples of Mexico; but there were *tlacotli*, or black slaves, owned by Spaniards with sufficient resources.[8]

African slaves became a strategic resource in the colonization process, because they were seen as at once more reliable, hardy and flexible than the indigenous populations, and capable of being directed to weak points in the imperial system. However, permission for their introduction was given cautiously and in small numbers, since there was always the risk that they would exacerbate the unsettled and delicate situation which prevailed in the early decades. Up to the year 1550 only some 15,000 African slaves were legally registered as entering Hispanic America. Some Africans accompanied the initial expeditions of conquest, in the retinue of the leading *conquistadores*. The first African slaves brought to the New World often came from the Canary Islands, or the Peninsula itself; in consequence they could speak Spanish and had adapted their skills to the colonizing society. In 1510 permission was granted for the export of 250 slaves from Lisbon, and in 1518 the first *asiento* was drawn up for slave trading. Slaves were admitted on a licence for which a fee had to be paid; by contrast Jews, Moors, foreigners and heretics – indeed, all those not subjects of Castile and of pure blood – were formally excluded from the Indies. It is quite possible that there was some contraband trade in slaves, since Portuguese traders were willing to sell them more cheaply than the official *asientistas*. The *asiento* has sometimes been described as an instrument of Spanish imperial manpower planning, but this is misleading, since the demand for slaves came mainly from individual colonists, for private purposes. African slaves were employed as servants, masons, carpenters, leather-workers, washerwomen and cooks, as well as on plantations and in the textile *obrajes* or workshops, where Indian labour predominated. Royal officials were certainly among those buying Africans, but these were for employment in their own households. Some African slaves were brought as *esclavos del rey* for work on fortifications and the like, but because they were expensive, such purchases were generally much less important than those made by individuals.

Bartolomé de Las Casas, the Dominican who campaigned against abuse of the Indians, found the enslavement of Africans in the early period acceptable, and proposed in a text of 1516 that the colonists should be permitted to introduce Africans in place of Indians. Las Casas recoiled against the utterly destructive impact of the Spanish colonists' exploitation of those entrusted to them, and vividly portrayed the *encomendero*'s greed, sexual rapacity and arrogance. The mass of those subject to *encomienda*, and even the Indian slaves brought from the mainland, had little commercial value; their lives were consumed in a year or two of forced labour, and they were prevented from caring for their families. There was a small population of the offspring of Spaniards and Indian women, but they were excluded from the *encomienda* system.

Las Casas wrote that he first 'began to consider' how unchristian was the treatment of the Indians when he heard a sermon in 1511 given on a text from Ecclesiasticus chapter 34, verses 21 and 22: 'The bread of the needy is their life. He that defraudeth him thereof is a man of blood. He that taketh away his neighbour's living slayeth him, and he that defraudeth the labourer of his hire is a bloodletter.' In the conditions of the early Spanish conquest the biblical imagery had a quite literal application. The colonists were destroying the Indians by brutality and overwork. As more and more were brought from the mainland simply to provide a labour force, and as resistance was cruelly crushed, the colonists themselves were clearly agents of destruction, without which the fevers, maladies or melancholy would have had no opportunity to cut down the Indians in such fearsome numbers. In 1516 the situation of the Africans seemed different to Las Casas. They survived life in the islands as well or better than Spaniards. They had a legal status with some rights, defined in Spanish law. They were treated like servants, but esteemed because they knew how to look after themselves and, by extension, how to look after their owners. Far removed from their native land, they were regarded by colonists as more dependable than the fickle and treacherous Indians; a few earned manumission and even minor office. When they were put to hard tasks, Africans carried them out effectively. But in the 1520s, when groups of Africans were put to the harsh labour of gold-panning or the sugar works, there were reports that they, too, had been driven to revolt or escape.[9]

Las Casas was to revise his views on the acceptability of African slavery as larger numbers became available, and as they were subjected to the most exacting employments. His change of heart represented partly a deepening of his hostility towards the colonists; but it was also in tune with the notion he had found in Ecclesiasticus that man should not be deprived of all benefit from his own toil. The 'humanist' inspiration of his views was rooted in a notion that 'all the nations of the earth are men', which entailed not only 'the faculty of reason' but also the ability and need to live by 'the sweat of their brow' and the right to receive at least a part of the fruit of their labour, as did the peasant or artisan. Since the urge to exploit was very evident in the demand for Amerindian and African labour, this emphasis lent significant reinforcement to the argument from reason. At the end of his life Las Casas wrote that he bitterly regretted ever having recommended the introduction of more African slaves, and was unsure whether God would pardon him for this. While the Dominican's representations on behalf of the Indian chimed in with royal concerns, his retraction concerning the Africans had no impact on imperial policy.[10]

The rate of importation of Africans increased as the century progressed, because Indian slaves were unavailable in the main centres and because the Spanish colonists had the money to pay for them. Since the authorities were slow to respond, privateers and interlopers from England and France began to practise a contraband slave trade in the middle decades. Yet the privateers' main interest was in attacks on silver and gold transports. The defensive reflex they engendered proved inimical to the interests of a broadly based exporting economy, and the more extensive slave trade that might have been linked to it.

While there had been a dreadful decline in the size of the indigenous populations, it is important to register that the latter still posed a potential threat to the conquerors. Moreover, for a considerable period their institutions preserved their vitality. The Spaniards had great need of intermediaries and subordinates. Africans often fitted the bill excellently: their facility with languages and lack of Castilian rigidity could make them particularly effective.

False Start in the Caribbean

The fate of New World slavery was to be bound up with the fortunes of plantation agriculture, yet in Spanish America plantation development stumbled after a modest start. From the early days of Columbus in Hispaniola the colonists sought to develop a commercial plantation agriculture, using mainly Indian slaves at first and then switching to Africans, some with experience in sugar-making. The Discoverer himself, and other members of his family, set up sugar plantations. There was nothing demeaning about engaging in such an enterprise. Columbus would have been aware of the illustrious and profitable precedents set by the Venetian Cornaro family, one of whose members reigned as Queen of Cyprus, and by Dom Henrique in Madeira. Cortés was to follow suit in Mexico, setting up sugar plantations in Morelos and near Veracruz. By mid century there were scores of sugar plantations in Spanish America, some of them worked by more than a hundred slaves, yet little sugar was dispatched to Europe. The *ingenios* of Hispaniola developed a capacity similar to that of the Canary Islands, but their early progress was hampered by Indian revolts, the expense of buying slaves and the danger of corsair raids. So long as they enjoyed special immunities and political influence, vice-regal families probably found plantation investment a reasonable proposition, but the cost of buying the slaves and sugar-making equipment for a plantation capable of producing the best sugar was immense.

The core of *ingenio* labour came to be supplied by several score of African slaves. The early *ingenios* consumed the lives of Indians, and they were subsequently banned from this work; even if they continued as an auxiliary labour force in the cane fields, it was deemed necessary to acquire an expensive African slave crew for the sugar works. Oviedo, writing in Santo Domingo in 1546, estimated the cost of setting up a sugar estate at 10,000–15,000 ducats, and estimated that one of the largest in the colony was worth 50,000 ducats. In the early years of Charles V the annual income of the Marquis of Mondejar, a grandee of Spain, was 15,000 ducats, while the income of the Duke of Medina-Sidonia, one of the two or three wealthiest magnates, was 55,000 ducats.[11] Such money could have been found if a reasonable calculation of risks, costs and revenues yielded satisfactory results. The authorities, aware of the difficulties of running a sugar estate, created the *privilegio del ingenio*, which prevented the assets of an *ingenio*, including its slaves, from being seized for debt. Prior to the silver expansion of the 1570s, official encouragement of the sugar industry

included special loans and tax exemptions, but such measures had few
lasting results. Once the dimensions of the silver flood became clear, the
perceived urgency of plantation development in the Caribbean declined. At
their peak, in 1558, the Spanish islands sent 60,000 *arrobas* of sugar to
Seville, but in the last decades of the sixteenth century Caribbean sugar
exports to Europe were negligible.[12]

The Caribbean sugar estates faced two big problems: defending the sugar
estate and marketing their sugar. French or English privateers were mainly
interested in gold or silver, but would happily plunder the *ingenios* and any
ship carrying sugar. The sugar estates set up in Peru and Mexico were
situated inland, and were far easier to defend. They catered essentially for
an American market, and their fortunes fluctuated with those of the new
colonial social formations. Indeed, it is a tribute to the wealth of sixteenth-
century Mexico and Peru that they could sustain even a modest sugar
industry. The mills established in Morelos, with an annual productive
capacity of 250 tons of sugar, were far from the sea but near Mexico City.
This orientation to an inherently limited colonial market was encouraged
by the workings of the metropolitan Casa de Contratación and by the
expensive and cumbersome *carrera de las Indias*, or fleet system. The
Spanish fleets, with their regular but infrequent sailings and high charges,
were geared to the transport of specie, not to a trade in plantation products.
One of the potential advantages of the Caribbean as a sugar-producing
locale, as compared with the Canaries or Madeira, was that the harvest
period extended over nearly six months; but a system of annual fleets could
not allow producers to exploit this. Official concern to sponsor a sugar
industry did not extend to a preparedness to disrupt the *flota* or tamper
with Seville's monopoly.[13] Space on the returning fleets often had to be
rationed. In the seventeenth century a modest sugar industry developed
under the protection of Havana's impressive fortifications; local officials
were, we learn, 'accused of permitting' the dispatch to Seville of 13,500
arrobas annually between 1635 and 1640. A study of twenty *ingenios* in
mid century finds that they had small slave crews: six had fewer than 9
slaves, ten between 10 and 19, two between 20 and 29 and two between
30 and 39.[14]

The silver of Peru had to be carried across the Central American Isthmus,
dispatched from there by means of a well-armed escort to Havana, where
it would meet the silver fleet from Veracruz on the Mexican coast and then
sail on to Spain. By mid century the swarm of French and English privateers
lay in wait to prey upon the fleets and to sack the ill-defended Spanish
Caribbean settlements. Having lost their indigenous population and modest
gold deposits, Santo Domingo and Cuba were abandoned by the mass of
Spanish colonists, who left to seek their fortune on the mainland. Away
from the direct line of the silver route, and sometimes even quite close to it,

the Spanish colonists lacked means of defence. By 1560 it was said that Santo Domingo, capital of Hispaniola, was the only municipality in the Spanish Caribbean whose militia could muster more than 200 men and boys. Some of the remaining population engaged in a smuggling or barter trade with the privateers, but the products involved were hides, provisions and tobacco; sugar estates were too vulnerable and too visible to sustain themselves mainly by contraband. Defiant Indians and runaway slaves, African as well as Indian, were to be found in many places, and they, too, engaged in exchanges with the privateers.[15]

In the first instance the *cimarrones* of the Caribbean were rebellious Indian slaves, but the term was soon extended to Africans who had escaped beyond the reach of Spanish power, whether or not they were linked to the Indian rebels. Spain controlled the core areas of the former Mexica and Inca empires, the mining districts and a series of strategic coastal regions and harbours. But there were large areas that they did not control. Many of the Indian nations of both South and North America had harried and expelled invading columns. For example, the resistance of the Araucanians denied Spain control of southern Chile. Outside the areas of Spanish conquest, the spread of herds of cattle and of horses furnished the Indian peoples with new resources which they quickly learned how to employ and mobilize against the invader. In the areas which had successfully repulsed the Spanish, fugitive blacks were often no more welcome than intruding Spanish colonists. But in several parts of the larger Caribbean and coastal area a *modus vivendi* was sometimes negotiated between hard-pressed Indian communities and groups of fugitive Africans. The latter were most often found adjacent to regions where slaves had been conscripted to the hardest labour, such as on the Caribbean islands, where slaves worked on sugar estates or construction projects, or near the central American Isthmus at Panama, where slaves were used as porters carrying heavy loads from one shore to the other. Inland from the salt pans and Tierra Firme, or the Spanish Main of South America, there were also groups of *cimarrones*. In some cases these fugitive Africans were said to be Muslims; certainly Muslim captives would have had an extra reason for escaping the clutches of the Spanish. In others escaped or shipwrecked Africans would ally with an Indian people, grateful for African help against the Spanish and other enemies, as happened in Esmeraldas on the Pacific coast of South America or in parts of the Lesser Antilles. The conflicts which erupted within the *república de españoles*, or between the *conquistadores* and the Crown, also furnished the occasion for revolt among slaves introduced to the mines, estates and workshops of New Granada and New Spain.[16]

The French and the English were greatly envious of Spain's mineral wealth. and continually sought to intercept it. The bolder privateers and pirates gradually came to develop contacts with several large communities of *cimarrones* in the vicinity of Panama, cemented by a trade of weapons and tools for victuals, skins and, perhaps, tobacco. By the 1560s French privateers, often Huguenots commissioned by Admiral Coligny, would raid the Spanish towns of the Isthmus in association with the *cimarrones*. Francis Drake's expedition to the Isthmus in 1572–73 was going badly until this former slave trading captain struck up an alliance with a force of thirty blacks who knew the country, had good intelligence of Spanish movements, and were connected to a mixed *cimarrón* and Indian community that was about three thousand strong. Their help was critical in an ambush which seized a mule train laden with silver and gold bound for Nombre de Dios. Later that same year, joined this time by the Huguenot privateer Le Testu, Drake and the *cimarrones* struck once again, making off with much of the specie carried by another mule train. The Spanish authorities in Panama reported: 'This league between the English and the Negroes is very detrimental to this kingdom, because, being so thoroughly acquainted with the region and so expert in the bush, the Negroes will show them methods and means to accomplish any evil design they may wish to carry out.'[17]

Acting on the correct supposition that Drake hoped to win local allies for further assaults on Spanish wealth, and that his example would inspire other predators, the Spanish authorities mounted savage attacks on those *cimarrón* settlements which they could reach, and apprehended some English sailors who had remained with them. After protracted and indecisive campaigns the Spanish commanders eventually offered a treaty to the *cimarrones* whereby they would be granted a self-governing *pueblo* on the Rio Chepo, on condition that they break relations with the English and agree to return any fugitive slaves who sought refuge with them. These terms were agreed to, and – at least so far as the first was concerned – complied with. When Drake returned to the Isthmus in 1596, the *cimarrones* refused to collaborate with him.[18] This satisfactory response no doubt encouraged the authorities to continue authorizing the large-scale import of Africans.

Between 1550 and 1595 only some 36,300 African slaves were imported by Spanish America, according to official records. But given the size of the African slave population of Mexico and other parts of Spanish America, it is certain that contraband increased the total by an indeterminate but possibly large number. Hawkins had little difficulty selling hundreds of African captives on each of his three voyages to the Caribbean; it is also known that there was much smuggling on the coasts of Tierra Firme and Mexico, with the involvement of Portuguese and Spanish traders as well as French and English. However, the really massive importation of slaves certainly did not occur until the period 1595–1640, during which time no fewer than 268,600 slaves were introduced to Spanish America, according to the official records. This large-scale influx reflects colonial demand for African slaves and the increased readiness of the Spanish Crown to cater to it. The Spanish authorities continued to regulate imports by means of *asientos*. In this case the *asiento* constituted a licence to sell a given number of slaves, and was sold to a foreign, usually Portuguese, merchant.[19] The same word was used to describe the great majority of contracts and loans negotiated to cover royal outgoings. Permission to trade in slaves was thus regarded as a tangible asset comparable to the right to receive the yield of a tax or of the royal fifth.

The Peninsular authorities were eager to maximize the flow of gold and silver across the Atlantic – in licensing a larger slave traffic they could do so in ways which, they believed, strengthened their hold on the New World. By this time Spanish America was reducing its purchases of Spanish foodstuffs and manufactures, because of the rise of local production – or because of a preference for luxury items produced in other countries. The slaves purchased from Portugal raised direct cash for the Crown, and enriched a kingdom now also ruled by the Spanish monarch. Some Africans were directly introduced to build fortifications, and reinforce the imperial communications, in areas of severe depopulation. Those slaves who had survived the march to the African coast and the 'middle passage' already had immunity to the most dangerous diseases. African slaves or their descendants came to comprise a third or more of the population in the colonized coastal lowlands of the circum-Caribbean region. They were engaged as an urban labour force or for work on plantations; those who gained their freedom could be enrolled in the militia. The absolute numbers of slaves in the Caribbean was considerably smaller than those absorbed by the great viceroyalties in the mainland, but they were of strategic significance.

Some idea of the overall contribution of African slavery to the colonization of the Hispanic New World Empire is gained by comparing slave imports to free Spanish immigration. In the early period the numbers of Spaniards entering the New World exceeded slave imports; while the latter totalled at least 60,000 up to 1595, net immigration of Spaniards was around twice as large. But from 1595 there is an official record of some 4,000 African slaves being sent to the New World each year, compared with Hispanic immigration of around 3,000 a year, some of whom would later return. Down to the 1640s African slave imports exceeded net European immigration to Spanish America by a considerable margin. Until 1596 the New World was kept as a Castilian preserve; other nationalities, including other subjects of the Spanish Crown, were formally excluded from settlement there. Even after that date no Spaniard legally travelled to the New World without a licence signed by the monarch himself; royal licences covered more than one person, but – soldiers and clerics excepted – averaged three per licence. The would-be emigrant needed to petition the *corregidor* or *alcalde* of his birthplace for proof of purity of blood, to supply testimonials from six witnesses, confirmed by three notaries, and to furnish the royal licence or a certificate establishing that it had been approved and awaited only the royal signature. Those prepared to take a risk, and at considerable expense, could acquire fake documents. Given these precautions, the cost of travel, and loss of earnings meanwhile, it is amazing that over 3,000 people a year left the Peninsula; a figure only to be explained by the excitement and resources associated with silver and gold, and the ability of those already in the New World to help their relatives.[20] Spain itself suffered a severe loss of population in the latter part of the sixteenth century, with particularly bad plagues in the 1590s, so there was less pressure to emigrate.[21]

African slaves had no prior entanglement in Europe's dynastic, religious or national rivalries: if they were properly handled they could buttress rather than undermine the power of Madrid. The Crown itself introduced slaves to the Americas for use in public works. Slaves constructed impressive fortifications throughout the Spanish Caribbean. They laboured in arsenals, chandlers, copper mines, logging camps, shipyards and provision grounds. Despite declining power in the Old World, and serious blows suffered in the New, Spain successfully defended the major sea lanes and Caribbean harbours. In the sixteenth century galleys were used to some effect against the privateers. In the early seventeenth century the *Armada de Barlovento*, whose warships were locally constructed out of hardwoods, continuously patrolled the Caribbean, and came to be feared by the smugglers and privateers. Cuban naval construction came to rival that of Northern Spain. In 1610 slaves comprised almost half of Cuba's population of 20,000, and furnished some of the skilled labour required by the royal arsenals and shipyards.[22]

Portuguese traders had always been essential to fulfilling the *asientos* even when these had been conferred on German Welsers or the Genoese. Following the Union of 1580 large contracts were sold directly to the Portuguese, to the considerable profit of the Crown. Finding ways to gather in as much as possible of the specie mined in the Americas was becoming ever more difficult. The colonists now produced their own wine, olive oil, leather goods and textiles, with results that undermined Spanish exports. But one transatlantic product – African slaves – was in ever greater demand as the Spanish confronted a worsening labour shortage. In 1561, as the first phase of the silver boom got under way, the value of Africans sold to Spanish America had been equivalent to 22.5 per cent of Peru's entire output of precious metal. In 1595 a Portuguese merchant contracted to pay 900,000 ducats to the Spanish treasury to acquire an *asiento* giving him the right to import 38,250 slaves over a nine-year period; around this time royal revenues from American silver were running at 2 million ducats annually.[23] The *asientista* himself sold shares in his licence piecemeal to particular slave traders and commercial backers. The terms of the *asiento* itself echoed the provisions of the original Portuguese slave trading licences; permission was granted for a given period to introduce for sale so many *piezas de Indias*, with each *pieza* supposedly equivalent to one prime male slave and infants and women as fractions of a *pieza*. Although male slaves outnumbered female slaves by about three to one, traders usually sought to exceed the numbers stipulated in their licence by invoking the *pieza* calculations.

The Antilles and Mexico had taken a large proportion of the slaves imported by the Casa de Contratación up to 1589. A survey of slave imports by port of entry for the years 1595–1640 (see Table III.1) shows a new pattern.

Table III.1   Spanish American Slave Imports 1595–1640

Port of Entry	Slave Imports
Cartagena	135,000
Veracruz	70,000
Other Caribbean	19,644
Buenos Aires	44,000
Total	268,664

Source: Enriqueta Vila Vilar, *Hispanoamérica y el comercio de esclavos*, Seville 1977, p. 226.

The slaves sold to the islands were few now compared with the numbers going to Mexico (Veracruz) and Cartagena, a port which supplied slaves to Peru, Venezuela and Columbia. No doubt the key reason for the salience of Mexico and Peru as destinations for African slaves lies quite simply in the fact that these were the centres of wealth and administration in Spanish America. Slaves helped to sustain the vice-regal capitals at Lima and Mexico City at a time when the indigenous population had suffered its severest decline. African slaves were employed as servants, overseers, skilled labourers, gardeners and general labourers, often in preference to Indians. The New World Spaniard regarded possession of African slaves as a badge of rank. They also worked as artisans and as labourers for construction projects. The textile workshops (*obrajes*) employed slaves, sometimes supervising the work of Indians, who were skilled weavers and cloth-makers. Another advantage of slave workers, whether in town or country-side, was that they could be subjected to continuous labour, while Indian *repartimiento* labourers had to be returned to their communities after an interval.

In 1636 the inhabitants of Lima numbered 27,394, of whom 14,481 were black or mulatto – that is, African slaves or their descendants. By 1650 the total black population of Lima had grown to 20,000, of whom about a tenth were free. Other towns and ports of South America, such as Cartagena, Arica and Quito, all had a high proportion of slaves in their populations. In 1570 the population of Mexico City was said to comprise

8,000 Spaniards, 8,000 black slaves and 1,000 mulattoes, with not dissimilar proportions in the smaller towns like Veracruz, Guadalajara, Merida and Puebla. Indians shunned the towns, whether for cultural or epidemiological reasons, leaving black slaves as the principal labouring force within them.[24]

Silver and Revenue: Exploitation without Enslavement

While most African slaves were to be found in the cities and along the lines of communication, they were also present in some of the mining districts. A census of those working in several important Mexican mines in 1570 notes the presence of 3,690 slaves, 1,850 Spaniards and 4,450 Indians; by 1597 the workforce of a similar list of Mexican mines comprised 296 Spanish mine owners, 1,022 slaves, 4,610 Free Indians, 1,619 *repartimiento* Indians, with a request for 2,544 more Indian workers.[25] In the Andean region the *mita* system of forced or tributary labour, a modified version of the Inca tribute system, supplied the basic labour force for the mines, though often not in sufficient quantity.

The *mitayos* were paid a daily rate in silver, linked to output targets, by the holders of mining concessions: access to this cheap labour was part of the value of a concession. Most of the *mitayo*'s silver earnings had to be passed over to the royal officials as part of the tribute owed by their community. The various Indian communities were obliged to send labourers for four-month stints in the mines to cover their quota; these labourers would arrive with some food for their stay, but in order to cover the costs of their subsistence they had to extend their period of work in the mines, working in rotation one week towards their *mita* service, two weeks as *mingados*, at a slightly better rate. The *mitayos* were allotted the hard but unskilled work of digging for the ore in shafts and galleries hundreds or thousands of feet into the mountain. The more skilled work of milling, treating and smelting the ore was performed by free workers. From the earliest days the Spanish relied on the *yanaconas*, bondsmen in the Inca system who had often rallied to the *conquistadores*, to provide skilled labour in the mines. A survey of the Potosí labour force in 1603 noted 4,780 *mitayos*, 11,020 *mingas* and 43,200 free workers; however, while all the *mitayos* and *mingas* were in the mining economy proper, this was the case for only 2,000 of the free workers.[26]

The Spanish authorities claimed the royal fifth from the mine owners, later reduced to a tenth, as well as collecting tribute from the *mita*. The tribute system also supplied a flow of basic foodstuffs and some clothing which, in turn, could be sold to the population of the mining districts. The free miner of Mexico or the Andes received a silver wage which would have looked impressive in Europe, but the miners and their families had to pay dearly for food, clothing, work tools, and shelter; any spare cash was spent on coca or chocolate. The political economy of the mining regions was such that the Indians who dug, smelted and refined the silver ended up with none of it, while the Spaniards, who did no productive work as such, ended up with all the precious metal. Around this time the Spanish *arbitristas* began to complain that Spaniards were the Indians of Europe, by which they meant that they did all the hard work of colonization while others, who supplied Spain with manufactures and foodstuffs, reaped all the profit.

The question must be asked: why were African slaves not more widely used in the silver mines? If the wages of a *mitayo* or *mingado* worker are compared with the price of a slave, then it could seem that there were some economic reasons why they should have been used. A *mitayo* had to be paid 3-and-a-half reales a day, the *mingado* 4 reales. Thus in one year the *mingado* cost/earned 1,224 reales or 154 pesos. The wages of free, skilled workers were considerably higher, though part of their reward was in the form of ore they kept. Before 1570 the price of a prime male slave in Spanish America was in the range 150–300 pesos, rising to 300–500 pesos over the subsequent half-century.[27] In Potosí slaves were never a significant part of the labour force, while in Mexico, where they once formed nearly a fifth of the mining workforce, their numbers dwindled after 1570.

It was said that Africans were unsuited to the climate of the Andes. But in addition to the cost of buying a slave, which might have been recovered in a few years, there were heavy subsistence costs that would have consumed most of the slaves' daily earnings. The mining city, with an estimated population of 160,000 in the early seventeenth century, was set on the barren *altiplano*, and most of its food had to be brought great distances; it could be fiercely cold, so heavy clothing was obligatory. The master who kept his slave at work in the mine would have to feed and clothe him at the high prices prevailing in the mining region, and could not expect the slave to fend for himself by gardening, as happened elsewhere. The small numbers of slaves brought to Potosí were servants or craftworkers. The economic motives prompting owners not to send their slaves to the silver mines also help to explain why this work, though paid, was unpopular with the Indians too. The colonial state itself profited from the high cost of living in the *altiplano* by selling clothing and provisions to the *mitayos* and free workers – this food and clothing having been extracted as tribute from the indigenous communities in the first place.

However, the intervention of the state, important as it was, did not fully solve the problem from the point of view of the holders of mining concessions, since it left them face to face with the demands of the free workers. While their profits were very high during the years of the early bonanzas, they later found themselves squeezed by taxes and wages. By the early seventeenth century several mine concessionaires did introduce Africans, partly as supervisors to extract more intense labour from their *mitayos* or *mingados* and partly as a lever to help them depress the wages of the free workers. This seems to have happened more in Huancavelica and Castrovirreyna than in Potosí, perhaps because living expenses were not so high in the former. Nevertheless, the African slaves still did not become the main labour force in any part of the Andes. The Spanish entrepreneurs found another way of lowering the cost of free labour by offering the usufruct of land to the free workers. The increasing numbers of *foresteros* – Indians who had deserted oppressively taxed communities – raised the competitive pressure within the ranks of the free workers, leading some to accept land in exchange for labour obligations. In this way the colonial entrepreneurs were able to turn to their own advantage the exploitative pressure of the colonial state through its taxes or levies.[28]

Although they were less renowned than the silver mines, the Spanish colonial *obrajes* were also a considerable economic feat, supplying most of the clothing used on the *altiplano*. A study of one centre of *obraje* production, Quito, reveals an industry drawing on the labour of 10,000 Indian workers and producing textiles worth a million pesos each year. In the late sixteenth and early seventeenth centuries Indian labour was communally supplied using the *mita* system, but as the industry developed labour was also drawn from so-called *voluntarios*, who were enmeshed in a system of debt-bondage and received only wages in kind. The *encomenderos* of Quito had rights either to communal labour or to a cash equivalent, with the existence of communal labour dues helping to depress the wages of other workers. Tyrer writes: 'The depressed wages of the obraje workers and payment in kind restricted the development of the cash economy in Quito and completely eliminated any possibility of the expansion of the domestic market which is usually associated with manufacturing.'[29]

One of the charges which the Indian communities were forced to pay, and which obliged them to find workers for the *obrajes*, was the salaries of the Spanish officials who organized labour conscription. A contemporary observer is quoted as commenting that for the community, 'to pay the foremen and impressor who brings the Indians, uprooting and violently incarcerating them, is like paying to be beaten, as they do in Turkey'.[30] This pointed observation testifies to the ruthless exploitation embodied by the *obrajes*, and to the Spanish attempt to manufacture a threadbare moral economy to cloak it. Among the personnel whose salaries had to be met were the *recogedor*, responsible for delivering the *mitayos*; the *alguaciles*, a steward or bailiff; the *protector de los naturales*, and the priest. The Indian caciques themselves could also share modestly in the *encomendero*'s profits. With tribute labour, or leveraged labour, available from the Indian villages, African slaves were rarely employed in Quito.

Slaveholding in a Baroque Empire

In one region African slaves did form the main labouring force involved in the extraction of specie: they panned for gold in the rivers and creeks of New Granada (Western Colombia). Around 1590 about a thousand slaves a year were purchased by those who owned the placer mines, presumably because Indian tribute or wage labour was not available here, and because slaves could grow their own food. The slaves were organized into *cuadrillas*, or labour gangs, under the direction of a *capitan*. They were permitted to work one day a week on their own account; they were also given plots of land, *piezas de roza*, on which they could grow food. At harvest time half the *cuadrilla* would be detailed to help bring it in. Ownership of labourers had priority over mining claims, and the *señor de cuadrilla* would be allotted stretches of land and river to work commensurate with his labour force. The slave population of the region did not grow as fast as might be expected – partly because of high mortality and sexual imbalance, but also, though to a lesser extent, because some slaves were eventually able to purchase their own freedom. Adult slaves were not expected to last more than seven or eight years in this work; if by the end of that time some had saved up enough to buy their freedom, the owner was doubly rewarded. The employment of slave labour in the placer mines was also assisted by the fact that gold, produced in more modest quantities than silver, maintained its value.[31]

The Spanish authorities liked to encourage each constituent caste – colonists, blacks and Indians – to maintain a distance from one another. There were laws banning Africans from Indian districts. Yet the shortage of Spanish and African women led to sexual unions and even marriage across the caste barrier. The children of Indian mothers and African fathers were, of course, free. Slave women were more likely to be manumitted than men; some married Spanish colonists, though there were regulations which sought to ban free black women from dressing like Spanish women. The regulations issued by the Spanish authorities were often ignored. In principle slaves enjoyed some of the provisions of the *Siete Partidas*, such as being able to appeal to be sold to another master because of unduly harsh treatment. In practice the slave needed the intercession of some powerful person or organization to have any hope of invoking such rights. The Inquisition very occasionally cited mistreatment of slaves in its indictments of those suspected of heresy. In other cases the baroque structure of Spanish administration, with separate instances encouraged to check and invigilate one another, offered opportunities to a few urban slaves to register a complaint. Thus the *audiencias* might sometimes appoint inspectors to investigate working conditions in the textile workshops in Mexico or the mines in Peru. In a study of hearings by the Holy Office in Mexico concerning mistreatment of slaves, only three cases between 1570 and 1650 resulted in a penalty for the master; two of these concerned the same master. Even extreme cruelty elicited only a fine and a recommendation that the slave be sold to another master. Two cases where slaves were killed led to no recorded sanction. Urban masters may have been a little less likely to abuse their slaves, aware that there was a slight chance of an embarrassing case being lodged against them by a neighbour or visitor; no cases were brought against rural slaveholders.[32]

In some parts of Spanish America slave cultivation of tropical staples did get under way, but little of it reached Europe. In the Caracas region of Tierra Firme slaves were put to work cultivating cacao. The slaveowners needed to own no more than a handful of slaves who could be offered the usufruct of a plot of land in exchange for tending the cacao bushes. During the intervals between harvests the bushes needed only weeding and watering; a detachment of slaves could be sent to plant more bushes. In the first place the market for cacao was, once again, mainly found in the Americas, with both Indian and *criollo* consumers. In Mexico cacao beans were widely used as a currency, with fifty beans counting as one real. The New World taste for chocolate spread gradually to the Old. Small and expensive quantities were dispatched via the *Carrera*, and some cacao was also sold to privateers. However, a taste for sweetened and spiced chocolate developed at the Madrid Court in the latter half of the sixteenth century, where it was both a drink permitted during periods of fasting and an accessory of aristocratic elegance. From Spain it spread to other baroque Courts, notably to the French Court after the arrival of Anne of Austria in 1615, retaining an aristocratic and clerical aroma for some time thereafter.[33] In the 1580s and 1590s the Dutch were barred from the salt of Setúbal, and sought to compensate for this by sailing to the large salt deposits along the Venezuelan coast; they supplemented the exploitation of this resource with a smuggling traffic in hides, tobacco and cacao.

The Spanish colonists in Central America also found it profitable to engage a parcel of slaves to gather and process indigo or logwood dye. These were products of the lowland tropical zone, to which it was thought Africans were acclimatized. The extraction of the dyes required harsh, unremitting labour, and could be easily invigilated, features which further adapted it to slave labour; in Amsterdam this work was reserved for prisoners.[34] In some areas of the Spanish Caribbean slaves may have been used to grow tobacco, though to begin with this was usually a crop grown by Indians or free settlers. Spanish Caribbean colonists had few qualms about smuggling, and were happy to sell tobacco, hides and skins to the Dutch and English. But the long-running battle between the Spanish authorities and the privateers made for an insecure environment which did not favour large-scale plantation slavery. Sugar plantations, with their costly and conspicuous equipment, were particularly vulnerable to attack, and mostly sheltered within range of the Spanish strong points. The seriousness of the inroads of corsairs and smugglers led the Spanish administration forcibly to evacuate the population of Northern Hispaniola in 1603, dismantling all buildings as they left; the Spanish settlements in this region were officially regarded as so many privateer and smuggling havens.

One of the principal products of contraband by this time was tobacco, much of it cultivated in Hispaniola itself. The Spanish authorities disapproved of this crop – partly because silver and gold were the only products thought to justify imperial investment, but also because the use of tobacco was associated with the despised culture of the Indians and blacks. Oviedo wrote in his *Historia General de las Indias* (1535): 'The Indians of this island, besides their other vices, possessed one of the very worst: that of inhaling smoke, which they call tabacco, for the sake of losing their senses.' Oviedo noted that the taking of tobacco was regarded as holy, and that the black slaves had adopted the habit of smoking it. While the smoking of tobacco spread from the Indians and the slaves to English, Dutch and French sailors, and from them to the European ports, it continued for nearly a century to be referred to very disapprovingly by the colonial authorities and by educated opinion. Carlo Ginzburg writes:

> . . . in the eyes of European observers, tobacco, in so far as it was an instrument of private pleasure and public ritual, semed like a wine which had lost its positive charge: a sort of sacred drink employed by natives in ceremonies that were considered idolatrous. Hence the distance between the detached response to opium, *bangue* and coca – intoxicating substances which the European observers associated (correctly or not) with a form of purely private consumption – and the manifest hostility to tobacco.[35]

When England's King James I came to write his 'Counter-blaste to Tobacco' (1604), he was at pains to stress its base origin:

> good Countrey-men, let us (I pray you) consider what honour or policy can move us to imitate the barbarous and beastly manners of the wild, godless and slavish Indians, especially in so vile and stinking a custom. . . . Why do we not imitate them in walking naked as they do? . . . It [tobacco] was neither brought in by King, Great Conqueror, nor learned doctor of physic.

He saw his subjects' rage for tobacco as 'the foolish affectation of any novelty', and lamented that accepting an offered pipe had become 'a point of good fellowship'. He claimed that even among the Indians tobacco taking was known to destroy good habits, and that they would offer 'no price for a slave to be sold, who is a great tobacco taker'.[36]

*

Down to the mid seventeenth century, about a third of a million African slaves were brought to Spanish America. Without them the Spanish authorities and colonists would have been obliged to fill their place by offering different and better terms either to free immigrants or to the Indians, or even to both. But Madrid could not weaken its grip on immigration without sacrificing the principles of the *monarquía española*, while the colonists were determined to maintain the mass of Indians in subordination. The availability of African slaves thus appeared providential, offering the powerholders the hope that their power would not have to be compromised, and literally sustaining and feeding the main centres of Spanish population. The imposing system of empire and its attendant caste arrangements were able to consolidate themselves, but at the cost of encouraging inertia and parasitism. The Spanish 'crisis of empire' was thus resolved in a conservative way.

The varied use of slaves in many functions did not create a self-sustaining slave population or slave economy. Slaveowners found that it could make sense to allow their slaves to buy their manumission over long years of service, or to allow them to buy their children's freedom. As a result there was a growing population of free persons of African or partly African descent. Most urban slaves, and the more fortunate rural slaves, were able to exercise their right to marry. In Mexico the union of African men with Indian women was seen as advantageous by both and, together with high slave mortality, helps to explain why the 35,000 African slaves reputed to be in New Spain in 1646 dwindled to a few thousand by the end of the seventeenth century.[37] In Cuba there were few remaining Indians, but the slaves of Havana began to enter marriages at a rate comparable to that of the white population. Some free mulatto men married slave women, but the male slaves wed only female slaves. Africans were prone to marry those from the same African nation as themselves, while American-born slaves preferred to marry one another. Through marriage the urban slave acquired some small accretion of rights. Where free blacks or mulattoes married a slave they frequently sought to purchase their spouse's freedom, usually paying a large price for doing so.[38]

Projects and Arguments

Spain's sponsorship of the African slave trade stimulated some soul-searching among a few of the moral guardians of the Empire, the members of the religious orders. The fact that leading and influential Spanish clerics were prepared to raise fundamental questions about the morality of the new Empire is a remarkable feature of Spanish imperialism. When Friar António de Montesinos had asked in 1511: 'Are these [Indians] not men?' he was formulating a question that could also be applied to the blacks. Las Casas, as we have seen, eventually challenged the colonists' right to enslave

Africans as well as Amerindians. Those friars who appealed to the royal power against the abuses of the colonists can be represented as more or less sophisticated advocates of Spanish or Christian imperialism. The faculty of reason detected in the Indians was to be exercised and, as it were, 'proved' by their conversion to Christianity. Indians who accepted baptism but continued 'idolatrous' practices would be thought no longer to be defended by a reasoning faculty they had betrayed. When the Crown, prompted by the clerics, suppressed the enslavement of Indians, it did so on the grounds that these Indians were its 'vassals', though most had made no such avowal.

In so far as such representations promoted the clerics' own role, or that of the orders to which they belonged, they can be seen as self-serving.[39] Yet the more radical of the clerical critics raised the question of Spain's right to conquer the New World. At a time when the mainland was still unconquered, Las Casas proposed that Spain should limit itself to establishing trading forts on the coast, and then confine itself to peaceful trade and attempts at proselytization. The continuing excesses of the *conquistadores* persuaded the Emperor Charles himself to request that the validity of the Conquest, and the proper rights of the indigenous peoples, be submitted to a 'great debate' at Valladolid in 1550 between the partisans of the conflicting schools of thought. Subsequently, the strenuous racism and imperialist apologetics of Sepúlveda were not permitted to be published, while Las Casas's views were broadcast in a number of trenchant and detailed books.[40]

Of course, the actual course of imperial policy and practice, as interpreted and modified by the colonists and colonial officials, was not to accord with the philosophy of Las Casas. It was closer to the doctrines of José de Acosta, a Jesuit who asserted the basic humanity of the Indians but insisted that they must undergo rigorous Spanish tutelage for an indefinite and lengthy period until they had proved that they were capable of fully receiving the Christian faith. The ban on the formal enslavement of the mass of Indians was upheld on the grounds that they were indeed legitimate vassals of the Spanish Crown. They could – and did – appeal to Spanish courts to vindicate their rights against arrogant colonists. Las Casas's campaign had been frustrated, but elements of a new 'public opinion' had been awakened. Among the Indians themselves there was a continuing disposition to rebel, and a new preparedness to press for their rights in both legal and illegal ways. The most remarkable expression of this was to be in the copiously illustrated representation compiled by Huaman Poma de Ayala; though this work never reached its intended destination, it did bear witness to an Indo-American consciousness and denounce Spanish oppressions.[41]

The supposed justification of Spanish rule had made much of the opportunities afforded for saving souls and spreading the Christian faith. In the early days in Mexico, Indians, especially those of the Mexica aristocracy, had been recruited to the clergy, and great efforts had been made to learn

Indian languages and customs. But in 1555 the First Provincial Council of the Mexican Church prohibited the ordination of Indians or *castas*, those of mixed descent. The Mexican bishops were here adopting a principle similar to that of the Spanish Church, which, stipulated that those of *linaje maculado* ('tainted lineage') could not enter the priesthood. Their option was further specified in a decree of 1585 which first excluded from the priesthood those with parents or grandparents who had been condemned by the Inquisition, then specified that the same exclusion related to those of mixed blood, whether from Indians or Moors or 'mulattoes in the first degree'. It was explained that possession of tainted or mixed blood was not in itself a 'personal fault', but that those advanced to sacred orders should not 'be held in contempt nor their ministry held up to censure'. The Vatican authorities were inclined to be critical of the workings of the *patronato*, and anyway the Mexican decree was contrary to a Papal brief. The Pope had wanted Indian priests because of the scarcity of Spanish clerics who knew the Indian languages. The version of the decree subsequently agreed by Rome gently qualified the exclusion of *castas* and mulattoes by saying that they should not be admitted to the priesthood 'without great caution'. It seems likely that the Spanish authorities were content with this compromise. Associated with these moves was a practice of using only Spanish for the rituals and catechism of the Church, since it was a 'Christian language', though unofficially some lay clergy and members of the orders continued to use Indian languages where they could.[42] Notwithstanding this the Church did put down some popular roots and the churches of the colonial baroque, with their special local virgins and plentiful gold or silver embellishments, testified to the syncretistic qualities of the social order.

A memorial presented to the Royal Council by the *Oidor* of Quito, Francisco de Auncibay, in 1592 furnishes an interesting glimpse of at least one Spanish official's attitude towards African slavery at a time when the outright enslavement of Indians was officially rejected. Auncibay urged the Crown to facilitate the purchase of 1,000 slaves for the mines of Zuruma, where there was an acute shortage of labour. The slaves were to be established in special hamlets, under the authority of mine owners who would themselves be ruled by a special code. He claimed that model communities could be built, echoing some of the ideas of Thomas More's *Utopia*. The purchase of Africans was acceptable, since:

> The negroes are not harmed because it is very helpful to these wretches to save them from Guinea's fire and tyranny and barbarism and brutality, where without law or God, they live like savage beasts. Brought to a healthier land they should be very content, the more so as they will be kept and live in good order and religion from which they will derive many temporal and, which I value most, spiritual advantages.

Auncibay added: 'even though the name of serf or slave offends my ears, this relationship has matured with the benefit of the laws of the Partidas and the equity of Castilian justice . . .'. He pointed out that freed slaves in the Americas sometimes found themselves reduced to misery and poverty because of the expenses of living. Slavery would also enable the Africans to benefit from paternal care and tutelage. However, he urged that they should live in their own houses and be encouraged to form families: 'from amongst them should be chosen the mayor, the foremen and the regidores; all this will ameliorate and correct the vices typical of the servile state'. The paternalist rhetoric is somewhat belied by proposed rules preventing them from learning to read, carrying arms or riding horses. If they failed to work or attempted to run away, then there was to be a tariff of punishments ranging from flogging, to cropping of the ears or hanging for persistent offenders. Slaves were to be allowed to purchase their freedom, but the new *libertos* would still be obliged to work as miners by taxes to be paid out of their wage. The slave hamlets themselves were to be kept in isolation from one another, and the conduct of the mine owners was also to be closely regulated. Auncibay's scheme required heavy initial investment, though he promised that it would bring the Crown great profit. The scheme was sidetracked by other pressing matters, but it shows that Spanish officialdom was capable of addressing the problems of large-scale slave enterprises with its own peculiar mixture of utopianism, practicality and concern for revenue.[43]

In Spanish America, as we have seen, African slavery remained limited in extent and varied in its settings. But the scale and character of the trade which fed it did provoke pointed and painful reflections from a handful of writers. In 1569 Tomás de Mercado published *Suma de Tratos y Contratos*, a treatise on the moral philosophy of commerce whose penultimate chapter offered a trenchant attack on the slave traffic. Mercado, a Dominican friar, wrote his book in Seville, but he had lived for many years in Mexico. His work sought to confront the impressive and disturbing workings of the Atlantic and European economies, to explain why gold or silver, which were used to measure value, commanded greater esteem (i.e. purchasing power) as they travelled from the places where they were mined to the great commercial centres of Europe. He draws attention to the disruptive effect on Spanish manufactures of an inflation which makes them seem costly compared to foreign products, and raises the cost of living. Mercado seeks to refine the notion of the 'just price' to take account of the new complexity of commercial and financial instruments. Values, based on natural law, reflect human efforts ('the sweat of the labourer's brow'), the differential fertility of different lands and the tastes of the consumer. But the interpretations proposed by merchants when they make prices require revision. It is the office of the public power to ensure that the self-interested calculations of the merchant do not prejudice human well-being or the legitimate demands of consumers. The chapter on the slave trade serves to highlight Mercado's message. He warns that it involves such cruelty that anyone who buys a slave is committing a mortal sin. He argues that the slave traders are notoriously unscrupulous and will have flouted the instructions of the Portuguese King, while the practice of baptizing embarking slaves with a sprinkler was a mockery. Mercado did not attack the notion of slavery as such, and was prepared to grant that there was such a thing as justified enslavement, but his concern was to argue that the Atlantic slave trade and the buying of Africans in the Americas did not come into this category.[44] Another Spanish writer who had worked in Mexico, Bartolomé de Albornoz, urged even more pointed conclusions in *Arte de los contratos*, published in Valencia in 1573, insisting that slave traders and slaveholders were violating the Africans' natural right to liberty, and attacking those clergy who condoned this.[45] Both these works appealed to a Thomist 'moral economy', which they saw as being violated by unrestrained and greedy commerce.

The sharp rise in the slave trade to Spanish America in the last years of the sixteenth century and the opening decades of the seventeenth inspired criticism of a different sort. The Spanish clerical authorities were not persuaded that the procedures of the Portuguese *asientistas* fully complied with their religious duties. The negligence of slave traders or perfunctory ceremonies by Portuguese priests, hosing down whole cargoes of uncomprehending captives, made some uncomfortable. Alonso de Sandoval, a Jesuit working in the port of Cartagena, decided to dedicate himself to working for the spiritual salvation of the African captives who were landed there in large numbers every year. He went on board the newly arriving slave ships and visited the depositories where the slaves were held as they recuperated from the rigours of the voyage. His first concern was to minister to those who might die. He would descend into the noxious stench of the slave holds and seek to revive those on the point of death by giving them honeyed water to drink. The last sacraments were administered to those about to expire. Sandoval, and a team of helpers which eventually numbered eighteen, likewise visited the newly landed slaves in the depository, ministering to their immediate physical needs with the aim of preparing them for catechism and baptism. To this end the team included several African interpreters, some capable of speaking eleven languages. Sandoval developed the idea that he would be able to save more of these Africans if he knew more of their customs and fears. He read as much as he could of what had been written about the 'Ethiopians', and wrote to co-religionists in Africa asking them to enlighten him on puzzles that remained. Sandoval's ministry attracted the criticism of local prelates who argued that the Jesuits were exceeding their authority and falling into the presumptuous error of rebaptizing those who had already received the sacrament. Sandoval declared that he was quite prepared to take a representative of the diocese with him to the slave holds whenever they wished – an invitation that was declined.

Sandoval began his ministry in 1605 and maintained it, with a couple of short breaks, until his death in 1652, of an illness that he may have contracted from the slave ships. In 1627 he published in Seville his work on how to convert Africans, later enlarged into a lengthy treatise entitled *De instauranda Aethiopum salute* (1647), in which he surveyed the variety of African peoples, questioned the practices of slave traders and condemned the treatment meted out to African captives. This work is not distinguished by the sharpness of its argumentation, but it furnishes a vivid account of the terrible conditions on the slave ships and the harsh fate that awaited most Africans in the Americas – unending toil, cruel punishments, meagre rations and an absence of religious instruction.

Sandoval recounts without criticism the theory that blacks, as descendants of Ham and Canaan, are inheritors of Noah's curse. He also speculates about the monsters to be found in Africa, apparently seeing them as proof of the demons active there. But he does also insist that the Lord God did not make humanity into masters and slaves, and gave each human an immortal soul. He likewise scorns the notion that the slave trader's trouble and expense by itself gives him any rights in the slave. One senses that Sandoval would have liked to reach a more robust judgement. But he cannot find an authority to justify a more clear-cut conclusion, and may anyway have been concerned to safeguard his opportunity to publish the book; the fact that the Portuguese had revolted against Spain in 1640 may have smoothed the way to publication of the longer version. In the end Sandoval's overriding concern is with the slaves' spiritual rather than temporal well-being.

The book concludes with a lengthy insistence that the manifold miseries of the Africans make them the best subjects for a ministry and that the Jesuits, with their special responsibility for the propagation of the faith, should be in the forefront of this work. Just as the merchants now have unprecedented quantities of silver and gold coins, so the Company of Jesus can save unprecedented numbers of souls. With St Ignatius as its Sun, the Company has sent his rays into far-flung and obscure kingdoms – China, Japan, Ethiopia and Monomatapa are all mentioned. While Sandoval was able to publish his work, he made no headway in the Society and lost his post as Rector of the College at Cartagena, in what may have been an unrelated incident (his Catalan assistant, Pedro Claver, was to be canonized in 1888, the year of Brazilian abolition, for his work in this ministry).[46] In evaluating the restraints placed on Sandoval, and the limitations of his work, it should be noted that the Jesuits owned a string of slave plantations.[47]

The preparedness of Mercado or Albornoz to attack the slave trade, or of Sandoval and Claver to minister to the arriving slaves, has something admirable about it, even if they never attacked slavery root and branch. But their work was carried out in obscurity, and came to the attention only of the limited circles able to obtain copies of books published in small editions, and in Sandoval's case in Latin – Albornoz's book was anyway soon placed on the Index. By contrast, Las Casas's criticism of the cruelty and destruction wreaked by enslavement of the Indians registered with the monarch himself, and helped to inspire the 'New Laws' which at least sought to suppress outright slavery. The writings of Las Casas had a huge impact, being translated into most European languages – especially Dutch, German, English and French – and becoming, after the Bible, a bestseller.

While the Spanish violation of the Indies had earned it a terrible reputation, its practice of African slavery was seen as comparatively unproblematic.[48] Indeed, together with the Portuguese example, it was to serve as a sort of model for other colonists and colonial powers – just as the term 'Negro' was adopted into English, with a heavy implication of enslavement. Those who colonized Providence Island, Jamaica, Virginia and South Carolina were very much aware of the Spanish practice of African slavery, even if their own adaptation of it was to transform what it meant to be a slave and a Negro – in both cases, as we will see in Chapters VI and VII, narrowing down and flattening the baroque features of Spanish notions of race and slavery. The attacks on the Atlantic slave traffic by Mercado and Albornoz were not translated into any other European language. They had been published at a time when the details of slave trading on the African coast were not the direct responsibility of the Spanish monarch; as we will see in the next chapter, once the Iberian crowns were united, an authoritative new doctrine of enslavement was produced which justified the African trade.

Notes

1. Pierre Vilar, 'The Times of Don Quixote', *New Left Review*, 68, 1971, pp. 59–71; Seed, *Ceremonies of Possession*, pp. 69–99.

2. John Lynch, *Spain 1516–1598: From Nation State to World Empire*, Oxford 1991, pp. 49–83. As Lynch makes clear, American revenues, though of rising importance, ran at an average of a fifth of Spanish revenues up to 1560 (p. 79). However, they did boost credit, and could be quickly mobilized in an emergency.

3. Lynch, *Spain*, pp. 32–3; J.H. Parry, *The Spanish Seaborne Empire*, London 1971, especially pp. 192–211; J.H. Elliot, 'Spain and America in the Sixteenth and Seventeenth Century'; and Joseph Leslie Barnadas, 'The Catholic Church in Colonial Spanish America', in Bethell, ed., *The Cambridge History of Latin America*, Cambridge 1984, vol. 1, pp. 287–341, 511–40.

4. I give only the most general orders of magnitude for the pre-Conquest period, but these are more likely to understate than overstate the devastation of the Indian populations. For references, see Leslie Bethell, 'A Note on the Native American Population on the Eve of the European Invasion', in Bethell, ed. *Cambridge History of Latin America*, vol. 1, pp. 145–6; the bibliography of vol. 2 of the *Cambridge History* gives references for recent work on the demographic impact of the Conquest. For an explanation of the catastrophe, see William H. McNeill, *Plagues and Peoples*, Harmondsworth 1976, pp. 185–200, 304–8; and Eric Wolf's discussion of the 'great dying' in *Europe and the People without History*, Berkeley and Los Angeles 1982, pp. 133–5. For a questioning of the higher estimates of the population of Hispaniola, see David Henige, 'On the Contact Population of Hispaniola', *Hispanic American Historical Review*, vol. 58, no. 2, 1978, pp. 217–37. For a critique of the higher estimates of the pre-Colombian Mexican population, and of the role of an early smallpox pandemic in reducing it in the first year or so, see Francis Brooks, 'Revising the Conquest of Mexico: Smallpox, Sources and Populations', *The Journal of Interdisciplinary History*, vol. xxiv, no. 1, Summer 1993.

5. Murdo MacLeod, *Spanish Central America: A Socio-economic History, 1520–1720*, Berkeley, CA 1973, p. 52.

6. Enrique Semo, *Historia del capitalismo en México: Los Orígenes 1521–1763*, Mexico 1973, pp. 60–92, 188–229; Silvio Zavala, *La colonización española en América*, Mexico 1972; C.S. Assadourian, 'Dominio Colonial y Señores Etnicos', *Revista Latinoamericana de Historia Económica y Social*, no. 1 (Lima 1983), pp. 7–20.

7. D.A. Brading, *The First Americans: The Spanish Monarchy, Creole Patriots, and the Liberal State 1492–1867*, Cambridge 1991, pp. 128–46; Steve J. Stern, *Peru's Indian Peoples and the Challenge of Indian Conquest: Huamanga to 1640*, Madison, WI 1982, pp. 40–44, 76–113.

8. James Lockhart, *The Nahua After the Conquest*, Stanford, CA 1992, pp. 111, 508–9.

9. Hugo Tolentino, *Origines du Préjugé racial aux Amériques*, Paris 1984, pp. 88, 106–11, 125–7.

10. Juan Friede and Benjamin Keen, eds, *Bartolomé de Las Casas in History*, De Kalb 1970, pp. 415–18, 291, 584–5. See also Brading, *The First Americans*, pp. 60–61; Anthony Pagden, *European Encounters with the New World*, New Haven, CT 1993, pp. 70–81; Gustavo Gutiérrez, 'Quien es el Indio? La Perspectiva teologica de Bartolomé de las Casas', in José O. Beozzo *et al.*, *La Iglesia y los Indios*, Quito 1990 (2nd edn), pp. 123–40 (p. 136).

11. Levi Marrero, *Cuba: Economía y Sociedad*, vol. 2, Madrid 1973, p. 313.

12. Eufemio Lorenzo Sanz, *Comercio de España con América Latina en la época de Felipe II*, vol. I, Valladolid 1979, pp. 614–17.

13. Ward J. Barrett and Stuart B. Schwartz, 'Comparación entre dos economías azucareras coloniales: Morelos, México y Bahía, Brasil', in Enrique Florescano, ed., *Haciendas, Latifundios y Plantaciones en América Latina*, Mexico 1975, pp. 532–72.

14. Alejandro de la Fuente Garcia, 'Los Ingenios de Azúcar en La Habana del Siglo VII (1640–1700): Estructura y mano de obra', *Revista de Historia Económica*, vol. IX, no. I, Winter 1991, pp. 35–67 (pp. 37, 46).

15. Paul E. Hoffman, *The Spanish Crown and the Defence of the Caribbean, 1535–1585*, Baton Rouge, LA 1980, p. 41.

16. Fernando Ortiz, *Los Esclavos Negros*, Havana 1916, pp. 425–9; David Davidson, 'Negro Slave Control and Slave Resistance in Colonial Mexico', *Hispanic American Historical Review*, vol. 46, no. 3, 1966, pp. 235–53.

17. Quoted in Kenneth Andrews, *Trade, Plunder and Settlement: Maritime Enterprise and the Genesis of the British Empire*, Cambridge 1984, p. 132.

18. Ibid., p. 134. Andrews points out that when he was in the Pacific in 1578, Drake abstained from any conflict with the Araucanians, who had captured two of his men, on the grounds that, as he explained, he 'would rather have beene a patron to defend them (the Indians), than any way an instrument of the least wrong that should have been done unto them' (quoted on p. 154).

19. For the organization of the trade, see Rolando Mellafe, *Negro Slavery in Latin America*, Berkeley, CA 1975, pp. 38–50; for figures, see Philip Curtin, *The Atlantic Slave Trade*, p. 25, and Enriqueta Vila Vilar, *Hispanoamérica y el comercio de esclavos*, Seville 1977, p. 226.

20. Anke Pieter Jacobs, 'Legal and Illegal Emigration from Seville 1550–1650', in Ida Altman and James Horn, eds, *'To Make America': European Immigration in the Early Modern Period*, Berkeley, CA 1991, pp. 59–85, especially 61–4.

21. For Spanish emigration, see Parry, *The Spanish Seaborne Empire*, p. 235; and Elliott, *Imperial Spain*, Harmondsworth 1970, p. 292; for slave imports see Marrero, *Cuba: Economía y Sociedad*, vol. 2, p. 356. According to the estimate of Vila Vilar cited in n.19 above, the annual imports of slaves in the period 1595–1640 was just under 6,000; though no exact estimate of Spanish immigration is possible, the hazards, expense and infrequency of the sea traffic between Spain and the New World virtually rules out a movement comparable to that of the Africans during the first half of the seventeenth century. Spanish immigration could have been fewer than 3,000 annually, but the American population of Spanish or partly Spanish descent grew rapidly none the less, favoured by its dominant social position in a fertile continent.

22. Marrero, *Cuba: Economía y Sociedad*, vol. 2, pp. 35–41; vol. 4, pp. 73–104; Parry, *The Spanish Seaborne Empire*, pp. 117–37.

23. Mellafe, *Negro Slavery in Latin America*, pp. 44–5, 74; Elliott, *Imperial Spain*, p. 286.

24. Frederick P. Bowser, 'The Free Person of Color in Mexico City and Lima', in Stanley L. Engerman and Eugene D. Genovese, eds, *Race and Slavery in the Western Hemisphere: Quantitative Studies*, Princeton, NJ 1975, pp. 331–68; Frederick P. Bowser, *The African Slave*

in Colonial Peru, 1524–1650, Stanford, CA 1974, Appendix 1; Colin A. Palmer, *Slaves of the White God: Blacks in Mexico, 1570–1650*, Cambridge, MA 1976, p. 46.

25. Palmer, *Slaves of the White God*, p. 76.

26. Carlos Sempat Assadourian, 'La producción de la mercancía dinero', in Enrique Florescano, ed., *Ensayos sobre el Desarollo Económico de México y América Latina (1500–1975)*, Mexico 1979, pp. 223–92 (p. 256). The account of the political economy of colonial mining which follows is based on Assadourian, but see also D.A. Brading and Harry Cross, 'Colonial Silver Mining: Mexico and Peru', *Hispanic American Historical Review*, vol. 52, no. 4, 1972, pp. 545–79. These authors note that the Peruvian *mita* raised a supply of some 13,500 labourers at any one time around 1574, based on the Indian communities of the region from Cuzco to Potosí supplying one-seventh of their adult labour for work in the mines. Even with much-reduced populations this levy was just about sustainable, and indeed lasted down to the end of the eighteenth century. The total labour force of the Mexican mines, where free labour came to predominate, was only a little larger, at 15,000.

27. Palmer, *Slaves of the White God*, p. 34; slave prices in Peru were a little higher; see Bowser, *The African Slave in Colonial Peru*, pp. 324–5. (A curious feature of Bowser's price series is that prices for African slaves were higher than those for slaves born in America; is this because the latter were more difficult to control, and would be more likely to seek manumission?)

28. Stern, *Peru's Indian Peoples and the Challenge of the Spanish Conquest*, pp. 138–57, 244. Stern writes:

> Alternative relationships arranged in 'civil society', which circumvented dependence on the labor patrimony of the state, represented the dynamic, growing forces of the future. . . .
> Thus even African slavery, relatively costly in a highland economy where profits depended on large inputs of cheap labour, grew into a significant economic force by the 1600s. . . .
> In the seventeenth century slave labor dotted the vineyards, sugar haciendas, and farms of prosperous zones. (p. 142)

In Mexico African slaves could also be used to improve the *hacendado*'s bargaining position *vis-à-vis* free workers, and Indian communal labour, by supplying a stable, core workforce on ranches and large estates. But the failure of slave populations to reproduce themselves made this an expensive expedient in the long run. See Lolita Guitiérez Brockington, *The Leverage of Labor: Managing the Cortés Haciendas in Tehuantepec, 1588–1688*, Durham, NC 1989, pp. 138–41, 143–58.

29. Robson Brines Tyrer, *The Demographic and Economic History of the Audiencia of Quito*, PhD thesis, University of California at Berkeley, 1976, p. 106.

30. Ignacio de Aybar, quoted in Tyrer, *Demographic and Economic History*, p. 125.

31. Robert West, *Colonial Placer Mining in Columbia*, Baton Rouge, LA 1952, pp. 83–90.

32. Palmer, *Slaves of the White God*, pp. 94–118.

33. Robert Ferry, 'Encomienda, African Slavery, and Agriculture in Seventeenth Century Caracas', *Hispanic American Historical Review*, vol. 64, no. 4, 1981, pp. 609–35; Murdo J. MacLeod, *Spanish Central America, 1520–1720*, Berkeley, CA 1973; Murdo J. Macleod, 'Spain and America: the Atlantic Trade 1492–1720', in Bethell, ed., *Cambridge History of Latin America*, vol. 1, pp. 341–88. For cacao as currency, see James Lockhart, *The Nahuas After the Conquest*, Stanford, CA 1992, pp. 177–8, 228–9.

34. Marrero, *Cuba: Economía y Sociedad*, vol. 3, pp. 3–5.

35. Carlo Ginzburg, 'The European (Re)discovery of the Shamans', *London Review of Books*, 28 January 1993, pp. 9–11 (p. 10). Ginzburg cites a Venetian traveller's report of 1565, according to which tobacco was 'very much prized by the slaves whom the Spaniards have brought from Ethiopia' (p. 9).

36. James I, 'A Counter-blaste to Tobacco', in *The Workes of the Most High and Mighty Prince, James by the Grace of God, King of Great Britain etc.*, London 1616, pp. 214–22 (214, 215, 220, 222).

37. Gonzalo Aguirre Beltrán, *La Población negra de México*, Mexico D.F. 1972, p. 234.

38. Alejandro de la Fuente, 'A Alforria de Escravos em Havana, 1601–1610: Primeiras Conclusões', *Estudios Economicas*, São Paulo, vol. 20, no. 1, January–April 1990, pp. 139–59.

39. For the argument that clerical philanthropy was largely vitiated by its ethnocentric and self-interested character, see Patricia Seed, '"Are These Not Also Men?": The Indians'

Humanity and Capacity for Spanish Civilisation', *Journal of Latin American Civilisation*, vol. 25, Part 3, October 1993, pp. 629–52.

40. Gines de Sepúlveda had asserted:

> with perfect right the Spaniards (españoles) exercise their domination over those barbarians of the New World and the adjacent islands, who in prudence, ingenuity and all human sentiments and virtues are as inferior to the Spaniards as children are to adults, women to men, the cruel and inhuman to the most refined, the hopelessly intemperate to those who are continent and moderate, finally I would say, monkeys to men.

(Gines de Sepúlveda, *Democrates Segundo o las justas causas de la guerra contra las Indios* [1545], Madrid 1986, p. 33)

41. Gustavo Gutiérrez, 'Quien es el Indio? La perspectiva teologica de Bartolomé de las Casas', in Juan Bottaso, ed., *La Iglesia y los Indios*, Quito 1990, pp. 123–41.

42. Stafford Poole, 'Church Law on the Ordination of Indians and *Castas* in New Spain', *Hispanic American Historical Review*, vol. 61, no. 4, 1981, pp. 637–50.

43. P. Jorge Villalba, 'Una República de Trabajadores Negros en las Minas de Zaruma en el Siglo XVI', in P. Rafael Savoia, ed., *El Negro en la Historia*, Quito 1990, pp. 121–5. See also *Anuario Columbiana de Historia Social and de la Cultura*, no. 1, 1963, pp. 197 ff.

44. Tomás de Mercado, *Suma de Tratos y Contratos*, vol. 1, ed. and intro. Nicolas Sanchez-Albornoz and transcribed by Graciela Sanchez-Albornoz, Madrid 1977, pp. 229–39. For the determination of value, see p. 61; for the fallible calculation of the merchant, see pp. 92 and 101; and for the necessary public role, p. 96. But note that while the common good is the greatest value, the merchant's profit, so long as it is not exorbitant, is justifiable, since it encourages him to meet public needs (p. 107).

45. Davis, *The Problem of Slavery in Western Culture*, pp. 212–13.

46. Alonso de Sandoval, *Un Tratado sobre Esclavitud*, Intro., transcribed and trans. Enriquetta Vila Vilar, Madrid 1987. Sandoval was removed from his post as Rector following three incidents: first, an accusation that he was uncooperative with the Inquisition; second, that he had allowed male students to dress as females in a play; third, that he had allowed a member of his staff to make a commercial visit to the Cape Verde islands with the aim of raising money for the College. Pedro Claver, a Catalan, was a generally safer candidate for canonization. He had vowed to make himself a 'slave to the slave', and was credited with the fantastic achievement of saving 300,000 souls. See William Bangert, *A History of the Society of Jesus*, St Louis, MO 1972, p. 256.

47. Nicholas Cushner, *Lords of the Land: Sugar, Wine and the Jesuit Estates of Coastal Peru, 1600–1767*, Albany 1980. When religious orders ran slave estates they tended to be just a little more attentive to the spiritual and temporal needs of the slaves than were other *hacendados*. But this is a very relative judgement. The Jesuit administrators were often recruited from the military or had run estates for a secular owner. Slaves were to be beaten with no more than 25 strokes of the lash for a minor offence and 50 lashes for attempted escape; however, Jesuits themselves were not to attend punishment sessions. The estates were not exceptionally profitable but Jesuit holdings grew impressively because of donations and bequests. While the estates of religious orders certainly furnished an example of plantation organization they did not lead break-throughs to new methods. To this extent the New World experience does not furnish further corroboration of the intriguing thesis of Randall Collins to the effect that monasteries and religious orders pioneered modern economic rationality (c.f. Randall Collins, *Weberian Sociological Theory*, Cambridge 1986, pp. 49–54). And such orders were absent from both the English countryside and the English colonies, which, as noted in Chapter I and as we will see in Chapter VI, did play an innovating role.

48. It is worth signalling that the distinctive skin colour of 'negros' or black Africans by making them more visible, rendered them easier to control. In the early decades colonists were permitted to bring 'white slaves' (i.e. *berberiscos* and *moriscos*) so long as they had been born in a Christian household, but it was found that, in New World conditions, they were soon able to loosen their bondage; while the marriage of female white slaves with colonists met with official approval it was feared that male white slaves were mischief-makers and they were consequently banned (Levi Marrero, *Cuba: Economía y Sociedad*, vol. 1, Rio Piedras, Puerto Rico 1972, p. 213). Some of the difficulties in stabilizing the condition of the white slave are indicated by the memoirs of Miles Philips, an English sailor taken captive, together with many of his mates, in the 1560s. After being subjected to captivity, and recanting his 'Lutheran'

heresy, he is sentenced to forced labour; after many sufferings and adventures he eventually makes his way aboard a returning fleet, pretending to be Spanish, subsequently regaining his native land and writing up his story. Philips's ability to pose as a colonist plays a vital part in his escape and could not have been matched by a black African. His story was published in Richard Hakluyt's collection and may be most conveniently read in the modern selection edited by J. Beeching: Richard Hakluyt, *Voyages and Discoveries*, London 1985, pp. 132–45.

IV

The Rise of Brazilian Sugar

[S]uch was their melody that – although they do not know what music is – those who have not heard them would not believe that they could make such harmony. At the beginning of the witch's sabbath, when I was in the women's house, I had been somewhat afraid; now I received in recompense such joy, hearing the measured harmonies of such a multitude, and especially in the cadence and refrain of the song, when at every verse all of them would let their voices trail, saying Heu, heuaure, heura, heuaure, heura, heura, oueh – I stood there transported with delight.

Jean de Léry, *History of a Voyage to the Land of Brazil*

Spain's overseas Empire was held together by the monarch, his civil servants, admirals, soldiers and clerics. At its centre was the artificial capital of Madrid, a small town near the imposing – even forbidding – edifice of the Escorial, a palace with a commanding view but the aspect of a headquarters building. Despite American silver, the taxes paid by Castile loomed largest in the royal revenues. By contrast, Portuguese absolutism depended for its lifeblood on commercial and colonial enterprise, to finance itself and to fix the loyalty of the privileged and possessing classes. While Spanish imperialism intervened within production, Portuguese colonialism organized monopoly profits in the realm of circulation. At its centre was the great port of Lisbon, and the ground floor of the Royal Palace was a commercial office and counting house. In the colonies there was no ramified bureaucracy but merchants, factors, planters and peasants tied to the metropolis by credit, sentiment and nautical skill. The acquisition of Portugal by the Spanish Crown was sealed by promises given to the Cortes of Tomar in 1581 that the structure of governance of the Portuguese possesions would be respected. Anyway, Madrid was preoccupied by European conflicts in the 1580s, and willing to be tolerant of Portuguese colonies and their trade so long as they yielded some revenue.

For a long time Brazil had been little more than a way-station and backwater within the Portuguese Empire, though this was to change in the 1570s and 1580s, possibly aided by the distraction of the metropolis. No large deposits of precious metals had been discovered; brazil wood, from which red dye could be extracted, gave the colony its name and remained the principal product for nearly half a century. Portuguese settlement was confined to a few coastal enclaves. Brazil's population of perhaps three million Indians were scattered over a wide territory, a circumstance which saved them, at first, the worst ravages of unfamiliar diseases. Some Indians were persuaded or forced to help cut down trees and transport wood, but contact was not extensive. Until the 1540s the loggers were often able to barter cloth, metal instruments and beads for the valuable hardwoods. But as the demand for Indian labour increased, so the Indians were able to bargain for better terms, and acquire the goods they wanted with less labour; the Indian communities did not have a limitless demand for European manufactures, and some which they wished to acquire, such as cutlasses and firearms, the Portuguese were reluctant to supply. Yet the Portuguese settlements were often dependent on the Indians for food supplies. In these circumstances resort to enslavement of Indians became more common. The setting up of a few sugar plantations in the 1540s accentuated the labour shortage.[1] In 1546 Duarte Coelho, the donatory of Pernambuco, explained the problem in a letter to the King:

> To get your brazil wood [the traders] importune the Indians so much . . . that my country is all in disorder. For it is not enough, Sire, to give them tools as was customary. To make the Indians fetch brazil wood it is now necessary to give

them beads from Bahia, and feather caps and coloured clothing that a man could not afford to buy to clothe himself and, what is worse, swords and arquebuses. . . . For when the Indians were needy and wanted tools they used to come and, in return for what we gave them, they did the carrying and all the heavy work, and used to come and sell us food which we needed rather badly. But now that they have plenty of tools they are becoming more useless than usual, are growing restless and proud, and are rebelling.[2]

The colony had been divided into twelve 'captaincies' at its original foundation, but plantation development took root in only a few of these, with Pernambuco making some headway. Only two of the donatories ever visited Brazil. However, some of the Portuguese colonists, stiffened by an admixture of peasants from northern Portugal, proved persistent, and for a while the barter system enabled the settlements to maintain themselves and send several shiploads of wood a year to Portugal. The Brazilian coast was long, and some of the best harbours had not been secured, enabling the French also to take off wood and bid for Indian labour. Bahia was made the administrative centre in 1549, when its nominal captaincy collapsed. Religious orders were encouraged to assist colonization by generous land grants. With Portugal encountering increasingly stiff competition in Asia and Africa, the authorities in Lisbon began to pay greater attention to Brazil. But in mid century the site of Rio de Janeiro still remained unsettled.

La France Antarctique

From the 1530s French ships from Rouen and other ports regularly called to acquire brazil wood from the Indians, and in the 1550s an attempt was made by a Breton adventurer, Nicolas Durand, Chevalier de Villegagnon, to found the colony of *France Antarctique* in the bay of Rio de Janeiro. This enterprise was supported both by Admiral Coligny, the French Minister, and by Calvin, a friend and former fellow student of the expedition's leader. At a pageant held in honour of Henry II and Catherine of Medici in Rouen in 1550, Tupinambá Indians were imported to mount an elaborate portrayal of episodes from their daily life staged in a little 'forest' assembled for the purpose; while some busied themselves in their huts or enacted a battle, others mimed their longing to carry brazil wood to the coast.[3] The French saw themselves as saviours of the Indians. However, Villegagnon and his followers soon discovered the hardships involved in the work of colonization, including the Indians' reluctance to play their allotted part in the pageant of French colonialism. Villegagnon reached Brazil in 1555, but before long he wrote to Calvin explaining the problems he encountered:

This country was all wilderness and wasteland. There were no houses or roofs nor any crops or cereals. On the contrary, there were fierce and savage people, strangers to any courtesy or humanity, totally different from us in their methods and education. They were without religion or any knowledge of honour or virtue ... the people of the country live from one day to the next, not troubling to farm the land. We therefore found no food supplies assembled in one place, but had to go far, hither and thither, to gather and seek it.[4]

Amerindians were taken as slaves by the colonists, but training them to labour proved very difficult; with an abundance of natural game, they saw no point in accumulating food stores. The natives, so the French alleged, were lazy and feckless; they tired easily, and would run away if they were not constantly watched. Villegagnon was also troubled by the Indian women's refusal to cover their bodies, and at the readinessess of his own colonists to establish sexual liaisons with them. His attempts to enforce restraint provoked a rebellion which he quelled with the aid of some Scots followers. France was asked to send more settlers, and Calvin to send some priests. Three hundred new settlers arrived in 1557, led by the Sieur Bois-le-Comte, Villegagnon's nephew, and two priests were sent by Calvin. However, violent religious disputes rent the small colony. The Calvinist priests urged that the celebration of the Eucharist should be modified or abandoned, since it might appear to give licence to the cannibalism of which they accused the natives. Villegagnon, at heart a traditionalist and disciplinarian, was scandalized by their arguments, and ordered their expulsion from the settlement. He then turned to the ultra-Catholic Duc de Guise for support, and soon left for France, entrusting the vulnerable and divided colony to the command of his nephew.[5]

The Portuguese authorities were greatly alarmed by the setting up of *France Antarctique*. Quite apart from Brazil's intrinsic value, it lay only a little off the route to the Indies, since the Cape was best approached from the South West Atlantic. A new governor with military experience was appointed: Mem de Sá. He assembled an expedition against the French, which captured their fortified base after a stiff fight and subsequently founded the ciy of Rio de Janeiro.

Since they had been driven out by the Portuguese, the French notion that they enjoyed a special rapport with the Indians was not punctured. The accounts of Léry and Thevet, especially the former, encouraged the view that despite their savagery and cannibalism, the Indians of Brazil were possessed of a natural virtue. The mixture is evident in the account of a Tupinambá ceremony by Léry given in the epigraph to this chapter.[6] Léry was fascinated by what he thought was a biblical echo, a reference in one of their songs to waters covering the world, though the Tupinambá believed that they had survived the flood by climbing tall trees.[7]

The Takeoff of the Sugar Economy

The period of the governorship of Mem de Sá (1557–72) marked the beginnings of a plantation economy in the colony. The Governor himself established two sugar mills staffed with a mixed Indian and African slave labour force. The foundation of Rio de Janeiro plugged a dangerous gap. Sugar *engenhos* multiplied in Bahia, and several were set up in Rio. In the course of the 1570s several sugar mill owners from São Tomé transferred operations to Brazil, attracted by security, good soil and communications. Mem de Sá participated in the sugar profits, and entrusted important commands to vigorous young relatives. But he did not seek to engross or control the sugar trade, or subject it to heavy taxation. Like Francisco de Toledo in Peru, he stabilized metropolitan rule and presided over an economic boom. While the Toledan regime was based on centralized control and enormously boosted the flow of specie to Madrid, the rule of Mem de Sá allowed the sugar and slave trades to flourish by giving entrepreneurs their head. The Jesuits, as reliable foes of any Protestant interloper, were given generous concessions and established colleges or schools in each of the major settlements; they also established ranches and mills on the land they had been given to help sustain their religious and educational mission.[8]

The development of sugar production had required the creation of an exacting regime of servile labour. Those who had received land grants [*sesmarias*] from the donatories, or proprietors of each captaincy, were theoretically entitled to claim labour services from its indigenous inhabitants, but this proved difficult or impossible to enforce, given the Indians' migratory inclinations, especially when they were confronted with a grasping landholder. Intermittent warfare with the Indian tribes, or simple raiding expeditions, produced a flow of enslaved Indians who, at the cost of much brutality, could be forced to perform some work.

In 1570 the royal authorities, acting in the name of the young King Sebastião I, decreed that the natives could be enslaved only if they were in open revolt, or if they were found practising cannibalism. They were placed under the protection of the Jesuits, who sought to resettle as many as possible in special hamlets [*aldeias*], where they could learn a craft but were obliged to abandon polygamy, cross-cousin marriage and ritual cannibalism, receive religious instruction in a Tupi-based *língua geral*, and live in rows of huts rather than long houses arranged in a circular plan. Both priests and Indians seem to have appreciated choral singing, Church music and participation in religious festivals. Under the watchful eye of the Jesuits the *aldeias* enjoyed limited self-government, and they supplied *forros* (freemen) to work for wages on neighbouring estates. After a few false starts the Jesuits ceased to train native priests, developing the notion that they were unsuited to the ministry and thus in some way less than fully rational. For their part many Indians avoided the invigilated life of the *aldeias*, with some even preferring to live attached to the estates of the colonists. Those who declined such shelter were exposed to continued slave-raiding. The colonists could be induced to serve in the militia against threatening Indian tribes only if they were offered the possibility of slave-raiding. Friendly Indians suffered several attacks, and many were enslaved on one pretext or another. The colony's early sugar mills were worked by enslaved or semi-free Indians, together with immigrants from Portugal and the Atlantic islands and a few African slaves.[9]

In 1570 there were only some 2,000–3,000 African slaves in the Portuguese settlements compared with ten or fifteen times that number of Indian slaves. However, the latter, unless they were especially skilled and trusted, were accorded a low value. 'Raw' Indians sold for one escudo each compared with a price of 13–40 escudos for an African slave; Indians trained for work in the cane fields or *engenhos* sold for about half the price of trained Africans.[10] On many estates little distinction was made between free Indians [*forros*] and those who were slaves, even though royal decrees stipulated that the former should be paid wages. While *forros* received only payment in kind, those who were enslaved sometimes ran away. Serious plagues in the 1560s and 1570s hit the Indians of the *aldeias*, encouraging would-be mill owners to search elsewhere for labour for the *engenhos*. From the outset the *engenhos* had been staffed by salaried immigrants and sugar experts from Portugal and the islands, some of the latter *mamelukos*, a name often referring to those of mixed ethnicity. Increasingly, African slaves were purchased as well. However, if Indian labour now declined in importance on the *engenhos*, this was a gradual process. In the interior, roving gangs of *bandeirantes*, freelance explorers, traders and predators partly composed of assimilated Indians and mestizos, continued to prey upon Indian tribes living beyond the coastal strip and beyond the range of the Jesuit missions.

The Jesuits themselves claimed in 1600 that the labour of 50,000 *forros* from the *aldeias* was available for hire. These workers would have been engaged in general agriculture and domestic service. The *senhores de engenho* wanted a permanent workforce, toiling throughout a nine-month-long harvest and available for preparatory and construction work at other times. They also wished to be sure that those who had learnt the necessary skills – the core of a dozen or fifteen sugar-makers – did not leave them; from this standpoint purchasing African slaves had distinct advantages over Portuguese immigrants or Indian *forros*. In 1571 the *Engenho Sergipe*, founded by Mem de Sá, had 21 Indian workers engaged in skilled sugar-making tasks; by 1591 no Indian workers were left in such posts, but there were 30 Africans, of whom thirteen were found in the key sugar-making posts – including the *mestre de açúcar*, his assistant, two *purgadores*, and three *tacheiros* (kettlemen, who had the delicate task of boiling the sugar until it reached the right consistency).[11] The Jesuits themselves, who drew the line at illegally holding Indians in slavery, purchased African slaves for their own sugar works. In this they faithfully reflected the official view that enslavement of Indians was wrong, but the purchase of African slaves was permitted.

Sugar brought Brazil prosperity in the last decades of the century, and for over a hundred years Africans were brought to the colony primarily to work on the sugar estates. The numbers of African slaves in Brazil grew from the 3,000 of 1570 to 9,000–10,000 in 1590 and to 12,000–15,000 by 1600; the 'white' population was estimated at 29,400 in 1585, mainly concentrated in Pernambuco and Bahia.[12] Most Africans worked in the *engenhos*, each of which needed between eighty and a hundred and twenty workers of different types. In 1600 the Africans were probably still outnumbered in the sugar sector by Indian general workers, whether slave or free; and their numbers were probably matched by free Portuguese or islanders, usually working in artisanal roles. But the proportion of Africans was steadily rising. In the whole period from 1600 to 1650, at least 200,000 Africans were to be brought to Brazil.[13]

Slave purchases on this scale represented an impressive – indeed, astonishing – investment, raising the question of why it occurred. Why were African slaves imported on such a scale, and how was it possible for the *senhores* and *lavradores de cana* to afford them? Evidently the demand for labour was voracious, and the earlier mixed system of labour recruitment was already proving inadequate. Under Spanish influence the royal authorities and the Jesuits continued to discourage enslavement of the Indians; while newly captured Indian slaves could still be purchased, such illegal or semi-legal captives lacked either the skills or the endurance required by the *engenhos*. Those of Indian or partly Indian descent who had acquired at least some of the agricultural techniques that were needed were either unresponsive or unsuitable. The nominal remuneration offered to the *forros* was insufficient either to secure their loyalty or to encourage more to come forward. Schwartz suggests that the failure to stamp out the illegal trade in Indian slaves itself undermined official encouragement that *forros* be paid wages 'like free men and treated as such.'[14]

The enthusiasm of *lavradores* and *senhores de engenho* for Indian slaves or *forros* was also diminished as servile Indian populations proved susceptible to the cult of *santidade*, in which Christian symbols were harnessed to Tupinambá beliefs in the coming of an earthly paradise in which, it was said, the hoes would till the fields by themselves, and arrows would find their mark as villagers rested. This cult, which clustered around a variety of 'bishops' and 'popes', emerged in the last decades of the sixteenth century. Its devotees, mainly former slaves, created villages of their own, organizing celebrations with tobacco, alcohol, dance, and song, which were regarded with fear and scandal by the colonists. In 1610 the Governor, who favoured re-enslavement of the Indians, warned that there were twenty thousand in the *santidade* villages, and that they were beginning to attract fugitive blacks. Those linked to the *santidade* were allegedly involved in attacks on *engenhos*, in which property was stolen and machines were broken. The representatives of the Crown were anxious that the *santidade* and rebel slaves could be a potential ally of an attacking force as had happened, they pointed out, in the Isthmus. In 1613 the Crown declared that it would take action against Indians and Africans who 'live in idolatry calling their settlements *santidade*, sallying forth from them often to rob and kill in the *aldeias* and *engenhos*'.[15] Caught between the military operations of the Governor and the freelance activities of the *bandeirantes*, such settlements led an unsettled and precarious existence. Although the Africans were evidently far from immune to the *santidade* movement, it was essentially based on the Indian and mixed population. Newly arrived Africans were sent straight to the *engenhos*, where they were subjected to a gruelling work regime; the minority who occupied artisanal roles were given petty privileges, while most were allowed to cultivate a small plot or *roça* to grow food for themselves. Such incentives meant more to the African captive than they did to the indigenous population.

During the years up to 1580 the mixed, but mainly Indian-worked, sugar estates were sufficiently productive and profitable to encourage investment in the industry. In fact the colony enjoyed striking natural advantages as a sugar producer, while the mother country had all the necessary commercial connections. Some slaves may have been brought to Brazil from Africa or the Atlantic islands on credit, or as an investment made by a slave trader. The complementarity of Portugal's various Atlantic possessions first hindered, then underwrote, Brazil's advance. Italian and Flemish merchants had long had a stake in the Atlantic islands, and only gradually discovered Brazil's advantages as declining yields and social problems reduced the sugar crop first in Madeira and the Canaries and then in São Tomé. The soil and climate of the Brazilian North East proved most hospitable to the sugar cane, with far more land available than there was on Atlantic islands, and a lengthy harvesting period. Sugar cane is an exhaustive crop, requiring constant fertilization of the soil; the cane can be cut many years running, but yields decline, as they appear to have done on the relatively small Atlantic islands. Coastal Brazil was also favoured by a multitude of small rivers and streams which could supply water power for the mills. While it was possible to grind the cane with ox-driven or even slave-driven mills, such as the *trapiche* used by producers in the Spanish Caribbean, the scale of output could be increased by using water power. A large water-powered *engenho real*, or 'royal mill', could produce eighty or even a hundred tons of sugar a year. A few mills in Morelos could match this capacity, but only by the extensive use of animal power: hundreds of oxen, with the grazing grounds and extra supervision they required.

The successes of Brazil's sugar industry did not all derive from scale. Indeed, the Brazilian industry had outstripped all other producers because its specific organization and the technical development of the *engenho* had permitted a medium scale of investment. The *senhores de engenho* had been able to reduce the costs of setting up a new mill by contracting for cane grown by *lavradores de cana*, independent cultivators or tenants. While the *engenho* would employ a dozen or so salaried Portuguese and scores of African slaves, the *lavradores de cana* would have a mixed labour force of Indian and African slaves, and could supply much of the cane needed by the mill. The *lavrador* received about a half of the sugar made from his cane if he owned his land, between a quarter and a third if it belonged to the *senhor*. From the earliest days of Brazil's sugar development those setting up a new mill were exempt from the *dízimo* for a ten-year period, and could purchase up to one hundred and twenty slaves at reduced duties. The religious orders and knights of the Order of Christ enjoyed further exemptions.[16]

Brazil's special advantages over the Caribbean at this time included readier access to markets and sources of slave labour. The sailing time from Brazil's North East to Lisbon was shorter than that from any other European settlement in the New World to the Old: about 45–55 days to Lisbon, compared with seventy from Havana to Cadiz and over one hundred and twenty from Veracruz.[17] Sailing times from Europe or Africa to the Brazilian North East were also shorter than those to the Western Caribbean. Since the slave trade was in the hands of the Portuguese, there were also fewer commercial intermediaries and fewer duties to be paid. Slave prices in Brazil were consistently lower than those in Spanish America: in the period 1574–1613 they ran at between a half and two-thirds of the prices in the Caribbean.[18] Brazilian sugar planters were meant only to trade with Portuguese merchants. By this time Lisbon had quite a flourishing and cosmopolitan mercantile community; it included natural-ized Italians and the so-called 'New Christians' – converted Jews, some of them refugees from Spain and several with experience or contacts in the Low Countries. Before 1591 foreign merchants, so long as they could claim to be Catholic, were permitted to own Portuguese trading vessels, and to accompany them, so long as they retained a Portuguese captain and crew. The sugar trade developed with the Atlantic islands was increasingly switched to Brazil when output faltered in the former. The Flemish merchant Erasmus Schest owned a mill at São Vicente, directed by his agent Jan van Hielst, whose revenues enabled him to buy the Duchy of Ursel in Brabant.[19]

At the Cortes of Tomar, Philip II had promised to respect the powers and privileges of the *Mesa da Conciência e Ordens*, a body concerned with both legal and religious affairs and with the administration of the assets of the Military Orders in both metropolis and colonies. A Spanish attempt to set up a *Conselho da India* for the Portuguese colonies was abandoned after opposition from the *Mesa da Conciência*. Portugal's colonial affairs remained the immediate responsibility of the kingdom's highest body, the *Desembargo do Paço*, which met in Lisbon. There were tensions with the *Junta de Fazenda de Portugal*, which met in Spain, but prior to the 1620s these did not significantly prejudice Brazilian colonial interests.[20]

Portugal had long pursued a lively commerce with the Low Countries and England. The Dutch revolt and Anglo-Spanish conflicts only intermittently jeopardized this. The main danger to Portuguese shipping came in European waters, especially in the years between the defeat of the Armada (1588) and the reconstruction of the Spanish fleet in the 1590s. In 1589 a large Anglo-Dutch expedition set out to establish a bridgehead in Portugal, or on one of its Atlantic islands, with a view to establishing Don António of Crato on the Portuguese throne and dismembering the Iberian empires. However, Queen Elizabeth I had to rely heavily on armed merchantmen, who lost sight of the strategic goal and devoted themselves to plundering the colonial trade. A contemporary explained the fiasco of the attempts to seize territory on the grounds that 'this army was levied by merchants; whereas in matters of this kind, princes only ought to have employed themselves'.[21] In the three years 1589 to 1591, English privateers seized sixty-nine ships engaged in the Brazil trade, carrying sugar reported to be worth £100,000. A decree of 1591, which argued that it was 'against all reason and sense' to allow foreign merchants to damage 'the trade of the kingdom', sought to ban foreign merchants from visiting the Portuguese colonies.[22] In 1592 a convoy system was established between Brazil and Lisbon, paid for by a 3 per cent duty on the sugar carried. The Brazil fleet adapted its schedule to the sugar harvest, and in this early form its charges were not too onerous. The security of the Brazil fleet was enhanced by Spain's major effort to protect the transatlantic sea lanes. Once the sugar arrived in Lisbon it could be transshipped for Genoa, Antwerp, Amsterdam or the Hanseatic ports by means of foreign merchantmen operating with a Portuguese licence. It was not unusual for trade to persist regardless of war.[23]

The Brazilian coast had less attraction for the privateers and corsairs than the Caribbean or the Atlantic approaches to the Peninsula. Those who did sail to the South Atlantic would often find smuggling more profitable than plunder, to the advantage of the colonists. From the mid 1590s onwards Dutch vessels became frequent visitors to the South Atlantic and South American coast. They were attracted by the salt pans of the Cape Verde islands and Tierra Firme as well as by commercial interloping, and avoided the well-escorted Spanish and Portuguese fleets. In 1598 there were said to be eighty Dutch ships in the South Atlantic zone.[24] In 1599 Dutch privateers captured São Tomé, but Brazil remained unscathed. The comparatively reasonable terms offered to the Brazilians for shipping sugar by the Portuguese convoy system may have reflected an attempt to undercut smuggling. Moreover, those who owned *engenhos* included colonial officials, members of the Military Orders and important merchants who would have exercised influence in Lisbon favourable to the Brazil trade. In

Portuguese terms the latter now merited the primacy accorded in Spanish America to the transport of specie.

Table IV.1 gives an indication of the qualitative advance represented by the rise of the Brazilian sugar plantations.

Table IV.1   Atlantic Sugar Production in the Sixteenth Century [*arrobas*]

	Madeira	São Tomé	Brazil
1507	70,000		
1570	200,000		
1580	40,000	20,000	180,000
1585	23,000		
1600		40,000	
1614			700,000

Source: Frédéric Mauro, *Le XVIᵉ Siècle européen: aspects économiques*, Paris 1966, p. 151 for all figures except that for Brazil in 1610, which is taken from Schwartz, 'Plantations and Peripheries', in Bethell, ed., *Colonial Brazil*, p. 76.

The Canary Islands produced about 70,000 *arrobas* annually, Cyprus about 30,000 *arrobas*, in the early part of the century; the North African states occasionally sent similar quantities to Europe. The combined sugar production of Spanish America oscillated somewhere within the range of output given for Madeira, with much being consumed rather than exported. In the latter half of the seventeenth century the largest annual shipment of sugar to Seville from Spanish America amounted to 60,000 *arrobas* in 1568, as noted in Chapter III. When Brazil reached an output of 700,000 *arrobas*, or 10,000 tons, around the turn of the century, it had broken through to a new order of magnitude. It reached about a million *arrobas* by 1620, since Brazil's sugar industry grew during the truce between Spain and the Netherlands (1609–21), and was boosted by the introduction of a cheaper and more effective mill for grinding the sugar cane.[25]

During the twelve-year truce, Atlantic shipping was safer, and therefore cheaper. The convoy system could be relaxed, and ships from Portugal's smaller ports such as Viana, Lagos, Faro and Oporto could take a share in the sugar trade, monopolized by Lisbon during the war. Before long Recife was loading 130 ships annually, Bahia around 75 and Rio de Janeiro 30.[26] Portuguese merchants still had the sole right to trade with Brazil, but they would enter into arrangements with English or Dutch partners who might supply the vessel and venture capital. The Madrid authorities must have known about this, but they were willing to tolerate it because they needed the truce with the Dutch and because the Spanish King had a stake in Luso-Brazilian prosperity.

✣

The standard sixteenth-century sugar mill had crushed pieces of cane between two horizontal rollers, with an extra press required to extract the remaining juice, which would then be boiled in a succession of copper vats, skimmed, purged and cooled in clay moulds that further purified the sugar. The mill introduced to Brazil around 1608–12, the *engenho de trés paus*, employed three vertical, collinear rollers, with the cane passing through the rollers twice and itself helping to transmit the motion of the machine. The new arrangement simplified the mill's traction, dispensed with the need for an extra press and allowed larger pieces of cane to be ground. The method of processing the cane juice was not affected, but because of increased yields, the new equipment put profitable sugar-making within the reach of the medium-sized producer. It was said that a Spanish priest from Peru introduced the new milling method to Brazil; it seems that a similar arrangement had been used for milling ore, and that the invention was an Indian one.[27] Between 1583 and 1612 the number of sugar mills grew from 115 to 192; by 1629 there were around 350 mills, capable of producing from 15,000 to 22,000 tons each year. The new *senhores de engenho* were of humbler social extraction than those who had built mills in the sixteenth century; sugar-making was no longer the special preserve of viceroys, aristocrats, merchant princes, and powerful religious orders, even if the latter had some fiscal privileges.[28]

Since Portugal had now lost much ground in the Asian spice trade, Brazil and its sugar, together with the slave trade from Africa, dominated its colonial commerce. In 1620 the Brazilian sugar crop amounted to 13,400 tons, worth £484,000 in Amsterdam; Deerr cites a Dutch document claiming that profits could be doubled if the Netherlands seized Brazil. In this same year England's total imports were worth £1,578,000, of which sugar imports were valued at £83,000.[29] Taxes were paid on Brazilian sugar both at the port from which it was dispatched and at its Portuguese destination; in the latter case a 20 per cent *ad valorem* duty on top of the normal sales tax. Over time the incidence of these duties drifted upwards as royal officials exploited the strength of Brazil's trading position. Brazil's sugar trade in 1627, worth about 3,500,000 cruzados, would have yielded over a million cruzados to the Portuguese Treasury, accounting for 40 per cent of total revenue.[30] The bureaucratic apparatus required to collect these duties from a few ports was much less elaborate than that of Spanish imperial administration in the New World, with its thousands of salaried *corregidores* and other officials stationed in hundreds of municipalities. Portugal's more economical colonial adminstration allowed the metropolitan Treasury to garner a larger proportionate contribution from the profits of empire than did Madrid; by this time sugar shipments had reached the value of those of Spanish American silver in the mid sixteenth century.

The growth of the sugar industry required more colonists and more slaves. Portugal, with a population one-tenth the size of Spain's, sent a larger stream of emigrants to its colonies: some 3,000–4,000 annually.[31]

The larger *engenho* engaged between ten and twenty salaried overseers, bookkeepers and craftsmen. Immigrants could also find employment with commercial houses or with the large ranches producing hides and dried meat for the plantations and ships. There was no shortage of land which could be acquired to grow foodstuffs or tobacco.

The Transatlantic Slave Trade and Africa

By 1630 there were 50,000–60,000 black slaves in Brazil. In some years 7,500 *peças de Indias*, perhaps 10,000 Africans, were sent to Brazil, 2,000 dying at sea. Since Portuguese traders were supplying unprecedented numbers of slaves to Spanish, as well as Portuguese, America, they brought 10,000–15,000 slaves each year from Africa.[32] Large contractors purchased the right to export and import African slaves, then sold these licences piecemeal to the actual traders. The traffic involved quite a large number of independent merchants in triangular voyages from Europe or the Atlantic islands to the African coast with trade goods, on to Brazil with slaves, and back again with Brazilian produce. On the African coast Brazilian rum and tobacco began to supplement trade goods originally acquired from Europe or the East.

The growth of the transatlantic slave trade transformed the nature of the Portuguese presence in Africa. Until the mid sixteenth century this had not gone beyond the maintenance of island trading bases and a few fortified coastal factories, established with the compliance of the local African monarch or chief. The forested coastal region of West Africa represented a most perilous disease environment for Europeans – or Africans from the interior. There was no overarching political structure, such as the Pre-Columbian empires in the Americas, but, rather, a host of small kingdoms and chiefdoms. The savannah posed a different problem for would-be colonizers and *conquistadores*. The larger states had achieved a formidable level of military organization, including the use of firearms, and there was no prospect of them falling to small European expeditions. The monarch of Bornu had a corps of musketeers, trained by Turkish instructors. The late sixteenth century witnessed a determined attempt by the Sultan of Morocco to regain control of the Africa trade – this culminated in 1590 in the seizure of Timbuktu by an expedition of 5,000 men, most of them musketeers and many mounted, who traversed the desert with the help of 10,000 camels carrying supplies. Even this formidable 'red fez' force defeated the army of Songhai only with the help of a renegade faction. Mounting an operation of this sort in West Africa was beyond Portugal's means, and was anyway rendered redundant by the opportunities for trading without conquest.

The slave traders visited small trading posts at the mouths of the rivers (the Gambia, the Senegal and the Niger, with its many outlets) and dealt through the established commercial networks, including the Afro-Portuguese *lançados*. The growth of the slave traffic gave resources to those states able to supply captives to the merchants. Among the latter were Mali, Allada, Denkyira, controlling the hinterland of El Mina, and the Yoruba Kingdom of Oyo. But other states withdrew from the trade, such as Benin on the Niger, whose king ordered, early in the sixteenth century, that no male slaves should be sold, and subsequently stopped the trade altogether. Faced with this obstruction, the Portuguese encouraged a more obliging break-away authority on the Forcadas river. According to Ryder: 'the young state appears to have enjoyed sufficient independence to follow policies different from those of Benin. It encouraged Portuguese trade, placed no restriction on the supply of slaves, and accepted Christian missionaries.'[33] While the Portuguese traders could gain some leverage in this way, it did not make them arbiters of the coast – Benin remained a more stable and considerable state than the new entity fostered by the Portuguese. Ryder observes: '"opening and closing the market" was to remain for centuries a standard Benin device for regulating trade with Europeans, and one suspects that it was practiced in local trade long before they appeared.'[34]

From the middle of the sixteenth century English and Dutch ships began visiting the Guinea coast in search of gold, and were able to offer an attractive array of merchandise – including weapons and firearms. On occasion they would also buy a cargo of slaves, though they did not yet establish a regular traffic. Squeezed by Morocco on land and the Dutch and English by sea, the Portuguese were thrown on to the defensive on the Gold Coast. Their forts dispatched a dwindling quantity of gold to Lisbon.[35] The Portuguese were still able to supply some of the trade goods which were important for the acquisition of slaves; Eastern textiles and spices were now as much in demand as European metals and manufactures. By the beginning of the seventeenth century, however, Portugal's dominance in the African slave traffic owed as much to its links with American markets as to its now threatened position in West Africa.

In South West and Central Africa there was a little more scope for direct Portuguese territorial encroachment. The African kingdoms of this region mainly took the form of quite large-scale confederations, with weaker military and commercial structures than were to be found in the savannah region of West Africa. The Portuguese had established advantageous treaties with the rulers of the Kongo, the Ngola of M'bundu, and other monarchs, enlisting them in the hunt for slaves. But such arrangements led to both internal strife and border conflicts. Portuguese intervention in favour of King Alvaro I had re-established the kingdom of the Kongo. While the Kongo began again to act as a slave mart, some freelance traders preferred to operate from Luanda, where they were less subject to invigilation and taxation. In 1571 the Portuguese Crown stepped in to establish a formal colony in the Luanda hinterland, among the Kimbundu on the territory of Ndongo. A Lord Proprietor was appointed, some peasant colonists were recruited, and Jesuits were charged with setting up a mission.

Portuguese pretensions were punctured by sustained African resistance and by the failure of the agricultural settlements attempted by the peasant colonists. Nevertheless, a small state mainly devoted to slave trading was set up among the western Kimbundu, sponsoring its own system of slave-raiding amd sending columns far into the interior. In 1591 the colonial charter of Ndongo was revoked and the beginnings of the Crown colony of Angola were laid, with its administrative centre at Luanda.

The Portuguese settlements were defended not only by a few hundred soldiers from the metropolis and a colonial militia but also by a locally recruited *guerra preta*, or black army. These African auxiliaries were themselves often purchased or captured; the would-be colonial power was thus adopting the 'army of slaves' employed by so many African rulers. Captives were acquired by two methods. Treaties with African kings or petty chiefs [*sobas*] required them to deliver a stipulated number of captives in return for some trade goods and continued good relations. Alternatively, freelance slave raids sponsored by Portuguese merchants would be permitted to ravage the interior. These raids were conducted by privately organized bands of local soldiers led by *tangomãos*, Portuguese who could speak African languages and had cultivated African contacts, and *Pombeiros* of mixed Portuguese and African blood.

Spain's *asiento* furnished large resources for equipping these forces, while the authorities in Madrid favoured territorial acquisition. But the blend of African and European, state sponsorship with private enterprise, remained more characteristic of Portugal. The numbers of slaves sent from Luanda and Benguela exceeded those purchased from the traders of West Africa, and reached almost 10,000 a year in the 1590s. Slave-raiding and trading on this scale began to depopulate the immediate hinterland, with some peoples seeking to move out of range. The Portuguese settlements around Benguela and Luanda were now colonies rather than simply trading posts. However, this did not mean that the state could impose a monopoly, since the trading and raiding network was in private hands, and spread far beyond the notional borders of the colonial enclave. In the direct hinterland some cultivation did develop to furnish provisions for the *tumbeiros*, the forbidding name given to the slave traders' caravels.[36] To the north Angola was shielded by the Christian kingdom of the Kongo, which occupied a territory about the size of Portugal itself. On Africa's East coast Portuguese forts at Kilwa, Mozambique and Quelimane played a role in the Indian ocean trade and were able to exchange cloth for gold in Matapa – but at this time they did not supply slaves to the Americas.

In the early seventeenth century the Portuguese still had a virtual monopoly on the supply of slaves to the New World; their skill at penetrating African commercial and political systems, and at constructing their own slave-raiding and trading networks, meant that they could take 10,000–20,000 slaves a year across the Atlantic. The slave commerce had a gross value of several million cruzados each year, as well as a manifest strategic significance for the linked Iberian powers. The trade to Spanish America, though smaller than that to the islands and Brazil, was much more profitable; those who secured the *asiento* entered a sellers' market, where the colonists' pent-up demand for slaves was backed by undervalued specie. By contrast, Brazil was more of a buyers' market so far as slaves were concerned, and it was often necessary to extend credit to *senhores* and *lavradores* who could buy from several suppliers and even make do with cheaper Indian labour: it is probable that some of the new *engenhos* were established by slave traders as a sideline.

To begin with, the Union of the Spanish and Portuguese Crowns in 1580–81 made little difference to the administration of the Portuguese Empire. As had been agreed, it was entrusted to Portuguese officials, and the Lisbon-based *Mesa da Consciência* continued to play an important part. But in the 1590s and after, there are indications that Madrid was taking positive steps to develop the Crown's Portuguese possessions. The commercial development of Brazil in the whole period 1580–1620 could scarcely have taken place unless it met with the approval of the Spanish King and his advisers. It seems likely that at some point the Spanish authorities grasped the fact that more revenue was likely to be derived from Brazil if it was encouraged to become Europe's main supplier of sugar. Likewise in Africa there are signs of a more forward policy of colonization, aimed at denying an opening to Dutch or English interlopers. Manifestly this could best be done by extending the range of fortified settlement, and by close treaties with African kings where this was impracticable. Cumbersome and expensive efforts were made to strengthen El Mina against Dutch encroachment; but though the fort was successfully defended, its trade in gold continued to languish. The new *asientos* granted to Portugal from the 1590s greatly stimulated the slave trade and encouraged the slave trading networks in Central and West Africa.

Arguments over Slavery

A memorandum prepared in about 1610 for King Philip found in the archives in Rio de Janeiro testifies to continuing problems with justification of the ever-rising tide of the slave traffic:

> Modern theologians in published books commonly report on, and condemn as unjust, the acts of enslavement which take place in Provinces of this Royal Empire, employing for this purpose the same principles by which the ancient theologians, doctors of canon law, and jurists had regulated legitimate and just acts of enslavement. According to these principles, only infidels who are captured in just wars, or who because of serious crimes have been condemned by their Rulers may be held as legitimate slaves, or if they sell themselves, or if they are sold by their own fathers who have legitimate need. And because, by the use of these four principles, great injustices are committed in the buying and selling of

slaves in our empire, as will later be seen, it is also certain that most of the slaves in this Empire are made so upon other pretexts, of which some are notoriously unjust, and others with great likelihood may be presumed to be so as well. Because on the entire Guinea coast and at Cape Verde those persons called *tangomãos* and other dealers in this merchandise, men of loose morals with no concern other than their own interests, commonly carry out raiding expeditions up the rivers and in the remote interior far from these areas that are frequented by the Portuguese, by His Majesty's officials, and by the priests of those regions. . . . Not even the merchants themselves deny that they collect the slaves in the ways described, but they defend themselves saying that they transport them so that they may became Christians, and so that they may wear clothes and have more to eat, failing to recognise that none of this is sufficient to justify so much theft and tyranny. . . .

The memorialist had clearly read Mercado, citing some of the same examples of abuse. He goes on to explain that 'ill-treatment and enslavement is scandalous to everybody, and particularly to those same heathens, because they abandon our religion, seeing that those who are supposed to convert them are the same persons who enslave them, as is witnessed every day'. He also argues that Portuguese practices of slave-raiding and slave trading had sabotaged the possibility of converting the ruler of Japan to Christianity. He concludes on an almost utopian note:

> And in regard to the justification of slavery through condemnation for the crime committed, the laws of China do not condemn people to slavery for any crime . . . there they do not have the practice of men selling themselves, nor does it appear that fathers sell their children during periods of great famine, as happens sometimes in Cambodia, since general famines do not occur in China, the laws of China not permitting them, everyone there being given what he needs to maintain himself, without working. So that on occasions the people of that nation are shocked by the way the Portuguese make slaves of them against the law of their land, who are not their legitimate masters. To which reasonable shock and dismay Your Majesty and your Ministers have an obligation to make a positive response.[37]

This memorial was as vigorous in its conclusions as Mercado or Albornoz – on the other hand, it remained a private communication to the King, who was now dependent as never before on revenues generated by the slave traffic. In a fatal concession the memorialist also unwisely allowed that there were valid procedures for enslavement.

The early years of union between the Spanish and Portuguese crowns saw an authoritative ideological ratification of the Atlantic slave complex with the publication of a new work by the Jesuit theologian Luis de Molina, already renowned for reconciling the doctrine of free will to salvation through Divine grace by arguing that God possessed foreknowledge concerning the free actions of human beings in the given circumstances. In his *De Justicia et Iure* (1592) Molina elaborated the theory of rights established by Gerson (to which reference was made in Chapter I). Richard Tuck summarizes a central argument of this work:

> Molina insisted that all rights must be active and that apparently passive rights are really rights to do things. But of course a right to beg is not the same as a right to be given alms: Molina's intensely active rights theory turned out unsurprisingly to be less interested in human welfare than in human liberty. This was a feature of his remarks about slavery also: 'Man is dominus not only of his external goods, but also of his own honour and fame; he is also dominus of his own liberty, and in the context of the natural law can alienate it and enslave himself. [The Roman law imposed conditions for voluntary servitude but they only applied to Rome.] It follows ... that if a man who is not subject to that law sells himself unconditionally in some place where the relevant laws allow him, then that sale is valid.' According to Molina the 'Aethiopians', that is the blacks, were in that position: there was no reason to suppose that they were not voluntary slaves, and they could have made themselves such for any sort of return, ranging from their lives to a string of beads. Molina's book ... was a consistent and comprehensive alternative to everything which Vitoria and his followers had been saying, and it paid little or no attention to the niceties of humanism. Coming from a country with a deep involvement in the slave trade and in colonial rivalry with other powers, his revival of Gersonian rights theory looks very much like an attempt to produce an ideology of mercantile capitalism. But its undoubted connection with his ideas on free will suggests also a much wider ideological scope: it was a theory of man as a free and independent being, making his own decisions and being held to them, on matters to do with both his spiritual and material welfare.[38]

While Molina's thought acknowledged the free will of the individual, his teachings on slavery and the slave trade show that he was not an individualist. Thus he acknowledged and deplored the fact that cruelty and violence often attended the slave traffic, as they did war and other undertakings. But, as Davis points out: 'Molina believed that in a just war even the innocent members of an enemy population might legitimately be enslaved as a way of punishing the entire population. Their children might also be enslaved to punish the parents . . .'.[39] The notion that since we owe our lives to our parents, and our faculties to the society which has nourished us, so our fate lies in their hands had wide resonance.

In contrast to the relative obscurity attending publication of those works in which the slave trade had been criticized, Molina's theories were debated at a special Congregation, described by Tuck as a sort of 'Catholic Synod of Dort', and achieved popularity 'particularly in the Spanish Netherlands'.[40] While the psychological doctrine of Molinism retained currency into the twentieth century, his teachings on slavery and the slave trade had a considerable impact on contemporary learned opinion, notably on Francisco Suárez, Hugo Grotius and Thomas Hobbes.

In *De Legibus ac Deo Legislatore* (published at Coimbra in 1614), Suárez refined Molina's work, reconciling it with Thomist orthodoxy, by showing that while 'natural law' permitted slavery, 'human law' could positively require it:

> it is manifest that a division of property is not opposed to natural law in the sense that the latter absolutely and without qualification forbids such division. The same is true with respect to slavery and other similar matters ... for the very reason that man is the *dominus* of his own liberty it is possible for him to sell or alienate the same.[41]

Once again, as with Molina, what is true of the individual is also true of an entire people, since peoples, through their rulers, were agents in the world and the source of the individual's faculties. Disconcertingly but significantly, Suárez uses the same approach to justify both wage labour and absolute monarchy.[42]

Another Molinian doctrine is worth mentioning since, though he might well not have been prepared to follow the line of thought, it did chime in with the practical attitudes of the new breed of slaveowner to be found in Brazil, a mentality with which Brazilian Jesuits were very familiar. The *senhor de engenho* who owned a hundred or so slaves tended to look on them as a species of domestic animal, to be inventoried and named like horses, oxen or cattle. The biblical doctrine, enunciated in Genesis, that animals were there simply for the convenience of mankind, or the formulas of Roman Law concerning the slave as a form of living property and speaking tool, to be compared with inert property and dumb animals, furnished the cultural background to such thinking. At all events, Molina went out of his way to exclude animals from the exercise of the rights which were enjoyed by rational beings:

> We must exclude from the area of ius those facultates by the contravention of which, for whatever reason, no injury can be done to their possessors. Of this kind are facultates of all beings deprived of reason and free will by their very nature, such as the facultates of animals to graze and use their limbs, or of stones to fall downwards, etc. Anything which is not endowed with free will is not capable of injury, so that anything which goes against their facultates for any reason is no injury to them, nor can their facultates be regarded as iura.[43]

The Jesuits of Brazil often braved planter hostility to insist that Indians and Africans were worthy of salvation, and it must be supposed that Molina would have supported them and regarded as blasphemous any equation between men and animals. Nevertheless, the Jesuits were also notable for a paternalistic view of the limited capacities of these same persons, who were not thought fit, even if they were free, for the exercise of religious responsibilities. In so far as they were beings of limited reason, then – according to Molina's argument – a restraint on their freedom was no injury. Similar reasoning, of course, was held to justify the lesser rights of women.

Slavery and the Looming Battle for the Americas

Despite the growth of Brazil, the supply of slaves to Spanish America under the *asiento* system furnished the Atlantic slave traders with their premium outlet. Some idea of what this meant is given by details for the operations of one of the largest *asientistas*, the contractor-financier Henrique Gomes da Costa, between December 1624 and August 1626. After disposing of *asientos* and contracts for the supply of 7,454 *peças* to Brazil, carried by 34 ships, he collected 539,000 cruzados; while for organizing the supply of 9,070 *peças* to Spanish America in 30 ships he collected 1,235,000 cruzados.[44] A part of these huge sums went to animate Portugal's slave trading network in Africa; they also meant that Portuguese *asientistas*, some of them New Christians, were playing a key role in Spanish finances. The traders who did the hard graft of acquiring and transporting the slaves thus operated in the shadow of financial and mercantile capital. The price of slaves rose in Brazil as well as Spanish America. Directly or indirectly the traders and planters also depended on the merchants of Northern Europe, who connected them with the most important markets and supplied them with trade goods and equipment.

To some extent the dependence was mutual: if the Luso-Brazilian trader or planter needed Dutch or English help in selling sugar or acquiring textile manufactures, it was also true that the Northern merchants needed access to a supply of tropical products, and welcomed new sales outlets. Until 1620 or thereabouts the Dutch, English and French had failed to establish viable American colonies and had made only the smallest inroads into the slave trade; most of the slaves smuggled into Spanish America were brought by Portuguese traders exceeding their *asiento* quotas, not by freelance smugglers. The trade in slaves could best be conducted by merchants who had the facility of African trading posts and island bases. Ready access to Eastern goods, much in demand in Africa, also assisted the slave trader. Once the Dutch and the English had broken the Portuguese monopoly of the Eastern commerce, the Atlantic trades in slaves and sugar were the next obvious targets.

It could be supposed that the emergent capitalist economy of Northern Europe, with its more or less autonomous dynamic, was bound, sooner or later, to acquire control of the colonial mining, planting and slaving economy of the South Atlantic and New World. The relationship between the emerging capitalist 'core' in Northern Europe, with its increasing incidence of waged or salaried labour, and the New World 'periphery', based primarily on coerced labour systems, was not symmetrical. The wider European demand for silver, spices and sugar sustained the colonial complex; without this demand, the colonial empires could not have existed in their given form. On the other hand, the emergent Northern core could certainly have survived, albeit with significant readjustments, if it had been deprived of New World silver and sugar. In the proto-capitalist core there was potentially a self-sustaining component in economic growth because it involved autonomous productivity gains, and because Say's Law had greater application – that is to say, production, through the disbursement of wages and the needs of reinvestment, would create its own demand. By contrast, the markets in the Iberian Peninsula and American colonies were increasingly cut off from one another, and stifled by bureaucratic regulation. The volume of transactions on the local markets in Mexico and Peru was, in fact, considerable, but little of it spilt back into demand for Spanish products.

This having been said, however, the new bourgeois forces in Northern Europe were in no position simply to await the working out of long-term economic trends in the hope that colonial sources of supply and markets would fall into their hands. Some of the liveliness of demand in Northern Europe was itself stimulated by exotic spices and drugs. Silver and gold were needed to help finance trade with the East, since there was little Eastern demand for European products. Spanish control of silver, and Portuguese control of sugar and slaves, reflected a formidable colonial mobilization. The Dutch and English faced the political and military task of throwing back the parasitical and obstructive apparatus of Iberian monarchy, and of its local allies, before they could gain proper access to the Atlantic trade, let alone develop it beyond the small beginnings seen in Brazil and a few other tiny enclaves. The eventual consolidation of the Dutch Revolt, effectively conceded by Spain in 1609, allowed capitalist accumulation to find and follow its own logic, without paying a ruinous tithe to support an obstructive swarm of royal bureaucrats and Court dignatories. Once the Dutch bourgeois had their own state, they naturally wished to use it to extend the circuits of commerce and accumulation. The defeat of the Armada and the provisional victory of the Dutch Revolt meant that the Habsburgs had suffered a major setback in the struggle for control of the Atlantic. But Spain and Portugal still possessed formidable resources, and their monarch had every intention of reserving the African coast, the Americas and the intervening ocean, with its islands, as his special patrimony.

More by happenstance than by design, the Spanish monarchy had permitted the takeoff of a slave plantation economy in Brazil. The critical transition had been made between 1575 and 1590, when the metropolis had more pressing preoccupations than detailed superintendence of Brazil. With Brazil flourishing, the concessions at the Cortes of Tomar had been adhered to. The crucial development registered in Brazil was the use of African slaves as shock troops of production, not simply as a prop or convenience, as they were in Spanish America. In Brazil there were certainly many slave domestics and artisans, but African slaves also furnished the nucleus of the workforce of the sugar mills. It is true that there were still Indian as well as African slaves, but by 1630, if not earlier, the Africans by themselves comprised around half of the population within the colonial jurisdiction – by contrast, the African slave population of Spanish America comprised no more than about 2 per cent of the total. The sugar mills had broken through to a new scale of production, and the sugar they produced had awakened the cupidity that had once focused only on silver and gold.

Notes

1. Alexander Marchant, *From Barter to Slavery: The Economic Relations of Portuguese and Indians in the Settlement of Brazil, 1500–1580*, Baltimore, MD 1942, especially pp. 69–71.

2. John Hemming, *Red Gold: The Conquest of the Brazilian Indians*, Cambridge, MA 1978, p. 37.

3. Marchant, *From Barter to Slavery*, p. 42.

4. Villegagnon to Calvin, 31 March 1557, in Jean de Léry, *Voyage au Brésil de Jean de Léry, 1556–1558*, Paris 1927, p. 28; Hemming, *Red Gold*, pp. 120–21; H.B. Johnson, 'The Portuguese Settlement of Brazil, 1500–80', in Leslie Bethell, ed., *The Cambridge History of Latin America*, Cambridge 1984, vol. 1, pp. 249–86.

5. Frank Lestringant, *Le Huguenot et le sauvage*, Paris 1990, especially pp. 32–6, 277–8. This book explores the significance of the rival accounts of *La France Antarctique* produced by the Protestant Jean de Léry and the Catholic André Thevet, both classic texts of colonial anthropology. The more austere Protestants, who left the island, made fewer demands on the Indians because of their willingness to work the land. They were also less preoccupied with converting the Indians, probably because they regarded them as anyway not among the Elect. Jean de Léry's initial report furnished a vivid picture of the Tupi which did not seek to assimilate them to European customs and prejudices. Following his experience of France's religious wars, he came to look back on his time with the Tupi with increasing nostalgia; his work helped to inspire esteem for the 'noble savage'.

6. Jean de Léry, *History of a Voyage to the Land of Brazil*, Berkeley, CA 1992, pp. 143–4.

7. Ibid., p. 144.

8. Johnson, 'The Portuguese Settlement of Brazil, 1500–1580', pp. 249–86; James Lockhart and Stuart Schwartz, *Early Latin America: A History of Colonial Spanish America and Brazil*, Cambridge 1983, pp. 192–3, 196.

9. Hemming, *Red Gold*, pp. 97–118; Lockhart and Schwartz, *Early Latin America*, pp. 196–7; Schwartz, *Sugar Plantations in the Formation of Brazilian Society*, pp. 40–41.

10. Hemming, *Red Gold*, p. 149; Barrett and Schwartz, 'Dos Economías Azucareras', in Florescano, ed., *Haciendas, Latifundios y Plantaciones*, p. 544.

11. Schwartz, *Sugar Plantations*, p. 67.

12. H.B. Johnson, 'Portuguese Settlement' and Stuart Schwartz, 'Plantations and Peripheries', in Leslie Bethell, ed., *Colonial Brazil*, Cambridge 1987, pp. 31, 72.

13. Mauricio Goulart, *Escravidão Africana no Brasil*, São Paulo 1949, pp. 106, 113.

14. Schwartz, *Sugar Plantations*, p. 43.

15. Quoted in ibid., p. 49 (see pp. 47–50 for an account of the movement).

16. Stuart B. Schwartz, 'Free Labor in a Slave Economy: The *Lavradores de cana* of Colonial Bahia', in Dauril Alden, ed., *The Colonial Roots of Modern Brazil*, Berkeley, CA 1973, pp. 147–97. See also Schwartz, *Sugar Plantations*, for the transition to African labour (pp. 65–72); though the discussion ranges over a longer period than that treated above; see also, for *lavradores*, pp. 295 ff., and for wage workers pp. 313 ff.

17. Pierre Chaunu, *L'Amérique et les Amériques*, p. 89; Pierre Chaunu, *Seville et l'Atlantique (1504–1650)*, Paris 1957, vol. VII, pp. 30–31.

18. Price series for, respectively, Cuba and Brazil are given in Levi Marrero, *Cuba: Economía y Sociedad*, vol. 2, pp. 357, 360–61; and Katia M. de Queirós Mattoso, *Etre Esclave au Brésil, XVIᵉ–XIXᵉ siècle*, Paris 1979, pp. 100–101.

19. José Jobson de Andrade Arruda, 'Colonies as Mercantile Investments', in James Tracy, ed., *The Political Economy of the Merchant Empires*, Cambridge 1991, pp. 360–420 (p. 362).

20. Mauro, *Le Portugal et l'Atlantique*, pp. 433–5.

21. *Adam's Chronicle of Bristol*, quoted in K.R. Andrews, *Trade, Plunder and Settlement: Maritime Enterprise and the Genesis of the British Empire, 1480–1630*, Cambridge 1984, p. 238.

22. Luiz Felipe de Alencastro, 'The Apprenticeship of Colonization', in Barbara Solow, ed., *Slavery and the Rise of the Atlantic System*, Cambridge 1991, pp. 151–77 (p. 160).

23. Mauro, *Le Portugal et l'Atlantique*, p. 447.

24. Cornelius Goslinga, *The Dutch in the Caribbean, 1580–1680*, Assen (The Netherlands) and Gainesville (FL) 1971, p. 52. Signs of Dutch/Flemish presence are also noted in the remarkable memoir of an English adventurer taken captive on the Brazilian coast and subsequently reduced to servile employment in the retinue of the Sá family. See 'The admirable adventures and strange fortunes of Master Anthony Knivet', in *Purchas his Pilgrimage*, pp. 177–289.

25. Stuart B. Schwartz, in Bethell, *Colonial Brazil*, pp. 75–6.

26. James Lang, *Portuguese Brazil: The King's Plantation*, New York 1979, p. 81; Vitorino Magalhães Godinho, *Os descobrimientos e a economia mundial*, vol. 2, p. 472.

27. António Barros de Castro, 'Brasil, 1610: mudancas técnicas e conflitos sociais', *Pesquiza e Planejamento Económico*, vol. 10, no. 3, 1980, pp. 679–712.

28. Evaldo Cabral de Mello, *Olinda Restaurada: Guerra e Açúcar no Nordeste, 1630–1654*, Rio de Janeiro 1975, p. 58.

29. Noel Deerr, *A History of Sugar*, I, pp. 104–5; Ralph Davis, *English Overseas Trade, 1500–1700*, London 1973, pp. 55–6.

30. Lang, *Portuguese Brazil*, p. 86.

31. Magalhães Godinho, *A estrutura na antiga sociedade portuguesa*, p. 43.

32. Lang, *Portuguese Brazil*, pp. 87–9.

33. A.F.C. Ryder, *Benin and the Europeans, 1485–1897*, New York 1969, p. 75.

34. Ibid., p. 45.

35. Vogt, *Portuguese Rule on the Gold Coast*, pp. 127–43. In the early decades of the sixteenth century as many as a dozen caravels a year plied between El Mina and Lisbon; by the last decades it was down to one or two.

36. David Birmingham, 'Central Africa from Cameroun to Zambezi', in Roland Oliver, ed., *The Cambridge History of Africa*, Cambridge 1977, vol. 3, pp. 519–66, especially 542–57; David Birmingham, *Trade and Conflict in Angola*, Oxford 1966; Joseph Miller, 'The Slave Trade in Congo and Angola', in Martin Kilson and Robert Rothberg, eds, *The African Diaspora*, Cambridge, MA 1976, pp. 75–113. Thornton stresses the considerable autonomy of the traders, despite official attempts to control their activity for the fiscal benefit of the Crown: *Africa and Africans in the Making of Atlantic World*, pp. 62–3.

37. 'Proposta a Sua Majestade sobre a escravaria das terras da Conquista de Portugal', in Conrad, *Children of God's Fire*, pp. 11–12, 14–15.

38. Tuck, *Natural Rights Theories*, pp. 53–4.

39. Davis, *The Problem of Slavery in Western Culture*, p. 127 footnote 37. Davis cites the following in support of this interpretation: Johan Kleinappi, *Der Staat bei Ludwig Molina*, Innsbruck 1935, pp. 145–6.

40. Tuck, *Natural Rights Theories*, p. 54.

41. Francisco Suárez, *De legibus ac Deo Legislatore*, published in Latin and English, 2 vols, Oxford 1944, English trans., vol. 2, pp. 278–9.

42. Tuck, *Natural Rights Theories*, pp. 53–7; W.A. Dunning, *A History of Political Theories: From Luther to Montesquieu*, New York 1928, p. 18.

43. Quoted from *De Justicia et Iure* in Tuck, *Natural Rights Theories*, p. 53.

44. Mauro, *Le Portugal et l'Atlantique*, p. 175.

V

The Dutch War for Brazil and Africa

God's fire impressed the mark of slavery upon you; and, granted that this is the mark of oppression, it has also, like fire, illuminated you. . . . Some religious orders are barefoot, others wear shoes; yours is one of bare feet and rags. . . . Your abstinences better deserve to be called hunger than fasting, and your vigils are not from one o'clock until mid-night, but the whole night without relief. Finally every religious order has a purpose and vocation and special grace. The grace of yours is whips and punishments. . . . Your vocation is the imitation of Christ's patience . . . ; and its purpose is eternal inheritance as a reward. . . . Oh, what a change of fortune will be yours at that time, and what astonishment and confusion for those who have so little humanity today.

Padre António Vieira, *Sermon to the Slaves*

Albert Eckourt, *The Kongolese Envoy to Recife* (The National Museum of Denmark, Department of Ethnography)

W erner Sombart has cited the formation and activities of the Dutch
West India Company (WIC) as proof of the emergence of a new type
of aggressive and plundering bourgeoisie.[1] While it lived up to this billing
in its early years, it was later to prove a disappointment to investors and
patriots alike. The WIC, formed in 1621, was partly modelled on its famous
and more successful precursor the VOC, or East India Company; founded
in 1602, the VOC had taken over much of Portugal's spice trade and seized
a number of its fortified islands. It had indeed brought businesslike methods
to the task of seizing and extending the spice trade of the East. In contrast
to Eastern traders, the well-armed Dutch vessels generally refused to pay
dues or tribute to local rulers; where necessary, they destroyed competitive
suppliers and established their own. Their ships also took on the pirates
who ravaged the trade of the Indian Ocean and China seas. On the other
hand, the Dutch VOC did not allow military expenses to outweigh the
profits of trade, as was happening with the Portuguese in Asia by the close
of the sixteenth century.

Fredrick Lane has analysed this distinctive pattern of the Dutch trading
companies in terms of an internalization, and hence a rationalization, of
the protection costs which all early modern trade incurred. Niels Steensgaard summarizes this view:

> [like] the trading empire of the Portuguese king, the [Dutch] companies were
> integrated, nonspecialised enterprises, but with one remarkable difference. They
> were run as a business, not as an empire. By producing their own protection, the
> companies not only expropriated the tribute but also became able to determine
> the quality and cost of protection themselves. This meant that protection costs
> were brought within the range of rational calculation instead of being in the
> unpredictable region of 'the acts of God or the king's enemies'.[2]

This judgement helps to illuminate the successes of the VOC, but it does
not confront the inescapable problems of sovereignty in a contested
multistate system. While the the rationalization of costs has no limit for a
commercial company, which can simply go out of business, a state may
wish to bear losses in the defence of sovereignty. When it came to
constructing and defending colonies, the Portuguese approach was to reveal
advantages in the Atlantic region which were not so evident in the East.
The Dutch focused on the rights of traders and the virtues of limited
sovereignty, while the Portuguese subordinated trade to a wider project
which, with the advantage of priority, could command allegiance from a
wonderfully motley colonial retinue. These were issues with which the
Dutch jurist Hugo Grotius grappled between the publication of his *Mare
Liberum* (1609), in which he eloquently attacked the colonial monopolies
of the Iberian *Mare Clausum*, advancing the rights of all other nations to
free trade on the high seas, and his *De Iure Bellis ac Pacis* (1625), in which,
as we will see, he discovered reasons why the defence of civil society itself
required upholding the claims of both sovereignty and slavery.

The first project for a West India Company had been aborted in 1607–08 because of the truce with Spain, and could not be resuscitated until it ended. The resources and commitment necessary to mount such a company were assembled in 1619–21 only after the ousting of the cautious oligarch Oldenbarnevelt, in 1618, and the rise to power of a militantly Protestant and anti-Spanish faction which opposed renewal of the truce. The new ruling faction promoted Prince Maurits to the office of stadholder in preparation for a resumption of hostilities. The new government's objective was nothing less than a global assault on the commercial and colonial system of the King of Spain and Portugal. The political logic of such an undertaking was that the time had come to go beyond the defensive Union of Provinces which had thrown off Spanish rule, and forge a central state strong enough to take on the global empire of the Habsburgs – in the New World as well as Asia. But the Provinces were imbued with a fierce spirit of independence; each jealously controlled their own finances and militia. Moreover, the construction of a central power seemed to imply acceptance of a proper monarchy in a country where many citizens felt more comfortable with a Republican polity or very limited monarchy.

The political revolution of 1618–19 had been supported by Protestants who had emigrated to the independent provinces from the still Spanish-ruled Southern Low Countries. But militant Protestantism was not a majority force, because of the division between strict Calvinists and the more tolerant Arminians, and because many in ruling circles were supporters of the Erastian doctrine that the government should control ecclesiastical matters, not priests the government. Oldenbarnevelt had been overthrown because he had failed to counter the threatening advance of Spanish forces – notably the seizure of Wesel in 1614 – and because of protracted diplomatic, religious and commercial disputes with England. If the England of James I could not be relied upon to resist Spain, as was clearly the case in 1618–19, then it was urgent for the United Provinces to strengthen their own capacity to take on Spanish might prior to the expiry of the eleven-year Truce in 1609.[3]

The West India Company

When the Estates General was brought to accept the establishment of the WIC, this was a compromise move, giving birth to a hybrid entity. The WIC was to be both an instrument of state policy and a commercial organization. This formula, which worked in the East, faced a more demanding test in the Atlantic, where the colonial and military competition was to prove stiffer, and the objectives of Dutch policy less consensual. The commercial privileges and opportunities conferred on the WIC certainly offered great potential, and its initial resources were formidable, but neither constituted the sort of guarantee of long-term support that the formation of a Dutch Atlantic fleet and colonial office might have represented.

The advocates of the WIC themselves pointed to the booming Atlantic trade in sugar and tobacco, and to the need to secure reliable supplies of the new staples. Dutch merchants were keenly aware of the value of the sugar trade, since Amsterdam was now the main European entrepôt; the number of sugar refineries in the city had grown from three in 1598 to twenty-nine in 1622. And independent Dutch traders already brought tobacco, dyestuffs, gold and ivory from the Americas and Africa, hampered only by the vulnerability of their trading posts and Atlantic sea lanes. The promoters of the West India Company believed they could bring about the same revolution in the Atlantic that the VOC was bringing to the Eastern commerce. The WIC was given a monopoly of all Dutch Atlantic trade, and the objective of plundering the Spanish, and replacing the Portuguese, in the New World. Spanish America was to be plundered since, in the first instance, it was too strong for there to be a hope of simply seizing it. Once sufficient damage had been inflicted and a new relationship of forces established, then, it was hoped, Spain would come to terms, ceding territory and admitting the Dutch to the trade of Spanish America. Brazil and Portuguese Africa were to be seized from the outset, just as Portuguese possessions and trade in the East had been. They were not only of great commercial significance, but also thought to be immediately exposed to Dutch maritime strength.

The foundation of the WIC was accompanied, as we have seen, by patriotic and religious justifications. Whatever its subsequent career, the WIC was conceived as an instrument of righteousness as much as a source of gain. The directors requested a clerical opinion upon whether it would be proper for the new company to engage in slave trading; when they were informed that it would not, they pledged the Company to abstain from the traffic. While there had been some freelance Dutch slave trading activity in West Africa, this had not enjoyed any public sanction. In 1596 a Dutch trader brought 130 Africans to Middelburg; following objections, the city decreed that slaves were not to be traded there, and that those on the ship should be freed.[4] Middelburg became a subscriber to the foundation of the WIC. Usselinx, the man who had campaigned for a Dutch American Company, had always supposed that colonization would be based on free emigration. The experience of the East India Company had precipitated controversy at the Synod of Dort over the baptism of children born to slaves, as mentioned in Chapter I. Dutch painting, the most luminous testimony we have to the mentalities of the Golden Age, supplied several fine portraits of Africans. One of the most striking was to be Jacob Jordaens's portrait of Moses and Zipporah, with Zipporah clearly represented as a black African woman – the more remarkable since the Dutch saw themselves as a people inheriting the traditions and character of Ancient Israel. Dutch art also betrayed unease with the spectacle of unrestrained consumption – though here it was the demoralizing effects of overconsumption, not the human costs of production, that were the focus of concern. Altogether, give or take the element of Puritan humbug, the moral climate of the United Provinces contained some impulses hostile to racial slavery, or at least favourable to its regulation.[5] However, the ethos of the plantation trades was positive and patriotic. While drunkenness and luxury were frowned upon, plantation products had other associations; they were easy to assimilate to a sober and hard-working lifestyle and to good housekeeping.[6] Although Africans could be portrayed with subtlety and humanity by some, Daniel Mytens and other portrait painters used African slave boys as mascots in the entourage of rich or royal personages, symbolizing both wealth and fidelity. Likewise, religious artists could render the equation of sin and blackness with a disturbing literalness.[7] In another ominous development, opening the way to theological justification of enslavement, prelates at the University of Leiden endorsed the notion that it was possible neatly to assign geographical areas to the sons of Noah.[8]

The East India Company, which in many ways furnished a model for the WIC, had adjusted itself to slaveholding and slave trading in the East. In 1622 it drew up an elaborate code, reflecting the more conservative view expressed at Dort, to regulate slavery and the slave traffic in its Eastern trading posts and colonies: Christian slaveowners were forbidden to sell slaves 'outside Christendom', but were permitted to purchase them from unbelievers. Masters were urged to treat their slaves in a kindly way, rigorously to abstain from sexual relations with them and to introduce them to the local Portuguese Protestant congregation (the slaves being more likely to speak Portuguese, though perhaps also because this was a somewhat isolated group, membership in which would confer little leverage on a slave). The Dutch colony at the Cape adopted similar temporizing measures, permitting slavery but hedging it around with rules which it was up to the slaveowners themselves to enforce.[9] In its early years, however, the WIC chose a different path from the VOC, and opted against slaveholding and slave trading.[10]

The Heeren XIX, as the directors of the WIC were known, included savants as well as merchants – one of their number was Joannes de Laet, who published a scholarly pamphlet arguing, *contra* Grotius, that the Indians of the Americas were not descendants of the lost tribes of Israel or, as others claimed, of Ham, but of people from Asia who had entered across the ice from Alaska (a conclusion reached by the Jesuit José de Acosta in 1570).[11] The writings of Las Casas and the vivid lithographs of Theodore de Bry inspired a sense of outrage at the sufferings of the Amerindians at the hands of the Spanish. Many agreed that it would be the task of the WIC to do what it could to elevate the condition of the Native Americans. The enlightened character of the WIC was also signalled by the fact that members of the Iberian Jewish community, refugees from the Inquisition, were openly numbered among its shareholders.[12]

In 1623–24 the VOC dispatched an expedition of eleven ships and 1,650 men to the Indian and Pacific oceans, while the WIC sent a reconnoitring squadron to the Caribbean and a larger force, comprising twenty-three ships, to capture Bahia, Brazil's capital. The Portuguese forces and Brazilian militia mounted a stiff resistance but could not prevent the city being seized, together with over 70,000 *arrobas* of sugar awaiting shipment. When news of the capture reached the Peninsula a large force was immediately assembled for the relief of Bahia, the so-called 'expedition of the vassals'. This expedition was commanded by a Spanish admiral, but was of overwhelmingly Portuguese composition. Numbering no fewer than 52 ships and 12,000 men, it recaptured Bahia after a Dutch occupation of less than a year. The speed and strength of the Portuguese response testified to a recognition of Brazil's importance shared by soldiers, traders, officials, and those wide social strata whose interests were connected to empire.[13]

The next major WIC coup was the capture of the Spanish silver fleet off the coast of Cuba in 1628 by a Dutch fleet of thirty ships; this was to be the only occasion on which the *flota* was lost to enemy action. Indeed, it represented a watershed for Spanish power in both the Old World and the New. In Europe the Genoese bankers who had been extending credit to the Spanish monarchy decided that enough was enough; the royal authorities in Madrid were thrown into a desperate search for new sources of revenue which was to drive the Catalans and Portuguese to revolt. In the New World Spain was now thrown comprehensively on the defensive, concentrating all its resources on convoying silver fleets of diminishing profitability.

The WIC had gained a famous victory, but it had also complicated its own position. With Spanish power weakened in the Atlantic, a part of its *raison d'être* was removed – at least in the eyes of those excluded from its privileges. The setting up of the WIC had been opposed by some of the independent traders to the Atlantic who were now expected to respect its monopoly privileges. Lack of enthusiasm for the WIC reduced the money it could raise from subscribers and increased its dependence on public subsidies. Hugo Grotius had defended the need for a *mare liberum*, or sea open to free commerce; he was in exile when the WIC was incorporated by a charter aiming to construct is own *mare clausum*. However, the WIC often found itself obliged to compromise with the independent traders. From the outset independent traders had been permitted to participate in the salt trade in South Africa. Subsequently, Dutch independent traders were behind the setting up of African or American trading concerns in Sweden, Courland and Brandenburg; sailing under these flags of convenience, they encroached on the WIC's trade where they could.[14]

The Dutch in Brazil and Africa

The Spanish silver allowed the WIC to resuscitate its plans to seize Brazil, demonstrating by so doing why its special privileges and powers were justified. It assembled an expedition for a renewed assault on Brazil in 1629–30, comprising 67 ships and 7,000 men. This succeeded in capturing the twin cities of Recife and Olinda, respectively the major port and the capital of the colony's most important sugar-producing captaincy, Pernambuco. The local forces retreated to the interior, tenaciously led by Matias Albuquerque, descendant and heir of the captaincy's founder. But the reaction of the Peninsula authorities was both tardy and inappropriate. The authorities in Madrid wished to avoid the charge that they had neglected the defence of Brazil, but they were desperately short of funds and faced threats on many fronts. With great difficulty and delay a mainly Spanish naval force, carrying regular troops commanded by an Italian general, was sent to Brazil, but failed to dislodge the Dutch, who themselves also received considerable reinforcement. While the troops of the WIC could handle the threat from Spanish warships and regulars, they did not pacify the interior of Pernambuco until 1636, when they obliged Albuquerque and his followers to withdraw to the South. The costs of replenishing the Dutch garrison were high, and the quantities of sugar sent back to Europe were disappointing: less than 25,000 *arrobas* annually in 1629–32 and 60,000–80,000 in 1634–37. Sugar output was hampered by continuing hostilities, destruction of mills, shortage of labour and the monopolistic privileges exercised by the WIC.[15]

The WIC conducted a vigorous trade to Africa in the years 1623–36, according to an account drawn up by de Laet, acquiring gold, ivory and other products in exchange for Dutch textiles and other European manufactures. Gold represented 75 per cent of the value of the returning cargoes, ivory 7.5 per cent, hides 7.3 per cent and Malaguetta pepper 2.6 per cent. The goods dispatched to Africa had a total value of 6.6 million guilders, while the returning cargoes were worth 15.5 million. The volume of this trade was no greater than that previously reached by independent Dutch merchants, but the trade mark-up, at 115 per cent, was probably higher – the WIC's formidable combination and concentration of naval and commercial resources might explain this.[16]

Reasonable though these results were, however, they were considerably inferior to those achieved in these same years by the Portuguese African traders supplying Brazil and Spanish America with slaves. Ernst van den Boogaart points out that 40,000 slaves were sold to Brazil and 45,000 to Spanish America during the period 1623 to 1632. He estimates that the Brazilians paid five million pesos – 12.5 million guilders – while the Spanish American slave purchasers paid around eight million pesos or twenty million guilders. In order to realize these sales the slave traders, nearly all of them Portuguese, acquired over a hundred thousand slaves in Africa for trade goods worth around three million guilders. While these estimates are framed in broad terms and do not take account of the cost of acquiring a share in the *asiento*, or special costs associated with the transport of slaves, they do indicate a trading mark-up very much higher than that achieved in the Dutch Africa trade of the same period – 983 per cent instead of 135 per cent.[17] The Dutch, whose commercial intelligence was generally excellent, will have been aware of this contrast.

As we have seen, the WIC was intended to be an arm of state policy as much as a trading corporation. It received a subsidy from the Estates General as well as the monopoly over the Atlantic trade, including that with West Africa. Nevertheless, its individual and corporate shareholders and the board of directors they appointed, the Heeren XIX, expected a positive return on their investment. Despite subsidies and privileges, they did not receive this in the early and mid 1630s. Outfitting fleets and establishing forts in Africa was very costly. The WIC accumulated a deficit of 15 million guilders by 1636. (Two guilders equalled one cruzado.) The merchants of Middelburg had subscribed to the Company in the hope of sharing in the profitable Atlantic trade, but had found that the WIC's monopoly was inimical to independent trading of the sort which thrived in Europe and within Asia. The Company's abstention from the slave traffic had been gradually and pragmatically eroded. In the first place, the WIC had to deal with the problem of 2,336 slaves found on board captured Spanish or Portuguese vessels in the years 1623–37 which had been sold – in the Americas, not Europe – to raise prize money. Once it was in control of a part of Brazil, it needed to take more deliberate steps to acquire slaves. A handbook published by Godfridus Cornelisz Udemans in 1638 to offer moral guidance to Dutch traders and officials doubted the claim that attached Noah's curse to all the sons of Ham, since in Genesis it had applied only to the descendants of Canaan, but deemed enslavement acceptable if it led to spiritual enlightenment.[18]

Hugo Grotius had already reached a conclusion supportive of slavery by a different route in his *De Iure Belli et Pacis* (1625). Prompted, perhaps, by the turbulence which had driven him into exile, he acknowledged the need for sovereigns and heads of families to dispose of absolute powers that would enable them to keep the peace. As part of this new understanding he insisted that liberty was the alienable right which people had in themselves. Thus he declares: 'It is lawful for any man to engage himself as a Slave to whom he please; as appears in both the Hebrew and Roman Laws'; and observes: 'Civilians call a *Faculty* that Right which a Man has to his *own*; but we shall hereafter call it a *Right properly, and strictly taken*. Under which are contained, 1. A power either over ourselves, which is term'd *Liberty*: or over others such as a *Father over his children*, or a *Lord over his Slave*.'[19] There are subtleties here which cannot be conveyed in a brief quotation, and passages in Grotius's work which later led others to different conclusions. But as Richard Tuck points out: 'It is significant that the first major public expression of a strong rights theory to be read in Protestant Europe should have contained both a defence of slavery and absolutism and a defence of resistance and common property *in extremis*.'[20] A new edition of Grotius's *De Iure Belli et Pacis* appeared in 1631 as the WIC was adjusting itself to the need to engage in the slave trade if it was to regain the initiative.

In an effort to retrieve the fortunes of the WIC, the Heeren XIX appointed Prince Johann Maurits of Nassau, nephew of the former stad-holder and a young man with a brilliant reputation, to be Governor of Brazil with plenipotentiary powers. The Prince arrived with reinforcements in 1637, and soon consolidated and extended the territory ruled by the Company in the North and North East of Brazil, until it comprised seven of the twelve captaincies. The Company was persuaded to relax its monopoly on the export trade in sugar and other tropical staples. More than a half of Pernambuco's *engenhos* had been abandoned and destroyed, with their former owners withdrawing to the Southern captaincies with as many slaves and as much equipment as possible. Prince Maurits confiscated abandoned estates and put them up for sale; credits to re-equip them could be obtained from private traders or, in some cases, the Company. The quantities of sugar exported, though modest, increased: the Company handled 60,000 *arrobas* in 1638 and 130,840 in 1639, while in these same years private traders carried 136,052 and 142,250 *arrobas* respectively.[21]

This seemed an encouraging start, and one which Prince Maurits carried off in fine viceregal style. He was accompanied by architects, naturalists, physicians and painters; he ordered palaces, forts, drainage systems, schools and orphanages to be built; he renamed the capital Mauritstad; he convened an assembly of those *moradores* who were willing to co-operate; a civilian militia was entrusted with the maintenance of law and order. As a graduate of the famous *schola militaris* run by his uncle, Prince Maurits promoted the drill and discipline of the early-seventeenth-century 'military revolu-tion', an example which had special implications for a plantation society. He was solicitous of the rights and properties of the planters. Portuguese Brazilians who returned could reclaim their property. Freedom of worship was offered to Catholics, and the civic equality of Jews and Indians was upheld. Special agents were entrusted with the well-being of the Indian nations and villages; some of these agents, betraying the trust put in them, connived at illegal forms of labour conscription. The different Indian nations were invited to send delegates to an Assembly which met in April 1645 in the *aldeia* of Tapisserica in Goiana. A resolution was passed declaring; 'Before all else we exhibit the Provision that was sent to us by the Assembly of the XIX ... referring to the liberty conceded to us, as to all other inhabitants of Brazil. Item I: Your Excellencies should deign to put this law into effect. Liberty should be immediately conceded to any of our race that might still be kept as a slave.'[22] Prince Maurits continued to exert his influence in favour of the Indians, but whatever success he had undermined his attempts to woo the Portuguese *moradores*.

Labour constituted a critical bottleneck, the more so as enslavement of Indians was more effectively banned than in the past. As a report to the Heeren XIX in 1638 succinctly noted: 'It is not possible to do anything in Brazil without slaves.'[23] In June 1637 an expedition had been dispatched from Recife to capture El Mina, now the most important Portuguese slave trading post on the West African coast. After a five-day siege El Mina was taken, and arrangements were put in train to acquire slaves for Dutch Brazil. The labour shortage in Dutch Brazil was eased, but recorded slave imports through Recife still numbered under 2,000 a year in the late 1630s, or less than half the rate prior to the Dutch occupation. The WIC still exercised a monopoly over slave trading, and only slowly acquired the necessary skills and connections. However, Dutch sea power permitted the WIC successively to oust the Portuguese from their main fortified trading posts on the African coast, eventually taking Luanda and Benguela in 1641.

The kings of the Kongo had long found their relations with Portugal frustrating, since the latter sought to monopolize the kingdom's relations with the outside world, whether commercial, political or religious. There had also been armed clashes between the Kongo and Luanda (Portuguese Angola) in 1621–24 which involved a loss of territory to the latter. The Kongo kings looked with cordiality on the arrival of the Dutch, who supplied trade goods on better terms and offered the possibility of escaping Portuguese tutelage. Indeed, the Dutch capture of Luanda in 1641 helped the Kongolese King, Garcia II, to negotiate with the Vatican the dispatch of a Capuchin mission which gradually displaced the Portuguese-linked Jesuits as the kingdom's main foreign clerical colony, and to secure a reorganization of the Kongolese Church, prising it away from the control of the Portuguese King. From the standpoint of the Kongolese monarch, however, there was a drawback to the strengthened position of the Dutch, since it also strengthened the autonomy of the breakaway province of Nsoyo, whose counts had tolerated contraband trade with the Dutch. With Luanda in their hands, and good relations with the neighbouring African kingdom, the Dutch were soon able to boost the numbers of slaves sent to New Holland. In 1642 the numbers of Africans sold in Recife rose above 2,000 annually for the first time, reaching a peak of 5,565 in 1644.[24]

The WIC urged Prince Maurits to capture Bahia. The stadholder of Brazil happily repulsed a Spanish attack on Recife in 1640, but he was not energetic in hostilities against the Southern captaincies. At least some of the sugar exported from Dutch Brazil may have been smuggled in from the South. He may also have been aware that tensions between Portugal and

Spain were coming to a head. By the late 1630s, increasing discord between the King of Spain and his Portuguese subjects was already apparent. Madrid had mounted costly – albeit unsuccessful – attempts to recapture Pernambuco; the expedition of the mid thirties cost over three million cruzados.[25] Madrid therefore felt entirely justified in levying extra war taxes on Portugal, such as the *real d'agua*. Throughout the 1630s trade between Portugal and Brazil became extremely hazardous, with dozens of caravels being lost each year to the Dutch.

The Union of the two crowns had never been popular in Portugal, and it became increasingly less so, as it was associated with the loss of half of Brazil and of El Mina and Luanda, with military failure and a multiplication of taxes. Economic woes prompted popular unrest in 1637, but the nobility declined to endorse it. Once popular turbulence had been suppressed, the dominant classes were more prepared to express their own dissatisfactions. The Union of the crowns had exposed Portugal's empire to damaging assault; before 1580 Portugal had successfully stayed out of European conflicts, apart from occasional clashes with its Iberian neighbour. In the face of the Dutch assault and the growing weakness of Spain, a return to the traditional stance became attractive. The Portuguese mercantile community had little reason to cherish the Spanish link, with the scope for new *asientos* dwindling. In 1640 Madrid invited the Portuguese military nobility to assist in the suppression of the revolt in Catalonia. Instead, it seized the opportunity to reject the rule of Spanish Habsburgs and to proclaim the Duke of Braganza King John IV of Portugal.

Since Madrid refused to accept Portuguese independence, the new regime in Lisbon found it prudent to offer a truce to the Dutch. During the early 1640s Dutch Brazil glimpsed prosperity for the first time. In 1641 the Company sent 94,000 *arrobas* of sugar, while private traders dispatched 353,000 *arrobas*, a combined total which at last approached prewar output. But Prince Maurits found himself increasingly at odds with the predatory and bigoted policy which the Heeren XIX and some Dutch in Brazil wished to impose upon him.

The rulers of the Dutch Republic saw little need to be overly attentive to Portuguese interests and sensibilities. The population of the two states might be similar, but the economic resources and development of the Dutch were vastly greater. The United Provinces possessed a fleet of two or three thousand easily armed ocean-going vessels, and could draw upon a pool of 80,000 seamen. The Portuguese had three or four hundred caravels and about a dozen galleons, most of them in the royal armada; there were only some 4,000–6,000 experienced Portuguese seamen.[26] In Ceylon, Africa and even Brazil the Dutch at first found a welcome from those previously exploited by the Portuguese. The Heeren XIX saw no need to conciliate the Portuguese; indeed, in 1640–41 they sent out messages to their representatives on both sides of the Atlantic to seize as much Portuguese territory as possible before the truce came into force. Prince Maurits readily supported the expedition to capture Luanda and Benguela, since the mills were still short of slaves. But this soldier was far more committed to the work of pacific construction and conciliation in Netherlands Brazil than the Dutch merchants and ministers.

Religious toleration had never been favoured by the Calvinist Predicants, whether in Holland or Brazil; it became increasingly unpopular when the Catholic Church in the colony made converts among the Dutch, while the Calvinists made none among the Portuguese. Some Indians accepted Protestantism, but immediately displayed an independence which attracted the hostility of the Predicants. The stadholder cultivated good relations with the Indian tribes, but he was also keenly aware that the colony's prosperity depended on continued collaboration from the remaining Portuguese *moradores*, merchants and planters who could not afford to abandon their property or were not so attached to the caste-ridden colonial order overthrown by the Dutch. The population of Dutch Brazil was over 100,000–120,000 at this time, but with fewer than 10,000 Dutch, including the garrison troops. The Dutch immigration had been distinguished neither by its quantity nor by its quality, as Prince Maurits never tired of complaining. The largest source of immigrants was the army of occupation, not all of them Dutch and none of them with the resources required to take over the economic leadership of the colony. The great majority of the mill owners and *lavradores* remained Catholic 'Portuguese' or Brazilians. There were still abandoned estates available in the early 1640s, but wealthy Dutchmen were evidently not attracted to the hazards of tropical colonization. The Prince patiently explained the problem to the Heeren XIX: 'Let me repeat again. Poor colonists are not adequate for a colony like Brazil. . . . Take care to colonize Brazil with men who dispose of resources – men who can buy blacks in order to establish cane plantations. To the capitalist all doors would be open.'[27]

There were Dutch commercial agents and Jewish 'New Christians' in the mercantile community but they were at loggerheads with the planters and *lavradores* who could not pay off the debts they incurred to rehabilitate their property. Prince Maurits was aware that planter indebtedness, stemming in good measure from the shortage and high price of slaves, was a delicate and explosive issue; at the cost of much unpopularity with the merchants, he prevented them calling in planters' debts, which amounted to 2 million florins (1 million cruzados) by 1644.[28] The small Dutch colony-within-a-colony found it easy to develop and display contempt for the Portuguese-speaking majority. Prince Maurits, by contrast, was most attentive to leaders of the Portuguese community, such as the planter João Fernandes Vieira, an arriviste reputed to be the illegitimate son of a Madeiran *fidalgo* and a mulatta.[29]

After clashes with both the Heeren XIX and the Dutch in Brazil, Prince

Maurits asked to be relieved. He left in May 1644, to be replaced by a committee that would be more attentive to the Company's Dutch masters. The WIC's resources were drained by efforts to break the Spanish hold on the Caribbean. The Prince had insistently requested reinforcements, but these were never forthcoming in sufficient numbers. So far as many in Dutch governing circles were concerned, the Portuguese revolt against the Spanish monarchy and a continuing conflict between Lisbon and Madrid meant that 'New Netherlands' was no longer a front in the overriding struggle against Spain.[30]

With Prince Maurits's departure, there was a rapid deterioration in the Dutch position. In June 1645 the *moradores* of Pernambuco rose in revolt against the increasingly intolerant and grasping policy of the Company. This was led by Fernandes Vieira, who formed a *terço* that came to number 1,800 men. The owner of a large estate in colonial Brazil would have his own armed henchmen [*agregados*] as well as *lavradores* dependent on him. Dutch attempts to foreclose on loans and to prevent Catholic worship in public in the capital alienated the *moradores*. The revolt acquired a distinctly Brazilian character, but no doubt it was also strengthened by the stronger claims on Portuguese loyalty that could be exercised by the restored monarchy in Lisbon. The Portuguese authorities did not publicly welcome the revolt, but after some hesitation they did extend clandestine support to the rebels, conferring commissions on the leaders and sending 150 experienced soldiers.

The Luso-Brazilian Recoil

From the outset the rebellion was strengthened by the adhesion of Indian and black commanders who had never reconciled themselves to the Dutch. The Portuguese had been in Brazil for well over a century, and the colonial social formation incorporated several thousands of Indians and free blacks, most of them Catholics, the former organized under their own chiefs and the latter with their own brotherhoods. In 1646 the black captain Henrique Dias led a column of 330 blacks, while the Indian Felipe Camarão led 460 Indian fighters; together they comprised nearly a quarter of the Portuguese forces at this time, and proved militarily very effective.[31] The Portuguese authorities were aware of the value of support from Indians and blacks, and made some ideological concessions to encourage it. The Jesuit priest António Vieira, already well-known in Portugal and Brazil for the brilliant oratory of his sermons, vigorously castigated the Portuguese colonists for the harsh way they treated Indians and blacks.

The participation of Indians and blacks in the 'liberation' struggle was subsequently to be the subject of much mythopoeic celebration by colonial and Imperial ideologists; an Henrique Dias regiment formed part of the Brazilian armed forces for over two hundred years. But both the Portuguese and the Dutch were most careful not to attack the institution of slavery. Some individual slaves were offered manumission if they would become soldiers, but the mass of slaves were kept hard at work. As the revolt unfolded it sometimes afforded slaves the opportunity to escape; *quilombos* of slaves who had freed themselves in this way formed in the interior, such as the famous black republic of Palmares. But these fissures in the slave system were no part of the plan of either side in the conflict.

The rebels repulsed Dutch columns sent against them, and greatly disrupted the sugar economy. By 1646 the Company sent back only 55,800 *arrobas* of sugar, while the private traders did even worse, with cargoes of just under 20,000 *arrobas*, representing a total harvest of less than a quarter of the yields achieved in the early 1640s. Since the WIC used profits on sugar sales to finance its operations, this was a heavy blow. The Regent oligarchs of Amsterdam held many shares in the WIC, and exercised a decisive influence in the Estates General. Their major interests lay in the Baltic, in the Mediterranean, or in the Far East. The Netherlands European trade was at least ten times as large as its transatlantic commerce, even at the best of times, while the Far Eastern trade offered opportunities for exceptional profits; by comparison, the Brazil trade was both small and – so far as the WIC was concerned – highly unprofitable. As the truce broke down the WIC was able to keep itself afloat mainly by preying on the Portuguese caravels and selling slaves in the Caribbean. The Company still received some backing, since it detracted from Portuguese attempts to recapture their Asian trading posts, and offered some outlets to the merchants of Zeeland, who had little stake in the VOC. In 1647 the Estates General dispatched a large fleet to the South Atlantic, with plans to capture Bahia and thus attack the rebellion in its rear. But supplies and reinforcements to the Dutch colony remained erratic and inadequate.

The Dutch occupation of Pernambuco had encouraged rather than prevented the development of the Southern captaincies. Émigré planters and their slaves helped greatly to boost the sugar industry of Bahia and Rio de Janeiro, which managed to outproduce Dutch Pernambuco even at its height. The sugar produced was sent to Lisbon, whence it would be sold to English or Dutch merchants. The boom in the South had partially reconciled the Portuguese authorities to the loss of the North; the immediate response to the 1645 revolt had been quite cautious. But the loss of Angola (Luanda and Benguela) had been particularly disturbing, since it threatened the supply of slaves upon which the prosperity of Portuguese Brazil was based. The breakdown of the truce after 1645 exposed Portuguese ships to seizure; 111 were captured in 1647.[32]

Finally, news arrived that a large Dutch fleet commanded by Witte de With had captured the island of Hisparica and was poised for an attack on Bahia. It was clear that accommodation with the Dutch was impossible.

The Portuguese King took the exceptional step of sending the entire royal armada to defend Bahia; on board were 462 gentlemen volunteers, 2,350 soldiers and 1,000 sailors.[33] The Dutch made no attack on Bahia, and evacuated Hisparica prior to the arrival of the armada, but the Portuguese declined to attack the stronger Dutch fleet. In Portugal another small squadron was assembled and dispatched to Rio under the command of Salvador de Sá, grandson of Mem de Sá and probably the richest man in Brazil – he owned 700 slaves. In Rio, Salvador de Sá enlarged his squadron at Brazilian expense and set sail for Angola. With 15 ships and 1,400 men, more than half of them from Brazil, he successively recaptured Luanda, Benguela and São Tomé. He was assisted in this feat of arms by the fact that pockets of Portuguese and their *guerra preta* had held out in the Angolan interior at Massange and a few other points – surviving, in some cases, by capturing slaves for the Dutch. In Africa as in Pernambuco the Portuguese colonial synthesis, implanted over many decades, was not easily uprooted.[34]

The signal victory of the Luso-Brazilian forces in Angola had been achieved only by dodging the Dutch fleet, which retained superiority at sea. In fact the sugar trade of Portuguese Brazil was brought to a halt in 1648, 132 caravels being lost to the enemy. Sugar seized from these caravels soon exceeded that produced in Dutch Brazil. The Portuguese Brazilian land forces inflicted defeats on the Dutch in 1648 and 1649, confining them to a tiny enclave around Recife which had to be expensively supplied by sea, and exported less than 16,000 *arrobas* of sugar in 1650.[35] In the South Atlantic zone Dutch sea power and Portuguese land power had stalemated one another.

In 1649 the Portuguese authorities, following a plan drawn up by Father Vieira, founded a new company which was to organize a convoy system and to receive a monopoly on Brazil's imports, and the right to levy a tax on the export of sugar and other colonial staples. Father Vieira, despite his inclination to scold the planters, knew Brazil's problems well, and received reports from his kinsmen there. His projected Brazil Company raised capital by promising New Christians immunity from the seizure of their property by the Inquisition. Vieira was sent to Amsterdam by John IV to undertake negotiations with the Dutch government, and used this opportunity also to reach an understanding with members of the Jewish community. Portugal's badly depleted mercantile marine was replenished by hiring English ships or giving them licences to engage in the Brazil trade. Already in 1648–49 twenty English ships had lent their assistance to the Portuguese in the South Atlantic – for a price. In 1650 the new company's first fleet, comprising 18 warships and 48 merchantmen, arrived in Bahia, to join forces with the royal armada and to escort the sugar harvest back to the Peninsula. A capital of 1,300,000 cruzados had been mobilized to achieve this. Following the outbreak of the First Anglo-Dutch War of 1652–54, the Brazil Company's armada blockaded Recife and forced a capitulation in 1654. However, hostilities between the Dutch and the Portuguese flared up again in other parts of the world, and a treaty formally laying to rest the Dutch dream of empire in the South Atlantic was not achieved until 1662, once again with England's self-interested assistance.[36]

Sources of Dutch Weakness

The defeat of the WIC in Angola and Brazil provoked intense resentment in the United Provinces: both de With and the directors of the Company were imprisoned for a time in consequence of their failures. Over a period of more than three decades huge resources had been consumed by this South Atlantic venture; in the end there was nothing to show for it beyond a couple of African forts and a handful of tiny Caribbean bases, such as the colony of Curaçao, established for tobacco smuggling and slave trading by the redoubtable Peter Stuyvesant. Even if the American trade was of less consequence than that of the Baltic or the Mediterranean, it remained highly complementary to the other Dutch trades: they needed American dyestuffs for their textile manufactures, and American sugar both for domestic consumption and as an additional means of gaining entry to European markets, where it remained much prized. There could be little doubt that the plantation trades had enormous potential – a potential which was partially stifled by the destructive conflict in Brazil, but was evident enough in the inflation of Amsterdam sugar prices, which rose by a third between 1644 and 1646. The failure to commit decisive forces to the WIC between 1645 and 1654 partly reflected the fact that Dutch independent traders ceased to rely on Dutch Brazil for sugar, tobacco or dyestuffs. An intermittent trade continued with Lisbon, where Brazilian products could sometimes be purchased more cheaply. Indeed, Dutch commercial exuberance itself sometimes conspired against the interests of the WIC, since Dutch traders also continued to sell the Portuguese naval supplies. During these years Dutch traders also found that they could sell supplies and buy produce from struggling settlements of English and French colonists which were being established in the Lesser Antilles.

The Dutch colonization effort in the South Atlantic lacked commitment, follow-through and clear strategic direction. Dutch superiority was never brought to bear upon Portuguese Brazil with tenacity and single-mindedness. The WIC itself, though it was an arm of state policy, was also expected to make a long-run profit; when it failed to do so, the Regent oligarchs simply cut their losses. The revolt of the Netherlands, the first successful bourgeois revolution, had not forged a new centralized political apparatus. It had

issued from a hydra-headed civic resistance to Habsburg heavy-handedness
and fiscal exploitation; it had drawn on the resourcefulness of the sea
beggars – a species of privateer – and the dynastic ambitions of the House
of Orange. This alliance was apt for the liberation and defence of the
United Provinces and for raids on the imperial Iberian trading monopolies,
but not for the setting up of new colonies. At crucial junctures in the
duel with the Portuguese the WIC and the Estates General were paralysed
by the veto power effectively wielded by one or other of the mercantile
factions, usually the Baltic trading interest of Amsterdam. In 1648 the East
India Company, aware of its stronger position, refused to join its forces
with that of the WIC to seek a common salvation. In 1650 the WIC's
prospects of receiving consistent and committed support were again diminished when the stadholder died without an adult heir; the Estates General
proclaimed a purer form of Republic in which the executive power was
further weakened.

Dutch failures in the Americas partly reflected successes in Europe. Once
independence from Spain had been achieved, the population of the Netherlands was too much at home in a prosperous and tolerant metropolis to
emigrate in sufficient numbers to found substantial new colonies. Dutch
women were not attracted by the prospect of making a new life in the
unfamiliar setting of a tropical slave colony. Those Dutch men who were
lacked that adaptability which enabled the Portuguese to find and keep a
foothold in the most inhospitable and unlikely terrain. For a time the Dutch
enjoyed the favour of the ruler of Kandy in Ceylon, of the King of the
Kongo and the Queen of the M'bundu in south central Africa, and of a
number of Indian tribes in Brazil, but they were less successful at spreading
their language and religion, or at creating lasting support for a colonial
presence, than the Portuguese. Dutch colonists hoped to return to Europe,
while those from Portugal were prepared to make a new life overseas.[37]

The Dutch also failed to send sufficient colonists to make its colony of
New Netherlands in North America a solid success. Dutch agriculture,
based on extensive land reclamation, shared with England precocious
features of an agrarian capitalism, but it did not create the same impetus to
emigration that was to sustain the English colonies in North America and
the Caribbean. The Dutch provinces made more generous provision for the
poor than did England, and there was no real equivalent to the expulsions
involved in English rural enclosure. Nevertheless, the Netherlands did
witness emigration and colonization in the seventeenth century; such was
the prestige of Dutch agriculture that attractive terms were offered to Dutch
settlers in many German principalities, in Scandinavia and, indeed, in
England. In such cases the Dutch colonist did not expect to encounter the
hazards of frontier settlement and unfriendly natives on the other side of
an ocean. Dutch emigration spread out along the pathways of its commercial network in Europe, just as England's was to be closely linked to
Atlantic commerce. Around mid century the WIC was sending only two

ships a year to New Amsterdam, which had a fur trade but no staple; the inhabitants of this North American colony also found the Company's monopoly and regulations irksome.[38]

Following the Restoration of 1640, the Portuguese state could again be directed with vigour and single-mindedness. Brazil was, of course, of greater significance to Portugal than any other colony – and also of greater value than Dutch Brazil could possibly have been to its far richer metropolis. In both metropolis and colonies there were powerful spontaneous forces making for colonial restoration. The Brazilians of Pernambuco found themselves driven to bankruptcy and treated with contempt; those in the Southern captaincies saw their further existence at stake when Angola was lost and the maritime link with Portugal was broken. The Brazilian planters undoubtedly hoped to emerge from the conflict with even greater powers and privileges. In the metropolis the colonial project unified nearly every stratum in society: royal officialdom and the *nobreza militar*, important merchants in Lisbon and potential emigrants from the North, members of the religious orders and ordinary seamen. The structures of Portuguese monarchy, despite their predisposition to the restrictive and cumbersome practices of feudal business, were strongly orientated to the defence of empire. Boxer comments: 'King John IV did not have to worry about obtaining the concurrence of the Algarve or the Alentejo before carrying out decisions which had been reached in his Council of State. Contrast this unified form of government with the chaotic situation in the self-styled United Provinces.'[39]

But though Portugal regained Angola and Brazil, the outcome was in other respects less clear-cut than this suggests. The underlying commercial strength of the Dutch derived from a many-sided exchange of agricultural and manufacturing products. The metropolis itself had an incipiently capitalist agriculture, food-processing industries, textile manufactures, and great naval construction yards and foundries. The tiny trading posts maintained by the Dutch in the Americas and in Africa long continued to be magnets for the slave-related and plantation-related trades because of this capacity to sustain a vigorous two-way maritime commerce. The Spanish authorities awarded large *asientos* for the supply of slaves to the WIC rather than to the Portuguese in the 1670s and 1680s. This Company, which had failed in its grand object of seizing Brazil or destroying the Spanish Empire in the Americas, was subsequently to find its main business in the slave traffic which it had started out by repudiating.

Portugal, by contrast, had a very modest internal market and little manufacturing, or even shipbuilding, capacity. The eventual defeat of the WIC in the 1650s was achieved with costly English support. Henceforth privileged English merchants were installed at the very heart of the Portuguese colonial enterprise. The Brazil Company was, in its own terms, a success, in that it furnished a safe and regular outlet for the Brazilian planters. In 1656, 107 ships carried nearly 2,000,000 *arrobas* of sugar to Lisbon, but this level of exports was rarely to be exceeded again. The Company and convoy system, and the alliance with England, imposed a straitjacket on the further development of the plantation economy. The WIC itself had shown that the great trading monopoly was not calculated to tap the expansive possibilities of the plantation trade. The Brazil Company eventually illustrated the same point. While other plantation producers entered the market, and showed that it was capable of a qualitative expansion, Brazilian sugar exports, confined to a rigid and expensive commercial formula, stagnated.

Yet given Portugal's resources, the resort to a company monopoly and convoy system did allow the metropolis to ensure that it received what it saw as its due. When Charles II of England negotiated for the hand of Catherine of Bragança in 1662, he asked his ambassador in Lisbon to find out 'whether it may be practical that the English may engross to themselves the sole trade in sugar, taking the whole commodity at a price, and we being bound to send our fleet to Brazil, and therewith to convoy such a proportion of sugar to Portugal as shall every year be assigned to that consumption, and may then transport the rest whither shall seem best'.[40] This proposal to liquidate the Brazil Company suggests that it was seen as an obstacle to British commerce. The Luso-Brazilian success in repulsing the Dutch in South America momentarily helped to preserve the original Iberian control of Northern Europe's access to New World produce. It was followed by a colonial mercantilist programme which sought to develop new industries in Brazil, and to foster expeditions for the discovery of precious metal.

Following the recapture of Angola and São Tomé, the Portuguese had experienced some difficulty in restoring the export of slaves to its former levels. The Dutch remained active all along the coast, and could still offer highly competitive trade goods. The governors in Luanda sponsored a series of local wars aimed at gaining control of the markets and trade routes linked to the slaving frontier of the interior. In 1665 they decided to take advantage of civil strife in the Kongo to launch a punitive attack against the former client kingdom. At the Battle of Mbwila the new monarch of the Kongo, António I, led his crack detachment of 380 musketeers, supported by tens of thousands of peasant soldiers, in a foolhardy attack on a Portuguese square of 450 musketeers, flanked by two cannon and the formidable *guerra preta*. The attack failed. António was killed, as were ninety-eight titled nobles and 400 lesser *fidalgos*.

This was to prove an even worse blow to the kingdom than Alcácer-Quibir had been to Portugal in 1578. The slaveowning aristocracy of the capital, São Salvador, was no longer able to impose itself on the villages or outlying regions, and the kingdom was torn by civil war. The Kongolese Crown was eventually seized by a Dutch-backed aristocratic faction led by the counts of Nsoyo. The Portuguese authorities eventually found a candidate they could support, and in 1670 they once more sent their musketeers and *guerra preta* into the Kongo. After scoring an initial success, the Portuguese forces fell into an ambush on 18 October in the course of which the Dutch-supplied Nsoyo force destroyed them, capturing their artillery and musketeers – as legend has it, the Nsoyo traders offered the Portuguese prisoners as slaves to the Dutch, who declined to purchase them. An entity known as the kingdom of the Kongo was to remain the object of aristocratic civil wars in the region for several decades. Thanks to a militant Afro-Christian popular religious movement led by a prophetess, Beatriz, who claimed that Jesus had been born in the Kongo, Kongo was eventually to achieve a semblance of its former self, but this was a peasant movement opposed to aristocratic strife. The Kongolese capital never again became an effective administrative centre capable of helping either Portuguese or Dutch, or of furnishing them with the stable commercial conditions that were best for the slave trade.[41]

The exact number of slaves in Brazil in the latter half of the seventeenth century is unknown, but with the restoration of the slave trade from Angola and Guinea after 1650 it must have risen to the range 60,000–100,000. In an obvious sense the rise of Brazilian sugar had been a harbinger of the future of New World slavery. Slaves played a critical part in processing the crop, and it was around this time that Father Vieira acknowledged the interdependence of the Portuguese Empire in a celebrated formula: 'without Negroes there is no Pernambuco, and without Angola there are no Negroes'. Nevertheless, the Brazilian *senhor de engenho* also engaged free workers for directly productive as well as supervisory tasks: as carpenters or boatmen, or even as general labourers. In sugar mill accounts, expenses for the salaries of free workers, running at a fifth or a quarter of total outlays, were greater than the expense of acquiring new slaves.[42] The *senhor* and the *lavrador de cana* also occasionally hired Indians, or slaves belonging to others, for the labour of cultivation and harvesting.

Thus the Brazilian sugar industry relied on a mixed labour force and, as yet, cultivation and processing were not fully integrated. Given this fact, it is difficult to see how more than 50,000 slaves were employed in the sugar sector; even at low levels of productivity a slave would produce a third of a ton of sugar each year, and Brazilian production rarely rose much above 20,000 annually. In the light of such admittedly rough-and-ready calculations, a quarter or more of Brazilian slaves are likely to have been employed outside the sugar sector. There was a pattern of slave employment in Brazil, as in Spanish America, which differed from pure plantation slavery. This pattern of slave employment outside export agriculture may even have borne some resemblance to a precedent which influenced Iberian culture: the pattern of slavery in the Ancient World. In the towns slaves supplied a host of services, handing over a proportion of their earnings to their masters. The colonists established towns and cities, but found that Indians were loath to live or work in them; in their stead African slaves and their descendants worked as carpenters, cobblers, candlestick makers, bakers, laundrywomen and truck gardeners. Since the price of slaves was comparatively low in Portuguese Brazil, they could be purchased by landowners outside the export sector, to work on cattle ranches or even subsistence cultivation. Importing foodstuffs from Europe was expensive and unsure; most of the colony's needs were met by local production.

Urban slaves and skilled slaves in Brazil would often have some hope of freedom for themselves or their children. As a consequence of the Dutch war, some freedmen could not only serve with the militia but also hope to achieve a commission: Henrique Dias became a knight in a military order. Both free blacks and some urban slaves could join religious fraternities which offered them some degree of insurance and protection. Both the *senhores de engenho* and the *lavradores* still engaged young Portuguese immigrants to work on their estates. Many still engaged *agregados* of mixed race, and held servile Indians of different sorts. The colonial officials who ran the colony were still *fidalgos*, while most *senhores de engenho* were denied *fidalguia*. Brazil was undoubtedly a slave society, but a baroque one based on a complex patterning of social and ethnic relations.

The struggle against the Dutch in Brazil and the Spanish in the Peninsula had severely tested the social order in both metropolis and colony. While it had dramatically mobilized mercantile and colonial support, the Portuguese monarchy was not directly answerable to these constituencies. The Cortes, which met three times between 1640 and 1656, gave generous representation to a conservative landholding aristocracy; Portuguese merchants and colonists had to be content to influence the King's advisers. In fact, the ejection of the Dutch from Brazil in 1654 came just in time, since the Portuguese soon entered a deeply troubled period. When John IV died in 1656, the royal power was exercised by his Spanish widow as Regent for his disturbed or retarded eldest son Afonso VI. A renewed Spanish attempt to invade Portugal was defeated with French help in 1662–65. Struggle between pro-French and pro-English factions at the Portuguese Court at first favoured the former, but was eventually resolved in favour of the latter in 1667, when Afonso's younger brother Prince Pedro seized power as Regent, declaring the King unfit to rule. Pedro favoured the English party and, with their help, negotiated Spanish acceptance of Portuguese independence in 1668. Pedro ruled as Regent until 1683 and as King until 1706. The English connection furnished an outlet for Portuguese wines and an element of security for its fleet system. In return the English merchant community in Portugal, known as the Factory, received commercial privileges and were allowed to have their own Protestant Church.[43]

The Portuguese colonial order remained less centralized than the Spanish imperial system from which it had escaped, and made more provision for incorporating colonial interests. Brazilian planters had played a significant part in the restoration of Pernambuco to the mother country, and could claim a special consideration. The Brazil Company was cumbersome, and did enable the metropolis to tax the colony, but its fleet system also furnished naval protection in dangerous seas. In the years 1662–64 the Company was put under the authority of a *Junta do Comércio*, following allegations that the stipulated number of galleons had not been maintained. Since the fleet had set sailing times, the Company's organizers feared that 'the greed of the growers' would lead to exaggerated prices as they withheld their crop until the last moment: 'Even though fixed prices are usually prejudicial to commerce, which increases with liberty, a fixed price is the only remedy for Brazil.'[44] Eventually a system was devised whereby the planters and merchants negotiated an annual price. While world prices set limits on the negotiation, both planters and merchants knew where they stood; in Schwartz's opinion, 'both sides probably gained something from the system, although in a particular year one side or the other felt disadvantaged'.[45]

Father Vieira, whose personal fortunes had been greatly affected by this turmoil, represented a remarkable expression of the contradictory tendencies at work in the new world of Atlantic slavery. Preaching to the newly installed Bragança King in the royal chapel in 1642, Vieira had developed the notion that John IV was the reincarnation of Sebastian, the King lost in the sands of Africa. In developing this idea Vieira was seeking to identify the monarch with a widely held notion of the return of a redeemer-king who would inaugurate a 'golden age'. The preacher, as we have seen, had used his influence with the King to secure a lifting of some of the disadvantages imposed on the New Christians – in return for which they had invested in the new Brazil Company. During his visit to Amsterdam in 1647–48 he had engaged in discussions with Jewish rabbis, and had the opportunity to study both Dutch and English Protestant teachings. Vieira's *História do Futuro* argued that Portugal's successes in converting heathens and Jews proved that it was destined to be the promised universal monarchy.

Following the death of his royal patron, Vieira was himself to become a target for the Inquisition. Returning from Brazil in 1661, he was subjected to a lengthy investigation and eventually sentenced by the Inquisition to perpetual silence and seclusion. The Inquisition's charges against him alleged that he was fascinated by every type of heterodoxy, and that his decision to wear layman's clothes in Amsterdam symbolized a deeper treachery. The Jesuit preacher's prophecy of the imminence of a *Quinto Império do Mundo* (Fifth Empire or Monarchy) under Lusitanian auspices was a particular target of the Inquisition's attack. Vieira liked to invoke the Old Testament and Revelations to celebrate Portugal's unique global destiny, looking forward to the day when the Portuguese King would 'subjugate all the regions of the earth under one sole empire, so that they may all ... be placed gloriously beneath the feet of the successor of St Peter'.[46] While the pro-French faction was in the ascendant, Vieira could do no more than suffer the investigation with fortitude. With the advent of Pedro's Regency in 1667 he succeeded in having his sentence commuted to a term of exile in Rome.

Vieira was allowed to leave Rome in 1675 with a Papal pardon, but he never again enjoyed the same royal influence. In 1681 he returned to Brazil, where he died in 1697. In Brazil he was again to become the scourge of the misdeeds of the planters and slave traders. In 1653, when he enjoyed great influence at Court, he had renounced the comforts of Lisbon for a mission to investigate the abuse of Indians in the then remote Amazonian provinces of Pará and Maranhão. He was appalled by the cynical way in which slaving expeditions were organized supposedly to rescue the slaves in the name of *resgate*. In this area of Brazil the Portuguese *moradores* found Indian slave labour preferable to African, since it was much cheaper and the Indians were skilled at collecting the gums, resins and fruits of the rainforest, this being the main activity. At Vieira's behest a new law of 1655 outlawed Indian enslavement and entrusted to the Jesuits a programme under which the native peoples were to be shepherded into mission districts. The Portuguese *moradores* nevertheless continued to prey on the hapless Indian communities, whose 'descent' to the missions had also exposed them to disease. Although Vieira's attempt to protect the Indians had disastrous results for many of them, it still greatly antagonized the *moradores*, who saw the Jesuit presence as a threat. In 1661 they mobilized gangs of their followers to arrest Vieira and the other Jesuit Fathers, who were then put on a boat for Portugal. Vieira arrived there to face the accusations of the Inquisition.[47]

Although his principal campaign had been in favour of the Indians, Vieira also took up the question of cruelty to African slaves. On one of his transatlantic voyages he had visited the Cape Verde islands and been impressed by the African clerics he met: 'There are here clergy and canons as black as jet, but so well-bred, so authoritative, so learned, such great musicians, so discreet and so accomplished that they may well be envied by those in our own cathedrals at home.'[48] In Brazil he preached sermons to mixed congregations of masters and slaves, one of which is worth quoting as a sample of his extraordinary style of reasoning. He evokes the spectacle of slaves arriving from Africa:

Now if we look at these miserable people after their arrival and at those who call themselves their masters [we see . . .] happiness and misery meeting on the same stage. The masters few, the slaves many; the masters decked out in courtly dress, the slaves ragged and naked; the masters feasting, the slaves dying of hunger; the masters swimming in gold and silver, the slaves weighed down with irons; the masters treating them like brutes, the slaves adoring and fearing them as gods; the masters standing erect, waving their whips, like statues of pride and tyranny, the slaves prostrate with their hands tied behind them. . . . Oh God! What divine influence we owe to the faith you gave us, for it alone captures our understanding so that, although in full view of such inequalities, we may nevertheless recognize Your justice and providence! Are these people the children of Adam and Eve? Were not these souls redeemed by the blood of Christ? Are not these bodies born and do they not die as ours do? Do they not breathe the same air? Are they not covered by the same sky? Are they not warmed by the same sun?

Having set up his problem, he has recourse to orthodox Christian doctrine to resolve it. But in the course of achieving this resolution, he manages repeatedly to scold the masters for a variety of offences:

Is it necessary that, in order to add another fathom of land to your cane fields, and another day's work each week on your plantation, you must sell your soul to the Devil? Your own soul, however, since it is yours, you may go ahead and sell and resell. But those of your slaves, why must you sell them too, putting your lust for gold . . . ahead of their salvation?

Turning to the slaves, and probably alluding to the carnal species of lust, he says:

If the master orders the slave to do something, or wants from a slave anything that gravely harms his soul and conscience, the slave is not obliged to obey. I have told you repeatedly that you must not offend God and if [the masters] threaten you because of this, and punish you, suffer it bravely and with a Christian spirit. . . .

Recalling the tribulations of the children of Israel, he points out that they were several times enslaved, and that on each occasion they freed themselves, since men are sufficient to liberate men from slavery of the body (the apposition being to enslavement of the soul to the Devil, which can be thrown off only through Divine grace). This sermon was delivered before members of the brotherhood of 'Our Lady of the Rosary', a self-help organization for slaves and people of colour, which sometimes helped the enslaved to buy their manumission, using a mixture of slave earnings and the savings of relatives. Finally, pushing a traditional conceit to its limit, Vieira offered the slaves the message of redemption given in the epigraph to this chapter.

Vieira wished to mitigate slavery, since its cruelties were likely to bring disaster to Portugal again:

Look to the two poles of Brazil, that of the North and that of the South, and see if there was ever a greater Babylon or a greater Egypt in the world, in which so many thousands of captives have been made, seizing those who were free in nature, with no more right than violence, and with no greater cause than greed, and selling them as slaves. . . . [B]ecause our own acts of enslavement began on Africa's shores, God allowed the loss of King Sebastian, after which came the sixty-year captivity of the Kingdom itself. I understand full well that some of these acts of enslavement are just; those which the laws permit, and supposedly also those slaves bought and sold in Brazil. . . . But what theology could justify the inhumanity and brutality of the exorbitant punishments with which these same slaves are mistreated? 'Mistreated' I said, but this word is totally inadequate. Tyrannized one might say, or martyrized; because they injure these miserable people, drop hot fat or wax on them, slash them, cudgel them, and inflict many other kinds of excesses upon them, of which I will not speak.[49]

The notion that the slaves were martyrized led Vieira to the exalted but unfortunate conclusion that they had been marked out for a special destiny by the Almighty. The reference to the 'mark' made by 'God's fire' (see epigraph) is, no doubt, to Noah's curse, and the illumination is the Christian faith and their own coming transformation. While this passage is expressed with his characteristic brio and sympathy, it is little more than an elaborate restatement of the Church's traditional position on slavery. Vieira consoles the African captives with the thought of heavenly bliss. However, he does not rule out the possibility that they may obtain some improvement in this world, arguing that this will depend on an earthly change, including the reformation or ruin of their masters. Such words, even coming from one of the most esteemed preachers in the Empire, are unlikely themselves to have had any impact on the planters or officials. But it is notable that a lay member of the Brotherhood of the Rosary began in the 1670s persistently to lobby the Holy Office of the Vatican for a ruling against the Atlantic slave trade and the holding of Africans in perpetual bondage in the Americas. Vieira may have assisted these representations (to whose fate we will return in Chapter VIII).

The terms of Vieira's reflections on slavery strikingly anticipate themes which were much later to be ventilated by Protestant critics – for example, by John Wesley in his *Thoughts on Slavery* (1774). In a somewhat muted way the Quaker leader George Fox came out against slaveholder cruelty around the same time as Vieira. What is puzzling is that no authoritative Dutch voice was raised against slavery and the slave trade in, say, the 1640s or 1650s. If the Dutch had declared freedom for the slaves in Brazil, they would have been able to go on the offensive against the Southern captaincies, as the Heeren had repeatedly urged. Their non-slave-related trade with Africa had proved far from negligible – if it was less profitable than the later slave trade it had, as we have seen, a two-way character. The price of sugar was high, and good wages could have been offered to former slaves and to European immigrants; New Netherlands could also have furnished tobacco grown by indentured servants offered their freedom after three years' labour – just as it was in most parts of the Americas at this time. Their failure in Brazil had itself reflected the absence of enough colonists with a wholehearted commitment to plantation slavery. But of course, none of this happened. As Seymour Drescher has pointed out, the seventeenth-century Netherlands, after brief hints of anti-slavery sentiment early in the century, failed to take up the cause,[50] even though to have done so might have transformed their chances of success in the Americas.

The considerable financial stake which the WIC developed in the slave trade certainly furnished a significant obstacle to enlightenment, but the WIC did not always get its own way. The Dutch republic did develop some elements of a humanitarian culture at this time, but not so far as slavery was concerned. The decentralized character of Dutch politics and the WIC's status as a commercial company tended to remove it from the domain of normal political concern; and anyway, Dutch politics were beholden to an inherently conservative and commercial oligarchy during these years, and were averse to radical measures or philosophies. When Spinoza published his *Tractatus Theologico-Politicus* in 1670, he did so anonymously and in Latin.

The crisis of 1672, precipitated by the French invasion, led to the overthrow of the conservative republicans. One of the arbiters of the country's fate at this moment was none other than the veteran Johann Maurits. The overthrow of de Witt led not to the sort of radical democratic interlude that might have given openings for attacks on slave trading, but to an Orange Restoration.[51] Nevertheless, before the century was out a few Dutch colonists in America, people sufficiently restive to have left their native land, did compose an eloquent and comprehensive condemnation of slavery – the Quakers of Germantown in 1688, several of whom were in fact Dutch. This famous declaration has the honour of being the first absolutely unqualified denunciation of slavery on record. Impressive as it was, theirs was the voice of a tiny minority.

The New Role of the Dutch

Dutch skill and success in Northern trades and in the Asian spice trade have encouraged the illusion that Dutch traders played an equally important role in the Americas. In effect the decision to capture Pernambuco, already the major sugar-producing area, meant that the entire Dutch effort arrested the New World's plantation development. While Bahia and Rio developed larger sugar industries, the output of Brazil as a whole was to remain stuck at the level already achieved in the 1620s, or even to fall below it. Pent-up demand in Europe sent the price up in the 1640s. Quite unintentionally, the Dutch also interrupted the growth of the Atlantic slave traffic. During the entire existence of Dutch Brazil, the WIC sent fewer than 26,000 slaves there. After the revolt in Pernambuco the WIC supplied slaves to the Caribbean and to Spanish America. Indeed, some Dutch leaders apparently believed that acquisition of the *asiento* was satisfactory compensation for the loss of Brazil. This was a profitable trade, but the numbers of slaves carried was probably below that reached in the days of the Portuguese *asiento*. In Surinam Dutch planters grew small quantities of sugar, but chafed under the tutelage of Company officials. After further reverses the WIC was wound up in 1673; its place was taken by a new Dutch slave trading concern, the Middelburg Company, which, like its predecessor, obtained the *asiento* to supply Spanish America.

It has been estimated that in the period 1680–90 European traders of all nations – the Dutch, Portuguese, English and French being those engaged, in order of importance – bartered goods worth 10.5 million guilders, or £919,000, to acquire slaves on the African coast, who were sold for 41 million guilders, or £3.6 million. The trading mark-up here was 290 per cent – lower than the nearly tenfold trading margin that can be calculated for the Portuguese traders in the 1620s, but higher than the 135 per cent margin achieved by the WIC in its African trade in ivory and gold in the same years. Competition between a multitude of traders from different nations had raised slave prices on the African coast and lowered them in the Caribbean. But since the Dutch had the most advantageous access to the European manufactures and Eastern goods demanded on the African coast, their profit margins remained good.

The Dutch continued trading in gold, ivory and other African products during the 1680s, but this traffic was still not as profitable as the slave trade. Van den Boogaart estimates that the different European traders exchanged goods worth 9.4 million guilders, or £825,000, to acquire African products which were sold in Europe for 19.7 million guilders, or £1.7 million.[52] The Dutch accounted for something over a half of the slave trade and Africa commodity trade. In addition, their slave ships will often have been able to pick up a sugar cargo in the West Indies. Thus the Dutch had lost a potentially rich colony, and their Atlantic trade was only a little larger than it had been in the 1620s – but it was very probably twice as profitable.

Under the terms of the Treaty of Breda in 1667, the Netherlands lost New Amsterdam, now renamed New York, but gained formal title to Surinam, a colony on the North East coast of South America which had been settled both by English planters and by Portuguese-speaking New Christians, originally from Dutch Brazil. Together with Curaçao, St Eustatius and a few other small islands, Surinam helped to supply the Netherlands with some plantation produce. While the scale of output remained modest, a distinctively multicultural slave society emerged in which the motifs of white racism were comparatively muted. The relatively small number of Dutch, English and Jewish whites were happy to concede at least some civic rights to free people of colour, as a guarantee against attacks by Indian peoples and maroon slaves. Even in this small colony the Dutch never reached the demographic density to hegemonize the social order. While the material treatment of African slaves seems to have been as harsh as it was elsewhere in the Americas, an Afro-creole culture developed embracing two languages which have persisted into the twentieth century: Sranam, now the national language and based on Neger-Engels, the seventeenth-century Anglo–African creole tongue, and Saramaccan, a Luso–African creole that developed among the Portuguese New Christian slaves and the maroons. The oral history of the Abaisa 'Bush Negroes' recalls a mass slave escape from a Labadist plantation in 1693 in the following terms:

> In slavery, there was hardly anything to eat. It was at the place called Providence Plantation. They whipped you there till your ass was burning. Then they would give you a bit of rice in a calabash. (That's what we've heard.) And the gods told them [the Africans] that this is no way for human beings to live. They would help them. Let each person go where they could. So they ran.[53]

The activity of maroons in the interior, sometimes in league with Indian peoples, helps to explain why Surinam never entered the big league of sugar producers. By 1700 there was a slave population of 8,000 in the colony, but growth lagged behind that of English and French producers, who had themselves been sponsored by the Dutch.

From the standpoint of the development of colonial America, the Dutch promotion of English and French plantation development was more significant than their own colonial efforts in the Americas were. The Iberian commercial and colonial monopolies had been broached, and conditions had been created whereby other European nations could enter the slave trade and plantation trade. Frustration in Brazil led Dutch merchants to look for other suppliers of plantation produce; long before the final débâcle independent Dutch merchants encouraged tiny bands of English and French colonists in an obscure corner of the Caribbean to take up planting.

Notes

1. Werner Sombart, *The Quintessence of Capitalism*, New York 1967, p. 75.

2. Niels Steensgaard, 'Violence and the Rise of Capitalism: Fredrick Lane's Theory of Protection and Tribute', *Review*, vol. 2, no. 5, pp. 257–73, 159–60. See also Fredrick Lane, *Profits from Power. Readings in Protection, Rent and Violence-Controlling Enterprises*, Albany, NY 1979. In the light of the story to be told in this chapter it is appropriate that it is a Brazilian theorist who has pointed out the theoretical flaws in this approach – See Roberto Mangabeira Unger, *Plasticity into Power*, Cambridge 1987, pp. 139–47.

3. Jonathan Israel, *The Dutch Republic: Its Rise, Greatness and Fall*, Oxford 1995,

pp. 276–306, 402–5, 472–4; V.G. Kiernan, *State and Society in Europe, 1550–1650*, Oxford 1980, pp. 75–8; Friedrich, *The Age of the Baroque*, pp. 144–50.

4. Drescher, *Capitalism and Antislavery*, pp. 15, 173.

5. Alison Blakely, *Blacks in the Dutch World: The Evolution of Racial Imagery in a Modern Society*, Bloomington, IN 1993. For unease at rampant consumerism, see Simon Schama, *The Embarrassment of Riches*, London 1988. Jacob Jordaens, though Flemish, was a Protestant and, as a recipient of several Amsterdam commissions, may be considered a contributor to the vision of Dutch patriotism.

6. Schivelbusch, *Tastes of Paradise*, pp. 96–110.

7. Examples of these various approaches are well illustrated in Blakely, *Blacks in the Dutch World*.

8. M. Chrétien, 'Les Deux Visages de Cham', in Pierre Giral and Emile Temime, eds, *L'Idée de Race dans la pensée politique française contemporaine*, Paris 1977, pp. 171–99 (174–5).

9. J. Fox, ' "For Good and Sufficient Reasons": An Examination of Early Dutch East India Company Ordinances on Slaves and Slavery', in Anthony Reid, ed., *Slavery, Bondage and Dependency in East Asia*, New York 1983, pp. 246–62.

10. W.S. Unger argues that it was the absence of outlets rather than religious scruple which stopped the early WIC from slave trading. See W.S. Unger, 'Essay on the History of the Dutch Slave Trade', in A.P. Meilink-Roelofsz, ed., *Dutch Authors on West Indian History*, The Hague 1982, pp. 46–98 (p. 50).

11. For the debate between De Laet and Grotius, see Lee Eldridge Huddleston, *Origins of the American Indians: European Concepts, 1492–1729*, Austin, TX and London 1967, pp. 118–27.

12. Johannes Menne Postma, *The Dutch in the Atlantic Slave Trade, 1600–1815*, Cambridge 1990, pp. 10–11, 18–22.

13. Pieter Geyl, *The Netherlands in the Seventeenth Century*, London 1961, vol. I, pp. 189–208; Geoffrey Parker, *Spain and the Netherlands, 1559–1659*, London 1979, pp. 55–6; C.R. Boxer, *The Dutch in Brazil: 1624–54*, London 1957, p. 25; Herman Wätjen, *O dominio colonial Hollandez no Brasil*, São Paulo 1938, pp. 85–94.

14. P.C. Emmer, 'The Dutch and the Making of the Second Atlantic System', in Barbara Solow, ed., *Slavery and the Rise of the Atlantic System*, Cambridge 1991, pp. 75–96 (p. 83).

15. Wätjen, *O dominio colonial Hollandez no Brasil*, pp. 95, 494–509.

16. Ernst van den Boogaart, 'The Trade between Western Africa and the Atlantic World, 1600–90: Estimates of Trends in Composition and Value', *Journal of African History*, 33, 1993, pp. 369–85 (pp. 374–5).

17. Ibid., pp. 376–7.

18. Blakely, *Blacks in the Dutch World*, p. 208.

19. Hugo Grotius, *The Rights of War and Peace*, London 1737, pp. 3–4, 64, quoted in Tuck, *Natural Rights Theories*, pp. 74, 78. For Grotius on slavery, see also Davis, *The Problem of Slavery in Western Culture*, pp. 133–5.

20. Tuck, *Natural Rights Theories*, p. 80.

21. Frédéric Mauro, *Le Brésil du XVᵉ à la fin du XVIIIᵉ siècle*, Paris 1977, pp. 105–6; Wätjen, *O dominio colonial Holandes no Brasil*, pp. 494–509. See also E. van den Boogaart, ed., *Johann Maurits van Nassau-Siegen, 1604–1679: A Humanist Prince in Europe and Brazil*, The Hague 1979.

22. Hemming, *Red Gold*, p. 294.

23. Postma, *The Dutch in the Atlantic Slave Trade*, p. 17.

24. John K. Thornton, *The Kingdom of the Kongo: Civil War and Transition, 1641–1718*, Madison, WI 1983, pp. 70–72; Wätjen, *O dominio colonial Holandes no Brasil*, p. 487.

25. Wätjen, *O dominio colonial Holandes no Brasil*, p. 487.

26. Boxer, *The Dutch in Brazil*, pp. 204–7.

27. Wätjen, *O dominio colonial Holandes no Brasil*, pp. 381–2.

28. Mauro, *Le Brésil*, p. 110.

29. C.R. Boxer, *Portuguese Seaborne Empire*, p. 113.

30. Jonathan Israel, *Dutch Primacy in World Trade, 1585–1740*, Oxford 1989, pp. 162–70.

31. Cabral de Mello, *Olinda Restaurada: Guerra e Açúcar no Nordeste, 1630–1654*, Rio de Janeiro 1975, pp. 172–3.

32. Ibid., p. 84.

33. C.R. Boxer, *Salvador de Sá and the Struggle for Brazil and Angola, 1602–1685*, London 1952, pp. 246–9.

34. Ibid., pp. 226–8, 242, 269–70.

35. Wätjen, *O domínio colonial Holandes no Brasil*, pp. 494–509.

36. George Winius, 'Two Lusitanian Variations on a Dutch Theme: Portuguese Companies in Times of Crisis, 1628–1662', in L. Blusse and F. Gastra, eds, *Companies and Trade*, Leiden 1981, pp. 119–34.

37. Charles Wilson, *The Dutch Republic and the Civilisation of the Seventeenth Century*, London 1968, pp. 218–23.

38. Gerald F. De Jong, *The Dutch in America, 1609–1974*, Boston, MA 1975, pp. 14–27.

39. Boxer, *The Dutch in Brazil*, p. 257. A judgement largely endorsed by Postma, *The Dutch in the Atlantic Slave Trade*, pp. 18–22.

40. Quoted in Carl Hanson, 'The European "Renovation" and the Luso–Atlantic Economy, 1560–1715', *The Review*, vol. VI, no. 4, Spring 1983, pp. 475–532 (p. 500).

41. Thornton, *Kingdom of the Kongo*, pp. 75–7, 79–80, 106–13.

42. Schwartz, *Sugar Plantations in the Formation of Brazilian Society*, p. 222.

43. Carl Hanson, *Economy and Society in Baroque Portugal*, London 1981.

44. Quoted in Schwartz, *Sugar Plantations in the Formation of Brazilian Society*, p. 198.

45. Ibid.

46. Quoted in Boxer, *The Portuguese Seaborne Empire*, p. 372. However, in a subsequent work Vieira denied many of the charges against him, and asserted that the advent of a fifth empire – the first four were, respectively, Assyrian, Persian, Macedonian and Roman – to consummate Christ's reign on earth had been predicted by many Fathers of the Church. See Padre António Vieira, *Defesa Perante o Tribunal do Santo Ofício*, 2 vols, Bahia 1957, vol. I, pp. 221 ff and António Vieira, *História do Futuro*, edited Maria Leonor Carvalhão Buescu, Lisbon 1992. This text, written between 1649 and 1664, was first published in 1718.

47. John Hemming, 'Indians and the Frontier', in Bethell, ed., *Colonial Brazil*, Cambridge 1987, pp. 145–89 (pp. 176–8).

48. Quoted in Boxer, *The Portuguese Seaborne Empire*, p. 259.

49. António Vieira, *Obras Completas de Padre António Vieira, Sermões*, 15 vols, Porto 1907–09, XII, pp. 301–34. Translation from Conrad, *Children of God's Fire*, pp. 163–74. See also Ronaldo Vainfas, *Ideologia e Escravidão*, pp. 95–7, 101, 125–9.

50. Seymour Drescher, 'The Long Goodbye', in Gert Oostindie, ed., *Fifty Years Later*, London 1996.

51. Israel, *The Dutch Republic*, pp. 799–809.

52. Ernst van den Boogaart, 'West African Trade, 1600–1690', *Journal of African History*, vol. 22, no. 3, 1992, pp. 378–9. Boogaart derives the slave trade values cited from David Eltis, 'Trade between West Africa and the Atlantic World before 1870', *Research in Economic History*, vol. XII, 1989, pp. 197–239.

53. Richard Price, *First Time: The Historical Vision of an Afroamerican People*, Baltimore, MD 1983, pp. 51–2, 70–72; Richard Price, *Guiana Maroons*, Baltimore, MD 1976, pp. 23–4; Natalie Zemon Davis, *Women on the Margins: Three Seventeenth Century Lives*, Cambridge, MA 1995, pp. 174–5.

VI
The Making of English Colonial Slavery

Be fruitful and multiply, and replenish the earth and subdue it; and have dominion over the fish of the sea, and over every living thing that moveth upon the face of the earth.

Genesis I: 28

In the afternoons on Sundays, they have their musicke, which is of kettle drums, and those of severall sizes; upon the smallest the best musician playes; and the others come in as chorasses: the drum all men know, has but one tone; and therefore varietie of tunes have little to doe with this musick; and yet so strangely they varie their time, as 'tis a pleasure to the most curious eares; and it was to me one of the most curious noyses that I ever heard made of one tone.

I found this Negro . . . being the keeper of this grove, sitting on the ground, and before him a piece of large timber, upon which he had laid crosse, sixe billets and having a handsaw and hatchet by him, would cut the billets by little and little, till he had brought them to the tunes, he would fit them too; for the shorter they were the higher the Notes which he tryed by knocking the ends of them. . . . When I found him at it, I took the stick out of his hand, and tried the sound, finding the sixe billets to have sixe distinct notes, one above another, which put me in a wonder. . . .

Though there be a mark set upon these people, which will hardly ever be wip'd off, as of their cruelties when they have advantages, and of their fearfullness and falsenesse; yet no rule is general, but hath his acception: for I believe, and I have strong motives to be of that perswasion, that there are as honest, faithfull, and conscionable people amongst them, as amongst those of *Europe*, or any part of the world.

Richard Ligon, *A True and Exact History of Barbados* (1657)

Richard Ligon, *A Map of Barbados*, 1657 (British Library)

In 1594 a pageant was enacted before James VI of Scotland, later James I of England, in which a 'Black-Moore', 'very richly attyred', pretended to haul a chariot on which was placed a table piled with a cornucopia of sweetmeats, confections and fruits of the earth, surrounded by the goddesses of Fecundity, Liberality, and so forth. The African who pulled the chariot, assisted by a 'secreet convoy', was standing in for a lion that had been thought too dangerous for the role. This tableau, upon which variations were to be played at such events as the London Lord Mayor's Show in the coming century, perfectly illustrates the Stuart sense that Africans were a sort of splendid but savage beast, who could be harnessed to bring forth the riches of the tropical earth.[1] But just as James's future English subjects were to defy his proscription of tobacco, so the dynamic of the plantation trades was to disappoint royal hopes that it would buttress the power of the Court.

The English success in establishing plantation colonies in the Americas in the seventeenth century critically depended on the fact that England itself was becoming the largest European market for tobacco, sugar, cotton, dyestuffs and spices; merchants who could acquire these from their own plantations proved able to undercut foreign suppliers, meet rising domestic demand, and even challenge the Dutch entrepôt trade. The burgeoning English market in its turn reflected the spread of capitalist social relations, with increasing numbers of workers selling their labour or service for wages, salaries and fees. The capitalist transformation of agriculture assisted colonial settlement in another decisive way by stimulating and permitting an exodus from the countryside, and furnishing at least some emigrants with the resources needed for colonial enterprise. English plantations in the Americas required colonists as well as capitalists.

While African slaves were to become the principal labour force on the plantations, there was a varying period of between twenty and eighty years when English servants filled the plantation colonies and comprised the principal workforce. The predatory but glamorous privateers of the sixteenth century, who harried Spanish or Portuguese shipping, sometimes made their fortune, but failed to found permanent settlements. Hawkins, Drake, Gilbert and Raleigh experimented with the slave trade and colonization, but they belong to the prehistory of English colonialism. Although the privateers practised some contraband trade, their gold lust and preference for booty were inimical to regular commerce. Colonization was an arduous undertaking, requiring in-depth support from merchants and an ability to attract the right type of emigrants. The problems that had beset Villegagnon in Brazil, notably those stemming from the Amerindians' failure to comport themselves as conquered peasants, also bedevilled the English attempts, such as the first attempt to establish an English colony at Roanoke.

Despite repeated setbacks, the colonial privateering impulse remained strong among England's fortune-hunting gentry. Rising rents, and under-employment for younger members of the landowning classes, meant that some had the material resources to meet the heavy outset costs of an ocean-going ship, and also a supply of younger sons and cousins to command them. If there were prospects of trade, then merchants might be persuaded to contribute to the costs of colonization. But the colonization projects that succeeded were to require something else: the support of thousands – eventually tens and hundreds of thousands – of colonists prepared to work: farmers, artisans and labourers, able to find a sponsor or to pay for some of the costs of setting themselves up in the New World. The colonies that failed contained too high a proportion of gentlemen adventurers, restless fortune-hunters, or those otherwise lacking appropriate skills or commitment.

The privateers paved the way for later settlement by creating a heroic myth of colonization, mapping the strengths and weaknesses of Spanish power, and identifying commodities that could be acquired and produced in the Americas. In England, especially the West Country, privateering reached its height in the late sixteenth and early seventeenth centuries. Quite apart from Drake's two large fleets, 183 other English ships, sailing in seventy-four separate ventures, were dispatched to Caribbean waters between 1585 and 1603. The quantities of hides, indigo, pearls, tobacco, sugar, salt, and other commodities they brought back were acquired as much by contraband or *rescate* as by the seizing of prizes. The advent of peace between England and Spain in 1604 meant the end of official sponsorship for privateering, but there was a lively continuing interest in opening up the New World to English trade and settlement.

In 1604, and again in 1614, no fewer than a third of all Members of the House of Commons were involved in colonial projects of one sort or another, though in this chancy field most opted for only a prudently modest investment. The large outset costs were usually spread among several participants and backers. The gentlemen adventurers and their mercantile sponsors still hoped to find gold mines, but they engaged in contraband, and even cultivation, in order to make some immediate returns. They looked first to acquire commodities, and even means of subsistence, by trade with the Native Americans or Spanish colonists. Footloose younger sons and gentlemanly adventurers usually lacked stamina and discipline, and expected routine labour to be performed by menials. While they preyed mercilessly on the Spanish Empire, they felt a certain sense of kinship with the Spanish *hidalgos* and their Portuguese equivalents. From them they learnt to accept African slavery as a matter of course. John Hawkins acquired his slave trading contacts and know-how in the Canaries and Azores, and many lesser privateers not only traded with the Spanish or Portuguese colonists but also learnt from them the unfamiliar customs of the New World, including smoking tobacco, drinking chocolate, sleeping in hammocks, eating barbecues – and holding slaves. They were to pass on a number of these habits to their fellow countrymen.[2]

The writings and compilations of Richard Haklyut and Samuel Purchas

chronicled the successes and failures of European exploration and colonization. In 1617 the revised third edition of Purchas's work supplied a
portrait of the entire globe, dwelling with particular emphasis on the
potential of the Americas and finding encouragement in the recovery of
Virginia from its many early difficulties. In his introductory first volume the
author notes the existence of a large slave trade in Angola and mentions its
connection with flourishing sugar plantations in Brazil; however, he also
notes the problem of slave unrest and of a 'mongrel sect' arising in the
latter colony. Purchas urges that the failures of English colonization have
been due to such avoidable errors as sloth and riot, ignorance of the
country and neglect of the appropriate seasons for planting and fishing:
'Maiz yeeldeth incredible recompense' in Virginia, he observes, and tobacco
'is known to be a vendible commodity'.[3] But while Purchas's compendious
volumes contained some useful recommendations and warnings they still
left a great deal to be learnt by trial and error, or by direct instruction from
the Dutch. As the various European social formations borrowed from one
another, the element of conscious calculation was often outweighed by
pragmatic experimentation. Like many colonial projectors to come Purchas
saw the future of the plantations in terms of a many-sided development of
farms, orchards and vineyards, mines and manufactures, and not the
merchant's single-minded attention to a few premium staples.

The fisheries of Newfoundland and the fur trade attracted an English
and French commerce, and the beginnings of settlement, to a northerly
region far removed from the main preoccupations of the Spanish monarchy.
Puritan and Huguenot emigrants, often travelling in groups of families,
were attracted by the prospect of being able to escape religious persecution
and build a godly community. But by themselves the fisheries, the fur trade,
and religious colonization would have established only small colonies in
the more northerly climes. A critical contribution to raising the overall
volume of emigration was made by the rise of the plantations in Virginia
and the Caribbean. To begin with, the term 'plantation' referred to any
project of settlement, but it was in these latter colonies that the term began
gradually to acquire its modern meaning, and to sustain a lively commerce
and demand for immigrant labour. Once ships were regularly plying back
and forth between a colony and the metropolis, the organization of a steady
stream of emigration became cheaper and easier.

Ireland was a rival destination for the intending English emigrants – much
closer but, as they discovered, stiffly contested. For England's monarchs the
conquest of Ireland remained a strategic priority, despite the difficulties
alluded to in Chapter I. The Protestant success in England and Scotland,
and rebuff in Ireland, made it even more important to crush and colonize
the Irish – and even more difficult to do so. The long and costly bid for
military control was eventually brought to success by General Mountjoy as

Elizabeth I lay on her deathbed. Some Gaelic chiefs chose peace with the English, and were confirmed in possession of what had been tribal land, but others went into exile. Much of Ulster and Munster was declared forfeit and made available for colonization. By making peace with Spain, James I deprived the Irish of a valuable ally. In 1609 English and Scots settlers were sent to the 'Plantation of Ulster' to develop Irish land, either by displacing the natives or by reducing them to the status of tenants and labourers. A thousand or so 'treasonous' Irishmen were shipped out to Sweden to serve its King as soldiers.

In 1602–22, 12,000 settlers established a Protestant colony in Munster, but the English plantation in Ireland did not prosper. The English could defeat the Irish in battles, but could not then fix and exploit them as peasants. The colonists became demoralized by the hostility of the natives and the desolation of the countryside; many returned to England. One-third of Munster reverted to native ownership, and some of the English, as a result of intermarriage, became Catholics. The Scots immigrants proved more tenacious and hardworking than the English, making good their claim to part of the projected plantation in Ulster.

The City of London backed the Ulster plantation, but found the greatest difficulty extracting profit from it. Land leased out to Irish Catholic tenants often reaped a better rate of return, thus undermining the colonization effort. In other parts of Ireland English notions of landownership and tillage clashed with Irish customs. Even when land was successfully brought under the plough, its main products competed with English agriculture. English policy continued to hold Ireland in a military grip and to whittle away the basis of Catholic power, since Ireland was seen as a vital flank exposed to renewed attack by Spain. For their part, the native Irish continually frustrated the would-be conquerors with sullen noncooperation or open outbreaks of revolt. For many intending English emigrants Bermuda, Barbados or Virginia came to seem more enticing destinations.[4] The two islands were uninhabited when the English arrived, while the Indians of the Chesapeake became the objects of a classical colonial romance, fêted when they were friendly and accommodating, mercilessly cut down when they resisted.

Whereas the might of the state was concentrated in Ireland, colonization projects in the Americas were obliged to make their own way. A new attempt to colonize Virginia was sponsored by the Virginia Company in 1608–09; the fertile island of Bermuda was settled as a by-product of this enterprise. After a few years, the settlers in first Bermuda and then Virginia found that they could grow the tobacco craved by English consumers. The settlement around Jamestown was consolidated. The Indian King Powhatan helped at critical junctures to secure food supplies. Before his death in 1618 there seemed enough room for both Algonquians and settlers, though the latter were beginning to expand. For a while Jamestown may even have offered advantages to the Algonquians as a trading post; not until it was too late did they discover that the consolidated settlement would also begin to seize their land. The Company held that it was making better use of the land than the natives; when the latter attacked the settlement under Powhatan's successor the Company declared a state of 'perpetual war' against them, a formula later endorsed by Sir Edward Coke. The Company militia went on the offensive against all the peoples linked to the Federation formerly headed by Powhatan, burning villages, uprooting crops and cleansing the Chesapeake of its native inhabitants.[5]

The First Colonies

By the 1620s the first successful English and French colonial settlements also established themselves at the eastern extremity of the Caribbean. In these settlements, too, the key to survival was the discovery that tobacco could be grown. English, French and Dutch merchantmen had successfully created and fed the taste for this product by means of the smuggling trade, and some direct cultivation, on the coast of Venezuela and Guiana. The insecure settlements on this coast had acquired the relatively simple techniques of tobacco cultivation, and helped to transmit them to the Eastern Caribbean and to Virginia. Spain's local *Armada de Barlovento* was to make smuggling increasingly risky, though it did not reach full strength until 1630. In the meantime the Spanish authorities on land attacked any attempt at settlement on the Caribbean coast, and sought to suppress or limit the cultivation of tobacco in the areas they controlled. In northern Santo Domingo (Hispaniola) they had even destroyed their own settlements to prevent the smuggling of locally produced tobacco and hides. In this way they indirectly encouraged their colonial rivals to undertake cultivation themselves, though not in regions close to the routes of the returning silver fleets. Small alien settlements in the Chesapeake or Eastern Caribbean did not seem to pose an urgent threat, and any sustained attempt to suppress them would have overstretched Spanish resources.

The trade in tobacco was still modest compared with that of American silver or the spices of the East, but quite substantial enough to be attractive to small independent merchants and to sea captains who preferred profitable trade to glamorous plunder. England's imports of tobacco were worth £60,000, over a quarter of a million pesos or cruzados, in 1610, and demand grew apace.[6] The Dutch and French also imported tobacco, but the English market was soon probably the largest. Tobacco was sold by medium-sized and small retailers, including many women, as well as by innkeepers and in taverns. By 1613 it was estimated that £200,000 was being spent on tobacco each year. As Carl Bridenbaugh observes: 'every effort to licence or regulate the tobacconists failed'.[7] The King abated his opposition to tobacco, and was later to protect the Virginian product in order to raise a revenue on it.

There was also a range of other crops that the new settlements could produce, such as cotton, indigo, and ginger. Indigo and the other new dyestuffs were revolutionizing the textile trades, contributing to the attractive styles and colours of the New Draperies. In 1614–17 the English monarch was persuaded by London merchants to ban the export of undyed cloth to the Netherlands: the failure of 'Alderman Cockayne's project' underlined the strategic significance of control over supplies of dyestuffs.[8] English merchants interested in Brazil helped to initiate settlement in the Eastern Caribbean. While the Netherlands opted, via establishment of the WIC, to take over Brazil, smaller merchants, including Dutch independents, were content to support attempts to colonize and plant on the outer fringes of the Spanish Empire.

The English attempts at colonization usually received little royal encouragement and no financial support. Indeed, royal charters were available only to those projects which promised to generate revenue and avoid major diplomatic problems. James I and Charles I followed Queen Elizabeth in accepting that the King of Spain could claim only territory in the Americas actually settled by his subjects and administered by his officials; other European monarchs – notably the rulers of France, Sweden, Denmark and Courland, all of whom hoped to establish colonies – concurred. Protestants naturally disputed the Pope's right to allot the Americas to Spain and Portugal. British public opinion warmed to the nationalistic, anti-Spanish and anti-Catholic rhetoric of the colonial propagandists, even at times of good relations between the Spanish and the English Court.

Neither James I nor Charles I committed resources to colonization, but if their subjects established productive settlements away from the areas of Spanish control, they certainly intended to profit from them. Colonial entrepreneurs sought out courtiers with the influence to obtain a royal charter. But the English Crown did little to protect even duly chartered colonies, which were left to fend for themselves. The survival of the English settlements owed much to the tremendous offensive of the Dutch in the Caribbean and Atlantic in the 1620s and 1630s. The Spanish were obliged to devote all their efforts to defending the main imperial arteries. While others engaged in arduous hostilities, the English colonized. England's lack of involvement in the Thirty Years War (1618–48) meant that its merchants were well placed to extend their trading networks; during this time the English merchant marine grew to over 150,000 tons, three times its size in the 1570s, boosting the resources which could be drawn upon by the colonization effort.[9]

In terms of sailing time, the islands of the Eastern Caribbean were often as close to Europe as they were to Havana or Veracruz. Knowing that it would take them a month or more to return, the Spanish squadrons based in these ports were reluctant to sail to the Eastern Caribbean. The potential of Barbados, at the extreme South East of the Caribbean, was noted in 1625 by the captain of an English ship returning from Brazil. This captain persuaded powerful and well-connected Anglo-Dutch merchants, William and Peter Courteen of London and Middelburg, to support the formation of a company to organize the settlement of the island. At this time Barbados was uninhabited, its original inhabitants having been enslaved or driven away by the Spanish in the previous century. Around the same time St Christopher, or St Kitts, in the Leeward Islands, which had intermittently served as a privateering base, was settled by English colonists under Captain Thomas Warner, who joined forces with French colonists, commanded by Sieur d'Esnabuc, to seize the island from the Caribs.

The settler populations of these colonies were modest, and to begin with there was no question of undertaking anything as elaborate as sugar cultivation and processing. Clearing the land for cultivation was itself a major task. Merchants were, however, willing to sponsor the work of colonization as a way of securing supplies of tobacco. Some of the first colonists were survivors from the early settlements on the South American coast, and some Arawak Indians from the same region were persuaded to help them acquire the arts of tropical cultivation. Tobacco grew quite easily, and did not require heavy investments in equipment; to produce a good-quality leaf on a large scale did demand skill and elaborate processing, but these could develop with practice. Small merchants from Middelburg, Flushing, Dieppe, Rochelle, Bristol and London advanced the colonists credit in return for a lien on their crop.

Thomas Warner on St Kitts acquired the sponsorship of a merchant syndicate headed by Ralph Merrifield of London. In 1626 Maurice Thomson, a merchant sea captain who had established himself in the Virginia trade, brought the first boatload of slaves to St Kitts; however, it was to be more than a decade before slave agriculture really took hold in the Eastern Caribbean, and in the interim tobacco, cotton and other crops were raised, with the help of servants brought over from Europe. To begin with, tobacco commanded a premium price, and land was available to those willing to clear and cultivate it. Merchants interested in the plantation trades sought to gain the patronage of courtiers who could obtain a royal charter for colonization. Puritan noblemen, notably the Earls of Pembroke and War-wick, and royal favourites, such as the Earl of Carlisle, lent themselves to these schemes and established a modicum of official cover for the colonization effort.

The first English settlement with predominantly slave-worked plantations, the Providence Island Company, was short-lived because it was too close to Spanish power. It was established on Santa Caterina and other islands near to the Central American coast, the most exposed end of the Caribbean, in 1630, following the defeat of the Spanish at the Battle of

Matanzas (Cuba) at the hands of Piet Heyn and the WIC. The backers of this Company – who included the Earl of Warwick and John Pym – have been described as a 'nominal roll of the Parliamentary Opposition'.[10] It attracted Puritan gentry rather than family groups. The Providence Island Company sent out indentured servants who were set to work producing small quantities of tobacco, indigo and sugar. But not all colonists liked being dependent on the Company for access to labour. Privateers who had captured slaves offered them at low prices, an opportunity seized by a number of colonists.

One of the Puritan colonists, Samuel Rishworth, challenged the holding of the African captives against their will. He also explained his views to the Africans themselves, encouraging them to abscond, which some of them did. Soon after this – and perhaps as a consequence – the Governor removed Rishworth from the council of the colony, though he was subsequently to be re-elected to it. The Company declared that slavery was lawful for persons who were 'strangers to Christianity', but urged the colonists to abstain from further purchases, since a growth of slave numbers would pose a security threat and deprive free colonists of gainful employment. Notwithstanding this advice, and the outbreak of a slave rebellion on May Day 1638, the planters of Providence Island continued to purchase Africans.[11] After more than a decade of privateering, smuggling and planting, this colony was destroyed by a Spanish attack in 1641, with the survivors retreating to the Bahamas, Eastern Caribbean or North America. They were to name one of the Bahamas Eleuthera, the Greek word for freedom, but nothwithstanding this biblical or classical echo they helped to diffuse and normalize the slaveholding habit, albeit on a still modest scale.

The King's failure to make defence of Providence Island a priority was one of the charges laid at his door by his opponents. In 1640 Pym urged a more aggressive policy:

> The differences and discontents betwixt his Majesty and the people at home, have, in all likelihood, diverted his royal thoughts and counsels from the great opportunities he might have . . . to gain a greater pitch of power and greatness than any of his ancestors; for it is not unknown how weak, how distracted, how discontented the Spanish colonies are in the West Indies. There are now in those parts, in New England, Virginia, and the Carib islands, and the Bermudas, at least sixty thousand able persons of this nation, many of them well armed, and their bodies seasoned to that climate, which, with a very small charge, might be set down in some advantageous part of these pleasant, rich and fruitful countries, and make His Majesty master of all that Treasure, which not only foments the war, but is the great support of popery in all parts of Christendom.[12]

Pym somewhat exaggerated the numbers of English colonists, and failed to notice that they went in serious numbers to those parts of the New World where there would be the least likelihood of having to fight the Spanish. It was the relatively remote situation of the colonies he mentioned which recommended them to ordinary planters and emigrants.

The most successful of the new tobacco colonies was Virginia, lying outside the zone of effective Spanish settlement and control to the North of 30° latitude. The profitability of Virginia directly assisted the development of the English Caribbean, since it was to be sponsored by merchants and sea captains who had thrived on the North America trade. The Virginia Company stumbled on the formula of successful colonization in the years 1618–24, after hopes of discovering gold had faded and it had become clear that the native Indians might barter food but not supply labour. In the years after 1618 the Company discovered that colonists given a plot of two or three acres could raise enough corn to feed themselves; those who wished for anything beyond the barest subsistence had to grow tobacco, if they had acquired land, or work for someone else, if they had not. The Company gradually eased the harsh obligations and strict controls which it had imposed on settlers in the early years.

Sir Edwyn Sandys, a leading member of the Virginia Company, pro-moted a policy which made land available at low rents to those settlers who had the resources to clear and work it. Land was offered on a 'headright' basis to whoever brought new settlers to the colony. Those who paid their own way could claim a 'headright' for themselves and for any servant whose passage they had paid. As if in obedience to the biblical maxim 'to him that hath shall be given', the 'headright' system allowed a planter with capital, and the necessary application, to accumulate both land and labour. This stimulated a two-way traffic in which the young colony exchanged tobacco for provisions, implements, building materials – and indentured labourers who bound themselves to labour for three, five or seven years for whoever had engaged their services; at the end of this time they would be free, and would normally receive a bounty – their 'freedom dues'. If they worked a little longer, they could buy land. When the new colony of Maryland was established, it was to offer 50 acres, clothes, tools and a gun to servants at the expiry of the indentures. At the English end ships' masters and smaller merchants organized the trade, entering into agreements with the more successful settlers and planters in the colonies.

The established merchants of the great trading corporations shunned this trade, giving an opportunity to a new breed of traders, many of them ships' captains with knowledge of both sides of the Atlantic. These men needed partners in both colony and metropolis. Their English sponsors were shopkeepers and grocers who were in touch with the eager demand for 'smoke' and other exotic products. In the colonies they needed to find reliable planters, capable of persevering in new and challenging conditions. The indentured labour system transformed Virginia's prospects, because the merchants and planters had good reason to seek out apprentices with the skills, commitment and sobriety that were needed in the raw and hostile surroundings of a new settlement. In the 1620s Virginia ceased to be a base for fortune-hunting gentry and a dumping ground for the destitute or criminal. In 1624 quarrels among the Company's sponsors led to the suspension of its charter and the colony's consequent reversion to being a simple possession of the Crown, under the authority of the Privy Council. However, neither the King nor his Council concerned themselves much with the colony beyond appointing a governor, who was in turn entitled to appoint his own advisory council from among the leading colonists. Those who had title to land, and had survived clashes with the Indians and the ravages of disease, could exercise considerable local power through their access to office within the parish and militia. The prospects for immigrants, whether free or indentured, improved, since the colony could pay its own way and was no longer subject to the draconian rules of the Company regime. The King was content to explore the revenue-raising possibilities of tobacco once it reached England.

Between 1607 and 1624 about 6,000 people had emigrated to Virginia; because so many died or returned, a census taken in 1625 showed only 1,200 people to be living in the colony. With the passing of Company control the 'headright' system was retained: it promoted the immigration of hundreds, sometimes several thousand, of indentured servants each year.[13] While tobacco cultivation rose in Virginia, there was still room for new Caribbean producers well into the 1630s; tobacco prices dropped from the absurd heights of the early days, but remained very profitable to planter and merchant alike.

John Rolfe reported that in August 1619 a 'Dutch man of warre . . . sold us twenty negars'.[14] In the following decade surviving registers show a black population in the colony of twenty-three one year, twenty-five the next, most of them listed like servants, but with no name, or only a first name, and often without an arrival date – an important detail in the case of servants bound for a term of months or years. A few of these 'negroes' or 'negors' were or became free, and at least one of them went on to own black servants himself. But those Africans who arrived in the colony did so not because there was a regular slave traffic, or a settled practice of slavery, but because there was a continual coming and going between different colonial ports and the metropolis in which a few black servants or slaves were involved. The supply of indentured servants from England was for several decades adequate to the planters' needs, but the latter were aware of the slavery alternative.

England was exceptional in the mobility of its population and in their willingness to emigrate. Somewhere between 170,000 and 225,000 emigrants left the British Isles for America in the years 1610 to 1660: 110,000 to 135,000 went to the Caribbean, 50,000 to Virginia and 20,000–25,000 to New England; 70,000 English and Scots left Britain for Ireland during the same period but, because it was easy to do so, many returned.[15] In the years which preceded the outbreak of the Civil War the annual emigration rate was between 5,000 and 8,500, more than double the numbers of emigrants from the Peninsula at this time. The fact that some hundreds of ships involved in the colonial trades crossed the Atlantic every year promoted the emigrant flow by reducing the costs of transportation: this factor also helps to explain comparatively high Portuguese, and low Spanish, emigration rates. Colonial emigration from France was also still a trickle, as we shall see in the next chapter.[16]

Did the English emigrate because there was a surplus of young men, together with a few young women, so poor and desperate that they were willing to take the big risks involved? Or was England able to send so many abroad because it was an economically buoyant society, with the resources to develop overseas plantations? The two types of explanation are not mutually exclusive; it was their conjunction that helped to stimulate emigration. In seventeenth-century France or Spain there was quite widespread poverty but not the commercial resources, or internal market, to sustain plantation development on the English scale. The development of England's distinctively capitalist agriculture was accompanied by rising productivity, rural enclosure and a strong internal market. Together with a rising population in the years 1550–1650 and a family structure that encouraged younger sons to move, economic buoyancy created a demand for plantation produce which, in turn, created a demand for plantation labour.[17] Thus the 'pull' factor should be given as much weight as the 'push' factors, especially since those who survived the difficult early period did, indeed, usually find a new and better life.[18]

Barbados and the Rise of Sugar

The tobacco of Barbados was of poor quality; smokers on the island preferred the imported Virginia leaf. Anyway, the island was not large enough for the extensive cultivation practised in Virginia. Some cotton, indigo and ginger were produced, but it was not until the introduction of sugar in the late 1630s or early 1640s that a really profitable staple was found. For a time Barbados and the Leewards attracted many settlers, for reasons that are not entirely clear. Virginia's Indian wars, autocratic governors and epidemics may have made the Caribbean seem more attractive. To begin with the squatter could find land on the islands quite easily. Moreover, the Caribbean still exercised a lure for fortune-hunters. More usefully, some slaves and sugar-making equipment arrived in the Leewards from those who withdrew from Providence Island.

Despite its tiny size – only 144 square miles – Barbados played an exceptional role in demonstrating the profitability of sugar plantations. Its soil was fertile and well watered, its climate comparatively healthy, with reliable sea-breezes. Above all, it was situated far out to windward from the main Caribbean chain, and had strong natural defences. Barbados suffered somewhat from being the disputed possession of rival proprietors;

on the one hand the Earl of Pembroke, backed by Sir William Courteen; on the other the Earl of Carlisle, backed by the London merchant Marmaduke Roydon. The claims of the Earl of Carlisle were upheld after Courteen had already spent £10,000 developing the colony. A dispute over Carlisle's will created further doubt about the island's status in 1635; Captain Henry Hawley, appointed Governor by Carlisle, convened an assembly of the freeholders in 1639 to boost his position, giving the colony an element of self-government.

In 1638 the population of Barbados was about 6,000, of whom 2,000 were indentured servants and only 200 African slaves.[19] While indentured servants owing four or five years' labour could be purchased for £12, a slave cost £25. Knowledge of the cultivation and processing of sugar seems to have been introduced to Barbados from Pernambuco by Dutch traders: in the first place by those who resented the WIC's privileges, subsequently by those withdrawing from the increasingly beleaguered Dutch colony. Barbados proved to be a haven for a curious assortment of refugees including Sephardic Jews and Dutch colonists or their collaborators from Pernambuco, members of Puritan English sects and subsequently English Royalists. They brought with them valuable resources, connections and know-how, and those from Pernambuco perhaps some *engenho* slaves as well.

Because of perennial labour shortages in Dutch Brazil, and because Indians were more effectively protected from enslavement than they were in the Portuguese captaincies, its planters had developed methodical styles of work and tighter invigilation; these techniques were to be imitated and improved upon in Barbados. In 1646–48 the WIC itself sold slaves on easy terms to the Barbadian planters, since they were unable to dispose of them in Brazil. Until the mid 1650s large numbers of white male indentured servants worked in the cane fields side by side with African slaves; it was not until the mid 1660s that whites were allotted only skilled or supervisory roles and blacks were organized in gangs. An outbreak of yellow fever in 1647 and certain later years carried off disproportionate numbers of servants; servant conspiracies and rebellion in 1649 and 1657 also made the owners of large estates increasingly nervous, prompting them to avoid bringing together large numbers of discontented servant menials, especially those who were of Irish extraction or sentenced to long penal terms.[20]

The costs of setting up a sugar plantation were such that those involved needed large resources from the outset; tobacco merchants and planters loomed large among those with access to the necessary land, finance and influence. On Barbados the sugar mill owners found it advisable and possible to grow the cane they needed on their own land, rather than purchase it from smallholders. The smallholders did not take to sugar cultivation because it was a new and unfamiliar crop, and because it could not be harvested for at least eighteen months after the first planting. The mill owner who cultivated his own cane was also secure in the knowledge that he could not be held to ransom by cane growers playing one mill off against another – an obvious danger on a small island.

The construction of plantations thus involved a process of concentration of land management and landownership. The planters had money to buy out the numerous smallholders or leaseholders dating from the early days of colonization; but the smallholder or tenant, satisfied with his position and with the rewards of a secondary staple, might be unwilling to sell. The larger planters held office as vestrymen in the parish councils, posts which they used to impose taxes and levies on the land. Smallholders were encouraged to sell both by the cost of landholding and by rocketing land prices. Between 1648 and 1656 a local statute enabled the Church vestries to confiscate and sell the land of any smallholder who had failed to pay the parish levies.[21]

Merchants who had advanced credit to landholders, whether large or small, were also in a position to amass land. In one way or another, scores of sugar plantations were set up, worked, to begin with, by a mixed force of indentured labourers and slaves. Emigration from Britain probably dropped in the 1640s, partly because of the Civil War and partly because Dutch ships were carrying much of the island's trade. Sugar prices were high, and the sugar trade was rich enough to bear the expense of importing Africans. The Earl of Warwick had been among the founders of the Guinea Company, one of whose objectives was slave trading, as early as 1618. But the Guinea Company had not prospered, leaving the field open to interlopers and Dutch traders. In 1631 Charles I granted a patent to trade with West Africa to Sir Nicholas Crispe, a courtier merchant. This renewed Guinea Company had more success, concentrating, in the 1630s, on the trade in gold and other African produce. From the 1640s a slave trade between West Africa and the English islands was organized by such interloping merchants as Maurice Thomson and William Pennoyer – the latter occasionally reached an arrangement with the Guinea Company.[22] Some Barbadian planters, such as James Drax, directly sponsored slaving voyages to the African coast. Traders, whether Dutch or English, could sell African captives on the island and pick up a returning cargo of sugar.

By 1653 slaves outnumbered indentured servants by 20,000 to 8,000; the rest of the island's population comprised 5,000 English freeholders and 5,000 freemen (former servants, of whom 2,000 were English, 2,000 Scottish and 1,000 Irish). No less than 7,787 tons of sugar – over a million *arrobas* – were dispatched to England in 1655, worth at least £380,000, since prices were high; further quantities may have been sent to other destinations. In 1657 Richard Ligon published an account of Barbados; though based on a visit in the previous decade, it furnished a vivid and well-informed portrait of the island's emerging sugar economy and slave society. The book included detailed descriptions of how to cultivate and process sugar cane, complete with technical drawings of the sugar 'ingenio' or mill and a map giving the location of the principal plantations. Ligon deplores mistreatment of white servants and observes that the African slaves, despite their growing numbers, remain in awe of the English, since they lack weapons, especially firearms, and 'are fetch'd from severall parts of Africa, . . . speak severall languages, and by that means, one of them understands not another.' Ligon found the Africans to possess positive qualities, as may be seen from the epigraph to this chapter, but most laudable of all was their capacity for hard work and loyalty – he cites the case of one 'Sambo' who not only informed on a slave conspiracy but declined, on behalf of the slave crew, the holiday offered as a reward on the grounds that they were just doing their duty. However, the author does note the reluctance of planters to allow the baptism of their slaves since they fear it might imply emancipation. Ligon's work stresses the huge economic potential of Barbados and would have given encouragement to intending investors. The island's exports began to rival those of Brazil in the 1650s. England's Civil War led to some factional tussles in the Caribbean but did not impede the advance of the plantations.[23]

The Role of Captains and New Merchants

According to a classic formula, merchants devoted themselves to buying cheap and selling dear; mercantile capital, therefore, would be unconcerned with directly organizing production. The colonization projects of the seventeenth-century Caribbean and North America did not conform to this view of the merchants' role. As we have seen, they reflected an interlacing of mercantile initiative with the entrepreneurship of sea captains and the land-hunger of a stratum of gentry, yeomen and peasants; without mercantile sponsorship, the latter's projects stood little chance of success. From about 1620 recession affected many branches of European economy but not the plantation-related trades. A long-term rise in the productivity of English agriculture helped to maintain and increase the level of English demand for imports of tobacco, sugar, indigo and cotton. Perhaps encouraged by these circumstances a new breed of merchant thrived in Northern Europe by supporting the new productive enterprises in the Americas. These men conducted themselves in ways quite distinct from the 'real merchants' or 'mere merchants' of the established guilds and trading corporations, who saw little advantage in plantation investment, when they could devote their resources to exploiting their commercial privileges, and who were formally debarred from engaging in the retail trade.[24] Plantation investment had an appeal to those who catered most directly to the new trades: shopkeepers, grocers, ships' masters or captains, chandlers and the like. Each of these categories numbered thousands: those who entered the American trade often acted as agents or ship's 'husband' for others, so that many shared in a particular voyage or enterprise and risks could be spread. The ship's master usually had a stake of his own in the venture and might be a relative of the sponsoring merchant or husband. By investing in the plantation colonies merchants could secure a source of supply of products for which demand was burgeoning: tobacco, sugar, cacao, cotton, ginger, dyestuffs. Another feature of the trade with the colonies was that the planters needed supplies of every sort: implements, household utensils, clothing, foodstuffs and, last but not least, labourers. The partnership between planter and trader was known as 'mateship' or *matelotage*.[25] The merchants' investment often took the form of advancing such supplies on credit in return for a lien on the crop. This was an extension of a mercantile practice which, on a more limited scale, was already present in those proto-capitalist branches of European agriculture where the farmer needed to purchase productive inputs in order to undertake cultivation.

Many of the new merchants were – or had been – ship's masters, giving them first-hand experience of problems of management and entrepreneurship. Other former masters became planters, while colonial proprietors often deemed it appropriate to appoint a captain to run their colonies. The ship itself was a productive enterprise and an investment; its operation required skilled co-ordination, a disciplined, methodical workforce. The ideal ship's master possessed integrity, managerial skills, commercial judgement and good seamanship. In the complex Africa trade 'super-cargoes' were sometimes to be engaged to superintend or check all commercial activities – but this meant an extra salary and was unusual in the American trades. In the latter merchants needed masters who were financially competent and trustworthy as well as good seamen. When looking for a partner to run a sugar estate or one of the larger tobacco plantations the trader-captain would look for similar qualities. The merchant depended on the honesty of his agents even more than on their technical skills; the latter could be supplied by the first mate or boatswain on a ship, or by an overseer or sugar master on a plantation. Merchants often looked to a nephew or cousin, or someone with whom they shared a religious bond, when sponsoring a voyage or setting up a plantation.

Merchants and shipowners in the colonial trades aimed at a bilateral or multilateral trade, since unit freight costs were thereby reduced and profit opportunities increased. With the growth in large-scale maritime commerce, the cost-effectiveness of shipping became a more crucial factor. In the first two decades of the Virginian tobacco trade there were dramatic improvements in cost-effectiveness, achieved by ensuring that vessels were well laden with provisions and servants on the outward journey, as well as improving the baling and packing of tobacco on the return to England.

The independent Dutch traders, whose origins lay in the Baltic and Mediterranean trades, fostered the early colonial settlements, whether Dutch, English or French: they offered Dutch manufactures and provisions, sometimes African slaves as well, in exchange for tobacco, cotton, indigo, sugar or cacao. The merchants of London, Bristol or Dieppe were also keen to secure supplies of these products. In the early years of colonization they were able to bring over indentured labourers somewhat more economically than was possible for the Dutch. In England – and to a lesser extent in France – traders found it possible to attract more such emigrants than were available in the Netherlands. Whatever the supply of servants from Europe, it could never be enough. Sugar could always command a good price, while that of tobacco still rewarded the efficient producer. The new merchants were directly tapping England's own large home market – and with or without Dutch help, they could always find a way to reach continental markets as well.

Tobacco and Sugar

Consumption of tobacco and sugar was becoming more widespread than that of traditional luxuries. In part this was testimony to the productive qualities of the plantations, allowing their staples to become cheaper rather than more expensive as demand grew. But it also testified to transformations within some European societies – foremost among them England and the Netherlands – that were putting money into the hands of new types of consumers. Higher agricultural productivity and better transport had boosted the standard of living of substantial sectors of the population. With England and the Netherlands leading the way, the smoking of tobacco was to become a popular luxury throughout Western Europe in the course of the seventeenth century; its price eventually dropped so much that it could be afforded even by urban or rural wage labourers. Other plantation products and their derivatives never became as cheap, and their consumption remained for a time more typical of the new middle classes. In the 1620s the price of tobacco fell from two or three shillings a pound (i.e. 24–36 pence per pound) to 3–5 pence a pound. With a few ups and downs the price settled at the lower end of the latter range. At this price the strange custom of pipe-smoking rapidly spread to many parts of Europe, with England and the Netherlands scoring the highest rate of consumption in per capita terms. By mid century or not long after about a quarter of the English population could have been smoking a daily pipeful of tobacco. In both England and the Netherlands annual consumption rose above one pound a head, and exceeded two pounds a head towards the end of the century.[26]

Despite continuing efforts by savants to vaunt the medicinal qualities of tobacco, its triumph was that of a popular pleasure. The spread of the custom owed most to sailors and the inhabitants of the port cities who eventually adopted it in preference to other drugs that could have been favoured, such as coca or marijuana. An account of the sailors' behaviour from 1570, cited by Jordan Goodman, gives a hint as to the reasons for this popular choice:

For you may see many sailors, all of whom have returned from there [the Americas] carrying small tubes ... [which] they light with fire, and, opening their mouths wide and breathing in they suck in as much smoke as they can ... in this way they say that their hunger and thirst are allayed, their strength is restored, and their spirits are refreshed; they asseverate that their brains are lulled by a joyous intoxication.[27]

Undoubtedly marijuana and coca were quite widely sampled by sailors and others, but their consumption did not travel so well or take hold so widely. Tobacco smoking did not stimulate appetite, as marijuana did; for sailors and other labourers this would have been a definite advantage. At the same time tobacco stimulated the spirits and brain without disorientating or befuddling – the latter conditions might expose those enjoying them to dangers in the Atlantic world of this time, and were anyway incompatible with many work roles. Tobacco, then, was a pleasure, but one that was more compatible with the conditions and demands of daily existence than potential rivals.

Sugar remained the most valuable of the plantation products. It began to be used in a wide variety of ways as both sweetener and preservative, in the making of jams, cordials, puddings and confectionery, in brewing and baking. Sugared foodstuffs, once tasted, easily became addictive. New World output of sugar in 1600 was around 10,000 tons; by 1660 it was around 30,000. Sugar prices dropped by a half between the 1620s and the 1670s: from about £56 a ton to about £28 as output continued to expand. Sugar was a townsman's luxury to begin with, consumed by nearly everyone in the great cities of Europe, especially those in the forefront of commerce, finance, administration and manufacture; as its price fell, the smaller towns and country folk could also occasionally indulge a sweet tooth.[28]

Plantation Labour, Slavery and Fear of Strange Women

Such a voracious demand for plantation products offered the new merchants and planters a bountiful prospect so long as they could find sufficient labour. This created pressure both to squeeze as much as possible from the indentured servants and to explore the use of Indian or African slaves. From the outset Barbados combined servant labour, as Henry Winthrop put it in a letter to Emanuel Downing in 1628, with that of 'slave negeres'. By the next year he was writing of '50 slaves of Indians and blacks', since the Guianese Araraks, who had voluntarily accompanied the English colonizers, had now – most disgracefully – been enslaved by those they had helped. In 1636 Governor Hawley announced that all Indian and African servants brought to the island, and their children, would be treated as chattel slaves unless they had a contract of service specifying otherwise.[29]

Hawley's legal improvisation showed the ease with which the English common law tradition, and practice of devolved colonial government, could begin to adapt to a new labour regime. Simply recognizing slaves and their children as property left issues to be decided – since unlike other property they could also carry out or resist orders, have sexual relationships and offspring with free persons, and so forth – but these further questions could be tackled in an empirical manner. The law relating to ownership of cattle and other domesticated animals offered some principles and precedents. Practice was relied upon to establish the 'customs of the country', themselves imbued with social assumptions, and only subsequently was a legal code enacted. Given the source of the slaves, Portuguese and Dutch example must have played some role in establishing the acceptability of slavery, but the fact of Iberian slavery was much better known than the details of its slave laws. In 1643 Dutch merchants called at Barbados with a parcel of fifty Portuguese prisoners from the war in Brazil, whom they offered for sale. The then Governor, Phillip Bell, was troubled by this, and forbade the sale to go ahead.[30]

If colonial lawmakers turned to English jurists for guidance on tied labour then they would find accounts of villeinage – though, as we saw in chapter I, this servile condition had died out some two centuries previously. Consulting Sir Edward Coke's authoritative *Institutes of the Laws of England*, published in 1628 and then much reprinted, they would find a defence of the legitimacy of private property in persons which directly echoed the *jus gentium* or Roman law of nations: 'then it was ordained by the Constitution of Nations ... that he that was taken in Battle should remain Bond to his taker for ever, and he to do with him, all that should come of him, his Will and Pleasure, as with his Beast, or any other Chattel, to give, or to sell or to kill.' Coke explained that Kings had subsequently arrogated the power to kill because of the cruelties of some lords but that otherwise the Bondman was entirely subject to his master. He also observed: 'This is assured, that Bondage or Servitude was first inflicted for dishonouring of parents: for Cham the Father of Canaan ... seeing the Nakedness of his Father Noah, and shewing it in derision to his Brethren, was therefore punished in his Sonne Canaan with Bondage.'[31] Coke's view chimed in with that of clerics like R. Wilkinson, who added that 'the accursed seed of *Cham* ... had for a stampe of their fathers sinne, the colour of hell set upon their faces.'[32] Furthermore the slave trade from Africa and the Iberian practice of slavery were registered in Richard Hakluyt's compilation of travel accounts which, together with Samuel Purchas's *Purchas His Pilgrimes*, did much to inform and shape projects of colonization. John Hawkins's slave-trading activities were recounted as something between heroic exploit and picaresque adventure, with his less fortunate companions being enslaved by the Spanish. The English perception of racial difference had a sharper edge to it than the Spanish or Portuguese, especially where people of colour were concerned. The Iberians were more familiar with Africans, more attentive to different shades and conditions of those of African or partly African descent; the tradition of the *Siete Partidas* had allowed for the emergence of a relatively large group of free mulattoes and some free blacks. In the early years of plantation slavery in the English Caribbean there was also an overwhelming concentration of blacks in menial employment, with very few admitted to the responsible or autonomous functions that were sometimes allotted to slaves in Spanish America. In the Caribbean colonies there was unpleasant work to be done and even tender-hearted whites would be grateful for a system of slavery which gradually allowed them to be relieved of it. This harsher variant of racial slavery was to be firmly established by the 1660s, and to exercise a direct influence on the English colonies of North America wherever there were significant numbers of slaves. The English sense of private property, sharpened by the rise of capitalist market relationships, was to put the accent on the slave as chattel and almost entirely to eclipse the notion that the slave was a human being.

The Puritans, who played such a large part in English colonizing, were inclined to take their cue from the Bible, which certainly sanctioned servitude, as we have seen. The conviction that it was the human creatures' lot to live by the sweat of their brow might discourage enslaving others in order to live in luxury and idleness – but the hard-working and hard-driving planter would be an instrument of God's purpose. Just as important in the construction of English colonial society was Protestant pride and self-regard, which could easily encourage ethno-religious exclusivism. Thus the Reverend William Symonds, one of the divines closely associated with the settlement of Virginia, warned:

> Out of the arguments by which God enticed Abraham to go out of his country, such as go to a Christian plantation may gather many blessed lessons. God will make him a great Nation. Then must Abraham's posterity keep to themselves. They may not marry nor give in marriage to the heathen, that are uncircumcised. And this is so plain, that out of this arose the law of marriage amongst themselves. The breakers of this rule may break the neck of all good success of this voyage, whereas by keeping the fear of God, may grow into a nation formidable to all the enemies of Christ and be the praise of all that part of the world. . . .[33]

The English colonists were inclined to distrust Indian conversions and to believe that Indian mothers would never bring up their children in a truly Christian way. Indeed, after initial enthusiasm only the most perfunctory efforts were made to convert the Native Americans, not because the latters' beliefs were respected but because they, and their whole way of life, came to be thought of as irredeemably heathen. John Rolfe had to struggle to overcome what he saw as biblically inspired precepts banning the marrying of strange women before he could wed Pocahontas. Some English writers argued that many of the problems of the colonization effort in Ireland came from the taking of native wives, or even nurses. Thus Edmund Spenser warned: 'the child that sucketh the milk of the nurse must of necessity learn his first speech of her, the which being the first that is enured to his tongue is ever after the most pleasing unto him. . . . For besides the young children are like apes, which will affect to imitate what they see done before them, specially by their nurses whom they love so well. They do moreover draw into themselves together with their suck, even the nature and disposition of their nurses, for the mind followeth much the temperature of the body . . . so that the speech being Irish the heart must needs be Irish.'[34]

The English had once thought of themselves as protectors of the indigenous peoples against Spanish rapacity. The first settlements in North America did achieve an uneasy but largely peaceful coexistence with the Indians, mainly because the settlements were small and insecure enough to feel the need for Indian goodwill and help. But as they expanded, there were increasing tensions and clashes as Indian communities resisted the loss of land they had hunted and rivers in which they fished. The condescending arrogance of most settlers turned to outraged ferocity if the Indians moved against them. In both Virginia and Massachusetts this furnished the occasion for reducing Indians to slavery, but made a negligible contribution to the local labour force. Thus, following the massacre of the Pequots in Massachusetts, seventeen surviving members of this Indian people were shipped out of the colony in 1638 and sold as slaves in Providence Island – the captain who undertook this voyage returned, according to the leading Massachusetts colonist John Winthrop, with 'cotton, tobacco, and Negroes etc.'. Although it is not known what became of these Negroes, their status in New England could have approximated to that of a servant, albeit on a long or indefinite contract.[35]

Writing to John Winthrop some years later, Emanuel Downing, now a leading member of the Massachusetts Company, ventured the following reflection:

> If upon a Just War [with the Narragansetts] the Lord should deliver them into our hands, wee might easily have men, women and children enough to exchange for Moores, whch wilbe more gayneful pilladge for us than we conceive, for I doe not see how we can thrive until we get a stock of slaves sufficient to doe all our business, for our children's children will hardly see this great continent filled with people, soe that our servants will still desire freedom to plant for themselves, and not stay but for verie great wages. And I suppose you know verie well how wee shall maynteyne 20 Moores cheaper than one English servant. These ships that shall bring Moores may come home laden with salt which may bear most of the chardge, if not all of it. . . .[36]

While this particular proposal was impractical, some of the reasoning behind it helps to illuminate the thinking of English investors. Both Downing and Winthrop had connections in the Caribbean, and sought a role in the overall development of English America. Seeing no prospect of finding enough servants or wage labourers for the plantations, many proprietors in English America shared Downing's desire to find unfree workers.

The generality of colonists in Massachusetts were more uneasy at the prospect of importing slaves. In 1641 the following awkward resolution was passed by the Court of the colony:

> That there shall never be any Bond-slavery, Villenage or Captivity amongst us, unless it be lawful Captives in Just Wars, (and such strangers) as willingly sell themselves or are sold to us, and such shall have the liberties and Christian usage which the Law of God established in Israel concerning such persons doth morally require; Provided this exempts none from servitude who shall be judged thereto by Authority.[37]

While this resolution allowed slaves to be brought in, it seems to promise them 'liberties and Christian usage'. Some years later the same body had to deliberate on the case of a shipload of Africans brought to the colony who claimed to have been abducted by violence – an African interpreter who had suffered the same fate put their case. The result was the following declaration:

> The General Corte, conceiving themselves bound by the first opportunity to bear witness against the hynes and crying syn of man stealing, as also to proscribe such timely redress for what is past, and such law for the future as may deterr all others belonging to us to do in such vile and most odious courses ... do order that the negro interpreter, with others unlawfully taken be, by the first opportunity, (at the charge of the country for the present,) sent to his native country of Ginny.[38]

Massachusetts never imported any large numbers of slaves, and those few brought in arrived from other English colonies where their slave status had already been validated. In the course of time the colony's merchants were to play a leading role in supplying provisions and slaves to the plantation colonies. The racial notions of Englishmen, and the leading colonists' willingness to buy slaves, were broadly the same in the different colonies. But in Massachusetts, and New England as a whole, there was no plantation staple. Without planter demand for slave labour, and planter domination of assemblies, the anti-slavery viewpoint was occasionally heard. The resolutions quoted above reflect these different circumstances. Popular anti-slavery was animated mainly – if these resolutions are anything to go by – by a fear of the logic of slaveholding rather than simple racial feeling, though the latter would not have been absent. It is worth remembering that slaves comprised at least a tenth of the population of the neighbouring Dutch colony of New Netherlands, which also lacked a staple. But New Netherlands was run in autocratic fashion by Peter Stuyvesant and other wealthy slave traders; the sort of religious dissidents who might have had reservations about slaveholding were excluded – first from any say in the government, then from the colony itself.[39] In 1652 the colonists of Rhode Island, whose ships had much intercourse with the Caribbean, decided that 'black mankind or white' were not to be held for more than ten years in servitude or beyond the age of twenty-four if they had been acquired when they were under fourteen. The most probable explanation for this resolution is that the mass of colonists had no wish to see the leading men being allowed to bring in large numbers of slaves with whom they could then overbear their neighbours.[40]

In Virginia the tobacco staple created an intense demand for labour, and the colony's leaders were far less responsive to the mass of colonists than those in Massachusetts. The first African captives were probably treated similarly to involuntary servants, such as convicts, since they lacked a contract. But in some cases the kindness or death of an owner may have furnished the opportunity for freedom to be negotiated. 'Antonio the Negro', sold as a slave in 1621, survived to become the freeman Anthony Johnson in 1650, married to an African woman and owning cattle and 250 acres. Some African slaves were able to accumulate the funds necessary to purchase their freedom, by cultivating a patch on Sundays or putting aside incentive money from their owners. Francis Payne saved up 1,650 pounds of tobacco, which he used to buy his freedom. For a time free African-Americans could bring lawsuits or bear arms in the militia. In 1656 a Negro woman wed a white colonist.[41] The arrival of large numbers of indentured servants meant that very few slaves were bought in Virginia until after 1661. Intending importers may have been deterred by doubts concerning the status of African slaves, who were sometimes believed to be entitled to their freedom after a reasonable interval and if they became Christians.

The lot of the servant in Virginia was easier than that of the servant in Barbados, and there were better prospects at the end of the term of service. In all the Caribbean colonies the planter enjoyed great power, subject only to the opinion of his fellows. In Virginia the emergence of a free population of ex-servants helped to create a certain further restraint: on completion of their contracts, West Indian servants often left for the mainland colonies because of the greater opportunities to be found there. The rise of sugar in the Caribbean also required or permitted a more gruelling work regime than was necessary for tobacco cultivation. But in principle all servants worked from sunup to sundown, and were subject to vicious punishment if they disobeyed their masters or tried to run away. Beating, the extension of their time of service, mutilation and branding were meted out as punishments to recalcitrant servants.

Under a Virginia law of 1642 servants who ran away were to serve double time – if they repeated the offence, they were to be branded with an R on the cheek. In theory they could appeal to the magistrates against extremities of abuse or violations of their contract, but the magistrates were themselves also proprietors. Particularly abusive planters might be reprimanded by their neighbours, but the condition of the servant remained highly vulnerable.[42] Another factor of restraint was that reports of bad usage of servants would discourage further indentures from signing on. The planters of Barbados drew up a Master and Servant Law in 1652 which supposedly offered both parties some guarantees, but it was admitted that planters could be very oppressive and negligent. English servants encountered several new and virulent diseases in the Caribbean, such as yellow fever. Planters were often unwilling to provide properly for such sick servants, and the Barbados legislature admitted that there had been cases of the 'malicious killing' of sickly servants 'up and down the colony'.[43]

The arrival of numbers of African slaves did not, to begin with, lead to an alleviation of the lot of the servants of Barbados or Virginia. Thus in Barbados in 1657 a law was introduced preventing servants from moving outside their plantations, unless they carried a ticket of permission from their owner. The dress of servants was distinctively meagre and drab, so that they would not generally be difficult to identify. But the system later revealed a flaw when it was discovered that forged tickets were circulating. The attempt to control servants' movements was deemed necessary in part because of the seditious activities of Irish servants – most of whom had been shipped to the colony as prisoners condemned to labour for ten years or so rather than under the voluntary indenture system. In 1657 the Governor warned that 'several of the Irish nation, freemen and women' were striving to sow unrest among the Irish servants, so stricter invigilation was necessary. In 1657 Captain Edward Thomson, a militia commander and one of several brothers of Maurice Thomson, reported that his men had found 'divers rebellious and runaway negroes lying in the woods and other secret places'. Slaves were also required to carry passes. As Hilary Beckles has observed, the methods of labour control developed for servants were soon applied to the African slaves.[44]

For much of the seventeenth century an indentured servant could be purchased for something like half the price of an African slave. There were both cultural and economic reasons for being satisfied with servant labour, so long as sufficient numbers of servants were available. The small planter making his first purchase of a servant or slave was taking a decision to share his life with that person; racial feeling, or a sense of ethno-religious exclusivity, could easily prompt a decision to opt for the familiar, especially if there was a reasonable economic case for doing so. Admittedly, the voluntary indentured servant was bound to work for only three, five or seven years. This could still seem cost-effective, since (1) mortality rates for new arrivals, whether servants or slaves, were so high that the planter could count on only a few years of service anyway – investing in four servants rather than two slaves spread the risk; (2) planters knew the language and habits of white servants, and could work them harder than in the Old World; getting work out of 'outlandish' African slaves, whose skills were unknown, was more of a challenge; (3) servants were not only cheaper than slaves but could often be acquired on credit more easily, since direct trouble, cost and risk to the trader who bought them was quite small –

African slaves had to be acquired for an outlay in trade goods on a far longer and more risky triangular voyage.

Of course the balance of these considerations shifted as the plantations grew, servants became scarcer and harder to manage, and Northern merchants became more adept at the African trade. The planters of the English Caribbean began to recruit a predominantly African slave labour force as early as the 1640s and 1650s – a move than was not made at all widely in Virginia or Maryland until the very end of the century. The English Caribbean sugar boom of the 1640s and later created such an intense demand for labour that the supply of servants could not satisfy it. Those setting up a sugar estate had large financial resources, and were apprentices to Dutch and New Christian merchants and planters who instructed them in the advantages of African labour.

The owners of sugar plantations in Barbados acquired African slaves simply to expand their labour force and raise output. Unlike the Virginian farmer, they were not going to live in the same cabin as those who worked their fields. In a rather short time they accepted that African slaves, though expensive, would comprise the bulk of their workforce. African slaves may have had a slightly longer life expectancy than English servants, being less vulnerable to some of the diseases prevalent in the Caribbean. The maintenance costs of Africans were generally lower – both because the clothing issued to them was cheaper, and because they were more adept at meeting their own needs. The African slaves had more knowledge of tropical agriculture and, without the prospect of soon becoming free, a greater motive for seeking to make the best of their condition. In the course of time sugar planters also came to value the fact that their slaves' skills in the complex tasks required of them accumulated to the benefit of their owners, rather than being lost every few years. But the Caribbean planters' discovery of these and other advantages in the acquisition of slaves did not mean that they ceased to request shipments of English servants. The pressure to find extra labour, whether English or African, was constant, because the scope for expanding output seemed to know no limit.

The planters of Barbados in mid century bought both Africans and English for work in the field. Salary-earning employees helped to run the plantation, though occasionally an English indentured servant was pro- moted to such a post, and Africans were sometimes found in the skilled work of sugar-making. So far as servants were concerned, plantation managers preferred Scots or English to Irish, because they were easier to handle, but if necessary they would take on even 'Papist' servants. Like slaves, servants were a species of property, their value rated in amounts of tobacco or sugar according to the unexpired portion of their indenture. They could be pledged or mortgaged like land, and were inventoried like livestock. An estate sold by Captain Hawley to a Captain Skeetle in 1640 described the 'goods and chattels' with their valuation in terms of cotton as follows: '40 sowes (12,000 lbs of cotton), 160 piggs (5,150 lbs of cotton),

2 hogs (3,000 lbs of cotton), 1 horse (700 lbs of cotton), 6 donkeys (3,600 lbs of cotton), and 28 servants (26 males, 2 females) 7,350 lbs of cotton)'.[45] When they were shipped, servants were rated as so many 'freights', with the underage as 'half-freights'.

Males comprised nearly three-quarters of the indentured servants sent to the English colonies in the seventeenth century. Those who shipped and bought women servants were particularly anxious to avoid acquiring a pregnant servant. Women and girl servants were sometimes subjected to intrusive medical examination before shipment; if they were thought to be pregnant, they would not be purchased. The planter did not wish to see the labour he had purchased swallowed up by pregnancy, childbirth and the nursing of infants. Women servants who became pregnant in the colonies, and the men involved – whether free or not – were subject to sanctions designed to make good the planters' loss, as well as to deter others. Women servants were not free to marry unless they had their owners' permission. However, there was a considerable shortage of women, so female servants, especially on the mainland, were often able to find a husband who would buy them out of servitude. The owner of a Virginia plantation wrote of women servants in 1649:

> if they come of honest stock and have good repute, they may pick and chuse their husbands out of the better sort of people. I have sent over many, but could never keepe one at my Plantation the Moneths, except a poor silly Wench, made for a foile to set of beauty, and yet a proper young Fellow must needs have her, and being but new come out of his time and not strong enough to pay the charges I was at in cloathing and transporting he, was content to serve me a Twelve month for a wife.[46]

Women and girls comprised nearly a third of the African slaves brought to the English colonies in the seventeenth century. It is probable that planters would have preferred fewer women slaves, since most saw little more advantage in a pregnant slave than in a pregnant servant. Slave women generally commanded a lower price than slave men. While the children of female slaves would, if they survived, themselves eventually add to the value of the slave crew, this was a risky and long-term investment. The majority of English planters in the seventeenth century were looking to recoup their investment in five years or less, given the uncertainties of the times. Women slaves were obliged to work in the fields, while this was less common for women servants, who were generally occupied with tasks in or near the household.

Civil War: Empire and Bondage

The rise of Barbados sugar plantations proceeded despite the onset of the Civil War in England. Indeed, the distraction of the metropolis allowed virtual free trade to its Caribbean colonies. Rival claimants to the proprietorship of the island appealed to King and Parliament, but only succeeded in undermining one another's claims. In 1643 the Assembly of Barbados declared that henceforth they would pay rent to no proprietor; for a decade the planters enjoyed virtual autonomy. The planter representatives sought to remain neutral between Parliament and King, insisting only that their growing wealth entitled them to special consideration and representation, perhaps on the model of a great municipality. There were three chief sources of planter concern: (1) because of the confusion over proprietorship of the colony, titles to land were unconfirmed; (2) English merchants and the English government might wish to curb free trade with the Dutch; (3) planters, outnumbered by a newly imported population of indentured servants and slaves, felt in need of a colonial regime guaranteeing authority and security. Different factions gave a different weighting to these concerns, or opted for different solutions. Most planters seemed to have favoured one or other proprietorial interest, so long as the latter was prepared to guarantee land titles and defend the colony's interests *vis-à-vis* the government, whatever that should turn out to be. On the other hand, some planters, including those most closely linked to English merchants, were prepared to see direct rule from London, in the interests of greater stability and security even if at the cost of commercial restrictions.

Political alignments in Barbados during the Civil War and Restoration period are linked in intriguing ways to metropolitan politics. Thus Barbados contained an influential group of planters linked to the 'new merchants' of the City, and to prominent representatives of the Parliamentary cause. Maurice Thomson, who played a major role in shaping the Commonwealth's colonial and commercial policy as a Member of the Commons Committee on Trade and Plantations, had several planter clients in Barbados.[47] Others strongly linked to the Parliamentary cause and the innermost counsels of its leaders included James Drax, probably the first planter to produce sugar; Stephen and Thomas Noel, planter brothers of the influential 'new merchant' Martin Noel; Thomas Kendall, a London grocer who also owned a plantation in Barbados; and John Bayes, a planter associate of Bradshaw, President of the Council of State. More ambivalent in their sympathies, but equally influential, were James Modyford, who fought for the King but then emigrated to Barbados where, as a cousin of General Monck, he played a key role in both Commonwealth and Restoration; William and Thomas Povey, merchants and office-holders; and Anthony Ashley Cooper, later Earl of Shaftesbury, an absentee Barbados planter with a lively interest in colonial projects. Finally, mention should be made of Lord Francis Willoughby, twice Governor of the island, who fought against the King but subsequently became the standard-bearer of the Royalist cause in the Caribbean.

The 'new merchants' had thrived principally on the tobacco and sugar trades, but this did not mean that Barbadian planters were happy about the growing influence of these men in the metropolis. Many new merchants in London and Bristol looked forward to the time when the English colonies would be barred from trafficking with their main rivals, the Dutch; they could point out that government would find it easier to tax the American trades if there was a colonial monopoly. The Embargo Act of 1650 and the Navigation Act of 1651 were inspired by such an outlook. It seems to have been this move to create an English colonial system, in which colonists would be required to ship their produce to England in English ships, which provoked the Barbadian planters, or a faction of them, to a belated Royalism in 1650. In May 1650 the General Assembly recognized Lord Francis Willoughby, nominee of the Earl of Carlisle, as Governor, and expelled those planters most clearly identified with the Parliamentary cause. Willoughby had broken with Parliament and rallied to the Royalist cause around the time of the King's execution in 1649. The dominant planter faction was prepared to accept a nominee of the proprietor so long as the latter would guarantee their lands, their security and their enjoyment of home rule. While the rumoured proximity of Prince Rupert's privateers gave courage to the Barbadian Royalists, the declarations of the planter Assembly left open the possibility of negotiation with the London government. This supposedly 'Royalist' body demanded representation in the metropolis, declaring: 'Shall we be bound to the Government and lordship of a Parliament in which we have no representatives or persons chosen by us?'[48]

Willoughby realized that he would gain planter recognition only by making himself the representative of their demands, displaying a willingness to negotiate and guarantee good order. In the uncertain conditions created by the victory of the Commonwealth, many Barbadian planters were alarmed that their indentured servants would seek to escape their bondage. In the colony's early days the important planters had arrested and executed a governor who had attempted to mobilize discontented servants against them. In 1649 eighteen servants were found guilty of conspiring against their masters, and executed; in May of the following year 122 Noncon-formists, and others deemed a threat to the peace, were deported. The pro-Parliament planters, who were also expelled, were rich men whose estates were worked largely by slaves rather than servants, which may have rendered them less fearful of servant rebellion.

Willoughby and the Barbadian Council may have hoped to strike a deal with the London government; they appointed as their agent there the brother of a regicide. They may also have hoped that the wealth and vulnerability of the plantations would imbue London with caution. The Council of State announced an immediate embargo on Barbados, and dispatched a large naval expedition there in 1652. The expedition's commander had orders to blockade the island, send raiding parties ashore, but be prepared to concede a negotiated surrender so long as Willoughby withdrew. The Barbadian militia, in which many colonists were loath to serve, was worsted in the only important clash. Eventually Modyford, the Royalist émigré and kinsman of Monck, organized a peace faction which delivered Barbados to the Commonwealth forces in January 1652.

During the Commonwealth the interests of colonial commerce were more vigorously asserted than ever before. The Navigation Act required colonial imports from England, and plantation exports to England, to be carried in English ships. However, it did in principle still permit a direct trade between the colonies and Europe, though the latter was interrupted by the war with the Dutch in 1652–54. The military and colonial policy of the Commonwealth was greatly influenced by what has been called the 'colonial interloping complex', comprising men such as Maurice Thomson and other members of the Commons Committee on Trade and Plantations. A powerful new navy was constructed to further English commercial interests. Advised by – among others – Thomas Modyford, Cromwell went to war with Spain and adopted the 'Western Design' of seizing further territory in the New World. A large expedition was sent to the Caribbean, and captured the sparsely inhabited island of Jamaica in 1655. War with Spain afforded new opportunities for privateering.

The new navy drew upon sea captains, especially those in the America trades, in replacing the many naval commanders who were Royalists. The able seamen were promised a wage of 24 shillings (£1.20) a month. This was lower pay than the privateers offered, but comparable to basic wages ashore – the able seamen had few expenses aboard and the prospect of a share in prize money. The hazards of life at sea still made recruitment difficult, so resort was made to the press gang, the involuntary enrolment of sailors by roving recruitment teams. The rate of pay of impressed sailors was somewhat lower than that of the able seamen, and conditions of service were less favourable. In 1654 a group of seamen in the Channel fleet produced a petition calling for improvements in the seamen's lot, and declaring impressment to be a species of 'thraldom and bondage' that was 'inconsistent with the principles of freedom and liberty'. The officers debated the issue and decided to support the petition by a vote of 21 to 4, with Vice-Admiral John Lawson, an associate of the Leveller John Wildman, lending his support. These proceedings threatened to delay the dispatch of the expedition to the West Indies, but the distribution of bounties to the seamen, promises to study their demands, and patriotic mobilization – with war looming – created conditions in which the fleet departed.[49]

Although the Commonwealth had asserted metropolitan control of colonial commerce and supported the projects of the 'new merchant', it had not chosen to dwell on the role of African slavery in the new order of things. While some Puritan leaders had happily invested in slave plantations and the slave trade, others had doubts about the justification for permanent enslavement. If the Parliament of the Saints had been persuaded to accept slavery, they might have encumbered it with conditions awkward for the slaveowner. In the heightened political atmosphere of the time, the most execrated condition was that of the slave, and to be a master of slaves was scarcely better.[50] Even – or perhaps especially – Commonwealth leaders who were themselves implicated in the slave economy avoided advertising the fact by legislating in favour of slaveholding.

The eminent savant Sir Thomas Browne, in his influential book on *Vulgar Errors* (1646), published a critique of the notion that Negroes had a black skin because of Noah's curse, and were hence condemned to servitude. Browne's chapter on this topic displays expert biblical scholarship that would have been likely to impress rather than offend religious radicals. He concludes: 'whereas men affirme this colour [i.e.blackness] was a curse, I cannot make out the propriety of that name, it neither seeming so to them, nor reasonably unto us'. He also considers human beauty as likely to be found in black as in white and, in connection with prejudices about Jews, offers the general warning that it is 'a dangerous point to annexe a constant property unto any Nation'.[51] However, the continuing depreciation of Africans was evident in the doggerel for the Lord Mayor's Pageant of 1657, where two Moors rode a leopard as the following sentiment was intoned: 'The ill-complexion'd Affrican into your Breast/Poures forth his Specie Treasure Chest.'[52]

The Parliamentary leaders acted cautiously with respect to the dispatch of Irish servants to the plantation colonies. After the defeat of the Irish Royalist forces, several thousand Irish prisoners were sent to America. The prospect of receiving further Irish convicts aroused alarm in Virginia 'till assurance be given of their not being carried where they may be dangerous'.[53] The Commonwealth authorities, who planned a sweeping expropriation of Catholic landlords, thought that their project demanded shipping out their large haul of captives in order to eliminate the danger of future resistance. But instead of sending all, or even the bulk, of the Irish prisoners to the plantation colonies, the British government arranged for some thirty-five thousand Irishmen to be sold as soldiers, via contractors, to Spain and other European armies. This extraordinary transaction may have satisfied the Puritan notion that Irish Catholics were really agents of the Spanish King but, given the likelihood of war with Spain, it was a strange proceeding all the same. The Committee of the Council of State adopted a more prudent approach to labour recruitment for the colonies, focusing mainly on young people. It asked Henry Cromwell, the commander in Dublin, for a thousand 'young wenches' and a thousand 'youths' to be collected for transportation. Henry Cromwell wrote: 'Concerninge the young women, although we must use force in taking them up, yet it being so much in their own goode, and likely to be soe great advantage to the publique, it is not in the least doubted that you shall have such number of these as you shall thinke fit to make use uppon this account.' Of the youths he later observed: 'who knows, but it may be a meanes to make them English-men, I meane rather Christians'.[54]

Following the suppression of a revolt at Salisbury in 1655, about seventy English Royalists were also shipped out to the plantations, where they were sold as servants to the planters. This proceeding was later to be attacked in Parliament when some of the victims managed to send back a pamphlet attacking the 'slavery' to which they were being subjected. Several had been sold to Martin Noel, where they worked a twelve-hour day in his sugar works. A parliamentary debate in 1659 echoed to calls from both Republicans and Royalists to end such a disreputable flouting of English liberties. A Republican MP warned that before long Roundheads might themselves be the victims of such high-handed procedures: 'Our ancestors left us free men. If we have fought our sons into slavery, we are of all men the most disreputable.'[55]

The commercial restrictions imposed on the colonies provoked a free-trading Royalism from many planters in Virginia, just as it had in Barbados. While Maurice Thomson and his associates aimed to tighten England's monopoly on the colony's trade, the Governor, William Berkeley, informed the Virginia Assembly:

> We can only fear the Londoners, who would fain bring us to the same poverty, wherein the Dutch found and relieved us; would take away the liberties of our consciences, and tongues, and our right of giving and selling our goods to whom we please. But gentlemen by the grace of God we will not so tamely part our king, and all these blessings we enjoy under him.[56]

Prompted by Thomson, William Claiborne and other 'new merchant' leaders, the English Parliament dispatched an expedition to restore Virginia to obedience to its laws. The Virginian planters prudently gave way, and Berkeley stepped down as Governor. The Commonwealth's assertion of English naval power – against the Dutch as well as its own colonists – made it clear that resistance would be fruitless. But the planters of Virginia also knew that England furnished them with a market and a supply of servants. Moreover, in any armed conflict with Parliament they could not count on the loyalty of the mass of poor freemen and servants. Yet many leading Virginians, including Berkeley, naturally welcomed the Restoration and hoped that it might provide an opportunity to loosen the regulations on their trade. Berkeley was again appointed Governor, and he issued a pamphlet in 1662 in which he attacked the mercantile regime of the Commonwealth: 'we cannot but resent that forty thousand people should be impoverished to enrich little more than forty merchants'.[57] Nevertheless, the Restoration regime could brook no relaxation of the colonial system, since this was now such a crucial prop of national commerce.

By 1660 London was on the way to overtaking Amsterdam as the leading entrepôt in Europe for the plantation trade, with significant quantities also passing through Bristol and other outports. In 1621 the Port of London had registered the import from Europe of sugar worth £83,000 and of tobacco worth £49,000; in this year no sugar and only £14,000 worth of tobacco had been imported directly from America. By 1660 London was no longer registering any imports of tobacco or sugar from Europe: sugar imports from the colonies were valued at £256,000 and tobacco imports at £69,000. London's combined imports of colonial produce from America totalled £344,000 out of its total import bill of £830,000. The rise of re-exports of colonial goods was even more striking. In 1640 re-exports accounted for about £100,000 out of a total export trade of around £3 million; by 1660 re-exports accounted for £900,000 out of a total export trade of £4.1 million.[58]

Prior to the Restoration there were important philosophical and legal speculations supportive of the colonial project. John Selden's *Mare Clausum* (1653) was to appear as *The Right and Dominion of the Sea* in 1662, justifying England's colonies and commerce, and tracing natural law back to a Noachid dispensation. The less discreet Royalist philosopher Jeremy Taylor published *Ductor Dubitandium* (1660), in which he boldly severed natural law from any necessary basis in events of the Old Testament. He maintained:

> The right of nature is a perfect and universal liberty to do whatsoever can secure me or please me. For the appetites that are prime, original and natural, do design us towards their satisfaction, and were a continual torment, and in vain, if they were not in order to their rest, contentedness and perfection. Whatsoever we naturally desire, naturally we are permitted to.... Therefore to save my own life, I can kill another or twenty, or a hundred, or take from his hands to please myself, if it happens in my circumstances and power: and so for *eating*, *drinking*, and *pleasures*.

While he was anti-Puritan, Taylor did not simply recommend libertinage. He urged merely that 'in those things where Christianity hath not interpos'd, we are left to our natural liberty, or a *Jus permissivum*, a permission, except where we have restrain'd ourselves by *contract* or *dedition*'.[59] So far as slavery was concerned, it was excluded neither by Christianity nor by contract. Taylor did not specifically praise it, but the philosophical trend represented by him and John Vaughan, the future Chief Justice in the Court of Common Pleas, offered no basis from which to criticize the slaveholder or slave trader, and some from which to recognize England's natural right to its new pleasures. Like their friend Thomas Hobbes, these men thought that the state of nature demonstrated the need for royal sovereignty, but their view of it was less bleak; consequently, an untrammelled royal power did not have to hold civil society entirely in its thrall.[60]

The Restoration and the Codification of Colonial Slavery

The Restoration confirmed and accentuated the colonial and commercial policy of the Commonwealth, while it discarded any lingering reservations about slavery or slave trading. Both metropolitan and colonial institutions moved under the Restoration to establish the legal forms of slavery, while monarch and Parliament promoted the slave trade.

During the last months of the Commonwealth, Modyford had been appointed Governor of Barbados. He speedily accepted the Restoration and was granted amnesty by his monarch; since his kinsman Monck was the chief instrument of the Restoration, this was not surprising. Modyford was replaced as Governor of Barbados by Willoughby, but soon appointed Governor of Jamaica, which was declared a Crown colony. In the last years of the Commonwealth Jamaica had become an important privateer base, seizing prizes worth £300,000 in 1659; Modyford soon reached an understanding with these men. Only two members of the Commons Committee on Trade and Plantations were former Royalist partisans. A new Navigation Act tightened up its predecessor, this time giving a monopoly of the major branches of colonial trade to English merchants and ships – though merchants in the colonies themselves counted as English, of course. Some half-dozen Barbadian planters were knighted by the King. In return for a confirmation of planter holdings, and in lieu of rent to a proprietor, Barbados was required to pay the monarch a 4.5 per cent duty on the colony's exports, some of which was to cover the expenses of defending and administering the island. Colonial administration in the Caribbean became more effective and vigorous than it had been under the Commonwealth, with governors and some other officers appointed by London. However, the colonists were still permitted to elect assemblies, which retained some powers over local finance. Wars with France, Spain and the Netherlands exposed the Caribbean settlements to special risk.

The Restoration's legislation for the mundane realities of tied labour in the colonies included clear recognition of the validity of slavery for Africans. In 1661 the Virginian Assembly extended statutory recognition to slavery, both African and Indian, and in the following year it ruled that all children born to slave mothers would themselves be slaves. The Master and Servant Act of Barbados in 1661 was meant both to ensure a due subordination among English indentured servants and, in the interests of encouraging indentures, to distinguish servitude from outright slavery. In the same year the Barbados Assembly also drew up an 'Act for the better ordering and governing of negroes'. While the preamble to the Master and Servant Act complained that the 'unruliness, obstinacy and refractioness of the servants' required that a 'continual strict course' should be taken with their 'bold extravagance', the preamble to the 'governing of negroes' Act described the latter as being 'heathenish' and 'brutish', a 'dangerous kind of people' who had to be watchfully suppressed at all times. In 1667 the English Parliament for the first time passed an 'Act to Regulate the Negroes on the Plantations', declaring that they had to be controlled 'with strict severity'. In the same year the English courts found that 'the Negroes being Infidels, and the subjects of an Infidel Prince, and are usually bought and sold in America as Merchandise, by the customs of Merchants', there could be 'a property in them' sufficient to maintain trover actions.[61]

In colonial legislation of this period servants were usually described not as whites but as Christians, to distinguish them from Indians and Africans, who were sometimes lumped together in the category 'all servants not being christians', though this was inaccurate, since some of the latter had been baptized, either in Africa or America, and thought of themselves as Christians. In 1667, following up its legislation of 1661–62, the Virginian Assembly ruled that 'the conferring of baptism does not alter the condition of the person as to his bondage or freedom'.[62] The Assembly was also concerned to deter servants from uniting in escapes with slaves:

> in case any English servant shall run away in company of any negroes who incapable of making satisfaction by addition of a time [i.e. slaves who were serving for life anyway]: ... The English soe running away in company with them shall at the time of service to their owne masters expired, serve the masters of the said negroes for their absence soe long as they should have done by this Act if they had not been slaves, every christian in company serving his proportion.[63]

If the runaway slave died, the complicit servants would have to serve his or her owner for four years or furnish them with 4,500 lb of tobacco. In 1667 the Virginian Assembly also decreed that masters who killed their slaves while punishing them should not be accounted guilty of murder:

> Be it enacted by this grand assembly, if any slave resist his master (or other by his masters correcting him) and by extremity of correction should chance to die, that his death should not be accompted Felony ... since it cannot be presumed that prepensed malice (which alone makes murther felony) should induce any man to destroy his own estate.[64]

The passage of new laws in Virginia and Maryland gave slaveholders in these states greater security, and encouraged an increase in the imports of slaves; they were preceded by legal cases – like that of Elizabeth Key in Virginia, the daughter of a slave, who had successfully sued for her freedom in 1656 on the grounds that she had been baptized – which had put some aspect of slavery in doubt. Likewise in 1664 the journal of Maryland's upper house noted:

Itt is desired by the lower house that the upper house would be pleased to draw up an Act obligeing negros to serve durante vita they thinking it very necessary for the prevencon of the damage Masters of such Slaves may susteyne by such Slaves pretending to be Christened And soe pleade the lawe of England.[65]

Following the Restoration, the leading men in Virginia and Maryland give repeated expression to such support for a racial slave system.

If Commonwealth policy bore the imprint of a 'colonial–interloping' complex, that of the Restoration reflected the restless and contradictory dynamic of a 'colonial–privateering' complex. Such Royalist champions as Prince Rupert, the Duke of York and Francis Willoughby had privateering antecedents, and a keen interest in the African and colonial trade. The privateering chief of Jamaica, Henry Morgan, had one uncle in the entourage of the King, another in that of General Monck, at the time of the Restoration. During the wars of the 1660s and 1670s he led a marauding force of around 15 ships and 1,500 men on an unparalleled campaign of plunder and mayhem throughout the Caribbean; the sacking of Panama alone netted five million pesos. Since Morgan's depredations were carried out under cover of an official letter of marque, the Governor of Jamaica (Modyford) and the Lord High Admiral (Duke of York) both received their share, as indeed did Charles II himself. Modyford argued that in Caribbean conditions attack was the best form of defence, and that the privateers supplied a self-financing means of defending colonies that were still highly vulnerable. Lord Francis Willoughby himself perished while defending the Windward Islands from a strong Dutch force; he was succeeded as Governor by his brother William. The two main English islands, Barbados and Jamaica, emerged virtually unscathed from the wars. Barbados even flourished, because of its exceptionally favourable geographical position, with two or three hundred vessels visiting the island annually and sugar output rising to 15,000 tons in a good year – almost as much as was being produced in the whole of Brazil.[66]

The smaller English settlements in the Leeward Islands (St Christopher, Nevis, Antigua) and Windward Islands (St Lucia, St Vincent) suffered attacks and invasions from the French and the Dutch which impeded plantation development. The ethos fostered by the privateers in Jamaica offered competition to settled agriculture and commerce. While the privateers were rampaging round the Caribbean, the Jamaican interior itself was not effectively pacified: the English invasion, and subsequent Spanish guerrilla resistance, had presented opportunities of escape to a number of slaves who held out in maroon communities in the interior. However, some of the gains of privateering went into plantations, with both Morgan and Modyford constructing large estates. Modyford brought 1,500 settlers from Barbados and made land available to those who had slaves or servants. The number of slaves in Jamaica grew from only 500 in 1661 to nearly 10,000 in 1673; in the course of the 1670s new slaves were introduced at the rate of about 1,500 a year. By 1683 Jamaica's development still trailed behind that of Barbados, despite its far larger size. In this latter year England imported over 18,000 tons of sugar from the West Indies: around 10,000 tons from Barbados, 5,000 from Jamaica and 3,300 from the Leeward Islands.[67]

The inventories of the estates of 198 Jamaican planters and farmers, who died between 1674 and 1701, suggest the pattern in the early phase of plantation development (Table VI.1):

Table VI.1   The Property of 198 Jamaican Planters/Farmers, 1674–1701

	Average Value (£)	Slaves	Servants
54 Sugar Planters	1,954	63	3
8 Ranchers	656	16	1
7 Cotton Farmers	356	12	0.5
20 Indigo Planters	310	13	0.5
109 Unidentified	306	8	0.6
Median	375	12	0

Source: Dunn, *Sugar and Slaves*, p. 171.

By Barbadian standards these estates were still of modest size, yet they reveal that the plantation's tied workforce was now overwhelmingly comprised of slaves – and the individual inventories leave no doubt that these slaves were overwhelmingly African captives. Only seven of the estates were worth more than £3,000. Two of the larger plantations belonged to Sir Henry Morgan, the privateer chief, who owned a total of 122 slaves; in Barbados this would be the crew of a medium to small plantation. The poorest 19 per cent of property-holders left estates worth less than £100. The value of estates was highly correlated with the type of cultivation. In the nature of things such inventories do not record the number of free, salaried or waged employees on the plantations, though other sources suggest that their numbers declined as slaves were gradually trained to take their place, eventually leaving only overseers, bookkeepers and maybe one or two specialist artisans.[68]

In Barbados 61 per cent of all slaves in 1679 were attached to plantations with a hundred acres or more and an average crew of 104 slaves and 2 indentured servants; there were English overseers and bookkeepers, but whites were outnumbered by thirteen to one on these plantations. About half of the larger planters owned estates that had originally been formed by members of their family in the tobacco era. The largest estates in Barbados had around 600 acres and 300 slaves; on other, less crowded islands plantations of over 200 slaves became common. A third of Barbadian slaves resided on smaller plantations with between 10 and 100 acres, and an average slaveholding of 14. Because of its early settlement and comparatively healthy climate and situation, Barbados was always to have quite a large population of white colonists, amounting to about a fifth or more of the total.[69]

The newly restored King, along with other members of his family, took an active interest in the supply of slaves to the plantations. On the one hand it promised to furnish the monarch and Royal Family with a badly needed source of independent revenue; on the other the African trade was thought to provide an appropriate outlet for the talents of royal or aristocratic privateers. The colonial demand for slaves was certainly strong. By the 1660s and 1670s indentured servants, if they had a choice, now signed on for Virginia rather than the Caribbean, as word got back of how hard life was on the large sugar plantations, and how tightly controlled these colonies were by the leading planters. Following the parliamentary scandals of 1659 over Royalist prisoners, and given the planters' lack of enthusiasm for English felons and Irish rebels, involuntary indentures could not solve the plantation labour shortage. In 1663 a monopoly in the supply of African slaves to the English colonies was awarded to the newly formed Company of Royal Adventurers to Africa, whose members and subscribers included the King, the Duke of York and Prince Rupert, with backing from the mercantile interest of London and Bristol. The Company issued a new gold coin – the guinea – to commemorate its activities.

The idea that slave trading was an activity worthy of Royal Adventurers must have helped to remove any lingering doubts as to the Company's legitimacy. However, its commercial organization was haphazard, and to begin with its enterprise had about it the aspect of a 'treasure hunt'. The impediments and temptations of war with the French, Dutch and Spanish distracted the Company from a large-scale slave trade, and lured some of its ships back into privateering. Independent traders made their appearance, and furnished the English colonies with clandestine supplies of slaves. In 1670–72, attempts were made to curtail the activities of the privateers and furnish more satisfactory conditions for colonial development. The death of the Duke of Albemarle (Monck), the dismissal of Modyford as Governor of Jamaica and the cancellation of letters of marque to Morgan signalled the swing of influence to a new faction. In the 1660s the Commons Committee on Trade and Plantations had been a dignified rather than an efficient organ of government. With the rise of the Earl of Shaftesbury, who had long been a member of this Committee, the needs of plantation development gained more consistent support.[70]

In 1672 the English slave trade was entrusted to a new monopoly, the Royal African Company. The shareholders of this Company still included the Duke of York, Prince Rupert and other members of the Royal Family. But allied with them were Shaftesbury himself; Sir Peter Colleton, a Barbadian planter; Thomas Povey, the colonial merchant; Sir George Carteret, a Lord Proprietor of the new colony of Carolina; and Shaftesbury's protégé John Locke, who was for a time the secretary of the Committee on Plantations. Leading City figures such as Sir John Banks and Sir Josiah Child also subscribed to the Royal African Company, which started with a capital of £111,100. The Company was to establish seventeen forts or factories on the coast of Africa, manned by two or three hundred Company servants. It dispatched some 500 ships to Africa in the years 1672–1713, and exported goods worth £1.5 million. During this period it was responsible for buying 125,000 slaves on the African coast, losing a fifth of them on the 'Middle Passage' and selling the remainder, about 100,000, to the English West Indian planters.

The Company pioneered an expensive and hazardous trade at a time when the supply of slaves was threatened by continuing warfare and the weakened capacity of other carriers (the WIC went bankrupt in 1673). It paid dividends and maintained the value of its shares, so that several of the original investors did well out of it – the Duke of York (James II) had made an annual 12 per cent return, if capital appreciation is included, by the time he sold his shares in 1689. However, the Company had heavy expenses and did not make a trading surplus. It allowed planters to run up debts of £170,000 by 1690.

Without the support of the Company, the English colonies would probably have put up a weaker and more uncertain performance in the 1670s and 1680s. Yet the Company was the target of widespread resentment from independent planters and merchants who attacked its 'foul monopoly'. After 1675 Shaftesbury and the Carolina promoters withdrew; henceforth the Company was directed by the London corporate establishment in league with certain favoured planters and governors in the West Indies; the English colonies in North America received very few slaves direct from Africa before 1698. Barbados was supplied with more slaves than any other colony, with the Leeward Islands kept very short. Even Barbados planters complained that the Company was discriminating against them: a number – Henry Drax, Christopher Codrington, John Hallet – commissioned their own slave trading voyages in violation of the monopoly. The prices charged by the Company were not high, but then many of its local agents were selling to themselves or to friends. Although the Company itself lost money, its servants often made a fortune. After 1689 the Company's monopoly disintegrated, and independent traders proved that they could carry two or three times as many slaves across the Atlantic each year as the Company had done. Not for the first or last time the Atlantic trade of this epoch proved its double character: as a potentially rich and rewarding trade, it could become a nesting ground for special interests; but at the same time its inherently expansionary impetus would eventually disrupt trading rings and cosy arrangements.[71]

Bacon's Rebellion and Virginian Slavery

The growth of English North America had been little disrupted by the Civil War, and was less constrained by the subsequent warfare and labour shortage which impeded the Caribbean colonies. Indeed, the war with the Dutch led to the capture of New Amsterdam and its transformation into New York in 1664. With the conclusion of the Civil War, a steady rise in 'headrights' register the increasing stream of indentured labourers to Virginia: some 45,000 between 1650 and 1674, and a total of no fewer than 75,680 between 1640 and 1699. Maryland received 31,100 indentured servants during this period. Virginia had produced about half a million pounds of tobacco in 1627, rising to 15 million in 1669, making the colony by far the largest Atlantic supplier. But at this level of output there was relentless downward pressure on the price of tobacco. Smallholders and medium-sized planters still retained control of much of the land in contrast to the Barbados pattern. The medium-sized planter would have between two or three and a dozen servants, with only a few having as many as twenty or thirty. But despite the continuing flow of indentured servants, the leading men in the colony owned some slaves, African and a few Indian, and wrestled with the problem of ensuring a proper rank and order among them. Around 1670 there were reckoned to be 2,000 African slaves in Virginia. One index of the wealth of the colony was that the English Customs were thought to raise £100,000 each year through the duty on tobacco, the latter being set at a higher *ad valorem* rate than the duty on sugar.

In 1676 there was a major revolt in Virginia, 'Bacon's Rebellion', directed against the veteran Governor Sir William Berkeley, who was accused of favouritism towards the large planters and merchants, and failure to defend the poorer, inland planters, who were, they claimed, exposed to Indian attacks and subjected to onerous taxes and restrictions. While the revolt began among the planters, it soon detonated explosive social antagonisms among the mass of free persons and oppressed toilers. The revolt was triggered when a group of proprietors and freemen urged a young member of the Governor's Council, Nathaniel Bacon, to lead them on an expedition against the Susquehanna nation, which had supposedly invaded the colony. The Governor valued the accord with friendly Indians, and rightly feared that the up-country vigilantes would kill indiscriminately.

The outbreak of the conflict with Indian nations further north, known as King Philip's War, added to Berkeley's caution. But the Governor's own profitable monopoly on trading in furs with friendly Indians attracted settler suspicion. And beyond the Indian issue there were, as the Governor himself was uneasily aware, a pent-up mass of problems waiting to destroy the good order of the colony. Tobacco prices had dropped, threatening many smaller planters with ruin; bad weather aggravated their plight. Agreements with the Indians did not harm the big tidewater planters, but did make it difficult for new men to acquire land. As the Governor wrote to London, he was also concerned at the disposition of the servants and slaves: 'Consider us as a people press'd at our backs with Indians, in our Bowills with our servants . . . and invaded from without by the Dutch.' In another pointed reflection he observed: 'Wee have at our backs as many servants (besides Negroes) as their are freemen to defend the Shoars and our Frontiers [against] Indians.' He feared that not only slaves and servants but many poor freemen would join a Dutch invader if doing so answered their 'hopes of bettering their condition by Sharing the Plunder of the country'. And he openly lamented: 'How miserable that man is that Governs a People when Six parts of Seaven at least are Poore Endebted Discontented and Armed and to take away their Armes now the Indians are at our throates were to raise an Universal Mutiny.'[72]

The Governor's foreboding proved justified, and before long he did indeed face a 'Universal Mutiny'. Bacon listened sympathetically to those who wished to fight the Indians, and urged the Governor to appoint him commander of an expedition. He pointed out that popular unhappiness with new taxes and the alleged neglect of defences could be alleviated by such a move. But Berkeley, distrustful of the 'Rabble Crue' demanding it, declined Bacon a commission and, when he mounted an expedition anyway, denounced him and all his followers as rebels. In June 1676 a newly elected House of Burgesses extended the vote to all freemen, opened up many offices to election, and removed tax exemptions from all officials. They also decreed that a militia of 1,000 men be raised, and offered the prospect of plundering and enslaving those Indians deemed rebellious. Under pressure from armed vigilantes Berkeley was obliged to issue Bacon a commission, only to retract it as soon as he was no longer surrounded by a hostile armed force.

Bacon, dubbed 'General by the consent of the people', now raised the standard of revolt against the Governor. While he gained the support of some self-described 'discreet and sober' men, the logic of the conflict with the Governor led him to enrol poor freemen in his armed force, and to offer freedom to servants and slaves owned by the Governor's supporters, if they would enlist in his ranks. Bacon seized and sacked Jamestown, obliging the Governor to seek refuge on the Eastern shore. For about three months Bacon controlled most of the colony. The authorities feared that he and his followers planned to appeal for help to the Dutch; it was considered a sign of treachery that the wife of one of the leading rebels had been heard to say that England's power was a broken reed. But before English forces could arrive, or Bacon reveal his larger strategy, the rebellion was thrown into a crisis when its leader caught dysentery and died. With vigorous help from the captains and crews of visiting English ships, order was restored. Most rebels were offered a free pardon in order to persuade them to lay down their arms. However, more than a hundred, many of them slaves or servants, held out at West Point for better terms, including guarantees of their own freedom. An energetic loyal captain offered negotiations to the rebels but, once they were within range of his guns, gave them no option but surrender. An expedition from England of 1,100 men aboard eleven ships arrived just too late to participate in the hostilities, but carried an instruction that Berkeley was to be replaced as Governor.[73]

The eight months of 'Universal Mutiny' gave spectacular evidence of the discontents of the servants and freemen. It showed how fragile a plantation colony could be if the leading men fell out with one another, and if they involved the servants and slaves in their quarrels. The colonial authorities insisted on concessions to the poorer freemen, replacing the hated poll levy with taxes on trade. The House of Burgesses sought to strengthen the racial barrier between English servants and African slaves. In 1680 it prescribed thirty lashes on the bare back 'if any negroe or other slave shall presume to lift up his hand in opposition to any christian'.[74] In the last decades of the century about 4,000 African slaves were purchased by Virginian planters, mainly from the West Indies. Slaves were more important in Carolina, a colony partly founded by Barbadian planters who moved with their slaves in the 1670s and 1680s in search of more land; indigo and rice eventually became the plantation staples in this colony, after a slow start. These planters naturally brought with them not only slaves but the practices and ideology of the English Caribbean's by now well-entrenched system of racial slavery. The 1669 Fundamental Constitutions of the Carolinas had stated: 'Every Freeman of Carolina shall have absolute power and authority over Negro slaves of whatever opinion or Religion soever.'[75] Altogether about 20,000 slaves were introduced into the North American colonies in the seventeenth century, the great majority of these in the last decade or two.[76]

The New Slavery and the Caribbean Plantation

The statute of slavery in England's mainland colonies was inescapably influenced by the ethos of its Caribbean colonies. In the latter the growth of sugar plantations and slave populations had led to a more pronounced degradation and racialization of slavery than had hitherto been seen in the New World. Large numbers of North American colonists, including not a few planters, had passed through the West Indies, and others maintained a reciprocal trade with them, selling provisions and buying plantation produce. Witness to the degradation of English slavery in the plantation colonies in general, and West Indies in particular, was the Anglican clergyman Morgan Godwyn, in his *Negro's and Indians Advocate* (1680) and other writings, in which he drew on experience he had acquired when he ministered in Virginia and Barbados in the 1660s and 1670s.

Godwyn attacks the planters' cruelty and negligence, both physical and spiritual, contrasting their insensate greed with what he sees as the more responsible attitude of Puritans in New England or even of the abominable Catholics in Spanish America. His main complaint is that the planters see their African slaves as beasts of burden, and actively oppose their evangelization, fearing that it might qualify or weaken slave subordination; the failure to introduce Indians to Christianity is also wrong, but in the case of the Africans they are under the planters' control. Godwyn supplies details of the cruel treatment meted out to the Africans. He observes that slaves often go hungry, being allowed too little time for cultivation; this problem is shared 'in a proportionable manner' by English and white servants also. Slave women are allowed no time to succour their infants properly, so that most of them die. Recalcitrant Africans are punished not just with flogging and the stocks but with cropping of ears or by 'emasculating' them. Naked female slaves are flogged in public. He writes of such punishments: 'their practice is so notorious, and there is no one not perfectly blind, that can avoid the feeling of it; nay even such cannot but know it'.[77]

In Godwyn's view the 'Planters chief Deity, Profit', blinds them to the common humanity of the Africans and leads them into the blasphemous notion that the Africans are 'brutes' or a species of 'pre-Adamite' subhuman:

> methinks, the consideration of the shape and figure of our Negro's bodies, their Limbs and Members; their Voice and Countenance in all things according with other Mens; together with their *Risibility* and *Discourse* (Man's peculiar Faculties) should be a sufficient Conviction. How should they otherwise be capable of *Trades*, and other no less manly employments; as also of *Reading and Writing*; or show so much Discretion in the management of business; eminent in divers of them; but wherein [we know] that many of our own people are deficient, were they not truly men?[78]

Godwyn quotes Holy Scripture to the effect that 'God had made (of one blood) all the Nations of Men' (Acts 17–26), and urges that Negroes from Guinea are 'not necessarily descendants of Canaan' and 'the curse said to be annexed thereto'; even if they are, this would not be a good reason to deny them baptism.[79] Godwyn does not challenge slavery, and argues that if the slaves were introduced to Christianity, this will promote their 'integrity and long-livedness' and render them less prone to rebellion.[80] In the sixteenth or early seventeenth century it is possible to find English authors who speculate that black Africans are not human, or are kindred to apes, but the portrait presented by Godwyn goes much further – he evidently feels that this view had become the consensus and practical wisdom of a whole community, that of the English in the plantation colonies.

In 1688 Godwyn was able to preach a sermon in Westminster Abbey, summarizing his advocacy of the need to evangelize the Negro, but after the Revolution he disappeared from public view. Around the same time Aphra Behn published *Orinooko*, in which she portrayed the noble resistance of an enslaved African prince in Surinam and the failure of his fellows to sustain the rebellion he launches. This work raises questions about slavery without quite attacking the very existence of the institution, especially if care was taken to enslave only commoners.[81]

In fact the British Caribbean was the setting for a prodigious new reality, a plantation system at a new pitch of intensive organization and commercialization. The integrated Caribbean plantation permitted – and, if the planter was to keep abreast of competition, required – the working of slaves in gangs, an incessant cycle of planting, weeding and harvesting, and night work in the mill, often adding up to eighteen-hour working days. Between fifty and three hundred slaves now lived and worked on each estate. Wind, water and animal power kept the mills working twenty-four hours a day in a six- or seven-month-long harvest season. There was heavy mortality among the slaves, very low rates of fertility for the women, and a consequent need for ever greater supplies of new slaves from Africa. By comparison with Brazilian methods, the new plantation required a more intensive, and a more closely invigilated, work regime. On the smaller Caribbean islands land was scarce, and the natural flora and fauna were soon destroyed. Bird species died out as the forest cover disappeared and rats multiplied. The planters needed new sources of fuel, and it was more difficult for their slaves to feed themselves. Exhaustive agriculture diminished cane yields.

The planters countered such problems by adopting new methods, nearly all of which raised labour requirements. Canes were planted in separate, deep holes rather than broad trenches. Dung farms were created for manuring the fields. The discarded cane tops were fed to cattle, and 'mill trash' was dried and used as fuel. New metal rollers were installed in the mills, and the train of seven coppers used to boil the sugar were heated by a single flue, in a system known as the 'Jamaica train', though it probably originated in Barbados.[82] All these processes called for skilled labour, but the pressure to bring in the biggest crop possible, to justify investments and meet the demands of creditors, was incessant and pervasive. The plantation was a total environment in which the lives of the captive workforce could be bent unremittingly to maximize output. While the importance of method had been imbided from the Dutch, England's experience of building a navy must have instilled further lessons in discipline, synchrony and co-ordination. The plantation and the ship-of-the-line were commanded by similar types of men, and on both obedience was exacted with the help of rations of rum and public flogging. The many problems and complications of the new plantation, and its difference from other coercive institutions of the day, will be explored in Chapter VIII and subsequently. Here it is simply necessary to register that the slave plantation had been completed and 'perfected' in the British Caribbean in the last decades of the seventeenth century.

The Glorious Revolution and the Colonies

In the last years of the Stuart kings, excessive government interest in the colonies actually impeded plantation development. During the latter years of the reign of Charles II, and the brief rule (1685–88) of his brother James II, formerly Duke of York, colonial planters and independent merchants were subjected to increasingly burdensome forms of royal administration and taxation. The rights of colonial assemblies were trimmed, and those of royal governors enhanced. A lasting consequence of this was a more uniform metropolitan authority throughout the New World colonies, but in the short run it favoured particular individuals at the expense of both smallholders and the majority of planters. From 1676 the commercial regulation of the colonies was entrusted to the Lords of Trade. Duties on tobacco and sugar were increased. Before his death in 1682 Shaftesbury, previously himself a royal monopolist, organized opposition to Stuart recidivism in religion, in the use of royal prerogative and in commercial policy. His Whigs – the first parliamentary opposition of the modern type – drew upon the support of landed magnates, independent merchants and outraged Protestantism. The assertion of royal power in the Caribbean drove many planters back to England, where they sided with the opposition. When James II raised the sugar duty in 1686, he completed the alienation of the West India lobby.

The 'Glorious Revolution' which removed James II in 1688–89 and installed William III and Mary on the English throne consolidated the commercial orientation of the English state. The foundation of the Bank of England in 1694, and of other core institutions of the City of London, reflected and facilitated a 'commercial revolution' closely linked to colonial trade and plantation development; the operations of the Bank were to be underpinned by an influx of Brazilian gold. In 1696 colonial administration and commerce was placed under the tutelage of a new department, the Board of Trade and Plantations. Colonial assemblies claimed to act as local parliaments, with control of local revenue and appointments, but still remained subject to the metropolitan 'Crown-in-Parliament'. A Society for Propagating Christian Knowledge established in 1699 aimed to promote conformity with the Church of England in the colonies. Two able Privy Councillors, Sir George Downing (son of Emanuel) and Sir William Blathwayt, created a professional corps of administrators to supervise the operation of the Navigation Acts, and their associated fiscal instruments in England and the colonies. The Treasury, the Board of Trade and the Commissioners of Customs and Excise severally superintended the financial and commercial workings of the colonial system. The Admiralty, with a naval establishment that absorbed a quarter of public revenues, often pioneered more effective methods of public administration. In this area the victors of 1688–89 rationalized the elements of a state apparatus and colonial system whose origins lay in the Commonwealth and which had been much elaborated as a consequence of Stuart attempts to assert royal authority. On the other hand, privateers were far more tightly controlled, and piracy was suppressed.[83]

Between 1693 and 1713 state revenue from Customs and Excise trebled, reflecting the buoyancy of Atlantic and colonial trade, the development of the internal market, the attainment of commercial objectives through war, and the consolidation of a more efficient administration. The state itself commanded great credit, because it was strongly committed to independent wealth and commerce within an imperial framework. The wars fought in the period 1690–1713 furnished both the occasion and the justification for naval expansion and the construction of an efficient fiscal apparatus. Yet the numbers of those employed by the great offices of state were not large, and most of them were concentrated in the metropolis itself. Revenues were not drawn directly from the colonies but, rather, levied on colonial imports or re-exports; this structure, so different from that of Spain, was made possible by the large size of the domestic market. In 1716 the Board of Trade had 65 employees and the Office of the Secretary of State 29; in the same year the employees of the fiscal bureaux, mainly Customs and Excise, numbered 5,947.[84]

The Glorious Revolution marked the beginning of a new epoch for colonies as well as metropolis. The news of the ejection of James II arrived first in Barbados, because of its close communications with London, and caused considerable satisfaction. So far as the West Indies were concerned, planter lobbies in London, rather than colonial rebellion, played the main role in 1688–89 in promoting the changes they desired. In Barbados slaves outnumbered free colonists by more than two to one. West Indian influence in London, reflecting as it did the greater wealth of the West Indian planters, rendered physical demonstrations redundant and secured a reduction of the sugar duty.

The pattern in North America differed from that in the Caribbean. New England, New York and Maryland had Glorious Revolutions of their own in which hated office-holders were ejected prior to receipt of official notification of their dismissal.[85] The transition in Virginia was less turbulent because the leading men, whether planters or officials, wished for no repetition of 1676. The active detachments of the reorganized militia were under their firm control. But the hegemony of the leading planters, merchants and officials did not preclude a certain populism.[86] Virginia's fairly numerous freeholders were allowed a say in deciding which of the gentlemen should govern the colony, while even the poorer freemen and servants were encouraged to feel superior to the blacks. All white Virginians could consider themselves 'free-born Englishmen' even if they had served an indenture. In many areas they had a 'freedom of the range' – access to grazing land and to hunting rights – which would have been the envy of an English cottager. The Virginia plantocracy did not enjoy the untrammelled local power and position of its Caribbean counterpart. The advent of more slaves in subsequent decades, until they became the major labour force in tobacco, never reached the point where it demanded the expropriation of the non-slaveholding farmers; rather, it remained at a level where it reduced social antagonisms within the white colonial community by removing the axis of exploitation from inside it. Indeed, the Englishmen of the North American colonies began to enjoy more ample liberties and rights just at the point when larger numbers of slaves were being brought to their shores.

The Glorious Revolution had been carried through in the name of English liberties, yet in the colonies it confirmed undisguised racial slavery. The work of John Locke wrestled with the resultant tensions. In his *Two Treatises of Government* he famously declared: 'Slavery is so vile and miserable an estate of Man, and so directly opposite to the generous Temper and Courage of our Nation; that 'tis hardly to be conceived, that an *Englishman*, much less a *Gentleman*, should plead for it.'[87] Locke meant that Englishmen, especially English gentlemen, should utterly reject the notion that they were slaves of the royal power, even in some metaphorical sense, but there were circumstances in which they might be forced to hold slaves. Every human had the innate capacity to develop their reason and industry to the point where they were qualified to enjoy natural liberty, but primitive peoples needed tutelage before this potential could be realized. He wrote of primitive man that 'to turn loose to an unrestrain'd Liberty, before he has Reason to guide him, is the not allowing him the privilege of his nature, to be free'.[88] For Locke, rational industriousness was the great virtue, and rational man had the right to make all living creatures the instruments of his satisfaction. When the Board of Trade and Plantations was troubled by crowds of able-bodied beggars and 'idle vagabonds' in England, Locke put forward a detailed plan for placing them in houses of correction and subjecting them to three years' compulsory labour: it stipulated regarding beggars '[t]hat whoever shall counterfeit a pass shall lose his ears for forgery the first time he is found guilty thereof; and the second time, that he shall be transported to the plantations, as in the case of felony'.

In Locke's view, 'the true and proper relief of the poor ... consists in finding work for them, and taking care that they do not live like drones on the labour of others'.[89] In Lockeian terms the new slavery of the British Caribbean was a phenomenon to be understood not only in terms of possessive individualism but also with reference to persons being forced to be useful to England, perhaps to their own ultimate benefit. Locke's famous definition of property could easily be extended to plantations and their products: 'Thus the Grass my Horse has bit, the Turfs my servant has cut; and the Ore I have digg'd in any place where I have a right to them in common with others, become my *Property*.'[90] The vocation of the colonial planter gave substance to the English right to possess what Locke once described as 'the vacant land of America', since he brought it into useful cultivation.[91]

Locke's summary defence of slavery was that it represented 'the state of war continued, between a lawful Conqueror, and a Captive'.[92] In fact this formula, which Locke did little to elaborate, really did capture some of the felt experience of colonial legislators who believed that Africans were dangerous to others and to themselves if they were not subject to the slave regime.

In the years 1696–1700 Locke was a member of the newly established Board of Trade and Plantations, a body with responsibility for – among other matters – revising the legislation of Virginia and the other colonies. Locke's notion of slavery as a state of war will have been confirmed by the colonial preoccupation with slave resistance. Locke's was not a formal appointment; he attended 372 meetings during a four-and-a-half-year stint on the Board.[93] The Board had only seven members. Among the mass of papers sent to the Board would have been information relating to the 1688 slave code in Barbados, a report on the slave conspiracy on that island in 1692 and of the 92 slaves executed together with four ringleaders following its discovery. Locke should also have seen the text of Virginia's 1691 'Act for Suppressing of Outlying Slaves'. This Act pointed out that since 'many times negroes, mulattoes and other slaves unlawfully absent themselves from their masters or mistresses service, and lie hid and lurk in obscure places killing hoggs and encouraging other injuries to the inhabitants of this dominion', it was lawful for the latter 'to kill and destroy such negroes, mulattoes and other slaves'. The same Act, whose wording assumes that all 'negroes' and 'mulattoes' are slaves, took steps to ensure that no free people of colour would be added to the population of the colony:

> for the prevention of that abominable mixture and spurious issue which hereafter may encrease in this dominion, as well as negroes, mulattoes and Indians intermarrying with English, or other white women, as by their unlawful accompanying with one another, be it enacted ... that for the time to come, whatsoever English or other white man or woman being free shall intermarry

with a negroe, mulatto, or Indian man or woman, bond or free, shall within three months of such marriage be banished and removed from this dominion for ever.

Any white responsible for the birth of a mulatto bastard was to be fined £15, a third of which would go to the parish, a third to the central government and a third to the informer; if the white could not pay within one month, then they would be sold as a servant for a five-year term. The Act also observed that 'great inconvenience may happen to this country by the setting negroes and mulattoes free, by their either entertaining negroes slaves from their masters service, or receiving stolen goods, or being grown old being a charge on the country'. To prevent this the Act stipulated a manumission fee or fine sufficient to pay for the transportation of the freed slave out of the colony.[94] The Board of Trade made no objection. As a member of the Board Locke became involved in the intrigues of James Blair, the Bishop of London's Commissary in Virginia and someone connected by marriage to the leaders of Virginian society. Locke's support does seem to have helped Blair's successful campaign to oust the Governor, attacking him for his high-handed way of ignoring the representations and rights of the Virginia Assembly. Locke seems to have sincerely believed that the best government of Virginia would be one most responsible to its propertied interests.[95]

Locke regarded the defence of colonial property against arbitrary encroachment as no less worthy a cause than the vindication of metropolitan liberties. The Board of which he was a member also recommended measures to suppress piracy and illegal trade, and to terminate or absorb colonial charters, which aroused his reservations. While Locke deplored the activities of the pirates, he was suspicious of the proposals emanating from some of his colleagues, notably Blathwayt, since they involved large extensions of the powers of the metropolitan state. Thus piracy was suppressed either by replacing colonial juries with London-appointed Vice-Admiralty Courts or by requiring the accused to stand trial in London. With some reluctance Locke eventually accepted the need for these judicial expedients, which did prove successful in stamping out the pirates, and furnished a facility for trade regulation. The proposal for the 'resumption' of the charters of the proprietory colonies did not come to fruition until after Locke retired from the Board in 1701. It is not surprising, perhaps, that Locke's legacy was to be cherished by future generations of independent-minded North American colonists.[96]

Although the Board of Trade had the right to object if it wished, the slave and race laws which now obtained in England's American colonies were regarded as matters for the colonists themselves to sort out. Yet the legislation of the colonial assemblies, and the workings of local courts, constituted substantial innovations which, in principle, were binding also upon metropolitan courts. Thus the law of slavery required that the inheritance of slave status should follow the mother's condition, not that of the father, which otherwise generally prevailed under English law. Similarly, the black person in North America was now generally presumed a slave, rather than presumed free, as was the case with Europeans. Virginia's ban on interracial marriage was echoed in the laws of Maryland, North Carolina, South Carolina and, perhaps less predictably, Massachusetts.[97] While there were fewer slaves in New York or Rhode Island, the institution of slavery was nevertheless still legal there, and the condition of free people of colour was increasingly precarious.

Ira Berlin has drawn attention to a layer of free 'Atlantic creoles' to be found on both sides of the ocean, and in all parts of the Caribbean, in the seventeenth century: African and mulatto merchants, sailors and interpreters, and in the Americas free people of colour who had managed to set themselves up in a trade or acquire a plot of land.[98] In Virginia as well as in New York the free people of colour were growing in number and social significance up to the 1670s. But the growth of the slave system doomed these small communities to an increasingly narrow and harassed existence. The free people of colour naturally wished to participate in local markets, yet as the slave populations grew, so did attempts to suppress petty trading by slaves.

The London governments formed after 1689 did gradually assert the rights of the metropolis, with Parliament concerned to establish its pre-eminence within the Empire. But in one important respect the new British authorities were inclined to defer to the representations of the planters: the suspension of the monopoly privileges of the Royal African Company, a body tainted by its association with the Stuarts. The metropolitan authorities wished to facilitate the supply of slaves to the colonies, as a way of simultaneously boosting the wealth of the plantations and encouraging the loyalty of the colonists. The planters had shown an independent mettle in 1688–89, and it seemed only wise to attach them to the new order. In the months immediately succeeding the ousting of James II, the African trade was opened to independent traders.

The Company itself survived the crisis of 1688–89 only because it maintained important facilities on the African coast and still incorporated influential interests associated with the City of London. The Company's backers tried to use its role as custodian of the English forts on the African coasts to recover its position. In 1699 Parliament instead voted that independent traders should pay a duty of 10 per cent on their exports from Britain, and a variable amount per slave purchased, as a contribution to the upkeep of the Company forts. Subsequently a battle was fought, with investors in and suppliers of the Company on one side, and a burgeoning alliance of independent manufacturers, merchants and planters on the other. The controversy aroused a stormy battle of pamphlets, newspapers and parliamentary petitions – over a hundred petitions opposing the Company's policy were presented to Parliament compared with fewer than twenty supporting it. Most manufacturers and most planters thought that they would gain better terms from the independent merchants than from a chartered monopoly. Up to 1712 the separate traders were still required to pay a commission towards the upkeep of the Company forts.

Eventually victory went to the more expansive mercantile faction, with its appeal for freer trade within the colonial system. The Company was compensated for its lost privileges by receipt of a contract from the newly formed South Sea Company to supply it with the slaves that were needed to fulfil the *asiento*. The terms of the *asiento* were drawn up in such a way as to maximize the opportunities for using it as a cover for contraband with the Spanish colonies: in this the *asiento* resembled the Methuen Treaty with Portugal, whose provisions were exploited to favour a semi-clandestine trade with Brazil, and to ensure that most of Brazil's gold ended up on board the Lisbon–London packet. More generally, this dispute helped to set a pattern whereby commercial and colonial groups openly lobbied Parliament, encouraged favourable press comment and stimulated public opinion.[99]

The evidence of trade statistics demonstrated the effectiveness of the new colonial system. The performance of the plantation colonies reflected both the new pattern of demand for colonial products and the development of the entrepôt trade. Retained imports of American sugar and tobacco were valued at £687,000 annually at the port of London in the years 1699–1701, amounting to 15 per cent of the capital's incoming trade.[100] Re-exports of these products earned an equivalent sum, and made the English merchants among Europe's leading suppliers of plantation staples at this time. If information was available for Bristol and other outports, the overall value of English colonial imports and re-exports might be raised by a fifth or a quarter.

Barbados was still the richest of the plantation colonies. Although it had little more than half the total population of Virginia in 1699–1701, its exports were worth nearly 50 per cent more. In 1665–66 the island's exports had been worth £259,600, dropping to £163,000 in the troubled years 1688 and 1690–91, but rising to £423,500 in 1699–1701, of which £289,900 was muscovado sugar, £86,100 rum and £36,600 molasses.[101]

The colonial trade broke the prior pattern whereby England possessed only one exportable manufacture: woollen goods. The colonies imported nails, pots, buckles, implements and utensils of every description, together with a variety of textiles. The Navigation Acts not only channelled plantation products to the metropolis but also ensured that the plantation colonies became major customers for English goods. They permitted a multilateral pattern of trade between England, Africa, the plantation zone and the more northerly American colonies. New England and Pennsylvania had few products which they could export to England; this could have made them poor markets for the English exporter. But the colonial system permitted them to earn a surplus, selling provisions to the plantations and building ships for the Atlantic trade; with this surplus they could and did buy English manufactures. By 1701 the English exporters shipped goods worth £542,000 to the American colonies and to Africa, representing about an eighth of total domestic exports. The special relationship with Portugal, cemented by the Methuen Treaty of 1703, also furnished a prime outlet for British manufacturers and exporters: the value of exports to Portugal and Brazil was soon running at around £600,000 a year, or slightly over an eighth of the total, with Brazilian sugar and gold making a major contribution to Portuguese purchasing power. Thus the Atlantic, slave-related trades accounted for at least a fifth of English exports, a proportion set to increase.[102]

The Commonwealth Act of Settlement in Ireland had introduced a new phase of English colonial rule there, which had been broadly ratified by the Restoration. Protestant ascendancy had briefly been put in doubt by the reign of the Catholic James II, but this was removed by William III's victory at the Battle of the Boyne (1690). When James's last Irish soldiers came to terms in the following year, it was agreed that as many as wished could leave for service in the French Army. English Protestant landlords now came to control over nine-tenths of Ireland's land, and had the power to impose onerous tenancies on Catholic Irish farmers, who were obliged to offer up two-thirds of their net product as rent. The demand for provisions from the plantation colonies furnished a helpful outlet for Irish produce, which might otherwise simply have depressed prices for English agriculturists. And when Irish producers sold to the plantations, they boosted Ireland's capacity to import from England. Irish linen could also be exported to the colonies, but wool exports were banned, as they competed with England's leading trade. However, the plantation colonies were not permitted to send their produce directly to Ireland, and Catholics were excluded from conducting Ireland's overseas trade, as they were from many advantageous employments. John Cary, a leading Bristol merchant, explained what he saw as the logic of colonial commerce:

> I take England and all its plantations to be one great Body, those being so many limbs or counties belonging to it, therefore when we consume their growth we do as it were spend the Fruits of our own Land, and what thereof we sell to our Neighbours for Bullion, or such commodities as must pay for therein, brings a second Profit to the Nation. . . . This was the first design of settling Plantations

abroad, that the People of England might better maintain a Commerce and Trade among themselves, the chief Profit whereof was to redound to the centre.[103]

When Gregory King estimated in 1696 that exports took as much as a third of English manufactures each year, he exaggerated, but the fate of the colonial and Atlantic trade was indeed of great interest to sections of the commercial and manufacturing classes. Woollen exports remained a major branch of trade, while wheat and flour became one, with the colonies being customers for both. Thus a significant stratum of England's landowners and tenant farmers also had a stake in promoting foreign trade. The English ruling class at this time was beset by intense factional battles, as Whigs and Tories fought over the precise shape of the post-Revolution settlement. But just as neither grouping seriously disputed the Protestant succession, so neither questioned the salience of commercial objectives. For political, 'anti-dynastic' reasons England was ranged against Bourbon France and Spain, and allied to the United Provinces and Portugal. England's commercial interests demanded that its allies should pay as heavy a price as its enemies for the wars of King William and Queen Anne. Although alignments were complex, the Dutch connection and the Methuen Treaty with Portugal, promoted by the Whigs, safeguarded the more traditional trades, while the Tory 'blue water' strategy – taking the war to the Mediterranean and Atlantic – though risky, ultimately favoured the newer colonial and commercial interests. In the negotiation of the Treaty of Utrecht in 1713 the Tories ensured that the *asiento* to supply slaves to Spanish America passed to England.[104]

The colonial trade boom had been made possible by a prior surge in slave imports to the English islands: these totalled some 263,000 in the years 1640–1700, about a half going to Barbados alone. A little over 20,000 slaves had been imported in the years 1640–50, and just under 70,000 in 1650–76. In the last quarter-century, 173,800 slaves were imported into the English colonies, with 64,700 going to Barbados, 77,100 to Jamaica and 32,000 to the Leeward Islands. Around 1700 the total slave population of the English islands numbered 100,000, with 40,000 apiece on both Barbados and Jamaica, and 20,000 on the Leeward Islands. The white population of Barbados had dropped to 15,000 by that year, but it was still as large as that of Jamaica and the Leeward Islands combined, each of which had about 7,000 white colonists. In 1650 the North American colonies had a population of 53,000 whites and 2,000 blacks; by 1700 the white population was 265,000 and the black population, nearly all slaves, numbered 31,000. The black population of the English West Indies grew from 42 per cent of the total in 1660 to 81 per cent in 1700; in Virginia and Maryland blacks grew from 2 per cent of the population in 1660 to 13.1 per cent in 1700.[105]

The construction of colonies in the Caribbean, where over four-fifths of the population were slaves, was a remarkable phenomenon; in North

America the enslaved proportion of the population later rose to a third or more in the Southern plantation colonies without ever reaching the Caribbean level. The English plantation colonies registered a greater concentration of slaves, and a more exclusive equation of slavery with dark skin colour, than had hitherto been witnessed in any European colony. The plantations themselves were now integrated units, combining cultivation and processing and worked by a menial labour force almost solely comprised of African captives and their descendants. While a very few estates of this sort might have been found in the sixteenth-century Spanish Caribbean or in Brazil, the English-style slave plantation, first appearing in Barbados and St Kitts in the 1650s, soon spread throughout those islands, to Jamaica, to South Carolina and to parts of Virginia and Maryland. Unlike the Brazilian plantations, it could not call on the labour of Indian villagers, and was beginning to engage fewer free workers; to compensate, it embodied a more intense model of labour mobilization. Last but not least, Britain's monarchy and Parliament had conferred respectability and legitimacy upon the institutions of colonial slavery, sanctioning slave trading and furnishing colonial proprietors with legal protection and slave codes.

Finally, English colonial development had slaked the thirst of the bourgeois and petty-bourgeois consumer. Fifty thousand Africans toiled in the sweltering sun of the Caribbean to produce twenty thousand tons of sugar a year for the English table. Over a hundred ships-of-the-line, requiring for their construction the felling of 2,500 trees and each capable of hurling half a ton of hot metal a quarter of a mile in broadsides every few minutes, patrolled the seas to make them safe for the English merchantmen. The broad domestic market for plantation produce of every type strengthened the hand of the merchants and helped them dictate state policy. The British Navy had battered the Dutch, the French and the Spanish in three wars apiece, winning valuable space for its new colonial system without achieving a knock-out blow. There were, of course, other stakes at issue, but the civilized appetites of the consumer were salient among them.

In *The Rape of the Lock* Alexander Pope showed how the drawing-room now commanded global resources to satisfy its whims and cravings. He observed that coffee was *par excellence* the beverage for those concerned with calculation, chocolate that of polite society; in both cases sugar would be added. The habit of smoking tobacco, using sugar and taking sweetened coffee, tea, and chocolate was spreading down through the social formation as urbanization proceeded, the professional and clerical classes grew, and waged or salaried labour became more important in both town and country. The serving of tea or coffee, with sugar, became a sociable and respectable domestic ritual. The new – and increasingly popular – luxuries baited the hook of greater dependence on stipends, fees, interest payments and wages. Sugar consumption per head in Britain rose from 2 lb in the 1660s to 4 lb in the 1690s, and to 8 lb in the period 1710 to 1719. Carole Shammas points out that retained imports of around 4 lb of sugar per head were sufficient to supply nearly 900,000 people, or a quarter of the adult population, with about half a pound of sugar a week, enough to be regularly sweetening their food and drink.[106]

The coffee-house milieu was responsible for sustaining the first newspapers, partly subsidized by advertising, and fostering oppositional politics under the last Stuarts. While financiers used the coffee shops, so did political radicals. During the Exclusion Crisis of 1679–81, several of the coffee houses in Bristol were closed down. A historian of popular culture in Bristol observes: 'Coffee house news was not absorbed privately but discussed publicly and indeed the cryptic, often allusive style of the reporting required such public interpretation.'[107] But after the Glorious Revolution a portion of this oppositional culture became the establishment. The salience of exotic produce in the new order of things is neatly symbolized by the fact that the newly established institutions of the City of London – the Bank of England, the Stock Exchange, Lloyd's Underwriters, several of the merchant banks – had been founded on the premises of coffee houses.[108] The only snag that might be detected in the new pattern of metropolitan consumption, imperial commerce and finance was a certain slackening in the tempo of agricultural advance, almost as if maritime and colonial ventures were drawing resources away from domestic development. Before investigating the colonial contribution to accumulation in general and British accumulation in particular it is necessary to scrutinize French competition – Chapter VII – and the general principles of the new plantation systems – Chapter VIII.

Notes

1. Peter Fryer, *Staying Power*, pp. 4, 26–7; Kim Hall, *Things of Darkness*, pp. 23–4.

2. Theodore K. Rabb, *Enterprise and Empire, Merchant and Gentry Investment in the Expansion of England, 1575–1630*, Cambridge, MA 1967, pp. 68–9, 93–5, 121, 127–8; Andrews, *Trade, Plunder and Settlement*, pp. 280–303. For demographic factors encouraging the privateering exploits of the gentry see Ralph Davis, *The Rise of the Atlantic Economies*, London 1973, p. 140.

3. Samuel Purchas, *Purchas His Pilgrimage*, 3rd edn, vol. 1, London 1617; for Angola and Brazil pp. 869–76 and 1040–43; for Virginia, pp. 940–47.

4. R.F. Foster, *Modern Ireland 1600–1972*, London 1988, pp. 13, 70, 130.

5. Angus Calder, *Revolutionary Empire: The Rise of the English-Speaking Empire from the Fifteenth Century to the 1780s*, London 1981, p. 153; Anthony Pagden, *Lords of All the World*, p. 96. Thomas Hobbes joined the Virginia Company as a director shortly after this, subsequently attending thirty-seven meetings of its council, including some concerned with its Somers Island subsidiary. His notion of the 'war of all against all', and the sanction this supposedly lent to absolute government, could well have echoed his knowledge of the establishment of Virginia as much as the English Civil War conflicts which are usually mentioned in this context. The Scriptural Leviathan was, of course, a sea-beast. For Hobbes

and the Virginia Company see Quentin Skinner, *Reason and Rhetoric in the Philosophy of Hobbes*, Cambridge 1996, pp. 222–4.

6. Andrews, *Trade, Plunder and Settlement*, p. 295.

7. Carl Bridenbaugh, *Vexed and Troubled Englishmen, 1590–1642*, New York 1968, p. 197.

8. Jonathan Israel, *Dutch Primacy in World Trade*, p. 410.

9. D.C. Coleman, *The Economy of England, 1450–1750*, Oxford 1977, pp. 67–8.

10. Christopher Hill, *The Century of Revolution 1603–1714*, p. 41.

11. Karen O. Kupperman, *Providence Island 1630–1641: The Other Puritan Colony*, Cambridge 1993, pp. 166–80.

12. Robert Brenner, *Merchants and Revolution: Commercial Change, Political Conflict, and London's Overseas Traders, 1550–1653*, Princeton, NJ 1993, pp. 30–39.

13. Wesley Frank Craven, *White, Red and Black: The Seventeenth Century Virginian*, Charlottesville, VA 1971, p. 3. Abbot Emerson Smith, *Colonists in Bondage: White Servitude and Convict Labor in America, 1607–1776*, Chapel Hill, NC 1947, pp. 307–37. In subsequent years some indentured servants could claim land for themselves once they had served out their contract.

14. Quoted in 'Blacks in Virginia: Evidence from the First Decade', in Alden T. Vaughan, *Roots of American Racism: Essays on the Colonial Experience*, Oxford 1995, pp. 128–35.

15. Estimates taken from Jack Greene, *Pursuits of Happiness: The Social Development of Early Modern British Colonies and the Formation of American Culture*, Chapel Hill, NC 1988, pp. 7–8.

16. Richard Dunn, *Sugar and Slaves: The Rise of the Planter Class in the English West Indies: 1624–1713*, London 1975, pp. 3–45, 65; Henri Blet, *Histoire de la colonisation française*, I, Paris 1947, pp. 107–10; Ralph Davis, *The Rise of the Atlantic Economies*, London 1973, pp. 125–42.

17. Allan Kulikoff, *The Agrarian Origins of American Capitalism*, Charlottesville, VA 1992, pp. 183–208.

18. This being one of Jack Greene's principal conclusions in *The Intellectual Construction of America: Exceptionalism and Identity from 1492–1800*, Chapel Hill, NC 1993.

19. Gary A. Puckrein, *Little England: Plantation Society and Anglo-Barbadian Politics, 1627–1700*, New York 1984, p. 31.

20. Beckles, *White Servitude and Black Slavery in Barbados 1627–1615*, Knoxville, TN 1989, pp. 103, 119, 121, 124.

21. Puckrein, *Little England*, p. 62.

22. Brenner, *Merchants and Revolution*, pp. 163–4, 174.

23. Richard Ligon, *A True and Exact History of Barbados*, London 1657, pp. 46, 86–98; Dunn, *Sugar and Slaves*, pp. 87, 203. For an informative survey of the early rise of sugar in Barbados and other Caribbean islands see Robert Carlyle Batie, 'Why Sugar? Economic Cycles and the Changing of Staples on the English and French Antilles, 1624–54', *Journal of Caribbean History*, no. 8, 1976, pp. 1–41.

24. The nature and significance of the new merchants is brilliantly illuminated by Robert Brenner, *Merchants and Revolution*, pp. 92–197; and David Harris Sachs, *The Widening Gate: Bristol and the Atlantic Economy, 1450–1700*, Berkeley, CA and London 1991, pp. 331–62.

25. Richard Pares, 'Merchants and Planters', *Economic History Review*, suppl. no. 4, Cambridge 1960, pp. 4–6; Robert Brenner, 'The Social Basis of English Commercial Expansion', *Journal of Economic History*, vol. 32, 1972, pp. 361–84; Ralph Davis, *The Rise of the English Shipping Industry in the Seventeenth and Eighteenth Centuries*, Newton Abbot 1962, pp. 159–74, 267–97.

26. Jordan Goodman, *Tobacco in History*, pp. 60–61; Shammas, *The Preindustrial Consumer in England and America*, p. 79.

27. Mathias de l'Obel quoted by Jordan Goodman, *Tobacco in History*, p. 47. For the spread of tobacco see Shammas, *The Preindustrial Consumer*, pp. 78–81.

28. Deerr, *A History of Sugar*, II, p. 528. See also Fernand Braudel, *Capitalism and Material Life*, London 1976, pp. 178–81; Sidney Mintz, *Sweetness and Power: The Place of Sugar in Modern History*, London 1985; Shammas, *The Preindustrial Consumer*, pp. 81–3.

29. Hilary Beckles, *A History of Barbados*, Cambridge 1990, p. 18; Beckles, *White Servitude and Black Slavery in Barbados*, p. 31.

30. Winthrop Jordan, *White Over Black: American Attitudes Toward the Negro, 1550–1812*, Chapel Hill, NC 1968, p. 65.

31. Sir Edward Coke, *The First Part of the Institutes of the Law of England*, fourth edn, London 1739, Lib. II, Cap. XI, p. 116. Coke's invocation of the *jus gentium* illustrates Perry Anderson's argument concerning the importance of Roman Law to the birth of early modern capitalism. See Anderson, *Lineages*, p. 422.

32. R. Wilkinson, *Lot's Wife: A Sermon Preached in Paul's Cross*, London 1607, quoted in Vaugn, *Roots of American Racism*, pp. 6, 255.

33. Ronald Sanders, *Lost Tribes and Promised Lands: The Origins of American Racism*, Boston, MA 1978, p. 287.

34. See also Jack Greene, *The Intellectual Construction of America*, Chapel Hill, NC 1993, p. 61 and Sanders, *Lost Tribes and Promised Lands*.

35. Quoted in Sanders, *Lost Tribes and Promised Lands*, p. 332.

36. Elizabeth Donnan, *Documents Illustrative of the History of the Slave Trade*, Washington, DC 1932, p. 8.

37. Ibid., p. 4.

38. Ibid., p. 8.

39. Gerald F. De Jong, *The Dutch in America*, Boston, MA 1975, pp. 14–25.

40. Sanders, *Lost Tribes and Promised Lands*, p. 358.

41. See T.H. Breen and Stephen Innes, *'Myne Owne Ground': Race and Freedom on Virginia's Eastern Shore, 1640–1676*, New York 1980.

42. James Perry, *The Formation of a Society on Virginia's Eastern Shore, 1615–1655*, Chapel Hill, NC 1990, pp. 106–8.

43. Beckles, *White Servitude and Black Slavery in Barbados*, p. 85; see also pp. 79–114.

44. Ibid., p. 103; Beckles, *A History of Barbados*, p. 37.

45. Beckles, *White Servitude and Black Slavery in Barbados*, p. 75.

46. David Galenson, *White Servitude in Colonial America: An Economic Analysis*, Cambridge 1981, p. 25.

47. Robert Brenner, *Merchants and Revolution*, pp. 316–92, 494–557.

48. Puckrein, *Little England*, p. 118. My account of events in Barbados largely follows this work but see also Vincent Harlow, *A History of Barbados*, Oxford 1926, especially pp. 10–20, 65; and Frederick Spurdle, *Early West Indian Government*, Palmerston North (NZ) n.d., pp. 12–20.

49. Bernard Capp, *Cromwell's Navy: The Fleet and the English Revolution, 1648–1660*, Oxford 1989, pp. 136, 262–73.

50. See, for example, the repeated invocation of slavery as the antithesis of the aspiration of Englishmen in Hill, *The Century of Revolution*, pp. 105, 106, 108; see also Christopher Hill, *Liberty Against the Law*, London 1996.

51. Sir Thomas Browne, *Pseudoxia Epidemica, Enquiries into Common or Vulgar Errors* (London 1646), Volume 1, chapter XI, Robin Robbins, ed., Oxford 1981, pp. 518–23. See also Joan Bennet, *Sir Thomas Browne*, Cambridge 1962, pp. 182–4. Kim Hall rightly draws attention to Browne's remark that Southern Europeans, while dark, 'do not deserve so low a name as tawny', and that the inhabitants of the 'torrid zone' 'descend not so low as unto blacknesse'. However, Hall does not perhaps sufficiently distinguish between George Best, with his phobic notion of the 'infection' of blackness and the curse of Noah, and Browne, who, while treating white skin as the norm, challenges the equation of hereditary sin and skin colour. See Hall, *Things of Darkness*, pp. 11–12.

52. Fryer, *Staying Power*, p. 27.

53. *Calendar of State Papers, Colonial Series, 1574–1660* (London 1860), pp. 324, 343, quoted in Peter Wilson Coldham, *Emigrants in Chains, 1609–1776*, Baltimore, MD 1992, p. 48.

54. Brownlow, *Lectures on Slavery and Serfdom*, pp. 23, 40. Clearly, if it was possible to turn Irish youths into 'Englishmen' then they could become loyal tenants or props of imperial expansion. Increasingly African slaves were being acquired as drudges in the Caribbean; though they might be described as 'English Negroes' this was not to mean that they or their descendants could ever become 'Englishmen'. However, at the limit, when colonial policy dictated, some recognition was offered to a group of Spanish Negroes and mulattoes who held out against the English conquest in remote or mountainous districts of Jamaica. A proclamation by the Governor of 1663 read: 'That Juan Luyola and the rest of the negroes of his palenque, on account of their submission and services to the English, shall have grants of land and enjoy all the privileges of Englishmen, but must bring up their children in the English tongue. ... That Luyola be colonel of the black regiment of militia, and he and others

appointed magistrates over the negroes to decide all cases except those of life and death.' Quoted in Michael Craton, *Testing the Chains: Resistance to Slavery in the British West Indies*, London 1982, p. 71. The English were here directly imitating Spanish tactics in a situation where there was great advantage in turning dangerous enemies into valuable allies. While there were intermittent agreements between the colonial authorities and one or another group of maroons it was not until 1739 that a longstanding treaty was achieved.

55. Godfrey Davies, *The Restoration of Charles II, 1658–1660*, London 1955, pp. 66–7; Hilary Beckles, *White Servitude and Black Slavery in Barbados*, pp. 52–4.

56. Quoted in Brenner, *Merchants and Revolution*, p. 593.

57. Stephen Saunders Webb, *1676: The End of American Independence*, New York 1984, p. 104.

58. Editor's Introduction in Walter Minchinton, ed., *The Growth of English Overseas Trade in the Seventeenth and Eighteenth Centuries*, p. 10; Ralph Davis, *English Overseas Trade, 1500–1700*, London 1973, pp. 55–6. See also J.E. Farnell, 'The Navigation Act of 1651, the First Dutch War and the London Merchant Community', *Economic History Review*, 2nd series, XIV, 1964, pp. 439–54.

59. Jeremy Taylor, *Ductor Dubitandium*, London 1676, pp. 167–8, 184, quoted in Tuck, *Natural Rights Theories*, pp. 111–12.

60. Hobbes's thought affirmed the right of the slaveholder on the grounds that the slave implicitly assented to bondage by not committing suicide. But *Leviathan* also recommended the need for a sceptical scrutiny of the Bible. In fact it was such a controversial work that even its pro-slavery conclusions did not offer colonial slavery the sort of practical legitimation which it required. In this respect the works of Selden, Taylor and Vaughan were far more important.

61. The above legislation, indicating the 1660s watershed, is detailed and discussed in John Hope Franklin, *From Slavery to Freedom: A History of American Negroes*, New York 1950, pp. 65, 71; Edmund S. Morgan, *American Slavery, American Freedom*, New York 1975, pp. 300–01, 312, 333; Helen Catterall, *Judicial Cases Concerning American Slavery and the Negro*, Washington, DC 1926, pp. 6, 9; Beckles, *A History of Barbados*, p. 33; Dunn, *Sugar and Slaves*, p. 246.

62. Helen Catterall, *Judicial Cases Concerning American Slavery and the Negro*, p. 57.

63. Ibid., p. 61.

64. Morgan, *American Slavery, American Freedom*, p. 312.

65. This remark is quoted by David Galenson in an essay which furnishes further reasons for believing that the new laws confirming slave property helped to clear the way for the expansion of slaveholding in these colonies; see David Galenson 'Economic Aspects of the Growth of Slavery in the Seventeenth Century Chesapeake', in Solow, *Slavery and the Rise of the Atlantic System*, pp. 265–93 (p. 274).

66. Dunn, *Sugar and Slaves*, pp. 87, 202.

67. Ibid., pp. 155, 203, 312.

68. Ibid., pp. 170–71; the trend for slaves to be trained to replace free employees as well as indentured servants is discussed in David Galenson, *White Servitude in Colonial America*, Cambridge 1981, pp. 134–41.

69. Puckrein, *Little England*, p. 155. Writing of the same period Dunn refers to the 'consolidated affluence' of the richest 175 planters; all seven of the colonels of the militia were drawn from this group. Dunn, *Sugar and Slaves*, p. 170. While Dunn stresses the evidence for high mortality among white colonists, Puckrein points out that, relatively speaking, Barbados was probably more healthy because of the absence of swamps and ponds in which disease carriers could establish themselves (pp. 181–94).

70. K.G. Davies, *The Royal African Company*, New York 1970, pp. 41–4, 63–5.

71. Ibid., pp. 62, 74, 319, 345–6. Galenson urges that, contrary to Adam Smith's belief, the Company never had a watertight monopoly and that, notwithstanding some insider dealing, its overall performance was impressively businesslike. Galenson, *Traders, Planters and Slaves*.

72. Quotes from Webb, *1676: The End of American Independence*, pp. 5, 16.

73. Morgan, *American Slavery, American Freedom*, pp. 260–70.

74. Ibid., p. 331. See also T.H. Breen, 'A Changing Labor Force and Race Relations in Virginia, 1660-1710', *Journal of Social History*, vol. 7, 1973, pp. 3–25.

75. Quoted in Donald Wright, *African Americans in the Colonial Era: From African Origins through the American Revolution*, Arlington Heights, IL 1990, p. 63.

76. James Lang, *Conquest and Commerce: Spain and England in the Americas*, New York 1975, pp. 105–27; Craven, *White, Red and Black*, p. 83; Paul E. Lovejoy, 'The Volume of the Atlantic Slave Trade: A Synthesis', *Journal of African History*, no. 23, 1982, pp. 473–501 (p. 478).

77. Morgan Godwyn, *The Negro's and Indians Advocate*, London 1680, pp. 39–40, 41, 82–4. For an informative essay on Godwyn see Vaughan, *Roots of American Racism*, pp. 55–81.

78. Godwyn, *Negro's and Indians Advocate*, p. 13. Similar points were made by Richard Baxter in *A Christian Dictionary* (1673) and Thomas Tryon in his *Advice to a Planter*. But the isolated nature of such representations is made clear by Lester B. Scherer, *Slavery and the Churches in Early America, 1619–1819*, Grand Rapids, MI 1975, p. 59.

79. Godwyn, *Negro's and Indians Advocate*, p. 19.

80. Ibid., p. 147.

81. For an illuminating discussion of Behn, see Moira Ferguson, *Subject to Others: British Women Writers and Colonial Slavery*, New York 1992.

82. These changes are analysed by David Watts, *The West Indies: Patterns of Development, Culture and Environmental Change since 1492*, Cambridge 1987, pp. 212–32, 319–447.

83. Ian K. Steele, *Politics of Colonial Policy: The Board of Trade in Administration, 1696–1720*, Oxford 1968, pp. 42–68.

84. John Brewer, *The Sinews of Power: War, Money and the English State, 1688–1783*, Cambridge, MA 1988, pp. 21–4, 66; Brenner, *Merchants and Revolution*, pp. 713–16; Dunn, *Sugar and Slaves*, pp. 102–3; Lang, *Conquest and Commerce*, pp. 159–71.

85. David Lovejoy, *The Glorious Revolution in America*, New York 1972, pp. 225 ff. See also Ian Steele, *The English Atlantic, 1675–1740*, Oxford 1976, pp. 94–110.

86. Morgan, *American Slavery, American Freedom*, pp. 338–62.

87. John Locke, *Two Treatises of Government: A Critical Edition*, edited by Peter Laslett, Cambridge 1960, p. 159.

88. Ibid., p. 55.

89. 'Draft of a Representation Containing a Scheme of Methods for the Employment of the Poor. Proposed by Mr Locke, the 26'h October 1697', in John Locke, *Political Writings*, David Wooton, ed., London 1993, pp. 446–61 (pp. 449, 452). The editor's suggestion that the draft represents a collective rather than individual view is belied by the fact that it was rejected by the committee. See also Paul Rahe, *Republics Ancient and Modern: Classical Republicanism and the American Revolution*, Chapel Hill, NC 1992, pp. 518, 1028–9 n.

90. Locke, 'Second Treatise', section 28, in *Political Writings*. The extent to which Locke's formulas correspond to the categories of a capitalist economy have been disputed, C.B. MacPherson seeing 'possessive individualism' as basically capitalist, James Tully pointing to non-capitalist elements in Lockian theory and Neal Wood urging that Locke was an advocate of the early, agrarian phase of capitalist development (Neal Wood, *John Locke and Agrarian Capitalism*, Berkeley and Los Angeles 1984, pp. 74, 86–90). Wood's conclusion has something to recommend it, but Locke's apparent endorsement of the development of the slave plantations does seem to argue the presence of what is, strictly speaking, a non-capitalist strand in his thinking.

91. Pagden, *Lords of All the World*, p. 77.

92. Locke, 'The Second Treatise on Government', *Political Writings*, p. 273. In the 1670s Locke had drafted 'The Fundamental Constitutions of Carolina' (*Political Writings*, pp. 210–32) in which it was stated: 'Every freeman of Carolina shall have absolute power and authority over his negro slaves, of what opinion or religion whatsoever' (p. 230).

93. I.K. Steele, *Politics of Colonial Policy: The Board of Trade in Colonial Administration, 1696–1720*, Oxford 1968, pp. 173–4.

94. William Hening, ed., *Statutes at Large*, New York 1823, vol. III, pp. 86–7.

95. Parke Rouse, Jnr, *James Blair of Virginia*, Chapel Hill, NC 1971, p. pp. 114–16. Blair was an unscrupulous and dissembling individual who was, in the course of time, to unseat no fewer than three governors. He gave Locke the impression that he and his friends favoured enlightened projects, such as the foundation of the college of William and Mary and the provision of independent stipends for priests. It is possible that he mentioned to Locke a provision for the 'Christian education of Indians, Negroes and Mulattoes' which was to be added to the draft of the proposed reform of the Virginian clergy which would be undertaken once Andros was out of the way. Whether or not this was the case, the provision for religious instruction soon disappeared without trace (p. 147).

96. Steele, *Politics of Colonial Policy*, pp. 42–83; Jerome Huyler, *Locke in America*, Lawrence, KA 1995.

97. William W. Wiecek, 'The Statutory Law of Slavery and Race in the Thirteen Mainland Colonies of British America', in P.C. Hoffer, ed., *Africans Become Afro-Americans*, New York 1988, pp. 262–84.

98. Ira Berlin, 'From Creole to African: Atlantic Creoles and the Origins of African-American Society in Mainland North America', *William and Mary Quarterly*, vol. LIII, no. 2, April 1996, pp. 251–88.

99. Davies, *The Royal Africa Company*, pp. 129–52; Alison Gilbert Olson, *Making the Empire Work: London and American Interest Groups, 1690–1790*, Cambridge, MA 1992.

100. J.H. Plumb, *The Growth of Political Stability in England, 1625–1725*, London 1969, pp. 24–6, 118–19, 129.

101. David Eltis, 'The Total Product of Barbados, 1674–1701', *Journal of Economic History*, vol. 55, no. 2, June 1995, pp. 321–38.

102. Davis, *English Overseas Trade*, p. 56; H.E.S. Fisher, *The Portugal Trade*, London 1971, p. 126.

103. John Cary, quoted in David H. Sachs, *The Widening Gate: Bristol and the Atlantic Community*, Berkeley, CA 1991, p. 340.

104. J.R. Jones, *Britain and the World, 1649–1815*, London 1980, pp. 149–79.

105. Dunn, *Sugar and Slaves*, p. 312; John J. McCusker and Russell R. Menard, *The Economy of British America, 1607–1789*, Chapel Hill, NC 1985, pp. 54, 222.

106. Shammas, *The Preindustrial Consumer*, pp. 81–2.

107. Jonathan Barry, 'Popular Culture in Seventeenth Century Bristol', in Barry Reay, ed., *Popular Culture in Seventeenth Century England*, London 1985, pp. 59–90 (p. 69).

108. Schivelbusch, *Tastes of Paradise*, pp. 15–79.

VII

The Construction of the French Colonial System

Thomas Le Gendre (1638–1706) was the coiner of the phrase *laissez-faire* as applied to politics and the economy. Le Gendre owned vast interests in Africa and the New World.

Murray Rothbard, *Economic Thought before Adam Smith*

The society of the Spectacle reached its apogee in the epoch of Louis XIV.

Régis Debray, *Remarks on Guy Debord*

The Coffee-Man

The development of the French-controlled Antilles lagged far behind that of the English islands during most of the seventeenth century. The ingredients for the spontaneous growth of plantation agriculture were considerably weaker in France than in England, though just strong enough to sustain the beginnings of colonization in the Antilles. Demand for plantation products developed more slowly, and despite the large size of the mother country, there was only a comparatively modest trickle of French emigrants. French agriculture was less buoyant, less commercial and less capitalist than that of England, with no equivalent to the enclosure of common lands, sale of Church property or extensive irrigation schemes which had helped to transform the English countryside in the sixteenth and early seventeenth centuries. Peasant landownership was more widespread, and the expectations associated with extensive family ties inhibited geographical mobility.[1]

In the longer run the French colonization effort was to depend more on the state and less on the spontaneous impulses of civil society than had been the case with England. But during the first half of the seventeenth century the French royal authorities were preoccupied by their attempts to strengthen the monarch's power against recalcitrant Huguenots and nobles. This Absolutist project detracted from French colonization in the New World, which – until the 1660s – was left largely in the hands of adventurers and missionaries, enjoying some official patronage but very little material support.

The persecution of the Huguenots blighted several key Atlantic ports, and sought to deny to the French colonies a promising source of immigrants. Some Huguenots went over to the Dutch or English; in 1628, the year of the siege of La Rochelle, a French Huguenot privateer, in the pay of the English, captured the fur-laden returning fleet of the newly formed Company of New France. Other Huguenots sought refuge in the Dutch colonies. The quarrels between the Crown and the nobility also took a toll. In 1632 the Duke of Montmorency, who had undertaken an effective reorganization of the French Navy, was executed for conspiracy. The authorities were subsequently distracted by the challenge of the Fronde and the Ormé of 1652, a popular revolt in Bordeaux which erupted in its wake. Such conflicts nourished royal distrust of the spontaneous impulses of Atlantic development. France's Catholic kings liked to recall the central role of the French kingdom in the Crusades; with the power of Spain faltering, they hoped to inherit its mantle and global responsibilities as the leading Catholic power. Richelieu and Mazarin were interested in colonial projects, but wished to be sure that they would remain under royal control and furnish an outlet for French Catholic proselytism. The Jesuits were given wide responsibilities in the French colonization of North America; with French help Capuchin missions were also mounted in Africa, with a Dominican mission in the Caribbean. The prominence of missionaries reflected the high-mindedness of the French colonial project and the belief that France was the native's best friend. In an effort to encourage colonization by Catholic families the French missionaries sent back glowing reports, stressing the fertility and beauty of the islands, their delicious fruits, fine palm trees, convenient beaches and friendly Indians. When published as brochures these furnished early examples of a modern vision of the Caribbean.

The case for a French colonial strategy was made by the Huguenot Antoine de Montchrétien in his *Traité de l'Économie politique* (1615), a work which influenced Richelieu. Montchrétien argued that a country the size of France needed colonies, and that they would strengthen national power. While it echoed some of the favourite themes of English colonial propaganda, Montchrétien's text envisaged something closer to the classic formulas of medieval colonization, such as had been practised on the European periphery, and the notion that France should reach out to the native peoples: 'Let us declare that the descendants of the French who live in these countries, together with those savages who have been brought to a knowledge of the faith, will be counted and reputed as native French, without needing to take out any letter of naturalization.'[2]

In North America the French made greater efforts than the English to cultivate friendly relations with the Indian nations. Since the fur trade furnished the main commercial resource of Quebec, and since French settlement remained very sparse – reaching only around 2,000 *colons* in 1660 – the competition for land which bedevilled relations between the English colonies and Indian nations was not so intense. In these circumstances French policy, guided by the Capuchins and Jesuits, cultivated a more tolerant policy towards the Native Americans. In the early days marriage between Frenchmen and Indian women was encouraged by the payment of a bounty. Enslavement of Indians was forbidden, and efforts were made to give them a Catholic and French education. The French developed good relations with an Indian people they called the Hurons, who practised agriculture, and many of them converted to Christianity. However, the alliance with the Huron entailed hostile relations with their enemies, principally the Iroquois federation. Following an Iroquois attack in 1649, the Huron settlements were largely overrun. With difficulty small groups of French colonists and friendly Indians were obliged to rebuild a trading network that reached far into the interior. Because of its own problems, French North America was unable to assist colonization efforts in the Caribbean, apart from some modest contribution from those involved in the fisheries.

In the Caribbean there was difficulty in finding the resources to sustain the arduous work of clearing a tropical island and defending its settlement against the native Caribs and the Spanish. The first royal patent, establishing a colony on St Christopher, was granted to Sieur d'Esnambuc, a privateer and Norman noble, who sailed with a group of colonists in the ships *La Catholique* and *La Cardinale* in 1626. D'Esnambuc proved a tenacious colonial governor, defending the St Christopher settlement and later supervising the colonization of the larger neighbouring islands of Martinique and Guadeloupe; a fragile *modus vivendi* with the surviving local Caribs was reached, though many withdrew to other islands. D'Esnambuc was succeeded by his nephew, Sieur Du Parquet, as proprietor and Governor of Martinique (1637–59), and the latter was succeeded as proprietor by his widow and other relatives (1659–64). The D'Esnambucs and Du Parquets were loyal servants of their King, but the colonies they commanded survived only through exchanges and understandings with the Dutch and the English in the Caribbean. For defence and the maintenance of order they relied on a militia recruited from the colonists.

In 1635 the royal authorities chartered a company trading with Guinea, and in 1648 Louis XIII specifically sanctioned a trade in African slaves so long as arrangements were made to bring them to Christianity.[3] But most slaves introduced to the French islands were sold by Dutch traders. The leading French planters still felt French and spoke French, but the society they governed was becoming creole. Interestingly, the Caribs, now increasingly crowded out of the larger islands, made a distinctive and enduring contribution to that society: a new creole language. A French priest who had lived for twelve years in Dominica and Guadeloupe wrote of the Caribs in 1647: 'They have a jargon or specific language through which they deal with us, which is Spanish, French, *Caraibe* pell-mell at the same time.'[4]

An Experiment in Mercantilism

The work of colonization was financed partly by the French *marine de guerre* and partly by merchants from Dieppe and Le Havre. But while the Navy continued to favour maintenance of French colonies in the Caribbean, the French merchants failed to keep pace with the growth of their plantations. The colonists soon learnt that tobacco cultivation was the best way of underwriting the costs of colonization, and that Dutch merchants would advance them supplies. The success of the St Christopher Company prompted incorporation into a wider entity, the Company of the Isles of America, which initiated the settlement of the neighbouring islands of Martinique and Guadeloupe. The new Company undertook to supply 4,000 *engagés* (indentured servants) to the newly settled islands as a basic labour force. Its sponsor and President in Paris was François Fouquet, a *conseiller du roy* and associate of Richelieu. The dispatch of a French naval squadron also gave evidence of official interest in the colonization effort. By the mid 1640s there were 5,000–7,000 French colonists in the Caribbean, about half of them *engagés*, and as yet few slaves. A total of some 20,000 French emigrants had left for the Caribbean and North America up to the year 1640, compared with four or five times that number of English emigrants over the same period.[5] Officially only good Catholics could settle in the French colonies; when a parcel of Huguenots were discovered on St Christopher they were sent to capture and colonize Tortuga, the buccaneer stronghold on the north coast of Santo Domingo.

In a familiar pattern the Company of the Isles of America did not thrive, though its governors prospered as owners of large slave plantations. In 1648 the Company went bankrupt after its authority had been defied by the governors. In an arrangement devised by Nicolas Fouquet, son of François and himself a high-flying royal official, the governors were allowed to purchase the various islands and become autonomous governor-proprietors. The French settlements flourished in the 1650s, beginning to cultivate sugar on a larger scale. When Recife fell in 1654 many Dutch traders and refugees turned to French rather than English planters, since the United Provinces were at war with England. By 1655 the French islands contained some 13,000 whites and 10,000 black slaves: Martinique and Guadeloupe had now overtaken St Christopher in size, accounting for about 5,000 each of the French colonists. By 1660 the trade of the French islands required over 100 ships a year, only four of these from French ports.[6]

The great Finance Minister Colbert was later to estimate, perhaps exaggerating a little, that sugar exports from the French Antilles at this time had been worth 2 million livres, or roughly £100,000 in sterling, and exports of other staples 1 million livres, roughly £50,000. Presiding over this colonial boom was the glittering figure of Fouquet, *surintendant des finances* of the kingdom, patron of the governor-proprietors, and himself the owner of plantations. After a lavish entertainment at Fouquet's Château de Vaux, Louis XIV complained that his minister lived in greater splendour than himself. The overmighty *surintendant* was dismissed and disgraced in 1661, leading to a new phase in colonial policy, implemented by Colbert. Fouquet was charged with self-enrichment – somewhat unfairly, since his whole fortune had been pledged to secure loans to the King; with his passing, colonial development lost its quasi-autonomous character and was subordinated to national objectives.[7]

In 1664 Colbert established the *Compagnie des Indes Occidentales*, or West India Company, enjoying a monopoly on all the trade with the French Antilles. Since France had been buying sugar from the Dutch at an annual cost of 1,885,000 livres, much of it originally produced by French colonists, the setting up of this monopoly is not difficult to explain. Colbert's Company ran into stiff opposition from the planters and colonists. But the dispatch of the Comte de Tracy as Governor General for the whole of French America, backed by a strong naval squadron, established a new metropolitan authority. The prospect of war with England persuaded recalcitrant proprietors to accept the protection the Company could offer; however, a planter revolt in Martinique in 1666 led to relaxation of the ban on trade with independent French merchants. The West India Company lasted only a decade, made no trading profits, and failed to expand basic plantation capacity. Nevertheless, it was highly successful, since during its brief existence the trade of the French islands was entirely rerouted; by 1674, 131 French ships sailed to the Antilles compared with the four of 1660. This increase in maritime traffic also helped to facilitate emigration. Colbert replaced the Company with the direct authority of the royal government. Colonial commerce was henceforth to be regulated by the principle of the *exclusif*. Only ships from designated French ports could trade with the colonies: duties would be payable at these ports unless the produce was to be re-exported, in which case a rebate of duty was forthcoming.

During the period of proprietary rule the larger planters had established refineries to make the finest white sugar. Colbert allowed the existing refineries to continue in operation, but discouraged further construction of refineries by placing a heavier duty on white sugar. His mercantilist policy boosted the commercial development of such ports as Bordeaux, Nantes, La Rochelle and St Malo. In one area a monopoly still reigned, at least formally: the supply of slaves. The Company had sent *engagés* to the islands, and contracted for slaves with two companies established for the Africa trade, the Sénégal and Guinea companies. These companies, in receipt of a royal patent and backed by the Navy, continued to enjoy a formal monopoly on slave supplies to the colonies. Nevertheless, since labourers were in short supply, French or foreign interlopers usually found little difficulty selling slave cargoes in the French Antilles. The winding up of the West India Company had a beneficial effect on colonial production. Sugar output in the French islands had totalled 5,800 tons in 1674: it rose to 8,700 tons in 1682, or just under half of the output of the English islands at this latter date. In 1660 there had been 2,642 African slaves on Martinique and 2,489 French colonists; by 1684 there were 10,656 slaves and 4,857 colonists; in Guadeloupe the slave population was recorded at 4,601 in 1687, with 3,210 whites.[8]

While all French colonists resented the controls on their commerce, those of Saint Domingue were the most assertive. Nearly every decade from 1670 witnessed a major rebellion or conspiracy in this colony directed at the metropolitan authorities. The Northern and Western parts of Santo Domingo, the deserted *bando del norte*, had originally been seized by French settlers from Tortuga without benefit of any colonial charter. In 1664 French Saint Domingue had been incorporated within the Charter of the West India Company, and a governor had been appointed to it. In 1670 the colonists rose up in arms against both Governor and Company, because of an attempt to stop them trading with the Dutch. This revolt was quelled only by sending a squadron from the Lesser Antilles. The West India Company had some success in promoting tobacco cultivation in Saint

Domingue – the colony produced 2.5 million lb in 1674, with half a million supplied by the other French islands – but thereafter the formation of a tobacco monopoly in France blocked further development. This monopoly, set up for tax-farming purposes, was initially made out in favour of Madame de Maintenon, who sold on the contract to a consortium.

The farm was initially obliged to purchase tobacco from French planters at prices it chose, and could resell it outside France if this offered greater profits. It could also buy foreign tobacco if it deemed this convenient. The production of tobacco in France itself was banned. However, the producers of Saint Domingue were unhappy with the monopoly's purchasing policies, and the monopoly complained about the poor quality of the French colonial product. Those running the monopoly discovered that the dry Virginia leaf was preferred by the French consumer and that it could be purchased cheaply in Europe, either directly from England, later Scotland, or via Dutch intermediaries. Until the early eighteenth century the monopoly was still constrained to buy French Caribbean tobacco, but the operators of this tax farm could prove that it was bad for revenues. In the 1690s the English government was able to raise around £200,000 annually from tobacco duties, while the net yield of the French tobacco monopoly was only 800,000 livres, or roughly £50,000.[9]

This remarkable violation of mercantilist principles – or rather, assertion of one mercantilist principle (revenue) at the expense of another (national production) – was a source of great bitterness to the French planters. If there had been only a tariff, instead of a monopoly purchasing organization, then the French colonial producers might have been able to find a market niche for their product – it did sell in Scandinavia. While there were real problems of quality and packing, the French planters were denied that free relationship with a multitude of traders which had educated the Virginian planters in the most advantageous product and practices. So far as the option for a monopoly rather than an English-style tariff is concerned, Jacob Price observes: 'It may well have been that the absence of a unified customs system in France precluded the collection of duties of such magnitude on tobacco. France, with treble the population, never in the eighteenth century achieved from *traites* the revenue which England obtained from customs.'[10]

With the decline of tobacco output in the last two decades of the seventeenth century, those proprietors with sufficient resources turned to the cultivation of cotton, indigo, or – if they were really rich – sugar. So far as these latter crops were concerned, the commercial structure introduced by Colbert still strongly favoured the French islands, allowing them something closer to imperial free trade. By 1681 the planters owned over 2,000 slaves in Saint Domingue, employing them mainly in the processing of indigo. The planters in Martinique and Guadeloupe complained about the difficulty of acquiring slaves. The Sénégal Company had established a trading fort at Gorée in 1671, but to begin with its operations were no match for the Royal African Company and the English interlopers. Colbert had encouraged eight ships to sail to Africa to buy slaves for the colonies in 1678–79, offering them tax and tariff rebates, but such piecemeal measures were not effective. During the whole period 1671 to 1693 Rochelle, a leading port in the French slave traffic at this time, sent only 43 ships to Africa, an average of about two a year compared to the 25 to 30 ships a year dispatched by the Royal African Company alone. Many of the slaves purchased by French planters – estimated to have totalled 124,000 in the last quarter of the seventeenth century – were probably supplied by English or Dutch traders.[11]

French slave trading activities at Gorée and Saint Louis in Lower Senegal were menaced by a widespread religious revolt within the neighbouring Wolof kingdoms of Kajoor and Bawol. Conflict within the ruling matrilineage led one faction to ally itself with the Muslim marabouts, leading to widespread strife in 1673–78. Louis Moreau de Chambonneau, director-general of the Sénégal Company, expressed surprise that a simple preacher could lead 'an uprising of the people and make them kill or chase their kings into exile under the pretext of religion'. What Searing describes as 'the first reformist jihad in West Africa' was led by Nasir ad-Din. According to Chambonneau, he and his disciples went round the villages urging that the kings were violating Islamic law and preying on their own peoples. In words which echo one of the themes of Ahmed Baba of Timbuktu, cited in Chapter I, the reformists declared, according to the director: 'God did not permit Kings to pillage, kill, or enslave their own peoples, that on the contrary, kings were required to sustain their peoples and protect them from their enemies, and that peoples were not made for kings but kings for peoples.'[12] The marabouts objected to the enslavement of Wolofs, but would not have protected the Sereer peoples of forests to the South.

The disarray of the Kajoor and Bawol was eventually overcome by the rise of Latsukaabe Faal, who united the kingdoms in 1695 and founded a dynasty which ruled them for most of the following century. Latsukaabe found Muslim allies in Kajoor, where the power of the marabouts was given official recognition, but the key to his success was the formation of a force of several hundred disciplined royal slaves armed with muskets; the latter were acquired by selling slaves, and training was requested from – and perhaps supplied by – the Company. However, Latsukaabe did not like the French Company's attempt to prevent him from trading with the English. In 1701 he arrested French personnel on the mainland and declared a boycott of trade with the Company. After an eight-month stand-off the Company agreed to give better terms to the King, while he agreed to trade only with the French. In subsequent decades most of the slaves taken from this coast, numbering between 1,800 and 5,000 annually, were bought by French traders.[13]

With the dissolution of the West India Company, the French Caribbean islands were directly administered by the Crown. Colonial trade was regulated by the *conseil du commerce*, while colonial revenues were gathered together in the *Domaine d'Occident* and put up to bids from the tax farmers. On each island royal administration took the form of a governor, representing the sovereign power and commanding the militia, and an intendant, responsible for finances, public works and the promotion of trade. These officials were constantly urged to enforce the *exclusif*, the reiteration of this advice suggesting that it was often flouted. The principal *habitants* were represented on a *conseil souverain* appointed by the Governor. Pluchon observes that the royal authorities were anxious to avoid re-creating in the Antilles the complex society of orders or estates to be found in the metropolis; there was to be the royal power, with its representatives, and then circles of loyal colonists. While the nobility and Church, especially the latter, had their place as props of royal power, they were not to constitute autonomous organizations of their own. In 1663 the new governor general had decreed that nobles and gentlemen would not be liable to pay a levy on the slaves they owned. Some privileges of this sort remained to encumber colonial administration, but they were discouraged and made difficult to claim (e.g. elaborate proofs, such as could not be acquired in the colonies, were required). The colonial administration itself was kept in the hands of career officials, with lesser nobles allotted roles as officers of the King in the colonies themselves. Colbert was followed as secretary of the colonies by his son Seignelay (1683–90) and then by Pontchartrain, whose family were to occupy important posts connected with colonial finances and administration until 1781.[14]

In the early years of the French colonies, as in the English, there are reports of whites working in the field side by side with blacks. An anonymous observer – probably Father Pacifique de Provins – wrote of the blacks: 'They are honestly treated, differing in nothing from the French servants, except that they were servitors and servants in perpetuity.' The Jesuit Pelleprat wrote that the *engagés* were 'worse treated than the slaves – they have to be forced to work, since they are so miserable and hungry – with blows from a stave'.[15] Africans were better at looking after themselves, building comfortable huts and finding food. The planters found that African slaves could be worked more intensely. In 1667 it was reported that

> in many of the estates in Martinique and Guadeloupe they teach the blacks how to twist tobacco, even though the profit to be gained is not so great, but it is still a large business because the planters can undertake it when they wish, something they could not do with the French tobacco workers who often engage in idle revelry and who can absent themselves when the needs are most pressing.

The Governor of the Îles du Vent in 1681 argued that there were many slaves in skilled and responsible posts – though undoubtedly where there were most slaves, they did all the hardest and most disagreeable work.[16]

The Testimony of Du Tertre

In the years 1667–71 the Dominican Father Du Tertre published a comprehensive three-volume report on the French colonies with a fifty-page section on the condition of the slaves, the most vivid and detailed such account available for any European colony in the seventeenth century. Both in these pages and elsewhere Du Tertre argued against the ill-treatment of slaves, drawing attention to what he saw as the main abuses, but apparently without questioning slavery itself or its racial presumptions. He alludes to the view that the 'laws of France', by which the colonists seek to live, abhor servitude more than those of any other country, so that slaves who land in France immediately acquire their liberty. The slave condition in the colonies is portrayed as a condition somewhere between the simple physical subjection of a captive and the outcome of an unequal and uneasy species of negotiation, in which the masters monopolize force, and control access to the means of livelihood, but nevertheless find limits to their power, since they need their slaves to work effectively. The small number of remaining Amerindian slaves were willing to fish or hunt for their masters, but only if they were asked to do so with tact and consideration. If they were shouted at, they would be overcome by melancholy; the Indian women made assiduous domestics, but the Indian men hated work in the fields, and would disappear if they were commanded to perform it. The more robust character of the Africans, according to Du Tertre, was their undoing. The 'blackness of their bodies' was a symbol of this, allowing the Europeans to use and abuse them as they wished:

> When they are treated with kindness, when they are well fed, they consider themselves the happiest people in the world, and are ready for anything. . . . It is true however that, speaking generally, they are proud, arrogant and overbearing [*superbes*]; and that they have so good an opinion of themselves, that they think themselves better than the masters they serve. It is this which obliges the European nations established in America, to treat them severely, and not to pardon their faults, as one might do with people one did not fear; because if the slaves have the least suspicion that one fears them they become more insolent, and more disposed to conspire together to free themselves from their captivity.[17]

In Du Tertre's view, the slaves often suffered greatly because they were given too little food by their masters. He deplored the 'Brazilian' practice of giving the slaves a day a week to work on plots of their own, then leaving them to fend for themselves so far as food was concerned. Hunger prompted many slaves to steal food, so that thefts became a bane of the colony; in some cases it drove them to escape into the mountains. Du Tertre favoured slaves raising chickens, tending gardens, and exchanging produce, but not as their sole source of nourishment. When drought struck, the condition of the Negroes [*nègres*] was particularly pitiable. Overworking and cruel punishments, especially the former, also afflicted too many slaves in Du Tertre's opinion:

> One can easily imagine the rigour of their work, by the strong passion which our colonists display for the amassing of wealth – they have come to the islands only for this reason and they obtain from their Negroes all the service they can. This is why they work not only from morning to noon but a good part of the night as well, especially when *petun* [i.e. tobacco] is in season.[18]

The heat, the beatings administered by the drivers, and, most of all, their own lack of any interest or possible gain from their toil, rendered it very oppressive [*insupportable*] to the slaves. Du Tertre itemizes the cruel punishments inflicted on the slaves – including mutilation, the rubbing of lemon or salt into wounds, the use of special metal instruments – and points out that their use follows no rule, but belongs simply to the arbitrary will of the master. The Negro who raised his hand against any Frenchman would receive severe punishment. Negroes found stealing in the daytime could be beaten by any colonist, and at night could even be killed:

> I know a very honest inhabitant of Martinique who dealt with theft in the following manner. Seeing that after several thefts which he had pardoned the thief continued to abuse his good will, he trapped him one day in his pig pen and cut off both his ears, without any form of trial, wrapped them in the leaf of a tree and ordered the thief to take them back to his master.[19]

Persistent runaways were often put in irons which they had to drag everywhere. Du Tertre concludes with a seemingly heartfelt but desperate appeal to the colonists to obey St Peter's injunction to treat their slaves with charity, and ensure that their overseers did likewise, because even though fortune had reduced the Negroes to servitude they remained their brothers by the grace of baptism, which made them God's children.

In Du Tertre's account the slaves, despite their afflictions, managed to develop a life of their own, and to exercise some pressure on their masters. Despite the pitifully few clothes given to them, they took pains to appear well dressed on Sundays and feast days. They displayed spontaneous family feeling and tenderness for their young. They preferred to marry Africans of the same nation, and liked to visit or receive their own people. Asked why he had used up all his precious store of food in offering hospitality, a slave replied that he had done so to prove to his fellow countrymen that he was living well. When slaves belonging to different masters wished to marry one another, arrangements would sometimes be made to allow this – though other masters would insist on imposing their own matches, if these were more convenient to them.

The Negroes loved dancing, singing and making music, we are not surprised to learn, and these activities seemed to refresh rather than tire them. As they worked in the fields they would chant songs, which often contained sarcastic comments on the weaknesses of the master or overseers. Occasionally the Negroes worked their hair into elaborate plaits until they looked like a Medusa's head, with snakes for hair. All spoke a 'baragouin' mixture of French, English, Spanish and Dutch. The newly arrived were often shocked at the amount of work expected of them, never having encountered anything like it in their life before. But others frequently told Du Tertre – or so he claims – that they did not want to go back to Africa because their life there had been miserable.

Du Tertre says the runaways were of two types: the first new arrivals, fleeing the unrelenting regime of plantation work; then slaves of longer standing, fleeing harsh treatment or starvation. He observes that the former often returned, finding life in the mountains too difficult. But those slaves who took with them tools and a store of food, occasionally replenishing the latter by theft, or intercourse with those who remained, had made *marronage* into a permanent and effective institution. In Du Tertre's view the success of the maroons in Martinique was encouraging the slaves to such an extremity that 'one does not dare to say a word against a Negro or give him the least correction'[20] – a judgement that is very much at variance with his observations elsewhere.

Du Tertre's response to what he describes is often apparently contradictory. He paints an affecting portrait of Negro mothers with their children, or of the children imitating the dances of the grown-ups. He pays tribute to the alertness of most Negroes, pointing to the advantages to be gained by teaching them a trade, or how to read and write. He is pleased that the Negroes – in contrast to the Indians – become sincerely attached to the Christian faith. Unlike many Frenchmen, they come promptly and reliably to Mass – and if they are absent it is usually the fault of their masters, who insist on keeping them at work. He explains that much can be learnt from the Africans and Indians, who know the uses of many plants alien to Europeans. But he then makes it clear that despite all this he nourishes a profound sense of racial difference. Thus he reprimands those whites who take advantage of the Negresses:

> One cannot have better verification of the saying that love is blind than the unregulated passion of some of our French who love the Negresses despite the blackness of their faces, which renders them hideous, and the unbearable odour which they exhale, which ought in my opinion to extinguish the fire of their criminal lust.[21]

He then goes on to explain that the offspring of these couplings are called *mulâtres*, 'making allusion without doubt to mules, since the mule is the product of two animals of a different kind [*deux animaux de différente espèce*].' It is as if the Dominican cultivated racial feeling as an aid to sexual continence and repression – he later concedes that some of the *mulâtres* are 'fairly well-made', and have married French colonists.[22]

The *Code Noir*

Louis XIV issued a decree in 1685 concerning the internal regime of the colonies, with particular attention to the regulation of slavery. It was based on a draft prepared by Colbert, who had sought colonial advice and who, in all in probability, had read Du Tertre (though the latter does not have responsibility for the use made by others of his observations). The preamble to the decree asserted that it would prove that the French colonies, no matter how far removed they were, were always the objects of royal solicitude – 'present not only to the reach of our royal power but also to our prompt attention to their needs'.[23] The first clauses of the *Code* display a concern with the religious integrity of the colonies. It ordered that Jews – 'declared enemies of the name of Christian' – be expelled from them. The second article declared that all slaves were to be baptized and instructed in the Catholic faith; the word 'esclaves' is used without circumlocution. No other religion than Catholicism was to be publicly celebrated, and marriages contracted through any other rite were to be null. Slaves were not to work on Sundays, or on any of the holidays observed by the Church. Only Catholic overseers were to be employed.

While religious preoccupations were present throughout the *Code*, it also attended to a range of secular matters. Freemen who had children by slave women had to pay compensation to the owner of the woman. If the father was the owner and a married man, then both the slave and child would be confiscated; if he was unmarried, then he would not be subject to punishment if he went through a proper marriage ceremony with the mother of his child, and she would be freed (Article 9). The consent of the master was required for the marriage of a slave. Slaves were in no circumstances allowed to sell sugar cane; they could sell other produce only if they had the written permission of their master. Officials were to be appointed to supervise markets in slave produce. Slaves were not to carry arms except – with the permission of their owners – for the purpose of hunting. Masters were not to permit gatherings of slaves of different masters; slaves illegally consorting together were to be subject to flogging or, in case of repeated offences, death. Each slave was to be issued with three cassava loaves weekly, each loaf weighing at least two and a half pounds, or the equivalent in manioc flour. They were also to receive two pounds of salt beef or three pounds of fish weekly. Slaves were to discharge no public office, and were deprived of autonomous civil capacity. Those who absconded for more than a month were to have one ear cut off and to be branded with the fleur de lys on one shoulder; those who ran away more than twice were to be put to death. Those who struck their masters and drew blood would also be put to death. Slaves were to be punished severely for theft, and if the master's negligence was responsible he was obliged to make restitution.

The penultimate Article (59) conferred on freedmen and women the same rights and privileges as were enjoyed by the freeborn. Taken as a whole, the *Code Noir*, as it was soon called, differed in several ways from the legislation of the English colonies. It was more systematic and comprehensive. In principle it did offer some protections to the slave, though often means of enforcement were lacking. A concern for security, subordination and religious propriety runs through the *Code*. In apparent response to a way of life already developed in the French colonies, slave participation in some local markets is envisaged. It is also accepted that there is a population of free people of colour, and that their rights should be under royal protection. These people of colour are, socially speaking, considered neither black nor white; eighteenth-century amendments to the *Code* eventually sought to outlaw marriage between whites and *mulâtres*. Overall, French law was to attempt to regulate slavery, just as French theologians, such as Bishop Bossuet, openly defended the institution:

> To condemn this state . . . would be not only to condemn human law [i.e. the Roman *jus gentium*] where servitude is admitted, as it appears in all laws, but also it would be to condemn the Holy Spirit which, speaking through St Paul, ordered slaves to remain in their condition and which did not in any way oblige masters to free them.[24]

Here Bossuet is trying to score points against Protestants, and does not directly justify any racial element in slavery. Both Bossuet and the *Code Noir* accepted that the legal codification of the condition of slaves would place them to some extent 'outside' the law, and in the sovereign power of their masters. But by anticipating the main ways slavery impinged on the wider society, French absolutism hoped to contain and direct the institution.

In the early decades of the French plantation colonies the numbers of male slaves outnumbered those of female slaves, and heavy mortality meant that slave numbers could be maintained only by continual new purchases. But to these undoubted facts must be added certain important qualifications. While adult men comprised just over 60 per cent of the slaves purchased by the French planters in the seventeenth century, the male proportion among the European immigrants was considerably higher. In Martinique between 1678 and 1709 there were about 110 male slaves for each hundred female slaves; among the whites in 1671 there were 2,182 men and 726 women. And while the slave population as a whole tended to decline every year, this was due to a high death rate rather than a low birth rate – the latter averaged annually around 30 births per 1,000, slightly above that in France. Those slaves born in the Americas had a life expectation of 34 years compared with 29 years for the slave population as a whole. The pretended official policy of encouragement for slave marriages in the French colonies had limited but not negligible results – a Jesuit report of 1681 in a district of Martinique found 1,480 slaves of marriageable age, of whom 720 were actually married, albeit 200 in 'bad relationships' (including concubinage).[25]

Royal Ambitions and the Spirit of Colonial Autonomy

While it was establishing common religious and legal principles, the French monarchy found itself obliged to treat colonial aspirations with unwonted respect. The rigid bureaucratism of the Spanish Empire did not fit the type of colonies France was developing, nor did the military situation recommend it. While the French King would have liked to take over Mexico or Peru, the real challenge he faced was that of developing the plantation colonies. These colonies did make provision for representing and incorporating settler opinion. The *habitants propriétaires*, or resident proprietors of the island, were represented on a *conseil souverain* or, in the case of Saint Domingue, two such bodies. The *conseils* had limited powers, and their composition was subject to nomination by the Governor and Intendant, but they nevertheless usually represented the standpoint of the larger planters. The economic strength of the latter was such that royal officials were obliged to acknowledge it if administration was to be effective. The colonial *conseils* claimed the right to determine the rate at which the *octroi* or export tax should be set, and this was usually respected. The governors appointed the principal colonists – planters and local merchants – to the *conseils*, and generally found it convenient to work with and through them.[26]

Colbert had planned and promoted the building of a long-distance commercial fleet and a formidable navy, as the necessary instruments of his colonial system. He encouraged those of noble extraction to participate in the strengthening of France's merchant marine by securing a guarantee that this would not derogate from their noble status, with its social cachet and tax privileges. When Colbert was first appointed to oversee the colonies, France had only a score of seaworthy warships. By 1683 the French *marine de guerre* counted 117 ships-of-the-line, thirty galleons and eighty privateers' frigates. A register of French seamen was established – the *inscription maritime* – and drawn upon to man the *marine de guerre*; in 1683 it counted 1,200 ships' officers and 53,000 mariners. The French merchant fleet had reached around 150,000 tonnes compared with about 340,000 tonnes for the English merchant fleet. In 1690 France achieved a naval victory at the Battle of Béveziers, but from 1693 onwards, following a subsequent setback, French naval strategy was to avoid set-piece encounters and concentrate on privateering attacks. The French Caribbean colonies became bases for the relentless *guerre de course* which represented a risk for them, but with the possibility of good plunder at the expense of England's richer and more developed plantation colonies. In the years 1689–97 the English Admiralty estimated that it had lost a total of 4,000 ships to attacks from the French, especially from privateers operating in the Channel, Atlantic and Caribbean.[27]

Until 1713 Saint Domingue was nest to swarms of French-commissioned privateers and buccaneers, the *flibustiers*. Privateering was regarded as a worthy occupation for a nobleman: sponsors were sought at Versailles for privateering expeditions, and among the privateer chiefs of the Caribbean were de Grammont and the Marquis de Maintenon. Vauban, the War Minister, believed that privateering, the *guerre de course*, could ruin English shipping and government finances; although the English did suffer badly, the worst hit were the Dutch. The privateer chiefs, operating with great independence themselves, helped to encourage the spirit of colonial autonomism in Saint Domingue. In the 1690s Governor Du Casse, an experienced captain whose Huguenot family had converted to Catholicism, welded the privateers into a formidable – and somewhat more disciplined – fighting force; following the Treaty of Ryswick (1697) he ensured that they received generous prize money. Subsequently the *flibustiers* were encouraged by Du Casse to invest their gains in plantations. As in the early stages of French colonization in the Lesser Antilles, land was generally available, under the terms of the so-called *droit de l'hache*, to those willing and able to clear and cultivate it. Those with the money to buy *engagés* or slaves could stake out a larger claim.

In 1698 an attempt was made to establish companies with a privileged lien on the colony's trade: this was abandoned in the face of colonial resistance. The prospect of being subject to a chartered company united the mass of colonists with all those planters and merchants who were not themselves shareholders in the project. Such companies paid poor prices for colonial produce, and charged excessively for metropolitan supplies. The royal authorities had to treat the planters of Saint Domingue with some respect – partly because they relied on mobilizing them as privateers when necessary, and partly because unless they were treated with consideration they could withdraw badly needed resources from the colony. In 1703 the King issued a Royal Instruction guaranteeing the colonists of Saint Domingue freedom from heavy-handed metropolitan tutelage: 'this colony established itself by itself; it has suffered losses during the last war; and in order not to impede its development, His Majesty wishes to leave its residents in an entire freedom of Rights'.[28]

The date of this handsome royal tribute helps to explain why it was issued. In 1703 Louis XIV was playing for much higher stakes than a few Caribbean settlements, most of them as yet less than half developed. The grand object of French royal policy was to place a Bourbon on the Spanish throne. The Spanish Empire in the Americas, despite a severe crisis and decline, was still a prize of immense value. Around 1700 the exchanges between Spain and America comprised about a tenth of total European commerce. If Paris was worth a Mass, then, at the inception of the War of Spanish Succession, the goodwill and loyalty of the redoubtable colonists and *flibustiers* of Saint Domingue were worth a gracious Royal Instruction.

Du Casse was appointed Admiral of the Fleet and loaded with honours and pensions; it fell to him to command the French escort which now accompanied the Spanish silver fleet. Saint Domingue's own development as a plantation colony received an unintended boost from the role conferred on it as a base of support and supply for the colonies of Spanish America, and for the French Navy operating in the Caribbean.

The Spanish Bourbon regime conferred the *asiento* on the French Guinea Company in 1702: according to this agreement, 48,000 slaves were to be sold in Spanish America over a ten-to-twelve-year period.[29] Thousands of Africans were brought to Martinique and Saint Domingue for shipment to the mainland, and to labour on fortifications and other public works. Among the promoters of the reorganized Guinea Company were the vastly wealthy Crozat, bankers and tax farmers. The Company commissioned many French merchants to help it fulfil this promising contract. When the war ended with transfer of the *asiento* to England, the French planters were able to buy slaves at good rates. The attacks on the English islands were another source of slaves, and of materials for the construction of plantations; there was little treasure in these plantation colonies, but slaves, cattle and equipment could be seized. In 1706 a raid by D'Iberville on the enemy islands led to the capture of 3,500 slaves. In an earlier raid Du Casse took 1,200 slaves from Jamaica.[30]

The French West Indian plantations were thus consolidated as a by-product of the otherwise hugely costly dynastic ambitions of *Le Roi Soleil*. Louis XIV had commissioned a formidable French navy numbering over one hundred ships-of-the-line, as well as – during the last years of war – integrating the privateers with the regular naval forces. This great effort had the more or less incidental consequence of securing the French islands and French Atlantic trade. The French title to Saint Domingue was formally recognized by Spain at the Treaty of Ryswick. Administration of the colonies was made the direct responsibility of the Ministry of Marine in 1699; in 1710 a special subdepartment, the Colonial Bureau, was formed within this Ministry. The Ministry of Marine and its Colonial Bureau were among the most efficient instruments of royal administration in France. The key offices in the Bureau were neither sold for profit nor donated to Court favourites but became the property of relatively conscientious and cautious royal bureaucrats, headed by the members of the Pontchartrain family. To begin with there was a risk that the advent of royal administration would lead to ferocious fiscal exploitation since, despite the rigours of war, the slave colonies seemed to be among the few royal possessions in a flourishing state.[31]

In 1700 there were about 30,000 slaves in the French colonies – 6,700 in Guadeloupe, 14,200 in Martinique and 9,000 in Saint Domingue – compared with 100,000 in the English colonies. While there were 30,000 whites in the English islands there were only about 14,000 whites in the

French. French sugar output was around 10,000 tons compared with the 25,000 tons exported by the English islands around 1700. By 1714–15, however, and despite warfare in the Lesser Antilles, the total slave population of the French colonies had grown to over 50,000, with 26,900 in Martinique and 24,000 in Saint Domingue.[32] The data in Table VII.1 are those given by Charles Frostin for the development of Saint Domingue in these war years.

Table VII.1   The Takeoff of Plantations in Saint Domingue: 1690–1713

	1690	1700	1713
Sugar Works	–	18	138
Indigo Works	–	–	1,182
Whites	4,411*	4,074	5,709
Slaves	3,358	9,082	24,146
*1687			

Source: Charles Frostin, *Les révoltes blanches de Saint Domingue*, Paris 1975, pp. 138–9.

It has been estimated that some 157,000 slaves were imported into the French American colonies prior to 1700, supplied by Dutch and English as well as French merchants. The reorganized French slave trading companies had about 250 employees on the African coast in the early years of the eighteenth century, and exported at least 30,000 slaves in the years 1703–10, and perhaps 45,000 in the years 1711–20. While more than half of those exported in the first decade went to Spanish America the great majority exported in the second decade were sold in the French colonies.[33]

The momentum of advance derived from a willingness to give a freer rein to French merchants, itself prompted by a keen sense that English planting successes were worth emulating. During the war years French colonial officials looked benignly on trade with foreign colonies, reckoning that on balance France had more to gain by interloping than did Spain or England. These practices persisted into the postwar period. By the 1720s French sugar output began to rival that of the English islands and, given France's more restricted consumption, furnished the basis for a major re-export trade. Indigo and other plantation products were also of increasing value and the cultivation of coffee commenced. The French and the English now dominated the plantation trade, with Brazil reduced to the second rank as a sugar supplier and modest quantities being produced from the small Dutch settlements, especially Surinam, and from the even smaller Danish island of Saint Thomas. The acquisition of large numbers of slaves produced huge slave majorities in the French islands, as it had in the English.

The conclusion of the Treaty of Utrecht in 1713 set the scene for a succession of sharp conflicts between the colonial authorities and the colonists of Antilles, as the former sought to capitalize on colonial prosperity by imposing new taxes and creating new colonial companies. The advent of peace made the authorities anxious to assert their authority, to enforce the *exclusif*, and, last but not least, to raise revenue. It was decided in 1715–16 to introduce an *octroi* levy on slaveholdings, and to require merchants or planters who wished to trade with foreign colonies to purchase a *passeport* from the royal officials. These proposals caused a storm of opposition from the colonists. The first opposition came in Guadeloupe in June 1715: a group of four or five hundred armed colonists drew up an appeal for the abandonment of the new measures, arguing that the *octroi* was beyond the capacity of an island which had been devastated by sieges and a bad hurricane, and presented it to the Lieutenant of the King, Coullet. The latter reported to Paris that he headed off the revolt by agreeing to endorse it; Malmaison, the island's veteran governor, privately distrusted the action of the Lieutenant, whom he believed to be in league with the rebels, but favoured avoiding a confrontation. In subsequent negotiations the levy on slaveholdings was replaced by a levy on the island's trade, a somewhat less visible tax but one which eased the situation of the planters who might have led disaffection.[34]

In Martinique the protests were not so easily contained. They were led, in the first instance, by Latouche de Longpré, a colonist of Martinique with two hundred family members and hangers-on. The mass of poorer and middling white colonists were told that the proposed measures would raise their cost of living. The colonial militia in Martinique, commanded by Colonel Jean Dubuc, sided with the protests, which soon became known as the *Gaoulé*, creole argot for rising. The authorities unwisely seized a Spanish ship which Latouche had chartered. Latouche and Dubuc proceeded to arrest the Governor and Intendant, accusing them of high-handed and oppressive behaviour, and deported them in an early ship to France. The colonial *conseil* even went so far as to open Martinique to the commerce of other nations. However, Dubuc did not favour any attempt at secession – some militia members cried out for 'independence and a republic' – but handed over his post to the lieutenant governor, with whom a compromise formula was agreed. Five marine companies were sent to bolster royal authority on the island but a general amnesty was extended to all except four of Latouche's nephews, who had to leave for a time. Dubuc was briefly detained but lived to become the island's most respected colonist and founder of a leading colonial dynasty.[35]

The Duc de Saint-Simon, himself a member of the Regency Council, describes these events in his memoirs in a surprisingly complacent fashion, relishing the discomfiture of the Governor and Intendant and admiring the decisive, and ostensibly loyal, conduct of the colonists. The whole affair was likely, he believed, to prove a 'good lesson' to the successors of the hapless officials.[36] As it happened the Regency was at this time embarking on a far grander attempt to profit from the colonies than the petty exactions of the colonial office – in the shape of John Law's System of colonial companies, the first of which was chartered in 1717. The new *Compagnies des Indes* were given extensive rights in the commerce and revenues of the colonies in America, Africa and the Indian Ocean. The new French colony of Louisiana was designated as a prospective Virginia, supplying all the needs of the tobacco monopoly. The sale of shares in these companies was to be used to amortize the royal debt and float a new paper currency. An attractive rate of interest and dizzying capital gains were predicted. Hasty plans were made to develop plantations in Louisiana and other colonies, including the dispatch of ships to obtain slaves from Africa, the recruiting of German specialists and draconian decrees ordering that all vagabonds able to work should be rounded up and sent to the colonies. This grandiose scheme was plagued by every type of disaster. Attempts to round up felons led to riot, with over 107 prisoners forcing their way out of confinement at St Martin des Champs in January 1720 and obliging the King to suspend the deportation orders in May of the same year. Law's companies were consumed by a fever of speculation and he was obliged to flee the wrath of investors in December 1720. The money raised by the companies was mostly absorbed by service payments and the currency débâcle, leaving too little for the schemes of colonization. The companies eventually sent some seven thousand men and women to Louisiana, of whom a thousand were soldiers and nearly four thousand *engagés* or deportees. Two thousand died of disease soon after arriving, while the bulk of the survivors were not considered *utils* by the Louisiana officials, who asked: 'What can one expect from a bunch of vagabonds and wrongdoers in a country where it is far harder to repress licentiousness than in Europe?'[37]

Attempts were made to relaunch a *Compagnie des Indes* following Law's flight and the collapse of his System, but these were no better thought out than their predecessor. Attracting sufficient numbers of colonists proved difficult – partly because of the colony's unsavoury reputation and partly because there was only a trickle of French emigrants anyway. The colonists resented the powers given to the new *Compagnie des Indes*, including both fiscal powers and a monopoly on the supply of slaves. When two directors of the new company arrived in Saint Domingue in 1722, they were briefly arrested by the *conseil* at Léogane to cries of 'Vive le Roi, sans La Compagnie'. On this occasion it was decided that the maintenance of royal authority required a show of strength. A squadron was dispatched to Saint Domingue. After the Regent's death in 1723, a more conciliatory spirit prevailed. In the following year the company's fiscal powers were withdrawn but its rights as sole supplier of slaves to the colony was maintained, at least nominally. Elaborate but ineffective measures sought to stimulate a new trade in *engagés* to the French islands. From 1698 onwards each ship leaving for the Antilles was meant to carry between three and six *engagés*, depending on its size; this legislation was tightened up in 1724, not for the first or last time, by imposing fines on those ships which failed to carry their quota. Very few Frenchmen, it seems, could now be persuaded to become servants in the plantation colonies. Some younger men hoping to make their way as *économes* or *gérants* still emigrated voluntarily to the French islands, but the total numbers remained modest.[38]

The reign of Louis XV witnessed a relaxation of French colonial policy. Grandiose schemes for colonial development were discredited and the argument for freer trade made headway. The royal bureaucrats realized that raising revenues directly in the colonies promised much wrangling for little gain. The metropolis could gain most from colonial development by controlling the trade in their plantation exports, thus making Bordeaux and Nantes into leading suppliers of sugar and coffee. When the metropolis could not supply the colonies with adequate supplies the local authorities would invoke 'emergency conditions' which permitted them to buy from foreign traders; officials were often induced to turn a blind eye to contraband. The colonists could not resist the squadrons sent by the metropolis and anyway relied on them for defence against hostile powers. But the colonial governors and intendants usually established a *modus vivendi* with the leading planters – indeed, despite a decree prohibiting it, most senior officials themselves became plantation owners. In Louisiana costly and fruitless efforts continued to be made to develop tobacco cultivation. Some of the new settlers found they could make a living raising provisions for sale in Saint Domingue but this humble activity, profitable though it was, did not appeal to the directors in Paris. In 1730 the Louisiana Company handed back its concessions to the Crown, having failed to produce tobacco at a reasonable cost, or of sufficient quality.

In the islands a new colonial model had taken hold. In a move away from official trading monopolies incentives aimed at individual merchants and planters were devised. The slave traders of Nantes and Bordeaux were offered a remission on duty payable on colonial staples if they could produce a certificate, the so-called *acquits de Guiné*, proving that they had sold slaves to the French islands. On a more *ad hoc* basis French planters could also often buy cheap supplies from North America, sometimes selling molasses in return. But this latitude was accompanied by strict control over the destination of the main plantation products which were sold to metropolitan merchants, often for processing and onward sale to other parts of Europe. Like their English counterparts the French 'new merchants' sought freedom of trade within a national monopoly.

Dynastic Calculation, Baroque Spectacle and Colonial Development

Colonial policy never enjoyed primacy at the French Court – dynastic advantage in Europe took pride of place, and until 1713 was thought to be the key to the New World anyway. Colonies had been acquired almost accidentally. At one point in 1672 Colbert had argued that French advances in the war with the Dutch dictated the seizure of the United Provinces: 'If the King subjects all these United Provinces of the Low Countries, their commerce becomes the commerce of His Majesty's citizens, and nothing could be more advantageous.'[39] The French were checked by Dutch resistance, as Prince Maurits fell back on prepared positions. The French King could, perhaps, have pressed his advantage, but he does not appear to have seen commercial hegemony as a prize worth aiming at. Instead he pursued the dynastic and national objective of extending and straightening France's frontiers, and reaching an understanding with the Habsburgs concerning Spanish succession.

Pierre Pluchon, who writes regretfully of France's failure to seize the leadership in European colonization in the Americas and elsewhere, sees Louis XIV as a man unable to see beyond Europe's narrow boundaries. In the secret agreement with Leopold of Austria in the 1660s 'the Ancien Régime was willing to renounce all colonial imperialism, all global strategy' for dynastic gain in the old continent. Once again in the 1690s Louis was willing to turn his back on American horizons: 'What a lack of a global vision of expansion was displayed by this sovereign so often denounced for his imperialist inclinations!'.[40] For Louis colonies in America were simply 'small change' to be bartered for the territory that really mattered – territory in Europe. Pluchon commends Colbert's success in building a French navy but condemns his preference for colonial companies and financial speculators – and his lack of appreciation for merchants and planters who, in his view, really built the colonies. That, somehow, France did end up with some fairly successful plantation colonies owed little to the cunning of mercantilism and imperial strategy, something to fortune, and much to the initiative of merchants, colonists and privateers.

The French monarch had found his dynastic objectives thwarted by the opposition of the other powers, and had been obliged to adopt a colonial and maritime strategy that was, in certain respects, the mirror-image obverse of English expansion. From the time of Colbert onwards French colonial and naval administration was more detailed and deliberate than that of England. While Colbert's colonial and slave trading companies imitated Dutch and English models his system of naval recruitment, the *inscription maritime*, was far more efficient than the arbitrary impressments relied on by the English Admiralty. While England's Navigation Acts permitted something approaching free trade within the boundaries of Empire the French colonial system included further carefully devised exemptions, privileges and bounties. There was no English equivalent to the bounty system which, in one form or another, was available to French slave traders with the express object of building up the colonial labour force and matching English plantation development. But the element of *dirigisme* in French colonial policy needed to be continually revised and tempered, as it was to be in the reign of Louis XV, so that it fostered the entrepôt trade in plantation produce.[41]

At the level of elemental social forces colonization had required a combination of 'bourgeois' enterprise and aristocratic land-grabbing. The territorial instinct of the noble cadet needed to be sustained by merchants who could supply a subject labour force and market the plantation produce. The spontaneous tendencies of commercial development needed to be anchored in colonial settlements which could survive the Hobbesian war of all against all that marked the seventeenth-century Caribbean. The tenacity of the Willoughbys and D'Esnambucs supplied the colonization effort with a necessary stiffening element.

The social basis and logic of the French and English state diverged sharply from the mid seventeenth century, yet their colonies bore a distinct resemblance to one another. In the course of England's seventeenth-century revolution the stratum of landlords and merchants resting upon new relations of production – proto-capitalist tenant farming, metropolitan manufacture and colonial planting – broke the power of the monarch and forged a new state machine and colonial system. This furnished an advantageous context for commercial agriculture, manufacturing exports and the plantation trades. A half or more of state revenue was derived, by means of Customs and Excise, from the sphere of exchange. The power of the monarch was circumscribed in ways that also limited the ability of the state to impose itself on civil society, most particularly in the colonies. In France royal power defeated its domestic antagonists and constructed a baroque model of the Absolutist, late feudal state. But the wars of Louis XIV took a heavy toll and then Law's system destroyed the credibility of corporate mercantilism. A hereditary aristocracy, both new and old, regained influence and power. The colonial merchants and planters gained from the partial retreats of a chastened Absolutism and from what appeared to be the wisdom, in the face of English colonial competition, of permitting a degree of autonomy to French colonial interests. In the *Esprit des Lois* Montesquieu was to express the view that the colonists of the plantations would never make good subjects, voicing a distrust of the planters which was widespread among his former colleagues of the Parlement of Bordeaux. The French monarchy continued to derive its principal revenues from direct taxation and levies but the entrepôt and Atlantic trades supplied a general economic stimulus. With a less monetized economy the French domestic market for plantation products was actually smaller than that in England even though France's population was four times as great. In France itself commerce, manufacture, and finances were still structured by corporate privilege, royal charters, and municipal or regional particularism. The French colonial producers and merchants enjoyed some privileges too but their enterprises were increasingly allowed to make their way in the competitive environment of the plantation trades. In the colonies cumbersome vested interests had less weight. Since colonial development was sited across the Atlantic it could be allowed to flourish in its own way without directly upsetting the social order of the metropolis.[42]

England and France had carved out prime positions in colonial development by combining commerce and public power, privateering and colonizing, in a complementary fashion. Eventually there was to develop a certain structural contrast between English 'bourgeois' colonization and French 'Absolutist' colonization, but the social forces involved in both – merchants and colonists – were comparable. In both cases the state was able and willing to shield its colonies and colonial trade, colonists were prepared to leave their homelands and merchants had sufficient resources to take advantage of the opportunities presented. Both states had the resources, the access to the Atlantic and the maritime potential required to make good their colonial claims. While colonial development vitally depended on the commitment of individual colonists, and the vitality of a new and more autonomous 'civil society', they did need a degree of state protection and state sponsorship.

The consolidation of an English empire in the Americas, as we have seen, owed as much to the later Stuarts as to the Puritans and Commonwealth, as much to the Duke of York as to Cromwell. While royal initiative had a role in French colonial development French merchants and colonists responded vigorously to every opening allowed them. Likewise industries brought into existence to supply the Army, the Navy or the Court acquired their own momentum and could find a profitable role in linking themselves to colonial development. The wine trade of Bordeaux and other ports gave French merchants some of the commercial experience and resources necessary for this: French wines and plantation products were soon reaching the same markets in Northern and Central Europe. The French textile industry and trade developed vigorously, encouraging the output of colonial dyestuffs and cotton.

The splendour of the French Court helped to advertise and promote French luxury products, setting a standard for the aristocracy and *haute bourgeoisie* throughout the continent. At Versailles Louis XIV, without intending it, had built a showcase for the exotic produce of the plantations: chocolate served from gleaming silver pots, snuff taken from elegant little boxes, banqueting tables spread with elaborate sugar confections. The plantations were to add mercantile zest to an Ancien Régime that might otherwise have sunk into lethargy. In the realm of economic theory Boisguilbert and Cantillon laid the basis for *laissez-faire*, a doctrine which could explain the vigour of France's entrepôt trade. Another crucial economic term – that of the entrepreneur or undertaker – was also conceived in France at this time. The merchants of Nantes and Bordeaux competed with one another even if they also benefited from bounties and privileges.[43]

In the early days the French and English colonial planters had made the breakthrough to economic viability on their own – and thanks to Dutch help – but, once this was established, the metropolitan authorities were able to assert a significant measure of control. The context of fierce military rivalry between the European powers in the years 1666–1714 helped to tame – but not extinguish – the autonomist inclinations of the colonists and to remind the French that they were, after all, French and the English were English. Both English and French colonists knew that the colonial order, including their title to land and their hope of securing a regime of dependent labour, ultimately depended on a power that could mobilize ships of war. On the other hand the authorities in London and Paris knew that they had to concede an element of local self-government and local initiative if their colonies were to prosper and to contribute to their own defence. Those colonists in the English islands who were not English and not Protestant, or those in the French islands who were not Catholic and not French, were often to experience problems with the test of identity posed by the military and mercantilist mobilizations of the period after 1650. Yet in the end those proprietors in the English colonies who were Catholic or 'New Christian', or those in the French colonies who were of Dutch extraction or supposedly 're-converted' from the Huguenot faith, rarely if ever engaged in collectively treasonable behaviour. Owning property, being a proper *habitant*, itself conferred an identity. Where they were wealthy, formal conversions and marriage alliances somewhat alleviated the situation, as did the simple passage of time, so that by the mid eighteenth century, if not earlier, the colonies were significantly more tolerant and pluralist than the metropolis.

Colonial identity problems proved to be at their most intense for national or religious outsiders who were not proprietors but servants or *engagés*, or convicts, or poor freemen and women. Thus the Irish indentured servants, or convict servants, of the English islands openly sided with the French on some critical occasions. The French seizure of the English part of Saint Christopher in 1689 was decisively assisted by the adhesion of one hundred and fifty Irishmen, most of them servants or convicts, who put themselves under the orders of the Comte de Blénac. The French also suffered from defections by Huguenots, especially those who were or had been *engagés* and convicts, who escaped to join the English or Dutch privateers or pirates. One of the most celebrated pirate captains was the freethinking former Huguenot Misson who, according to Captain Johnson, established the colony of Libertalia in Madagascar in the early eighteenth century.[44]

In this context African slaves seemed potentially more reliable than persecuted religious or national minorities. In Barbados, in the 1690s and after, some blacks were armed at times of military emergency while Irish servants were not. Likewise the militia in Guadeloupe, as in other French islands, included some blacks, while Huguenots were strictly excluded. In fact the French plantation colonies began to differentiate themselves from the English; in addition to the free white population there was also a significant free coloured population. According to official returns they only comprised a tenth of the free population in 1700 but this proportion was to grow steadily in subsequent decades. Many of the free people of colour were American-born and all creoles had a greater capacity to reproduce themselves in the colonies. Also the manumission of slaves, though taxed, was legally established and acceptable to the colonial authorities. The free people of colour were good Catholics and felt a greater need to display loyalty to the colonial regime than was always the case with the free white colonists.[45]

The plantation colonies evinced a keen desire for autonomy, but eventually found that they could not refuse the authority of the metropolis, especially if some concessions were made to them. The Caribbean was a dangerous place. The slaveholding colonists presided over too fragile a social formation to dispense with metropolitan support and protection. The planters of Barbados and Martinique had discovered that they could influence the metropolis but not defy it outright. Thus they did succeed in defeating colonial monopolies which would have smothered plantation development. Such monopolies had a role to play in the Africa trade and in initiating, or asserting metropolitan control over, colonial development. But in the medium and long run the slave trade and plantation development thrived best when propelled by a multitude of competing entrepreneurs. The central Government's role was to supply a favourable context, financing the costs of administration and defence out of taxation, not to supplant the free spirit of the slave and plantation trades.

The privateers had contributed to the defence and development of particular colonies but in the long run they were the source of such destruction, disruption and uncertainty that they checked the growth of the plantations. After the Treaty of Ryswick European diplomacy no longer excluded the Caribbean, and other territory 'beyond the line', from the terms of international agreements. As the size of naval squadrons in the Caribbean grew larger, and the more notable *flibustier* were conscripted into regular commands, the days of the English and French privateers drew to a close. Morgan had been knighted, Du Casse ended his days at Versailles, de Grammont and de Maintenon acquired sugar plantations. But it was not until several years after the Treaty of Utrecht that the Caribbean and Atlantic was cleared of the most dangerous privateers and pirates. These seas were still not to be completely safe, partly because of a succession of Anglo-French and Anglo-Spanish wars and partly because the Spanish Caribbean *guarda costas* were liable to seize merchantmen even in peacetime on real or invented charges of smuggling. But from around 1720 widespread, and almost random, privatized violence was replaced by the more orderly and predictable manoeuvres of the English, French and Spanish navies.[46]

Indeed, war-making in the Caribbean often seemed to obey an even more decorous etiquette than in Europe. While the military commander in Europe might invite the enemy to fire first – 'Messieurs les Anglais, c'est à vous de tirer' – the Caribbean colonial governor was often pressed to come to terms with an enemy squadron in order to save the plantations from the disturbances of war. English squadrons seized Saint-Louis in the south of Saint Domingue in 1748, Martinique in 1759 and Havana in 1762, with little more than token resistance from the land forces. Leading planters were willing to collaborate with the occupation authorities, while British merchants did a brisk trade. There was, it would seem, a consensus that making plantation colonies into battlefields was in nobody's interest.

By the early eighteenth century the English and French colonial systems rested on an increasingly distinct, though not absolute, division of labour between the state and economic agents. The owners of ships and plantations were now *primarily* economic agents; thus, while armed themselves, they knew the force they disposed of was inadequate and that they might need the colonial state to defend them, either from their rivals or from their slaves. If, unlike the feudal serflord, the planters and merchants needed a modicum of protection, they were also in a good position to pay for it out of the extraordinary surplus generated by the slave plantations. Military and economic competition operated in different but complementary ways. A military contest had marginalized the Dutch and established the French in possession of Saint Domingue. On the other hand, economic competitiveness had given an edge to the English tobacco and sugar colonies. The French colonial establishment had been obliged to abandon company rule in its Caribbean islands and allow elements of commercial competition, albeit within a neo-mercantilist framework.

Notes

1. Bartolomé Bennassar, 'L'Europe des Campagnes', in Pierre Léon, *Histoire économique et sociale du monde. Tome 1. L'Ouverture du Monde, XIVᵉ–XVIᵉ siècles*, Paris 1977, pp. 449–92.

2. Quoted in Robert and Marianne Cornevin, *La France et les Français Outre-mer*, Paris 1990, p. 79. For colonial propaganda see M. Devèze, *Antilles, Guyanes, la Mer des Caraïbes, de 1492 à 1798*, Paris 1977, pp. 138–9.

3. Henri Blet, *Histoire de la Colonisation Française*, Paris 1947, pp. 63–5; C.A. Banbuck, *Histoire de la Martinique*, Paris 1935, pp. 24–7, 319; P. Butel, 'Les Temps de Fondations: les Antilles avant Colbert', in Pierre Pluchon, ed., *Histoire des Antilles et de la Guyane*, Paris 1982, pp. 53–78.

4. Raymond Breton, 'Relation', in Peter Hulme and Neil L. Whitehead, eds, *Wild Majesty: Encounters with Caribs from Columbus to the Present Day*, Oxford 1992, pp. 108–16 (p. 111). This language of contact was different from the Carib language – or languages – themselves. (Breton, who produced a dictionary and a grammar, reported that men and women each had their own language, p. 153). The Kréyole languages spoken to this day in much of the Caribbean were to receive a strong African influence but the Carib patois referred to by Breton and others is likely to have been the pre-Kréyole about which linguists speculate. Lambert-Félix Prudent, *Des Baragouins à la Langue Antillaise*, Paris 1980, pp. 23–5.

5. Henri Blet, *Histoire de la Colonisation Française*, I, pp. 107–10; Ralph Davis, *The Rise of the Atlantic Economies*, London 1973, pp. 123–42.

6. Gaston-Martin, *Histoire de l'Esclavage aux Colonies Françaises*, Paris 1948, pp. 130–31; Banbuck, *Histoire de la Martinique*, pp. 26, 35, 58–9.

7. Stewart L. Mims, *Colbert's West India Policy*, New Haven, CT 1912, pp. 14–53; D.H. Pennington, *Seventeenth Century Europe*, London 1970, p. 427.

8. Mims, *Colbert's West India Policy*, pp. 180, 280. Robert Stein, *The French Slave Trade in the Eighteenth Century*, Madison, WI 1979, p. 13; P. Butel, 'Un Nouvel Age Colonial: Les Antilles sous Louis XIV' in Pluchon, *Histoire des Antilles*, pp. 79–108 (p. 92).

9. Jean Meyer, *Les Européens et les autres de Cortès à Washington*, Paris 1975, p. 197; Jacob Price, *France and the Chesapeake: A History of the Tobacco Monopoly, 1674–1791, and of its Relationship to the British and American Tobacco Trades*, Ann Arbor, MI 1973, pp. 53, 73–115.

10. Price, *France and the Chesapeake*, pp. 15–16.

11. K.G. Davies, *The North Atlantic World in the Seventeenth Century*, London 1974, pp. 119–21; Pierre de la Vassière, *Saint-Domingue, la Société et la Vie Créole sous l'Ancien Régime*, Paris 1909, p. 164.

12. Quoted in James Searing, *West African Slavery and Atlantic Commerce: The Senegal River Valley, 1700–1860*, Cambridge 1993, p. 25.

13. Ibid., pp. 18–26, 34.

14. Pierre Pluchon, 'Les Blancs des Îles', in Direction des Archives de France, *Voyages aux Îles d'Amérique*, Paris 1992, pp. 189–97 (p. 189); Lucien Abénon, *La Guadeloupe de 1671 à 1759*, Paris 1989, pp. 43, 217.

15. Quoted in Arlette Gautier, *Les Soeurs de la Solitude: la condition féminine dans l'esclavage aux Antilles du XVIIᵉ au XIXᵉ siècle*, Paris 1985, p. 191.

16. Ibid., p. 193.

17. R.P.J.B. Du Tertre, *Histoire générale des Antilles habitées par les françois*, 3 vols, Martinique 1973 (Paris 1667–71), Volume II, pp. 453–501 (p. 465).

18. Ibid., p. 488.

19. Ibid., p. 494.

20. Ibid., p. 500.

21. Ibid., pp. 477–8.

22. Ibid., pp. 478–9.

23. Louis Sala-Molins, *Le Code Noir ou le calvaire de Canaan*, Paris 1987, p. 90. This work contains the full text of the *Code Noir*, together with commentaries and notes.

24. *Avertissement aux Protestants*, quoted in Sala-Molins, *Le Code Noir*, p. 65.

25. Gautier, *Les Soeurs de la Solitude*, pp. 72–3, 80; Myriam Cottias, 'La Martinique: Babylone fertile ou terre stérile? Des discours sur la fécondité aux indicateurs démographiques et sociaux (XVIIᶜ–XIXᶜ siècle)', *Annales de Démographie Historique*, Paris 1992, pp. 199–215, 205, 207–8.

26. D.K. Fieldhouse, *The Colonial Empires: A Comparative Survey from the Eighteenth Century*, London 1965, pp. 34–41.

27. P. Butel, 'Un Nouvel Age colonial'; Pluchon, *Histoire des Antilles*, p. 103; Cornevin, *La France et les Français Outre-mer*, p. 103.

28. Quoted in Fieldhouse, *The Colonial Empires*, p. 41; Charles Frostin, *Histoire de l'autonomisme colon de la partie française de St Domingue*, Paris 1972, pp. 77–115, 125–32. For the wider context see Nellis Crouse, *The French Struggle for the West Indies*, London 1966, pp. 178 ff.; Geoffrey Symcox, ed., *War, Diplomacy and Imperialism, 1618–1763*, New York 1973, pp. 24–6, 239–42.

29. C.W. Cole, *French Mercantilism: 1683–1700*, New York 1943, pp. 255–60. The French companies had a slave trading factory at Ouidah by 1671, converted to Fort Saint-Louis in 1703; Ouidah was strategically located on the Bight of Benin, which accounted for nearly a half of all African slave exports around this time.

30. Davies, *The North Atlantic World in the Seventeenth Century*, pp. 121–2. The war years saw contraband flourish; see Clarence J. Munford, *The Black Ordeal of Slavery and Slave Trading in the French West Indies*, Lewiston, NY 1991, vol. II, pp. 374–97.

31. Blet, *Histoire de la Colonisation Française*, I, pp. 107–17.

32. For slave populations, Leo Elizabeth, 'The French Antilles', in D.W. Cohen and Jack P. Greene, eds, *Neither Slave nor Free*, Baltimore, MD 1973, pp. 148–51; for sugar output Dunn, *Sugar and Slaves*, p. 205.

33. Davis, *The Rise of the Atlantic Economies*, p. 135; Curtin, *The Atlantic Slave Trade*, Table 63, pp. 170, 210–11; Lovejoy, 'Volume of the Atlantic Slave Trade', pp. 482–6; Serge Daget, *La Traite des Noirs*, Paris 1990, pp. 102–3.

34. Abénon, *La Guadeloupe*, pp. 212–35.

35. Charles-André Julien, *Les Français en Amérique de 1713 à 1789*, Paris 1977, pp. 72–3; M. Devèze, *Antilles, Guyanes, la Mer des Caraïbes de 1492 à 1789*, Paris 1977, pp. 229–31.

36. Duc de Saint-Simon, *Historical Memoirs, 1715–1723*, edited and translated by Lucy Norton, 3 vols, vol. III, New York 1992, pp. 131–2.

37. Quoted in Gwendolyn Midlo Hall, *Africans in Colonial Louisiana: The Development of Afro-Creole Culture in the Eighteenth Century*, Baton Rouge, LA and London 1992, p. 7; see also Price, *France and the Chesapeake*, I, pp. 302–60.

38. Pluchon, *Histoire de la Colonisation Française*, pp. 129–34; Christian Hertz de Lemps, 'Indentured Servants Bound for the French Antilles in the Seventeenth and Eighteenth Centuries' in Altman and Horn, eds, *'To Make America': European Emigration in the Early Modern Period*, pp. 172–203, especially pp. 183–90.

39. Quoted in Pluchon, *Histoire de la Colonisation Française*, p. 90. For contrasting approaches to taxation see: Peter Mathias and Patrick O'Brien, 'Taxation in Britain and France, 1715–1810', *Journal of European Economic History*, vol. 5, no. 3, Winter 1976, pp. 610–50, especially p. 617. For the overall orientation of the English state see Christopher Hill, *Reformation to Industrial Revolution*, London 1967, pp. 123–34,144–51; and Calder, *Revolutionary Empire*, pp. 251–429; for the relationship between French Absolutism and colonialism see Anderson, *Lineages of the Absolutist State*, pp. 40–41, 103–4; Elizabeth Fox Genovese and Eugene Genovese, *The Fruits of Merchant Capital: Slavery and Bourgeois Property in the Rise and Expansion of Capitalism*, Oxford 1983, pp. 61–75.

40. Pluchon, *Histoire de la Colonisation Française*, pp. 89, 95.

41. Jean Meyer, 'Des origines à 1763', in Jean Meyer *et al.*, *Histoire de la France Coloniale*, pp. 103–6; Symcox, *War, Diplomacy and Imperialism*, p. 24; Cole, *French Mercantilism*, p. 94.

42. For the retreats of French Absolutism after Louis XIV see Anderson, *Lineages of the Absolutist State*, pp. 106–12. I discuss the peculiar formation of the Hanoverian regime in England, seen as a species of 'illegitimate monarchy', in *The Overthrow of Colonial Slavery*, pp. 69–75; Montesquieu's position on the colonies is discussed pp. 36, 47–8, 154.

43. The precocity of French economic thinking is stressed by Murray Rothbard, *Economic Thought before Adam Smith*, vol. I, Cheltenham 1995, pp. 253–74. That the France of Louis XIV and Louis XV should have been the cradle of *laissez-faire* economics thus testifies not only to the continuing obstacle of French Absolutism but also to the commercial vigour of its leading ports, a vigour which derived much from the colonial and re-export trade. Colonial appeals for free trade are cited in Munford, *The Black Ordeal of Slavery and Slave Trading in the French West Indies*, II, pp. 418–30.

44. Captain Charles Johnson, *A General History of the Robberies and Murders of the Most Notorious Pirates*, second edition, London 1726.

45. Jean Meyer, 'Des origines à 1763', in Meyer *et al.*, *Histoire de la France Coloniale*, pp. 11–197 (pp. 124–6, 165–8).

46. Foucault argues that the idea of the nobility as a 'conquering race' expressed by the Comte de Boulainvilliers in the closing years of Louis XIV's reign fostered the notion of an 'aristocratic liberty' which proved itself not by respecting the freedoms of others but precisely by trampling upon them. Certainly the planter elite, however parvenu its origins, eagerly associated itself with this notion of aristocratic liberty. See Michel Foucault, *'Il Faut Défendre la Societe', Cours au Collège de France (1975–76)*, Paris 1997, pp. 139–40. The English legal codifier Edward Coke opened out the notion of aristocratic liberty by claiming it as a national patrimony in an extended commentary on Magna Carta. Thus Englishmen could not be exiled or sent abroad without Parliament's approval; see Coke, *Institutes of the Lawes of England*, II, London 1642, p. 47. The doctrine of metropolitan liberty was to inspire some audacious slaves to claim their freedom if they were taken to England or France. For French examples see Sue Peabody, *'There Are No Slaves in France': the Political Culture of Race and Slavery in the Ancien Régime*, Oxford 1996.

VIII

Racial Slavery and the Rise of the Plantation

All servants imported and brought into this country, by sea or land, who were not Christians in their native country, (except Turks and moors in amity with her majesty, and others that can make due proof of their being free in England, or any other Christian country, before they were shipped, in order to transportation hither) shall be accounted and be slaves, and as such bought and sold nothwithstanding a conversion to Christianity afterwards.

An Act Concerning Servants and Slaves, Virginia 1705

Fortune never exerted more cruelly her empire over mankind, than when she subjected these nations of heroes to the refuse of the goals of Europe, to wretches who possess the virtues neither of the countries which they come from, nor of those which they go to, whose levity, brutality, and baseness, so justly expose them to the contempt of the vanquished.

Adam Smith, *Theory of Moral Sentiments*

Upon one of their Festivals when a great many of the Negro Musicians were gathered together, I desired Mr. *Baptiste*, the best Musician there to take the Words they sung and set them to Musick, which follows.

You must clap Hands when the Base is plaid, and cry, *Alla, Alla*.

Jamaican music, from Hans Sloane, *Voyage to the Islands* (British Library) (see also p. 348)

The slave systems of the Americas embodied a new type of slavery and plantation, constituting, by 1714, a major source of colonial wealth. The events recounted in Chapters II–VII meant that the Atlantic slave trade, the ideologies and codes legalizing racial slavery, and the slave plantation as an enterprise, were all now in place. The Portuguese had established themselves with great tenacity on the African coast, in the Atlantic islands and in Brazil, trafficking in slaves and experimenting with improved versions of the sugar plantation. The Spanish had lent the prestige of *conquistadores* to slaveholding. Both Iberian powers supplemented medieval and classical laws, and traditional religious justifications, with new slaveholding doctrines, though the latter did not yet hermetically enclose all those of African descent in slavery.

The plantations of Brazil achieved a scale and autonomy that had eluded the overregulated Spanish. The Dutch sought to capture Brazil, failed, but broke the Portuguese slave trading monopoly and greatly weakened Spanish power in the New World. The English and French merchants and planters exploited this situation. Instructed by the Dutch and refining the example given by the Atlantic islands and Brazil, they had elaborated a potent new species of slave plantation agriculture. By 1700 the word plantation, eclipsing previous meanings, now commonly referred to an overseas settlement producing a tropical cash crop, with tied labour, and by extension to an estate producing such crops, increasingly through the mobilization of black slaves. In contrast to the Brazilian prototype, cane cultivation and sugar-making were integrated on the Caribbean plantations. Wherever plantations flourished, African captives and their descendants had replaced – or were soon to replace – Indian slaves or European indentured servants as the principal labour force.

In this chapter I will explore the reasons for the emergence of the American plantations and their reliance on tied labour, examine the switch from indentured servitude to slavery and its racial basis, and ask whether alternatives to racial slavery could have been devised. This will entail analysing the strengths and weaknesses of the slave plantation, explaining how such a wasteful institution could be profitable and such an oppressive one comparatively secure. Without profitability and security, the plantations would not have been able to make their way in the competitive and dangerous climate of the seventeenth- and eighteenth-century Atlantic, nor would they have received the backing of governments.

The plantations had been brought into existence by Europe's powerful and seemingly limitless appetite for their products – once the full harshness of unregulated plantation labour was manifest, racial slavery had recruited people to occupy the vacant occupational slots. Given the presence of alert and acquisitive entrepreneurs, whose actions were primarily dictated by competitive pressures and the desire for gain, this development could not have been avoided unless slavery and racial super-exploitation had been outlawed by some powerful sanction.

As it was, the new plantations supplied European markets with products that commanded a premium price, since Europe itself could not produce them, or could not produce them competitively to the required levels of output and quality. The sea lanes of the Atlantic brought the Americas closer to Europe than potential alternative suppliers in Africa or Asia. Political conditions in the New World – the spread of European control – also favoured it as a supplier for European markets. It is true that warfare sometimes interrupted Atlantic trade, but the routes to Africa and Asia were, if anything, even more dangerous. From the standpoint of European settlers the New World was more favourably situated, less well defended, and more fertile than other areas to which they might have been drawn. Sugar and other plantation crops could be most swiftly produced by mobilizing slave labour.

These exotic items might have been secured in some other way (a point we will explore later in this chapter), but the acquisition of African captives, and their treatment as slaves, certainly proved itself a practical and profitable solution in a context where finding voluntary labourers would have been difficult and expensive. The merchants and planters responsible for purchasing Africans did so in order to boost their fortunes; other colonists had little say in the matter, but were content to leave harsh toil to the slaves. The metropolitan states, having discovered the advantages of a plantation development they had done little to assist, granted considerable autonomy to the planters and merchants involved: so long as reasonable access to markets was not denied the plantation trades could be taxed and channelled, yielding an impressive revenue.

The Spanish monarchs had found that outright slavery enriched their colonists while ruining their new lands. Banning the further enslavement of the hugely depleted indigenous populations, they instead levied communal tribute labour and taxes, and fostered an intermediary layer of mestizos, ladinos and unattached *indios*. The apparatus of imperial rule, staffed by nobles and *hidalgos*, aimed to extract specie by means of an extensive system of exploitation – even communities far from the mining centres were required to pay tribute in silver, obliging them to produce goods which could be sold or to supply labour to textile workshops. The Spanish monarchy had also been prompted to sell ever more permits to import slaves – the *asientos* – as another way of recouping silver from the colonies. Spanish imperial power had been forced to give ground in the Caribbean and North America, and the costs of imperial defence had absorbed much of the colonial surplus. Yet it held on to all its principal holdings and, as Bourbons succeeded Habsburgs, contrived to raise once again the level of mining output and colonial revenue. The imperial power and its colonial entrepreneurs constituted an extensive, non-capitalist apparatus of exploitation but one which, as the price of survival, had to produce an economic surplus.

The English and French plantation colonies represented a different formula of exploitation, though it too was based on extra-economic coercion. While Madrid awarded mining concessions and rights of *encomienda*, the planters and merchants of the English and French colonies constructed intensive systems of exploitation largely through their own efforts. The English and French settled parts of the Caribbean and North America inhabited by tribes and confederations which practised shifting cultivation, hunting and gathering. Unlike the Aztec and Inca empires, the colonial incorporation of these peoples offered prospects of continuing resistance, and little gain. The English had first bargained and traded with these native peoples, then massacred, expelled or marginalized them; the French followed this cycle more slowly, developing colonies of settlement in the Caribbean but retaining the emphasis on trading networks in North America. The planters' gain from maximizing production of a cash crop meant finding as many labourers as possible as quickly as possible. Amerindian captives were difficult to capture and difficult to keep, and the men were unused to agricultural routines. At first the planters found European servants to work their plantations, but between 1640 and 1715 they were replaced by Africans who were acquired by purchase, not subjugated by conquest.

Attempts to convert the Africans were desultory, and were not allowed to stand in the way of their mobilization for slave labour. The slaves were not offered even partial assimilation, whether or not they converted; the slave community had its own hierarchy but no public representatives or leaders, such as the native caciques and Indian aristocracy of Spanish America. Far from being expelled from the land claimed by the Europeans, Africans were imported to work it and to make good the expulsion of Indians.

The plantations produced premium cash crops in an intensive system of exploitation; the colonizing powers did not need to raise large revenues within the colony, since they could impose customs and excise on the resulting trades. The colonial systems had a certain baroque complexity, with newly elaborated social distinctions and racial identities. In the Hispanic case state initiative played a key role in co-ordinating production and defining an ethno-social hierarchy. In the slave colonies the imperial states furnished some legal codification and external protection but the complex of planters/ merchants/ free colonists had to have a coherence and dynamic of its own. In the Spanish case slavery acted as an element in the construction of overseas empire by an absolutist state; in the other colonies plantations were the project of a new type of mercantile-planting capital responding to the increasing commercialization of social relations in the metropolis.

*

As we have seen, African slavery was first thrown up by Iberian colonization and then, on an increasing scale, extended and fixed by the demand for plantation labour. The racial doctrine which saw African captives as made for slavery was the work of no one social category or European nation and continued to exhibit different patterns, interpretations. The Portuguese and Spanish principle of formally confining slavery to Africans had furnished a precedent which the Dutch, English and French had made far more systematic. By closing off nearly every avenue to manumission the English produced the sharpest polarization between free whites and black slaves. For most Europeans the Africans' lack of Christianity and 'savage' nature was thought to explain the need to keep them in bondage. The story of Noah's curse, and the theory that blackness constituted the symbol of this curse, furnished justification for the permanent enslavement of blacks regardless of their faith or conduct. But it did not supply legal formulas for treating slaves as property – these were furnished by residues of Roman Law, with Coke as well as Bossuet invoking the *jus gentium*, as we have seen. Where capitalist relations had emerged the sacred aura they gave to private property cast a cloak over chattel slavery, while the biblical injunction to bring forth the fruits of the earth was harnessed to accumulation and slave planting. As the new slave systems were consolidated they thus combined the secular and the sacred, the new and the old.

The rise of the slave colonies took place in and through economic, military and social competition. A complex of exploitation and oppression which nobody had foreseen seemed to be delivering the goods, and even reproducing itself in dangerous and unstable conditions. If heavy military outlays are included, then it might well be that none of the colonial powers had yet secured a real surplus. But none doubted that, in themselves, the plantations of Brazil, the Caribbean and North America could be worked profitably for the owners, the merchants and the metropolitan governments. The willingness of the governments of England and France to anticipate future profit from Atlantic hegemony explains their commitment of huge resources to the task in the period 1650–1713 and later. If the ultimate resolution of this military competition was as yet in doubt, the same could not be said for the slave plantations, which had already more than proved their economic viability and were now the dynamo of colonial development. Who were the architects of this new enterprise? Why were African slaves rather than European servants increasingly purchased to staff them? What productive possibilities did the plantation realize? How did it meet the formidable problem of security in colonies with a large black majority?

Planters, Merchants, Captains

The planters and merchants of the early years anticipate features of the modern entrepreneur. They had to be resourceful, businesslike, lucky and ruthless. Resources and luck were needed to survive the many accidents and disasters that attended long-distance trade and life in the colonies: wars, revolts, hurricanes, epidemics and other 'acts of God'. Entrepreneurial and managerial qualities could help the planter anticipate, overcome or minimize the hazards of boom and slump, of thieving partners or underlings, of soil erosion and declining yields. Knowledge of the more commercial branches of European agriculture would have afforded some advantage. The experience of a ship's captain would have been even more relevant, as we have seen, because of the varied skills involved – judging the best cargo and most advantageous ports of call, forecasting the needs of crew and ship, ensuring discipline and application among an unwilling and wayward labour force. Early Caribbean planters were indeed drawn from nautical, privateering, gentry and mercantile backgrounds, to which was later added a sprinkling of overseers and bookkeepers. A sample of free male emigrants to seventeenth-century Virginia and Maryland found 30.6 per cent claiming membership of the gentry, 27.6 per cent entered as merchants, only 4.4 per cent mariners and a bare 3.2 per cent claiming an agricultural occupation. Most of these men, as free emigrants able to claim land, would have become planters, albeit small planters to begin with. A minority would eventually have ascended in the ranks of those owning slave plantations.[1]

In well-established colonies plantation managers and owners were drawn from quite diverse backgrounds. Planting was a *carrière ouverte aux talents*. The plantation manager or attorney, if he was skilful, industrious and healthy, was very well paid, and had a prospect of acquiring his own plantation. While some of the early planters could boast gentle birth, later generations of planters in the large new colonies of Jamaica and Saint Domingue often rose from the ranks of bookkeepers and *gérants*. In the English colonies Quakers and other Nonconformists owned plantations, as did Sephardic Jews, though all of them might have started off with mercantile resources. In both English and French islands colonial officials, from a gentry background, were well placed to build large plantations; but so were lawyers and merchants' clerks of plebeian or bourgeois extraction. There were even some cases of former Scots indentured servants, or Breton *engagés*, entering the planter class. And while those of gentle birth were more likely to start out as proprietors, they were also more likely to return home. Whatever his origins, the large planter could assume the style or dignity of a gentleman. He would be expected to play a part in colonial self-government, as a justice of the peace or militia colonel or, in the French colonies, as a member of the *conseil*.

Generally, the possessing classes were more fluid and open in the colonies than they were in the metropolis. Du Tertre observed: 'There is no difference between the noble and the commoner, amongst the inhabitants; he who owns more is more esteemed; only the royal officials possess rank and only the rich have distinction among them.'[2] In Maryland the proprietor made an effort to create a hierarchical society, 'based on land and rents duplicat[ing] the social system familiar to the lords of Baltimore as English landowners and colonizers of Ireland'. But the project foundered: 'The effort to promote a rigidly stratified society crumbled as new wealth led to the emergence of a "home-grown" elite who challenged the political power of Baltimore's aristocracy.'³ In Brazil, where a patrimonial ethos was to linger, the mill owners unsuccessfully strove to assert noble status in order to 'dissociate themselves from the stains of religious heterodoxy, mechanic origins, or links to the "infected races" of Moors, Jews, or Mulattoes (as the prescription ran)'. But as Stuart Schwartz adds: 'Some of the Bahian planter families, in fact, were not free of such association, begun as they were by New Christians, merchants, and occasionally even artisans.'⁴ While a few Brazilian *engenhos* were owned by members of noble families, no commoner *senhor de engenho* was ever raised to the nobility before the nineteenth century.

The planters and their commercial sponsors had to innovate and adapt. They rearranged traditional institutional and moral codes to solve their problems – to meet the keen demand for their products, to overcome the shortage of labour, to assemble a properly skilled crew at an affordable cost, and to govern the resulting colonial society. They needed a streak of opportunism and ruthlessness to overcome scruples concerning the buying and selling of servants and slaves, and their subjection to a destructive regime of forced labour. The notion that the Atlantic slave trade or plantation slavery was a means of Christian evangelization could scarcely survive knowledge of their reality, but the early slave traders and slaveholders were not regarded as monsters. After all, the generality of European merchants, landlords, military officers and ship's captains often did not treat the lower orders at home with any tenderness or consideration. They could be particularly harsh with underlings of another nationality or religion. In the wars of religion in Europe atrocities were frequently committed against those deemed to fall outside the moral community. The daily working of houses of correction, workhouses, or military or naval units often involved physical degradation and abuse. Those considered to have offended against property or order could be publicly flogged, placed in the stocks, subjected to branding and exemplary punishment. Young people without property or gainful employment were encouraged to sell themselves into several years of dependency. Plantation labour in the Caribbean made a system of such techniques. It also proved the effectiveness of labour under the direct control of the planter. The merchants and planters discovered the advantages of tied labour first; only gradually did they develop the logic of racial slavery and foster identities supportive of it.

Plantation Labour: From Indenture to Slavery

Why did the Caribbean sugar planters come to rely on tied rather than free labour? And once they did so, why buy African slaves, not European prisoners or indentured servants? I will argue that the option to buy Africans was made on economic grounds by merchants and planters who found out, by trial and error, that a construction of the economic based on racial exploitation served their purposes well.

Those who invested in plantations counted on a return because of the high price their crop commanded. Slaves, indentured servants and *engagés* had in common that, in principle, they could not legally desert the planter, or ask for extra money when the harvest had to be brought in, or decline to be rehired. The sugar or tobacco planter was running an enterprise where the demand for labour was intense and timing was critical; he needed to be able to rely on sufficient hands being available when required. Achieving all this co-ordination by voluntary means would have been difficult and expensive. It would have required considerable outlays in wages or purchases from smaller suppliers, and a different type of entrepreneur. Neither Native Americans nor Africans were used to wage labour; even the French or English, given the choice, would aspire to work the land independently. The common European willingness to disregard Amerindian claims to land meant that white colonists could usually acquire it on advantageous terms. The shortage of free labourers meant that wages were high. The planters thought it best to take advantage of labourers who were in no position to claim land or demand wages. To begin with they made little of the distinction between servants and slaves, putting the two to work side by side. But as the scale and intensity of plantation labour grew, African slaves were preferred to servants.

Philip Curtin has suggested that the preference for African as against European tied labourers reflected, in large part, the formers' greater chance of survival in the Caribbean disease environment.[5] The evidence is patchy, but it seems that immigrants from Europe had a mortality rate about twice as high as did Africans in the first year or so following their arrival in the Caribbean, and contemporaries were aware of this discrepancy. However, this by itself does not offer sufficient explanation; servants were used in both Virginia and the Antilles during the early phase of tobacco farming, and were largely replaced by African slaves with the transition to sugar or indigo, or more intensive tobacco planting. The epidemiological factor was reinforced by other considerations which recommended African slave labour to the owner of a plantation, if expansion was to be pursued.

The numbers of indentured servants or *engagés* available for purchase was chiefly influenced by social and economic conditions, and these began to discourage emigration just at the point when the planters sought to expand. Convict labour could not supply a remedy. Some involuntary servants were dispatched following such events as the English campaigns in Ireland, the defeat of the Monmouth Rebellion, the suppression of the Fronde, the 'dragonnades' at places like Poitou and the Revocation of the Edict of Nantes (1685). Servitude was sometimes granted to lesser offenders as an alternative to the death sentence. To those charged with recruiting convict labour for the plantations on the British Leeward Islands in the 1680s the discovery of the Rye House Plot 'appeared a very Godsend, as providing a large number of prisoners'.[6] But even in this case the harvest was a few hundreds at a time when the Leewards' planters were looking for thousands of forced labourers.

Penal servitude was found to be an unsatisfactory source of labour for the plantations; it was unpredictable and dangerous, and the prisoners were unsuitable in terms of numbers or quality. The planters did not wish to recruit their labour force mainly from the criminal stratum, while the authorities were unwilling to concentrate too many political or religious opponents in the plantation colonies, where they might lend assistance to hostile powers: the English worried about Irish Catholic assistance to French attacks; the French about Huguenots joining up with Dutch or English privateers. African captives might escape or revolt, but so long as the various rival colonial states all held Africans in slavery, they had no motive for a commitment to the enemy. African runaways were much less likely to find shelter or support from colonists than European indentured servants. Wherever they went the darkness of their skin would prompt the presumption that they were slaves, while the absconding servant had some chance of merging with the free white population.

The numbers of slaves brought across the Atlantic were to reach levels that could not have been equalled by an influx of forced labourers from the European metropolis, unless this were preceded by some improbably draconian social convulsion. The majority of indentured servants and *engagés* had not been reduced to actual slavery, and even these semi-servile labourers were in short supply by the end of the seventeenth century.

The main supply of indentured servants to the English colonies had come from England itself. The consolidation of the English bourgeois state involved no drastic deprivation of personal liberty for the mass of English subjects; indeed, the Civil War and Glorious Revolution were accompanied by a celebration of civic liberties that could not be entirely empty because the new arrangements required a modicum of civic endorsement. The same can be said for the Restoration, heralded as it was by parliamentary speeches in favour of English liberties and attacking the fate of servants in Barbados. 'We are the freest people in the world', Sir John Lenthall told the English Parliament in 1659, speaking in defence of the Royalists who had been sold into servitude in the Caribbean.[7] Those English youths who were still willing to go as voluntary indentured servants to the colonies saw this as a ticket to eventual fortune and liberty.

In order to guarantee their control of Ireland, Britain's rulers periodically organized or encouraged the deportation or exile of tens of thousands of Irishmen. The celebration of liberties for Englishmen went hand in hand with their denial for Catholic Irish. In the 1650s about eight thousand Irish captives were sent to the American colonies, many of them on ten-year penal contracts. More could have been sent, but two circumstances limited their numbers. On some occasions, such as the Treaty of Limerick in 1701, the commanders of Irish troops negotiated terms which allowed for the honourable exile of their men; leaving to become plantation menials would not have been an acceptable alternative to those who comprised the celebrated Irish Brigade of the French Royal Army. However, there were certainly Irish captives who had little choice. In England there were influential personalities, like Sir William Petty, who speculated about the forced deportation of larger numbers of Irish. But while a few thousand prisoners were sent to the plantations the authorities were reluctant to send too many for security reasons. As Catholics the Irish would be prone to ally with the French in the case of war, as they did on St Kitts in 1666–67; moreover, this danger was almost as bad in the case of voluntary Irish servants and worse in the case of those who, having served their time, had the free run of the colony. Irish servants, especially those condemned to many years' servitude, were known to be capable of conspiring with the Negroes, as they did in Bermuda in 1661. Irish servants in Barbados in 1686 were accused of 'being concerned or privy to the late intended rising of the negroes to destroy all masters and mistresses'.[8] In the 1690s Irish servants and freemen in Barbados were imprisoned on charges of aiding the French and of being prepared to support rebellious slaves; the Catholic Irish were generally excluded from the militia, while some blacks were armed.

The French colonial authorities had an even more pressing need to find labour for the plantations, because of low levels of emigration. France had a large population, but, as Le Roy Ladurie has pointed out, the metropolitan rural regime was labour-retentive and did not produce the voluntary migration seen in England.[9] Moreover, the monarchy claimed to uphold the liberties of its French Catholic subjects, limiting its ability to foster an involuntary emigration. This royal guarantee was part of the King's unwritten compact with his people against the power of the great nobles. Indeed, the personal liberty of the subject was the more important to recognize, since political participation was so narrow. The seventeenth century was notable for the welling up of an ethnocentric popular consciousness in France as well as England which held that members of the national and religious community were guaranteed certain essential minimum civic rights. The withering-away of forms of direct servitude in the metropolis had been appropriated as a popular conquest, and freedom from slavery was held to be the birthright of every true Christian and loyal subject. The Bishop of Grenoble had described France in 1641 as 'the freest monarchy in the whole world', while Massillon declared that monarchs must remember: 'You do not rule over slaves, you rule a free and fiery nation, as jealous of its liberty as of its loyalty.'[10] The building of a fully absolutist state under Louis XIV heavily qualified the notion of personal freedom, and events such as the suppression of the Fronde generated a few prisoners who could be sent to the galleys or the colonies. But the aim was to win over and integrate the recalcitrant nobility and their followers; once chastened, they might supply cadres for colonization, but not a menial labour force. In the late seventeenth and early eighteenth centuries the trend in the French countryside was still away from the direct personal subjection of the peasant or labourer. The countryside was depopulated by terrible famines in 1693 and 1707, by epidemics and by warfare. Both nobles and peasants were short of the hands needed to work their land. In these conditions there were very few voluntary emigrants. When the Regency Council instructed the intendants to round up supposed vagrants in 1718–20 there was a storm of opposition because this measure threatened to deprive landholders of badly needed labourers. The resulting outcry contributed to Law's downfall and chimed in with the notion that the sovereign confirmed the social liberty of the subject.[11]

In Christendom's religious feud opponents were prepared to starve, burn and massacre one another. They would seek forced conversions and, failing that, expulsion. But given the intermittent paranoia of the French royal authorities concerning the heterodoxy of their colonists, they were not inclined to trust them with the custody of heretics. Following the suppression of Huguenots in Southern France in 1703 a total of some five thousand Camisard rebels were sent to the galleys. At around this time the authorities were making every effort to recruit for the plantations, but understandably drew the line at shipping out vigorous Huguenots who would look for the first opportunity to link up with their English and Dutch co-religionists, or with the pirates, many of whom were themselves Huguenots.

The planters were demanding in their labour needs. The Atlantic slave trade supplied them with vigorous young adults, most aged between sixteen and twenty-five and, in contrast to many European convicts, possessed of useful agricultural skills. While voluntary indentures were desirable, planters were not keen to acquire those categories the metropolis found it easiest to spare: the halt or the lame, elderly beggars or hardened criminals. Anyway, it was rare for more than a trickle of ordinary criminals to be available as involuntary servants. The young men who fell foul of the new order in Scotland were exceptional, in that planters had a high opinion of their potential; even in the aftermath of rebellions or clearances, the numbers available rarely exceeded a thousand or two a year.

If the planters wanted European labourers, then they had to attract them by means of voluntary contracts. For reasons noted above the French planters never attracted a large stream of *engagés*. Those leaving for the British colonies declined from the 1660s onwards. However, this decline at first mainly affected the Caribbean. The small and medium planters of the

English North American colonies continued to rely mainly on servants until the first decades of the eighteenth century. So long as there was an adequate supply of young men and women willing to sign up as indentured servants, they were thought preferable to the raw African. The servant or *engagé* knew the language of his or her master, and was familiar with European implements and customs. The numbers attracted by the prospect of life in the English colonies during the half-century or so after 1624 meant that indentured labour was cheaper than that of African slaves. The tobacco planters found indentured labour well adapted to this type of cultivation, as well as cheap and reasonably plentiful. The servants themselves seem to have been more willing to go to Virginia, or to the early Caribbean settlements – partly because they believed land would be available on completion of their service.

But even in the cultivation of tobacco, there was a substitution of slave for servant labour in the last decades of the seventeenth century and the early decades of the eighteenth. Because land varied in fertility, and was more fertile when it was first planted, making comparisons of productivity is difficult. But Lorena Walsh, after making allowances for such factors, has found that 'output per worker peaked during the year in which the proportion of slaves rose to a half or more . . .'.[12] The superior productivity of the slaves stemmed both from the fact that they were kept more intensively at work and from a lower turnover in the workforce with, in consequence, less time lost training newcomers. According to Walsh, Virginian slaves were given fewer holidays in the year – with time off only at Christmas, Easter and Whitsun – and worked in the evenings and, during the harvest, sometimes even on Sundays. Slaves also accumulated expertise at the intricate tasks of tending, harvesting and processing the main staples. This was as true of tobacco cultivation as of sugar or cotton, even if the processing was not as elaborate as the boiling and purging of cane juice.

The majority of European servants and *engagés* submitted to their condition voluntarily, if not without misgivings, as young men or women exchanging a few years of hard labour for hopes of a better future. The indenture system was represented as the colonial equivalent of apprenticeship; in some cases the indenture would stipulate that the servants could be required to work only at a given trade. Like the lower order of apprentice in Europe, they could be punished physically. Unlike such apprentices, they could be sold without their consent. News of bad treatment on the plantations eventually discouraged all but the desperate – a feedback effect which, of course, had no African equivalent. The indentured servant retained some rights, and a real prospect of freedom, and for both these reasons he had a different status from the slave. Neighbours, many of them former indentured servants themselves, probably acted as a restraining factor on the mainland.

The lot of the indenture or *engagé* in the Caribbean is invariably described in bleak terms by contemporaries. Richard Ligon writes:

The slaves and their posterity, being subject to their master for ever, are kept and preserved with greater care than the servants, who are theirs but for five years, according to the law of the Island. So that for the time, the servants have the worser lives, for they are put to very hard labour, ill lodging and their diet is very light.[13]

Du Tertre claims a similar pattern for the French islands:

The harsh manner of treatment meted out by the masters to their French servants indentured for three years is the only thing that seems to me to be worrying; for they are made to work to an excessive degree, are very badly fed and are often obliged to work in the company of the slaves, which afflicts these poor people more than all the excessive hardships they suffer.[14]

The racial feeling evident in this last remark partly explains the perception of the servant condition as actually worse than that of the African captives, since the latter were assumed to be more fitted for their role. But the European servants may well themselves have been betrayed by their own expectations of reasonable or customary treatment. They often believed that their employer was bound to feed, clothe and house them, as stipulated in their contract. Since they lacked subtropical survival skills, the alternative of fending for themselves was arduous. The planters found that the Africans were cheaper to maintain because they were more self-reliant – better able to build a hut suited to the climate, and more adept at cultivating a garden. The Caribbean slave would be unlikely to count on their owner to furnish adequate means of subsistence, even if they believed their masters had a duty to make sure they did not starve in times of drought.[15] Faced with an indefinite prospect of servitude, the African captive had more of an incentive to seek to make the best of things, bad as they were.

Indentured servants could and did claim protection from the courts, appealing on the basis of their contract, which indicated general conditions of service and its terminal date. In all probability their case would be heard by another planter who would lean towards his fellow proprietor in deciding the case. But, health permitting, the term of service would end. It has been calculated that of every ten servants sent to the English colonies in North America, one was destined to become a relatively prosperous farmer, one an artisan, the remaining eight to die in service, return to England, or become a 'poor white'. About a third of Virginia's landholders in 1666 were former indentured servants. In the Caribbean the overwhelming majority of servants either died or emigrated; among the very few to become proprietors were those who became pirates or privateers.[16]

If the labour regime was very hard, many indentured servants would abscond. Their bondage was less durable, in every sense, than that of the African – more friable as well as shorter. Escaping slaves and servants sometimes helped each other, but the servant had the better chance of establishing freedom. Compared to the escaping slave, the refugee European servant had a good chance of finding anonymity, or even solidarity, within the population of free colonists. Many of the latter were, of course, themselves former indentured servants. The European labourer was the beneficiary of a colonial 'moral economy' which planters found it prudent to accept. The exemplary punishments which forced the African slaves to work in the most atrocious conditions could not be normally be visited upon white, 'Christian' servants who had committed no offence. In times of danger the latter would often be enrolled in the militia, while African plantation slaves would not.

The decline in the numbers of indentured servants shipped from England after 1660 reflected the fact that the population was no longer growing so fast. It may also be that there was less willingness to undergo the rigours of colonial servitude – or so, at least, is suggested by the defensive remarks of those who vaunted the necessity of the system. Writing after the Restoration, a proponent of the servant system declared:

> Why should there be such an exclusive Obstacle in the minds and unreasonable dispositions of many people, against the limited time of convenient and Necessary servitude, when it is a thing so requisite, that the best of Kingdom's would be unhing'ed from thier quiet and well-settled Government without it. Which levelling doctrine we here of England in this latter age (whose womb was truss'd out with nothing but confused Rebellion) have too much experienced, and was daily rung into the ears of the tumultuous Vulgar by the Bell-weather Sectaries of the Times.

This author insisted that it was a calumny to claim that indentured servants 'are sold in open market for slaves', or made to draw carts like horses.[17] But such assertions did not restore the falling supply of English servants; the supply of French *engagés* was always rather modest, and did not increase.

The fact that servants would claim their freedom after a few years became a more important disadvantage for planters as the time horizon of the plantation was extended. While the tobacco farmer thought of this year's and next year's crop, the sugar planter liked to plan three, four or five years ahead. Slaves helped to constitute a permanent and collective labour force – the crew – whose efficiency would grow over time. The indentured labour force had to be continually formed and re-formed as indentures expired. The former servants were unlikely to offer themselves for future employment on the plantation, or would do so only for very good wages. Such considerations were particularly salient in the case of skilled work. The rewards for training a slave to a skill would continue to be reaped for the rest of his or her working life. Although whites were employed on the plantations as craftsmen as well as supervisors, bookkeepers, doctors and engineers, they had to be paid high annual salaries – often as much or more than the purchase price of a slave. Economies could be made by training slaves for skilled work; planters would encourage slaves to become carpenters, masons, and carters as well as specialist craftsmen in the sugar works. Both the colonial authorities and the mass of free colonists sought to restrain this promotion of slaves to skilled work, since it led to the exclusion of whites from good jobs and to fears concerning security. The colonial assemblies passed 'deficiency laws' stipulating a minimum proportion of whites that had to be employed on each plantation; but like other attempts to regulate the plantations, it was not very effective where it conflicted with the individual planter's own calculations. Slavery, perhaps not surprisingly, enabled the planter to garner the fruits of the formation of 'human capital' among his workforce. In Chapters X and XI details will be given of the rising proportion of skilled slaves on the eighteenth-century plantations.[18]

So long as the servants constituted a large component of the menial workforce, there was a potential axis of solidarity between them and African slaves. In Barbados in the 1650s and Virginia in the 1670s the combination of large numbers of white servants and growing numbers of black slaves proved – perhaps not only for political reasons – particularly unstable. In the case of even momentary alliances servants and slaves sometimes had complementary assets, just like creoles and Africans or blacks and Indians, since in such cases they were less likely to be trapped in one social milieu. There were several instances of servants and slaves helping one another against the planters and authorities in Virginia and the West Indies. During the Dutch wars there were reports of servants and slaves in Virginia combining to escape their masters, or to steal hogs, or simply to get drunk together, rather than apply themselves to their tasks.[19] The last days of Bacon's Rebellion witnessed a joint act of servant–slave resistance, while in the Lesser Antilles there were instances of co-operation between escaped slaves and the Caribs.

But of course, prevailing circumstances did not favour a 'rainbow alliance' of all the oppressed and exploited; Indians were the ostensible target of Bacon's Rebellion, and the 'black Caribs' of the Lesser Antilles were not always kindly disposed towards the remaining Arawaks. The consolidation of slavery was increasingly to be based on a racial bloc. Cases of joint slave–servant resistance became rare in Virginia after the 1670s and in Barbados after the 1690s. By this time those committed to slaveholding and slave trading controlled great wealth and power, including the ability to divide servants from slaves, and slaves from one another. Both poor whites and privileged slaves could win some concessions within the system of colonial slavery, but since the slave system concentrated real wealth and power in a few hands, these concessions had a necessarily limited character.

African slavery in the Caribbean brought out the crippling racial qualification of the popular European attachment or aspiration to personal freedom.

The mass of free colonists could easily admit a community of interest and civic belonging with the indentured servants. Fellow feeling for the enslaved African was much rarer, though not entirely absent; with the establishment of the slave system it was suppressed by fear and the rewards of racial privilege. Prior to the construction of the new slave systems Europeans were certainly prone to racist sentiment, but the common people were also generally hostile to allowing their superiors to own slaves. Slaveowners sought to mobilize racial animosity in favour of slavery, but it could also lend an extra dimension to hostility to slaveholding. The white colonists of North America, discounting the claims of the savage Indians, were inclined to see the continent as destined by the Almighty for settlement by themselves. There was no very strong reason for most of them to welcome the introduction of African slaves who would only further aggrandize a few wealthy colonists. One of the earliest pamphlets attacking slavery in North America was Samuel Sewall's *The Selling of Joseph*, published in Boston in 1700. This work contained some reasonable arguments against the personal and social morality of slaveholding, but it also appealed to aversive notions of racial difference: 'there is such a disparity in their conditions, color, and hair that they can never embody with us and grow up into orderly families to the peopling of the land, but still remain in our body politic as a kind of extravate blood'.[20]

In New England and the Middle Atlantic colonies, as in Europe itself, hostility to slaveholding acted to limit the introduction of slaves. Sometimes this was reinforced by racial antipathy, though free blacks were certainly more acceptable than enslaved ones. In the plantation colonies those who did not own slaves had little political or economic power, and were in no position to stop the planters doing as they wished; if they disliked slavery or slaves enough, then they could leave. The small planter who bought a few slaves and prepared in some sort to share his life with them was himself at least rising above the aversive species of racial prejudice, while still counting on the racial solidarity of his neighbours.

Of course, racial feeling did lend itself to strengthening slavery once a sizeable slave population was already in place. When they made the transition from servants to slaves, planters traded on the fact that the mere presence of the African captives was seen as a threat by nearly all white colonists, with the exception only of the occasional desperate rebel or religious radical. The slave trader and slaveholder introduced to the colonies a category of person who – they themselves insisted – was dangerous, capable of any atrocity if not closely watched and controlled. Once it reached a certain threshold, the introduction of Africans as slaves stimulated a racial fear and solidarity which helped to secure the slaveowner in possession of his property. Racial fear was probably as important as white privilege in rallying the support of independent white smallholders. Fear and privilege, both constituted with reference to black slaves, possessed the ability spontaneously to 'interpellate' white people, making them see themselves as slaves might see them – that is, as members of a ruling race – and thus to furnish them with core elements of their social identity.[21] Slave resistance and rebellion very rarely led to much loss of life among whites, while the suppression of rebellion was always followed by blanket reprisals. Whites would also entertain sometimes extravagant fantasies concerning the intentions of the slaves. Their fear psychology generated a species of 'rational' paranoia. Richard Ligon had warned that if the slaves of Barbados ever had the 'power or advantage' they would 'commit some horrid massacre upon the Christians, thereby to enfranchise themselves, and become masters of the island'.[22]

Those who built plantations worked by slaves and those who sponsored them did so to make or improve their fortunes; a preparedness to inflict great suffering on black slaves was a concomitant of this wealth strategy. The original proponents of English, French or Dutch overseas settlement had not envisaged estates mainly staffed by African toilers, nor colonies where whites were in a minority. But merchants and planters found that the formula worked. These men were often willing to subject defenceless Europeans to degradation and mistreatment as well. What they saw as the racial otherness of the African and black removed any remaining scruples. The economic motive, using slaves as means to a fortune, was strengthened and generalized by commercial competition. Some planters persuaded themselves that they were doing their slaves a favour, but whatever their excuses, economic rivalry dictated resort to slave labour for survival, let alone profit.

With the rise of the Dutch slave trade and English plantations, secular and utilitarian practices of racial slavery emerged which were codified in laws rather than religious injunctions; the French *Code Noir* was a sort of uneasy halfway house. The slave laws updated Roman and medieval legislation treating the slaves as private property, as a permanent menace to civil order, as equivalent to the more feckless and recalcitrant servant so far as authority was concerned, and as equivalent to beasts of burden in most other respects. Seventeenth-century gentlemen were possessed of strong class as well as racial prejudices, such that the two were at least half-assimilated to one another. The slave condition could also be understood within the terms of patriarchal ideology as one which was emasculated and 'feminized'; the 'scold's bridle' used to gag impertinent women was to reappear on the plantations, as did ducking or burning as weapons of 'correction' or terror (slave punishments are discussed below in the section on plantation security). But while European women's virtue was fiercely protected, that of the women slaves was casually violated, or harnessed to crude natalist policies.[23]

The widespread practice of seeing slaves as beasts of burden is revealed by inventories where slaves and animals are listed side by side. When

Scold's bridle (England) and iron mask (Caribbean)

Morgan Godwyn urged slave baptism, planters would insist that the blacks 'were beasts and had no more souls than beasts'. Planters gave slaves names normally used for dogs, horses, donkeys or cows ('Jumper', 'Gamesome', 'Ready', 'Juno', 'Caesar', 'Fido', and so forth). Alternatively, the adult slave would be known by a diminutive and would often lack any family name. In the Caribbean a higher proportion of slaves had African names, though usually this was a minority, while in the colonies of the Catholic powers priests sometimes insisted on 'Christian' names. As Ira Berlin points outs, some planters, like Robert Carter, keenly appreciated the importance of naming their slaves.[24]

Access to a large-scale Atlantic slave trade meant that African slaves could be purchased in quantity by planters who found an apparently inexhaustible demand for their products. Once the switch was made to slaves there was, in effect, no longer any labour constraint on the expansion of plantation production. It will, therefore, be appropriate to consider the new scale of the Atlantic slave trade before delineating the new plantation regime itself. As we will see, the peoples of West and West Central Africa were vulnerable to entrapment in ways which did not apply to Europe.

The Supply of Slaves and the Turn to Slavery

The timing of the transition to slave labour was strongly influenced by the price at which slaves could be purchased relative to increasingly scarce alternatives. Thus slavery spread from the Caribbean to the English North American colonies with a lag of three or four decades, reflecting the higher transport costs involved, the more modest labour requirements of tobacco and the greater willingness of indentured servants to bind themselves for work on farms in North America. The turning point came in the 1680s. The planters of the Chesapeake needed more field labourers to expand output: European servants were unavailable in sufficient numbers, and willing to sign on only if good conditions and land were available. Slave prices were dropping, while European wage rates were rising. The numbers of slaves introduced to the Chesapeake rose from 1,700 in 1670–80 to 7,300 in 1680–90, 7,700 in 1690–1700 and 10,700 in 1700–10. In the 1690s the supply of servants temporarily dried up, with slaves supplying some of the deficiency; when servants again arrived in large numbers after 1700, they were far less likely to be bound for field labour. So far as the French islands were concerned, the flow of *engagés* had always been insufficient, and their colonists were ready to buy slaves as soon as they had the resources and opportunity to do so. In the French Caribbean, as in English North America, the turn of the century marked the transition to a new type of slave trade in which the monopoly privileges of the old Africa Companies were relaxed in favour of independent traders, sometimes operating with a licence from the Companies and often flouting even this formality.[25]

It is clear from Table VIII.1 that the rise of the English and French plantations was predicated upon the increased supply of slaves.

Table VIII.1   Slaves Taken by the Atlantic Trade from Africa in the Seventeenth Century

	No. of Captives	Average Price (£)
1601–25	225,400	4.27
1625–50	218,800	4.27
1651–75	442,200	5.26
1676–1700	723,000	3.67

Source: H.A. Gemery and J.S. Hogendorn, 'Elasticity of Slave Labour Supply and the Development of Slave Economies in the British Caribbean', in Ruben and Tuden, eds, *Comparative Perspectives on Slavery in New World Plantation Societies*, New York 1977, pp. 72–83.

The declining tendency of slave prices on the African coast, crudely indicated by the average in Table VIII.1, is particularly remarkable in view of the doubling and trebling of the size of the traffic in the third and fourth quarters of the century. The price drop must have encouraged the planters' shift to slavery.[26] It testified to the increasing cost-effectiveness of the arrangements for capturing, selling and transporting the slaves, despite high slave mortality at every phase of the translation from African captivity to New World slavery.

The conflict between the Dutch and the Portuguese in the second quarter of the century diminished American demand for slaves and disrupted the supply routes. The rise of the new plantation colonies from around 1650 boosted demand and raised prices as English and French traders bid for slaves. The Dutch introduced a more enticing and variegated array of trade goods to the African traders and chiefs, including firearms, gunpowder and more sophisticated metal manufactures and textiles. The other European powers followed suit. The forts and trading factories set up by the slave trading companies proved expensive to maintain, without offering any guarantee of better terms of trade. Competition was now much keener, and at several points on the coast, African merchant princes – men such as Edward Barter, John Konny, John Kabes and Asomani – constructed and fortified trading posts of their own, and happily engaged in trade with the interlopers. In 1693 Asomani captured the Danish castle of Christianborg at Accra, and set himself up there as its Governor; although he did not stay at Christianborg, he built a castle of his own further down the coast, defended by cannon.[27] The merchant princes generally needed a good relationship with one of the rulers of the large states, which thereby acquired economic resources and firearms on better terms.

The merchant princes also had their own agents on different parts of the coast and at strategic points up-river. The French reported that such men would typically inhabit a *case à la portugaise*, which appears to have been a typical product of the Afro-European creole culture which had grown up in the centres of the African trade. Because of their priority on the scene and their greater inclination to mingle with the Africans, the cultural matrix on most parts of the coast had a Luso-African character, with Portuguese-based creoles being common. However, the so-called 'Portuguese house' was, in fact, a structure unknown in Portugal itself. It was generally oblong with an open vestibule, or roofed porch, at the front and a large, airy veranda all the way round; the walls might be constructed of stone or wattle-and-daub, and would be handsomely whitewashed. Both Africa and India would appear to have supplied elements of the *case à la portugaise*, a structure which was to be imitated throughout the colonial world and make its contribution to the Brazilian *casa grande*.[28]

In the early decades of the eighteenth century the American planters' thirst for slaves was slaked by further increases in the numbers shipped as prices on the African coast began to climb steadily. This produced the strange result that European slave merchants felt exploited by the Africans with whom they dealt. In 1705 the Royal African Company complained in a memorandum to the British Parliament that the local merchants were 'so insolent that they are not to be dealt withall under any reasonable terms', adding: 'under the present establishment [the trade] is onely advantagious to the natives of Guinea and prejuditiall to the Company and Plantations'.[29]

This extraordinary locution captures only one aspect of the double-edged relationships on the coast. The various African states involved in the slave trade were now less dependent on any one European power, though they were sometimes increasingly dependent, like the other Atlantic states, on resources which could be acquired only by responding to market demand. The expansion of the slave trade was now associated with the growth of African states whose *raison d'être* was increasingly penetrated by the need to secure fresh supplies of slaves via tribute, warfare, distortion of judicial processes or degradation of dependent kin. In South West Africa the restoration of Portuguese control boosted slave exports as the colonial governors reconstructed the networks of slave tribute: other European slave traders could acquire slaves from this region at the port of Luango, just north of the Congo river. In West Africa the multiplication of trading posts, improved commercial facilities, and continuing political fragmentation favoured a rise in the export of slaves from areas such as the Bight of Benin, where the local states had hitherto sought to limit the traffic. The unification of Kajoor and Bajo (Senegambia) in 1695, under the rule of Latsukaabe and his army of slave musketeers, consolidated a slave-raiding regime which thrived on Atlantic exchanges, even if there was stiff bargaining over the terms. The monarch of Dahomey withdrew from the slave traffic for several years in the early eighteenth century, but the combination of intensive military and economic competition was eventually to break down such resistance. In the period 1640 to 1800 West Africa dispatched some 4 million slaves, with 1.5 million coming from the Bight of Benin. This compares with a total of around 3.2 million slaves exported from South West Africa during the three centuries 1500 to 1800.[30] Winthrop Jordan, a writer who stresses the racial animosities of Europeans in the pre-slavery period, nevertheless writes of the earliest years of colonization:

> There is no reason to suppose Englishmen eager to enslave negroes, nor even to regard Richard Jobson eccentric in his response to a chief's offer to buy some 'slaves': 'I made answer, We were a people, who did not deale in any such commodities, neither did wee buy or sell one another, or any that had our owne shape.'[31]

Yet Jobson's boast of 1623 proved empty, and the English became the largest carriers in an eighteenth-century slave traffic which was itself vastly larger than the sixteenth- or seventeenth-century trades. The Dutch, the English and the French all displayed some initial scruple in the matter, but before long competitive pressure, and the logic of Atlantic trade, made the slave trade widely acceptable – indeed, a commerce to be patronized by royalty, blessed by the clergy, and practised by the aristocracy and gentry, as in England's Royal African Company.

The desire for gain prompted slave trading; racial exclusion made it acceptable for Africans to be treated in ways that would not have been allowed for Europeans; Africans were packed so tightly into the slave trading vessels that a given ship would carry three or four times as many slaves as it would indentured servants or even European convicts; higher mortality on the slave ships did little to diminish this huge cost advantage to the merchants. Racial sentiment was integral to the functioning of the plantations, furnishing the basis for the fear and privilege which united the white colonists. But the merchants who sponsored the Atlantic traffic in slaves, and the statesmen and philosophers who endorsed them, often had no first-hand experience of slavery at all. Their judgement of personal or national or class advantage, underpinned by a sense of racial and religious superiority, sufficed to confer this decisive facility to the planters. I have found no evidence that those most concerned with the construction of the slave systems were primarily animated by racial feeling. Take the case of John Locke. As we have seen, he was an investor in the Royal African Company; as an active member of the Board of Trade and Plantations he must certainly be accounted one of the founders of English colonial slavery. Yet he regarded any attempt to exclude Negroes from the human race as a childish delusion, writing: 'a Child having framed the Idea of Man, it is probable, that his idea is just like that Picture, which the Painter makes of visible Appearances joyned together, and such a Complication of Ideas together in his understanding, makes up the single complex Idea which he calls Man, whereof white or Flesh-colour in England being one, the child can demonstrate to you, that a Negro is not a Man, because white-colour was one of the constant simple ideas of the complex idea he calls Man: And therefore he can demonstrate by the Principle, *It is impossible for the same thing to be, and not to be, that a Negro is not a Man*; the foundation of his Certainty being not that universal Proposition, which, perhaps, he never heard nor thought of, but the clear distinct Perception he hath of his own simple ideas of Black and White.'[32] Of course this reflection has the abstracted quality of a philosopher's example, but its force comes from acceptance that Negroes are indeed men. As I have suggested in Chapter VI, Locke endorsed colonial slavery because he thought it an institution necessary to the productive exploitation of English colonies and because he saw in the planter-colonists a counterweight to royal power.

Anti-slavery impulses should be noted, though they were easily contained. The belief of some Protestants that baptized slaves, or their children, should be offered eventual manumission had been overcome in every plantation colony; reference to Noah's curse as well as to the injunctions of St Paul helped to stifle the residual Protestant commitment to the freedom of all true believers. For their part Catholic clerics had been exercised by the validity of the original act of enslavement, leading them to question the legitimacy of the Atlantic slave trade as well as to raise issues connected with the right to baptism. The Holy Office in Rome briefly endorsed a sweeping condemnation of the Atlantic slave trade in 1686, following representations from Capuchin missionaries in the Kongo and from Lourenca da Silva de Mendouça, representative of an African Brotherhood in Brazil.[33] The fact that there was tension between Spain and Portugal, and that Protestants now loomed large in the trade, may have allowed these voices to be heard in Rome. But the condemnation was shelved and individual Catholic powers were urged to take their own measures to reconcile religion and slavery; the French *Code Noir* was probably one result. In Brazil the Jesuit Jorge Benci published a treatise on the Christian management of slaves in 1700 in which he condemned planter excesses, overwork and cruelty, urging that not more than forty blows be administered as punishment at any one time.[34] The Spanish maintained that their practice of slavery was legitimate, because Africans were introduced to the Catholic faith, but that other powers, especially the Protestant English, either failed to baptize the captives at all, or introduced them to heresy. In 1693, and on several later occasions, the Spanish authorities in Florida offered a haven to Africans unjustly held in slavery by the English; those fleeing to St Augustine (Florida) and willing to undergo religious instruction were offered manumission and a place in the militia.[35] The English authorities believed that the Jamaican maroons also received encouragement from the Spanish authorities in Cuba or Puerto Rico. The intermittent refusal of Spain to accept the legitimacy of the slavery practised by other powers, especially England, furnished only a hairline fissure in the carapace of the slave systems, though one which, by the last decade of the eighteenth century, was to acquire greater significance.

Women and children loomed larger in the Atlantic slave trade than they did in the traffic in indentured servants and *engagés*, and they comprised a higher proportion in the seventeenth century than they did in the eighteenth. The indentured servants and *engagés* were generally between fifteen and twenty-three years old, though convicts could be older; just over three-quarters of the servants introduced to the English colonies were male, a proportion rising to over 90 per cent for the *engagés*. Of the slaves sold in the Caribbean between 1663 and 1700, men comprised 50.5 per cent, boys 8.4 per cent, women 37.0 per cent and girls 4.0 per cent. Thus although male slaves outnumbered female slaves by a ratio of 59 to 39, the female contingent is still comparatively large.[36] Female slaves were often as valuable, or more valuable, than male slaves in Africa, since they had usually been raised to work in the fields, as well as to bear children and attend to domestic tasks. The European traders refused to pay any premium for women and usually offered less, on the grounds that they were purchasing slaves for the harsh toil of the sugar works and cane field. But the slave trading captain had only so much leeway when he was making up his human cargo. Female slaves could be sold to planters, generally at a price somewhat below that of the male slaves.

The seventeenth-century planters did see some advantage in encouraging their slaves to have children. They were also willing to pay premium prices for creole slaves; Debien reports that the owners of the larger *sucreries* favoured a high proportion of creole slaves, in some cases reaching a third as early as 1670.³⁷ While the planters were immersed in a world of business calculation, those who wrote about encouraging slave families did not usually calculate returns to an investment in children but, rather, spoke of the positive moral effects of permitting elements of family life among their slaves. An investment in a human child takes rather a long time before it begins to pay off – say fifteen or twenty years when, as pointed out in Chapter VII, the planter was thinking only five or eight years ahead, given Caribbean mortality rates. Women were made to work during pregnancy, almost until they gave birth; they would often be back in the fields within a month or so. The extra expense of having children on the plantation was not great, since all their food and clothing would be supplied from within the plantation, much of it by their mother working in her spare time. Small children were looked after by older and infirm slaves; by the time they were six or seven they would be carrying out light tasks themselves.

So long as it did not detract from a ferocious work regime, the planters liked to think of themselves as people who favoured family values. The real threat to the development of family life among the slaves was the sexually predatory behaviour so common among the white males on the plantations and, to a lesser extent, black males in authority positions. Of course, overseers and drivers were also capable of forming relatively permanent unions with female slaves; these sometimes contributed to the slave children born on the plantations. While the live birth rate on the Caribbean plantations was quite low, it was probably higher than that among female slaves in Africa – Claude Meillassoux claims that the true female slave in Africa was generally 'sterile', lacking conditions for having children unless, by becoming a wife, she partially elevated her status.³⁸ As we will see in Chapter X, slave women practised forms of birth control and abortion, and some may have had resort to infanticide. But slave women were also to find consolation in having children – as American-born slaves their children had a better chance of reaching a relatively privileged position. The older colonies like Barbados and Martinique had growing creole minorities within their slave populations which had a positive natural growth rate. This was significant for the future, even though the maintenance – let alone expansion – of overall slave numbers still heavily depended on importing more African captives.³⁹

The New Plantation

The late-seventeenth-century plantation, and its successors, integrated aspects of production that had previously been separate: cultivation, processing, transportation. This was an Anglo-French refinement of the Brazilian example. The Brazilian *senhor de engenho* purchased much of the cane that his mill ground from the *lavrador de cana*, and generally sold his sugar to a merchant in the nearest port. By contrast, the West Indian planters grew all their own cane supplies, and many English planters sold their sugar in Europe. The Brazilian estate was worked by a mixed labour force of Portuguese employees, African slaves, and Indian day labourers; the Portuguese and Indians might outnumber the African slaves. In the early days of English and French planting, estates were small and the labour force was mixed; by the late seventeenth century over nine-tenths of the menial labour force would be slaves. In Brazil and North America black slaves never comprised a majority of the population; in the Caribbean plantation colonies, by 1700 or soon after, they comprised three-quarters or more of the total.

According to Richard Sheridan, 'the merchant system of finance played a key role in the transition from small to large units of production'.[40] A significant proportion of planters were themselves merchants, or relatives or partners of merchants, revealing the new scope of mercantile initiative in a colonial and slave trading context. Whatever their background, successful planters would be tempted to undertake some mercantile as well as productive functions. Early plantation profits were often used to enlarge the plantation or to acquire satellite farms. The sponsorship of plantations by mercantile capital did not mean that they were thereby technogically conservative or stagnant. The merchants supplied equipment to the planters, and were interested in boosting their output. Those involved in the plantation trade were 'new merchants', concerned to organize and improve transport, cultivation and processing – not simply, as in the classical formula, to buy cheap and sell dear. For the same reason successful planters could become successful merchants; some notable examples will be supplied in Chapter X.

Richard Dunn writes:

> The seventeenth century Caribbean colonists built a truly impressive sugar-producing system, especially when one considers the tradition-bound character of English farming at this time. The sugar planters utilized agricultural techniques radically different from those they knew at home and learnt how to manipulate men, beasts and machines on a far larger scale than their cousins in Virginia or Massachusetts.... In the pre-industrial world of the seventeenth century, the Caribbean sugar planter was a large scale entrepreneur. He was a combination farmer-manufacturer.[41]

Gabriel Debien, historian of French colonial slavery, is equally insistent on both the scale and the novelty of the Caribbean plantation:

When the large sugar works appeared after 1690 agricultural colonisation was combined with industrial colonisation. The making of sugar, even the simplest raw sugar, requires, if undertaken on any scale, the rotation of numerous disciplined work teams, a regime of punishing toil, closely supervised by day and by night. This was a new type of work, an element of social revolution.[42]

In Europe it was the tenant farmer or peasant who organized the great bulk of agricultural production. In acreage the landowner's home farm or demesne would be larger than a plantation, but the numbers of labourers employed on it would be smaller. In England the landlord's home farm would not regularly engage more than two or three dozen labourers, if that.[43] As an integrated unit Caribbean plantations came to be five or ten times as large as their metropolitan equivalents, with a crew of two or three hundred slaves. While the European landlord employed a steward or bailiff to look after his estate and collect rents, the Caribbean planter required the functionally more specific services of the bookkeeper and supervisor, or *économe* and *gérant*. Plantation labour was intensive, closely invigilated and coerced.

The plantation evidently belonged to the world of manufacture as much as to that of commercial agriculture. The plantation crops, especially sugar and indigo, required elaborate processing, and both permitted and required the intensive exploitation of labour. Cottage industry was not, of course, uncommon in the European countryside. But unlike many contemporary European manufacturers the planter, or his manager, organized the labour process, and thus had a direct stake in the productivity of his workforce. Under the 'putting-out system' the European manufacturer was not immediately responsible for production, which was carried out by cottager families or craftsmen. The Caribbean planter was responsible for purchasing equipment, implements, provisions, and a supply of new slaves to replace those who died, or were worn out by toil. He or his overseer was also responsible for organizing some production of foodstuffs on the estate or on satellite farms, and for building work and maintenance. Apart from the overseer, hired staff could include sugar-boilers and craftsmen; the services of doctors, lawyers and bookkeepers would also be engaged.

The complexity of the Caribbean plantation as an integrated unit meant that the planter had manifold outgoings: for slaves or servants, for domestic animals, foodstuffs, clothing, implements, processing equipment, construction materials, packing cases, and the payment of wages and salaries to employees, taxes to the state, commission and fees to lawyers, brokers and merchants. Plantation profits were dependent on good timing in making shipments and sales, and on skill in deriving revenue from subsidiary crops or products – rum and molasses made a crucial contribution to the sugar planter's revenue. On the productive side, the plantation required the co-ordinated and meticulously timed activities of between 10 and 300 workers. Specialist slaves, working long hours but receiving some small privileges, came to work in the responsible positions in the sugar works, as planters discovered that this was cheaper than hiring specialized employees. So far as field work was concerned the slaves were organized into gangs to facilitate their unwilling incorporation into a tightly controlled and exorbitant labour regime. Responsible slaves were found to replace the white servants as drivers of the slave gangs in the fields. Eventually the planter or overseer came to rely considerably on the 'head people', who would also supervise the distribution of clothing or supplementary provisions, and would have their pick of available dwellings and garden plots.

Debien writes that by the end of the seventeenth century the *commandeur*, or driver, was also generally a slave:

> He was responsible for the work and discipline of the slaves. A large authority was left to him in this. Since he knew their ethnic origin, their seniority, their health, one could say that their disposition and application depended on the driver. He was the centre of distribution. A driver was not changed unless in some extremity. His stature, his energy, his sense of command were the qualities which recommended him, not preference of 'nation' or age. However one very often found a creole in this function, sometimes a new slave as a second driver, but almost never a mulatto.[44]

The slave-driver or *commandeur* was thus the hinge of the plantation system, and necessarily enjoyed considerable privileges. He was himself responsible for allocating tasks and provisions among the generality of the slave crew. His juridical status as a slave imposed real limitations on him, but within the plantation he – drivers were overwhelmingly male – had authority over scores of people, while he was subordinate to only one or two. The conscientious overseer or planter would continually tour the estate, whip in hand, pistol at his belt, during the harvest and planting season. He would calculate the size of tasks and assign them to the drivers, check that animals and equipment were working properly, and supervise punishment. But with only a handful of whites among a few hundred blacks, he necessarily depended on his 'head people'.

The Barbadian planter Colonel Henry Drax of Drax Hall wrote that the organization of slaves into gangs was the best way 'to prevent idleness and make the Negroes do their work properly'. At Drax Hall the slaves were divided into five or six gangs according to their strength, sex and age, ranging from the 'ablest and best' reserved for 'holing and the stronger work', through 'the more ordinary Negroes in a gang for dunging', down to the children's gang, which might be assigned weeding. During the harvest a 'running gang' was charged with keeping the furnaces supplied with fuel. A responsible slave, the driver, would be placed in charge of each gang, and required to keep a 'list of the gang under his particular care that he may be able to give a particular account of everyone, whether sick or how employed'. These lists were brought to Drax every fortnight so that he could check on the performance of every slave in the crew, and identify 'lazy Negroes absenting [themselves] from their work'.[45] Once the cane had been brought to the mill, it was subjected to a quasi-industrial division of labour as some tended the mill while others boiled and purged the juice. The mills themselves were increasingly effective, powered by wind, water or animals, and helping to maintain intense work rhythms. A Barbadian slave was quoted as saying: 'the devil was in the Englishman that he makes everything work; he makes the negro work, he makes the horse work, the ass work, the wood work, the water work and the wind work'.[46]

The simplification and repetition of tasks, the co-ordination of labour between different categories of labourer, the imposed rhythm of the gangs, seem to represent a form of organization which echoes not only shipboard life but also the perhaps related revolution in seventeenth-century military training and tactics associated with Maurits of Nassau, Prince of Orange and uncle of the Prince Maurits who governed Dutch Brazil. Drilling or 'square-bashing', standardized methods of loading and firing, closer super-vision by NCOs, had created a new type of fighting force, and greatly boosted firepower. William McNeill notes a concomitant which might have caused problems: 'when a group move their arm and leg muscles in unison for a prolonged period of time a primitive and very powerful social bond wells up among them'.[47] The slave gangs usually sang as they worked. There are regrettably few accounts of their songs in the early period, but if those of colonial forced labourers in Africa are a guide, they will have included vigorous lampoons and poignant laments.[48] In exceptional circum-stances the *esprit de corps* of the slave gang did erupt in rebellion, but normally it possessed a disciplining function which, like military discipline, was carefully trained on the targets prescribed by those who ran the apparatus.

The enterprise under the planter's management, denying the individual producer control over much of the labour process, anticipated some of the features of capitalist industrialism. But it has often been argued – especially by those working in the tradition of classical political economy or Marxism – that slavery remained a wasteful and inflexible form of labour. In this view the plantations' basis in slave acquisition and domination set narrow limits on profitability and productivity, which were not normally encoun-tered where wage labour was employed. The slave plantation has been seen as overcapitalized and rigid, with planters being unable to vary the size of their labour force at will, and lacking this spur to economy. The labour of slaves has also been thought to have been suboptimal: as forced labourers slaves lacked motivation, and were apt to be careless with their masters' property and equipment, thus further inhibiting improvements. Partially offsetting such drawbacks were the slaveowners' access to (1) the advan-tages of the slave gang; and (2) the defraying of some costs by self-provision ('natural economy').[49] As we will see, this classical critique poses many relevant issues. But in the specific conditions of the New World in this epoch, the balance of advantage from slave acquisition and use was still very much weighted in favour of the merchants and planters.

The construction of slave plantations did indeed require large fixed investments. Whether the planter acquired his labour force by outright payment or on credit, the purchase price of the servile labourer, whether enslaved or indentured, represented a prior claim on the output of his enterprise. Even provisions bought for the slaves had to be purchased many months before they would be eaten. The planter was paying for labour long in advance of that labour being brought into production; the capitalist employer of the future was to be in the happier position of paying the direct producer only after he had possession of the product – though he might have to wait many months before a sale was made. The planter who borrowed money to buy slaves or servants would be responsible for interest charges arising from the point of purchase onwards. Labour for the planter was an investment made with years of anticipation: it was part of his fixed, not circulating, capital. The price of the slave or servant constituted discounted future surplus product that the slave or servant might be expected to produce. The planter would hope to extract a large surplus product from his slaves, who covered their own subsistence costs in one or two days each week, but his profits were shared in advance with the merchant and slave trader.

In the early days of a colony, records often show the planter making large profits, but after a few decades profits tend to decline. New plantations were generally established when prices were high, but the pattern of declining profitability also reflects such factors as reduced cane yields, expenditure on fertilizers, the cost of replacing equipment and slaves, and sundry 'acts of God'. The planters' profits were greatly affected by the fortunes of war. On the one hand, war raised the price of sugar; on the other, it prevented some planters from producing, or from getting their sugar to market.[50] But beneath the interplay of such contingent factors the tendency of the planters' rate of profit to decline to a 'normal' level simply reflected the competitive nature of the business. So long as profits remained above normal, there was an incentive for more plantations to be brought into production. While financing the acquisition of a slave crew did represent a heavy charge on the income of a plantation, it should not, in principle, have reduced profits below a normal level.[51]

A second potential limitation of the use of slave labour concerns the seasonally uneven labour requirements confronting even the best-organized plantation. Generally the size of the slave crew was determined by the peak requirements of the harvest period; the intensive labour of processing coincided with that of bringing in the harvest, thus raising the number of hands required at this time. During the rest of the year the crew could be underemployed; from the investment point of view, unused slave labour time was a form of idle capital. Subsistence and subsidiary crop cultivation, which could be timed to complement that of the main crop, somewhat mitigated this problem, as did the practice of hiring out slaves for construction or public works during the dead season. Sugar, the most valuable crop and the one employing the majority of slaves, had a harvest period in the Caribbean of five or six months, from December to May; the Brazilian pattern of separate slave-worked *engenhos* may have partly derived from the fact that the climate of Pernambuco permitted the cutting of cane over a nine-month period, thus keeping the mill slaves toiling most of the year.

West Indian planters deliberately prolonged the harvest to get the most out of their crew, but since yields declined sharply, the problem could not be evaded. The main crop did require heavy work in the planting season, and there was always a need for weeding, dunging, repairs to buildings, and so forth, but these tasks might not fully occupy the slaves. As a consequence, the planter's concern with labour productivity was selective: methods of improving the efficiency of processing, the 'bottleneck' in the flow of production, aroused much more interest than those relating to methods of cultivation, especially preparation of the soil and planting. As a way of reducing underemployment in the off-season, and because of mortality among the slaves, the planters were often short of hands during the harvest. This led both to overworking and to neglect of subsistence production.[52]

During the harvest period the organization of labour was at its tightest, and there was an incentive to economize upon it – outlays on equipment were considerable. The use of slave labour did not inhibit planters from improving and enlarging the mill machinery. As early as 1653 a Barbadian planter was ordering iron casings for his mill rollers from an Oxford foundry. Metal implements raised working capacity and were more resistant to hard use. Some idea of plantation demand for metal manufactures is given by the following order sent to England by a Barbadian plantation manager before the 1693 harvest: 50,000 nails, 10 brass fittings for the mill frame, 12 ladles, 6 skimmers, 3 sheets of lead, 600 hogshead and barrel hoops, and a 70-gallon copper. Outlays on equipment for the planting season were, however, more modest. The soil was laboriously worked by means of metal hoes: neither horse nor plough was put to this work, since surplus slave labour was available. Cultivators equipped with hoes could be worked as a gang; ploughing teams could not be organized and invigilated in the same way.

The agricultural tools used by an English agricultural labourer would be worth about £1, while the planter could equip fifty slaves for £5.[53] But the slave gangs used up their equipment at a much faster rate; a large plantation might order 20 dozen hoes, weighing half a ton, each year.[54] All such items could be ordered on account from the merchants. Planters sometimes suggested that hoes were best for slaves, since they were closer to the

implements they knew from Africa; since African slaves picked up the
unfamiliar and complex techniques of sugar-making, this explanation is
not decisive. Watts points out that the cultivation methods used caused less
erosion and loss of soil moisture than ploughing, an important consideration with a highly exhaustive crop like sugar cane. The Caribbean planters
had an incentive to see that the quality of the soil was protected by cane-
holing and manuring, because land on the islands was scarce, even if labour
out of season was not. After noting the advances in husbandry achieved by
the seventeenth-century planters, Watts concludes: '[m]ore resistance to
innovation was displayed in the realm of field implement revision than in
any other aspect of West Indian estate life', which could have resulted both
from the absence of pressure to economize on labour and from the slaves'
lack of concern for productivity.[55]

Each of the above limitations may have constrained plantation productivity to some degree, yet in the end, the plantation systems survived and
prospered. What seem like drawbacks from the somewhat anachronistic
standpoint of a fully functioning capitalist system (such as did not then
exist) were accompanied – and largely neutralized – by characteristics of
slave labour which brought compensating gains, together with limitations
of a different sort. So far as production was concerned, the slaveowners
could exploit the resources of gang labour as a way of boosting output;
they could also have recourse to so-called 'natural economy' or autosubsist-
ence as a way of reducing costs. The organization of slaves in gangs allowed
an exceptionally intense rhythm to be maintained; it was a special form of
the coerced co-ordination which, as Marx observed, slavery could facilitate.[56] This way of organizing work was well adapted to cutting cane and
several other species of plantation labour, but it required close supervision
and delivered exceptional results only where cultivation was concentrated
in a small compass.

Slaves could be used in general farming, as the Dutch showed in North
America and the Brazilians in South America. Slave cattlemen and urban
artisans were common in Spanish America. In such cases slaves were not
organized in gangs, and their work situation often dictated elements of
autonomy. If they were offered some chance of buying themselves out of
slavery, they could be induced to work very hard. But this offered no firm
basis for a permanent slave regime. The British and French slaveowners
preferred to find ways of obliging their slaves to work hard without offering
them freedom – and this meant, above all, resorting to gang labour. In
suitable employments the momentum and rhythm achieved by carefully
graded slave gangs yielded formidable results.

Planters had to develop a special apparatus to extract labour from the
slaves, but once they had done so they had an asset that gave, as we will
see below, a reasonable return. Their real problems arose from the slave
response to the rigours of gang slavery. While the traders, the colonial
officials, planters and overseers might all agree that the slave owed labour

to his or her owner, the slave had not been consulted. It was down to the planter and overseer, and their team of drivers, to extract work from slaves who would always be more or less unwilling to exert themselves. The salaries paid to overseers reflected this consideration, as did sundry small incentives offered to the drivers and 'head people'.

The gang slaves on a sugar plantation were forced to work extraordinarily long hours. During the harvest the mill would be kept working all night if there was cane still to be ground. The stronger slaves were expected to work a full day in the cane fields – sunup to sundown, with a two-hour break at midday – followed by an alternating shift in the mill at night. The night shift, sometimes known as a 'watch' or 'spell', would last from six to twelve or twelve to six, and would be worked every other night. Thus the prime slaves would be working ten hours one day, sixteen the next, not including the lunch break. This would be the regime in a 'well-run' plantation, and some planters would have tried to extract even more from their captive labour force. During harvest time the slaves were usually allowed to drink as much raw cane juice as they wanted, boosting their calorie intake, though it was not otherwise a particularly nutritious addition to their diet.

The regime of plantation labour had dire effects on slave mortality and fertility. Notwithstanding African slaves' somehat greater resistance to the disease environment, mortality rates were very high. The sugar plantations on which over three-quarters of all Caribbean slaves worked consumed the lives of slaves almost as voraciously as the mills ground the mounds of cut cane. Planters estimated that the young African brought to their estates had an average life expectancy of little more than seven years. The planters' calculations were certainly influenced by the fact that slaves could be bought cheaply in the seventeenth century. In 1695 a Jamaican planter would have to pay around £20 for a slave who, on a well-run plantation, would produce sugar worth this amount each year; there were other expenses to meet, but the scope for profit was still enormous. Looked at from another point of view, however, the value of a slave crew was, in contemporary terms, very great: a crew of 100 or so slaves was worth at least £2,000, or more than twenty times the annual income imputed by Gregory King in 1688 to the family of a naval officer, clergyman, prosperous farmer or tradesman, all of which were in the range £44–£80.

The high capital value of a Caribbean slave plantation put pressure on the planter to maximize output from a given crew; since he had often borrowed at high interest to complete preparations for the harvest, the pressure was all the greater. The planters were willing to protect the lives of their slaves by all measures short of abandoning slavery or sugar cultivation, the only actions which might have lowered the death rate. The slaves were fed a high-protein diet, and doctors were engaged to tend them, but they died none the less. The slave population's 'depletion rate' (i.e. negative 'growth rate') of 2–4 per cent annually reflected low fertility as well as high mortality. The planters did buy female slaves, albeit in lesser numbers than male slaves, and sometimes even encouraged them to have children, but the plantation regime placed great pressure on family life and child-rearing. The failure of slave populations to reproduce themselves, however, did not prevent the growth of the plantations so long as the revenues generated by the sale of slave produce sufficed to purchase more Africans. Moreover, merchants were often willing to advance credit themselves as a way of disposing of slaves or obtaining a lien on the produce of the plantation. So far as the plantation system is concerned, the traders were as much part of it as the planters.

The viability of the plantations did not rest only on the destructive profitability of gang labour. The planters could also defray some costs by relying on slave labour to meet them without the need for cash outlays. The slave could produce food as well as the cash crop, and could work on investment projects as well as the final product. Once again these potentials were double-edged, since they permitted an excessive degree of autarky. While planters or their managers did not stint on outlays directly related to bringing in the cash crop, they were parsimonious when it came to providing clothing or extra food for their slaves; and what might be a bare sufficiency in a normal period would turn into a starvation ration if the food crop was destroyed by drought or pest. The Caribbean plantations were more reliant on external supplies and more exposed to the vagaries of war than those in North America, where there was more land and the average size of slaveholdings remained much smaller. Whether his plantation was small or large, the Virginian tobacco planter had fewer outgoings for equipment, and sought to reduce direct outgoings on food by organizing work on the main food crops himself. While the slave plantations everywhere in the Americas had to justify themselves in commercial terms sooner or later, they retained a basis in the 'natural economy' of self-provision. In Brazil and most of the Caribbean, slaves were expected to produce the bulk of their own food supplies on plots given them for the purpose.

The agricultural techniques known to Africans were of considerable help in the Americas. African slaves grew maize or manioc, potatoes or vegetables, and raised chickens or pigs. The planters and overseers sought to set strict limits on the energies spent on anything other than the cash crop, yet they also saw the advantage of slaves meeting most of their own food needs. In principle the planters would allow their slaves to work on their plots for a day, or a day and a half, a week. Thus during the slaves' 'free time' they worked to feed themselves, but during the harvest the planters might begrudge them even this.

In the Caribbean the planters were forced to buy in dried meat or fish to supplement the slave diet, as the land available for slave plots was scarce and distant, but in North America planters generally achieved a high level of self-sufficiency. In 1726 William Byrd, one of the largest Virginian planters, described his situation:

> Besides the advantage of a pure Air, we abound in all kinds of Provisions without expense (I mean we who have Plantations). I have a large family of my own, and my Doors are open to Every Body, yet I have no Bills to pay, and half a Crown will rest undisturbed in my Pocket for many Moons together. Like one of the Patriarchs, I have my Flocks and my Herds, my Bond-men and Bond-women, and every soart of Trade amongst my own Servants, so that I live in a kind of Independence of everyone but Providence. However this soart of life is attended without expense, yet it is attended with a great deal of trouble. I must take care to keep all my people to their Duty, to see all the Springs in motion and make everyone draw his equal Share to carry the Machine forward. But then 'tis an amusement in this silent country and a continual exercise of our Patience and Economy.[57]

This vision of patriarchal virtue and plenty portrays the ideal of the resident planter. The numerous struggling small planters of Virginia were able to achieve only a penurious and stunted version of it – partly because their larger neighbours, if they were self-sufficient, bought little from them. Moreover, even the large tidewater planters of Virginia and Maryland very frequently managed to accumulate large debts. Byrd himself was driven into debt by the cost of making good the acquisition of huge tracts of land. However self-sufficient they were they did hire some help, and buy some equipment, manufactures and building materials. If their slaves wove cloth or made shoes – as they did – they would still need tools and machines. They and their families also ordered, usually on credit, the necessary appurtenances of gentle living. Such outgoings dictated the need to practise 'economy', and to 'carry the machine forward'. In times of difficulty, when warfare disrupted communications, many slave plantations could live on their own, with more land and labour devoted to subsistence. As Jacob Gorender puts it, they could withdraw 'within the shell of natural economy'.[58] But in more normal times the commercial value of the slaves owned by a planter weighed on him to some extent – if he could not find profitable employment for them, then he could sell them.

The English and French plantations made more intense use of slaves than the traditional Brazilian pattern of ownership and production. Stuart Schwartz cites a report of the 1660s urging that those running Sergipe do Conde, a mill now owned and rather poorly managed by the Jesuits, should buy more cane land to ensure supplies, and that slaves should be trained to take over from expensive salaried workers. Competition from new producers did encourage Brazilian planters to copy where they could, but the cane growers often clung on to their land, while the workers earning a salary were often people towards whom the owner of the *engenho* felt some obligation.
  The organization of the 'noble business' of Brazilian sugar-making was

modified, but not transformed, in the late seventeenth century. While the English and French planters now outproduced those of Brazil, Brazilian sugar, despite high freight charges and onerous colonial levies, retained an important niche in the European market. The Brazilians mills produced a good-quality 'clayed' white sugar, while the English and the French were dissuaded from doing so by colonial authorities who wished to foster the development of refining in the metropolis. The traditional Brazilian *senhor de engenho* did not get as much work out of his slaves as did the French and English planters, who could switch them at will between field and mill according to the cycle of planting, maintenance, harvest and processing. On the other hand, the Brazilian sugar industry by no means disappeared – sugar continued to be the colony's most valuable export even during the eighteenth-century gold-mining boom.[59]

The Brazilian, North American and Caribbean slave plantations, despite real differences, shared the characteristic that their property was only half-inserted in the circuit of commodity exchange. A significant part of the value of the plantation derived from an input of slave labour removed from the realm of commodity relations. Slave labour was used to improve land and to erect fine buildings. The larger planters everywhere built themselves splendid residences – the Big House, or Grand 'Case – often embellished with elaborate woodwork and stone, their imposing Palladian or baroque exteriors and staircases pointed up by African detail craftsmanship. The availability of slave artisans for work on such houses during the quieter months meant that their costs of construction were considerably below what they would have been in Europe. It is striking that even absentee owners generally found it agreeable to have a fine mansion constructed to house them on their visits to their property, rare though these might be.

The strictly agricultural dimension of the plantation also revealed its essentially hybrid character, and complicates the task of calculating planter profits. Such profits are usually assessed by first placing a value on the estate. The value of improved land and of the buildings housing the sugar works invariably boosted the estate's value by a quarter or a third, yet these had been constructed by slaves, whose value was also entered as part of the value of the enterprise. While the planter would generally have invested real resources in buying slaves, he had been able to build up the productive potential and market value of his estate, using slave labour, with little further expenditure. The fillip given by slave labour to the value of the estate has the effect of reducing the apparent rate of profit, if the latter is established on the basis of the former rather than the planter's cash outlay. Schwartz points to a feature of planter accounts in Brazil and North America which may well have been linked to these peculiarities, since they were also to be encountered in the business practices of Caribbean planters: while planters could estimate the value of their estates, and kept track of cash coming in and going out, they did not distinguish between capital and current expenditure, or make provision for amortization of capital items.[60] Another way of putting this point would be to say that the planters lacked a modern concept of capital, despite the many modern features of their enterprises.

J.R. Ward has calculated the rate of profit for some seventeenth- and early-eighteenth-century British West Indian sugar plantations in a way which bears out the anecdotal evidence that they were financially a good investment. He finds that the Parham plantation in the Leeward Islands, with 150 slaves, made an annual average of £694 profit in the years 1689–97, representing a 10.3 per cent return on outlay; in the peacetime years 1698–1702 the profit rose to an annual average of £915, or a 13.6 per cent rate of return; in the wartime years 1703–13 it was £561 annually, or a rate of return of 8.3 per cent. The Bybrook estate in Jamaica had a more chequered record, partly in consequence of the attack suffered by the colony. In 1687–91, with 139 slaves, it made an annual average profit of £520, representing a 6.6 per cent rate of return; in 1697–98 it suffered a loss of £410, and the slave crew dropped to 103. In 1698–1702 there was a modest recovery: an annual average of £297 profit was earned, representing a rate of return of 4.8 per cent. Plantation profits in the English islands subsequently settled into the range 5–12 per cent, which would certainly have been accounted a good rate of return in the metropolis.[61]

These are, of course, planters' profits; the plantation trade also yielded a surplus to merchants (especially if they were also creditors) and revenues to colonial governments. There were elements of monopolistic 'rent' in the overall surplus relating to the natural advantages enjoyed by the plantation colonies and, in some cases, an element of colonial protection as well. But undoubtedly the ability to mobilize, and batten upon, slave labour furnished the lion's share of the surplus (as we will see in Chapter XII). While it yielded access to premium crops, it also permitted a degree of technical advance.

The performance of the early-eighteenth-century sugar plantation embodied technical improvements in nearly every aspect of cultivation and processing as well as a ferocious mobilization of labour. Some of these improvements have already been noted. The planting of cane in holes rather than trenches reduced erosion and counteracted declining yields, so long as manure was applied. The integration of farm animals as suppliers of dung, as a means of transport and sometimes as a source of mill power, added a further vital element to raising output, though it required more space to be made over as grazing land. With their relative abundance of land, the Virginia planters could always switch from exhausted to fertile 'sections', and it was to take longer before they introduced such improvements. The sugar planters of the Caribbean, especially on the small islands, had to learn a careful husbandry which saw the advantage of conservation. Inside the mill the juice was more efficiently expelled by means of metal-cased rollers; inside the boiling-house fuel was conserved by use of a single flue to heat the coppers. Bagasse, or mill trash, was widely used to feed the furnaces. The technical advances in cultivation and processing encouraged twenty-four-hour production in the harvest season, and were compatible with intensified labour at all times. In the early days, when the new methods were introduced in Barbados, the sugar plantations still engaged many servants, and at least some of the slaves had responsible and artisanal roles. The slave-worked estates were perfectly capable of adopting these innovations, but did not substantially add to them; only this latter point hints that the oppressive nature of the plantation labour process exacted a certain toll on productivity.[62]

The British and French islands where sugar cultivation spread had strong natural advantages. Although the Lesser Antilles were cramped, by the same token they had readily available maritime transport. The phenomenal rise in production which had just begun was the result of a multiplication of Barbados-style plantations throughout the British and French Caribbean, staffed by an ever-rising number of slaves. Some advances were to be made in crop types and irrigation, but the essentials of the productive system were all in place by the beginning of the eighteenth century. Those Portuguese and Spanish colonies which were also suitable for sugar cultivation still lacked the requisite commercial facilities and outlets. The discovery of gold fields in Brazil in 1687, and of new silver seams in Spanish America, led to neglect of plantation possibilities until the latter half of the eighteenth century. In Surinam, and for a while even in Jamaica, plantation development was restricted because bands of maroons had established themselves in the interior.

The Plantation Regime and the Question of Security

The plantation agriculture which developed in the Caribbean required exacting standards of security. The founding of colonies where slaves comprised four-fifths of the total population was unprecedented in the prior history of enslavement. The small size of the Caribbean islands facilitated invigilation of the slaves, and made escape more difficult. The planters and their free employees were always well armed and organized into militia regiments, for the purposes of internal as well as external security. So long as the free employees were treated with a minimum of consideration, they could be relied upon to rally to the defence of the social order of the colony, racial fear and privilege cementing their loyalties. Colonial powers could guarantee their Caribbean possessions only by stationing naval squadrons and garrisons in the region; this helped to suppress buccaneers, encourage the loyalty of their own colonists, guard the plantations and deter colonial rivals. The captive Africans cannot fail to have been impressed by the concentrated firepower upon which their masters could draw in an emergency. Mounted teams of slave-catchers, accompanied by tracker dogs, dealt with the problem of runaways. Life for a runaway was exceptionally hard and hazardous unless they could find or found a maroon community.

The whip and the stocks were ever-present reminders of the punishment that would befall the slave who failed to work hard or show respect. The routine punishments meted out to the slaves were severe and humiliating, and could include cropping of the ears or other mutilation. The severed head of a rebel would be placed on a pole outside his or her plantation. The owners of slaves executed for sedition could claim £25 compensation in Barbados; forty-two slaves were executed in the years 1685–88 and ninety-three in the year 1691 alone.[63] The slave suspected of a rebellious act was subject to extreme and elaborate violence. Hans Sloane writes:

> The Punishments for Crimes of Slaves, are usually for Rebellions burning them, by nailing them down on the ground with crooked sticks on every Limb, and then applying the Fire by degrees from the Feet and Hands, burning them gradually up to the Head, whereby their pains are extravagant. For crimes of lesser nature Gelding, or cropping off half of the Foot with an axe. These punishments are suffered by them with great constancy. For running away they put Iron Rings of great weight on their Ankles. . . . For negligence they are usually whipt by the overseers with hard-wood switches, till they be all bloody. After they are whipped till they are Raw, some put on their skins Pepper and salt to make them smart. . . . These punishments are sometimes merited by the slaves, who are a very Perverse Generation of People, and though they appear harsh, yet are scarce equal to their crimes, and inferior to what punishments other *European* nations inflict on their slaves in the *East-Indies*. . . .[64]

Father Labat found that the English in Barbados treated the slaves with great cruelty, but he quickly adds:

> I admit the punishments are cruel, but one must consider before condemning the inhabitants of the islands that they are often constrained to abandon moderation in the punishment of their slaves, in order to intimidate them, to impress on them fear and respect, and to prevent themselves from becoming the victims of the fury of a people who, being one against ten, are always ready to revolt, to take over everything and to commit the most horrible crimes in order to liberate themselves.[65]

These two passages, written by supposedly civilized and humane individuals, testify to the fear, rage and racial hatred directed at slaves who simply resisted slavery.

While the apparatus of coercion was always visible, other factors helped to forestall or fragment slave resistance. Efforts were sometimes made to assemble slaves from different African peoples, though the trader's scope for doing so was limited while there were some planters who preferred to buy slaves from a few favoured nations. Undoubtedly cultural and linguistic fragmentation undermined the spontaneous solidarity of slave crews wherever there was a large proportion of newcomers. In 1680 the Gentleman Planters of Barbados produced a memorandum opposing the religious education of their slaves, urging that there was 'no greater security than the diversity of our negroes' languages which would be destroyed by conversion, in that it would be necessary to teach them in English'.[66]

The whole sequence of capture, transport to the coast, middle passage and sale in the Americas was traumatic and demoralizing. Most of the victims of the slave trade knew slavery as a familiar condition, which certainly helped to reconcile them to it, albeit with great anguish and without renouncing all hope of escape. But though slavery was known to the captives, the sugar plantation and its demands would have been something else. The extraordinary discipline, hierarchy and productive exertion of the plantation bore down relentlessly on the slave. During the harvest season the plantation built up a fierce momentum, whose pace was set by the need to keep the mill fed with cane and the furnaces with fuel, and which the individual could scarcely resist outright. If the slave survived the first years, then they would have acquired a plot of land, formed friendships, possibly found a spouse; for a sizeable minority of the men there was the prospect of joining the elite of slave-drivers, craftsmen, and 'head people'. These might receive extra rum or clothing, or a separate dwelling-place or larger garden plot; they were also better placed to find a companion. Such attachments and privileges helped to secure the adhesion of a vital layer of slave adjutants to the plantation regime. A few women became housekeepers and others acquired the often dubious privileges of the household slave. Those with children were much less likely to run away. Most plantations were a world of their own, with communication between different slave crews forbidden or kept to a closely controlled minimum.

The African captives possessed some knowledge of what it meant to be a slave. While they would have hoped to escape the rigours of enslavement, they immediately found themselves inserted into a fully functioning slave system, with a calibrated range of sanctions and incentives. Those who had arrived ahead of them had usually carved out some small space for themselves and the slave community. Nearly everywhere the slaves managed to establish customary usages which offered them a little time and some access to a patch of land. They usually picked up something of the language of the whites, but in most slave colonies new tongues developed – pidgins, patois and Kréyoles. These new languages were little spoken by the planters, and even overseers often had scant command of them. However, the colonial sailors, dockers, craftsmen, smallholders, poor whites and free people of colour spoke the patois or Kréyole, which developed precisely in the space between these various social layers and the slave community. While European and Native American languages contributed much to the lexicons of the patois and Kréyoles, their grammatical structure and rhythms had important African elements.[67]

There was a continual struggle between overseers and slaves over time. It is significant that in most parts of the Americas Sunday was eventually – if insecurely – established as a free day for the slaves. This practice was to be zealously defended by African slaves, whether or not they were Christian or familiar, as Muslims would also have been, with the seven-day week. Religious observance in the plantation zone was slack, and little attempt was made to proselytize the slaves, but the idea of Sunday as a day when they did not work for the planter was certainly very attractive to them. That it had a cultural-religious sanction was clear from the behaviour of indentured servants and free employees, and from observation of the rituals of colonial society. On many early plantations it would have been impractical to put the slaves to work but not the servants. Supervisors and drivers would also generally be reluctant to lose their own rest day. Sometimes owners might wish to work on a Sunday at harvest time – especially the small planters who predominated in Virginia and Maryland. But in the Caribbean planters saw advantages, as was noted above, in allowing free time to their slaves. Sunday work and Sunday markets gave a small opening to slaves and the slave community which they eagerly filled. Working on their plots and provision grounds, the slaves of the Caribbean not only fed themselves but also produced crops for sale. Indeed, slave-grown produce soon furnished the main supply for the local markets on many islands.

The slaves' ability to sell the food they grew inevitably became a source of tension. Colonial officials and planters sought to control slave markets, fearing them as a source of unrest and conspiracy. There was also a potential for clashes with poorer white farmers who resented black competition. Regulations were enacted requiring that markets be policed by whites, that they end at ten in the morning and that the goods for sale be cleared by the slaves' overseer. In 1714 the Antigua Assembly passed a law 'for the better regulating Negroes and the suppressing their Conspiracies and Profanation of the Lords Day'. But this attempt to control the Sunday slave markets was found 'highly inconvenient', and the Act was repealed seven years later.[68] If they were allowed to conduct their own markets, the slaves could feed the colony – a satisfactory arrangement that cumbersome attempts at regulation threatened. Planters recognized that permitting their slaves access to markets allowed them the diet they needed even if it could also divert energies – and furnish an outlet for stolen produce.

In each colony there was a running struggle between overseers and slaves over the extent of the latters' free time, and access to land and markets. Slaves were able to make gains partly because a gain for the slave was often, indirectly, a gain for the planter too. The Reverend Robert Robertson, a slaveowner of Antigua, claimed in 1729 that so far as slaves were

Koromanti.

Jamaican music, from Hans Sloane, *Voyage to the Islands* (British Library) (see also p. 308)

concerned, Sundays were 'peculiarly their own', and that 'this unbounded Liberty of doing what they listeth on the Lord's Day made their Slavery fit the easier all the rest of the week'. He also observed: 'Slaves have (or, which is the same, think they have) some Rights and Privileges, of which they are as tenacious as any Freeman upon Earth can be of theirs, and which no Master of common Sense will once attempt to violate.'[69] Robertson's claims were doubtless overpitched for apologetic purposes, but they refer us to the intimate contest where some slave gains were favourable to the planters' interest.

The slaves' subsistence cultivation was limited on Barbados and other smaller islands by the shortage of land, leading to heavy food imports; nevertheless, slaves still covered at least half their own food requirements, with the masters supplying dried fish or meat as a supplement. The slaves of Jamaica and Saint Domingue met even more of their own needs. The Caribbean practice of issuing clothing and provisions to the elite of head slaves, who would then distribute them as they saw fit, helped to strengthen the authority structure of the plantation. In Virginia the planters and farmers asserted even greater control by allowing less space to the slaves' garden patches and instead organizing much of basic food production themselves, in the intervals of the work required by tobacco cultivation.

At night, even after a gruelling day in the fields, the slaves made music and danced. While he was working as secretary to the Governor of Jamaica in the 1680s, Hans Sloane visited a plantation in the company of a French musician. With the help of the latter he noted down various slave songs which displayed a strong African character – 'Angola', 'Papa' and 'Koromanti' – though he also opined that 'their songs are all bawdy and tending that way'. He describes the slaves playing instuments of their own manufacture resembling lutes, harps and guitars. Gourds were used as drums, though drums of any size were banned by the planters, since the slaves 'making use of these in the Wars at home in Africa, it was thought too much inciting them to Rebellion'.[70]

It is by no means the case that Africans were less prone to resist or escape enslavement than European labourers. It is simply that, once in the Americas, their opportunities for so doing were more tightly circumscribed. The slave factories on the African coast witnessed repeated revolts and break-out attempts. The slaves were chained on board ship and often kept in manacles or leg-irons after landing. The planters' monopoly of firepower and organized force secured outward compliance with the plantation regime, but many issues remained to be negotiated between overseer and driver, driver and gang. The regime accepted under the threat of the lash would be contested by non-cooperation or escape, flouted or denied in song, dance and story. The slaveholders rarely or never felt safe on their own estates and could easily be panicked by real or invented slave conspiracies. Most whites carried a pistol or a sword in the country districts. The sanctions controlled by the slave regime were so considerable that even the reality of negotiation did not prevent its results being highly unequal and oppressive for the slaves. But the couplet accommodation/resistance does not exhaust the gamut of slave experience, since there was always the middle term of sheer survival, for both the individual slave and a slave community which pieced together its own new conditions of life, its rules as to provision grounds and burial grounds, the mutual support of 'ship-mates' (who had arrived together), and its reconstructed memories and stories, many of which stressed the advantage of patience, persistence and slyness over brute strength or arrogant self-regard, as in the talks concerning Brer Rabbit or Anancy the Spider Man. Even the most heroic dimensions of slave resistance usually had some relationship to strategies of survival.

Runaways and maroons gave continual evidence of rejection of the plantation regime, but they usually engaged in an irregular intercourse with those who remained on the plantations as well as with pedlars to whom they sold honey, herbs or fruits. The colonial wars of the seventeenth century gave the opportunity for larger-scale revolts or escapes. In Brazil the 'black republic' of Palmares in Pernambuco (mentioned in Chapter V) was only one of a dozen or more large *quilombos*. While it first flourished during the war between the Dutch and the Portuguese, it survived for several decades thereafter. Between 1672 and 1694 it withstood, on average, a Portuguese expedition every fifteen months; its eventual dispersal was achieved only after the deployment of six thousand troops and a siege of forty-two days. The *esclavos del rey* of the copper mines of Eastern Cuba refused to continue supplying this metal unless they were offered possession of land for subsistence cultivation and guarantees against sale to any private owner; the representatives of the Spanish King were obliged to accede to these demands. As previously noted, maroon communities held out in

Jamaica from the time of the English conquest; after repeated unsuccessful attempts to suppress the maroons the colonial authorities instead entered into a treaty with them in the 1730s. Maroon communities appeared in Saint Domingue and inland from the Caribbean coast of South America. The predatory bands of buccaneers and 'brethren of the coast' occasionally supplied an opportunity for a slave breakout, or even admitted escaped slaves to their ranks. Jamaica was the scene of repeated slave revolts, because its terrain offered scope for escape.[71]

Awareness of the fragility of the slave regime prompted due caution in the warring European powers. Attacks were made on the plantation colonies in the course of the Wars of Spanish Succession, but no attempts had been made to incite slaves against their masters. The main island colonies – Barbados and Martinique, Jamaica and Saint Domingue – were strongly enough defended to repel or deter any invader during the whole cycle of wars which ended in 1713, though Jamaica did suffer one destructive incursion. The agreement at Ryswick and Utrecht to extend peace agreements to the Caribbean and the New World – ending the tradition of tolerating unending warfare 'beyond the line' mentioned in the Introduction – signalled the intention of the authorities in Paris and London that the ravages of the privateers and *flibustiers* should now be ended. The brief war that flared in 1718 set the scene for an agreement between the powers that did at last end the worst ravages of the pirates.

Alternatives to Slavery?

The slave plantation was the most distinctive product of European capitalism, colonialism and maritime power in the late seventeenth and early eighteenth centuries, with racial sentiment acting as a crucial binding agent. Without the rise of new markets and new circuits of accumulation, without mercantile sponsorship, and without preparedness to flout a traditional 'moral economy', the slave plantations could not have been constructed. Moreover, these plantations played a role in social conflicts in Europe itself by outflanking the popular prejudice against enslavement. But a recent essay by David Eltis seeks to present the role of capitalism in a quite different light, pointing out that its deference to shared values in Europe protected Europeans from enslavement, and that in the course of time the descendants of the slave would also benefit from the emancipatory influence of market relations.[72]

While my account accords considerable weight to cultural assumptions, they could not have produced the tragedy alone. Slaves were not acquired to grow sugar or tobacco out of a desire to punish Africans for their black skin. On the other hand, without racist assumptions the Atlantic trade would not have been permitted, nor would it have seemed right to subject Africans to treatment and toil that would have been deemed excessive for

Europeans. The growing demand for tobacco, sugar and other plantation products itself reflected a new culture of consumption. The culture of the new consumerism and cash dependence broke with the traditional moral economy which had been theorized by St Thomas Aquinas, according to which any purchase or sale had to be regulated by norms of justice, not simply the possession of desires and the cash to satisfy them. This traditional moral economy faced a challenge in an epoch when long-distance trade began to involve large sections of the population. The critique of the slave trade made by Fernão Oliveira or Tomás de Mercado had been an attempt to renew and extend Thomist principles to the era of Atlantic trade, but their voices had been drowned by the clamour for commercial gain and the sophistry and apologetics of Luis de Molina and Suárez, or the perilous reasoning of Jeremy Taylor and John Locke.

The emergence of the plantation systems and the practice of subjecting only Africans to the extreme rigours of plantation toil evidently reflected European conceptions of the Other to which attention has been repeatedly drawn. Planters did experiment with white servant labour in the most menial roles but, given the wider availability of African slaves, were eventually drawn to construct a racial bloc of free whites against enslaved blacks. So while we should continue to assert the presence, and from certain points of view the primacy, of economic forces and motives, it is also necessary to register the reworking of given identities and the new emphasis on 'race'.

Alden Vaughan has pointed to the widespread evidence of racial sentiment hostile to Africans and blacks in the early days of the English colonies. But not all of these racial sentiments were useful to slaveholders or importers of Africans, as I have argued, and Vaughan himself does not contest the fact that racial sentiment was transformed and partially redirected by the rise of the slave systems. In a review of the link between racism and slavery, he quotes J.R. Pole to the effect that racism was not 'as profound at the beginnings as it latter became', but that nevertheless '[i]t was only necessary that racism should be sufficient, and that visible identification – already a cause of racial repugnance – should make slavery so easily practical'.[73] But while historians should certainly pronounce racism guilty in the matter, this does not mean that its accomplices, rampant capitalism and the free market, and their accommodation to slavery, are not co-responsible. If power is highly unequal, and practically unaccountable, then racial feeling will have great scope to become racial exploitation, and may even be magnified by the opportunity.

David Eltis argues that most modern writing on the construction of slavery in the Americas has wrongly focused on economic motives. In his view the slave systems contradicted such motives, since the colonial powers could have extracted more profit by shipping out European slaves to the plantations; both shipping and acquisition costs would have been lower. They declined this opportunity because other Europeans were deemed to be members of their own moral community.[74] This sense of moral community, in its turn, is traced both to Christendom and to the emergence of generalized market relations in early modern Europe. Given time, a wider Atlantic market would also generate a new sense of moral community, and Africans would be emancipated, in ways that have been outlined by Thomas Haskell.[75] Curiously, this supposed critique of economic causation actually proposes that the capitalist market was ultimately the decisive moral and political force. This being the case, its proponents are perplexed that market relations should be conducive to racial slavery in the seventeenth century but not, apparently, in the nineteenth.

I have tried to show that the construction of colonial slavery involved a reworked racial ideology as well as new economic forces. But in so doing I find more merit in previous accounts of the construction of colonial slavery by Edmund Morgan, Richard Dunn and K.G. Davies than does Eltis, and am led to propose a different counterfactual possibility to highlight the role of racial ideology.

Richard Dunn sums up the making of plantation slavery: 'Whites enslaved blacks because they found this labour system worked very well. Economic exploitation seems to me the prime motive: racism conveniently justified and bolstered the use of forced labour.' He adds:

> The rape's progress was fatally easy: from exploiting the English labouring poor to abusing colonial bond servants to ensnaring kidnaps and convicts to enslaving black Africans. . . . Once Barbadians took the plunge and began importing Negroes from Africa by the boatload, they never looked back. Nor did they pause to consider whether these black labourers had to be enslaved, whether they might not be organized as indentured servants or wage workers.[76]

English traders and planters held slaves in order to produce commodities for the market. Unlike African slaveholders, they did not buy slaves for military reasons or with the intention of marrying them, or even for reasons of display. Some Caribbean planters no doubt gained satisfaction from lording it over slaves on the plantation, but many returned to England, without slaves, as soon as they had made a satisfactory fortune. The Virginian planters came to value their patriarchal role, but they too had to adapt continually to market forces or see themselves driven into debt. The slave enterprises were profitable – indeed, they had to be profitable or they would gradually have ceased to exist, profits being needed to buy new supplies of slaves. As we will see in Chapter XI, even planters who felt that they were gentlemen first and foremost discovered that heavy debts destroyed their aspirations.

The economic benefits of the new colonial slavery to planters, merchants and the colonial state were to be enormous. But it will be worth considering the possibility that in the long run racial slavery was costly and inflexible, even in ways that could be measured by the market, let alone in more general human terms. If such a view can be sustained, then the economic motives which impelled the resort to racial slavery would themselves have been short-sighted, though no less effective for all that.

There was an ideological and extra-economic component in the decision to opt for African slavery, since colonial settlement could have proceeded in a more humane fashion, as the more imaginative and generous-spirited members of the slave societies occasionally argued. The decision for slavery was implicit in the competitive commercial structure of planters and merchants; servants, *engagés*, smallholders and metropolitan governments were not consulted. Once planters and merchants competed to bring plantation produce to the market by the swiftest means possible, with a free hand to import slaves and exploit them, the transition to the slave-worked plantation was inevitable. The Atlantic slave trade option was supported by governments, deferring to the wishes of the main actors in the matter. For the planter who was seriously interested in maximizing output, and in the fortune this promised to make him, the decision to buy African slaves became a natural one. In all the European colonies there were people who declined this temptation, contenting themselves with farming their land with family and hired help. While they did produce provisions for the market, and even some cash staples, they were not numerous enough to match the phenomenal increase in the plantation output.

As Dunn rightly points out, there is no sign that the larger planters seriously considered any alternative to enslavement, such as recruiting extra African labourers by offering them indentured service or wages. Had they done so it would have demanded innovation, but so did their practice of the slave trade. Left to themselves, individual planters would have had difficulty devising a feasible alternative, since it would have required an institutional and regulatory framework implemented by a public authority. But the merchants and planters were influential men; and since these were systems of colonial slavery, the metropolitan governments could also have stepped in to change the context in which merchants, planters and potential plantation workers took their decisions. In effect this is what Spanish colonial officialdom had done in the sixteenth century, devising, as we have seen, circumstances in which free and semi-free waged labour was available to the owners of mining concessions. Likewise, in the aftermath of emancipation, colonial government devised a series of alternatives to slavery which, though they were often objectionable in various ways, still allowed more autonomy, and better prospects, to the plantation labourers than did the slave systems.[77]

It might be thought that the harshness of plantation labour, or the difficulty of devising alternatives, rendered outright slavery more or less inevitable in seventeenth-century conditions. This option corresponded well to the outlook of those who had gained the upper hand in the Atlantic world. But the criticism of Mercado or Vieira, or the early reservations of the Dutch WIC, pointed in another direction. After all, the colonial systems also showed that they could rise to the challenge of staffing even very onerous employments without recourse to slavery when they deemed it necessary. The work of the seaman could be almost as harsh as the toil of a slave in a sugar plantation, and his living conditions were in some ways even worse. The ruling authorities used some convicts and slaves in their ships, but they never became the principal labour force for the ships-of-the-line or, for that matter, the merchant marine. While galleys in the Mediterranean were staffed mainly by convicts and slaves, this type of labour did not seem suitable to the ocean-going sailing ships, because of the demands made on the sailors of such a vessel and the opportunities open to them. The English and French navies both resorted to compulsion in manning their ships, but this compulsion stopped way short of enslavement. The press-ganged or conscripted sailor was paid some wages, accorded some rights and dignity, and had some prospect, however uncertain, of regaining his liberty. When slaves were recruited as sailors it was normal for them to be offered similar conditions. While the lash was a constant presence, a real attempt was made to encourage a positive commitment among the crew – a commitment that would be badly needed when supplies ran low, or hostile engagements loomed, or a ship was stranded or becalmed, or there were good prospects for deserters. Seventeenth-century merchants and sea captains also had to overcome such problems of motivation and labour control in very demanding conditions.

The fact that it was possible to man the Royal Navy or the *marine de guerre* without recourse to outright slavery suggests that a means other than slavery could have been found for producing the plantation crops. Why did those very same merchants and sea captains who conducted an arduous transatlantic trade without slavery resort to it for the sugar plantations? The navies were constructed by means of an extraordinary effort of the public power. A notably efficient system of inspection was required simply to ensure that the contractors who supplied provisions to the warships maintained demanding standards of quality and durability.[78] When Louis XIV sought to regulate the plantations, he neglected to stipulate any effective system of inspection and enforcement. The construction of the navies involved conceding some elementary rights to sailors against abuse – concessions of any kind were not at all welcome to the wealthy or powerful in the seventeenth century.

The captains of merchantmen wielded great power; nevertheless, the seamen held formal and informal rights protective of their interests. Perhaps the most significant right was that on an English ship the payment due to the sailors had first claim on the value of the vessel. While sailors had to vow obedience to their captains, they negotiated a contract of engagement in advance, stipulating their monthly wage, the size of advance they would receive, and their share (if any) of the proceeds of the voyage, provisions for various contingencies and perhaps some basic stipulations as to 'necessaries of life', though some of these were customary.[79] Merchants and captains needed to offer some guarantees simply to man their ships; since shipboard life was known to be unpleasant and dangerous, wages were often a little above those of unskilled workers ashore.

It may be imagined that planters would have seen little advantage to themselves in offering similar guarantees and contracts to their workforce. Yet had they been willing to do so, they might have found it much easier to recruit wage labour or indentured labour to the plantations. Of course the planters of Virginia and Maryland did cultivate their estates mainly with free or servant labour for more than half a century by offering freedom dues or the prospect of claiming land. Work on the sugar plantations was harder but instead of, say, doubling the freedom dues or land, planters offered the same or less. They successfully recruited craftsmen and specialist labourers by offering premium salaries, but gradually found it cheaper to substitute slaves for free workers in many posts requiring skill. From the standpoint of the individual planter such a decision made economic sense, but enslavement was costly or fatal to much larger numbers of Africans, and while some of these improved their material position this could have been achieved without the degradation of enslavement; likewise a large number of consumers made immediate, but small, gains, while a little patience could have brought a more rounded and humanly sustainable economic pattern, as we will see.

The fact remains that Britain and France probably could not spare the very large numbers of able-bodied workers that would have been needed to produce sugar, tobacco and other plantation products on a contract labour basis: that is one reason why the numbers of indentures dwindled. Yet it would also have been possible for British and French entrepreneurs to have signed up labourers in Africa or Asia, offering them freedom, or return passage, after five years or so. Assuming that coastal contractors received a commission considerably below slave prices, the slave trading and slave-raiding nexus would have been at least discouraged. The sophistication of social relations in West Africa could very possibly have accommodated arrangements for the export of migrant workers, some of whom could then send back remittances, much as happens now at the close of the twentieth century.

While some of the slaves brought to the African coast had been enslaved directly or indirectly because of the vigorous demand created by the Atlantic trade, as I have argued above, John Thornton has urged that there was in any case a large potential source of slaves in Africa, independent of transatlantic demand, because of such factors as dynastic or territorial wars, generating captives whom it was convenient to dispose of, and famine, which could spur the afflicted to sell themselves or their children.[80] These slaves could have been bought from the merchant princes of the coast, then given contracts as indentures. The inducement to sign up for three or five years would have remained very great, since the African captive or 'pawn' would not have been welcome where they came from, and their only alternative would have been some African variant of slavery.

Of course transport of such workers would have been more expensive, since none could have been enticed voluntarily to put up with the tight packing of the slave ships. Likewise living and working conditions on the plantations would have had to be improved. By reducing mortality such measures would also have reduced the need for such a large influx of labour as that represented by the Atlantic slave trade. Planters and merchants would have had to pay good money up front to acquire these contract workers. But they would have had the resources to do this because labour productivity in the New World was certainly higher than labour productivity in Africa – partly because of natural endowment, partly because of new crops and partly because of new agricultural techniques. Such a system would probably have led not to the integrated plantation but to a system whereby cane cultivation was separated from processing – as had been the case in Brazil and as happened in parts of the Caribbean in the aftermath of slavery. The success of slave-dominated subsistence cultivation in much of the Caribbean shows the potential for a more decentralized model. Finally, respect for the territorial rights of the Native American peoples could have greatly limited access to land by indentured servants who had served their time, making them more willing to accept waged employment. Las Casas had pointed out that trade was quite highly developed among the Indian nations and could have been extended to promote peaceful agreements on land use.

The possibilities canvassed above may seem far-fetched. But what would have happened if, for some reason, slaves had not been available from Africa? If Islam had established effective control of the African coasts, there might have been a ban motivated by a desire to weaken Christendom as well as religious scruple. Or if a major European power had also found some mixture of religious and geopolitical motives for bringing the Atlantic traffic to a halt and attacking any slave colony, it might have been very difficult for others to embark on constructing slave systems. The Papacy's short-lived ban on the Atlantic slave trade of 1686, and the reservations of some Puritans and Quakers, show that the seventeenth century did produce impulses of this sort. In such a case I believe that the merchants, colonists and planters would have been driven to find alternative sources of labour that would have fallen far short of outright slavery, and would even have been obliged to improve rather than degrade the status of the indentured servants. An effective ban on the Atlantic slave trade would have probably required a concert of the major powers, and redefinition of European identity, of the sort canvassed by William Penn in *The Peace of Europe* (1693) and by the Abbé Saint Pierre after the Treaty of Utrecht.[81] Had such a concert been brought into existence some of the resources and manpower devoted to the military could have been devoted to organizing alternative ways of securing a supply of exotic products. If the heavy duties payable on sugar had been reduced then higher production costs need not have pushed up consumer prices much, if at all.

If this line of thought is valid – and reasons for it will be given below –

then an interesting conclusion follows. From traditional accounts it could be inferred that the role of economic forces was to create a large number of very onerous productive roles, fit only for slaves; and the role of racial ideology was to reserve those roles for Africans. But if a ban on the purchase of slaves would eventually have prompted the emergence of a differently shaped productive apparatus then ideology – respect for private property, concern to extend national wealth, patriarchal notions as well as stereotypes of Africans as beasts of burden – did, in the context of an emergent capitalism, make a contribution to the selection of the slave plantation system as well as to the allocation of roles within it. Max Weber's claim for the role of ideas as 'switchmen', selecting different paths of historical development, or Antonio Gramsci's argument that ideas have the capacity to become a material force, could help to explain how acceptance of slavery allowed colonial development to be driven by the slave plantation.[82] I have assumed, however, that enslavement of Europeans would not have ensued if slaves had not been available on the African coast.

Edmund Morgan presents an account of the formation of English–American slavery which is broadly congruent with the picture painted by Dunn but which also stresses the role of class ideology in the development of the slave systems. He points out that the English ruling class of the period often pronounced in favour of the most rigorous systems of subordination, inspired by disdain for the lower orders. They believed that the English poor were 'vicious, idle, dissolute', and addicted to 'Laziness, Drunkenness, Debauches and almost every kind of Vice', including 'mutinous and indecent Discourses'. It was therefore best to find ways to oblige them to work, whether through incarceration in a domestic 'workhouse', or transportation to the plantations, or the press gang. Bishop Berkeley was to recommend making 'sturdy beggars ... slaves of the public for a term of years',[83] echoing Protector Somerset and John Locke's proposal of 1696–97 mentioned in Chapter VI.

French aristocrats and bourgeois shared many of the sentiments of the English gentlemen on these points. As we have seen, the period of the Regency and of Law's colonial projects witnessed unsuccessful attempts to round up beggars for the plantations. While African slaves were too expensive to be purchased by metropolitan proprietors, even some remaining enclaves of medieval serfdom belonged to the most stagnant sector of French agriculture. The metropolitan authorities and possessing classes were sometimes ready to envisage forced labour or transportation for undesirables; but this was a reflex of social revanchism rather than a considered contribution to colonial development. Planters did not want troublemakers or the halt, the lame, the criminal and the mentally unstable. They wanted strong young men and women capable of following orders and meeting their own elementary needs. Legislation which really pinpointed such people would have been – as was indicated above – prejudicial to the interests of metropolitan employers. Either it would directly take away some of their own apprentices or farm labourers, or it would push up their wages by creating a labour shortage. Moreover, beyond a certain point, forcible labour conscription provoked too much popular resistance, or accumulated too much combustible social material in the colonies. Even those who were unlikely to become its victims themselves recoiled from constructing an apparatus of enslavement in the metropolis.

Perhaps some English or French planters would have declined European slave labour if they had been offered it, though the harsh treatment they meted out to many servants and *engagés* does not warrant much optimism on this score. The real obstacles to such a development, I have argued, related, rather, to the relationship of social forces in West Europe and to the lack of all-round, long-term advantage such a system of slavery would have represented. Together, it is true, such considerations helped to comprise a powerful ideology of civic liberty to which nearly all paid tribute on appropriate occasions.

The enslavement of African captives also entailed costs and risks, but for the time being these seemed more manageable. The disruption caused by enslavement was kept well away from Europe. Barbara Fields argues that cultures of solidarity and resistance have a historically formed and accumulative character:

> when English servants entered the ring in Virginia, they did not enter alone. Instead, they entered in company with the generations that had preceded them in the struggle; and the outcome of those earlier struggles established the terms and conditions of the latest one. But African and Afro-West Indians did enter the ring alone. Their forebears had struggled in a different arena, which had no bearing on this one. Whatever concessions they might obtain had to be won from scratch, in unequal combat, an ocean away from the people they might have called upon for reinforcements.[84]

When English migrants felt and claimed the rights of 'christians' and 'free born' English men and women, they had a lever they could use against their exploiters, or would-be exploiters. The African slave might claim – and feel no less intensely – the respect due to the Akan, or Mandingo, or people of Kongo. While this could – and did – inspire some epic instances of resistance, it could not prevent the consolidation of English colonial slavery.

Even in terms of the restricted horizon of a defence of 'English liberties', the rise of the colonial slave system had been a defeat for popular traditions. For some considerable time the common people in England had opposed not only attempts to enslave them but also attempts by the powerful or wealthy to own any slaves, of whatever nationality. They often suspected that their own liberties and conditions would be degraded if they had to live in the shadow of slaveholding magnates. Hilary Beckles makes it clear that the generality of white servants or smallholders in Barbados gained little or nothing by the rise of slavery. This is why they left in droves, and could be persuaded to stay for a year or two only by high wages. As late as 1695 the Governor complained that planters' attitudes to white servants and poor whites – their habit of 'domineering over them and treating them like dogs'[85] – was undermining the morale of the militia.

In Virginia the lot of the poor white was certainly better, but the large planters held a more complete sway over the colony than did the leaders of more northerly colonies where there were few slaves and no large slave-owners. Thus in New England and Pennsylvania slaveowning remained marginal, and the slaves to be found there were more likely to be treated like servants. There were certainly some significant gradations of wealth in these colonies, but they were far less marked than they were in Virginia, let alone South Carolina or the West Indies. In Virginia by 1700 the richest 5 per cent of free adults owned two-thirds of all land and, as Jack Greene observes, '[w]ith the transition to slavery, the large landowners acquired even further advantages over their poorer neighbours'.[86]

Europeans were protected from enslavement at home not only by their immediate capacity for resistance – though this was important – but also because the rulers themselves found slaveholders awkward subjects: their power over their slaves tended to remove them from the reach of common laws. The sovereigns of both England and France were thus content to accept and uphold the 'free air' doctrine that had been adumbrated by many late medieval and early modern municipalities. Slaveholders in distant colonies were less of a threat, especially if they required protection from actual or potential enemies, but they were still treated as potentially wayward subjects. The rulers of the different European states respected norms of conflict among one another, so that prisoners of war were exchanged or ransomed rather than subjected to enslavement. The common heritage of Christendom provided some rules governing such matters, with an implicit assumption that only Europeans were true Christians. But the practice of not enslaving captives also reflected the power and prestige of their monarch: it was out of respect for him that a prisoner was not enslaved. Turkish prisoners would also be exchanged or ransomed because of the imposing might of the Ottoman Empire. The Christian kings of the Kongo, as we saw in Chapter II, were often unable to protect their subjects from enslavement, unlike the Islamic rulers of Turkey. When Virginia revised its slave legislation once more in 1705, it stipulated that servants from Turkey who entered the colony, even though they were not Christians, should not be accounted slaves unless they had been slaves in Turkey, since the Prince of this country was recognized by England. On the other hand, no infidel – 'Jews, Moors, Mahometans' – and no person of African descent was to own a 'christian servant', though they could own a servant 'of their own complexion'. Thus the law thoroughly confused race and religion, in such a way that those of a darker complexion were excluded from the category of Christian.[87]

Racial solidarity did act as a force protecting those with white skin, but the spread of slavery in the plantation colonies brought little benefit to non-slaveholding whites, since they were bound to be overshadowed by the large slaveholders. The tendency of non-slaveholding free emigrants to leave the Caribbean for North America was a response to this. The non-slaveholders in the plantation colonies, many of them 'poor whites', had significant skin privileges to console them, but they were not much envied by other colonists. In the Caribbean both smallholders and artisans found their position undercut, as slaves furnished the market with their own produce and were promoted to the employments requiring craft skills. In the North American plantation colonies non-slaveholding whites clung on to a more considerable role as supervisors and slave-drivers, or as farmers supplying some foodstuffs. But their existence was still constrained by the planters' power and, so far as farmers were concerned, preference for self-provision.

The fact that European planters began to batten upon the labour of tens, then hundreds, of thousands of African slaves leads K.G. Davies to conclude: 'As the blacks poured in a version of capitalism evolved, virtually outside public control and untrammelled by tradition or social constraint, which swamped all other influences and put political power firmly in the hands of a few great slave owners.'[88] This conclusion, and many of the arguments presented above, are challenged by David Eltis. The fact that the planters resorted to African, *but not European*, slaves seems to him to demonstrate a self-imposed restraint that is at variance with unfettered capitalism. He argues that

> seventeenth century capitalism, mercantile or not, was hardly as unrestrained and voracious as many students of early modern Europe have portrayed it. Profit-maximising behaviour occurred within agreed-upon limits defined as much by shared values as by the resistance of the less propertied classes.[89]

He is led to this view because he believes that resort to a supply of European slaves would have been the more profitable, because less costly, option for the planters. He writes that 'Europeans, and in particular the English', passed up an economic opportunity because of their refusal to enslave their own peoples:

> if they had emulated the sixteenth century Russian aristocracy by creating an ideological distance between the common people and themselves and enslaving some members of their own society, they would have enjoyed lower labour costs, a faster development of the Americas, and higher exports and income levels on both sides of the Atlantic.[90]

I find this conclusion erroneous and perverse. For reasons already given, it would scarcely have been possible to reintroduce slavery to England or France by the seventeenth century, even if the champions of such a project had been able clearly to identify a suitable group of victims. And even if it had been possible this would not have been, as Eltis suggests, favourable to European or American development, as the very example of Russia itself shows. It is true that a layer of power-holders and wealth-holders dreamt of the advantages of reducing sections of the European population to abject servitude. In Ireland the English attempted something like this and, after a succession of bloody struggles, expropriated many Irish landholders and imposed oppressive leases on the Catholic peasantry. While individual Protestant landlords grew rich, their success constrained the purchasing power of Irish peasants and, by denying Catholic Irish tenants the benefits of agricultural improvement, discouraged advances in productivity. Outright enslavement of the Catholic Irish – even supposing it to have been possible – might have boosted some individual fortunes, but it would have fostered a pattern of social relations that was even less conducive to a properly capitalist accumulation process, let alone any more balanced and egalitarian development. Alternatively, shipping fit young Irish or French peasant slaves to the New World would have deprived European landlords of their workforce. There was economic and social progress in the Netherlands, England and some other parts of Western Europe precisely because they were not mired in an Eastern European morass of peasant servitude. On the other hand, as we shall see, they did undeniably derive economic benefit from exchanges with, and investments in, the new colonies of the Americas. But this was because the colonies presented a significantly different social panorama from the 'cheap' servitude of Eastern Europe.

Paradoxically, it was the 'expense' of purchasing and equipping African labour which helped to stimulate the English economy; odd though this may sound, the even greater expense of being forced to rely on free labour would have been even more stimulating. And this is not only a happier counterfactual speculation than the one proposed by Eltis, but one which was to some extent realized, since a sizeable part of the colonial social formation in North America, where slavery was marginal, did vigorously contribute to Atlantic advance. The New England and Middle Atlantic colonies played a large part in widening the colonial market for English manufactures and furnished supplies, foodstuffs and shipping services to the plantation colonies.[91]

In many parts of Western Europe, and in much of North America, there was a growing sentiment that – as the philosophical Bristol merchant John Cary put it in 1697 – 'the Freedom and Liberty of the subject' was vital to the wealth and prosperity of the nation, and that ultimately 'everyone lives by each other'.[92] Wealthy proprietors and landlords often still hankered for a supply of completely servile labour, but it was the frustration of such inclinations which allowed for economic advance on a broader basis, encompassing both a wider internal market and a more flexible ensemble of producers. The writers of the Scottish school of moral philosophy and political economy were to draw out the implications of this. Likewise, in the first volume of *Capital*, Marx drew attention to the paradox that the regulation of the length of the working day – opposed by many individual capitalists on the grounds that they made their profit in its last hours –

nevertheless encouraged the raising of productivity and the attainment of a higher rate of accumulation.

While English and French plantation development in the New World represented a dynamic element of Atlantic economy based on slave labour, it is worth noting that the Portuguese and Spanish Atlantic islands also became highly productive in employing varieties of free and independent labour. Madeira and the Canary Islands produced wine, while the Azores supplied wheat to Portugal and its dependencies. The intensive agriculture of these islands was based on independent craft labour and wage labour, not slaves. The islands furnished convenient stopovers and revictualling points for Atlantic commerce, with opportunities for some entrepôt and contraband traffic. They also exported domestic animals to the Caribbean. The population of Madeira and the Azores was around 109,000 in 1650 and rose to 149,000 in 1720. The tariffs levied in the Atlantic islands constituted 14 per cent of Portugal's total tariff revenues, not including the considerable sums raised on the islands' trade in Lisbon.[93] To a lesser extent the Spanish Caribbean, parts of Brazil, French Louisiana and even Surinam were sheltered from the full rigours of commercialized and racially mobilized enslavement. The development of full-blown racial slavery was held back in these colonies by colonial and corporate regulation. The resulting baroque species of slavery allowed greater opportunity for subaltern identities to emerge and receive some recognition, in the form of African Christian brotherhoods and social rights for free people of colour. The creolizing tendencies of New World slavery were more evident in these colonies – partly because they were culturally less intolerant, and partly because their slower rate of development meant that their population was renewed more by natural reproduction than by the advent of newly uprooted forced immigrants. But while the development of these colonies was slower, it was not nugatory. In Cuba, as we will see below, tobacco was still cultivated by free labour and produced a valuable product, while ranching was another major industry partly based on free labour.[94]

The Puritans of New England and the Middle Atlantic colonies were, as we have seen, averse to employing slaves. Ethno-religious exclusivism played some part in this, as did disapproval of idleness and luxury. The better-off colonists engaged a few servants or slaves, while those who were merchants played a role in the Atlantic slave traffic. But public opinion in these colonies was hostile to the creation of a large, permanent stratum of subordinate slaves or servants. The Dutch of New York and New Jersey owned quite a few slaves, but the practice did not spread. Pennsylvania gained a reputation as the 'best poor man's country' precisely because there were few slaves in this colony. But the fact that slavery remained legal there, and that leading colonists were active in the slave trade, was enough to stimulate uneasiness. In 1688 opposition to slavery was given eloquent form by the Quaker group in Germantown, and further expressed by the Scottish Quaker George Keith in his *Exhortation and Caution* (1693).

Following the eruption of slave resistance in New York in 1712, the future of slavery and the slave trade became an issue of public controversy in Pennsylvania. A petition to free all slaves in the colony was rejected by the Assembly, but a proposal to place a prohibitive £20 tariff on each slave entry was accepted. The colonial authorities vetoed this measure, accepting only a lower tariff. These events have significance because they are the first occasions on which slavery and the slave trade were challenged as matters of public policy by a representative assembly. Since leading colonists were well represented in the Assembly, and most likely to be implicated in slavery, it is not surprising that these first initiatives failed. But long before the first Abolitionist successes there was a diffuse prejudice against slavery which could – and in parts of the Atlantic world did – constrict its development.[95]

Stanley Engerman and Kenneth Sokoloff have recently drawn attention to the fact that those American elites which resorted to unfree and tied labour gained an immediate ability to exploit the natural resources and advantages of their continent. But, they argue, the highly unequal pattern of society thus produced was to prejudice later economic development because its characteristic forms of labour control – whether slavery or labour tribute, debt peonage or sharecropping – were not conducive to broad participation in 'commercial economy, markets and technological change'.[96] This conclusion chimes in with the broad argument presented above, but I will be proposing that the slave plantations, while they were not as fully integrated into commercial circuits and technological change as enterprises employing formally free wage workers might have been, were nevertheless, in seventeenth- and eighteenth-century conditions, relatively adapted to enlarged circuits of accumulation, and capable of absorbing at least some technological changes. Thus, having stressed the economic as well as human disadvantages of the slave plantation option, it will be necessary in what follows to trace the huge contribution they nevertheless made to Atlantic accumulation. Engerman and Sokoloff themselves contrast the negative legacy of slavery and *encomienda* with the buoyant economy of farmers, small producers and merchants which developed in the North-ern colonies of the United States. While this contrast is indeed a striking one, the fact remains – as we shall see in Chapter XI – that the New England and Middle Atlantic colonies themselves broke out of an initially rather autarkic pattern of economic activity by finding markets and sources of supply in the plantation regions. The actual, rather than counterfactual, contribution of slavery to Atlantic accumulation will now form the main burden of what follows.

Notes

1. See James Horn, '"To Parts Beyond the Seas": Free Emigration to the Chesapeake in the Seventeenth Century', in Altman and Horn, eds, *'To Make America': European Emigration in the Early Modern Period*, Berkeley, CA 1991, pp. 85–131 (p. 92).

2. Du Tertre, *Histoire générale des Antilles habitées par les françois*, vol. III, p. 445. On planters more generally see Sheridan, *Sugar and Slavery*, p. 267; Gabriel Debien, *Les Esclaves aux Antilles françaises, XVIIᵉ et XVIIIᵉ siècle*, Basse Terre (Guadeloupe) / Fort-de-France (Martinique) 1974, pp. 105–17.

3. Horn, '"To Parts Beyond the Seas"', in Altman and Horn, eds, *'To Make America'*, p. 93. Horn is here summarizing the conclusions of Russell Menard, 'Economy and Society in Early Colonial Maryland', Ph.D. dissertation, University of Iowa, 1975, pp. 32–6.

4. Schwartz, *Sugar Plantations in the Formation of Brazilian Society*, p. 274.

5. Curtin, 'The Atlantic Slave Trade', in Ajayi and Crowder, *A History of West Africa*, I, pp. 252–3; Philip Curtin, 'Epidemiology and the Slave Trade', *Political Science Quarterly*, 83, June 1968, pp. 190–216.

6. C.S.S. Higham, *The Development of the Leeward Islands under the Restoration*, London 1921, p. 172. If, as recent work by Richard Ashcraft suggests, John Locke was a participant in the Rye House Plot, this sponsor of the Royal African Company might conceivably have found himself shipped off to St Kitts to work on a plantation – though generally gentlemen were punished in some other way, in accordance with prevailing class ideology.

7. The debate of 1659 is cited in a paper on the notion of the 'freeborn Englishman' in Keith Thomas, National and Local Feeling in England: c.1550–1750, History Department, Oxford University, 1985. For an impressive vindication of the rights of the 'freeborn Englishmen' see William Penn's account of his success in winning over a jury in 1670: William Penn, 'The People's Ancient and Just Liberties Asserted', in *The Peace of Europe, The Fruits of Solitude and other Writings*, London 1993, pp. 135–52.

8. Beckles, *White Servitude and Black Slavery in Barbados*, p. 111.

9. Le Roy Ladurie explains the lack of emigrants mainly by reference to the logic of smallholding: 'in the eighteenth century, despite the permanent incursion of land-buyers … the multiple archipelago of family plots managed to defend itself fairly well. … This is one reason why France, unlike Great Britain or Spain, was not a land of emigration: the French-type small-holding, almost endlessly divisible, provided the increasing number of peasants with a relatively open and available outlet.' Le Roy Ladurie, *The French Peasants, 1450–1660*, London 1987, p. 410.

10. Blandine Barret-Kriegel, *L'Etat et les Esclaves*, Paris 1979, pp. 51, 75–6.

11. Pluchon, *Histoire de la Colonisation Française*, pp. 132, 135. For the ideological tenor of the Absolutist monarchy see Daniel Gordon, *Citizens without Sovereignty: Equality and Sociability in French Thought, 1670–1789*, Princeton, NJ 1995. For the decay of forms of personal bondage see Jean Bart, *La Liberté ou la Terre: la Mainmorte en Bourgogne au Siècle des Lumières*, Dijon 1984.

12. Lorena Walsh, 'Slaves and Tobacco in the Chesapeake', in Ira Berlin and Philip D. Morgan, eds, *Cultivation and Culture: Labour and the Shaping of Slave Life in the Americas*, Charlottesville, VA 1993, pp. 170–201 (p. 176). Walsh adds: 'Black slaves, not white servants, made most of the largest individual crops recorded, and most of these efficient workers were Africans not creoles.' But, as she points out, the better score of the African compared to the creole could simply reflect the greater fertility of virgin soil – a point, however, which does not undercut the comparison with white servants who also had this benefit.

13. Richard Ligon, *A True and Exact History of the Island of Barbados*, London 1673, pp. 43–4.

14. Du Tertre, *Histoire générale des Antilles*, vol. I, quoted in Huertz e Lemps, 'Indentured Servants Bound for the French Antilles', in Altman and Horn, eds, *'To Make America'*, p. 175.

15. The planters of South Carolina particularly appreciated the self-reliant qualities of the African. See Peter Wood, *Black Majority: Negroes in Colonial South Carolina from 1670 through the Stono Rebellion*, New York 1974, pp. 95–130.

16. Smith, *Colonists in Bondage*, pp. 243–4, 257–9, 279, 291–306. On the relationship between the numbers of French *engagés* and political repression in the metropolis see Gabriel Debien, *Les Engagés pour les Antilles*, Paris 1952, pp. 247–61.

17. George Alsop, 'A Character of the Province of Maryland', in Clayton Colman Hall, ed., *Narratives of Early Maryland: 1633–1684*, New York 1910, pp. 335–406 (pp. 354, 359).

18. But see also Galenson, *White Servitude in Colonial America*, pp. 134–41.

19. Morgan, *American Slavery, American Freedom*, p. 327.

20. Samuel Sewall, *The Selling of Joseph*, Boston, MA 1700.

21. For the dynamics of interpellation see Louis Althusser, 'Ideology and ISAs', in Slavoj Žižek, ed., *Mapping Ideology*, London 1994.

22. Richard Ligon, *Barbados*, p. 54.

23. For the 'scold's bridle' see Anthony Fletcher, *Gender, Sex and Subordination in England, 1500–1800*, New Haven, CT and London 1995, pp. 273–4. For its use in the New World see Olaudah Equiano, ed. Vincent Carretta, *The Interesting Narrative and Other Writings*, London 1995, pp. 62–3; Ortiz, *Los Negros Esclavos*, p. 261.

24. Godwyn, *The Negro's and Indians Advocate*, p. 111. For slave names see Michael Craton, *Searching for the Invisible Man: Slaves and Plantation Life in Jamaica*, London 1978, p. 157; Berlin, 'From Creole to African', *William and Mary Quarterly*, April 1996, pp. 251–2, 286.

25. On the transition to slavery in North America see Richard Bean and Robert P. Thomas, 'The Adoption of Slave Labour in British North America', in Gemery and Hogendorn, *The Uncommon Market*, pp. 377–98. For a more extended examination of the comparative economic costs of slavery and indentured labour see David Galenson, *White Servitude in Colonial America*, New York 1981; with figures and a summary on pp. 154, 217. So far as the French Caribbean is concerned the increasing availability of slaves around the turn of the century and after is evident from the *Memoirs* of Père Labat.

26. A point elaborated by William A. Green, 'Race and Slavery: Considerations on the Williams Thesis', in Barbara Solow and Stanley Engerman, eds, *British Capitalism and Caribbean Slavery*, Cambridge 1987, pp. 25–50.

27. Kwame Yeboa Daaku, *Trade and Politics on the Gold Coast, 1600–1720: A Study of African Reaction to European Trade*, Oxford 1970, pp. 96–143.

28. Peter Mark, 'Constructing Identity: Sixteenth and Seventeenth Century Architecture in the Gambia-Gebu Region and the Articulation of Luso-African Ethnicity', *History in Africa*, vol. 22, 1995, pp. 307–27. For the Brazilian *casa grande* or Big House see Gilberto Freyre, *The Masters and the Slaves*, New York 1956, pp. xxxii–xxxv.

29. Quoted in Davies, *The Royal African Company*, p. 140.

30. James Searing, *West African Slavery and Atlantic Commerce*, Cambridge 1993, pp. 18–25; Paul E. Lovejoy, *Transformations in Slavery: A History of Slavery in Africa*, Cambridge 1983, pp. 66–87.

31. Richard Jobson, *The Golden Trade*, London 1623, quoted in Winthrop Jordan, *White over Black*, p. 63.

32. John Locke, *An Essay Concerning Human Understanding*, Oxford 1975, pp. 606–7; quoted in Hannaford, *Race*, p. 195.

33. Richard Gray, 'The Papacy and the Atlantic Slave Trade', *Past and Present*, 115, May 1987, pp. 52–68. Examples of Spanish incitement to slave insurrection will be found in Part Two, Chapter XI and in *The Overthrow of Colonial Slavery*, chapters V and IX.

34. Jorge Benci, *Economia Christão dos Senhores no Governo dos Escravos*, São Paulo 1977 (original edition Bahia 1700; this work was denied a licence at Rome in 1705).

35. John TePaske, 'The Fugitive Slave: Intercolonial Rivalry and Spanish Slave Policy, 1687–1764', in Samuel Proctor, ed., *Eighteenth Century Florida and its Borderlands*, Gainesville, FL 1975, pp. 1–12.

36. David Eltis and Stanley Engerman, 'Was the Slave Trade Dominated by Men?', *The Journal of Interdisciplinary History*, vol. XXIII, no. 2, Autumn 1992, pp. 237–258 (pp. 241, 243).

37. Debien, 'Les Esclaves', in Pluchon, *Histoire des Antilles*, p. 142.

38. Meillassoux, *The Anthropology of Slavery*, Part One, chapter 3.

39. Myriam Cottias, 'La Martinique: Babylone fertile ou terre stérile?', *Annales de Démographie Historique*, 1992, p. 204; Gautier, *Les Sœurs de solitude*, pp. 62–78; Richard Ligon, *A True and Exact Account of the Island of Barbados*, London 1657, p. 113. Barbara

Bush-Slimani, 'Hard Labour: Women, Childbirth and Resistance in British Caribbean Slave Societies', *History Workshop*, Autumn 1993, pp. 83–99.

40. Richard Sheridan, *Sugar and Slavery: An Economic History of the British West Indies, 1623–1775*, Baltimore, MD 1974, p. 23.

41. Dunn, *Sugar and Slaves*, pp. 188–9.

42. Gabriel Debien, *Les Engagés pour les Antilles*, p. 257.

43. C.P. Timmer, 'The Turnip, the New Husbandry, and the English Agricultural Revolution', *Quarterly Journal of Economics*, vol. 83 (969), pp. 375–95 (p. 394).

44. Gabriel Debien, 'Les Esclaves', in Pluchon, ed., *Histoire des Antilles*, pp. 141–62 (p. 146).

45. Henry Drax, 'Instructions for the Management of Drax-Hall and the Irish-Hope Plantations', quoted in Puckrein, *Little England*, pp. 82–3.

46. Quoted in Puckrein, *Little England*, p. 77.

47. William McNeill, *The Pursuit of Power: Technology, Armed Force and Society since AD 1000*, Chicago 1982, p. 129. See pp. 126–33 for a general description of the new military techniques.

48. Vividly evoked and quoted in Leroy Vale and Landeg White, 'Forms of Resistance: Songs and Perceptions of Power in Colonial Mozambique', *American Historical Review*, vol. 88, no. 4, October 1983, pp. 883–919.

49. For analysis along these lines within the Marxist tradition see Eugene Genovese, *The Political Economy of Slavery*, New York 1968; Jacob Gorender, *O Escravismo Colonial*, São Paulo 1988; G.A. Cohen, *Karl Marx's Theory of History: A Defence*, London 1978. The critique of the economics of slavery made by the classical liberal economist John Cairnes in *The Slave Power*, London 1862, coincided on a number of points with the analysis that Marx was making around the same time in the *Grundrisse* and *Capital*. For a review of the latter see also Robert Miles, *Capitalism and Unfree Labour: Anomaly or Necessity?*, London 1987.

50. J.R. Ward, 'The Profitability of Sugar Planting in the British West Indies: 1650–1834', *Economic History Review*, 2nd series, XXI, no. 2, May 1978, pp. 197–213.

51. Those who wrote on the expense of slave labour had this aspect in mind. In his discussion of the genesis of capitalist ground rent in volume 3 of *Capital* Marx argues that the price paid for the slave, based on anticipated surplus value to be produced by the slave, is effectively subtracted from production, that is from the resources available to the slaveowner to build up the plantation. Cf. Karl Marx, *Capital*, III, London 1981, Chapter 47, section v, p. 945.

52. This problem is indicated by Eugene Genovese, *The Political Economy of Slavery*, p. 49; for an extended discussion see Gorender, *O Escravismo Colonial*, pp. 192–240.

53. Dunn, *Sugar and Slaves*, pp. 197–200.

54. Sheridan, *Sugar and Slavery*, p. 267.

55. Watts, *The West Indies*, pp. 403–4, 429.

56. Karl Marx argued that: 'The sporadic application of cooperation on a large scale in Ancient times ... and in modern colonies, rests on direct relations of domination and servitude, in most cases on slavery,' Karl Marx, *Capital*, vol. 1, p. 452. He wrote as follows about the US South: 'The cultivation of the Southern export articles, cotton, tobacco, sugar etc, carried on by slaves is only remunerative as long as it is conducted by large gangs of slaves, on a mass scale and on wide expanses of a naturally fertile soil, that requires only simple labour. Intensive cultivation, which depends less on the fertility of the soil than investment of capital, intelligence and energy of labour is contrary to the nature of slavery.' Karl Marx and Frederick Engels, *The Civil War in the US*, New York 1937, p. 67.

57. Letter to the Earl of Orrery, quoted in Pierre Marambaud, *William Byrd of Westover, 1674–1744*, Charlotteville, VA 1971, pp. 146–7.

58. Gorender, *O Escravismo Colonial*, p. 142.

59. Schwartz, *Sugar Plantations in the Formation of Brazilian Society*, pp. 193, 231–2. According to surviving records Jesuit estates were neither profitable nor well-run; however Schwartz cites information showing that the Benedictine estates made a reasonable return and also made above average provision for their slaves (pp. 222–3, 236).

60. Ibid., p. 218.

61. J.R.Ward, 'The Profitability of Sugar Planting in the British West Indies, 1650–1834', in Hilary Beckles and Verene Shepherd, *Caribbean Slave Society and Economy*, London 1991, pp. 81–94 (pp. 85, 91–2). This valuable study was first published in the *Economic History Review*, vol. 31, no. 2, 1978.

62. Watts, *The West Indies*, pp. 391–447.

63. Hilary Beckles, *Black Rebellion*, Bridgetown 1984, p. 51; Beckles, *History of Barbados*, p. 40.

64. Hans Sloane, *A Voyage to the Islands*, London 1706, vol. I, p. lvii.

65. Jean-Baptiste Labat, *Voyages aux Îles de l'Amérique*, Paris 1979 (originally 1722), p. 248.

66. *Calendar of State Papers, Colonial*, 10: 611, 8 October 1680.

67. Lambert-Félix Prudent, *Des Baragouins à la Langue Antillaise*, Paris 1980.

68. David Barry Gaspar, 'Sugar Cultivation and Slave Life in Antigua before 1800', in Berlin and Morgan, eds, *Cultivation and Culture*, pp. 101–23.

69. Robert Robertson, *A Letter to the Bishop of London*, London 1730, quoted in Gaspar, 'Sugar and Slave Life in Antigua', in Berlin and Morgan, eds, *Cultivation and Culture*, p. 117.

70. Hans Sloane, *A Voyage to the Islands*, vol. 1, pp. xlvii, lii. See Richard Cullen Rath, 'African Music in Seventeenth Century Jamaica', *William and Mary Quarterly*, October 1993, pp. 700–26, especially pp. 710–12.

71. For obvious reasons it is difficult to document the outlook of African slaves and rebels in the earliest period. The history of the maroon rebellions and communities remains the best evidence that Africans rejected the utilitarian nightmare of American slavery. See Orlando Patterson, 'Slavery and Slave Revolts: A Socio-historical Analysis of the First Maroon War', in Richard Price, ed., *Maroon Societies: Rebel Slave Communities in the Americas*, New York 1973, pp. 246–92; R.K. Kent, 'Palmares: An African State in Brazil', in Price, *Maroon Societies*, pp. 179–90; Debien, *Les Esclaves aux Antilles*, pp. 411–69; José Luciano Franco, *Las minas de Santiago y la rebelión de los cobreros*, Havana 1975.

72. David Eltis, 'Europeans and the Rise and Fall of African Slavery in the Americas: An Interpretation', *American Historical Review*, December 1993, pp. 1399–1423 (p. 1423).

73. J.R. Pole, *Paths to the American Present*, New York 1979, p. 71, quoted in Vaughan, *Roots of American Racism*, p. 173.

74. David Eltis, 'Europeans and the Rise and Fall of African Slavery in the Americas: An Interpretation'.

75. Eltis cites Thomas Haskell, 'Capitalism and the Origins of Humanitarian Sensibility', parts one and two, in Thomas Bender, ed., *The Antislavery Debate: Capitalism and Abolitionism in Historical Perspective*, Berkeley, CA 1992, originally published in the *American Historical Review*, April and June 1985.

76. Dunn, *Sugar and Slaves*, pp. 225–6.

77. In the late eighteenth and early nineteenth centuries the English government bought thousands of slaves in Africa, enrolled them in special West Indian regiments and offered them some wages and the prospect of emancipation in return for loyal service; at the end of their period some remained in the Caribbean, others returned to Africa. Henry Christophe, the King of Haiti (1807–21), also recruited soldiers in this way. Both the British and the French recruited indentured servants in the aftermath of emancipation, the British from India and the French from Africa – in the latter case those recruited were almost certainly slaves in Africa and only achieved some prospect of eventual freedom in the New World after an abolitionist outcry. In the 1850s and 1860s, prior to the abolition of slavery, the Spanish authorities in Cuba permitted the introduction of Chinese indentured servants, who served for three years for nominal wages. In all these instances the pressure on the servants to sell their future was severe and their condition in the New World oppressed and vulnerable. But it lay somewhere between that of the European indentured servant and the European convict, and closer to either than to that of the slave. Those who survived became free persons, but, as with Europeans who had been convicted, without the promise of land or freedom dues.

78. See N.A.M. Rodger, *The Wooden World: An Anatomy of the Georgian Navy*, London 1988. Even though this work is determined to present a rosy view of life aboard vessels of the Royal Navy, it cites more than enough solid evidence to show that the world of the naval rating and that of the slave were indeed quite different.

79. Marcus Rediker, *Between the Devil and the Deep Blue Sea: Merchant Seamen, Pirates and the Anglo-American Maritime World, 1700–1750*, Cambridge 1988, pp. 116–52. See also Arthur L. Stinchcombe, *Sugar Island Slavery in the Age of Enlightenment: The Political Economy of the Caribbean World*, Princeton, NJ 1995, pp. 57–88. Stinchcombe stresses the functional complexity and mobility of ships which, he believes, dictated the offer of reasonable terms to secure the willing labour required. For the risky but sometimes rewarding experiences of a black seaman see Equiano, *The Interesting Narrative*.

80. Thornton, *Africa and Africans in the Making of the Atlantic World*, pp. 98–128. Thornton is sceptical that Atlantic demand had any large impact on slave supply. While I find Thornton's argument persuasive for the pre-1680 period, the prodigious levels of the trade in the late eighteenth century, outside Thornton's period, are another matter (compare Manning, *Slavery and African Life* and Lovejoy, *Transformations in Slavery*). However Thornton does usefully explain why large numbers of slaves were available for purchase in Africa.

81. William Penn, 'An Essay towards the Present and Future Peace of Europe', in William Penn, *The Peace of Europe*, pp. 5–22. Abbé Saint Pierre urged that the powers should conclude an undertaking that 'No sovereign shall take up Arms or commit any Hostility but against him who shall be declared an Enemy of the *European* society ... [T]he Union shall make, if possible, with its neighbours, the Mahometan sovereigns, Treaties of League offensive and defensive, to keep each of them in Peace within the Bounds of his Territory.' See Denis de Rougement, *The Idea of Europe*, London 1964, pp. 112–20. William Penn also envisaged Ottoman participation. The international pact proposed by these writers, designed to avoid new wars, was a scarcely less radical proposal than the possibility canvassed above.

82. Thus Weber writes: 'Not ideals, but material and ideal interests, directly govern men's conduct. Yet very frequently the "world images" that have been created by "ideas" have, like switchmen, determined the tracks along which action has been pushed by the dynamic of interest.' H.H. Gerth and C. Wright Mills, eds, *From Max Weber: Essays in Sociology*, London 1948, p. 280. The 'track laying' function of religious ideas and norms is elaborated by Michael Mann, *The Sources of Social Power*, I, pp. 341–72, 376–9. And for the specific proposal that 'anti-slavery' could function as a crux see Runciman, *A Treatise on Social Theory*, II, *Substantive Social Theory*, pp. 133–4. For Gramsci on ideas as a material force see David Forgacs, ed. *The Gramsci Reader*, London 1978, p. 200.

83. Morgan, *American Slavery, American Freedom*, pp. 319–24.

84. Barbara Jeanne Fields, 'Slavery, Race and Ideology in the United States of America', *New Left Review*, no. 181, May/June 1990, pp. 95–118 (p. 104).

85. Beckles, *White Servitude and Black Slavery in Barbados*, p. 113.

86. Greene, *Pursuits of Happiness*, p. 92.

87. Jordan, *White over Black*, pp. 94–5.

88. Davies, *The North Atlantic World in the Seventeenth Century*, pp. 211–15.

89. David Eltis, 'Europeans and the Rise and Fall of African Slavery in the Americas: An Interpretation', *American Historical Review*, December 1993, pp. 1399–1423 (p. 1423).

90. Ibid., p. 1422.

91. See Allan Kulikoff, *The Agrarian Origins of American Capitalism*, Charlottesville, VA 1992, pp. 34–43. Evidence on these points is also given in chapters XI and XII below.

92. Quoted in Sacks, *The Widening Gate*, p. 341.

93. T. Bentley Duncan, *Atlantic Islands: Madeira, the Azores and the Cape Verdes in Seventeenth Century Commerce and Navigation*, Chicago and London 1972, pp. 243, 256.

94. Hall, *Africans in Colonial Louisiana*, pp. 119–201; Berlin, 'From Creole to African', *William and Mary Quarterly*, April 1996; Davis, *Women on the Margins*, pp. 166–98. Some of the work inspired by Frank Tannenbaum's thesis that Latin and Catholic slavery was fundamentally different in ethos from Anglo-Saxon Protestant slavery helps to point the difference between what I prefer to call baroque and commercial slavery. See, in particular, Herbert Klein, *Slavery in the Americas*, Chicago 1967, and Herbert Klein, 'The Coloured Freemen in Brazilian Slave Society', *Journal of Social History*, vol. 3, 1969, but note that where and when plantation slavery really developed – e.g. in nineteenth-century Cuba and Brazil – there was a hardening of the racial system. The writings of the Cuban anthropologist Fernando Ortiz and the Brazilian historian Gilberto Freyre likewise draw attention to significant features of the slave regimes while failing properly to grasp that peculiar dynamic of the commercial plantation slavery that is analysed with such insight by Manuel Moreno Fraginals in *El Ingenio* and Jacob Gorender in *O Escravismo Colonial*.

95. Gary B. Nash and Jean R. Soderland, *Freedom by Degrees: Emancipation in Pennsylvania and its Aftermath*, New York 1991, pp. 41–6.

96. Stanley Engerman and Kenneth Sokoloff, *Factor Endowments, Institutions, and Differential Paths of Growth among New World Economies: A View from Economic Historians of the United States*, National Bureau of Economic Research Inc., Historical Paper no. 66, 1994.

Part Two

Slavery and Accumulation

IX

Colonial Slavery and the Eighteenth-Century Boom

When I recovered a little, I found some black people about me, who I believed were some of those who brought me on board, and had been receiving their pay; they talked to me in order to cheer me but all in vain . . . amongst the poor chained men, I found some of my own nation, which in a small degree gave ease to my mind. I inquired of these what was to be done with us? they gave me to understand we were to be carried to these white people's country to work for them. I was then a little revived, and I thought, if it were no worse than working, my situation was not so desperate: but still I feared I should be put to death, the white people looked and acted, as I thought, in so savage a manner; for I had never seen among any people such instances of brutal cruelty; and this not only shewn to us blacks, but also to some of the whites themselves. . . . At last, when the ship we were in had got all her cargo, they made ready with many fearful noises, and we were all put under deck, so that we could not see how they managed the vessel.

The Interesting Narrative of the Life of Olaudah Equiano

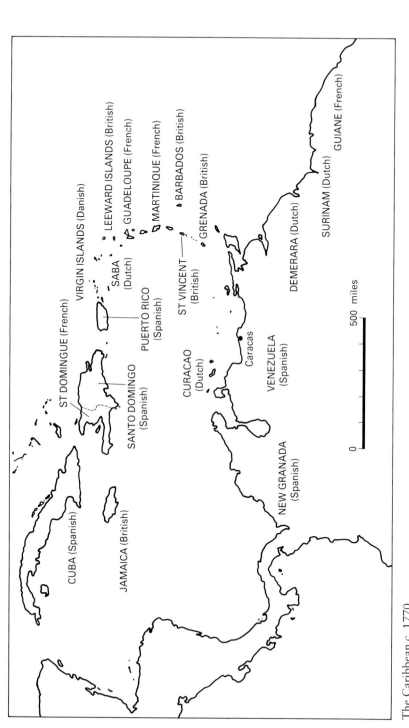

CUBA (Spanish)

JAMAICA (British)

ST DOMINGUE (French)

SANTO DOMINGO (Spanish)

VIRGIN ISLANDS (Danish)

LEEWARD ISLANDS (British)

SABA (Dutch)

GUADELOUPE (French)

PUERTO RICO (Spanish)

MARTINIQUE (French)

BARBADOS (British)

ST VINCENT (British)

GRENADA (British)

CURACAO (Dutch)

Caracas

VENEZUELA (Spanish)

NEW GRANADA (Spanish)

DEMERARA (Dutch)

SURINAM (Dutch)

GUIANE (French)

0   500 miles

The Caribbean c. 1770

By the end of the seventeenth century the New World was still only on the threshold of an enormous boom in plantation production, with its attendant slave trade. The rise of the slave plantation in the English and French Caribbean in the period 1650–1720, despite the adverse impact of war and piracy, was significant because of the uneven or hesitant record of most other branches of European commerce in the century after 1620. During this period there had been stagnation or decline in the transatlantic shipments of bullion, in the Baltic grain trade, in the North European trade in woollen textiles, and in the French wine trade and the South European trade in luxury manufactures. The development of the mercantile, manufacturing and agricultural capitalism of the Netherlands was hemmed in by this secular recession.

As E.J. Hobsbawm argued in a classic essay, 'The Crisis of the Seventeenth Century', the uncertain cross-currents of European economics and politics in this period amounted to an impasse of the previous formula of predominantly feudal expansion and business. In the sixteenth century a dramatic increase in the grain trade had been based on an intensification of feudal exploitation in Central and Eastern Europe: this had restricted the purchasing power of the peasantry, diminished the number and wealth of the minor nobility and enriched only the comparatively small number of exporting landlords. East European imports of manufactures became correspondingly depressed. The display of the Renaissance and baroque courts encouraged luxury and craft production rather than wide markets for manufactures and the introduction of industrial methods. As Hobsbawm observed: 'the future industrialist required not an infinite willingness to keep scores of chefs, stucco artists, and perruquiers employed, but mass demand'.[1]

The expansion of trade with the East could not remedy this deficiency in the structure of demand, since the East had no interest in European products and exchanged its own for bullion or for the mercantile services offered by the Europeans in the Indian Ocean. With the decline of American silver output after the 1620s, Europe had difficulty financing its Eastern trade; the Spanish American colonies had less purchasing power and, as local manufacture and commercial agriculture developed, less need to import from Europe. Of the various European states England and the United Provinces were best placed to resist the recessionary climate because of a developing internal market sustained by the exchange between town and country, agriculture and manufacturing. Yet this domestic buoyancy was not impervious to stagnating foreign markets, or to costly commercial wars. Hobsbawm suggested that colonial and plantation demand acted as a 'forced draught' fanning the flames of metropolitan accumulation. The trade to Africa and the Americas, as noted above, did indeed take increasing quantities of manufactures of every type. The planters bought much themselves, and their need for supplies helped to boost the ability of other transatlantic markets to pay for their imports.

Yet it could be – and has been – maintained that the New World plantations were in the long run no more congruent with capitalist accumulation than the feudal estates of Eastern Europe.[2] Although they were involved in cash crop production for the European market, both were based on direct, essentially pre-capitalist, forms of exploitation and domination: both involved the extra-economic mobilization of labour, with consequent limitations on the type of demand generated. The planters and colonial merchants certainly consumed luxury goods themselves, and were to give employment to a not inconsiderable army of chefs, perruquiers, and stucco artists. Just as the serflord battened on the 'natural economy' of peasant subsistence, so the slaveowner was battening on the production of captive young adults in Africa and the daily reproduction of the slave crew thanks, at least in part, to the slave plots.

Marx wrote of the way in which production for the voracious new capitalist market in such a context 'grafted the civilised horrors of overwork onto the barbaric horrors of serfdom and slavery.'[3] But this observation did not lead him to consider serf or slave estates to be capitalist, since he regarded wage labour, exchanging against capital, as essential to the circuit of fully capitalist accumulation. The proletarian, who needed to sell labour-power in order to survive, would create a wider market and the basis for mass production. Moreover, looked at from the side of production, an enterprise which rested on some species of forced labour, and relied on 'natural economy' for the renewal of labour-power, would have only a limited possibility of raising the productivity of labour. To the extent that the market did not incorporate the process of reproduction, the pre-capitalist enterprise did not need to respond to market pressures by improving efficiency. As for boosting the surplus product, this could be done directly by raising the rate of exploitation.

However, the undoubted fact that neither the feudal estates of Eastern Europe nor the slave plantations of the Americas can properly be regarded as capitalist enterprises should not lead us, as it has led some writers, to regard them as *equivalently distant from the capitalist mode*.[4] The feudal estates of Eastern Europe were a product of the manorial reaction of the fourteenth and fifteenth centuries – sometimes referred to as Europe's 'second serfdom'. In the first instance they were created not in response to the dictates of cash crop production but as the lords' answer to the impact of the demographic crisis in the Eastern marchlands. Their subsequent orientation to cereal exports required very few productive inputs from the West, and encouraged no reciprocal exchanges. The American slave plantations, by contrast, were set up directly for the purpose of supplying the European market, and had no other *raison d'être*. In their operation, as in their foundation, they remained intimately geared to exchanges with European merchants and manufacturers. Even at the height of Polish grain exports they accounted for only 10–15 per cent of total production, with luxury items dominating imports.[5] In the New World by far the greater part of plantation output was exported, and many productive inputs were imported from European manufacturers: equipment, implements, construction materials, clothing, foodstuffs; as for the African slaves, they also were acquired increasingly in exchange for manufactured trade goods. Western Europe's trade with the slave plantations was thus less unbalanced and more conducive to cumulative, reciprocal expansion.

The output of the slave plantations could be raised both by increasing the supply of slaves and by the introduction of better equipment. By contrast, the Eastern European serflords faced a demographic limit, set by the size of the serf population and its requirements for natural reproduction. The serflord could not raise the rate of surplus extraction above a certain point without threatening the food supply needed by his serfs to maintain numbers. Moreover, if too many of his villagers were reduced to a very miserable condition, he might be more vulnerable to the test of war or revolt. The serflord had direct responsibility and control over a smaller proportion of total output than did the planter, who permitted only minimal possession of land to his slaves and forced them to work on one or another aspect of cash crop production for by far the greater part of the year. The planter claimed and exercised a more concentrated and unlimited social power. In conjunction with material conditions of production that repaid continuous labour, this was bound to produce a higher rate of surplus extraction than was possible on a feudal estate. This certainly created a security problem on the plantations, but the slaveowners guaranteed security and subordination by relying on racial privilege and fear binding non-slaveholding free persons, a labour force lacking pre-given collective cohesion, the plantation hierarchy and the firepower of the colonial state.

Since the slave trader and the colonial merchant played a vital role in reproducing the slave plantation, they were well placed to siphon off a portion of the super-profits it generated. Mercantile initiative and credit could, given the transatlantic slave trade, directly sponsor the expansion of the plantation, enabling the planter to ignore any restraint which natural reproduction would have imposed. Thus while the planter was less 'hemmed in' by natural economy than the serflord, he was goaded further down the path of accumulation by the eager demands and exactions of merchants who were also suppliers and creditors.

Both the serflord and the American planter had an interest in fostering domestic manufacture and self-provision within their estates. But full self-sufficiency could never be a rational objective for the planter, as it often was for the serflord. Since plantations were constructed by means of cash outlays, it made sense for the planter to think in terms of expanding his productive purchases to the point where they yielded no additional surplus product. There was no equivalent to this quasi-capitalist form of calculation on the Eastern European estate, however complex its regulation of a large labour force. Since the Eastern European estates did not purchase means of production from the West, they were slow to adopt technical advances made there (e.g. metal implements). Moreover, the feudal estate did not have to justify its use of resources in economic competition with other estates. Its performance could not be compared with an 'average rate of profit', nor could it be 'forced out of business'. The merchant could not take over an indebted estate, or appoint a new serflord to run it.

The American plantation might withdraw for a time within a shell of 'natural economy' if the market for its products was temporarily disrupted, but this could not be done indefinitely without devaluing and decomposing the plantation. Planters sought to obtain legislation protecting their estates from seizure for debt, but they could never keep creditors wholly at bay if they wished to continue in business. Foreclosure, distraint and bankruptcy all made their appearance in the plantation colonies, and helped to reorganize production. Planters calculated profit using rough-and-ready calculations which invariably revealed that their estates needed to raise their output of cash crops by maintaining or increasing their outlays on slaves, equipment, fertilizers, new crop types and technical help. Such expenditures seemed to them a heavy charge on their profit – but if they refused them, their profits would drop even further. And taken as a whole, these expenditures stimulated the circulation of Atlantic trade. Paradoxically (as we saw in Chapter VIII), the offer of wages to their labourers could have furnished an even greater stimulus.

The American slave planter of the seventeenth century and after was not a capitalist – in the strict sense of the term, the species was only just coming into existence – but neither was he as far removed from capitalism as the feudal lord or the Ancient slaveowner. Until shortly before 1600 American slavery was a relatively modest adjunct of feudal business and feudal imperialism. But following the rise of the slave plantation – first in Brazil around 1580, and then, in a more sustained way, in the British and French colonies from about 1650 – American slavery became an outgrowth and adjunct of the European transition to capitalism. This transition did not choose the optimum path, as was argued in Chapter VIII, but at least it did not relapse into a bog of slavery and serfdom. The oxygen required by the European furnace of capitalist accumulation, if it was not to succumb to auto-asphyxiation, was supplied by the slave traffic and the plantation-related trades.

The slave plantations were dependent and hybrid socioeconomic enterprises, not animated by a pure capitalist logic but closer to it than European serfdom and slavery would have been, or were. Plantation slavery was an artificial extension of mercantile and manufacturing capital in the age of capitalist transition, extending their reach at a time when fully capitalist social relations were still struggling into existence. The salience of the merchant in the creation of the slave plantations, and in the politics of some of the metropolitan states, was in striking contrast to the relative social and political insignificance of merchants in Ancient Rome. In the Ancient World the slave mode of production may be regarded as dominant because it supplied the strategic surplus of the ruling class.[6] The social character of the European states which colonized the New World was principally determined by metropolitan social forms; slavery was important in the colonies, but not at all important in the metropolis. Yet, paradoxically, there was to be more slavery in the New World than in the Ancient World, even though it was now only a subordinate mode of production. The slave plantations not only swam against the stream of the seventeenth-century crisis; they also became a dynamic pole of Atlantic economy in the period 1700–1815. The next two chapters survey the slave colonies in the eighteenth century and bear out the claims made above for the socioeconomic character of the plantations. In Chapter XII I show that the plantation-related trade did make a crucial contribution to British industrialization, helping Britain to escape the fate of the United Provinces, which remained overreliant on the commerce of the Baltic and Eastern Europe. But before substantiating the argument sketched above, it will be useful to outline the European context and the dimensions of the Atlantic slave trade, which furnished the planters with the labour required to expand their operations.

Europe and the Atlantic

The eighteenth century witnessed rapid growth in the slave-related trade of the Atlantic and in the size of the slave populations of the Americas. In the sixteenth century some 370,000 people had been taken from Africa by the Atlantic slave trade; in the seventeenth century the number rose to 1,870,000; in the eighteenth the captives taken from Africa by the Atlantic trade totalled no fewer than 6,130,000. In the Americas the overall slave population of African origin or descent grew from about 330,000 in 1700 to over three million in 1800.[7] In South Carolina, the frontier regions of Spanish America and much of Brazil, there were still some Native American slaves at the beginning of the century, but by its end the slave labour force was overwhelmingly African or of African descent almost everywhere in the Americas. As we have observed, the Native American peoples who were most resistant to European colonization, and thus the most exposed to enslavement, were also those whom the planters found unproductive and troublesome. Africans, torn from their society of origin, disorientated by the Atlantic crossing and often inured to agricultural labour, provided colonial landholders with the captive labour force they felt they needed to exploit a fertile continent where it was difficult to find a free and willing labour force in any numbers.

The plantation form of organization drove up the volume of slave produce in keeping with slave numbers and, as productivity gains were exploited, sometimes a little more rapidly. The commercial and naval strategies of such statesmen as Walpole and Chatham, Choiseul and Pombal, concentrated on the New World as much as the Old. Britain's rulers wished to avoid the domination of continental Europe by a single power, but were themselves quite prepared to aim at hegemonizing the Americas. However important Europe might be to France, its rulers never felt that they could allow the British a free hand in the New World. To do so would have been to renounce not only fabled riches but also something that held out extraordinary promise for the future and distinguished the modern from the classical age. Louis XIV, Choiseul and Napoleon were prepared to make very considerable efforts to advance French interests in the Americas. The French sought to maintain a mighty fleet of eighty or a hundred ships-of-the-line whose main purpose was to dispute British control of the Atlantic and its adjacent seas. France's rulers devised complex dynastic and diplomatic scenarios in order to win Spain or neutralize Portugal. In the 1750s, 1770s and 1800s military expeditions were sent across the Atlantic at huge expense. But every competent statesman was aware that the economic strength of colonies and commerce was not only a prize in the struggle but also itself a vital resource of power. Colonial commerce translated into several sorts of state revenue, while a vigorous merchant marine was twinned with naval potential.

The more astute statesmen grasped that the surge of Atlantic commerce was essentially a spontaneous economic fact, with governments needing only to supply security, and otherwise to practise a policy of 'salutary neglect' or 'mitigated' mercantilism. The spectacular collapse of 'Law's System' and the puncturing of London's 'South Sea Bubble' cleared the way for individual investors rather than chartered companies to take the lead in colonial development. The European governments still sought to direct the trade of their colonies, but the logic of the struggle led them to undermine and destroy the commercial system of their rival. This European state competition was eventually to help American planters, farmers and merchants to shake off the tutelage of the Old World – as the Virginians did in 1776, the French Antillian planters in 1793, or the planters of Gran Colombia in 1812 and Brazil in 1821. But the capacity of the new American elites to claim self-government in politics was rooted in the independent strength of their local economy. The importation of African slaves enabled some of those elites to construct strategic enterprises that exploited those New World resources that were most in demand in the Old World.

Slavery certainly appeared to such elites as a providential short cut, but as they were to discover, reliance on enslavement carried risks and costs of its own in the longer run. New World elites that relied too much on imperial privilege or protection – as did the British West Indian sugar planters or the mine owners of Mexico or Peru – would find their capacity for independent action severely constrained. As the eighteenth century progressed, planters throughout the Americas strove to increase their autonomy and productivity. Underlying the ebb and flow of political conflict was a keen awareness among wealth-holders, especially those owning slaves, that the existence of their enterprises depended on being able to raise marketable output and guarantee the renewal and replenishment of the forces of production – above all labour and soil – which they exploited so prodigally. In the eighteenth century those types of rational calculation and mobilization which had appeared in the slave plantation (discussed in Chapter VIII) were to be considerably refined and developed.

In the past, both liberal and Marxist political economy was inclined to view the New World slave economies as not only extraordinarily wasteful but also economically irrational; if they were profitable, this was simply because of the distorting effects of colonial mercantilism. Assigning the slave systems to the murky world of mercantilism implied that they were removed from that of rational commercial calculation. Slave plantations were seen as an aberration, an atavistic survival due to be superseded by the rise of industrial capitalism, a blind alley leading off the highway of economic growth. Some reasons to doubt this picture have already been indicated. Modern research into the operation of the slave trade and slave plantations in the eighteenth century amply bears out such doubts. It reveals that they were run according to business principles which were very advanced for the epoch. They were indeed prodigiously wasteful of human life, but did not flout commercial calculation. They were profitable, but not excessively so, and the actions of planters and traders can best be understood as reflecting narrow economic calculations and a market rationality rather than delight in dominion or cruelty for its own sake.

Indeed, the business of traders, captains, factors and planters was conducted with such routine and regularity that it could seem humdrum were it not for the fact that the slave plantations were also a dynamic pole of Atlantic economy, pioneering commercial and productive arrangements, and well attuned to the new market conditions. Colonial protectionism distorted rather than revealed the logic of plantation commerce. Colonial mercantilism, far from being virtually synonymous with plantation slavery, became an obstacle to its further development. Mercantilist policies were sometimes to be pursued with success in the eighteenth century so long as they conformed to certain rigorous conditions. Naval power, and all the huge expenditures this entailed, was certainly needed to protect shipping and to batter down obstacles erected by colonial rivals. State contracts or colonial companies could bring new branches of production into being, and protect them in their infancy. There was even a case for protective tariffs so long as they were part of an overall system of exchanges that put a premium on reciprocity. The British Royal Navy sponsored the provision of naval supplies in North America, while both Spain and Portugal (as we will see in Chapter XI) used colonial companies to establish new export industries. London governments offered tariff protection to British West Indian sugar; this probably made sense in imperial terms, but did not prevent the French sugar islands overtaking the British. Strict mercantilism often involved absolute trade bans rather than tariffs – in the course of time both were eroded by the surge of Atlantic commerce, and the colonial companies were wound up.

The very fact that the operation of the slave systems can be illustrated with an abundance of statistics is indicative of the instrumental rationality they embodied. It is true that the forward plunge of the slave economies was exceedingly wasteful of human life, and that by the second half of the century the question was posed of whether they were sustainable, given the negative growth rate of the slave populations, the exhaustive effects of plantation agriculture and the violent conflicts to which colonial develop- ment gave rise. But the rational attention paid to the reproductive capacity of the slave plantations, and the attempt to devise strategies to boost it, was another sign of their modernity. The slave-based enterprise had to maintain a certain forward momentum to reproduce itself. Not infrequently it succeeded in escaping the consequences of its own destructiveness, replenishing its labour force at the cost of African peoples and its land resources at the cost of dispossessed Native Americans. The projects of the slave traders and slaveowners were plagued with risk, which they sought to meet by taking out insurance of one sort or another. While some addressed prayers to their God, they put their main trust in practical remedies and precautions. Thus insurance at Lloyd's was a precaution taken by French slave traders if they could, even when their country was at war with England.

The expansion of the eighteenth-century slave-worked enterprises of the Americas depended on a steadily rising supply of captives from Africa, a widening area of European control, and some advantageous exchanges with American farmers, ranchers and fishermen who did not use slave labour. But the Atlantic boom should be seen as rooted in, and contributing towards, the sustained economic advance of the European metropolis. By the end of the century exchanges within the Americas were not insignificant. But it was European demand for their produce which brought the planta- tions into existence in the first place, and well into the nineteenth century it continued to furnish the impetus to expansion.

The years after about 1720 witnessed a general European recovery from the preceding downturn. The population of Europe rose from 100 million–120 million in 1700 to roughly 180 million–190 million by 1800. The wars which were fought between 1713 and 1789 were less destructive than those of the seventeenth century. The middle decades of the eighteenth century witnessed a long succession of good harvests. Mortality rates declined in mid and late century, probably because of increasing immunity to the worst plagues. In 1700 France's population was about 20 million, and it even fell below this in the disastrous last years of Louis XIV; by 1800 its population had reached around 27 million. The population of England and Wales rose from 5.8 million in 1700 to 9.1 million in 1800. Spain's population rose from approximately 7.5 million in 1700 to 11.5 million in 1800. Portugal's population of 1.7 million in 1700 had risen to 3.4 million by the year 1800.[8] While these population figures can be no more than approximate estimates, it is far more difficult to give precise data for overall output; in many parts of Europe, a significant proportion of this was not recorded or not marketed. Nevertheless, there can be little doubt that there was a generalized economic advance during most of the eighteenth century. One indicator is the growth of international trade in which all European nations participated, as Table IX.1 shows:

Table IX.1   European Trade 1720–1800

(Millions of pounds sterling)	1720	1750	1780	1800
Britain	13	21	23	67
France	7	13	22	31
Spain	10	14	18	12
Portugal	2	3	4	4
Low Countries	4	6	8	15
Germany	8	15	20	36
Russia	8	14	17	30
Europe (incl. others)	62	103	137	228

Source: Michael Mulhall, *Dictionary of Statistics*, p. 128.
Note that 'trade' is the sum of imports and exports, including re-exports; the latter comprised as much as a half of the trade of some important states in this century (e.g. France). Figures are given in terms of current values of the £ sterling; between 1713/16 and 1750 prices declined by about 10% in Britain, while in the latter half of the century they rose by over a third.

By 1720 Britain's Atlantic exchanges had already pushed the value of British trade ahead of that of larger countries like France or Spain. Over the whole period from 1720 to 1800 Britain's trade grew more rapidly, multiplying over fivefold, while that of other European countries or regions grew over threefold. Between 1720 and 1750 Britain more or less maintained its initial lead. However, French trade subsequently grew at a greater rate, so that across the years 1720–80 it gained on that of Britain; the latter's trade was, of course, depressed by the American War of Independence in 1780. Starting from the war-afflicted early years of the century, the agriculture and manufactures of France advanced as swiftly, and overall perhaps more so, than those of a Britain experiencing the onset of both agricultural and industrial revolution. The output of the French Caribbean plantations overtook that of the British West Indian plantations around mid century, and maintained a faster rate of growth until the outbreak of the Revolution in 1789. But in the last two decades of the century British cotton manufactures did spurt ahead. Cotton consumption in France grew from half a million lb in 1700 to 11 million in 1780; British cotton consumption grew from 1.1 million lb in 1700 to 7.4 million in 1780, and reached no less than 42.9 million by 1800.[9] And in this latter year, Britain's colonial and Atlantic trade loomed larger than ever in its overall exchanges.

The generalized nature of the economic advance in Europe puts in context the growth of the slave-worked plantations and gold mines; the latter, of course, were producing directly for European markets. The economic expansion of eighteenth-century Europe translated into a more than proportionate rise in the demand for luxuries, especially the produce of the New World plantations. Plantation products entered the trade of all European states. European consumers preferred American tobacco, and taxes on its entry proved a convenient fiscal instrument. From about 1720 the New World plantations began to supply coffee in ever-increasing quantity. Somewhat later the Americas were also to become Europe's principal source of cotton.

By 1720 slave colonies were producing about 80,000 tons of sugar a year. Sugar loomed large in the trade of every state. Its consumption was most intense and widespread in Britain, with its growing middle classes and wage-earning proletariat. Annual sugar consumption in England rose from around 6 lb per head in 1710 to 23.2 lb per head in the 1770s.[10] Sugar prices dropped by about a third in the aftermath of the Peace of Utrecht, helping to spread its use from London to the provinces and from the middle classes to the lower strata. The subsequent steady growth in the consumption of sugar reflected the expansion of England's internal market. French sugar consumption ran at 1.5 lb to 2 lb per head per year in the early part of the century, and rose to a maximum of 3 to 4 lb per head in the 1780s. France had the larger population, but even in absolute terms the English market for sugar was more extensive and pulled further ahead, growing from a total of a little over 30 million lb in the 1710s to some 175 million lb by the end of the century, compared with a French market that grew from 25 million lb in the 1730s to a peak of 57 million in the 1780s.

The roughly tenfold advance of American slave-based commerce was premissed upon a geopolitical circumstance that should be briefly mentioned. If there was a demand for subtropical products in Europe, then the Americas were best situated to supply it. Attempts to establish plantations on the African coast or in the Indian ocean, or in the Far East, ran up against a host of problems. Those who attempted to sponsor plantations on or near the African coast, as the Royal African Company did, discovered that they confronted too many hazards and inconveniences for the intending planter, ranging from slave escapes or revolts, and heavy losses of European personnel from disease, to lengthy sailing times and hostile neighbours.[11] The Dutch produced some sugar in the Far East, and established a small slave colony at the Cape, but they were in no position to compete with the New World producers. The Caribbean and circum-Caribbean had everything required by plantation development: territories cleared of native peoples, fertile land, good harbours, favourable winds, high-yielding local subsistence crops, appropriate climatic conditions, manageable security problems – the only thing missing was a labour force.

The Slave Trade in the Eighteenth Century

The eighteenth-century slave trade was among the least effectively regulated of all branches of colonial commerce. The planters were usually eager to buy slaves and the slave traders to sell, regardless of the nationality of the buyer or seller. Moreover, the sale of a cargo of slaves involved such a considerable sum that it could easily bear the cost of any necessary bribes to local officials. The colonial authorities themselves recognized that slave purchases enabled their planters to boost production, so they were less concerned to suppress slave smuggling. The three principal slave trading nations in the eighteenth century were England, Portugal and France; Table IX.2 shows the numbers of slaves taken from Africa over the century:

Table IX.2   Atlantic Slave Trade, 1701–1800

Carrier	Total
English	2,532,300
Portuguese	1,796,300
French	1,180,300
Dutch	350,900
North America	194,200
Danish	73,900
Other (Swedish, Brandenburger)	5,000
Total	6,132,900

Source: Paul E. Lovejoy, 'The Volume of the Atlantic Slave Trade: A Synthesis', *Journal of African History*, 1982, p. 483.

These estimates are based on export shipping data: of the total about 40 per cent came from West Central Africa (Angola and the Kongo), about 40 per cent from the Bights of Benin and Biafra, about 15 per cent from the Gold Coast, Sierra Leone and Senegambia, and the remainder from unknown places of embarkation, including South East Africa and Madagascar. About 15 per cent of those who embarked on the African coast failed to survive the crossing – thus nearly one million Africans perished during the middle passage in this century. Although data on the immigration of free persons to the Americas are much less precise, it seems probable that enslaved African immigrants to the New World outnumbered Europeans by about four or five to one during the eighteenth century.

As will be seen, however, the slaves' chances of surviving and reproducing themselves were much lower. The British colonies of North America grew rapidly in the course of the eighteenth century, but this had as much to do with their high natural reproduction rates as it did with the receipt of some 322,000 immigrants from Britain and about 100,000 immigrants from Germany and German-speaking lands.[12] The discovery of gold in Brazil, combined with lack of opportunities in the metropolis, helped to stimulate an emigration from Portugal that has been roundly estimated at 300,000 during the course of the century as a whole; Spanish emigrants may have numbered nearly 200,000, but there were many fewer French emigrants. The European emigrations were somewhat reduced by those who returned – something which was rare indeed for the Africans.[13]

The single largest slave purchaser was probably Brazil, accounting for 31 per cent of the total; followed by the English Caribbean, taking 23 per cent; the French Caribbean, taking 22 per cent; Spanish America, with a little less than 9.6 per cent; the Dutch Caribbean, with 7.6 per cent; English North America, purchasing only 6 per cent; and the Danish Caribbean, 0.4 per cent. A colony's purchases from the Atlantic traders relied both on the vigour of plantation development and on the extent to which its slave population reproduced itself without such purchases. English North America was the only sizeable territory where the natural increase of the slave population came to sustain significant plantation growth. Some 30,000 to 40,000 slaves reached the Americas each year in the first three decades of the century; from 1730 to 1780 about 60,000 to 70,000 arrived each year; in the last two decades of the century 80,000 or more slaves were landed each year.[14]

There are breakdowns by age and sex for about a tenth of the 27,000 slaving voyages which took place between 1667 and 1867. The eighteenth-century slaving voyages – totalling nearly 17,000 – carried slightly more men and quite a few more children than had the slave trade of the previous century. The proportion of males rose from 60.3 per cent to 65.0 per cent, while the proportion of children rose from 12.2 per cent to 22.7 per cent. The children were those thought to be under fifteen, with few younger than ten, and of both sexes. David Eltis and Stanley Engerman have been able to establish a positive relationship between the rising proportion of children and declining costs of passage, due in the main to more efficient shipping. The cost of shipping a child was conventionally the same as the cost of shipping an adult – and amounted to nearly half of the slave price at the beginning of the century – so when shipping costs declined, the traders were able to offer slave children at a better discount. Eltis and Engerman point out that sugar planters would have found some advantages in acquiring children, because they were more easy to train in the complex techniques of sugar cultivation and processing.[15] The sugar plantation of this epoch was to be a striking embodiment of the importance of 'human capital', as we will see in Chapter X.

To varying degrees England, Portugal, and France all possessed the preconditions for a successful slave trade: a ready supply of the trade goods in demand on the African coast, access to markets in the Americas, and a vigorous merchant marine. The main carriers all possessed colonies of their own, with the possibility of a smuggling trade to neighbouring territories. English shipping was the strongest, and was backed up by the most considerable sea power; however, colonial development itself encouraged quite an impressive growth of the French and Luso-Brazilian merchant marine. The most acceptable items on the African coast were European manufactures (iron bars, metal implements, firearms, cloth, paper, etc.), East Indian textiles and spices, American plantation produce (rum, tobacco), and gold, silver, or currency equivalent (such as cowrie shells). The slave trading vessels needed a well-judged 'assortment', with each of the foregoing broad categories comprising between a fifth and a third of the total.[16] East India goods were initially indispensable, and every slave trading power had direct access to them via their own East India Companies. The slave merchants on the African coast were quite fixed in their attachment to these, but eventually the European manufacturers learnt to make textiles which would be acceptable substitutes. Portuguese traders acquired English or Dutch manufactures without much difficulty, and created a specialized demand on the African coast for Brazilian tobacco cured in molasses. The Dutch had no problem acquiring the necessary trade goods, but were hobbled by their continuing reliance on the trading company formula.

The slave trade was able to thrive because it was backed by the most dynamic commercial and manufacturing resources Europe had to offer. With the exception of the Portuguese enclave in Angola, the Europeans still commanded very little territory in Africa, but the Atlantic commerce gave a tremendous boost to the enslaving networks of the hinterland. By the end of the century the English alone were exporting an average of around 300,000 guns to West Africa each year.[17] This flood of firearms – albeit of fairly low quality – helped to stoke the furnace of internecine conflict. Conversion to Islam sometimes reflected the resistance of particular African peoples to enslavement, but the Muslim jihads also swelled the intake of the coastal slave factories. The leading African states and empires, and the sophisticated trading complex stretching back from the coast, were encouraged to supply ever larger numbers of captives by a dazzling array of commodities.

Persistent European representations of the slave trade portrayed African merchants and chiefs as lacking rational concepts of economic value. Africans, dwelling in the realm of fetishes, had no grasp of the true value of material things. Even such an astute observer as Willem Bosman could not resist contrasting the calculating ways of the Western traders with the impulse and superstition of the Africans with whom they dealt.[18] Europeans were not unused to estimating the worth of human beings in cash terms – whether as marriage partners or servants – and were aware that they themselves were both buyers and sellers in this context. But they suggested that Africans were so in thrall to fetishistic notions that they would part with slaves for baubles. In fact the notion that an African captive could be acquired for a handful of beads was fanciful, and modern econometric history has reconstructed consistent and systematic equivalences such that series of slave prices can be established in terms of contemporary European currencies. On parts of the coast slaves were themselves a species of currency; in Luanda the Portuguese merchants would advance imported goods to the Luso-African traders in return for promissory notes that stipulated their value in terms of so many slaves to be supplied.

The outset cost of a ship on the Africa run – that is, the value of its trade goods – was two or three times as great as in most other branches of European or Atlantic commerce. The acquisition of 180 slaves on the Gambia coast in 1740–41, long before slave prices reached their peak, required the following assortment of goods: 1,179 silver coins, weighing 17 kg, 430 iron bars, weighing 4,730 kg, 92 cutlasses, 430 gun flints, 1,162 kg of salt, 300 kg of linen cloth, 130 kg of Manchester textiles, 108 kg of Indian textiles, 219 kg of woollen cloth, 47 reams of paper, 164 guns, 71 pairs of pistols, 518 kg of gunpowder, 16 kg of lead balls, 102 brass pans weighing 457 kg, 301 kg of pewter ware, 2 rods of copper, and 119 gallons of rum.[19] In this instance the assortment also included beads and shells, which served as currency on some parts of the coast: to be precise, 15,195 finely worked cornelian beads, 60,000 crystal stones, and 17 kg of cowrie shells. The economic or military significance of this single consignment for an African merchant or monarch is evident enough. In addition to the trade goods there would be special presents for the African monarchs, merchant princes and their officials: firearms, wines and brandy, fine clothes, and perhaps a clock or lamp.

*

There was an underlying tendency for the prices of slaves on the African coast to rise from the late seventeenth century to the end of the eighteenth, reflecting growing demand, tougher bargaining and increasing costs of enslavement and transport, some stemming from resistance to enslavement. In the years 1676–79 a slave could be purchased on the African coast for trade goods worth a little over £3; by 1698–1707 this had risen to £8–£12, and by 1763–88 to £12–£15.[20] An alternative series cited by Gemery and Hogendorn gives the following average worth of trade goods per slave: 1701–10: £12.6; 1711–20: £16.8; 1721–30: £14.2; 1731–40: £20.2; 1741–50: £17.7; 1761–70: £20.0; 1771–76: £21.0; 1777–80: £11.4; 1781–90: £29.1; 1791–1800: £25.3.[21] If exception is made of periods when the slave trade was interrupted by war – especially during the American War of Independence, when the major slave carrier was threatened by an unprecedented coalition of foes – there was a constantly rising tendency of slave prices. They rose in the New World, too: from £15–£17 in 1676–78 to £28–£35 in 1763–88; by the last decade of the century the average price of an African slave, newly landed in the West Indies, had reached £50. This increase reflected the productivity and profitability of the plantations, as well as the craving for exotic produce in Europe. On the West African coast actual prices were set in terms of a local *numéraire* – bars of iron, ounces of gold, etc. – which mediated between European and African valuations of each commodity. By the late eighteenth century gunpowder and firearms offered good value to the European trader, metal implements bad value – but no assortment could be offered which omitted the latter, or no deal would be struck.[22]

Another indicator of the rising demand for African slaves is the increase in the average value of an investment in a slave trading vessel: for English merchants this doubled from about £4,000 in the 1730s to around £8,000 in the 1780s. The outset cost of a 200-ton ship sailing from Nantes around mid century was reckoned to be rather costly at 120,000 livres, though Pluchon suspects that the principal undertaker of the voyage could have exaggerated in order to reduce eventual profits.[23] Furthermore, the cost of a slaving voyage was boosted by the need for a large crew. The Middelburg Company's ships carried a crew of fifty or sixty. Paying and feeding such a complement for a year or more was costly, but the control of three or four hundred captives was demanding, especially if an epidemic cut the size of the crew, as could easily happen.[24]

By the latter half of the eighteenth century, when 80,000 or even 100,000 young men and women were taken from the African coast annually, the Atlantic trade was responsible for a subtraction that could have taken each year's natural population increase in West and Central Africa. Particular peoples and nations seem to have been entirely destroyed by the traffic, others greatly weakened. A large number of captives died before ever reaching the hold of a slave trader's vessel; and of course, countless others died in wars principally conducted to feed the slave traffic.

In the course of the eighteenth century, as the slave traders penetrated deeper into the continent, the slaves' march to the coast became longer – and, for that reason, more deadly for the captives and costly for the traders. In narrowly economic or demographic terms, those directly responsible for capture and enslavement received means of production which would have partially offset the loss to Africa of human productive and reproductive resources.

Patrick Manning has estimated that in order to deliver nine million slaves to the coast in the entire period 1700–1850, some twenty-one million people were probably captured – the gap between the two figures is explained by the death of five million within a year of capture and the reduction of a further seven million to slavery in Africa, helping to sustain the African-based apparatus of capture and commerce. Manning has also attempted a careful quantitative assessment of the relationship between the slave trade, on the one hand, and the population of the principal exporting regions as a whole, on the other. While the size of African populations can be only broadly estimated, the well-established information on slave exports combines with demographic models of reproduction to allow relatively firm conclusions. Manning argues that population dropped in each of the major West and West Central African zones involved in the Atlantic slave trade in the period 1720–1850. And, as we have seen, he concurs with Paul Lovejoy's thesis that the trade was greatly boosting the numbers of slaves being held in those regions of Africa which supplied it. Since slaves in Africa also had a lower propensity to reproduce themselves, this would have had a depressive effect on population levels.[25]

The European traders' avid demand for human captives, channelling a flow of resources to those most willing to satisfy it, fostered a virulent and predatory involution of many of Africa's political formations. The very fact that in African societies a relatively high value was placed on the ownership of slaves, with few opportunities for the private ownership of land, suggests that there was a strictly limited 'natural' pool of slaves available to merchants, and that it was only higher prices and intensified conflict which raised the volume of the trade so greatly in the eighteenth century. While the weight within Africa of predatory social formations increased, so did social and natural obstacles to their activities.[26] The rising price of slaves on the African coast reflected the increasing difficulties of the slave traders and slave-raiders as well as the strength of American demand. The continent, vast as it was, was not a limitless pool of human resources; each slave taken represented a decade or two of nurturance by their society of origin. The rising price of slaves eventually itself stimulated concern among planters and colonial officials, prompting them to look for ways to reduce dependence on the Atlantic traffic. As we shall see, many slaveowners deemed it impossible to dispense with slave imports – instead, they hoped to boost the productivity of their estates so that they could afford escalating slave prices.

The English pre-eminence in eighteenth-century slave trading was based on sea power, financial and maritime resources, colonial development and manufacturing strength. The trade was a competitive one, and the risks it entailed were considerable, so average profits were not greatly out of line with other branches of commerce. Roger Anstey has calculated an annual average profit of 9.5 per cent accruing to British slave traders in the years 1761 to 1807. Gross receipts from voyages entailing the sale of 1,428,701 slaves totalled £60 million during this period (worth approximately £6 billion in 1996 terms). There was wide variation in the profitability of individual voyages, but much of the trade was engrossed by traders who had a long-term commitment to it. The meaningfulness of Anstey's 'average rate' is enhanced by the fact that each voyage was financed by a multitude of investors, who would themselves be interested in a number of slaving expeditions. The annual rate of return on slave trading compared well with other contemporary investments, such as consols, which yielded around 3.5 per cent a year in this period; or real-estate mortgages, which yielded 4.5 per cent a year; or investment in West Indian plantations, which might yield 6–11 per cent yearly.

The English slave trade was certainly more profitable than that of the Dutch Middelburg Company, the successor of the WIC, which achieved an annual average profit of only 2.58 per cent in the period 1761–1800. The Dutch average did represent a spread of results, with a small majority of voyages making between 5 and 10 per cent while about 40 per cent made a loss. In peacetime overall profits sometimes depended on gains from the trade in goods other than slaves; Dutch traders found acquiring a timely return cargo more difficult, and often sailed back to Europe in ballast. Roughly three-quarters of the slaves brought over by the English traders went to English planters, with the remainder sold to Spanish or French colonists; in the years 1740–60 British naval strength made it possible for English slave traders to supply about half the slaves purchased by French planters.[27]

David Hancock's study of a group of London merchants explains how they acquired Bance Island, a former Royal African Company base and fort fifteen miles upstream from the mouth of the Sierra Leone River, in 1749. They rehabilitated the fort, built dwellings for local factors and slave pens; eventually they constructed Africa's first golf course in the 1770s, making the island, so far as visiting merchants and captains were concerned, the most agreeable spot for slave trading on the coast. One visitor described the sportsmen dressed in whites, attended by African caddies in tartan loincloths; golf was, he declared, 'very pretty exercise', after which they would repair to a meal of roast ape, antelope or boar washed down with

Madeira wine.[28] Such recreations did not get in the way of businesslike attention to the buying and selling of slaves. Bance Island became the linchpin of a wider slave trading operation that dispatched 12,929 slaves from West Africa to the Americas between 1748 and 1784. Hancock reports that the overall commercial balance of this trade was as follows: 'the net contribution from the sale of slaves and other goods in Africa, the West Indies, and North America totaled £61,133, facilities expenses £30,292, and overall profit £30,841 on an initial fixed investment of £4,000'.[29] However, the annual rate of profit on the slave trading voyages of Hancock's twenty-three merchant associates ran at an annual average rate of return on capital employed of only 6 per cent, considerably below the profits they made on trade with or investment in the plantations, which in the case of one associate ranges as high as 29 per cent and 44 per cent respectively.[30] However, slave trading profits fluctuated widely, and those associates who were able to integrate different aspects of their activities – for example, by buying slaves with their own goods or supplying their own plantations with slaves – would be able to set poor returns in one sector off against higher returns in another.

The French slave trade may have been a little less profitable than the English, but more profitable than the Dutch. The French *négriers* did not have effective legal recourse against the indebted planter, since the latter's land, machinery and slaves were protected against seizure for debt by colonial statute. The planters of the English colonies had enacted similar statutes, but this colonial legislation was overridden by the Credit Act of 1732, which included slaves among the assets that could be recovered in lieu of a debt; the English colonial merchants and big planters shared an interest in strengthening the position of creditors, since they acted as bankers and merchants to smaller planters. Investment in the French slave trade brought a return of 7–10 per cent annually, somewhat less than that reaped by French tax-farmers but quite satisfactory none the less. While it is reasonable to compare English slave trading profits with the yield of other investments, this is a less appropriate exercise in the case of France, where investment opportunities were bounded by special exclusions and privileges. While anyone could purchase consols, the same could not be said of entry into French tax-farming. Likewise, investment in land was more straightforward in England than in France, where its value would vary according to the precise status of the landowner.[31]

The relatively high rate of return in slave trading compensated for the high risks for each voyage. For some this return could be boosted if they were in a position to make an investment 'in kind' by contributing surplus stock, or their own manufactures, to the outset cargo. The French slave traders were encouraged by special privileges. First they received *acquits de Guiné* for slaves they sold to French planters, entitling them to remission on the duty on the colonial produce they brought to France – this scheme was adjusted in various ways in the course of the century, but usually it was possible to sell the *acquits*. This incentive helps to explain the rapid build-up of the French slave trade in peacetime conditions, or in the years 1778–83, when Britain lost naval supremacy. A second privilege enjoyed by the leading French slave traders was possession of a title of nobility, granting exemption from many taxes; these titles were distributed to the *négriers* to reward them for their crucial part in promoting colonial development.[32]

The Luso-Brazilian slave trade may have been the most profitable branch of the eighteenth-century slave traffic. The Luso-Brazilian merchants had skill in assembling a cost-effective assortment of trade goods, and benefited from Portugal's long-established presence in Africa. In Angola the inland slave trading complex was in the hands of Afro-Portuguese merchants who took trade goods to the inland slave fairs and brought back caravans of slaves. Joseph Miller has shown that the circuits of merchant capital reached far into the interior, as credit was extended by Portuguese or Brazilian traders to their local counterparts, who in turn extended credit to the African chiefs in the tangible form of cloth and other trade goods.

While predatory slave-raiders operated in the interior, so did strictly commercial mechanisms. The African chiefs had to find supplies of slaves, or they would cease to receive the trade goods they needed to attract and satisfy followers. The rivalry among different African chiefs put a premium on access to fine cloth, metalware, rum and other trade goods; yet the chief who availed himself of such supplies would quickly find that only human tribute would satisfy his creditors. The Lisbon merchants who transported slaves from Angola to Brazil did not themselves purchase the slaves but, rather, charged the Angolan slave traders for the cost of transport and the price of trade goods which had been supplied on credit. In this way they minimized their own risk and secured payment for their services either in specie, or in bills drawn up by Brazilian purchasers. The slave traders of Luanda were thus as much enmeshed in a constricting circle of credit as the African chiefs – though of course it was the captives who were the real victims of the 'way of death'. Miller also confirms the trend to larger numbers of children, especially boys, in the trade; the African chiefs kept back numbers of adult female slaves to be given to followers or to form part of their retinue. And the traders, for their part, found that the acquisition of child slaves did facilitate tight packing of their *tumbeiros*.[33]

The Brazilian economy itself supplied certain vital trade goods (sweet tobacco, gold and cowries), while the slave carrier of Bahia or Recife also usually purchased quantities of English cloth and metal manufactures, or East Indian textiles. A major advantage enjoyed by the Luso-Brazilian branch of the trade was the relatively short sailing times between Africa and Brazil compared with the often protracted triangular voyages of the English and French traders. Whereas the latters' investment usually took two years to be realized, that of the former took from six months to a year; and because the carriers did not buy the slaves themselves but, rather, extended trade goods and transportation costs on credit to the African coastal suppliers, they insulated themselves from some of the risks of the trade. On other parts of the coast European traders were much less inclined to extend credit to local traders because they had no recourse in case of default; because the Portuguese controlled a sizeable stretch of the Angolan coast, this was a more manageable risk for the Luso-Brazilian slave carriers.[34]

Slaves were hauled across the Atlantic in atrocious conditions. The detailed records left by the slave traders reveal that within the prevailing limits the tight packing of the slave ships had little impact on shipboard mortality rates. Of course, if the slave traders had been willing to allow each slave as much space and food as were generally offered to Europeans making the transatlantic voyage, the mortality rate of between 9 and 18 per cent could have been halved; but to do this would also have nearly halved the number of slaves landed in the Americas for each voyage, transforming a reasonable profit into a significant loss. However, the slave traders did gradually bring down the mortality rate as they discovered that a more varied diet helped to keep valuable slaves alive. The main killers were disease and poor nutrition, neither of which was necessarily linked to the variation in the numbers of slaves per ton. The length of the voyage explains some of the variations in mortality rate, probably because the longer voyages exhausted food supplies and gave more time for the incubation of disease. There is some evidence that mortality on shipments from Angola was lower than on those from West Africa, reflecting both a better provisioning system and a less severe disease environment in the Portuguese colony.

Mortality rates averaged around 13 per cent per voyage in the French eighteenth-century trade and 17 per cent in the Dutch trade. In the latter part of the century, mortality rates in the English slave trade fell from 8.5–9.6 per cent in 1761–90 to 3–5 per cent in the decade after 1794.[35] This decline probably reflected the important advances made by the British Navy in preventing the illnesses which plagued shipboard life. Between the American War of Independence and the Napoleonic Wars the length of time a British fleet could be kept continuously at sea rose from six weeks to six months because of improvements in nautical diet and medicine. The sharp drop in slave mortality in the English slave trade in the 1790s is almost certainly to be explained by similar factors. It was in this decade that the protective value of concentrated orange or lemon juice was first widely appreciated, becoming compulsory issue in the British Navy in 1795. Since slaves cost much more than oranges and lemons, some traders adopted this practice.

By the latter part of the eighteenth century it was quite common for

English traders to have slaves inoculated against smallpox before bringing them on board. Although slave cargoes were often insured – itself a sign of the relative modernity of the slave traffic – the slave trader still had most to gain from landing as many live slaves as possible; measures such as inoculation could also be used to bargain for lower rates. The French Navy and slave traders also displayed an interest in using appropriate medical knowledge. The great French discoverer of this epoch, Admiral Bougainville, shared with Captain Cook, his English counterpart, a keen interest in improving the diet and health of seamen; their innovations were not neglected by slave traders or planters. The European crews of the slave trading vessels seem to have suffered a heavier shipboard mortality than the slaves because of the greater time they spent on board: as many as a hundred thousand sailors died on the slaving ships in the course of the century. On the other hand, shipboard mortality among the slaves, even when it was reduced, remained higher than for European migrants, whose mortality rates dropped to 1–3 per cent or less.[36]

The African captives had little idea of what lay in store for them. By the time they were driven on board the slave trading vessel, if not before, they would have realized that they were in the hands of white men rather than being kept as part of the slave labour force on the coast. In some African cultures whites were believed to be the spirits of dead people, who needed the living for their own obscure but ominous ends.[37] While there is often a fatalistic streak in surviving oral testimony, there is other evidence of resistance and desperate attempts to escape. Thus the records of the WIC list fifteen major revolts aboard their ships in the years 1751–75, most of them occurring while the vessel was still close to the African coast. In 1770 the slaves, led by one Essjerrie Ettin, seized control of the *Guinniese Vriendschap*, but the Dutch warship *Castor* succeeded in recapturing it. On another occasion when an entire ship, the *Neptunius*, was seized, in 1795, an English warship suppressed the mutiny, though only by blowing up the ship.[38] A British slaver, Captain William Snelgrave, explained that there were always dangers in keeping war captives on the coast, or on ships close to land, while waiting to complete an advantageous cargo. He recounts one mutiny involving Coromantins – 'the stoutest and most sensible Negroes on the coast', who were 'resolved to regain their liberty if possible' – which was quelled by a display of firepower in which he himself felled a leading rebel with a pistol shot. In Snelgrave's view, 'mutinies are generally occasioned by the sailors' ill usage'.[39] The Dutch WIC asked slave captains to protect the slave women:

> We also seriously demand that you do not permit any Negroes, slaves or slave women to be defiled or mistreated by any of the officers or crew members. And if such should occur anyway, this should be noted in the log book, an affidavit

signed, and the offender punished by the ship's council according to the offence, including confiscation of salary.[40]

Once the slave ship had left the coast, the danger of full-scale mutiny diminished, but there was still scope for conflict over mistreatment, food, and exercise periods. The famous Abolitionist diagram of the tight packing of a slave ship represented the slaver's ideal; feeding and exercising the captives could afford opportunities for greater communication between them, and for some disorder. Equiano remarks that the captives were kept below decks to prevent them seeing how the ship was managed. 'Shipmates' – that is, slaves brought over in the same ship – were often sold to the same or neighbouring estates and often kept in touch with one another, becoming a sort of surrogate family.

From the 1770s onwards there was a chain of movements of Muslim renewal in West Africa which reflected a form of resistance to the Atlantic trade. They began in the area of the Wolof kingdoms, triggered by crises related to drought and famine as well as slave-raiding and warfare. This movement was able to draw support from regions which specialized in growing grain and provisions for the Atlantic coast and islands, and for the slaving ships. Thus the peoples of Fuuta Tooro had been able to develop a more settled pattern of existence based on a trade in products of the soil rather than slaves. Islamic education made considerable strides in these regions. When they found themselves the target of raids by the hard-drinking and brutal soldier slaves of the King of Fuuta Jallon, the people rose in rebellion and succeeded in overthrowing him in 1776. In the 1790s the kingdom of Kajoor was swept by a similar revolt, and was to smoulder with conflict for another twenty years, but eventually the King managed to suppress it. As pointed out above, however, the pressure for Muslim reform protected particular peoples, but did not reduce the overall flow of the slave traffic.[41]

Gwendolyn Midlo Hall cites a Louisiana folk myth concerning the creation which, she believes, had Senegambian origins:

> The creation myth conveys a reverence for all forms of life. God had ordered the animals not to destroy or eat one another but to eat only grass and fruits. 'That was better, because they were all his creatures and it pained him when they killed each other; but as quickly as they would eat the grass and fruits, He, God, would take pleasure to make them grow again to please them.' But the animals refused to obey. The lions ate the sheep, the dogs ate the rabbits, the serpents ate the little birds, the cats ate the rats, the owls ate the chickens. To stop them from destroying themselves and to punish their cruelty God sent a great drought.[42]

As Hall observes, drought was a marked feature of Senegal, not Louisiana; likewise lions; however, the story could also echo passages from Genesis, with which Muslims as well as Christians would have been familiar.[43]

Whatever its origin, this African-American folk tale reflects the memory of people who had passed through the ordeal of enslavement and the Middle Passage.

The Pattern of Trade and Shipping

The trade generated by the slave plantations was roughly ten times as valuable as the trade in slaves themselves, and since – unlike the Eastern trade – it involved quite bulky products, it made correspondingly large demands on shipping. In around 1800, when Britain was by far the largest slave trading power, only 4–5 per cent of its merchant marine were engaged in the slave traffic. But as Table IX.3 shows, the colonial trade required a massive and growing volume of shipping:

Table IX.3   Tonnage of Shipping in the British Overseas Trade (000 tons)

	1663	1686	1771–72
Northern Europe	16	28	78
British Isles and nearby	39	41	92
Southern Europe	30	39	27
America and West Indies	36	70	153
East India	8	12	29

Source: Ralph Davis, *The Rise of the English Shipping Industry*, Newton Abbot 1972, p. 17.

Shipbuilding was a major national industry, and the Atlantic trade made a strong contribution to it. As privateering and piracy were gradually suppressed, it was possible for ships on the West India run to be purpose-built. The main innovations were made in vessels weighing 150–450 tons: they ranged from the replacement of the tiller by the steering wheel early in the century to copper-sheathing of the ship's bottom to check the ravages of the teredo worm in the last decades. Before about 1740, merchantmen on the Jamaica run required a manning ratio of one seaman for every 9 tons; Spanish privateers were still a danger at this time. Prior to the American War, manning ratios dropped to 14.5 tons per seaman.[44] The French also undertook a vast programme of naval construction, since over 600 vessels a year were arriving in their colonies by the 1780s. However, manning levels did not fall so much on the French ships, since a law required apprentices to sail with every vessel.

The English deep-sea merchant marine employed about 25,000 sailors in mid century, and gave employment to similar numbers of dock workers and shipbuilders. In the American ports free persons of colour also worked in the docks, and by the second half of the century many also worked as sailors. Given the value of the cargoes, and the need to bring them to sale at advantageous times, dockers constituted a strategic workforce wielding some bargaining power. Slaves also sometimes worked on the docks, or on ships as servants, sailors or interpreters. But the circumstances of shipboard life, and the dispositions of their workmates, often undermined the slave condition in the long run. Slaveholders found that the best way to motivate their slaves for individual employment was to offer to let them buy themselves out of slavery, using their accumulated savings or any money they could borrow for the purpose. In North America such offers gave rise to 'freedom suits' as slaves, calling on the testimony of workmates, petitioned the courts for their liberty. In Brazil it was said that the urban slave was already half-free; there and in Spanish America the practice of offering slaves the opportunity to buy their own freedom was even more common, with African *cofradias*, or Christian brotherhoods, helping to bring social pressure to bear to ensure that agreements were kept. The ports and ships engaged in the Atlantic trade were a slave frontier and, given the slaves' powerful urge to freedom, often a porous one. But if this frontier permitted some slaves to gain their freedom, there was also the risk that a free coloured sailor would be seized as a slave if his ship was captured in war near the slave zone; and even if they were spared such a disaster, free persons of colour did not enjoy legal equality with whites, even in such a relatively tolerant colony as Pennsylvania, while in all the English ports white sailors themselves were subject to impressment by the Royal Navy.[45]

By the middle of the eighteenth century, half of all Britain's overseas trade consisted of shipments of sugar or tobacco; sugar and coffee comprised more than half of all French overseas commerce. These same plantation products loomed large in the intra-European re-export trade. In the third and fourth decades of the century, French sugar largely displaced English from the principal European markets. However, the overall pattern of British exchanges in the Atlantic zone was more diversified, and the commercial mechanisms involved, including the new bill of exchange, were increasingly efficient:

> it was the South Atlantic system, which presaged the multilateral character of English trade more than any other branch, that brought the bill system to the peak of its development. By contrast with the payments problems involved in trade with the East, which for so long was essentially a bullion trade, long distance traffic on the Atlantic brought several diverse interest groups together in a pattern of trade which achieved overall balance by means of indirect settlements between its constituent parts. The bulk growing and marketing of raw materials in exchange for manufactures produced under regimes of considerable specialisation, together with the purchase and re-sale of supplies of slave labour, could not have been carried out with any facility without an efficient clearing system.[46]

Each of the imperial powers sought to prevent merchants of other nationalities from engaging in any direct trade with its colonies. However, Atlantic exchanges exhibited a definite impetus to freer trade as smuggling qualified protectionist restrictions. The Dutch colonies, especially St Eustatius and Curaçao, were centres of a thriving contraband trade in which merchants of all nationalities participated. The English merchants used the *asiento* to penetrate Spanish commercial barriers, while the French gained access to the legal Spanish American trade. Britain's naval and commercial aggressions in the Seven Years War (1756–63) led both France and Spain to inaugurate a 'free port' system in the Antilles which opened up further loopholes in the system of colonial protection. However, contraband made really large inroads only where there was a degree of official connivance, or where large comparative advantages were being suppressed.

The British and French authorities created difficulties for themselves by seeking to enforce their own restrictions while breaking those of other powers. The French colonial authorities often turned a blind eye to North American or English ships bringing provisions to their islands and buying plantation products in contravention of England's Molasses Act of 1733 and similar prohibitive legislation. On the other hand, the French and English authorities could, if they wished, exercise reasonably effective control over their own islands and over entry to metropolitan ports. Metropolitan invigilation was facilitated by naval patrols, the small size of many colonies, the visibility of the plantations' operations, the relative bulk of the cargoes and the limited number of ports of entry in Europe for ocean-going ships. Eighteenth-century Atlantic commerce was thus very far from effective free trade, but this was the direction in which it pressed. Even where contraband flourished, it was not so secure as to permit the use of the more flexible and sophisticated commercial methods being developed by the English colonial trade.[47]

At their height, in around 1750, Brazilian exports of gold were worth over £1 million annually. If we add this to the other important slave-produced commodities – sugar, coffee, tobacco, rice, cotton, indigo, pimiento, dried meat, and so forth – the total value of American slave produce cannot have been much below £15 million annually around mid century. In 1774 the exports of the French slave colonies were worth £5.5 million on arrival in Europe, of the British West Indies £3.5 million, of the Southern slave colonies of North America £1.8 million, of Brazil about £2.5 million, of the Dutch Caribbean £1 million and of the slave products of the Spanish Caribbean £0.4 million: a grand total of £15.7 million.[48]

The swelling eighteenth-century Atlantic slave trade, and the keen demand for plantation products, were linked to a proliferation of plantation cultivation. The productive prowess of the slave plantation was the driving force behind the commercial booms. Beyond the archipelago of Caribbean islands was a wider archipelago of slave plantations stretching from Maryland in the North to São Paulo in the South. Brazil imported more slaves than any other single colony – indeed, slightly more than all the English colonies put together. English North America was by far the largest supplier of tobacco and was notable for the positive growth rates of its slave population. Under Bourbon rule the Spanish Empire staged a recovery, and the Spanish colonies eventually imported slightly more slaves than English North America. But until nearly the end of the century the British and French West Indian islands remained the pacemakers, producing the most valuable cargoes for the Atlantic trade, developing the most commercialized plantations, and together importing more slaves than any other region of the Americas.

Notes

1. E.J. Hobsbawm, 'The Crisis of the Seventeenth Century', in Trevor Aston, *Crisis in Europe: 1560–1660*, London 1965, p. 46. This essay first appeared in *Past and Present*, 5 and 6 (1954).

2. This is the implication of the argument advanced in two influential articles, Robert Brenner, 'The Origins of Capitalist Development', *New Left Review*, 104, July–August 1977, pp. 72–3, 84–5; and Ernesto Laclau, 'Capitalism and Feudalism in Latin America', *Politics and Ideology in Marxist Theory*, London 1978, pp. 30–32, 38–9.

3. Karl Marx, *Capital*, vol. I, London 1976, chapter 10, 'The Voracious Appetite for Surplus Labour', pp. 344–5.

4. The authors indicated in note 2, for example.

5. Witold Kula, *An Economic Theory of the Feudal System*, London 1976, pp. 89–91.

6. Geoffrey de Ste Croix, *Class Struggles in the Ancient Greek World*, London 1982; Perry Anderson, *From Antiquity to Feudalism*, London 1974.

7. The slave population estimates are my own. For 1700 they are based on sources given in earlier chapters with the following breakdown: British colonies 110,000; French colonies 30,000; Spanish America 70,000; Brazil 100,000; Dutch and Danish colonies 20,000. The breakdown of slave populations for 1800 will be given below.

8. André Armengaud, 'Population in Europe 1700–1914', in C.M. Cipolla, *The Fontana History of Europe*, vol. 3, *The Industrial Revolution*, pp. 22–76, especially pp. 27–9.

9. François Crouzet, 'England and France in the Eighteenth Century', in R.M. Hartwell, ed., *The Causes of the Industrial Revolution in England*, London 1967; W.W. Rostow, *How it All Began*, London 1975, p. 168. For the unevenness of European economic advance in this period see Immanuel Wallerstein, *The World System*, volume III, Cambridge 1978, chapter 2, and Carlo Cipolla, ed., *The Fontana Economic History of Europe*, vols 4 and 5, London 1974 and 1976.

10. David Richardson, 'The Slave Trade, Sugar and British Economic Growth 1748 to 1776', in Barbara L. Solow and Stanley L. Engerman, eds, *British Capitalism and Caribbean Slavery*, Cambridge 1987.

11. This was a problem, which had also beset England's 'new merchants' when they attempted to set up plantations off the African coast: Brenner, *Merchants and Revolution*, pp. 177–80.

12. Altman and Horn, 'Introduction', *'To Make America'*, p. 3.

13. Nicolás Sánchez-Albórnoz, 'Las Migraciones Anteriores al Siglo XIX', in Birgitta Leander, ed., *Europa, Asia y África en América Latina y el Caribe*, Mexico D.F. 1989, pp. 61–88 (pp. 82–3).

14. Paul Lovejoy, 'The Volume of the Atlantic Slave Trade', *Journal of African History*, 23, 1982, pp. 473–501.

15. David Eltis and Stanley Engerman, 'Fluctuations in Age and Sex Ratios in the Transatlantic Slave Trade', *Economic History Review*, XLVI, no. 2, 1993, pp. 308–23 (pp. 310, 318). These authors also suggest that children may have been less susceptible to some Caribbean diseases than adults.

16. David Richardson, 'West African Consumption Patterns and their Influence on the Eighteenth Century English Slave Trade', in Gemery and Hogendorn, *The Uncommon Market*, pp. 303–30; Pierre Verger, *Flux et reflux de la traite des nègres entre le golfe de Bénin et Bahia*, Paris 1968, pp. 117, 306.

17. J.E. Inikori, 'The Import of Firearms into West Africa, 1750 to 1807: A Quantitative Analysis', in Inikori, *Forced Migrations*, pp. 126–53 (pp. 134–5).

18. Willem Bosman, *A New and Accurate Description of the Coast of Guinea*, London 1725, translation from a Dutch original of 1703.

19. Philip Curtin, *Economic Change in Pre-colonial Africa: Senegambia in the Era of the Slave Trade*, Madison, WI 1974, p. 172.

20. Sheridan, *Sugar and Slavery*, p. 252.

21. Gemery and Hogendorn, *The Uncommon Market*,

22. For West Indian slave prices, Sheridan, *Sugar and Slavery*, p. 252; for trade goods, Richardson, 'West African Consumption Patterns', in Gemery and Hogendorn, *The Uncommon Market*, p. 309.

23. Pierre Pluchon, *La Route des Esclaves: Négriers et Bois d'Ébène au XVIIIe siècle*, Paris 1980, p. 286.

24. Postma, *The Dutch in the Atlantic Slave Trade*, p. 281.

25. Patrick Manning, *Slavery and African Life: Occidental, Oriental, and African Slave Trades*, Cambridge 1990, pp. 60–96. See also Paul E. Lovejoy, 'The Impact of the Atlantic Slave Trade on Africa', *Journal of African History*, no. 30, 1989, pp. 365–94, who reaches substantially similar conclusions.

26. The data cited are taken from Gemery and Hogendorn, 'The Economic Costs of West African Participation in the Atlantic Slave Trade', in Gemery and Hogendorn, *The Uncommon Market*, pp. 143–61; Martin Klein and Paul Lovejoy, 'Slavery in West Africa', in Gemery and Hogendorn, *The Uncommon Market*, pp. 181–212; Charles Becker and Victor Martin, 'Kayor and Baol: Senegalese Kingdoms and the Slave Trade in the Eighteenth Century', in Inikori, ed., *Forced Migrations*, pp. 100–25. See also Lovejoy, *Transformations in Slavery*.

27. Roger Anstey, *The Atlantic Slave Trade and British Abolition, 1761–1810*, London 1965, pp. 47, 57; David Richardson, 'Profitability in the Bristol–Liverpool Slave Trade, La Traite des Noirs par l'Atlantique', *Revue française d'histoire d'outre mer*, Paris 1975, pp. 301–8; Sheridan, *Sugar and Slavery*, pp. 381–2; J.M. Postma, *The Dutch in the Atlantic Slave Trade*, pp. 276 ff.

28. David Hancock, *Citizens of the World: London Merchants and the Integration of the British Atlantic Community, 1735–1785*, Cambridge 1995, pp. 1–2.

29. Ibid., p. 423.

30. Ibid., pp. 415, 423–4.

31. Robert Stein, *The French Slave Trade in the Eighteenth Century: An Old Regime Business*, Madison, WI 1979, pp. 14, 26, 40; Jean Meyer, *L'Armement nantais dans la deuxième moitié du XVIIIe siècle*, Paris 1969, p. 244.

32. François Thesée, *Négociants bordelais et colons de Saint-Domingue*, Paris 1972, pp. 120, 145; Herbert Klein, *The Middle Passage: Comparative Studies in the Atlantic Slave Trade*, Princeton, NJ 1978, pp. 203–6.

33. Joseph Miller, *Way of Death: Merchant Capitalism and the Angolan Slave Trade*, Madison, WI 1988, pp. 135–9, 159–65.

34. Klein, *The Middle Passage*, pp. 46–8; Miller, *Way of Death*.

35. Klein, *The Middle Passage*, pp. 64–5, 86–90, 229–41; Anstey, *The Atlantic Slave trade*, p. 31.

36. J.H. Parry, *Trade and Dominion: European Expansion in the Eighteenth Century*, pp. 292–3; David Eltis, 'Europeans and the Rise and Fall of African Slavery in the Americas'.

37. Fritz Kramer, *The Red Fez*, London 1993, explores a number of African myths relating to the slave trade.

38. Postma, *The Dutch in the Atlantic Slave Trade*, p. 166.

39. Captain William Snelgrave, *A New Account of Some Parts of Guinea and the Slave Trade*, London 1734, pp. 146–9, 172, 186–7. See also Winston McGowan, 'African Resistance to the Atlantic Slave Trade in West Africa', *Slavery and Abolition*, vol. 11, no. 1, 1990, pp. 5–29 and Searing, *West African Slavery and Atlantic Commerce*.

40. Postma, *The Dutch in the Atlantic Slave Trade*, p. 366.

41. Searing, *West African Slavery and Atlantic Commerce*, pp. 91–2, 155–62.

42. Hall, *Africans in Colonial Louisiana*, pp. 193–4.

43. For the vegetarian theme in Genesis see Alexander Cockburn, 'Carnivores and Capitalists: A Short History of Meat', *New Left Review*, 215, January–February 1996.

44. Parry, *Trade and Dominion*, pp. 278–84.

45. The milieu of British seamen is comprehensively explored in Marcus Rediker, *Between the Devil and the Deep Blue Sea*, Cambridge 1987; and that of the London dockworkers much illuminated by Peter Linebaugh in *The London Hanged*, London 1992. For Philadelphia see the opening chapters of Gary Nash and Jean Soderland, *Freedom by Degrees: Emancipation and its Aftermath*, New York 1991.

46. B.L. Anderson, 'The Lancashire Bill System and its Liverpool Practitioners', in W.A. Chaloner and B.M. Ratcliffe, eds, *Trade and Transport*, Manchester 1977, pp. 64–5.

47. For the limits of smuggling see John J. McCusker, *The Rum Trade and the Balance of Payments*, New York 1991, pp. 301–10. However, R.C. Nash finds reasons to suppose that there was considerable under-reporting of Scottish tobacco imports for some time after 1707, 'The English and Scottish Tobacco Trade in the Seventeenth and Eighteenth Centuries: Legal and Illegal Trade', *Economic History Review*, vol. 35, 1982, pp. 354–72 (p. 364).

48. Richard Sheridan, *The Growth of the Plantations to 1750*, Barbados 1970, pp. 29, 35, 41, 49; R.M. Robertson and G.M. Walton, *History of the American Economy*, 4th edn, New York 1979, pp. 128, 130; Roberto Simonsen, *História económica do Brasil 1500–1820*, vol. II, Rio de Janeiro 1937, table facing p. 222. Brazil's gold exports in the years 1730–60 averaged about £750,000 annually. The broad estimates given here indicate the size of the colonial branches on European trade, not the monies received by planters.

X

The Sugar Islands

I was shock'd at the first appearance of human flesh exposed to sale. But surely God Ordained 'em for the use and benefit of us: otherwise his Divine Will would have been made manifest by some particular sign or token.

John Pinney, planter and merchant, 1760s

It was on the Gallifet estate in the parish of La Petite Anse that there took place an aeronautical experience, the second in Saint Domingue. This was in 1784. . . . The height of the balloon was 30 feet, the average diameter eighteen, and its circumference 57. It went up in a spiral path, leaving people time to consider the ornaments with which they had decorated it, including the coats of arms of the two chiefs of the Colony. . . . The ascencion took five minutes, the stationary phase three. . . . It was estimated to have gone up 1,800 ft. This phenomenon so new to the American world, had brought together a great crowd of persons. . . . The negro spectators seemed as if they would keep crying out forever over the insatiable lust of man to bring nature within his power.

Moreau de St-Méry, *Description de Saint Domingue*

ÉLÉVATION DE LA PRISE D'EAU AU PIED DE LA MONTAGNE DE LA TRANQUILLITÉ.

Dam in Saint Domingue, where irrigation schemes fostered the plantation boom

Towards the middle of the eighteenth century sugar overtook grain as the most valuable single commodity entering world trade. Around mid century total annual American exports were worth £7.5 million at wholesale prices in Europe; if the commerce in the increasingly sought-after by-products – rum and molasses – is added, the total rises to £9 million, or nearly a fifth of European imports.

The British and French Caribbean colonies supplied 70 per cent of all sugar entering the North Atlantic market in 1740, rising to 80 per cent by 1787; Brazil continued to be a significant supplier, though good figures are lacking and the estimates quoted in Table X.1 may overstate the level of exports achieved. The Americas as a whole supplied nearly all of Europe's sugar imports, with modest quantities arriving from Java, Bourbon, Réunion and the Atlantic islands. Table X.1 sets out the broad pattern of growth of sugar exports in the eighteenth century:

Table X.1 New World Sugar Exports 1700–1787

000 tons*	1700	1720	1760	1787
Brazil	20	20	28	19
British Islands	22	24	71	106
French Islands	10	24	81	125
Dutch West Indies	5	6	9	10
Danish West Indies			5	8
Cuba			6	18
Total	57	74	200	286

Sources: Roberto Simonsen, *História econômica do Brasil*, vol. I, facing p. 170, for Brazil 1700 and 1720; Deerr, *History of Sugar*, pp. 530–31, for Brazil 1760; for other figures 1700 and 1720, Davis, *Rise of the Atlantic Economies*, p. 257; for French and British islands 1760 and 1787, Seymour Drescher, *Econocide*, pp. 48, 78; for other data, Moreno Fraginals, *El Ingenio*, I, p. 41.

As we will see, on the larger 'sugar islands' the sugar plantations might engage only half, or less than half, of all slaves, with others working on secondary crops, or livestock, or gardening pens. The build-up of the slave populations in the British and French Caribbean is set out in Table X.2 (see page 404).

While the British and French islands had much in common as slave plantation societies, their pattern of development was naturally much affected by the military and commercial fortunes of the empires of which they formed a part. They will be considered separately in order best to bring out their distinctive features.

Table X.2   Slave Population of the Caribbean Islands

	French	British
1680	11,000	64,000
1690	27,000	95,000
1710	60,000	130,000
1730	169,000	219,000
1750	265,000	295,000
1770	379,000	428,000
1790	675,000	480,000

Sources: Mims, *Colbert's West India Policy*, pp. 336–7; Dunn, *Sugar and Slaves*, p. 312; Seymour Drescher, *Econocide*, p. 34; Gaston Martin, *Histoire de l'esclavage dans les colonies françaises*, pp. 24–6, 103, 124–5; Frostin, *Les Révoltes blanches à Saint Domingue*, pp. 28–9.

Economics and Demography in the British Caribbean

The development of the British West Indian plantation colonies poses several puzzles: (1) why did Jamaica take so long to fulfil its potential?; (2) why did islands which received a stream of one-and-a-half million slaves in the course of the eighteenth century have a total slave population of less than half this number at the end of the century?; and (3) given heavy costs of slave replenishment, and with unwilling and unhealthy labourers, how could the plantations be profitable? The answers to these questions will require a deepening of the lines of analysis suggested in Chapter VIII concerning plantation security, productivity and profitability.

The problems of plantation development were most sharply posed in Jamaica. At the beginning of the eighteenth century it was already clear that this island, with its far larger size, could easily outproduce the older colonies of the Eastern Caribbean. But before 1740 the development of Jamaica was held back by its poor internal and external security. The success of several thousand maroons in fighting off many attempts to suppress them encouraged slave revolts and runaways. Even though maroon settlements, like Nanny Town, could be captured, the maroons would regroup elsewhere. To the alarm of the authorities and planters the maroons often fought with firearms; the latter were probably stolen, or purchased on the 'black market', though Spanish agents were also suspected. The maroon threat was eventually contained when the colonial authorities came to terms with the main maroon forces, led by Colonel Cudgoe and Captain Accompong, in 1739, as war with Spain loomed; the freedom of the maroons was recognized, as was their tenure of 1,500 acres of land and the right to engage in local trade; in return they agreed to return runaways and defend the island against foreign invasion.[1]

The security problem had been compounded by the fact that Spanish *guarda costas* based on Cuba frequently seized ships on the Jamaica run; their cargoes would be sold on the real or alleged grounds that these ships were engaged in smuggling. From mid century onwards external security also improved as the *guarda costas* were intimidated by Britain's sustained naval deployment in the Caribbean. Jamaica was never the target of an invasion attempt, but the war of 1756–63 stimulated several alarms. In 1760 a string of ultimately unsuccessful slave revolts following 'Tacky's Rebellion' and mainly involving 'Coromantins' (Akans from present-day Ghana) were ferociously repressed with the help of colonial troops and maroon auxiliaries. A further period of tribulation followed in 1777–83, when the cessation of supplies from North America caused starvation among the slaves and communications with Britain were occasionally severed. With all these problems the development of Jamaica's population and economy was a little slower than it might have been, but impressive nevertheless:

Table X.3 Jamaica: Economy and Population 1673–1800

	1700	1734	1750	1774	1789	1800
Whites 000	7	8	9	19	23	27
Free Coloured	–	1	2	4	–	10
Slaves 000	40	80	122	190	256	337
Sugar Mills	150	300	525	775	710	800
Sugar Output (000t)	5	16	20	40	50	70
Exports £000	325	625	1,025	2,400	–	3,854

Sources: Eighteenth-century export values are taken from Richard Sheridan, *Sugar and Slaves*, pp. 216–17; the export value for 1800 is taken from B.W. Higman, *Slave Population and Economy in Jamaica, 1807–1834*, London 1976, p. 213; the figures for the free coloured population are from David W. Cohen and Jack P. Greene, eds, *Neither Slave nor Free*, Baltimore, MD 1972, p. 336. All other data are from Michael Craton, 'Jamaican Slavery', in S. Engerman and E. Genovese, eds, *Race and Slavery in the Western Hemisphere*, p. 275, supplemented by Michael Craton, *Searching for the Invisible Man: Slaves and Plantation Life in Jamaica*, London 1978, pp. 34–5, 37.

Jamaica pulled ahead of the other British islands only in the 1750s. The slave population and sugar economy of Barbados had reached a plateau. There was little possibility of raising sugar output further, and slave imports began to decline. The planters turned instead to increasing the value-added of their final product by 'claying' the muscovado – this process yielded both white sugar and molasses. The white sugar commanded a higher price and was less bulky to ship. The molasses could be sold in the North American colonies in return for plantation supplies. Some slaves had to be trained for the skilled work of claying, but in an old colony with an experienced labour force this posed no problem. Consequently, Barbadian planters earned more from crops the size of which rose little.[2]

In the early decades of the eighteenth century the most rapidly developing British colonies were the Leeward Islands; unlike Barbados, the planters had not yet cultivated all suitable land. The combined slave population of the Leewards overtook that of Barbados in 1730 and reached 73,000 by 1750. The planters of Antigua had a reputation for staying on their estates and taking an informed interest in improved methods of cultivation. There were 10,000 whites in the Leeward Islands in 1750. Barbados long continued to have proportionally the largest white population, with 15,000 whites, 2,000 free coloured and 64,000 slaves in the 1780s.[3] Britain acquired a number of other islands in the Eastern Antilles at the conclusion of the Seven Years War – the Ceded Islands – but their development was halting, partly because of the uncertainties created by French proprietors and the formidable resistance of the Black Caribs of St Vincent. The latter, descendants of Caribs who had intermixed with shipwrecked and runaway African slaves, occupied some of the best land in St Vincent in 1764, when the British took over. Rapacious planter-speculators sought to drive them away, but did not succeed in securing the major military operation necessary to attack them until 1773–74. After many Black Caribs made common cause with the Jacobins in the 1790s, the whole community was transported to the Western Caribbean.[4]

The ownership of both land and slaves in mid-century Jamaica was even more concentrated than it was in the other plantation colonies. In 1754 there were 467 large planters, owning more than 1,000 acres each and accounting for 77.8 per cent of the land available for cultivation.[5] The commanders of the militia and the leaders of the colonial assembly were both drawn from the ranks of the large planters; they thus dominated the social life of the colony despite a very high absentee rate. The Jamaican Assembly claimed – usually with success – to control local revenues; the Governor was often chosen from the ranks of planters.

The planter who returned to Britain would leave an attorney or a relative in charge of his estate; he would usually correspond with them regularly, and often supervise plantation sales and purchases from England. From 1740 the Jamaican Assembly established machinery for monitoring the performance of estates owned by absentees. The absentee's agent or attorney was required to file comprehensive information relating to the estate they managed with the Secretary of the island's Accounts Produce Department; every year they had to supply an inventory, a breakdown of output and financial accounts. In 1770 about a third of Jamaica's estates, accounting for 40 per cent of sugar output, were administered by agents or attorneys on behalf of absentee owners. It is a remarkable tribute to the effectiveness of this system of long-range devolution that average profits on agent-managed were the same as those on owner-managed estates. By the end of the century, when the colony enjoyed remarkable prosperity, only one in ten of the Great Houses was occupied by its proprietor.[6]

Beneath the 467 large Jamaican planters of 1754 there were 303 landholders with between 500 and 999 acres, enough for a medium-sized estate; 566 landholders with between 100 and 499 acres, enough for a small estate; and only 263 landholders with less than 100 acres; not included in these figures were farmers who leased land and supplied the internal market. Cattle pens occupied an important niche in the island's domestic economy; slaves from the pens would also be hired out as job-bing gangs when new land was to be cleared or planted. Most large plantations were devoted chiefly to sugar, though they would often be attached to satellite stock farms and provision grounds. A sugar estate could not usefully exceed 2,000 acres in extent, or the cane could not be brought to the mill before its sucrose content had dropped below the level of profitable extraction. Thus the 214 landholdings of 1754 which exceeded this limit probably included satellite farms; others were certainly holding land in reserve or for speculative purposes. The trebling of Jamaica's sugar crop in the second half of the eighteenth century was achieved by an increase in the number of sugar estates from 535 in 1750 to 900 in 1790, together with a doubling or trebling of the size of the average estate. By the last decade of the century investment in elements of a 'new husbandry', with more livestock and manure, led to an improvement in yields per slave.[7]

Towards the end of the eighteenth century Jamaica had only a few of those poor whites who could be found in larger numbers on some of the smaller islands. The white population of nearly 30,000 at the end of the century included 3,000 troops and 1,000 shopkeepers, merchants or urban craftsmen. There were some 4,000 farmers and small planters, many of whom lived by supplying the large plantations. The great majority of the whites were directly dependent upon the plantation system, whether as professionals (doctors, attorneys, bookkeepers) or overseers, craftsmen and technical specialists, or as owners of cattle pens supplying the big estates. The generality of whites enjoyed some political influence, chiefly because the large planters relied on their loyalty and expertise. Most adult white males had the vote, but were not eligible as office-holders, since the income qualification was too high.

In the 1780s their numbers were swelled by refugees from the Northern colonies; numbers of free coloured also arrived from this quarter. The whites sought to insulate themselves from competition from slaves and freedmen by calling for legislation to reserve responsible posts for them-selves, and generally foster racial caste privileges. Planters or overseers who had children by slaves sometimes sought to free them and endow them with property. If a white employee formed a lasting liaison with one of their master's slaves, as the overseer Thomas Thistlewood did with Phibbah, this increased the planter's leverage over them. Phibbah's owner was able to retain Thistlewood's services for longer than he wished by refusing to hire her out; subsequently he refused to manumit her, and instead charged Thistlewood heavily for her rent and for the manumission of their child. Phibbah's owner did not consent to her manumission until after Thistlewood's death.[8]

After establishing in 1762 that mulattoes owned four sugar estates, seven cattle pens, thirteen houses and other property, the Jamaican Assembly enacted a law limiting the amount that could be bequeathed to a free person of colour to £2,000. Attempts were also made to make manumission more difficult and to enforce more strictly the 'deficiency' laws which stipulated the minimum numbers of white staff to be present on the plantations.[9] Despite the presence of the garrison the security of Jamaica, as of all the other British colonies, also depended on the militia, which was simply the male white population in arms; a variety of black auxiliaries, such as the maroons and the 'Black Shot'; and – last but not least – the internal reserves of the plantation regimes themselves.

In order to underline this latter point, it is worth considering a first-hand account of the unrest connected to 'Tacky's Rebellion' in 1760 in the diary of Thomas Thistlewood, at that time overseer of the Egypt plantation, some three or four miles from Savannah la Mar in Jamaica's Westmoreland parish. At the time Thistlewood was living with one other white man on an estate with a complement of about a hundred slaves. When the alarm was given he could, in theory, rely on support from the militia – indeed, he was expected to rally to it himself. However, whites were far from punctilious in performing their militia duties, and when the estates they were responsible for were in danger, they had good reason to remain on them. Thistlewood was grateful for the occasional patrols of colonial troops, and reported that in the first clashes 'Col Cudgoe's Negroes behaved with great bravery'.[10] But as the revolts spread, he became greatly alarmed:

> When the report was of the Old Hope Negroes being rose, perceived a strange alteration in ours. They are certainly very ready if they durst, and am pretty certain they were in the plot, by what John told me on Sunday evening, that they had said in the field on Saturday in the Pawpaw tree piece, that he, what signified him, he would dead in a Egypt &c.&c., and from many other circumstances, Lewie being over at Forest's that night, &c. Coffee and Job also very outrageous.

A white man had been killed at Forest's 'that night', and the phrase 'dead in a Egypt' is evidently a directly reported patois phrase, *dead eenna Egypt*. While he was suspicious of certain named individuals – with good reason – Thistlewood's response to another reported rising was perhaps surprising: 'Immediately armed our negroes and kept a strict guard and look out'. He quickly adds: 'our Negroes have good intelligence, being greatly elevated and ready to rise, now we are in the most imminent danger'. The slaves feared by Thistlewood and those armed by him appear to have been an overlapping category. While those he armed were the slave elite and their immediate retinue rather than known troublemakers, matters got serious in such a situation, when the slave elite itself defected. The loyalty of Cudgoe's men might be appreciated, but they were believed to be an inspiration to some rebels who intended to 'kill all the negroes they can, and as soon as dry weather comes fire all the plantations they can, till they force the white men to give them free like Cudgoe's Negroes'.[11]

Two of the slaves of Thistlewood's estate left, supposedly to join the rebels, but the slave elite remained loyal and helped to guard the estate. They may well have doubted both the aims of the rebellion and its chances of success. The rebellion in Westmoreland was led by Apongo, a prince of a Guinea people tributary to the King of Dahomey, and the insignia of the rebellion was a wooden sword adorned with parrot feathers. Creole slaves and those who were not from Guinea might not have been much attracted to a rebellion whose aim was sometimes said to be that of constructing an African kingdom which would take over and run the plantations. Even more tangible than such speculations would be Egypt's proximity to a town, with patrols calling quite frequently, and the sight of captured rebels being burnt over a slow fire – eventually four hundred died in this way, or with some other type of exemplary violence. Finally Thistlewood himself, though he had vicious qualities – he punctiliously records merciless floggings and relentless fornication – and was a prey to some fanciful ideas – he was on the lookout for Jesuits, white or black, whom he believed to be behind the rebellion – was neither a coward nor lacking in self-composure. In normal times, confident that the force of colonial society was within him, he would tackle runaways even if they were armed with a bill; his slave 'wife', the housekeeper Phibbah, later told him that his name among the slaves was 'No Play With'. During and after this crisis, as his editor writes, he became more attentive than usual in the discharge of his duties:

> He kept the Egypt slaves as busy as he could; he tended them when sick; he flogged them when he thought they erred; he regularly gave them their allowances of food and clothing and liquor, and sometimes extras for unusual labour or good performance; he allowed them, even in the midst of rebellion, their Sunday tickets to move about: but he held them in strict control: 'Wednesday December 24th: Driver Johnnie drumming at the Negro House last night. Flogged him for it.'[12]

The productive regime of the plantation itself, as we will see, incorporated disciplines and privileges which constituted a rampart of defence against slave insurgency. And its evident value and scale must have made it clear that the whites would not abandon their plantations without calling on all the considerable resources at their disposal.

A 'medium-sized' Jamaican sugar estate in 1774 was almost twice the size of the average large estate on Barbados a century before. One such was inventoried as in Table X.4:

Table X.4   Inventory of a Medium-Sized Jamaica Estate 1774

	Number	Average Value	Total
Value			
Total acres	600	£10 0s	6,001
Acres in cane	266	£16 1s	4,273
Sugar Works			3,962
Realty Total			9,963
Negroes	200	£35 14s	7,140
Livestock	95	£15 9s	1,495
Utensils			429
Personality Total			9,064
Grand Total			19,027

Source: Sheridan, *Sugar and Slaves*, p. 231.

Among the characteristic features of this inventory would be (a) the itemizing of slaves together with livestock; (b) slaves comprising about a third of the value of the estate; (c) the significantly higher value attributed to land planted with cane, reflecting an investment of slave labour; (d) the utensils and sugar works, the latter constructed by the slave crew, comprising between a fifth and a third of the total value. Livestock – tended, of course, by the slaves – played an important part in the plantation economy, furnishing animal power for the cane carts and mill, manure for the fields and a source of fresh meat for the white employees.

This sort of valuation would approximate to what an estate would fetch if it were sold. But most of the capital represented by the buildings and improved acreage would represent the value added by slave labour, with only modest outlays on tools and materials. Jamaican eighteenth-century accounts, despite being more detailed and abundant than those available for the seventeenth-century Brazilian plantations, shared with them the failure (noted in Chapter VIII) to distinguish between capital and current expenditures. In both cases slave labour could be applied to capital items such as building and opening up new land without visible extra expenditure. On the other hand, the purchase of slaves, though clearly an investment, was also often seen as an urgent item of current expenditure, required to bring in the harvest.

The overall expansion of Jamaica's sugar output was accompanied by an increase in both the scale and intensity of plantation labour. Between 1741 and 1775 the median size of slave crews on inventoried estates rose from 99 to 204; most slaves, therefore, were on estates with more than 204 others.[13] The largest estates had a slave crew of over five hundred. An attorney who managed five or six estates would gross the princely salary of between £2,000 and £4,000 a year. The salaries of the other white employees ranged between £50 and £200 a year, so – as noted in Chapter VIII – planters had a great incentive to encourage slaves to carry out skilled work. On a plantation with a slave crew of 256 there was a slave elite comprising four drivers, for goading the slave gangs; six carpenters; four coopers; three distillers; two masons; two wheelwrights; one boiler; one ropemaker; three mulemen; three cartmen; and so forth.

On Worthy Park, a large estate, there were 577 slaves in 1793 and only 10 white employees who included an overseer, a head bookkeeper, three under-bookkeepers, a head boiler, a head distiller and a doctor. Under-bookkeepers were often required to supervise work in the field as well as to keep records. At Worthy Park there was a slave elite of twenty-one, many of whom directed a team of craftworkers and apprentices: they included seven slave-drivers and driveresses, two head housekeepers, a head cooper, head potter, head boiler, head mason, head sawyer, head carpenter, head blacksmith, head cattleman, head muleman, and two head wainsmen. Slaves with special skills – carpenters, masons, boilers, and so forth – comprised a secondary elite of 95 workers.[14] Thus specially skilled or responsible workers comprised a fifth of all slaves and over a quarter of the active labour force. The training and skill embodied in these slaves were reflected in the premium prices they could command – though few would ever be sold.

The procedures for organizing the slave crew, while they echoed prin-ciples of 'gang labour' noted for the seventeenth century, became far more elaborate and intense in the course of the eighteenth-century boom. According to Samuel Martin's handbook of plantation management – first published in 1754 and much reprinted thereafter – the plantation should be a 'well constructed machine, compounded of various wheels, turning different ways, and yet all contributing to the great end proposed; but if any one part turns too fast or too slow in proportion to the rest, the main purpose is defeated'.[15]

Apportioning slaves between the cane fields, the mill, the boiling house, the distillery, the provision grounds, the cattle pen, and so on, required good judgement and timing, especially during the hectic harvest season. Worthy Park's 365 field workers in 1793 were divided into five gangs, not including those tending cattle. Slaves aged between sixteen and forty made up the 'Great Gang'; on Worthy Park at this time 60 per cent of the Great Gang were women. While slave men rose to the ranks of craftsmen, the women were left to predominate in field labour. The Second Gang comprised 67 slaves aged sixteen to twenty-five, the Third Gang 68 slaves between twelve and fifteen. Slaves aged between five and eleven made up the Grass or Weeding Gang, while a residual 13 slaves of various ages were assigned to the Vagabond Gang, since they were persistent runaways or miscreants.[16]

The overseers had to work closely with the slave-drivers to ensure precise co-ordination and good order; likewise, the drivers needed to command the obedience or respect of their gang. Slave-drivers would be armed with a whip as standard issue, but this was far from being their only instrument for eliciting obedience. The overseer kept a close watch on the stores, making sure that supplies of foodstuffs, clothing and rum were distributed to slaves in accordance with their position in the plantation hierarchy, with a discretionary bonus often channelled via the slave elite or 'head people'. When he was choosing slaves to appoint as drivers, the overseer would not have a completely free hand; while he would certainly want a tough taskmaster, it could be counterproductive to appoint a driver whom the slaves hated and despised.[17]

The records for the Jamaican plantation Mesopotamia give an interesting picture of the internal stratification of the slave crew by gender, origin, age and colour (i.e. shade). This stratification distributed crucial privileges, helping to secure the compliance – if not loyalty – of the slave elite, their immediate dependants (members of the slave elite were likely to have one or more wives and several children) and, through them, the slave community. The plantation was fashioned as an elaborate hierarchy in which each would know their place. The 'outsider's' view of the plantation sees a mass of black slaves juxtaposed against a few white managers, technicians and owners. From the 'insider's' point of view the difference between one type of slave and another must often have appeared more immediately significant. Thus on Mesopotamia over the period 1762–1831 there were 16 mulatto craftworkers, another 16 mulatto domestics, 18 mulatto 'non-workers' (children, old people) and only two mulatto field workers. This contrasted with 403 African slaves and 329 black creole slaves of whom, in each case, 66 per cent worked in the field gangs.[18] It was common for about a tenth of the children born on Jamaican plantations to be mulattoes. These descendants of 'free born Englishmen' (or Scotsmen or Irishmen) had been cheated of their fathers' birthright but, in recompense, were destined for a privileged niche in the plantation hierarchy. They were also more likely eventually to obtain manumission, though this would require both their fathers' willingness to come up with the price and the planter's willingness to manumit.

On many plantations Africans might have predominated over creoles in the field gangs, but the owner of Mesopotamia deliberately bought many creole women in the hope of raising reproduction rates. If we turn to the slaves' primary occupations, it is notable that all craftworkers were male, while 61 per cent of domestics were women; of the slave-drivers, 71 per cent were male, while 29 per cent were female. No less than 55 per cent of the prime field hands were women. Planters generally favoured placing men in the field gangs but, as on Mesopotamia, often found that they ended up with a high proportion of women. This was partly because mortality, especially in the first year or so, was higher for men, and partly because men were promoted out of the field gangs to craft occupations while women were not.

Table X.5 gives the mean age at death for various categories of slave:

Table X.5   Age at Death of Mesopotamia Slaves

Males		Females	
Drivers	58.2	Drivers	59.3
Craftworkers	48.6	Domestics	59.0
Field Workers	43.4	Field Workers	47.0
All men	45.3	All women	47.7

Source: Richard Dunn, '"Dreadful Idlers" in the Cane Fields: The Slave Labor Pattern on a Jamaican Sugar Estate, 1762–1831', in Solow and Engerman, eds, *British Capitalism and Caribbean Slavery*.

The slave-drivers had usually been promoted from the cruel labour of the field gangs after a less than average stint, though no doubt the small privileges they enjoyed also contributed to their greater longevity. Since there were no female craftworkers, all those women slaves who were not domestics toiled in the field gangs. Neither male nor female slaves worked in the main field gang for much more than fifteen years; this spell would have such a negative effect on their health that they would then have to be moved to somewhat lighter work. But women worked longer in the field, being relegated to the second gang when the state of their health required it. The only women slave-drivers were those placed in charge of the children's gang. The high proportion of women in the field gangs, and the fact that they spent longer there than the men, contributed to problems of low fertility (which will be explored below). The absentee owner of Mesopotamia did urge that women slaves should not be worked too hard, in the interests of raising the birth rate, but evidently the overseers believed that female labour could not be stinted without damaging output. Maintaining the requisite numbers for the main gangs was always difficult because of the high incidence of sickness: the 333 female field slaves at Mesopotamia were categorized as 'able' only 54 per cent of the time compared with 57 per cent of the time for the 257 male field gang slaves. The higher proportion of 'sickly' or 'invalid' female field slaves seems in part to have reflected the fact that fewer other employments were deemed suitable for them: male slaves who were often sick were more likely to be assigned to specialist or miscellaneous work.

Male prominence in the slave elite and the male monopoly over craftwork reflected gender stereotypes held by both Europeans and Africans. The sexual division of labour on the plantations was also functional for the plantation's security and production regime. Slave-drivers had to be physically imposing. African women worked in the field, traded, and had children – but with rare exceptions they did not command groups of men.

So far as craftwork was concerned, men also probably had a small edge of physical advantage, because they were stronger and did not get pregnant. Craftworkers embodied years of training, and needed to be kept continuously employed and always available at critical phases of the production process. Their quite low mean age at death shows that the sugar works took its toll – it required effort of such intensity and in such conditions that it would have been no better, and probably worse, than work in the field so far as pregnant women were concerned. While craftworkers commanded a mean price of £125 each, the price of slave-drivers was £115, the price of prime field hands £102, of secondary field hands £58 and of domestics £74. Female slaves who were thought to be fertile attracted a slightly higher price for this reason – so long as they were also fit for work in the field. But slave women's capacity to bear children did not by itself rank high in the plantation manager's scale of values, for reasons which will be explored below.[19]

While the slaves' differential life expectations reveal a pattern of privilege, the ages at which they died were, in all circumstances, rather advanced. Life expectancy in Europe was generally under forty years in the eighteenth century. Of course the slave figures given above do not reflect mortality in infancy or childhood, or during the Atlantic crossings, but they still gave slaveowners the prospect of twenty-five or thirty-five years of exploitation across the lives of their slaves – a fact which also helps to explain slave prices.

Stratification was scarcely a novel means of labour control. One of the most 'modern' features of the plantation and mill was the variety of devices for regulating and monitoring overall performance. The ringing of a bell or blowing of a horn would signal the transition from one phase of the working day to another. In the sugar factory itself there would often be, as there was at Worthy Park, a raised dais from which all parts of the works were visible. The proprietor of Worthy Park left instructions which point to the integration of labour allocation and financial control at which planters aimed, and also explain the presence of all those 'under-bookkeepers' noted above: 'There are always five separate books to be kept on Worthy Park, viz: a great Plantation Book, a store book, a Boiling House Book, a Still House Book, and a Daily Labour Book.'[20] These books gave the planter or his attorney an exact picture of the operation of the estate on a day-by-day basis; Henry Drax, over a century before, had been content with one plantation book and fortnightly reports on the deployment of labour.

In principle, the planter or overseer was the master of the process of production; in this respect the slave plantation shared, or anticipated, a novel feature of the capitalist factory as compared with peasant agriculture or craft manufacture. Few other productive enterprises of this epoch would aim at such detailed financial regulation; the owner of a large estate, especially if he owned several or was an absentee, had an exceptional need for financial control. Towards the end of the eighteenth century a sugar plantation could be worth well over £30,000, and some were worth as much as £70,000. This compares with the value of an Arkwright water-powered cotton mill: between £3,000 and £5,000; or a steam-driven multistoreyed cotton mill: £10,000–£20,000.[21] While a sugar estate counted on the coerced and co-ordinated labour of 200 or more labourers, a large farm in England would engage between 15 and 21 full-time labourers and an extra 30 or 40 part-time workers at the peaks of the planting and harvesting seasons.[22]

The planters' concern for productivity was still highly uneven and selective, reminding us of the hybrid social character of the slave plantation. In the processing phase planters were prepared to experiment with, and adopt, machines that raised cane yields and labour productivity. In 1754 a new horizontal arrangement of the mill rollers, permitting increased scale, was adopted by some planters in the Leeward Islands, though it was to take several decades to perfect. In 1768 a Jamaican planter patented an application of the steam engine to the sugar mill, but the project failed.[23] The interior of the eighteenth-century sugar works remained closer to large-scale, integrated manufacture, with its teams of craftsmen, than to a fully industrialized process.

Two circumstances inhibited industrial advance within the sugar works. First, the established planter possessed skilled teams of workers, over whom direct control was exercised; he therefore had no urgent need to mechanize; moreover, the planter's skilled labour force, unlike that of the cotton master, could not unionize or threaten to withdraw labour. The early cotton master's incentive to mechanization was thus stronger than that of the planter. The second consideration which favoured the cotton masters as industrial pioneers is that there was no yawning social gulf between them and the specialist workers. The small cotton master was far more likely to have a rapport with his skilled workforce than the planter, attorney or overseer with the skilled slaves. The planters' mechanical experiments were usually dilettantistic and their innovations impractical, even when they were informed by a promising intuition.

If the planters were not good at developing productive innovations, they were willing to adopt them quite speedily if yields were improved or bottlenecks reduced. Plantation handbooks invariably stressed the import-ance of conserving the fertility of the soil. In the later decades of the eighteenth century a new plant variety, the Bourbon cane, was generally adopted by Caribbean planters; Admiral Bougainville had encountered this higher-yielding variety in the Orient, and it was taken over by the English from the French sugar planters. But while a new cane variety was welcomed, the cane fields were still laboriously prepared by use of the hoe; Edward Long pointed out that ploughs would lighten this labour, but most planters still saw no need to economize on slave labour outside the harvest period.[24]

The slave plantation was multilayered: sophisticated methods of financial control; elaborate manufacturing techniques; close invigilation of labour on the cash crop. But underpinning the whole was a process of daily reproduction which depended heavily on slave initiative. The slaves grew much of their own food, made garments out of the cloth they were given, manufactured household utensils and built their own dwelling-places as well as the stone houses of their masters. Their quarters often resembled an African village with a circular or semicircular arrangement of thatched, earth-floor huts. They had small gardens close by, and might keep a few chickens and pigs. They were also allotted provision grounds, but usually some distance away, since cane had priority in the land adjoining the mill; the distance to be travelled and the difficulty of protecting crops from theft or damage could greatly reduce the value of this concession. The slaves were allowed to cultivate their provision grounds, out of crop time, on Saturdays: either for a half-day every Saturday or for a full day every fortnight. Depending on the location of the grounds, they also stole away in the evenings and on Sundays to tend such crops as yams, plantains, cassava and beans.

If they were lucky a slave would receive half an acre, or find a fertile gully in a neighbouring mountain, but where land was scarce – on Barbados, for example, slaves would be allotted no land at all – the planter was responsible for supplying more food. The planters also set aside grounds for slave burials; as a plantation got older this could become a source of tension, as the burial ground expanded and overseers wished to maximize the land available for cultivation. The provision grounds and burial grounds were looked on by the slaves as their land; they were handed on from one generation to the next according to rules devised by the slave community itself. Most planters and overseers accepted this state of affairs, recognizing that it would be counterproductive not to. The growing proportion of internal commerce and currency in the slaves' hands was another development encouraged by the provision-ground system which neither planters nor officials could halt. Long estimated that a third of Jamaica's currency was in slave hands by the 1770s.[25]

To the extent that children were born and raised on the plantation, it came to encompass a sphere of reproduction partly under slave control, albeit also semi-collectivized, with communal nurseries, medical attention, and the like. It was rare for plantation slaves to receive any formal instruction, whether secular or religious. Slaves elaborated a syncretistic culture, blending several African themes with European elements and American innovations. The patois spoken by the majority of the slaves in Jamaica and the older British islands was based on an English lexicon, with additional words from Spanish, Portuguese, Celtic, Dutch and several African tongues. While many overseers and slaves could communicate perfectly well in a pidgin based on patois, the slaves could often speak to one another in ways that most whites could not understand. The slave religious practice of obeah – the raising of spirits and casting of spells – was also not infrequently resorted to by poor whites. Christianity did not make much headway among the slave populations until the end of the eighteenth century, with the arrival of missionaries and 'African Methodists' or Baptists from North America. From the 1760s, however, a new African-based religious movement, Myalism, appeared in Jamaica and claimed to be able to counter the sorcery of both obeah-men and Europeans. It seems possible that the eclipse of the Akan-led revolts laid the way for a more pan-African sensibility, preoccupied with neutralizing European sorcery and preferring – at least for the time being – nocturnal dances to open rebellion.[26]

Death also furnished a rallying point, enabling the nascent slave community to assert new as well as old ties. The funerals of slaves who had established themselves would be marked by a numerous gathering of friends and relatives, the former including 'shipmates'. In Antigua these events were perceived as a threat to the social order, and an Act attempted to ban ceremonies which were 'pompous and expensive': 'No Slave or Slaves in any of the Towns shall be buried after Sun-set . . . or in any other than plain Deal-board Coffin, without any Covering or Ornament, neither shall there be worn any Scarfs or Favours at any of their Funerals.'[27] It is probably no coincidence that the colony which enacted this legislation had been profoundly shaken a few years earlier, in 1736–37, by the discovery of a widespread slave conspiracy aimed at seizing the island. This conspiracy had been preceded and prepared by a series of nocturnal feasts and public parades in which prominent slaves had assumed the style of Akan kings and generals, or even of planters and colonial officials. At the trial of the conspirators it had been reported that the slaves Court and Tomby (Thomas Boyd) had used grave-site oaths to bind their followers to them. Alternately they added grave dirt and other 'Oaths Ingredients' to rum before drinking a toast to the overthrow of the whites at a feast:

> Tomby then took up a bottle and fill'd into a glass and Said Gentlemen, I am going to Toast a Health, & Damnation to them that wont pledge it or wont give their Assistance. . . . Said he we are going to Attack the Town and Kill the Baccarraras and Everybody must join Court and me to do it. . . .[28]

The rebels planned to blow up the Governor and the chief planters at a ceremony to be held on 11 October 1736, to commemorate the coronation of George II. To impress potential supporters they staged their own war-dance on 3 October. The changed demeanour of slaves alarmed the authorities, and the plot was discovered when the Governor's ceremony was postponed. This precipitated panic among the planters, and vicious reprisals followed against all real or supposed accomplices; by the end of December there had been executions and forty-eight deportations. Torture was used to extract incriminating information; by May 1737 the total of executions had risen to eighty-six, of which seventy-seven victims had been publicly burnt.[29]

In his report on the affair, the Governor wrote:

> As this horrid conspiracy cannot but be heard of wherever people hold correspondence with Antigua, it will no doubt be variously animadverted upon; and as slavery is the very odium of the Englishmen some of our countrymen may do it to our disadvantage. Yet slavery is among us not of choice but of necessity, and unless (as it is not to be imagined) our mother country should quit the trade of the sugar-colonies Englishmen must continue to be masters of their slaves.

He sought to minimize the use that had been made of torture to extract information: 'we three times made fruitless experiment thereof and then declined further use'.[30] The investigating magistrates had no doubt that in the view of the ringleaders: 'Freedom and the Possession of their Masters' Estates were to be the Rewards of their [the slaves'] perfidy and treachery.' Since so many of the instigators were skilled slaves, it was recommended that henceforth slaves should be barred from becoming distillers or tradesmen. The magistrates also explained the legal condition of the slave, no doubt with the aim of excusing the ferocity with which an unsuccessful conspiracy had been suppressed:

> a slave is not a Person known by the Law of England, and in the Eye of the Law is the same Person after conviction as before; Slaves being incapable of giving Evidence, except against each other, (which is always done without Oath), or being sued, having no inheritable blood, Masters of no considerable Property, and being the Estate and Property of others; so that they can lose no Credit, nor have their blood tainted, nor forfeit any Property, nor suffer any disability by any attainder.[31]

It was, of course, true that the slave was already legally a prisoner and forced labourer, so these were not sanctions that could be applied to malefactors. To the extent that slaves exercised petty rights or privileges, they did so because planters or overseers found it convenient or prudent to let this happen. Despite being warned that this 'corrupted' their slaves, they continued to do so whatever the advice of Governor Matthew and his magistrates.

The bloody panic which had gripped Antigua revealed the vice of fear in which both whites and blacks were caught. Any personal autonomy allowed to – or won by – the slaves was restricted by the ferocious labour demands of the plantation, by detailed rules of conduct and by the ever-present fear of savage sanctions in the case of any real or imagined transgression. Offenders would be mercilessly flogged and deprived of all petty privileges or extra rations. Slaves could not set foot outside the plantation without express permission; however, some of the slave 'elite' might regularly be able to obtain chits permitting them to go to neighbouring plantations or the local township, either to visit relatives or to buy or sell provisions. On most of the islands the slave produce markets, usually held on a Sunday morning, became a crucial part of the local economy, enabling slaves to earn a little money and furnishing the main source of fresh produce for most of the free population. At the larger of these markets a profusion of vegetables and fruits was available, as well as fish and fowl. However, slaves were strictly prohibited from cultivating or selling sugar cane or any of the other export crops – this discouraged theft and asserted planter control of the colonial staples. Slaves would also occasionally be paid small sums for working on holidays or for running special errands. Thistlewood's slave 'wife' Phibbah was able to lend him over £66 when he set up a pen of his own (nearly £5,000 in 1994 values).[32] In Jamaica the small population of free coloured people were often petty traders or pedlars; they were sometimes allowed to visit the plantations and trade with the slaves.

The comparative 'modernity' of the plantation was bought at a high price by the planter. The plantation was always at risk of becoming hypercapitalized with respect to the flow of sales and profits. Thus a sugar estate on Antigua worth £20,000 at mid century had a revenue of £3,600 and operating expenses which came to the quite manageable total of £1,272, including £300 for extra provisions, £290 for other supplies, £320 for salaries, £254 for colonial and parish taxes, and £110 for Crown fees and duties. While the surplus of revenue over expenditure was large, the planter had to discount this against the high capital value of the plantation and heavy depreciation charges; the manufacturer or improving landlord of the time would not have to contend with such considerable deductions. The cost of maintaining slave numbers, in the case cited, might well have added a further £400 annually. Together with duties payable in England, the various charges on this plantation eventually produced a rate of return on capital of about 8.5 per cent per year.[33] The value of a plantation would often be hard to maintain after its first decade or two, as yields of old cane declined and the soil became exhausted.

In their eagerness to deflect taxation, West Indian planters went out of their way to emphasize the hazards they faced. Thus Edward Long pointed to the many risks which threatened high short-run profits. He calculated that a large plantation worth some £30,000 in 1770, and with 300 slaves, might make its owner 10 per cent a year. He adds:

> This although a large interest, yet will not be thought too exorbitant by those who candidly consider, that the proprietor is subject to a great variety of risks, and accidental losses, by dry years, hurricanes, fire, mortality of Negroes and cattle, the sudden rise of those necessary articles which he is obliged to buy every year, or the sudden fall at market in the price of sugar and rum: for all these casualties and vicissitudes he stands his own insurer.[34]

Planters' profits undoubtedly dropped below 10 per cent in bad years; but then (as evidence to be cited below will show) they exceeded this level in good years. The element of incalculability in plantation prospects set limits to the economic rationality they could achieve. Provision made for depreciation might be inadequate. Slave prices were difficult to anticipate; rises increased the book value of a plantation, but also boosted replacement charges. Planters had little difficulty keeping track of their income, since this came largely from sales of sugar, rum and molasses, supplemented by occasional sales of livestock, or income from hiring out slaves for work on minor products or public works. Outgoings were subdivided between 'Island Expenses', payable locally; the 'Invoice', submitted by the metropolitan merchant or factor; and the costs of freight, since many British planters shipped their own produce for sale in England. Planters usually hoped to cover all 'island expenses' through sales of rum and molasses to North American merchants; they would cover freight and the 'Invoice' out of the proceeds from the sale of the main crop in England, retaining the considerable balance themselves. In this way the cash earned by the absentee never left the metropolis, and there was usually a shortage of currency in the colonies.

The themes of Edward Littleton's *The Groans of the Plantations* (1689) was often to be echoed – the groans were not those of the slaves but those of planters crying out against the difficulty of making a profit. But modern research has shown that these self-interested lamentations were misleading. Working from plantation accounts, J.R. Ward has calculated the series for British West Indian planting profits in Table X.6:

Table X.6   British West Indian Planting Profits

		Average Annual Profits %	No. of Sample
1689–97	War	6.2	2
1698–1702	Peace	9.4	3
1703–13	War	5.2	4
1714–38	Peace	11.9	4
1739–48	War	14.9	2
1749–55	Peace	10.1	4
1756–62	War	13.5	7
1763–75	Peace	9.3	9
1776–82	War	3.4	11
1783–91	Peace	8.5	10
1792–98	War	12.6	10

Source: J.R. Ward, 'The Profitability of Sugar Planting in the British West Indies', *Economic History Review*, 1978, pp. 197–213 (pp. 204, 207).

Wars put up sugar prices but also raised the cost of provisions, supplies, insurance and freight. If war went well for the British Navy, then the British planters' gains outweighed their losses; the British market by itself was large and buoyant enough to sustain demand. Peacetime brought stronger competition, especially outside the home market. The revolt of the Northern colonies in 1776 and the reverses suffered by the British Navy in the following period led to a drastic contraction of plantation profits, not fully registered in the averages in Table X.6, since there were certainly many bankruptcies at this time. Every year several hundred 'execution orders' were made out against people unable to pay their debts, which often reached hundreds of thousands of pounds a year.[35]

The high cost of acquiring and maintaining a slave crew made it necessary for the planter to have more or less constant access to risk capital. The latter was supplied at annual interest rates of around 18 per cent by larger planters, factors or merchants. While it was standard practice to insure the cargo of a slave trading vessel, the planter did not have access to insurance for his crew; those with larger and more diversified slaveholdings were best placed to withstand disaster. The leading families of the British West Indies – the Beckfords, Lascelles and Pinneys – combined banking and mercantile functions with the ownership of plantations, some acquired through foreclosure. One of the most striking features of the British eighteenth-century Caribbean, as we have noted, was the success of the practice of absentee proprietorship. In the seventeenth century the planter who became an absentee invited disaster – a fact Dunn vividly illustrates in *Sugar and Slaves*. No doubt some British absentees in the late eighteenth century led a dissipated and feckless existence, but probably not the most successful. West Indian proprietors found that residence in the United Kingdom made sense because it gave them cheaper access to capital and commercial resources than could be found in the Caribbean – this consideration was especially relevant for proprietors who owned several estates and for those who also had important investments at home. Highly paid attorneys and the Accounts Produce Department afforded reasonably effective estate management. But while such arrangements gave the owner overall financial control, they were not calculated to achieve sustained agro-industrial advance, in the absence of better-motivated and free craftworkers.

David Hancock's study of twenty-three merchant associates centred on London gives a vivid idea of the strategic role played in their activities by plantations and colonial trade. In 1750 the associates severally owned 9,000 acres in the plantation colonies, rising to 21,000 in 1763 and reaching 130,000 at the end of 1775, with estates in Jamaica, the Leeward Islands, South Carolina, Georgia and Florida. The Caribbean sugar plantations were their most profitable possessions. While a few of these estates were acquired by inheritance or at auction, many came into their hands through foreclosure on debts. Six of the associates had a slave trading factory on Bance Island in Sierra Leone, and were able to restock their estates from this source.

One of them, Sir Alexander Grant, had seven Jamaican plantations in the years 1766–71 which dispatched sugar worth £152,828 on which, according to Hancock's calculations, he earned a profit of £20,000, or £3,450 per year, representing a return on capital outlay of no less than 29 per cent. Grant's mercantile profits on the West India trade excluding slaves, however, were even better: £6,118 per year over a twelve-year period in which thirty voyages were undertaken, representing a rate of return of 44 per cent on capital employed. (Hancock points out that Grant's profit of £20,000 in 1766–71 would represent about £1,326,094, or $1,972,405, in 1994 values, and that the £6,118 annual mercantile profit would represent £467,314, or $695,074, in 1994 values.) Grant was a keen 'improver'; he sent two steam engines to his West Indian estates in 1767, together with a host of other ideas and gadgets, both good and bad. However, inattentiveness to local conditions, unsuitable subordinates and lack of consistency led him to lose large sums on planting experiments in Florida. Like most of the associates, he made a more modest profit on the slave trade, averaging about 6 per cent, than on either West Indian planting or colonial trading.[36]

Hancock's associates rose to considerable social eminence but came from middling Protestant families, with a Scottish, provincial English or colonial background. They generally lacked inherited wealth and started out as small tenant planters, plantation doctors (Alexander Grant) or commercial clerks. They owed their eventual success to careful commercial planning and integration, advantageous acquisitions from planters in difficulty, and lucky timing. When Sir Alexander Grant died in 1772 his estate was valued at £95,000 – an impressive sum, but overshadowed by the estate of £500,000 left by his erstwhile associate Richard Oswald in the subsequent decade.[37]

If Richard Pares's classic study *A West India Fortune* is representative, this pattern was repeated in the subsequent generation. John Pinney inherited a sugar estate in Nevis in the 1760s. In 1783, having built up experience and connections in the Lesser Antilles, he left to set himself up in business as a merchant in Bristol. Although he was not anxious to own plantations himself, he did lend money to planters as well as buying their sugar and selling them supplies. In 1782 his fortune was worth £70,000, with £60,000 represented by his West Indian estates. By his death in 1818 the overall value of his estate had grown to £340,000, with £146,000 in West Indian properties and more in floating mortgages. If inflation is taken into account, he had still more than tripled the value of his estates, with the interest and profits on his West Indian business furnishing the main source of his success.[38]

The economic, demographic and technical information relating to the performance of British West Indian plantations is more abundant and

detailed than that available for the slave colonies of other European powers
in the eighteenth century. One salient quality they displayed may be taken
as typical: a seemingly limitless capacity for quantitative expansion. The
improvements in cane yields due to improved varieties, the modifications
made to the mills and the generally enlarged size of the plantation led to
greater output, but output per slave or per acre remained static until 1800.
Throughout the century planters obtained somewhere between 7 and 11
cwt, or a little under half a ton, of sugar per slave, and about one ton per
acre of cane land.[39] Variations usually reflected the fertility of the soil, the
age of the cane 'ratoons', and rainfall. As the plantation grew, the cane had
to be brought to the mill over longer distances, at greater cost and with a
loss in sucrose content. In the mill itself grinding was more effective, but
this enlarged the area of cane land it needed; thus expansion in output per
mill was likely to lower output per slave and per acre. The slave crew
would have to work harder to sustain this classic instance of extensive
development, hauling the cane further. Likewise, the boiling process,
employing up to seven separate copper vats, was cumbersome. Accidents
were not uncommon when desperately tired slaves fed cane to the mill or
poured the boiling cane juice from larger to smaller vats until sugar could
be 'struck' from the syrup. Cane feeders could lose an arm, or worse, while
a splash of boiling syrup could maim or kill.

The cost of making regular slave purchases simply to maintain, let alone
expand, output refers us to what was perhaps, after plantation security, the
most important, and often the most intractable, problem besetting the
Caribbean planters. The growth of Caribbean slave populations was slow
and modest if it was measured against massive and rising imports. The
British Caribbean imported about 1.6 million slaves between 1700 and
1800, yet the slave population was under 600,000 around the end of the
century. Barbados, as the oldest plantation colony, had a growing population of American-born 'creole' slaves with greater immunity to local
diseases and a greater propensity to reproduce; even so, in the mid
eighteenth century it still required huge annual imports simply to replenish
the slave population each year. Thus between 1712 and 1734, 75,893
slaves were introduced to Barbados, yet the island's slave population rose
only from 41,970 to 46,373. Records of a Barbadian plantation during this
period show only one slave birth for every six slave deaths. Disease and
accident inflicted quite a high death rate, but population levels could have
been maintained if only there had been a reasonable birth rate. Males
outnumbered females by a ratio of about 65:35 in the Atlantic slave trade,
but the impact of this gender imbalance on the birth rate was not as
significant as the low fertility of slave women, practically none of whom
was past child-bearing age at the time of purchase. On the plantation
already cited there was only one birth each year for each hundred slaves. In
England at this time the birth rate was 33–38 per thousand. Birth rates of
10–15 per year per thousand slaves were to be quite common for first-

generation slave populations in the Caribbean, and rose only slowly thereafter.[40]

Jamaica repeated the characteristic pattern: the introduction of nearly half a million slaves between 1700 and 1774 raised the slave population by only a little over 150,000. The Jamaican planter Edward Long observed: 'those Negroes breed the best, whose labour is least, or easiest'.[41] Women slaves who worked in the household, in some skilled occupation or on cattle ranches tended to have more children; those condemned to the menial work of the cane fields and sugar mills had fewest. In the course of the eighteenth century there was a drop in the depletion, or 'negative reproduction', rate of the Jamaican slave population from −3.7 per cent a year around 1700 to −3.4 per cent a year around 1734, −2.5 per cent around 1750 and −2.0 per cent around 1774. This improvement in the reproduction rate, limited as it was, would reflect both the 'creolization' of the slave population and some reduction in the proportion on sugar estates. Once sugar mills were established, it made sense to engage more slaves on ranches to supply the sugar estates with food: livestock on Jamaica grew from 10,000 head in 1673 to 193,000 in 1774. With more plentiful land than the smaller islands, Jamaica also had room for a more diversified range of crops. In 1768 there were 166,000 slaves, of whom 99,000 worked on sugar estates, nearly 6,000 in Kingston, and 62,000 on ranches or estates devoted to secondary crops or foodstuffs. In the last decades of the century there was also some expansion of cultivation of secondary crops, notably coffee. While conditions for slave mothers were a little better outside the sugar sector, the large size of this sector, and the special demands it placed on women, set strict limits to improvements in slave reproduction rates.[42]

On the sugar estates young men and women in the main gang worked an average of seventy to eighty hours a week, often continuing at night in the mill after a gruelling day in the field. As we have seen, women often remained longer in the main gang, since they had much less chance of promotion than the men. Pregnant women worked in the fields until shortly before they gave birth, and returned to the gangs within a few weeks. Among the various factors which contributed to lower the Caribbean slave birth rate the rigours of women's existence, especially in the sugar plantations, were significant. The slaves were kept at work with the help of whips, and ferociously punished for misdemeanours small and large – women slaves, even if they were pregnant, could receive fifty lashes for such common crimes as absenting themselves or pilfering food. The field worker had to stoop to cut the cane; others had to carry and load it. This was heavy work.[43]

The owners of the sugar estates were drawn from a stratum of British society that was beginning to cultivate what it saw as a more refined sensibility. In the mid 1770s Janet Schaw, a 'Lady of Quality', composed an account of a visit to Antigua and St Christopher, where she was the guest or companion of such agreeable persons as Mr Halliday, with his five plantations, Lady Ogilvy, Mr Martin, Lady Payne, and other leading lights of planter society. Janet Schaw confesses herself gratified by the sight of Negroes attending a church service and entranced by the spectacle of a happy throng all clad in white muslin 'on their way to town with their Merchandize'. She explains that 'at this season the crack of the inhuman whip must not be heard'. A few pages later she describes slaves at work:

> The Negroes who are all in troops are sorted so as to match each other in size and strength. Every ten Negroes have a driver, who walks behind them, holding in his hand a short whip and a long one. You will easily guess the use of these weapons; a circumstance of all others the most horrid. They are naked, male and female, down to the girdle, and you constantly observe where application has been made. But however dreadful this must appear to a European, I will do the creoles the justice to say, they would be as averse to it as we are, could it be avoided, which has often been tried to no purpose. When one comes to be better acquainted with the Negroes, the horrour of it must wear off. It is the suffering of the human mind that constitutes the greatest misery of punishment, but with them it is merely corporeal. As to the brutes it inflicts no wound on their mind, whose Nature seems made to bear it, and whose sufferings are not attended with shame or pain beyond the present moment.

Since nobody is obliging the 'Lady of Quality' to be consistent, she does not have to explain why she is pleased to see brutish Negroes at a church service, or why, granted that they are mere animals, they nevertheless have to be flogged in ways that would be thought excessive for a dog or for cattle. Schaw did not attend a flogging, but she was present at a slave sale, prompting the following further reflection:

> Since I am on the chapter of Negroes feelings, I must tell you I was some days ago in town, when a number for market came from on board a ship. They stood up to be looked at with perfect unconcern. The husband was to be divided from the wife, the infant from the mother; but the most perfect indifference ran thro' the whole. They were laughing and jumping, making faces at each other and not caring a single farthing for their fate. This is not, however, without exception, and it behoves a planter to consider the country from whence he purchases his slaves; as those from one coast are mere brutes and fit only for the labour of the field, while those from another are bad field Negroes, but faithful handy house-servants.[44]

The planters and their overseers must, at some level, have been aware that their harsh regime was damaging the capacity of slave women to bear children and to nurse them properly in the first year or two. The customs of the planter could reflect some such crude, 'unthinking' calculation as the following. The annual cost of maintaining a slave averaged between £4 and £5, though infants and children would be much cheaper. Even if the direct cost to the planter of rearing a slave child to the age of ten was no more than, say, £10, he would also consider that the cost of lost output from the mother, assuming a loss equivalent to, say, one season's output, would be around £5, plus a contribution towards the cost of the mother's upkeep for one year (£4–£5), plus interest accruing on all these amounts until the child began to make a net contribution to the plantation budget. Altogether the expenses per child could easily total £40, including accrued interest, especially if the cost of infant mortality was factored in, as it would have to be. Throughout most of the eighteenth century the Caribbean planter, as noted above, could buy a young adult slave for between £15 and £40, with the range £28–£35 being common in the period 1763 to 1788. The slave trade was thus a cheaper source of slaves than natural reproduction.[45]

Some planters, however, were not happy about being so heavily reliant on the slave trade. Slaves born on the plantation would be more adapted to its regime and less prone to illness – or to the melancholy which seemed to kill quite a number of slaves newly arrived from Africa. Moreover, the incidence of war and the rising tendency of slave prices gave further inducement to planters to encourage their slaves to reproduce. Some bought more slave women and made greater provision for child-care, but improvements were slow. Evidently, the whole experience of enslavement and captivity had a deleterious impact on the women's desire or ability to have children. African women had lower fertility than did creole slave women; very rarely did they have any children at all during their first five years in the Americas. On the other hand, because African women survived in somewhat larger numbers than the men, planters were often left with a workforce about a half or more of which was female.

The African women had suffered the shock of capture and shipment. With no delay they were conscripted to the unremitting toil of the slave gangs. They probably still bore within them African notions of whom they should mate with, just as many carried tribal scars on their faces. Some will have left spouses in Africa, others must have been inclined to reject any partner not of their own nation. In most African cultures slavery did not consort with childbirth, except in the case of formal marriage and concubinage. A relatively high proportion of African women never had a child, while others eventually had children in their late twenties and thirties but ceased child-bearing earlier than creole women. On average Africans tended to be about two centimetres shorter than slaves born in the Americas, so it is possible that African women were sometimes physiologically less strong – though, of course, others did have many children and lived to their seventies or eighties.

A high rate of infant mortality and miscarriage depressed the recorded birth rate for all slave women; the problem was common to African and creole women, and generally more pronounced on sugar estates. Recorded infant death gives evidence of heavy losses due to tetanus (lockjaw), infant beriberi, diphtheria and protein deficiency.[46] Planters or overseers alleged that the scourge of such complaints was compounded by the ill or 'evil' disposition of the slave women. Barbara Bush is convinced that the low live birth rate on the Caribbean plantations reflected slave women's ability to regulate their own fertility. Certainly many contemporary European observers believed this. Bush argues that the low live birth rate could be the result of deliberate 'abortion, contraception and infanticide'.[47] While there is widespread evidence for practices of contraception and abortion, the allegation made by overseers and planters that their slave women practised infanticide could well have been designed to divert attention from their own treatment of slave mothers. Yet such was the slave condition that, in Barbara Bush's opinion, infanticide may quite often have been practised. Between a quarter and a half of the newly born died within ten days, very often of identifiable diseases such as infant tetanus. Until infants had survived this very early period they were not deemed to have arrived, either by overseers or, perhaps, by their mothers – in these early days the newborn infant was still a 'ghost' or angel, which for one reason or another could be left to die.

Planters also claimed that 'promiscuity' among the slaves was responsible for low rates of child-bearing. Barbara Bush is inclined to defend the women slaves from this charge, but she does not sufficiently consider one possible meaning of the planters' allegation. The authority structure of the Caribbean slave plantation offered little protection to female inmates. Thomas Thistlewood's account makes it very clear that women slaves in Jamaica, perhaps especially the younger ones, were sexually vulnerable to exploitation by whites and, to a lesser extent, by black men in positions of authority. He records warning his nephew not to molest Little Mimber, the wife of 'driver Johnnie'; but the nephew persisted and was drowned on a river expedition in an odd 'accident'. With no tangible evidence of foul play, the coroner declined an inquest. A few days later, Thistlewood adds: 'heard a shell blow on the River, and afterwards in the night, 2 guns fired with a loud Huzza after each, on the river against our Negro houses, for joy that my kinsman is dead, I imagine. Strange impudence.'[48]

This was an exceptional episode in which a junior white suborned the wife of a member of the slave elite, and his death may indeed have been accidental, though welcome to the slaves nevertheless. Thistlewood makes it clear that most slave women, especially the young ones, were deemed fair game, and itemizes his own extensive sexual depredations. Many women on the plantations lacked even that degree of patriarchal protection against sexual exploitation which would be implicit in a kinship system. These were not conditions likely to encourage childbirth. Slave women would have had good reason to wish to have an acknowledged partner before having children. The children born to younger slaves were often mulattoes; mulatto children comprised about a tenth of live births. While slave women sometimes secured advantages from liaisons with white overseers, book-keepers and drivers, this was far from always being the case – there was a high turnover among such personnel, so the slave mother would be left with the burden of child maintenance and, no doubt, a certain stigma in the eyes of fellow slaves. Edward Trelawny, a former governor of Jamaica, had his own backhanded way of acknowledging this situation: 'what chiefly contributes to their being so few children among the English Negroes is the Practice of the Wenches in procuring Abortions. As they lie with both Colours, and do not know which the child may prove of, to disoblige neither, they stifle it in birth.'[49]

Even if such an occurrence was relatively rare, the vulnerability of slave women is likely to have somewhat inhibited – though not, of course, prevented – the formation of families within the slave community. As a slave plantation matured, a more elaborate pattern of slave attachments developed. In a study of three early-nineteenth-century Jamaica plantations, Barry Higman found that 'the most fertile women were those who lived with a mate and their children'.[50] However, he also found quite a number of slave mothers living in their own households, but without a mate; in a few cases he was able to establish the likelihood of a polygynous relationship. Contrary to what might be expected, African slaves were often found in a 'modern' family structure, with monogamous unions and nuclear families, while a few creoles practised polygyny. The African slaves were uprooted, first-generation immigrants who, for this reason, lacked extended family ties on arrival; by the second and third generations creole slaves had built up a more complex kinship network. Polygyny on the slave plantations was usually the prerogative of the elite slaves, many of whom were creoles.

Higman has also identified another feature associated with the slave mother's disinclination to have many children. Women were likely to have more children where they were less reliant on slave provision grounds. In Barbados and in Vere, an old-established parish of Jamaica, there was little land for allotments and the slaves received a high proportion of their food from their owners; they also registered a positive rate of natural increase. Female domestics, who were less reliant on distant provision grounds, also tended to have more children. Although the slaves appreciated the provision grounds, and were glad of the element of autonomy they made possible, the effort of cultivating them often aggravated the problem of overwork, especially when they were several miles from the estate. Masters who had allotted provision grounds to slaves were thereafter inclined to believe that the problem of slave subsistence had been largely met, ignoring the frequent loss of crops due to typhoons, droughts, stray cattle and theft. Apart from such common problems slave women may well have seen a disadvantage in having more than two or three children since the arrival of extra mouths would not increase the crops in the provision grounds or the labour immediately available to cultivate them, and a woman with six children was not allotted twice as much land as one with three. Sidney Mintz has described Caribbean slaves as a 'proto-peasantry' partly because of their attachment to the small plots of land given to them. The reproductive pattern of many Caribbean slaves – child-bearing in the twenties, not teens;

careful mating strategies and limited number of children – would all be quite consistent with such a description.[51]

In the later eighteenth century shortages and rising slave prices led to greater concern with 'ameliorative' practices that might raise the slave birth rate. Small cash premiums were offered to women bearing children; those who had as many as five living children might, in some cases, be excused further work in the main field gangs. The effects of pro-natalist policies were often modest – as were, indeed, the concessions generally offered to slave mothers. However, on Barbados in 1786 a group of leading planters jointly urged the provision of better perinatal facilities, and a lightening of tasks allotted to pregnant and working women; subsequently they also advocated paying mothers and midwives for successfully 'bringing out' children, and awarding mothers of three or more children a regular Christmas bonus. This barrage of natalist policies was widely adopted, and by the 1800s the Barbadian slave population displayed positive natural growth rates. As an old-established colony Barbados had a quite high proportion of creole slaves, a circumstance that would have favoured higher reproduction rates. But the importance of sugar on Barbados militated against positive natural growth. It seems that the amelioration measures aimed at giving slave women positive support and encouragement, even at some little expense, were more systematic and consequential than on other sugar islands. And since Barbados planters provided a large proportion of their slaves' food, the 'proto-peasant' restriction suggested above would not have been so strong.[52]

Positive natural growth rates for the slave population, it seems, could be achieved only by a cluster of favourable circumstances and policies which, in combination, were able to triumph over slavery's tendency to depress them. In the Barbadian case the favourable cluster may have included a further circumstance. We have argued that the degrading conditions to which women were subject on large sugar estates were a factor inhibiting family formation, and hence reproduction. Abolitionist attacks on the sexual exploitation of slave women could have helped to reduce its incidence on the Barbados plantations because of the presence of much larger numbers of white women, spouses of the planter and his employees, than were to be found on the other islands. Resident wives had a lively objection to their husbands forming attachments to women on the plantation.[53] At all events Barbados, with its considerably larger and more balanced white population, responded to the policies of 'amelioration', and the slaves of Barbados achieved a sustained positive natural birth rate in the first decades of the nineteenth century.

The same happened in the Bahamas, where birth rates rose even higher than in Barbados. Among the factors explaining the strong increase of the Bahamanian slave population were the absence of sugar plantations or other similarly destructive employments, measures encouraging marriage and families, and the circumstance that the Bahamas had experienced an influx of Loyalist slaveholders and their slaves from North America in the mid 1780s. As we will see below, positive natural growth rates had also appeared among the slave population in the North American colonies, for a similar variety of reasons.[54]

So far as the Caribbean was concerned, the experience of Barbados and the Bahamas was exceptional. Elsewhere the planters' usually half-hearted efforts to encourage slave reproduction were not allowed to stand in the way of mobilizing all hands for the sugar harvest. Planters and overseers may have thought ahead a few years, but – as already pointed out in Chapter VIII – not the twenty years which it would require for an 'investment' in slave children to mature. However, while their demand for slave labour did not abate, they did seek to bring down mortality rates, since this seemed to promise immediate returns. They furnished their crews with a comprehensive medical service, hired doctors and constructed sick bays or hospitals on every plantation. Nevertheless, mortality rates were highest precisely on those estates, the large sugar plantations, which were most likely to have a full-time doctor and a hospital. Although it was not completely useless, the medical knowledge of the time could not counteract the severe effects of overwork – and of the undernourishment that so often accompanied overwork during the harvest, since less time was available for cultivating food. Smallpox inoculation, a medical practice known in parts of Africa and the Middle East, was quite widely employed in eighteenth-century Jamaican plantations, and proved very effective. But for the most part the European doctors lacked knowledge and medicines appropriate to Caribbean conditions. As for the slave hospitals, few of these were well run, and many doubled up as prisons for slaves who had committed some infraction and places of confinement for mothers who had just given birth.

The general level of health on the plantations was poor; large numbers of slaves reported sick as a consequence of yaws, ruptures, elephantiasis, ulcers, sores and a variety of other highly unpleasant conditions. Sheridan cites a typical statement of the condition of slaves in 1789 at Rose Hall plantation, Jamaica, where out of a potential labour force of 163, 57 were 'able and healthy', 42 'healthy', 22 'weak, healthy but weak, or very weak', 9 afflicted with 'ulcers and sores', 8 'sick', 8 'invalids, all very old and weak', 4 'useless or almost useless', 4 'in the yaws', 4 'blind or almost blind', 2 'ruptured', and so on and so forth. The hospitals sought to patch up the sick, but they were also designed to deter the malingerer. One of the more remarkable features of the Caribbean plantations is that their calibrated mobilization of a very diverse labour force managed to extract the maximum from the labourers available, male or female, old or young, sick or healthy. The 'labour force participation ratio' they achieved can rarely have been equalled.[55]

The French West Indies

Although research into the internal functioning of the French plantations is less extensive, there is no doubt that their overall performance in the eighteenth century was superior to that of the British plantations. The periods of most rapid growth were 1713–40 and 1765–90, with French naval reverses weakening the position in the middle decades. In all plantation products except one, tobacco, the French islands outproduced the British. They not only supplied the metropolis with all the sugar, coffee and indigo it needed, but also established a pre-eminent position in these products in continental European markets. While the British West Indian planters exercised a comfortable monopoly within a protected and expanding home market, the French planters were delivered to the entrepôt skills of the Bordeaux merchants. When conditions were favourable, the latter proved able and willing to make large investments in colonial trade, dispatching every sort of provision and equipment to the islands and marketing their products with considerable flair; together with the merchants of Nantes, they also brought huge numbers of captive Africans to the French colonies. However, planters had some reason to resent the colonial merchants. The rules of the *exclusif* forced them to deal only with the merchants of the metropolitan ports, on terms that were less favourable than those they would have been offered by the Dutch or North Americans.

The social structure of the French islands, with their slave plantations, bore a strong family resemblance to that of the British islands. Colonial society was dominated by *les grands blancs*, owners of the large sugar estates, while slaves comprised four-fifths or more of the population. Absenteeism was a little less extensive than with the British planters. While sugar was by far the most important product, the pattern of plantation development was somewhat more diversified than that of the British islands, as Table X.7 suggests:

Table X.7   Exports from the West Indies 1770

% of Total	British Islands	French Islands
Sugar, rum, molasses	81	49
Coffee	11	24
Indigo	–	14
Cotton	3	8

Source: Davis, *The Rise of the Atlantic Economies*, p. 261.

The preferential treatment given to British colonial sugar in the expanding home market made it the most profitable crop for British planters, and encouraged sugar monoculture. If they had sufficient resources, French planters usually devoted their estates to sugar cane, but smaller planters cultivated coffee, indigo and cotton. By 1770 the French islands produced more sugar than the British islands, though since they received lower prices for it, their income from sugar sales may have been lower.

The French Antilles were favoured by geography and, for much of the eighteenth century, by international alignments as well. The total land area of the French island colonies was over twice as great as that of the British islands. The Spanish *guarda costas* did not harass French colonial shipping as they did that of Britain; this reflected friendly relations between the two Bourbon kingdoms and the undoubted fact that British ships were far more likely to be engaging in contraband with the Spanish colonies. In the mid 1740s and early 1760s, communications between France and its Caribbean possessions were difficult or impossible; but for by far the greater part of the period 1713–90, French colonial shipping had little to fear. France maintained a larger military establishment in its islands than did Britain. While slave runaways and *petit marronage* were always a problem even on Saint Domingue, there was nothing like the scale of the revolts or maroon activity which had impeded the development of Jamaica.

In the first half of the century Martinique and Guadeloupe retained a strong position in French colonial development. Martinique had the distinction of its own refining industry, enabling it to produce the finest white sugar. In 1755 Martinique supplied 91.7 per cent of the white sugar arriving at Bordeaux, leaving Saint Domingue to supply 98 per cent of the raw sugar or muscovado; the sugar of Guadeloupe was often processed in Martinique.[56] This pattern was a vindication of the tenacious defence of their refining privileges by the *colons* of Martinique. Following the introduction of coffee in the 1720s, Martinique also became the leading Caribbean supplier of this valuable crop. In 1740 Martinique dispatched 6.5 million lb of coffee to Europe, and began to drive the Arabian and Moroccan product from the markets of Western and Northern Europe. In 1743, 97.3 per cent of the West Indian coffee arriving at Bordeaux was dispatched from Martinique, the main commercial centre in the French Antilles and the base of operations for many *commissaires* or merchants in Bordeaux and Nantes. While British planters often shipped their own sugar for sale in the metropolis, this was unusual for French planters, who instead sold direct to the *commissaires* in the islands.[57]

The scope for development in Saint Domingue was naturally much greater than it was on the more easterly islands. Saint Domingue had a heavily indented coastline, facilitating the loading of cargoes. It had four extensive and fertile plains: around Le Cap in the North, Antibonite and Cul-de-Sac in the West, and the Plain des Cayes in the South. Standing behind these plains were wooded hills from which a multitude of streams and rivers flowed down through the plains to the sea. Wood and water supplied vital inputs needed by the sugar mills. The number of sugar mills in Saint Domingue rose from 138 in 1713 to 339 in 1730, and reached 793 in 1790; in 1787 Saint Domingue's sugar output reached 87,000 tons, compared with an output of around 49,000 tons in Jamaica in the same year. In the aftermath of the Seven Years War the *colons* of Saint Domingue were permitted to clay their own sugar; in 1775, 260 out of 459 *sucreries* had refining facilities, and by 1790 the number had grown to 431 out of 793 sugar mills.[58]

The refining process allowed the French planters to produce more rum and molasses, without sacrificing sugar output. Since the refined sugar was about a third less bulky than the raw muscovado, there were significant savings on freight costs. The availability of more rum and molasses made possible a two-way trade with the British colonies in North America, and later with the United States; in return for these products the planters of Saint Domingue were able to acquire North America's reasonably priced plantation provisions and supplies. British planters were galled to see the French islands drawing off North American custom and reducing the price of sugar by-products. They themselves were prevented from producing refined sugar by protectionist legislation favouring the metropolitan refineries. But the West Indian planters exercised their influence in London to sponsor provocative – and much-evaded – British legislation prohibiting the North American molasses trade with Saint Domingue and Martinique.

The French sugar estates and refineries were highly productive and co-ordinated compared with other contemporary enterprises, as Robert Stein observes: 'few industrial workplaces were as tightly controlled as the plantation and the large refinery where on one estate, or under one roof, up to several hundred workers might be ruled by one foreman or manager'. However irksome it was for the planters to ship their produce to French ports, they benefited both from the subsidized slave trade and from the excellent commercial connections of the French merchants. Stein argues, however, that the advanced features of the production and marketing of French sugar were still yoked to property arrangements which belied them. The planters' dependence on merchants, and the vulnerability of both to French inheritance laws, which required the equal division of an estate among heirs, obliged the French sugar magnates to formulate careful marriage strategies and commercial partnerships if they were to ensure a future for the enterprises they had built up: 'In spite of ... significant modernities, the sugar business was still firmly rooted in the Ancien Régime.'[59]

Estates devoted to secondary crops grew as rapidly as the sugar plantations. Thus the number of indigo estates on Saint Domingue rose from 1,182 in 1713 to 2,744 in 1730, and reached 3,445 by 1739. The

metropolitan textile industry furnished a sizeable market for both cotton
and indigo. During the eighteenth century French cotton exports rose as
rapidly, sometimes more rapidly, than those of Britain. Moreover, by the
1780s the cotton of Saint Domingue was being bought in large quantities
by English as well as French manufacturers. While some cotton was grown
in the British West Indies, the British manufacturers acquired indigo from
the North American colonies before 1776.[60]

From around mid century Saint Domingue began to produce increasing
quantities of coffee. By offering beans from Saint Domingue at prices some
5–10% cheaper than those of Martinique, the latter's position as a coffee
supplier was squeezed. In 1767 Saint Domingue exported a little over 12
million lb, rising to the impressive total of 72 million in 1788–89. The
coffee estates were generally smaller than sugar plantations. A *caféière*
whose records are investigated by Debien had a slave crew ranging from 60
to 114, with an output of roughly 1,000–1,500 lb annually for each of the
nègres de jardin. The coffee bushes had to be carefully tended and weeded;
the beans, once harvested, had to be husked and dried. The slaves were
divided into work gangs or *ateliers*, as on a sugar plantation.[61]

While the French plantation regime generally resembled that of the
British islands, its overall performance, as we have seen, was superior. The
sucreries probably achieved higher yields, and certainly produced more and
better sugar, than did the British mills. It is no doubt significant that French
planters were responsible for the introduction of new cane varieties. The
integration of milling and refining stimulated interest in sugar chemistry,
and paved the way for later advances in sugar-making. The data cited
above on the number of mills and the rise of sugar output in Saint
Domingue, compared with those given earlier for Jamaica, suggest that the
average production of the estates in the French colony was significantly
greater. The average output per mill in Saint Domingue appears to have
been at its height in the 1760s, when mills had an average annual output of
about 124 tons; by 1787–89 this had dropped to 104 tons per mill, as more
sucreries were built to cash in on the French sugar boom of the 1780s.
Output per mill in Jamaica was roughly 70 tons annually in 1789; with the
virtual elimination of Saint Domingue in the subsequent decade, Jamaica's
output rose from 50,000 to 75,000 tons, and output per mill climbed to 94
tons annually. But Jamaica's product was still unrefined muscovado with
fewer by-products, especially molasses, than had been produced in Saint
Domingue. The *sucreries* of Saint Domingue do not seem to have had larger
slave crews than those in Jamaica; Geggus cites a sample of 100 between
1745 and 1792 with a mean slave complement of 177, whereas the
Jamaican sugar plantations already averaged slave crews of 200 in mid
century.[62]

The French planters took advantage of the relative abundance of water
and land on their islands to elaborate a more intensive and comprehensive
agricultural system than was found on the British islands. While Saint

Domingue had many streams and rivers, rainfall was reliable only on the Northern coast and in the mountainous districts. Irrigation schemes enabled the planters to ensure a larger and more predictable crop, and to use water-powered mills. Such schemes enjoyed official patronage and were assisted by the engineering skills of the military, a number of whom came to own or run plantations. During the 1740s and 1750s these schemes led to the irrigation of 100,000 acres of land in Saint Domingue.[63]

The inventories of estates in Saint Domingue reveal that the value of improved cane land could be as large as that of the sugar works and slave crew put together; though, of course, these improvements were themselves the product of slave labour. Thus *La Sucrerie Cottineau* in 1784 was estimated to be worth £45,167, of which £19,983 represented the value of 453 acres of cane land, compared with the value of 173 slaves listed at £8,423 and the value of the sugar buildings at £9,593. The cane land comprised 44 per cent of the total value of this estate, compared to 22 per cent in the inventory of the Jamaican estate given above. Since slave labour was not fully used in cultivation outside the harvest period, construction and irrigation projects allowed the planter to make more intensive use of the slave crew's total labouring potential. Once a well-irrigated and water-powered *sucrerie* had been constructed, it was highly productive and profitable. J.-B. Say estimated that a sugar plantation in Saint Domingue returned its purchase price to its owner within six years, compared with an estate in France, which might not return one twenty-fifth or thirtieth part of its value each year; though such calculations did not take account of the much heavier depreciation charges relevant to a slave plantation, where the labour force was wasting away every year.

In the early and mid 1780s French sugar-planting in Saint Domingue was regarded by Jamaican planters as distinctly more profitable than their own undertakings: an annual profit range of 8–12 per cent, they claimed, was standard for the French colony, in their view, compared with only 4 per cent for Jamaica. (J.R. Ward's figures for Jamaican plantation profits are close to those claimed in this estimate: only 3 per cent a year in the difficult wartime years 1776–82, climbing to 6.4 per cent in 1783–91: see p. 420 above.) Often the French planters had borrowed heavily, or entered an *affirmage* agreement, to buy slaves and construction materials, in which case planting profits were drawn off by commercial entrepreneurs. As in the British islands, the hypercapitalized structure of the slave plantation meant that good profits could be soaked up by interest charges. In the 1740s and 1750s the Superior of the Jesuit Order in Martinique had run a bank which had offered cheap credit to the planters, but this rare experiment came to grief in 1757.[64]

Jacques de Cauna's study of the *Sucrerie Fleuriau* argues that it was highly profitable, but these results may understate some costs. The owner incurred 'plantation expenses' of around 60,000 livres in 1787 and transport costs of 3,500 livres set against an income of 144,000 livres. The largest items of expense were usually slave purchases (20–35 per cent) and taxes and the irrigation levy (15–30 per cent). If the performance of the *Sucrerie Fleuriau* in the 1780s is compared with that of Worthy Park, then it appears that the former achieved slightly higher sugar output per slave (1 ton against 0.9 of a ton) and considerably higher output per acre (1.5 tons against 1 ton). In 1777 *Sucrerie Fleuriau* had been valued at 700,000 livres; the estate's *produit net* was reckoned to furnish a rate of return of 18 per cent per annum in the 1780s. David Geggus has analysed the accounts of the sugar plantation of *Saint Michel* at Quartier-Marin which appear to tell a different story, since its annual rate of return in the 1780s was only 4.9 per cent which, as he points out, was distinctly lower than the 8–10 per cent rate of return which has been found by other studies of sugar estates of the Plain du Nord during this period. However, much of the revenue of *Saint Michel* plantation during this time was devoted to building up a satellite plantation with a crew of 131 slaves; over the whole period 1765 to 1790 *Saint Michel* yielded an average of 100,000 livres each year to its proprietors. In the mid 1780s, with an average crew of 246 slaves, this plantation remitted 463 livres or a little over £18 per slave compared with net revenues per slave of between £12 and £25 at Worthy Park in the late 1780s. These calculations are based on all slaves, including children, the elderly and the sick; profits per field slave were approximately twice as great in both Saint Domingue and Jamaica, while the gross value of the output per field slave reached 2,490 livres or £98 at *Saint Michel*, and £100 per field slave at Worthy Park, in the late 1780s. The absentee proprietor allowed the *procureur*, or attorney who supervised the estate, 10 per cent of its receipts, with a fixed, usually much lower salary for the overseer. The profitability or otherwise of all plantations depended crucially on the costs of their acquisition; and, on a year-to-year basis, they depended on fluctuations caused by losses at sea, droughts, epidemics, and so forth. Geggus points out that those who sold their estates for cash often realized only a half of their nominal value while those who extended credit to the purchaser might well have difficulty securing full payment.[65]

On the eve of the Revolution the planters of the French Caribbean were said to owe 99 million livres, or some £4 million, to the merchants of Bordeaux and Nantes.[66] The operating expenses of a prime estate were so considerable that even those rich or influential enough to have acquired one outright would have some recourse to credit to finance their first crop. The inheritance laws contributed to these problems by saddling the son who took over an estate with obligations to other heirs. Anxious to secure a lien on the sugar crop, merchants would offer credit for supplies or the purchase of extra slaves. The Baron Wimpffen observed in July 1790:

> The appetite grows with eating, as the old saying has it . . . so that most of the proprietors, instead of using the receipts of their first crops to pay off ruinous debts, use them instead to buy more Negroes, that is to say, to contract new

debts, without having calculated in advance whether the profit they anticipate from raised output will compensate them for the very considerable difference between what they borrow and what they will have to repay.

Pluchon comments: 'The proprietor was caught from the first day in a trap whereby he indebted himself in order to make more income with the aim of wiping out his debts more quickly and making a net profit.'[67] While colonial debts were certainly large, so was the value of the colonial estates. Merchants regularly extended credit to the planters, as this was a way of securing their custom on advantageous terms. Plantation property enjoyed some legal protection, but if the merchant found that the planter became so indebted that he owed a sum close to the value of the property, then the merchant was able to foreclose. In other cases heavily indebted planters would sell out to the merchant, realizing what was left of their asset before it all disappeared. Thus Romberg, Bapst et Cie of Bordeaux owned 16 *sucreries*, 31 *indigoteries* and 16 *caféières* by the end of the Ancien Régime. Indeed, by this time a high proportion of the larger estates were owned either by merchant families – Gradis, Journu, Chaurand, Bouteiller, Lantimo, Begouen, Feger, and so on – or by families of high officials.[68]

Indebtedness was also an affliction of British West Indian planters. Hurricanes, slave revolts and epidemics could ruin a planter, while a bad war could depress even the luckiest and best-managed estate. Mercantile families such as the Beckfords and Lascelles, or mercantile 'associates' like Sir Alexander Grant, came to own strings of plantations. The problems of the Jamaican planters in the 1770s and 1780s led to a rising incidence of bankruptcy – figures that did much to persuade Lowell Ragatz and Eric Williams that the onset of West Indian decline should be traced to these years.[69] But the occurrence of bankruptcy was in itself evidence that the market mechanism was transferring plantation resources from those who had not proved able to manage them successfully to new, and possibly more competent or luckier, hands. The sugar estates of the British and French islands were very large enterprises anyway. While the problem can, from one point of view, be seen to stem from the high value of the slave crews, from another it stemmed from the fact that such large enterprises really required a 'joint-stock' pattern of ownership, so that risks could be spread between several proprietors, as happened with most slave trading voyages.

However, it paid the merchants to let the planters stand in the front line and bear the initial impact of risk. If they fell into ruin then the merchants took over, sometimes sharing ownership of a particular estate with other merchants or with the planter on a *contrat de liaison* basis. While there were bad years in both Jamaica and Saint Domingue, average profits were positive. The splendour of eighteenth-century Bordeaux scarcely suggests a merchant class which was being systemically defrauded by feckless planters. The fate of French colonial proprietors and merchants was to be decided by the course of Revolution, not the tallying of accounts (and even many who were expropriated were eventually to receive some compensation in return for French recognition of the Republic of Haiti). Likewise, as J.R. Ward and Seymour Drescher have shown, the British West Indian planters enjoyed great prosperity for nearly thirty years after 1790 – in this case helped by the removal of their more productive French rivals.[70]

The relative productive inferiority of the plantations on the British islands must be attributed both to natural endowments and to the social institutions which managed them. The British islands generally lacked the water resources to match the irrigation schemes of Saint Domingue or Martinique; but those British planters who bought estates at Essequibo were obliged to devise irrigation schemes, and found that they boosted both productivity and profits. The French colonial and maritime authorities were in general more willing to spend money on roads, port facilities and canals than those of the British islands; the planter-dominated assemblies of the British islands were often quite narrow in their approach, and refused to tax themselves for improvements which might only assist new planters. On the French islands each estate owed *corvée* labour to the extent of its slave complement; those planters who did not wish to lose the services of some of their slaves would pay for the hire of substitutes. The French Ministry of Marine backed numerous scientific expeditions aimed at discovering new or improved plant varieties; they also sponsored botanical gardens and attempts to improve hydraulic and processing techniques.[71]

Both geography and politics meant that the French planters commanded more adequate food supplies than did the planters of the British islands. Richard N. Bean has calculated that the British islands typically relied on overseas imports to supply some 500 calories per day per inhabitant – that is, about a quarter of food consumption needs. In the period 1777–83 there were many interruptions in this import trade to the British islands, and many thousands of slaves died as a result. The French, lacking extensive mainland colonies and always aware of the vulnerability of maritime links, never relied on imported foodstuffs as much as the British. Saint Domingue, on the other hand, could purchase foodstuffs securely and on a large scale from the Spanish half of the island, Santo Domingo, with its extensive ranches and *estancias*.

The French islands were larger, and had a more varied topography, than the British. The French colony of Saint Domingue was 10,714 square miles compared with 4,411 square miles for Jamaica; Martinique (425 square miles) and Guadeloupe (583 square miles) were considerably larger than Barbados (166 square miles) or Antigua (108 square miles). Greater variety of terrain on the French islands meant that there was land unsuitable for cane which could be devoted to provision grounds. This was, of course, a mixed blessing for the slaves who, as in many parts of Jamaica, were left with the arduous and uncertain work of feeding themselves. On the smaller French islands planters took more responsibility. In 1736 there were 4,800 banana trees and 34,000 trenches of cassava on Martinique. French planters or *gérants* were more inclined than their British counterparts to organize slave labour for the provision grounds themselves: *commandeurs* (slave-drivers) marshalled slaves for the cultivation of maize and beans. Although French planters might hope to acquire North American provisions, they did not count on this and saw the cost advantage in minimizing purchases. Gabriel Debien argues that this emphasis on self-provision required tighter co-ordination of slave labour, with an integration of cash crop and subsistence work, and concludes that it was a 'product of the increasingly industrial character of large scale cane cultivation'. However, Debien's account makes it clear that despite greater emphasis on food cultivation, the essential features of the labour process were common to both French and British plantations: coerced gang labour, constant supervision, use of the hoe and not of the plough, uneven mechanization, co-ordinated manufacture, and night work in the *sucreries*.[72]

Pierre Pluchon observes:

> The plantation economy brought to Saint Domingue, and more modestly to the Îles du Vent, the agrarian capitalist revolution which England had undertaken in the seventeenth century and which France had barely begun. The creole estate was built by means of capital accumulation, by amassing land; it adopted the division of labour and that early machinism illustrated by the sugar mill, driven by animal or hydraulic energy. It comprised an agro-industrial structure, when it turned out a product like sugar or indigo. In the case of the *caféteries* and the *cottoneries* it involved embryonic mechanisation. The agriculture of Saint Domingue, in advance of that of the metropolis, excluded the autarchic reflex . . . .[73]

While the features mentioned by Pluchon did not, in fact, add up to a fully capitalist type of enterprise, he is right to stress their comparative modernity.

From quite an early period the French colonies had a somewhat larger population of free people of colour than did the British islands, and it was partly thanks to their economic contribution that French plantation agriculture advanced on such a broad front. Thus many of Saint Domingue's coffee estates were owned by free people of colour; they also owned small estates or farms producing other secondary crops, and furnished many urban services. The comparatively low level of French emigration to the New World, compared with that of Britain, helps to explain the original emergence of a recognized caste of free blacks and mulattoes. In the late seventeenth and early eighteenth centuries both the planters and the colonial authorities encouraged the social promotion of some of the people of colour. Taxes on manumission had made this more difficult, but free people of colour still exercised a number of civic rights, including property ownership. Since there was a relative scarcity of white colonists, the recognition of a free coloured caste gave added social insurance to the colonial slave regime. French planters were more likely than British planters to reward the long service of elite slaves with a grant of manumission. Since more of them were resident in the Caribbean, they may have had more natural offspring by slave women and were inclined to manumit both mother and child, bequeathing some property to them. Fathers of illegitimate children by a slave mother were liable to payment of a fine to the Church, but this apparently did little to discourage them. In the British colonies there were just as many mulatto children fathered by white colonists, but the latter were more likely to be slaves or employees rather than planters.

By the latter part of the century the free coloured population of the French colonies comprised nearly 5 per cent of the total compared with about 2.5 per cent for the British islands around mid century. In 1775 there were 6,897 free people of colour in Saint Domingue compared with a free coloured population of 3,700 in Jamaica, comprising, respectively, 2.4 per cent and 1.7 per cent of the total population. The social visibility of the free coloured in the French colonies owed as much to relative economic success as to absolute numbers. Many ran a small business or owned property – typically a house and garden, or a small estate, with a few slaves. The mulatto coffee planters in South and West Saint Domingue had estates worked by from 10–15 to a hundred or more slaves each. Moreover, unlike the French immigrant *petits blancs*, the free coloured population was rooted in the Antilles and had little or no prospect of going to live in France; in 1776–77 metropolitan decrees sought to exclude blacks and mulattoes, whether enslaved or not, from the metropolis. French migration to the Antilles rose somewhat after the Peace of Paris in 1763, as the loss of French Canada was combined with the boom in Saint Domingue, Martinique and Guadeloupe. By 1789 the French West Indian colonies had a total white population of 54,000, many of them *petits blancs*, compared with 36,000 free people of colour and no fewer than 675,000 slaves.

In the mid eighteenth century the French colonial authorities saw in the free coloured population a valuable military resource; a coloured militia could, they thought, strengthen colonial defences and furnish a counterweight to the not wholly trustworthy white colonial militia. While garrisons of metropolitan troops were stationed in the Antilles – with an establishment of at least 3,000 – they were expensive to maintain and, thanks to corruption and the ravages of disease, often not up to strength. The colonists had never been easy to handle and became less so as their wealth grew. Thus the white colonists of Guadeloupe had collaborated cordially with the British when their island was occupied in 1759–62; the 'autonomist' inclinations of the French *colons* were notorious, and much encouraged by resentment of the *exclusif*. In 1769 the Governor of Saint Domingue aroused vigorous protests from the white colonists when he sought to reorganize the militia. While the initial protest targeted the imposition of both taxes and militia obligations, opposition grew when the Governor announced the formation of a coloured militia; after bitter conflicts the latter were included in the forces sent to fight with the expeditionary force in North America. The success of the free coloured in economic activities aroused the antagonism of the *petits blancs*. The colonial authorities eventually appeased the white *colons* by enacting a series of discriminatory decrees barring people of colour from official employments, stipulating minimum numbers of whites to be employed on large estates and discouraging intermarriage between whites and coloured. As noted in the Introduction, Moreau de St-Méry, the 'enlightened' colonial authority on Saint Domingue, devoted many pages in his classic study of the colony dividing people of colour into no fewer than 110 different categories according to their degree of white ancestry; the last-named category of 'mixed blood' had only one part black to 127 parts white.[74]

While the free coloured had conquered for themselves an important position in the economic life of the colony as small proprietors and urban craftworkers, the *petits blancs* were the backbone of the regime inside the large plantations, where they worked as bookkeepers, engineers and overseers. Concessions had to be made to the *petits blancs*, since, as Charles Frostin explains with reference to Saint Domingue:

> In order to keep control of the socio-economic apparatus the white oligarchy had the most pressing need of the *petits blancs* as agents of transmission, execution and above all surveillance. The colony was organized like a 'disciplinary battalion' which cannot function without the vigilant loyalty of its non-commissioned officers: if the latter wavered, the troops would soon mutiny.[75]

The conditions of existence of the mass of slaves in the French colonies were no better than those of slaves in the British islands. Certainly the pattern of high mortality and low fertility was strikingly similar. Thus between 1680 and 1776 about 800,000 slaves were introduced to Saint Domingue, yet the slave population numbered only 290,000 in the latter year. It is true that the slave population of the French islands somewhat exceeded that of the British islands by 1790, despite a slightly lower total of slave imports; but this discrepancy is to be explained by the fact that French slave imports were particularly concentrated and heavy in the 1770s and 1780s. Debien suggests that mortality rates of 5–6 per cent were quite usual for the slave crews.[76] There was always the danger that *gérants* desperate to bring in the harvest would so overwork their slaves that the latter would neglect their gardens and provision grounds. On most sugar plantations, whether French or English, the slaves were generally allowed to drink as much cane juice as they wished during the five or six months of the harvest, but they often lacked a balanced diet, and fell victim to a variety of deficiency diseases.[77] Stealing food – including cane that was growing in the fields – was a common slave crime. Slaves who deserted their estates for a short period – the practice known as *petit marronage* – might be punishing their owners for failing to feed them properly. Large-scale slave revolts were less common in Saint Domingue than in Jamaica; on the other hand slave runaways were quite numerous and it was probably easier for them to blend in with the free coloured population – the latter included the so-called *libres de savanne* who had not been given manumission papers, usually because the formalities were expensive. However, the runaways ran the risk of encountering the *marechaussée*, a well-organized rural police force, who used tracker dogs. The effectiveness of the *marechaussée*, which included veterans of the coloured militia, helps to explain why maroon activity was small in scale. Poisoning and arson, weapons of the weak, were the forms of slave resistance most feared by French proprietors.[78]

In the 1780s the African slaves comprised about two-thirds of the slave population with a wide range of African nations represented. Bantu-speaking Africans described as Congos comprised 40.8 per cent of the African slaves on the sugar estates and no less than 63.9 per cent of the African slaves on the coffee estates. This category included such peoples as the Mayombe, Moussondi, Solongo and Mayaque, but nevertheless repre-sented a considerable concentration of Africans from a single cultural group. The sugar planters preferred to buy the taller slaves from the Senegambia and the Bight of Benin. The slaves drawn from particular African peoples tended to acquire a reputation for one or another special-ized type of work: those from Senegal as domestics or stockmen; the Bambaras as craftsmen; the Congos as domestics, craftsmen and fishermen; the Hausas as sugar-boilers. As in the British islands, creole slaves were overrepresented in the elite positions. On a sample of 34 sugar estates David Geggus found that 87 per cent of drivers were creoles, as were 90 per cent of master carters, 100 per cent of coachmen, 100 per cent of housekeepers and 88 per cent of wheelwrights; on the other hand, Africans comprised the majority of sugar-boilers, fishermen and carters' mates, and 34 per cent of all craftsmen. As on the British islands, African female slaves were less fertile than creole female slaves, and slave women on coffee estates more fertile than those on sugar estates. Geggus comments:

> To a striking degree slave women on coffee estates gave birth at much younger ages than in the plain. . . . In other words the adverse effect of sugar cultivation on fertility was not uniform, affecting young women, especially young African women, with particular severity.[79]

In Saint Domingue as in Jamaica a significant proportion of the children born to young slave women on the sugar estates were mulattoes born to creole mothers; while the fathers would have been whites, the mothers would have been domestics, not field workers.

The markets of Saint Domingue were just as vigorous as those of Jamaica, and they were vital meeting-points for a stratum of the slave population. Most planters did little or nothing to introduce their slaves to Christianity, and the charges levied by priests could easily place their services beyond the reach of most slaves. Nevertheless, at least for the slave elite, baptisms, marriages and funerals could all be important occasions. The voodoo ceremonies and practices that emerged among the slaves of Saint Domingue combined Christian and African elements in a new synthesis. Some of the large numbers of slaves of Congo extraction would already have been acquainted with versions of Christianity in Africa. Michel-Rolph Trouillot contends that the high concentration of slaves from the Congo on the coffee estates of Saint Domingue, combined with the relative isolation of those estates in mountainous regions, favoured the survival of African cultural motifs. He also points out, however, that these estates were smaller and conducive to a more intense cultural negotiation and interaction – presumably processes which included the large numbers of resident, often mulatto, proprietors.[80]

The birth rate among French slaves was probably somewhat lower than it was for the British slaves, reflecting the higher proportion of Africans, though exactly comparable information is lacking. Myriam Cottias has reconstructed birth rates for the slaves, the free people of colour and the white population of the old colony of Martinique, using the proportion of children in each group as a basis. She reaches the interesting conclusion that there was a convergence of birth rates among the three populations, with the free coloureds and whites declining by about 1800 to the rather low levels reached by the slaves. While there were certainly strong and specific reasons for a low slave birth rate, the atmosphere and conditions of Caribbean slave society were not, it seems, conducive to a high birth rate among any social group. Cottias's method of deriving a birth rate from surviving children cannot, by its nature, yield information concerning infant mortality, though other evidence suggests that it was high.[81] Slave women probably had the same motives for restricting the numbers of their children as they had on the British islands. The Jesuit plantations of Martinique had a reputation for achieving a positive natural growth rate among their slave complements – something which, as we have seen, eluded the English Society for the Promotion of Christian Knowledge – and drew the following tribute from a freethinking governor:

> I have observed that on estates belonging to religious houses (it is the only good thing that can be said of them) . . . they feed the slaves well, they take care of the mothers and their infants, and that the population is so considerable that they rarely purchase new negroes . . .[82]

The overall configuration of the French slave colonies, and the extent of their commercial edge over the British, will emerge more clearly from a comparison of French and British Atlantic trading patterns. Paradoxically, while the French plantation colonies were more productive and competitive than those of Britain, the latter's orientation to Atlantic trade was more favourable to metropolitan economic growth. A significant part of the explanation of this paradox lies in the special contribution of North America, which will be considered after presentation of the broader picture.

Anglo-French Patterns of Colonial Trade

In assessing the reasons for the generally superior performance of the French plantations, the relevant macro-economic context must be borne in mind. The colonial mercantilist systems were rigorous enough to mean that French and British plantations belonged to different economic systems, if by this we understand economic zones not only defined by the exchange of commodities but actually integrated by investment decisions and the movement of capital. The British plantations had to compete for funds with investments in British agriculture, manufacturing, commerce, and public bonds. The evidence cited above on the profitability of British plantations suggests profit-taking as well as profit-making, in so far as the calculated 'rate of return' was net of new investment in the plantation. Of course there were phases of plantation expansion in the British colonies when profits were ploughed back into them, but the tariff protecting the British market gave British planters premium profits which they saw no reason to reinvest in the plantations. Fearing the impact of higher British output on London prices, British planters were quite happy to see Guadeloupe handed back to France under the Treaty of Paris. In Chapter XII we will assess the extent of net disinvestment in the British plantation colonies during much of the eighteenth century.

A number of the peculiarities of the British plantation colonies, such as the factor system and the conversion of successful planters into merchants and bankers, would certainly have been favoured by a flow of capital from colonies to metropolis. Another sign of the decision by British planters and colonial merchants not to plough back gains would be their failure to raise slave numbers as rapidly as did the French planters: while French Caribbean populations rose by 78 per cent between 1770 and 1790, those of the British Caribbean rose by only 14 per cent. The workings of the bounty system did little to reduce slave prices in the French colonies; nevertheless French planters acquired many thousands of slaves from the British islands in the 1780s.

The build-up of the French colonies involved a different commercial pattern by which merchants directly sponsored plantation development. So-called *liens d'habitation* and *affirmage* agreements led to mercantile capital being deployed in the construction or enlargement of estates. In some cases these investments were involuntary, since they represented planters' debts which, under prevailing legislation, could not be recouped by means of forced sale of the estates. But the very fact that French merchants were willing to extend large credits to planters testified to their belief in colonial prosperity. While returns from planting probably compared well enough with other possible metropolitan investments – as suggested above in the discussion of the French slave trade – the link between merchant and planter also gave rise to commercial profits in the marketing process.

French colonial trade in the eighteenth century was a spectacular success. The high proportion of French colonial produce entering European trade is evident from Table X.8:

Table X.8 French Colonial Re-exports

% Re-exported	Cacao	Coffee	Cotton	Indigo	Sugar	Total
1775–77	48	85	–	53	75	77.3
1785–89	64	89	32	60	70	72.8

Source: Jean Tarrade, *Le Commerce colonial de la France à la fin de l'Ancien Régime*, Paris 1972, 2 vols, II, p. 753.

The main immediate destinations for French colonial re-exports were the Hanseatic towns (34.4 per cent), Holland (19.4 per cent) and Austria (16.1 per cent). The pre-eminence of French plantation produce in European markets reflected not only the productivity of the French colonies but also the comparatively small size of the French internal market. Thus France, with two or three times the population of Britain, consumed only half as much sugar. It also signalled the success of French merchants in dominating the European market for luxury products of all types.

In 1716 France's export trade was valued at 50 million livres, with imports worth approximately the same amount; in this year imports from the Antilles were worth only 4.5 million livres and exports to the Antilles a mere 2.1 million. By mid century the American colonies supplied France with imports valued at 65.2 million livres annually, and colonial re-exports accounted for half of all France's export trade. In the years 1784 to 1790 France's average annual imports of colonial goods were valued at 203.3 million livres (£8.3 million), of which goods worth approximately 148 million livres (£6 million) were re-exported, somewhat more than half of all French exports.[83] It should be borne in mind that these figures are based on official valuations and concern colonial produce which, in some cases, was processed in the metropolis. Nevertheless, the picture they present of the colonial contribution to the rise of French commerce in the eighteenth century must be approximately correct, and does not include the colonial element in textile exports. The surge in colonial commerce and re-exports created brilliant fortunes in the Atlantic ports, and alone permitted France to balance its international exchanges. Sixty-four merchants from slave trading Nantes received titles of ennoblement; thirty-seven Bordelais merchants were similarly honoured.

The price of sugar in France was raised by a series of taxes and imposts which inflated it by 50 per cent. Together with the cost of carriage, this meant that the price of sugar in Paris was double that in Bordeaux. The merchants who dominated the sugar trade found their main market in the capital, and in many parts of France the mark-up in price was much steeper. Higher prices and the greater weight of subsistence cultivation meant that the market for sugar in France was smaller than it was in England, but the export market made up for this. Aided by tariff rebates and established trade networks in brandy, wine and high-quality textiles, the French merchants exported sugar all over Europe.[84]

The French colonies were a protected market as well as a source of supply. The French *colons* chafed at the restrictions of the *exclusif* in part because it obliged them to buy expensive French provisions and manufactures. Around mid century North American flour cost 45 livres a barrel, French often sold at 70 livres. In the 1760s the provisions of Choiseul's so-called *exclusif mitigé* permitted the French colonies to purchase some supplies from North America, though duties were payable, while still reserving the colonial market for manufactures to the metropolitan producer. While the planters were reasonably happy to buy luxury goods for their own consumption from France, they resented paying high prices to French traders for provisions or tools and equipment; they became notorious for their preference for contraband dealings with English, Dutch or North American traders.

The celebrated Physiocrat economist Mercier de la Rivière, Intendant at Martinique in the 1760s, composed cogent memoranda on the advantages to France itself of allowing freer trade to her West Indian colonies. His reasoning had some impact on official thinking, in the shape of Choiseul's *exclusif mitigé*, though his argument favoured a more sweeping approach.[85] Mercier de la Rivière also had proposals to reform the law of inheritance and colonial taxation, in both of which he laid out important new principles. He urged that the inheritance of sugar estates should not be allowed to provoke the break-up of the enterprise. Instead he proposed that the eldest son (or daughter, if there were no sons) should inherit the sugar works and those slaves who mainly worked in processing, and that the land and remaining slaves should be equally divided among the remaining heirs. The latter could, if they wished, sell their portion to the eldest, after an independent valuation, or cultivate it on their own account. This proposal might seem to echo the traditional structure of Brazilian sugar estates. In fact it also prepared the way for the model of a central sugar mill, surrounded by satellite cane farms, which was to figure in the writings of Condorcet, though in his case the idea was to transcend the need for slave labour, something barely hinted at by the Intendant at Martinique.

Mercier's proposed reform of colonial taxation had a wider relevance to the vexed issue of taxation in the metropolis, since he advocated taxing people and enterprises on the basis of their ability to pay. He argued that a prudent fiscal system should levy taxes only on the *produit net* of an estate, not on its gross revenues, so that account would be taken of the fact that planters had heavy expenses to meet. He offered calculations showing that estates of different kinds had to make different provision for the purchase of current supplies and inputs to the production process, and that the large sugar estates could bear a higher rate of taxation than the smaller ones. He also urged that the rate levied on the net product should take account of the scale of investment needed to purchase the necessary slaves and equipment to keep the enterprise in business. Thus he estimated that on estates with more than forty-five slaves the net product of each *nègre* was at least 250 to 260 livres (a little over £10). The planter would need to spend the equivalent of 100 livres per slave to make up for mortality. Mercier advocated that the tax rate should be no more than one-seventh of the net product – a level which approximated, he believed, to the levy prevailing on the English islands. He added: 'It must be observed that a rich planter is in a better position to pay 2,000 livres on a net revenue of 14,000 livres than another proprietor would be to pay 200 livres on a revenue of 1,400 livres.'[86]

Mercier was, in fact, outlining the basis for a value-added taxation system; he pointed out that the net product should be traced through the system of exchanges so that those who supplied the plantations should also be taxed on their surplus of revenues over costs. The 'progressive' element which he also advocated was to shield smaller estates and enterprises from the danger of being driven out of business. Such a proposal was, perhaps, a little at variance with pure *laissez-faire* principles. It may well have been prompted by the feeling that the social order of a slave colony needed support from a stratum of small proprietors. The circumstance that colonial wealth was newer and heavily commercialized meant that the Intendant's proposals were less than revolutionary; to have advocated a uniform valued-added rate – or, still worse, a progressive schedule – in France itself would have been an attack on the privileges and exemptions upon which the Absolutist regime was based. On the other hand, it might have offered the Royal Exchequer a means of tackling its mounting financial problems. Mercier's proposals, which circulated among influential officials and fellow economists, can almost be regarded as a time bomb since, if other all expedients failed, it would be tempting to apply their principles to the metropolis.

✳

Despite the impressive performance of the French colonies in mid century, Britain still derived more overall benefit from Atlantic exchanges on the eve of the American Revolution. A tour of duty in the Antilles or ownership of a plantation by a cadet member saved the fortune of a number of the *noblesse d'épée*, while the profits of colonial commerce swelled the ranks of the *noblesse de la robe*. But the prosperity of colonies and of the exporting enclaves had a more limited impact on the metropolitan economy than it did in the case of Britain, because they were not part of a rounded and well-integrated system of exchanges. Britain's colonial and Atlantic trade, and the manufacturing regions which served them, together loomed larger and were to have a broader impact. This is not immediately apparent if the commerce with the Caribbean colonies is not put into a wider perspective, and if the focus is mainly on imports.

The share of the West Indian colonies in Britain's total imports rose fairly steadily from 17.9 per cent in 1713–17 to 27.6 per cent in 1798–1802, but never reached anything like the level of the colonial contribution to French overall imports: 46 per cent in 1789. Britain's West Indian colonies were useful markets, taking 5.0 per cent of all exports in 1713–17, 7.1 per cent in 1753–57 and 14.3 per cent in 1798–1802.[87] But these figures cover only direct exchanges, and do not reveal the extent to which Britain's colonial system had an integrated and multilateral character. Thus the planters' outgoings for new slaves boosted Britain's manufacturing exports to Africa, while their acquisition of North American provisions raised the purchasing power of New England and Middle Atlantic farmers. Likewise, West Indian expenditure on Irish foodstuffs, or wines from Madeira, or dried fish from Newfoundland, enabled these various suppliers to buy British goods.

The British West Indies had a nominal surplus in their exchanges with the metropolis, but a deficit in trade with the Northern colonies. The earnings of the Northern colonies on the West Indian trade in turn helped them to finance a deficit in exchanges with Britain. Table X.9 gives the pattern of British West Indian trade with North America:

Table X.9   British West Indies Trade with North America

Annual Average in £000	Commodity Exports	Commodity Imports
1699–1701	100.0	110.0
1726–30	139.5	190.0
1748–50	241.5	313.5
1773–74	420.0	725.0

Source: Sheridan, *Sugar and Slaves*, p. 315.

The West Indian planters, whether French or British, found that the provisions and supplies they could buy from North America were excellent value, enabling them to economize on the costs of slave upkeep and acquire such essential items as the wooden boxes and barrels needed to pack their produce. The North American merchants also made a considerable contribution to the carrying trade, whether within the Americas or between America and Europe and Africa.

Of course, the buoyant growth of the North American economy, to which such contributions were linked, was to encourage a momentous colonial challenge to Britain's rulers, threatening the pleasing symmetry of the colonial system. English North America developed an increasingly versatile slave-based sector in the eighteenth century, as we will see in Chapter XI. And in North America, as throughout the hemisphere, Anglo–French rivalry was to be pursued in a variety of military, diplomatic and commercial forms. The prize of this great contest was that of dominating Atlantic exchanges and the commerce of the plantations. The experience of the French Antilles during and after the American War of Independence seemed to offer French strategists the opportunity not only to push the French islands still further ahead of the British but also to create a French-led trading zone that could outcompete what was left of the British Empire. In 1778 a treaty was concluded between France and the rebel Confederation which relaxed the remaining restrictions on trade between the French colonies and the North Americans.

The Brilliance of French Creole Society

Together with the dispatch of a French army, some of it drawn from and based in Saint Domingue, the new alliance between France and the Confederation set the scene for a boom in trade between North America and the French Caribbean. With the ending of the war, and even while it was still in progress, the French planters acquired freer access to cheap supplies of such vital plantation inputs as wooden casks and staves, flour and dried fish, rice and dried meat. They could also pay for these inputs by selling molasses, a by-product of the sugar-making process. The resulting boom in French plantation output, nourished by large-scale slave purchases, also strengthened French colonial trade.

The advance of the plantations and of the slave trade led to French exports to Guinea worth 17.5 million *livres* annually, and exports to the Antilles worth 70.3 million *livres* annually, in the years 1784–90. In 1789, 19 per cent of all France's exports were sent to the colonies; together with the Africa trade, the plantation-related component of French commerce was not much short of a quarter. Thanks in part to protectionist commercial restrictions, a high proportion of France's exports to the colonies were of textiles (37.6 per cent in 1788), or of other manufactures (23.6 per cent in

1788). The French planters, and those merchants who were based in the Antilles, would still have liked to see complete free trade, but the relaxation of the French colonial system as a consequence of the *exclusif mitigé* and the American War left them in an apparently strong position. By contrast, the American War and the North American victory had raised the expenses of the British planters, cut them off from a significant market, and imposed great hardship and losses on the slave populations, because planters and overseers skimped on their rations.

In 1784 Saint Domingue was the site of the first balloon ascent in the Americas, an event carried off with the stylishness and scientific enthusiasm one might expect in this epoch of Enlightenment. In the French Caribbean of the 1780s what had for some time been called creole society was in full flower. Nothwithstanding the elaborate distinction it was possible to draw between *grands blancs*, *petits blancs*, the many types of *mulâtres* and *mulâtresses*, and the great mass of *noirs*, colonial society appears to have acquired its own distinctive dynamism and character. Visitors from France were immediately impressed by the free-and-easy ways and casual cruelty of this slave society. They were struck by the informal, loose-fitting garments worn by free men and women, which, together with cooling drinks, seemed so suited to the climate. Baron Wimpffen confessed that he was both impressed and disturbed by the languor and sensuality of the *mulâtresses*. The sons and daughters of the *grands blancs* often sympathized with the most advanced ideas. Several planters followed the advice of the Abbé Raynal, and permitted their slaves to organize their own entertainments and festivities outside the harvest season, with frequent African motifs.

The relative shortage of whites, even compared with the British islands, the huge mass of Africans and blacks and the extensive mulatto slaveowning elite, gave creole society in the French Caribbean a markedly Afro-American character. The term 'creole' derived from the Portuguese *crioulo*, for an American-born slave, or from the Spanish *criollo*, which, at least by the eighteenth century, usually referred to an American of mainly European ancestry – as noted in the Introduction the *criollo* had been suckled by an Indian or African *criada*, or nurse. Even when it was used of aristocratic white women, the term creole somehow carried with it suggestions of a temperament nourished by tropical miscegenation. The tone of French island culture was indeed set by the mingling of different African peoples with *gens de couleur* and the comparatively small numbers of native *blancs*. As on most of the English islands, the slave markets furnished the great bulk of foodstuffs, and creole cuisine already displayed an original repertoire.

The everyday language of the native-born residents, whether free or slave, was the local version of that patois we now call Kréyole. The Kréyole tongue stemmed from the jargons noted by Du Tertre and other seventeenth-century French priests – with, no doubt, further accretions from the dialects of the African coast. While French supplied much of the vocabulary, it also contained Carib, Portuguese, Dutch, Wolof and Kongolese terms, knitted together by an original grammatical structure, with pronounced African features. Although it was not written down until the revolutionary epoch, Kréyole was now a fully fledged language. In his monumental description of Saint Domingue, published just after the revolutionary upheaval, Moreau de St-Méry drew attention to voodoo as well as Kréyole. Voodoo or vodun was fairly widespread and, as noted above, occasionally patronized by the more enlightened planters. The great slave rebellion of August 1791 seems to have been planned at a voodoo gathering. Popular songs, such as the meringues, were also flourishing by the end of the colonial period; the patriotic anthems of the Jacobins were each to be reworked in Kréyole versions and with distinctive musical elaboration.[88] By the 1780s eight towns in Saint Domingue had their own theatre with the largest, that in Le Cap, having capacity for an audience of 1,500 – whites, mulattoes and free blacks were each accommodated separately. The theatrical company at Le Cap – *Comédie du Cap* – comprised twelve men and eight women. Port au Prince had its own eleven-man orchestra. 'The Marriage of Figaro' received its première in Saint Domingue in 1784 only weeks after its first presentation in Paris. There were three *cabinets littéraires*, or reading clubs, in Cap François and ten different editors and publishers in the colony as a whole. However the weekly newspaper *Affiches Américaines* was a staid publication dedicated to official bulletins, commercial intelligence and advertisements giving information about runaway slaves. There were some twenty Freemasons' lodges. The *Cercle des Philadelphes* brought together those dedicated to scientific improvements, their aims supposedly including that of improving the lot of the slaves 'without harming the interests of the colonists'.[89] In 1784 a Watt-style steam engine built by the Perrier brothers was installed on the Bertrand plantation.

The successes of the French colonial formation – both the fortunes it created and its role as advanced support base for the victorious French expedition in North America – enormously stimulated the confidence and expectations of the planters and merchants, ensuring that representatives from the islands, Bordeau and Nantes would play an outstanding part in the drama of 1789. This revolutionary turmoil was in turn to give openings first to the *petits blancs*, then to the *mulâtres* and finally to the *noirs*. This remarkable sequence derived impetus from the extraordinary dynamic of the most brilliant creole society in the Americas.

Notes

1. Michael Craton, *Testing the Chains: Resistance to Slavery in the British West Indies*, Ithaca, NY and London 1982, pp. 81–98.

2. John J. McCusker and Russell R. Menard, *The Economy of British America, 1607–1789*, Chapel Hill, NC 1985, pp. 164–5.

3. Cohen and Greene, eds, *Neither Slave nor Free*, pp. 194, 218–19.

4. J. Paul Thomas, 'The Caribs of St Vincent', *Journal of Caribbean History*, vol. 18, no. 2, 1984, pp. 60–73.

5. Sheridan, *Sugar and Slavery*, p. 219.

6. J.R. Ward, 'The Profitability of Sugar Planting in the British West Indies, 1650–1834', *Economic History Review*, 2nd series, XXXI, no. 2, May 1978, p. 208; Sheridan, *Sugar and Slavery*, pp. 385–7.

7. Craton, 'Jamaican Slavery', in Engerman and Genovese, eds, *Race and Slavery in the Western Hemisphere*, pp. 276–80; Sheridan, *Sugar and Slavery*, p. 231; J.R. Ward, *British West Indian Slavery, 1750–1834*, Oxford 1988, pp. 80–91.

8. Douglas Hall, *In Miserable Slavery: Thomas Thistlewood in Jamaica, 1750–86*, London 1989, pp. 60–61, 66–7, 148, 215.

9. Bryan Edwards, *The History, Civil and Commercial, of the West Indies*, London 1793, vol. II, IV, pp. 7–8; for Jamaican social structure see Edward Braithwaite, *The Development of Creole Society in Jamaica, 1770–1820*, Oxford 1971, pp. 135–6. For legal discrimination against free people of colour see Elsa Goveia, *The West Indian Slave Laws of the Eighteenth Century*, Barbados 1970.

10. Hall, *In Miserable Slavery: Thomas Thistlewood*, p. 101.

11. Ibid., p. 110.

12. Ibid., p. 111.

13. Sheridan, *Sugar and Slavery*, p. 251.

14. Craton, 'Jamaican Slavery', in Engerman and Genovese, eds, *Race and Slavery in the Western Hemisphere*, pp. 276–80.

15. Samuel Martin, *An Essay upon Plantership*, London 1773, pp. 57–8.

16. Craton, *Searching for the Invisible Man*, pp. 176–7.

17. Richard Dunn, '"Dreadful Idlers" in the Cane Fields: The Slave Labor Pattern on a Jamaican Sugar Estate, 1762–1831', in Barbara Solow and Stanley Engerman, eds, *Capitalism And Slavery*, Cambridge 1987, pp. 163–90. On Worthy Park mulattoes also had privileged access to craft and domestic employment.

18. One indicator of the pressure exercised by the field slaves on the choice of driver is that Africans, while denied other privileged posts, were appointed as slave-drivers, as the Worthy Park data make clear. The sometimes precarious authority of the overseer, his need to select 'confidential negroes' and to negotiate with especially recalcitrant slaves, is suggested by J.R.Ward in 'A Planter and His Slaves in Eighteenth-century Jamaica', in T.C. Smout, ed., *The Search for Wealth and Stability*, London 1979, pp. 1–20.

19. Dunn, '"Dreadful Idlers" in the Cane Fields'.

20. Michael Craton and James Walvin, *A Jamaican Plantation: The History of Worthy Park, 1670–1970*, London 1970, p. vii.

21. The numbers common on a slave plantation, in the range 200–400, were, however, quite similar to the number of hands required by an early factory: Maxine Berg, *The Age of Manufactures, 1700–1820*, London 1985, pp. 230–31. And for further data on cotton factory values François Crouzet, Introduction to Crouzet, ed., *Capital Formation in the Industrial Revolution*, London 1972, p. 37.

22. Such a labour force was recommended by Arthur Young for a farm of 500 acres. C.P. Timmer, 'The Turnip, the New Husbandry, and the English Agricultural Revolution', *Quarterly Journal of Economics*, vol. 83, 1969, pp. 375–95, p. 394.

23. Deerr, *A History of Sugar*, II, pp. 460–71, 534–95; Sheridan, *Sugar and Slavery*, pp. 377–81.

24. Edward Long, *History of Jamaica*, vol. I, London 1774, pp. 448–52. The hoe was probably more suited than the plough to co-ordinated gang labour, which thus would not fully exploit the advantages of slave mobilization. When Long noted that 'one mode of management is too indiscriminately applied to every species of soil' (p. 448) he was referring to the fact that there were branches of cultivation for which hoe cultivation by slave gangs was ill-adapted.

25. Sidney Mintz and Douglas Hall, 'The Origins of the Jamaican Internal Marketing System', in Beckles and Shepherd, *Caribbean Slave Society and Economy*, London 1992, pp. 319–34; Woodville K. Marshall, 'Provision Ground and Plantation Labor in Four Windward Islands', in Ira Berlin and Philip D. Morgan, *Cultivation and Culture: Labour and the Shaping of Slave Life in the Americas*, Charlottesville, VA 1993, pp. 203–22.

26. The first references to Myalism are by Thistlewood in a 1769 entry (see Hall, *In*

Miserable Slavery: Thomas Thistlewood, p. 217) and Edward Long, *The History of Jamaica*, 3 vols, London 1770, vol. 2, pp. 416–17. While Long stresses that Myal was open to all, Thistlewood's entry implies an element of clandestinity: 'Egypt Lucy acquainted Phibbah privately, that the Myal dance has been held twice in Phibbah Coobah's house, at Paradise Estate, as also Egypt Dago, and Job, who are both Myal-men attend these dancings.' Thistlewood was inclined to use words like 'odd' and 'strange' about 'Negro Diversions', implying a certain sense of unease. He was here learning that his wife's daughter was sponsoring Myal and that suspect characters like Job attended. For an interpretation of Myalism's significance see Monica Shuler, *Africa and the Caribbean: The Legacies of a Link*, Baltimore, MD 1979, pp. 65–78.

27. David Barry Gaspar, *Bondmen and Rebels: A Study of Master–Slave Relations in Antigua*, Baltimore, MD 1985, pp. 144–5.

28. Ibid., pp. 243–4.

29. Michael Craton, *Testing the Chains*, pp. 121–4.

30. Report of Governor Matthew of an enquiry into the negro conspiracy, Antigua, 30 December 1736, *Calendar of State Papers*, colonial series, America and West Indies, vol. 43, London 1737.

31. *A Genuine Narrative of the Intended Conspiracy of the Negroes of Antigua, Extracted from an Authentic Copy of a Report, made to the Chief Governor of the Carabee Islands, by the Commissioners, or Judges appointed to try the Conspirators*, Dublin 1737, p. 19.

32. Hall, *In Miserable Slavery: Thomas Thistlewood*, p. 125.

33. Sheridan, *Sugar and Slavery*, p. 269. In calculating the rate of profit planters often deducted 'interest', in the form of 6 per cent on the capital value of the plantation, from their net revenues. This custom was also to be found among early manufacturers. This seems to have been a rough-and-ready way of measuring the return on capital compared with a supposedly natural 'rate of interest'; however, it had the function of anticipating depreciation and compensating for the slow rate of circulation of capital in a pre-industrial economy.

34. Edward Long, *History of Jamaica*, London 1774, I, pp. 462–3.

35. Drescher, *Econocide*, p. 42. Ward calculates the capital of a plantation from the inventory value of slaves, equipment and land. J. R. Ward, 'The Profitability of Sugar Planting in the British West Indies', in Beckles and Shepherd, *Caribbean Slave Society and Economy*, pp. 84–5.

36. David Hancock, *Citizens of the World: London Merchants and the Integration of the British Atlantic Community, 1735–1785*, Cambridge 1995, pp. 143–71,409–11.

37. Hancock, *Citizens of the World*, pp. 40–84, 383–98. According to the conversions previously cited these fortunes would have been worth approximately £6.5 million (Grant) and £33 million (Oswald) in 1994 terms; however, such a valuation, based a general index of price inflation, does not fully register the size of these fortunes in relationship to eighteenth-century scales of wealth nor the value that might be placed today on the landed estates possessed by Grant or Oswald.

38. Richard Pares, *A West India Fortune*, London 1950, pp. 163, 320–21, 332.

39. J.R. Ward, *British West Indian Slavery, 1750–1834: The Process of Amelioration*, Oxford 1988, p. 91.

40. Bennett, *Bondsmen and Bishops: Slavery and Apprenticeship on the Codrington Plantations of Barbados, 1710–1838*, Berkeley, CA 1958, pp. 14, 44–53, 61–2; Michael Craton, *Sinews of Empire: A Short History of British Slavery*, London 1973, pp. 197–8.

41. Edward Long, *A History of Jamaica*, vol. II, London 1774, pp. 432–3.

42. For reproduction rates see Craton, 'Jamaican Slavery', in Engerman and Genovese, eds, *Race and Slavery in the Western Hemisphere*, pp. 251, 275; for the distribution of the slave work force see Sheridan, *Sugar and Slavery*, p. 231.

43. The deleterious consequences for child-bearing of overwork and cruel punishment are stressed by Richard Dunn, 'Sugar Production and Slave Women', in Berlin and Morgan, eds, *Cultivation and Culture*, pp. 49–72.

44. Janet Schaw, *Journal of a Lady of Quality; Being the Narrative of a Journey from Scotland, to the West Indies, North Carolina and Portugal in the Years 1774 to 1776*, edited by E.W. and C.M. Andrews, New Haven, CT 1923, p. 128. This account may be compared with Equiano, *The Interesting Narrative and Other Writings*, p. 110.

45. For slave prices, Sheridan, *Sugar and Slavery*, pp. 247, 252; for an attempt to estimate Jamaican slave rearing costs see R.W.Fogel and S.L. Engerman, *Time on the Cross*, New York 1974, vol. II, pp. 120–22. However, Fogel and Engerman here place the emphasis on the costs

of the child's upkeep and not, as I have done above, on the costs of allowing potential and actual mothers an easier work regime.

46. Kenneth Kiple, *The Caribbean Slave: A Biological History*, Cambridge 1984, pp. 120–34.

47. Barbara Bush, *Slave Women in Caribbean Society, 1650–1838*, London 1990, p. 137. Bush's discussion of 'slave motherhood' is thorough, see pp. 120–50. The possibility of infanticide as a response to want and abuse is illuminated by Nancy Scheper-Hughes, *Death Without Weeping*, Berkeley, CA 1992, though this work is based on Brazil in the twentieth century.

48. Hall, ed., *In Miserable Slavery: Thomas Thistlewood*, p. 133. Barbara Bush's study is based on thorough and wide-ranging research but was completed before the publication of these extracts from the Thistlewood diaries. Some of Bush's generalizations are questionable in the light of the diary, e.g. 'the number of slave women involved in sexual relationships with whites most likely was limited to a small percentage of the total population of slave women.' (*Slave Women in Caribbean Society*, p. 117.) During more than thirty years in Jamaica as Overseer and small planter he describes having sexual relations with twenty or thirty slave women a year, on an almost daily basis; in his account other whites also interfered with large numbers of slave women. Barbara Bush herself quotes the impressive, if qualified, proscription enacted by a quite exceptionally scrupulous planter, 'Monk' Lewis: 'any white person who can be proved to have had an improper connexion with a woman known publicly to be living as the wife of one of my negroes, is to be discharged immediately.' Mathew Gregory Lewis, *Journal of a Residence Among the Negroes of the West Indies*, London 1845, p. 122.

49. Edward Trelawny, *An Essay Concerning Slavery*, London 1746, pp. 35–6. Quoted in Richard S. Sheridan, *Doctors and Slaves: A Medical and Demographic History of Slavery in the British West Indies, 1680–1834*, Cambridge 1985, p. 224. See also Richard S. Dunn, 'Sugar Production and Slave Women in Jamaica', in Berlin and Morgan, eds, *Cultivation and Culture*, pp. 49–72, especially pp. 70–71; and Ward, *British West Indian Slavery*, pp. 171–2.

50. Barry Higman, 'Household Structure and Fertility on Jamaican Slave Plantations: A Nineteenth Century Example', in Beckles and Shepherd, *Caribbean Slave Society and Economy*, pp. 250–72 (p. 270). (This study originally appeared in *Population Studies*, November 1973.) The dire record of sugar plantations as regards both birth rates and death rates is documented in Higman's subsequent study, *Slave Population and Economy in Jamaica, 1807–1834*, Cambridge 1976.

51. Barry Higman, 'The Slave Populations of the British Caribbean', in Beckles and Shepherd, *Caribbean Slave Society and Economy*, pp. 221–7 (p. 223). Sidney Mintz, *Caribbean Transformations*, Chicago 1974, pp. 151–2.

52. Hilary Beckles, *Natural Rebels: A Social History of Enslaved Black Women in Barbados*, London 1969, pp. 97–113.

53. As is clear from the comments of Mrs A.C. (Emma) Carmichael, *Domestic Manners: and the Social Condition of the White, Coloured and Negro Populations of the West Indies*, 2 vols, London 1833. Beckles refers to widespread prostitution of slaves in Bridgetown, the capital of Barbados. This would not have been so damaging to the prospects for general slave reproduction as sexual exploitation of the much larger numbers of slave women to be found on the plantations. However, Beckles is surely wrong if he means to imply that the slave prostitutes themselves had many children (Beckles, *Natural Rebels*, pp. 141–51).

54. The Bahamanian experience is discussed by Michael Craton, 'Changing Patterns of Slave Families in the British West Indies', in Beckles and Shepherd, *Caribbean Slave Society and Economy*, pp. 228–49.

55. Michael Craton, *Searching for the Invisible Man: Slaves and Plantation Life in Jamaica*, Cambridge, MA 1978, pp. 94–9, 112–13. For the medical system developed by the planters and its limitations see Richard Sheridan, *Doctors and Slaves*, especially pp. 42–71, 192 (condition of the Rose Hill slaves), 268–320.

56. Paul Butel, *Les Négociants bordelais, l'Europe et les Îles au XVIIIᵉ siècle*, Paris 1974, pp. 15–35.

57. Ibid., pp. 212–51.

58. Frostin, *Les Révoltes blanches à Saint Domingue*, pp. 144–5; Butel, *Les Négociants bordelais*, pp. 26, 28.

59. Stein, *The French Sugar Business*, p. 170.

60. Frostin, *Les Révoltes blanches à Saint Domingue*, pp. 114–15; Moreau de St-Méry,

Description . . . de la partie française de l'îsle Saint Domingue, Paris 1958 (1st edn Philadelphia 1797), vol. I, p. 111.

61. For commercial data on coffee see Butel, *Les Négociants bordelais*, pp. 26, 31; for the *caféières* see Gabriel Debien, *Études antillaises: XVIIIe siècle*, Paris 1956, pp. 1–137, and Gabriel Debien, *Les Esclaves aux Antilles françaises: XVII–XVIIIe siècles*, Guadeloupe 1974, pp. 140–46.

62. David Geggus, 'Sugar and Coffee Cultivation in Saint Domingue', in Berlin and Morgan, *Cultivation and Culture*, pp. 73–98 (p. 74).

63. Watts, *The West Indies*, pp. 299, 444–6.

64. For a most informative comparative survey, stressing the contribution of irrigation to the productivity of the French plantations, see Richard Sheridan, *The Development of the Plantations to 1750*, Barbados 1970, pp. 48–55. For the *Sucrerie Cottineau* see Gabriel Debien, *Plantations et esclaves à Saint Domingue*, Dakar 1962, p. 18. For French and British planting profits, as estimated by British planters in a representation to Parliament, see Seymour Drescher, *Econocide*, Pittsburg 1977, p. 51.

65. Jacques de Cauna, 'Les Comptes de la Sucrerie Fleuriau' in Paul Butel, ed., *Commerce et plantation dans la Caraïbe: XVIIIe et XIXe siècles*, Actes du Colloque de Bordeaux, 15–16 March 1991, Bordeaux 1992, pp. 143–67; Jacques de Cauna, *Au Temps des Îles à Sucre; histoire d'une plantation de Saint-Domingue au XVIIIe siècle*, Paris 1987, p. 196; Robert Forster, 'Two Eighteenth Century Plantations', in Patricia Galloway, ed., *Proceedings of the Seventeenth Meeting of the French Colonial History Society*, Chicago, May 1991, Lanham, MD 1993, pp. 71–8. For *Saint Michel* at Quartier Marin see David Geggus, 'Une famille de la Rochelle et ses plantations de Saint-Domingue', *Proceedings of the Twenty-Second French Colonial History Society*, publication forthcoming. For Worthy Park see Craton, *Searching for the Invisible Man*, pp. 138–40.

66. Pierre Pluchon, *La Route des esclaves: négriers et bois d'ébène au XVIIIe siecle*, Paris 1980, p. 292.

67. Alexandre-Stanislas de Wimpffen, *Haïti au XVIIIe siècle*, edited by P. Pluchon, Paris 1993, p. 246.

68. Wimpffen, *Haïti au XVIIIe siècle*, p. 104 note k, p. 245 note c.

69. Lowell Ragatz, *The Fall of the Planter Class in the British West Indies, 1763–1833*, New York 1928, and Eric Williams, *Capitalism and Slavery*.

70. Seymour Drescher, *Econocide*; Ward, 'The Profitability of Sugar Planting in the British West Indies', *Economic History Review*, 1978.

71. James McClellan, *Colonialism and Science: Saint Domingue under the Old Regime*, Baltimore, MD 1992, pp. 71–4, 147–62.

72. For Martinique data see Sheridan, *The Development of the Plantations to 1750*, p. 36. For the organization of foodstuffs cultivation see Debien, *Les Esclaves aux Antilles françaises*, pp. 182–3. Debien discusses other aspects of slave work on pp. 119–63 and the limits of mechanization on pp. 163–9. See also Gaston Martin, *Histoire de l'esclavage dans les colonies françaises*, pp. 122–8.

73. Pierre Pluchon, Introduction, Wimpffen, *Haïti au XVIIIe siècle*, p. 44.

74. Moreau de St-Méry, *Description . . . de . . . Saint Domingue*, I, pp. 83–111. The difficult situation of the free people of colour is examined in Leo Elizabeth, 'The French Antilles', and Gwendolyn Midlo Hall, 'Saint Domingue' , in Cohen and Greene, eds, *Neither Free nor Slave*, pp. 137–71, 172–92. Acquiring documentary proof of free status was neither easy nor cheap, as these authors make clear; it is possible that the official data on the size of the population of the free people of colour were understated for this reason (these data are cited pp. 146–51).

75. Frostin, *Histoire de l'autonomisme colon de la partie française de St Domingue*, II, p. 703.

76. Gaston Martin, *Histoire de l'esclavage*, p. 139; Debien, *Les Esclaves aux Antilles françaises*, p. 345. Debien compares this 5–6 per cent mortality rate with an upper limit slave birth rate of 3 per cent per annum.

77. Frantz Tardo-Dino, *Le Collier de servitude: la condition sanitaire des esclaves aux Antilles françaises du XVIIe au XIXe siècles*, Paris 1985, pp. 129–42. See also Sheridan, *Doctors and Slaves*, pp. 185–219 and Kenneth F. Kiple and Virginia H. Kiple, 'Deficiency Diseases in the Caribbean', *Journal of Interdisciplinary History*, vol. 11, no. 2, 1980, pp. 197–215.

78. David Geggus argues that maroon activity was relatively small-scale in Saint Domingue

in the latter half of the century: see Geggus, 'Slave Resistance Studies and the Saint Domingue Revolt', Florida International University, Winter 1983, p. 7. In 1784 an agreement was concluded with the Maniel maroons, one of the few stable and large groups. A legend grew up around Macandal, a slave who had lost his arm in the sugar works and was reputed to be behind a large-scale poison plot in 1757. The great fire in Port au Prince in 1787 was blamed on slave arsonists. See Moreau de St-Méry, *Description*, I, pp. 247–56.

79. Geggus, 'Sugar and Coffee Cultivation in Saint Domingue', in Berlin and Morgan, *Cultivation and Culture*, pp. 92–3.

80. For voodoo see Alfred Métraux, *Voodoo in Haiti*, London 1959, pp. 25–40; Leslie G. Desmangles, *The Faces of the Gods: Vodou and Roman Catholicism in Haiti*, Chapel Hill, NC 1992, pp. 15, 25–8. For the coffee estates see Michel-Rolph Trouillot, 'Coffee Planters and Coffee Slaves in the Antilles', in Berlin and Morgan, *Cultivation and Culture*, pp. 124–37, especially pp. 133–4.

81. Myriam Cottias, 'La Martinique: Babylone fertile ou terre stérile?', *Annales de démographie historique*, Paris 1992, pp. 199–215.

82. The Marquis Fénelon quoted in Frantz Tardo-Dino, *Le Collier de servitude*, p. 168.

83. Data on French eighteenth-century trade from Comte Chaptal, *De l'Industrie française*, Paris 1819, pp. 79, 134–5; and Jean Tarrade, *Le Commerce colonial de la France à la fin de l'ancien régime*, Paris 1972, 2 vols, vol. 2, p. 123. For the relations between merchants and planters see Butel, *Les Négociants bordelais*, pp. 239–45; Pierre Léon, *Marchands et spéculateurs dauphinois dans le monde antillais du XVIIIe siècle: les Dollé et les Raby*, Paris 1963, pp. 50–89, 122–6, 171–4. However, the institutional and geographical limitations on the impulse given to the French economy by colonial trade are stressed by Pierre Boulle in 'Slave Trade, Commercial Organisation and Industrial Growth in 18th Century Nantes', *Revue française d'histoire d'outre mer*, 1972.

84. Robert L. Stein, *The French Sugar Business in the Eighteenth Century*, Baton Rouge, LA 1988, pp. 160–63.

85. Mercier de la Rivière, *Mémoires et textes inédits sur le gouvernement économique des Antilles*, avec un commentaire et des notes de L. Ph. May, Paris 1978.

86. Ibid., p. 208.

87. Data on Britain's eighteenth-century foreign trade are available in B.R. Mitchell and P. Deane, *Abstract of British Historical Statistics*, Cambridge 1962, pp. 309–11; see also P. Deane and D. Cole, *British Economic Growth*, London 1967, p. 89. Some refinements to these figures will be considered below but do not affect the broad comparison made here.

88. Pluchon, 'Des Colonies en lutte avec leur métropole', in Pluchon, ed., *Histoire des Antilles*, pp. 225 ff.; Lambert-Félix Prudent, *Des Baragouins à la langue antillaise*, Paris 1980, especially pp. 19–34; Moreau de St-Méry, *Description*. See also Hall, *Africans in Colonial Louisiana*, especially pp. 156–200. There were, of course, parallel cultural developments on the English islands, notably Jamaica: see Richard D.G. Burton, *Afro-Creole: Power, Opposition and Play in the Caribbean*, Ithaca 1997, pp. 13–46.

89. McClellan, *Colonialism and Science*, p. 292.

XI

Slavery on the Mainland

Stratford 31.st of Aug.t 1754

Aron

You were very Saucy while you were in England, and Resisted me twice. There must be no more of that; for if you offer to Strike your overseer, or be unruly, you must be tyed up and Slasht Severly and pickled: and if you Run a way you must wear an Iron Pothook about your Neck: and if that don't tame you, you must wear Iron Spaneels till you Submit; for as you are my Slave you must and Shall be obedient. But if you behave your Self well you Shall be used kindly. If I hear a Good Character of you, I will Send you Some of my best Old Cloths; and other things. Take Warning and don't Ruin yourSelf by your folly. I rec.d your Letr. If you will be good I Shall be Yr. Loving Master

Jos. Ball

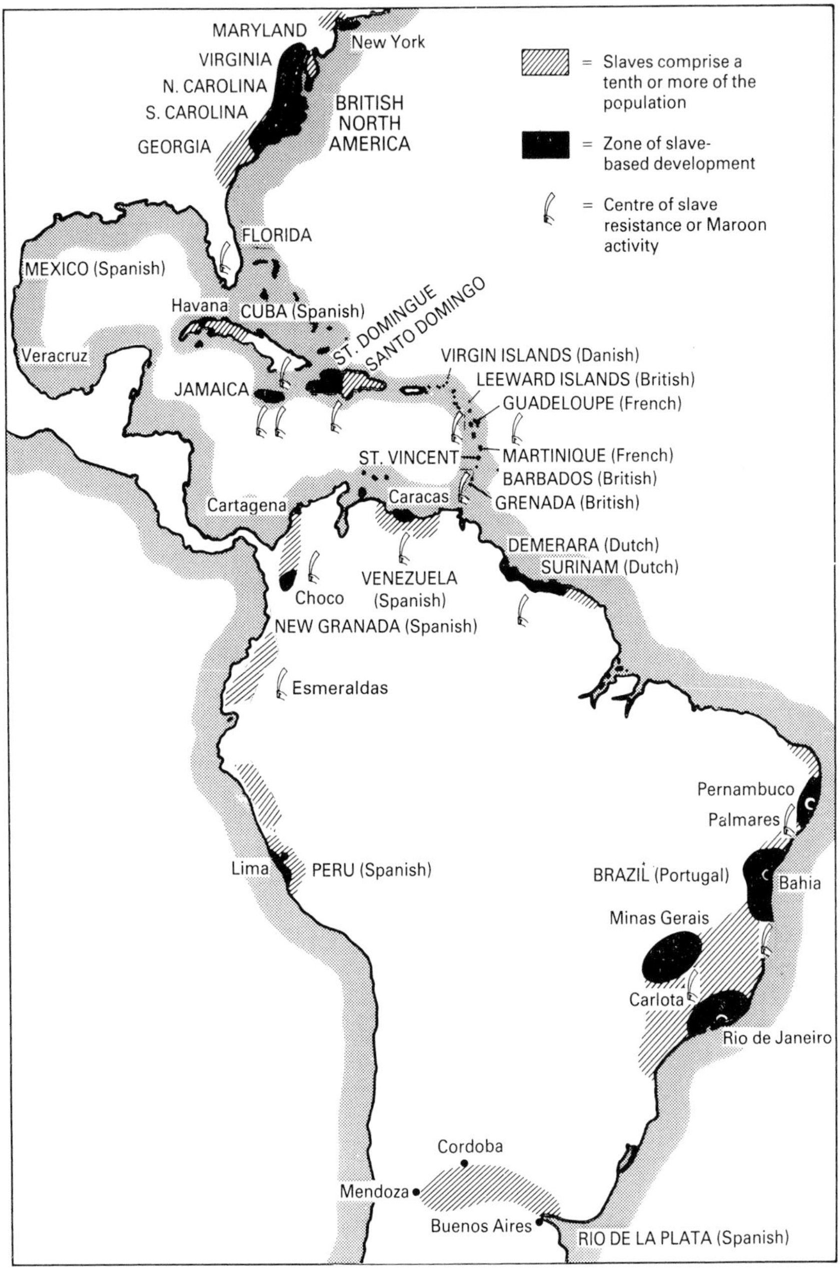
= Slaves comprise a tenth or more of the population
= Zone of slave-based development
= Centre of slave resistance or Maroon activity
MARYLAND
VIRGINIA
N. CAROLINA
S. CAROLINA
GEORGIA
New York
BRITISH NORTH AMERICA
FLORIDA
MEXICO (Spanish)
Havana
CUBA (Spanish)
ST. DOMINGUE
SANTO DOMINGO
Veracruz
JAMAICA
VIRGIN ISLANDS (Danish)
LEEWARD ISLANDS (British)
GUADELOUPE (French)
ST. VINCENT
MARTINIQUE (French)
BARBADOS (British)
GRENADA (British)
Cartagena
Caracas
DEMERARA (Dutch)
SURINAM (Dutch)
VENEZUELA (Spanish)
Choco
NEW GRANADA (Spanish)
Esmeraldas
Pernambuco
Palmares
Lima
PERU (Spanish)
BRAZIL (Portugal)
Bahia
Minas Gerais
Carlota
Rio de Janeiro
Cordoba
Mendoza
Buenos Aires
RIO DE LA PLATA (Spanish)

The Americas c. 1770

The mainland colonies were also the theatre of a momentous conflict between Britain and France, or between Britain and the Bourbons. Britain's colonial exchanges crucially depended on North America, and on the dynamic amalgam found there between farming, petty commodity production, commercial capital and slave plantations. The purchasing power of New England, New York, Pennsylvania and Charleston partly derived, as we have seen, from the carrying trade to the British and French West Indies. Britain's advantageous agreements with Portugal tended to bring it within the British sphere, while the dynastic links between France and Spain gave the French some advantages in the official Spanish–American trade. The presence of unaligned Dutch and Danish colonies facilitated smuggling and hence commercial competition.

Within the North American colonies themselves a novel slave plantation system developed around the Chesapeake and in areas to the south, the earnings of which greatly contributed to the buoyancy of North American demand. Thus in 1768–73 three slave plantation products – tobacco, indigo and rice – accounted for three-quarters of all exports to Britain from the North American colonies.[1] In addition a proportion of the wheat exported by these colonies was also slave-produced, as we will see. The North American pattern deserves attention in its own right, since it produced the most original, successful and expansive system of slavery in the Americas.

The contribution of slavery to the fortunes of the colonies of Portugal and Spain will be analysed in the latter half of this chapter, enabling comparisons concerning the role of the imperial state as well as the prevailing character of the slave system. The rapid growth of the thirteen British colonies owed little to state sponsorship, something to a framework of free exchanges within the British–Atlantic sphere, and a lot to the independent initiative of North American planters and merchants. The economies of the Portuguese and Spanish colonies also developed quite rapidly in the course of the eighteenth century, but here development owed much to a species of neo-mercantilist state co-ordination. Slavery had a role in all three colonial systems, but its strength tended to vary in inverse proportion to direct state involvement.

North America and the Reproduction of Slavery

The economic significance of plantations, and the plantation-related trade, in North America developed in the context of a colonial society profoundly different from the sugar colonies of the Caribbean, even in the Southern colonies, where there was the highest concentration of slaveownership. While black slaves produced three-quarters of exports around 1770, they comprised 18 per cent of the colonial population and 40 per cent of the population of the Southern colonies. Both white and black populations displayed positive natural growth rates, further boosted by continuing free and forced immigration – the uncounted populations of the Indian nations were displaced rather than subjugated. The demographic pattern is evident enough from Table XI.1:

Table XI.1   The Population of the Thirteen North American Colonies by Region in 1700 and 1770

Region	1700		1770	
	White	Black	White	Black
New England	92,000	1,700	581,000	15,500
Middle Colonies	54,000	3,500	556,000	35,000
Southern Colonies	104,000	22,400	1,010,000	409,500
Total	251,000	27,800	2,148,000	460,000

Source: US Bureau of Census, *Historical Statistics from Colonial Times to 1970*, Washington, DC 1975, p. 1168.

Thus the slave population of North America was larger in 1770 than it had been throughout the Americas in the year 1700; and while the latter had required the introduction of over two million Africans, the slave imports into the North American colonies totalled perhaps 340,000. Slaves introduced to the mainland colonies of Spain or Portugal evidently faced a very different destiny from those brought to North America: they were far more likely to be delivered from slavery, by death or (for the lucky few) manumission, than their cousins in the North; likewise, the slaves of Latin America were less likely to have children, but those they had were more likely to be or become free. The social formation of North America was more apt for the reproduction of slavery, in both a social and demographic sense, than those of Central and South America. Like the sugar islands of the Caribbean, the North American colonies were deeply implicated in the whole system of Atlantic exchanges; unlike them, they were potentially autonomous and freestanding within that system, capable of surviving without metropolitan defence, supplies and services.

Although there were some large landowners, especially in New York, and in the towns a number of officials, lawyers, merchants, tradespeople, artisans and labourers, nine-tenths of the white population of the Northern colonies were farmers. The North American farmers acquired an even more pronounced taste for plantation produce than did the European agriculturists of the epoch – and with the aid of local merchants, they could sell their own surplus production to the plantations. During the first half of the eighteenth century Britain was a large-scale exporter of wheat, and had no need for North American supplies; other temperate farm products could be imported from Ireland more readily than North America. The demand generated by the plantations of the Caribbean made possible a strong development of the commercial agriculture of New England and the Middle Atlantic colonies. The agricultural productivity of Northern farmers and fishermen was such that the plantation colonies of the West Indies, whether British or not, all found their supplies the cheapest.[2]

In the Southern colonies slave plantations developed side by side with small farms. The slave-worked estates were first consolidated in the tidewater region where transport posed the least problem, gradually extending further inland along the navigable rivers; but farmers with few or no slaves predominated further inland and in the dangerous frontier zones. The North American tobacco plantation might occupy as much land as a Caribbean sugar plantation, but it employed far fewer slaves. Because tobacco exhausted the soil, the planter would shift to a new 'quarter' every seven years or so, allowing the used land to lie fallow for twenty years. The medium and large tobacco plantations would have crews of between ten and fifty slaves, and many small planters had fewer. In lowland South Carolina and in Georgia there were rice plantations which supported a pattern of slavery closer to that of non-sugar crops in the Caribbean, with some slaveholdings of 60–120 and slave majorities in some counties. Charleston in South Carolina was the largest slave market in North America; the slave population of the rice zone approached a positive natural reproduction rate only in the 1770s. Before considering the reasons why the North American slave population achieved a positive natural growth rate – something which occurred around the beginning of the century in Maryland and Virginia – it will be appropriate to consider other aspects of the strong performance of the slave colonies of British North America.

As North American planters purchased more slaves and fewer servants in the early eighteenth century, the labour regime became more exacting. And later, as these planters became more sophisticated agriculturists in the course of the century, they again boosted the workload extracted from their workforce. Tobacco production grew from 30 million lb in 1710, reaching around 50 million in the 1730s and over 100 million in 1775; North America's main competitors, Brazil and the Netherlands, each produced around 8 million lb annually during the whole of this period.[3] While the large tidewater planters prided themselves on the quality of their oronoco or sweet-scented tobacco, cultivation spread inland to the piedmont, where small planters or farmers were able to raise large harvests from virgin soil, initially using few or no slaves. In the middle decades of the century the Scottish factors purchased large quantities of tobacco from the smaller planters, often for onward sale to the French tobacco monopoly, while the large tidewater planters sold their crop through London commission agents. The rise of tobacco cultivation in the piedmont also led to an increase in slaveholding there. In one such region of Southern Virginia, Amelia county, the percentage of households owning slaves rose from 23 per cent to 76 per cent between 1736 and 1782, and the median number of slaves held rose from two to six.[4]

On the North American tobacco plantations heavy work was performed in the 12–14 hour period 'sunup to sundown', with a two-hour lunch break. As the century progressed, the planters of Virginia and Maryland also increased the intensity of labour, both by growing other cash crops – especially wheat and corn – and by introducing or extending evening work, processing or packing tobacco. With low tobacco prices, many slaveowners in Virginia and Maryland turned to the production of wheat and corn as cash crops. While they did not usually abandon tobacco, they did convert their plantations to a more diverse pattern of cultivation. In order to cultivate wheat on an extensive scale the slave labour force operated animal-drawn ploughs rather than the hoes that were used for tobacco. Corn or hay was also grown to furnish forage for the draught animals, while the latter supplied manure which increased wheat, corn and tobacco yields. Lorena Walsh describes this as the development of a 'second system of agriculture', and observes that it was the big slaveowners who took the lead. It certainly represented a more sophisticated pattern of cultivation than had prevailed hitherto on the shifting tobacco 'quarters'. The more complex combination of tobacco, grains and some animal husbandry gave greater revenue and flexibility to the planter in the face of changing market conditions, even if it too, in the course of time, was to be exploited so intensively that it created ecological problems of its own.[5] In 1773, Virginia exported tobacco worth £337,391, grains worth £145,360 and wood products worth £31,740, the latter mainly destined for the Caribbean.[6]

The diversification of the plantations of Virginia and Maryland boosted the planter's marketable crop by extracting more labour from the slaves. The precise mix of crops varied according to region and the planters' strategy, but invariably one result of the mixture was to occupy more of the slaves' available work time. Wood products could be garnered and prepared in winter. Wheat and tobacco or wheat and maize had partially complementary planting and harvesting cycles. The planters also economized by promoting household manufacture of clothes, candles and dairy products, which gave openings for an extension of evening work. Wheat farming, and the animal husbandry that accompanied it, created a demand for new types of skilled labour which was met by male slaves – the women were left with traditional tasks: household manufacture and more of the demanding field work required by tobacco. While the reproductive capacity of the slave women was not destroyed, they worked harder and – at least in the field – at tasks allowing less autonomy. Michael Mullin points out that the records of the larger planters show that they were continually engaged in calculation, working out, say, the number of hills that could be planted each day by one hand.[7] Confronted with his failure to make money out of cultivating hemp, William Byrd wrote:

> labor is not more than tuppence a day in the East country [i.e. the lands on the Baltic] where they produce hemp and here we cant compute it for less than

tenpence, which being five times as much as their labor, and considering besides that our freight is three times as dear as theirs, the price that will make them rich will ruin us, as I have found by useful experience.[8]

From around mid century there were also examples of attempts to introduce a form of work study calibrating what could be extracted from each slave. Landon Carter wrote:

> as to all work I lay down this rule. My overseers tend their foremen close for one day in every Job; and deducting 1/5 of that day's work, he ought every other day to keep up to that. Therefore by dividing every gang into good, Middling, and indifferent hands, one person out of each is to be watched for 1 day's work; and all of the same division must be kept to his proportion.[9]

So far as the planter was concerned, the changes had much to recommend them. Their more diversified output helped them to survive the troubled years of Revolutionary war and tighter organization laid the basis, when foreign markets beckoned once again, for gross crop revenues per hand of some £25 sterling in the years 1790 to 1807. This impressive figure began to compare with the results achieved by Caribbean sugar planters.[10]

The development of rice cultivation in South Carolina also demonstrated the versatility of the slave plantation and its capacity to extract more work from the slaves by means of more complex organization. In the case of the other main staples, the owners of the slave plantations were catering to strong demand which they were in a good position to supply. In the early eighteenth century rice was regarded as an inferior crop, a substitute for other grains. The Carolina planters began to cultivate rice in the period 1690–1720, when prices were high because of crop failures and war in Europe. But they continued to expand production in 1720–60, when prices dropped. Indeed, it was the cheapness of rice which won new markets for the product in the West Indies and elsewhere. Not until 1767 did the British government remove high duties payable upon imports of colonial rice, following which Britain also bought a portion of South Carolina's crop. The planters raised productivity by transferring from upland meadows to coastal swamps, and subsequently from intermittent to tidal irrigation. The latter method tended to boost rather than exhaust the fertility of the soil. They used wind fans to winnow their grain, hand mills to husk the rice, and from mid century experimented with a variety of large-scale rice-pounding machines.

By the late colonial period the slaves were set to work using the task system rather than gangs, reflecting the more complex nature of the productive system. This system would also have allowed planters to draw more effectively upon the agricultural expertise of African slaves who, as Peter Wood has suggested, were familiar with rice cultivation. In the 1720s 29 per cent of the slaves were employed on estates with a complement of thirty or more. This proportion rose to 54 per cent by the 1740s, then stabilized, though some planters owned more than one estate. South

Carolina's exports of rice in 1768–72 averaged £305,533 annually. The colony's 70,000 slaves also produced most of the indigo it exported to an annual average value of £111,864 in those years. Nash calculates that the volume of exports per slave in this colony rose by a third between 1750 and 1770.[11]

By the 1750s and 1760s rice cultivation had spread from South Carolina to Georgia, a colony comprising the territory between South Carolina and Spanish Florida. Those responsible for founding this colony in the 1730s had decreed that its lands should be reserved to free white colonists, and that 'black slaves and Negroes' should be banned. Georgia was to be, its Trustees hoped, both a place of salvation for England's poor and a strategic buffer against Spanish power to the South and West. However, the chances of success for the colony as a haven for free colonists were not increased by the Trustees' own heavy-handed paternalism. Until 1742 there was a ban on spirits and rum, together with other regulations designed to instil good habits in the settlers. A five-hundred-acre ceiling was set on landholdings, and a quit rent of 4 shillings per hundred acres charged. Despite the Trustees' regulations immigrants from South Carolina began to encroach on Georgia's coast and petition for an end to the ban on slaves. In defiance of the ban, these 'Malcontents' actually introduced teams of slaves, sometimes thinly disguised as contract labourers, together with overseers and drivers. However, both Scots settlers in the county of Darien and the German or Dutch Protestants at Savannah supported the principle that Georgia should remain a colony based only on free labour. In 1739 eighteen Scots immigrants drew up a vigorous manifesto pointing out that legalization would benefit only the wealthy, would pose a serious security problem which Spain would exploit, and was anyway 'shocking to human nature'.[12] The ban on slaves inhibited the development of a plantation staple economy.

By the late 1740s the colony had a white population of only 4,000, and produced no export surplus – the Trustees had hoped it would establish a valuable trade in silk and wine, but this did not happen. Subsidies from England were needed to cover its expenses. If Georgia's first decade-and-a-half is compared with that of Virginia or the New England colonies, then its record was quite reasonable. But the 'Malcontents' from South Carolina commanded resources and painted a rosy picture of the future that would beckon if only slavery was legalized. Joyce Chaplin explains their arguments:

> The Malcontents drew mostly on the English tradition of law that gave subjects the right to manipulate their property free from interference by the state. Malcontents also used liberal assumptions that individuals, acting independently, were the best support of a prosperous and improving economy. Georgian settlers also argued for their right to hold slaves, which British subjects had elsewhere. . . . Malcontents who argued for slave labor drew extensively on modern defences of individuals' economic rights.[13]

In 1750 the Georgia Trustees were eventually persuaded to allow slavery, though following representations from a Dutch pastor, the institution was supposed to be regulated by greater consideration for the slaves' religious and physical well-being than obtained elsewhere. Many of the owners of the plantations which spread in low-country Georgia ignored such rules, but some – including several Dutch and German colonists – did not. The black population of Georgia, including some free blacks, subsequently made an important contribution to the development of African–American Christianity. In 1776 there were 17,000 whites and 16,000 slaves in the colony.[14]

There can be no doubt that North American planters found ways to make their slaves work very hard, and that they had far greater success in producing a marketable surplus than the farmers who used only family and free labour. The planters' skill at extracting work from their slaves increased in the course of the eighteenth century, yet the North American slave populations achieved positive natural growth rates. Most North American slaves were concentrated in Virginia and Maryland, where positive reproduction rates prevailed from the 1720s or 1730s.[15] Such a development, contrasting with Caribbean slavery and most slave systems, reflected factors related to climate, work and plantation regime.

The disease environment in North America, with the more temperate climate of even the Southern colonies, favoured lower mortality rates, among both whites and blacks, than were to be found in the Caribbean or tropical mainland. More plentiful and fresher food supplies enhanced resistance to disease. The relative abundance of fertile land and good grazing grounds, once the Native Americans had been driven back, helped to make the North American colonies a most propitious environment for the white colonists; the small size of its towns, and the modest incidence of landlordism and taxation, further favoured demographic growth. In Europe large towns and cities had high mortality rates; indeed, the new manufacturing and commercial centres of the Old World exhibited the negative natural growth rates typical of the sugar colonies of the New.

High birth rates were probably even more important than low mortality rates in explaining the strong natural growth which came to characterize both white and black populations in North America. It should be borne in mind, however, that a high recorded birth rate in this period often meant a low incidence of infant mortality, since no record might be made of infants who died soon after birth, especially if they were children of slaves. The natural and social environment of the tobacco plantations was conducive to a far higher live birth rate than that of the sugar plantations. Slave women still lost more children in infancy than did white women, but they were more fertile, and their children more healthy, than the slave women and infants of the Caribbean: in Prince George, a Virginia county, the number surviving rose from between two and three in the 1740s to around four in the 1770s.[16]

One feature of slave recruitment to the North American plantations may have favoured higher reproduction rates from the outset. In the early decades the North American tobacco planters, lacking a well-established slave trade from Africa, were more likely to buy already 'seasoned' or creole slaves from the West Indies. By itself this was conducive to somewhat lower mortality rates and somewhat higher fertility. On the other hand, the proportion of females purchased by North American planters was little different from that obtaining in other parts of the Americas.

The positive natural growth rates must have been favoured by a less destructive work pattern than was found in the Caribbean. In North America, despite fairly intensive work rhythms, there was still no equivalent to the labour regime of the sugar estates. Tobacco cultivation required care and attention spread throughout the year. Seedbeds were planted in January, the seedlings were transplanted in May and June, the growing plants were weeded and topped in July and August, the tobacco leaves cut in September, then cured, stripped, stemmed and prized in the last three months of the year. This was an exacting schedule, but it had nothing to compare with the sustained and unremitting toil, day and night, of the five-month sugar harvest.[17] Even the late colonial tobacco/wheat plantations did not involve anything like the night work of the sugar estate, with its 16–20-hour shifts, when day work in the cane fields was followed by a night-time 'spell' of six or eight hours in the mill.

Night work on the sugar estates was dictated by the continuous process character of sugar-boiling; if the sugar train was allowed to cool, there would be considerable trouble and expense in getting it started again. Of course the sugar planters could have organized a shift system which obliged no slave to work more than twelve hours in any one day, but the very possibility of working slaves as hard as they did proved an irresistible temptation – one which was doubtless reinforced by competitive pressure from other plantations. There was no technical need for all-night labour on the tobacco, wheat or rice plantations. This certainly greatly reduced both the temptation for and the competitive pressure upon planters to emulate the work regimes of Caribbean sugar. During certain critical periods lasting a week or two – when the time was ripe for transplanting, or at the end of the year when the crop was prized or packed into hogsheads – planters would force or bribe their slaves to work on Sunday or late into the evening, but all-night work seems to have been unknown. Arranging for the invigilation of slaves working all night would itself have been expensive, requiring, as in the Caribbean, teams of overseers and substantial cash payments.[18]

On the Caribbean sugar plantation, lighter tasks, such as tending livestock, were given to maimed or sickly slaves – often casualties of years of gang labour or accidents on the night watch. On the tobacco plantation fewer slaves were disabled or worn out, and lighter tasks could be given to children and nursing mothers. While gang labour was employed for basic cultivation on the tobacco plantations, it was supplemented by the 'task' system for processing work, such as stripping and prizing the tobacco. Depending on whether the slave was assessed as a 'full hand', 'three-quarter hand' or 'half hand', he or she would be expected to get through so much work; male and female slaves, if they were healthy adults, would both count as a 'full hand'. Within strict limits the 'task' system allowed slaves to set their own pace of work; this did not apply in Caribbean sugar production, where the pace of work was set, in effect, by the grinding capacity of the mill.[19]

In North America, female slaves were conscripted for field labour, as they were in the Caribbean. But planting tobacco seeds, or even transplanting the young plants, though demanding enough, was not nearly as gruelling as digging cane holes. Likewise harvesting tobacco leaves was hard work, but not as hard as bending to cut six-foot-long canes near the root with a heavy machete, stripping the cane and loading it on to carts. The weight of cane cut and carried by the Caribbean slave would have been eight or ten times that of the tobacco picked by the Virginian slave. Lorena Walsh cites tobacco output per labourer in eighteenth-century Virginia ranging from 400 to nearly 1,600 lb in a year. Jamaican slaves generally produced 8–12 hundredweight of sugar a year; thus the weight of the finished product could be roughly similar. But in the case of tobacco the leaf was simply dried and cured, while to produce a given quantity of muscovado sugar fifteen to twenty times the weight of cane had to be cut, carried and crushed. (To make 100 lb of sugar it was necessary to boil 100 gallons of cane juice, and to obtain this quantity of juice it was necessary to cut one ton of sugar cane.[20]) The introduction of secondary crops certainly boosted the workload of the slaves of Virginia and Maryland, but it was still probably less onerous than that on the sugar plantations, where ancillary and subsistence cultivation also had to be undertaken.[21]

Because the North American estates were smaller, and because the planter class was resident rather than absentee, there was more scope for the household employment of female slaves – not simply as personal servants but also as spinners, weavers, seamstresses, dairymaids, washer-women, cooks, ironers and nurses. In these capacities they catered to the needs of their fellow slaves as well as those of their owners. The climate of the Chesapeake was much colder in winter than the Caribbean. The slaves needed more and heavier clothing; much of this was spun and weaved on the plantation. A study of the work of slave women shows that the proportion engaged in non-field occupations on larger estates rose from under 15 per cent in the early decades to about a quarter after mid century, and reached a third or more by 1800; the proportion of males in non-field occupations was about the same, or slightly greater. Combined with the inherently lighter labour of the tobacco plantation, this pattern of female employment would have contributed to the reproduction of the slave labour force, both by raising the birth rate and by furnishing more adequate conditions of existence. While the data cited are for larger plantations, there can be little doubt that housewifely labour also fell to female slaves on the smaller estates. A survey of inventories cited in the study mentioned above shows that 71.4 per cent of households in Virginia and Maryland had spinning wheels in 1774, 14.4 per cent had brewing or cider-making equipment, and 9.4 per cent had butter- or cheese-making equipment.[22] Those slaves who worked primarily to reproduce the plantation as such had to work hard, but they produced specific use-values for the slave community; they were not subject to the market's limitless demand for commodities. While many of their evenings were taken up, there was neither a technical nor an economic reason to make them work all night, like the slaves of the sugar mills.

The North American regimes of plantation work can have offered few positive incentives for slave women to have children, but at least it did not directly destroy their fecundity. Other aspects of plantation life, however, probably played a part in persuading them to have children. In the North American context of relatively small-scale, semi-domestic slavery, the resident planters and their spouses were more appreciative of the economic and moral advantages of permitting family life among their slaves, and better placed to protect it, than the absentees of the British West Indies. The North American planters, large and small, constructed a colonial society that was itself at once familistic, conjugal and patriarchal. In the seventeenth century women who survived their husbands and remarried had played an important part in founding several fortunes. In the eighteenth century, American-born planters lived longer and aspired to patriarchal authority over wives and children. But the ideal of companionate marriage and marital fidelity was widely celebrated, so long as racial boundaries were strictly observed. A white woman who had sexual relations with a black man in Virginia would be condemned to five years' servitude. White men certainly did not flaunt their illicit relations with slave women, as commonly happened in the Caribbean. The overall incidence of such relations was less than in the Caribbean, and the mulatto population was smaller.[23]

The small and medium planters of North America lacked both the wealth and the apparatus of coercion available to the sugar magnates of the Caribbean. A slave with family attachments was less likely to run away, would be easier to motivate with petty concessions, and would work on the provision grounds more willingly. In North America planter, overseer and slave were far more likely literally to 'speak the same language' than was the case in the Caribbean; since slaveowners always had the whip-hand in any 'negotiation' they could invariably strike an advantageous verbal bargain. The letter quoted in the epigraph to this chapter gives an interesting example of the threats, pleading and promising this involved, rendered the more striking by the slave's literacy. The larger planters in North America, as resident proprietors, were more likely to see themselves in a patriarchal role and to be able to influence the conduct of their overseers. Joyce Chaplin writes of the planters' increasing tendency to subscribe to an ideal of 'humane' treatment while strengthening the bonds of enslavement. The correspondence of North American planters and merchants reflected a concern with slave reproduction and a willingness to adhere to verbal agreements. Thus Henry Laurence writes to his overseer: 'I send up a stout young woman to be a Wife to whom she shall like best among the single men. The rest of the Gentlemen shall be served as I have opportunity. Tell them that I do not forget their request.' Another planter, an absentee, writes to a friendly colonial official:

> And I shd be obliged to Yr Excellency, for advising those who may be concerned for me, in such Encrease of Negroes, not so much to consult my own Immediate Profit, as to render the Negroes I now have more contented and happy, wch I know they cannot be without having each a wife. This will greatly tend to keep them at home and to make them regular and tho the Women will not work all together so well as ye men, yet Amends will sufficiently be made in a very few years by the Great Encrease in children, who may be easily trained up and become fruitfully attached to the Glebe and their master.[24]

It would be possible to find Caribbean proprietors announcing similar wishes, but the overall context in North America was different. The physical demands of production were less ferociously destructive and the cultural context was more adapted to direct bargaining between master and slave.

The rudiments of family life encouraged slave women to have more children; doing so would offer some solace in the heavily circumscribed world of the slave. It has also been suggested that conditions in North America may have persuaded slave women to abandon practices that inhibited childbirth, such as lengthy breastfeeding, associated with long intervals between conception.[25] The abundance of foodstuffs in North America made unnecessary practices which had arisen where food shortage was a constant danger, as could be the case in both the Caribbean and Africa. The culture of the North American colonies was strongly familistic and monogamous. The North American plantations were generally smaller, and anyway better regulated, so they did not need to give special mating privileges to a male slave elite; polygyny was less common than it was in the West Indies.

Higman cites three Jamaican plantations where slave households comprising a male and a female, with or without children, constituted 38.5 per cent of all slave households. The reconstructions of Herbert Gutman imply a higher proportion of clearly conjugal households on North American slave plantations. Even on South Carolina plantations, which were closer in size and regime to the Caribbean pattern, the evidence of inventories cited by Philip Morgan shows that 66 per cent of slaves had stated family ties in 1760–69, rising to 79 per cent in 1790–99.[26] Allan Kulikoff cites information for Robert Carter's plantation in 1736: 70 per cent of the slaves lived in households with kin. But while 95 per cent of children under nine lived with their mothers, this proportion dropped to 61 per cent for those between ten and fourteen. For a sample of small plantations in 1776 cited by Kulikoff, 41 per cent did not cohabit with others, while 43 per cent of ten-to-fourteen-year-old slaves lived in separate dwellings. Thus while small children invariably lived with their mothers, this ceased to be true for youths. The sale of slaves, or their transfer within their owners' families, led to the break-up of slave households. Even though they were no longer resident on the same property, such slaves did their best to keep in touch with their kin.[27]

The presence of larger numbers of nursing slave mothers and their children on the North American tobacco plantation implied its own costs, but in prevailing conditions this was a less expensive way of reproducing the labour force. African slaves were more expensive in North America because of the longer voyage, and for those with reasonable security, interest rates ran at about half the level of those in the Caribbean. It seems unlikely that planters themselves computed the accrued interest on the money spent rearing infants, but in the climate engendered by lower interests rates there would have been a less hectic concern to recoup outlays than was common for West Indian planters.[28] In any case, the North American plantations were more self-sufficient in foodstuffs than the sugar plantations, a circumstance that reduced the costs of slave-rearing all the more in that most bought-in supplies would appear to have been of supplementary foodstuffs and clothing, mainly consumed by working slaves. The North American model of slave reproduction meant, in the abstract, that a somewhat higher proportion of the slaves were unavailable for production than might be the case for Caribbean plantations; in practice, however, the latter had their own burden of unproductive workers, since it was common for a quarter of the crew or more to be unable for work because of sickness. Altogether the emergence of positive reproduction rates among North American slaves was encouraged by a more favourable conjunction of climate, crop requirements and plantation regime, and was confirmed and consolidated by a more effective familistic regime. But perhaps the single most important consideration was supplied by the collective arrangements made for feeding the slaves, since these both reduced the chance of famine and encouraged child-rearing.

North American slaves were usually allowed to keep a few chickens and cultivate small garden plots near their huts; sometimes they could supplement their rations by fishing or hunting. But they were not given provision grounds and then expected to fend for themselves, with all the risk and extra toil that involved in the West Indies. Instead the planter or overseer would direct slave cultivation of maize and other foodstuffs on collective provision grounds. Likewise, slaves would weave cloth and tend livestock as part of the co-ordinated routine of the plantation. In Chapter X we saw that Caribbean slaves who received larger rations from their owners had a higher reproduction rate, and it was suggested that slave women, under these circumstances, saw the raising of children as less of a burden. The same considerations could well have encouraged North American slave women to have children. Slaveowners often found that the slaves worked more enthusiastically when put to the task of raising their own food. Reports of corn-shucking, and other activities linked directly to slave consumption, suggest that it was undertaken in a positive communal spirit, with singing or the telling of stories.[29]

If the material conditions of life of the North American slaves were somewhat easier than those of the Caribbean slaves, the same cannot be said for every aspect of their situation. The arrangements described above reduced the scope for autonomous economic activity by slaves. The planter might purchase a few items – eggs or vegetables – from his slaves, but rarely were they able to buy and sell as they pleased in a local market. Planters would themselves dispatch an overseer or responsible slave to market to buy little extras on behalf of those who remained on the plantation. On the South Carolina coast the slave community was in a majority, worked on large estates and had somewhat greater autonomy – here slaves spoke Gullah, a distinctive patois such as was spoken in Jamaica. The slaves of South Carolina also had better chances of effecting an escape, because Spanish territory was nearer and because Charleston was the only town of any size in the Southern colonies.

However, most North American blacks were inserted into a majoritarian white society that was neither disposed nor required to make concessions to an alien people or culture. From the earliest times the English colonists in North America were remarkable for their rigid attachment to their own way of life, their failure to find a *modus vivendi* with the Indians and their stolid confidence in their own superiority; they might display scientific curiosity about flora and fauna, but not the sympathetic interest in the indigenous population displayed by many Portuguese and Spanish clerics. In the Caribbean the English, Scottish and French planters and overseers confronted such a massive African presence that they were obliged to negotiate with, and make concessions to, the slave elite. In the Southern colonies an already consolidated white colonial society had a greater opportunity to impose itself on a fragmented slave population. There were initially fewer elite positions for slaves to occupy, and little need to promote a more favoured stratum. Very few slaves were ever manumitted, though a small free coloured population, dating from the days before a functioning slave system had existed, enjoyed a few civic rights.

Since the few Southern towns to be found were very small – Charleston, with 8,000 inhabitants in 1760, was the only exception – there was no significant urban milieu to qualify the self-enclosed rural world of slavery. The racial code operated in simple black-and-white terms, without those elaborate distinctions of shade and shape found in other New World slaveholding societies. All people of colour were 'blacks', and about 98 per cent of 'blacks' were slaves. The numbers of mulattoes seem to have been somewhat lower than elsewhere; but those there were had little likelihood of recognition or freedom from their white parent, even if the latter was their owner. In the Caribbean it was not unusual for slaves to be branded; on the Codrington plantations, bequeathed to the Society for the Promotion of Christian Knowledge, each slave was marked 'SOCIETY' with a red-hot iron. In North America branding appears to have been much rarer, but dark skin itself branded the slave more thoroughly.[30]

Mechal Sobel has argued that the culture of North American whites, despite its rigidity, did acquire strong African inflections because of the negotiations, however unequal, between slaves and the surrounding white population. Planters and overseers needed a *modus vivendi* with the key slaves on their plantation. The large planters increasingly came to rely on slave craftsmen, while their wives needed much slave help in bringing up their own children. Landon Carter chronicled in his diary his fraught relations with his manservant, the family slave Nassau Carter. When Nassau ran away, he complained: 'I have been learning to do without him, and though it has been but very badly yet I can bear it and will.'[31] When Lord Dunmore, Governor of Virginia, offered freedom to those slaves who would desert rebel planters, Nassau responded – but within a few months he was back bickering with his master. In many spheres of Virginian life – architecture, woodwork, cuisine, and even religion – the African presence made itself felt. Often this meant simply that slaveowners, with all too little acknowledgement, drew on slave know-how.

In the case of religion, the slaves demonstrated that their memories and experiences were still informed by an African matrix which was at variance with the repressed personality and utilitarian philosophy of so many of their owners. Sobel suggests that African conceptions of non-linear time and proper work rhythms had something in common with popular traditions among the poorer whites who did not subscribe to the latitudinarian rationalism of the large planters or the obsessive instrumentalism of the overseer stratum. The years 1740–70 were marked by a Protestant 'New Awakening' in which there was widespread involvement by both blacks and whites. This revivalist movement spoke to the spiritual needs of people who had been uprooted by the Atlantic boom, yet had not found a safe harbour. Thomas Rankin, a Methodist preacher, reported of one service:

> I preached from Ezekiel's vision of the dry bones: And there was a great shaking. I was obliged to stop again and again, and beg of the people to compose themselves. But they could not: some on their knees, and some on their faces,

were crying mightily to God all the time I was preaching. Hundreds of Negroes were among them, with the tears streaming down their faces.[32]

The slave appropriation of Christianity – or what George Whitefield once referred to as the 'miraculous compound of Paganism and Methodism' – aroused misgivings among many planters. The nature of such long-standing apprehensions had been expressed, not for the first time, by a colonial correspondent writing to the Bishop of London in 1710. Having heard of the Bishop's wish that slaves be taught the Christian religion, he lamented the 'confusion' that 'the best Negroe scholar was likely to create among his fellow Slaves for having put his own construction upon some Words of the Holy Prophet's that he had read'. This fear was well grounded, since in 1723 the Bishop of London received a letter from a Virginian slave who appealed to him to 'Releese us out of this Cruell Bondegg'. Since there are so few documents written by slaves at this early period, it is worth quoting at length:

> here it is to bee notd that one brother is a SLave to another and one Sister to an othe which is quite out of the way and as for mee my selfe I am my brothers SLave but my name is Secrett . . . wee are commanded to keep holey the Sabbath day and we doo hardly know when it comes for our task mastrs are has hard with us as the Egypttions was with the Childdann of Issarall god be marcifll unto us
>
> here follows our Sevarity and Sorrowfull Sarvice we are hard used on Every account in the first place wee are in Ignorance of our Salvation and in the next place wee are kept out of the Church and matrimony is deenied us and to be plain they doo Look no more upon us then if we ware dogs which I hope when these Strange Lines comes to your Lord Ships hands will be looket into. . . .
>
> we desire that our Childarn be putt to Scool and and Larnd to Reed through the Bybell which is all at prasant with our prayers to god for itts good Success before your honour these from your humbell Servants in the Lord my riting is vary bad I whope yr honour will take the will for the deede I am but a poore SLave that writ itt and has no other time butt Sunday and hardly that att Sumtimes
>
> September the 8th 1723
>
> To the Right Reverrand father in god my Lord arch bishup of J London these with care wee dare not Subscribe any man's name to this for feare of our masters for if they knew wee have Sent home to your honour wee Should goo neare to Swing upon the gallas tree.[33]

James Blair, the Bishop of London's Commissary in Virginia, seems to have been intermittently troubled by the restiveness of Virginia's slaves. William Byrd noted in his diary that on one occasion when he visited the Commissary he was treated to the recitation of a poem in Latin concerning the suppression of a rebellion among the Northern Neck slaves. In 1731 Blair reported to London:

> there was a general rumour among them [the slaves] that they were to be set free. And when they saw nothing came of it they grew angry and saucy, and met

in the night-time in great numbers, and talked of rising; and in some places of choosing their leaders. But by patroulling; and whipping all that were found abroad at unseasonable hours, they quietly broke all this design, and in one County, where they had been discovered to talk of a general cutting off of their Masters, there were four of the Ring-leaders hanged.[34]

A few years later Byrd wrote of his own presentiments of slave rebellion in a letter to the Earl of Egmont:

We have already at least ten thousand men of these descendants of Ham fit to bear arms, and their numbers increase every day, as well by birth as by importation. And in case there should arise a man of desperate courage among us, exasperated by a desperate fortune, he might with more advantage than Cataline kindle a servile war. Such a man might be dreadfully mischievous before any opposition could be formed against him and tinge our rivers, wide as they are, with blood.[35]

As it happens, a serious slave rebellion was to break out in South Carolina just three years after the composition of this letter.

Rising tension between Spain and Britain, leading to the outbreak of war, led the Spanish Governor at St Augustine, Florida, to revive the offer of freedom to slaves who escaped from the British North American colonies. This appeal seems to have been an extension of the standing promise to free all those who were Catholics, or willing to convert to Catholicism. The Governor of South Carolina reported the incitement 'for the Desertion of Negroes' in January 1739. A few months later it was reported that four slaves and one Irish Catholic had made good their escape to St Augustine. In September, events of a rather different description took place. Twenty slaves – predominantly Angolans and therefore putatively Catholic – commanded by one Jemmy rose in rebellion at Stono: 'Several Negroes joined them, they calling of liberty, marched on with colours displayed, and two drums beating, pursuing all the white people they met with, and killing Men, Woman and Child.' One innkeeper was spared by the rebels on the grounds that he was a good man. As the troop marched southwards, crossing the border with Georgia in the direction of Florida, the rebel troop swelled to sixty or a hundred, all 'Dancing, Singing and Beating Drums'.[36] The rebels decided to make camp in Georgia, and wait for other blacks to join them, but by this time the South Carolina militia attacked them, killing many, though a few, nevertheless, escaped. The British then sought to mount a land attack on Florida. This was repulsed at the strong point of Mose with the help of a coloured regiment commanded by Francisco Menéndez, a freedman.[37] Britain's acquisition of Florida under the terms of the Treaty of Paris (1763) enabled this threat to the North American slave order to be removed.

The Stono uprising fed the hopes and fears of colonists who looked askance at the transformations overtaking their society, and stimulated interest in George Whitefield's evangelical Christianity. One of Whitefield's followers, Hugh Bryan, a member of a prominent planter family, forecast the destruction of the colony by a slave revolt if there was not an immediate shunning of wickedness; he camped out in the woods with both white and black followers, arousing the hostility and suspicion of the generality of planters.[38] Whitefield himself urged that slaves should not be treated like brutes, but he certainly counselled slave subordination and became a slaveowner himself. Once the Great Awakening was under way, it inspired some attempts to catechize blacks; the Reverend Seward, sponsor of a Negro school, was killed by an anti-revivalist mob. The instructors of slaves invariably urged that it was better to suffer than to sin, and that they should unfailingly adopt a loyal and respectful demeanour towards their owners; but their students could draw their own conclusions. The advertisement for a runaway slave called Caesar, published in 1772, observed of him: 'can read, is a great professor of religion and has much to say on the subject'. An anonymous author in the *South Carolina Gazette* was alarmed that plans for religious instruction could open the floodgates, so that

> every idle or designing person that pleases, shall be at liberty to pursue Attempts not of this but of *another* and most dangerous nature: viz. gathering *Cabals* of negroes about him, without public authority, at unseasonable times, and the Disturbance of the Neighbourhood; and instead of teaching them the Principle of Christianity, filling their heads with a parcel of *Cant-Phrases*, *Trances*, *Dreams*, *Visions*, and *Revelations*, and something still worse which prudence forbids to name.[39]

Important though it was, the black appropriation of Christianity did not remove the gulf between black and white, nor displace the practical control exercised by the planters. The gentry stratum retained ultimate hegemony through all vicissitudes. Patriot planters like Patrick Henry spoke the language of popular enthusiasm, but incorporated it in the secular objective of the Patriot cause. While the drudgery of plantation labour fell to the slaves, the non-slaveholding majority of white colonists could sell some of their produce to the planter, or earn a little extra by working for him during the harvest. These economic opportunities had to compensate them for the fact that farmers without slaves could no longer hope to make much money out of cultivating tobacco, though they could cash in when prices rose, as they did in the 1750s. Another compensation available to the free white was the freedom to graze livestock on open ranges; while common land was subject to enclosure in England, in the Southern colonies unfenced backlands provided an axis of alignment between planters and yeomen. It made sense for the non-slaveholding white to raise hogs and grow vegetables, giving him both a minimum subsistence and a surplus commodity to sell to the planter or trader. While all the crops cultivated by slave labour required fairly constant and continuous labour, the farming activities of whites could be more intermittent. And of course, adult white males enjoyed far more extensive political rights in colonial America than their counterparts in

Europe. Intense ethnic conceit formed a bond between slaveholding planters and other whites, reinforced by the patronage the former were able to bestow on the latter, and by the dispersal of slaveownership.[40]

While a successful slave society flourished in the Chesapeake and further south, slavery remained modest or marginal in most of the Northern colonies. In the Middle Atlantic and New England colonies slaves comprised between 1 per cent and 5 per cent of the population. In these colonies there was, of course, no single export crop as important as tobacco, which could have meant that there were fewer resources with which to buy slaves. However, the Northern farmers did produce a marketed surplus for the towns and for the carrying trade to the plantation colonies. If slave labour could have been profitably engaged in Northern farming, then the farmers had enough cash to begin the construction of a slave system. In the years 1768–72 the thirteen colonies as a whole exported goods and provisions to the West Indies worth £775,000 annually, with about two-thirds coming from the Middle Atlantic and New England colonies.[41]

It has been argued that slave labour did not fit the work requirements or scale of production prevailing in the North, and there is some evidence for this. The climate of the Southern colonies meant that there were about 220–40 frost-free days in the year, during which slaves could be working the fields; in the Northern colonies there were only 160–80 frost-free days, giving less scope for slave toil. The general farming of the North needed much less continuous and co-ordinated labour, and was less easy to invigilate. In some parts there were pockets of slavery: by the 1770s slaves constituted 7 per cent of the population of Rhode Island and 8 per cent of the population of New Jersey. The Rhode Island slaves worked as porters, craftsmen or domestics; many were owned by merchants or richer citizens emulating the grand lifestyle. In New Jersey and New York, however, many Dutch farmers owned a few slaves and kept them reasonably busy. As Ira Berlin points out, these slaves 'worked at a variety of tasks and never labored in large gangs'.[42]

There was no absolute incompatibility between general farming and slavery, but it offered few advantages. There could, perhaps, have been some scope for the employment of slaves in manufacturing and construction. In the absence of any social pressure against slaveholding, there would probably have been more slaves in the North generally, especially in Massachusetts and Pennsylvania. The timber industry and the making of casks for the West Indies demanded fairly continuous labour; in the Southern colonies slaves were engaged in it, but not to any significant extent in the North. The absolute numbers of slaves in the Northern colonies increased in the course of the century but the enslaved proportion of the population fell nearly everywhere. In 1741, during the war with Spain, an extensive conspiracy was discovered in New York, involving Irish and free people of colour as well as slaves, some of the latter being troublemakers who had been offloaded by West Indian owners. An outbreak of fire was believed to be the work of slave arsonists. Even short of such dangerous proceedings the ethos of the towns was not favourable to slavery, since slaves inescapably had more autonomy while the generality of the free population had little incentive to maintain the privileges of slaveowners. In Spanish or Portuguese America it was said that the urban slave was half-free; in the English colonies institutions for regulating urban slavery were less developed (and in the Southern colonies few so-called towns had a population over a thousand). Following events such as the conspiracy of 1741 there was reluctance to buy West Indian blacks, and from mid century the overall proportion of slaves in the population fell – from 14.4 per cent in New York in 1750 to 11.7 per cent in 1770, or from 2.4 per cent in Pennsylvania in 1750 to 2.1 per cent in 1780. These were times when Northern slaveholders might incur a degree of unpopularity if they used slaves in ways that seemed to threaten or undercut the position of free workers. It was also a period when numbers of those held as slaves came forward in the North, pleading that they had been unjustly cheated of a manumission due to them. The fact that juries could be sympathetic to such appeals must have been a deterrent to Northern slaveholding.[43]

Favoured alike by their natural setting and by the circuits of Atlantic trade, the North American mixture of social relations produced what was already one of the richest societies in the world. With a total population of under two-and-a-half million, the thirteen colonies could afford to import goods worth nearly four million pounds sterling in the years before the Revolution. With a highly productive domestic economy, foreign trade per capita was around £2.4 in 1769, just a little behind the mid-century figure for Britain (£2.8), well ahead of Holland and Belgium (£1.7), Spain (£1.6), Portugal (£1.1), and France (£0.5).[44] The commodity exports of the North American colonies were worth some £2.8 million, of which £1,528,000 went to Britain and £759,000 to the Caribbean; the other main trade outlet was Southern Europe (notably Portugal and Spain) and the Atlantic or Wine Islands, to which just over £400,000 of fish, rice and wheat were exported. In the years 1768–72 the main export commodities were as in Table XI.2:

Table XI.2   Exports of the Thirteen Colonies 1768–72

In £			
Tobacco	766,000	Fish	154,000
Wheat and Flour	410,000	Indigo	113,000
Rice	312,000		

Source: G.M. Walton and J.F. Shepherd, *The Economic Rise of Early America*, Cambridge 1979, p. 81.

The West Indian islands were supplied with livestock and wood products as well as dried fish and cereal products. On the eve of the Revolution the provisions trade to the West Indies, especially the foreign West Indies, was rising more rapidly than the already established tobacco trade. The Navigation Acts had long diverted the tobacco of Virginia and Maryland to British ports – with Glasgow gaining on London – even though nine-tenths was destined for resale to Europe; about a quarter of the crop was purchased each year by the French royal monopoly. The commercial operations of the British factors lowered the price planters received by as much as a third; the price obtained by the planters for Virginian tobacco sold outside Britain was about £3 a ton less than could have been realized by a direct trade.[45] Resentment at this was intensified by the steady decline of tobacco prices after about 1750. The rising sales of wheat and maize gave some relief; nevertheless, many planters were indebted to the British factors or commission agents, and this exacerbated bad relations with the metropolis. Timothy Breen has shown how deeply the larger planters identified with tobacco. They took pride in the quality of their product – it would often carry their own mark. They were pained if merchants and factors they looked on as friends pressed them for payment. The tobacco crises of the 1760s and 1770s did not signal the exhaustion of the slave economy – its vigorous contribution to wheat, rice and indigo cultivation was proof of that – but did stir the planter's ire and direct it at the mother country.[46]

Breen's reading of the mentality on the great tidewater portrays it as innocent of well-founded economic reasoning. Some of the large Virginia planters whose correspondence he cites were extravagant or improvident, and no doubt most of them cultivated values different from those of the urban merchant. But their complaints that the British merchants were not prepared to share more risks with them, and were overeager to get them to produce tobacco to the neglect of other crops, had substance. One such planter wrote to London with a scheme to make his creditors his partners: 'if you'll advance me a Sum of Money, at 3½ or 4 per cent to be laid out in Negroes, their Crops shall be mark'd with a distinguishing Mark from the rest, & the Produce annually remain Untouched & go to discharge the Money so advanc'd.' He had just informed the merchants: 'I have been & still am, Very unfortunate in my slaves dying, having lost as many of my Men, with these ten years, as would Amount to 1,000 pounds.'[47] In this view, while the merchants reaped the profits, the planters were left with risks – such as slaves so inconsiderate of their masters' welfare as to die on them. Of course the merchants could burn their hands too, but they rarely allowed debts to go above the value of an estate. Since they knew what a planter could produce, and what he was spending his money on, they had an excellent basis on which to formulate their credit policy, and had only themselves to blame if they made a mistake. John Robinson, Speaker and Treasurer of Virginia's House of Burgesses between 1738 and

1768, developed his own way of meeting the credit needs of fellow planters who were in temporary difficulty: he lent them used notes which the Treasury was meant to destroy. Discovery of this practice precipitated a scandal, paralleling that in Martinique, and showed the planter's thirst for credit.

The British merchants' preference for tobacco was easily explained: although they acted as bankers and suppliers to the planters, they were essentially tobacco traders and had no use for other Virginian products. The planter might have a financially cogent scheme for restocking his plantation, and devoting half his resources to wheat or hemp, when the latter's price rose, but the British merchant would not be impressed, since there was only one crop he was interested in. As one Virginian put it, the British merchants 'take every step in their power to keep the Planters imploy'd in the Commodity [tobacco], and often refuse to purchase their Hempe, by which means many people are deterred from cultivating it . . .'.[48]

The selective and prejudicial policy of the British merchants created openings for local merchants. The growing role of colonial merchants in the Southern colonies, carrying Virginian wheat or corn and South Carolina rice to purchasers in Portugal, Spain, the Wine Islands or the foreign Caribbean, helped to promote the diversification of Southern slave agriculture. Jacob Price describes the 'growth of the independent indigenous merchant' as 'the most dynamic feature of the Chesapeake economy during the 1760s and 1770s'.[49] The Scottish publishers of John Mair's much-reprinted guide to double-entry bookkeeping and mercantile practice, *Book-keeping Methodiz'd*, later retitled *Book-keeping Moderniz'd*, added a chapter on the colonial merchant.

Protectionist legislation, enacted to assist the British West Indies, notoriously interfered with the carrying trade to the foreign Caribbean. According to Shepherd and Walton, the registered imports of the Northern colonies in the years 1768 to 1772 included an annual average of goods worth £771,000 from the West Indies (mainly British), of which no less than £606,000 was accounted for by sugar, molasses and rum. Coffee was officially entered at the modest total of £15,000. The significant contraband trade with the French islands in these products shows up only to the extent that false origins were given for declared goods.

If the Navigation Acts and other commercial restrictions constituted a burden on the plantation and provision trades, they were far from crippling colonial wealth. The commission taken by the Scottish or English tobacco factors declined over time as they increased the efficiency of their operations: whereas Amsterdam tobacco prices were 83 per cent higher than those in Philadelphia in 1720–24, they were 51 per cent higher by 1770–72.[50] Exports of indigo rose in response to the payment of a bounty by the British Exchequer from the 1740s onwards. A variety of manufactures were discouraged, or even prohibited, by British regulations, mainly non-perishable consumer goods; the extent of home manufacture on farm and plantation also limited demand for such items unless they were of superior quality or mass produced, in which case they were generally imported. Twenty-five sugar refineries and 140 rum distilleries met much of local demand, albeit with the help of contraband supplies of molasses. The average size of saw mills and flour mills was rising. Some 82 furnaces and 175 forges produced as much simple ironware as was being turned out in Britain itself. Colonial shipyards built 40,000 tons of shipping a year in the decade before the Revolution.[51]

The Navigation Acts permitted colonial earnings from shipping, seamen's wages and the sale of naval stores. In the years before the Revolution the Northern colonies earned some £600,000 annually from shipping and £140,000 from the sale of ships.[52] Intercolonial trade, the West Indian carrying trade, and the South European trade were almost entirely conducted in North American ships. In this epoch ownership of ships was highly correlated with mercantile enterprise, since it was the chief capital cost the merchant had to face. While the tobacco trade was in the hands of British merchants, the West India trade was engrossed by American merchants; some of the latter also traded with Africa.

Alice Hanson Jones's research indicates that the private physical wealth per free person in North American colonies in 1774 was £76, and their per capita income was in the range £14–£25 a year.[53] In Britain at this time per capita income was £18, according to Arthur Young's estimates. In North America the average holdings, and estimated income, of the free colonists of the South were nearly three times as great as those in New England and the Middle colonies. The slave plantations were the source of this contrast, as Table XI.3 shows:

Table XI.3   Wealth per Free Person 1774

in £	New England	Middle Col.	Southern Col.	Overall
Land	27	28	55	38
Slaves/Servants	0	2	58	21
Livestock	3	5	9	6
Tools/Equip.	1	1	3	2
Crops, etc.	1	3	5	3
Total	38	46	137	76

Source: Alice Hanson Jones, 'Components of Private Wealth per Free Capita for the 13 Colonies by Region, 1774', in US Bureau of Census, *Historical Statistics: Colonial Times to 1970*, Washington, DC 1976, p. 1175.

The figures for per capita wealth include children and women, though 90 per cent held no wealth in their own right. The average value of slavehold-ings in the South for each wealth-holder was £132.6: in Virginia the average wealth-holder owned seven slaves, while in Charleston he owned 33 slaves. There was, of course, considerable inequality within the ranks of the wealth-holders and slaveholders. Just over 40 per cent of Southern wealth-holders, and 36 per cent of farmers, owned no slaves at all. The richest 10 per cent of wealth-holders accounted for nearly half of all net worth in the Southern colonies. Mercantile fortunes in New England, New York and Philadelphia also yielded quite high indices of inequality, yet overall inequality was much greater in Britain or in the West Indies. Average wealth-holding per free person in Jamaica reached £1,200 around this time, even though many white employees owned no slaves. It was a measure of the relatively egalitarian pattern of slaveholding that three-quarters of all Virginian slaveholders owned between 3 and 25 slaves, and that 59 per cent of all Southern wealth-holders owned a slave.[54]

Stanley Engerman and Kenneth Sokoloff have produced estimates for wealth per capita in British America in 1774 which somewhat extend and refine the above contrasts. They calculate that if slave wealth is excluded and if total wealth is divided up among all persons, whether free or slave, then the wealth-holding per capita of the British colonies came out at £36.6 for New England, £41.9 for the Middle Atlantic colonies, £54.7 for the Southern colonies and £84.1 for Jamaica. Of course, the rather high score of the plantation colonies, even with slave property excluded – and the total remaining wealth spread over all inhabitants – still reflects the value conferred on agricultural property because of the presence of the unfree workers.[55]

The distribution of wealth in colonial North America encouraged a widespread sense of confidence and independence among citizens who prided themselves on their role in checking royal tyranny in 1688–89 and who, after the Seven Years War, no longer needed to fear the French. The metropolitan government taxed the North Americans very lightly; on the other hand, it performed very few services for them. The colonists actively resented imperial attempts to restrain their westward expansion at the expense of the Native Americans. While English forms of law and self-government were highly appreciated, they did not require the remote authority of a British establishment. Given their aspirations to a civilized existence, the Southern gentry were concerned at the tiny size of their towns and the absence of such civic institutions as universities and theatres. In the economic sphere the colonial government made only a modest contribution – it did not even furnish an adequate currency, so that Spanish silver dollars, or even tobacco, had to act as the circulating medium. Average wealth-holdings were high, while the combination of planting, cash crop farming, naval construction and trading gave an autonomous basis to the economy for which there was no parallel in the West Indies. The fact that there was a large white presence in the plantation zone meant that the planters' security was in their own hands. If free North Americans suffered some disabilities within the British colonial system, they had a solid base from which to attack it. In doing so they represented the revolt of colonial wealth against the conditions which had given it birth.

The American Revolution was certainly something far more than simply a rejection of colonial mercantilism – as the ideals proclaimed in the Declaration of Independence made clear. From the outset the colonists announced a boycott of the Atlantic slave trade, while at its most radical the Revolution even provoked the first legislative attacks on slavery (notably Pennsylvania's Emancipation Act of 1780). But the main thrust of the Revolution was obviously not aimed at plantation slavery; indeed, its most prominent champions included slaveholders and carrying-trade merchants who looked forward to an unfettered advance of the North American involvement in plantation commerce. In 1779 the British renewed the offer, first made by Dunmore in 1775, of manumission to slaves who abandoned rebel masters. This offer was made simply with the intention of disrupting the rebel forces, and any wider anti-slavery message was scrupulously avoided. But it had the effect of rallying wavering planters to the side of the rebellion. The great majority of slaves stayed on the plantations, using the disturbance of the times to win easier conditions for the duration; only a minority of perhaps twenty thousand or so found the opportunity and confidence to respond to the British appeals, or to seek escape to Florida or the North. During the war years the great bulk of the white population in the South was armed and organized, ready to suppress servile resistance with great harshness; at the same time the regime of slave work and punishment was considerably eased, both because crops could not be sold and because such a concession seemed advisable in the circumstances.[56]

The War of Independence, and the difficult years which immediately followed the War, severely tested the institution of slavery in North America – yet it survived. The pressures and cross-pressures of political, social and military conflict created a climate in which moderate anti-slavery made some gains. Many tens of thousands of slaves were offered manumission by their owners during, or immediately after, the conflict and slavery itself was ended in some Northern states. The recovery from the wartime disruption of trade and of plantation discipline took time. Even with the advent of peace, exports of indigo and rice did not recover, as new producers had established themselves in the market. North American tobacco now moved directly to its European markets and in the late 1780s it was worth a quarter more than in 1768–72; but the wars of 1793–1815 created many difficulties for the tobacco planters, with European conflicts disrupting access to major markets. The slave trade itself had been suspended at the outset of the War, and was only partially reinstituted at its close.

Yet despite such difficulties the numbers of slaves in the United States continued to grow. According to the Census of 1790 there were 658,000 slaves in the Southern states, their number having nearly doubled in two decades; this was repeated in the next two decades with 1,164,000 slaves in the South by 1810.[57] The slavery of the Southern United States proved able to survive difficult times because of economic versatility, relative security and demographic buoyancy. When trade links were cut, slaves could be put to subsistence cultivation and household manufacture. When they were restored, there were new as well as old crops that could be cultivated for sale. After public advertisement in the Southern states offering a reward for a method of ginning inland cotton, a suitable gin devised by Eli Whitney in 1793 permitted the construction of a promising new sector of plantation production. Although they were still in their infancy, the US cotton plantations raised output from 2 million lb to 48 million lb in the course of the 1790s.[58] By the turn of the century the United States was supplying a third of the cotton required by Britain's rapidly expanding cotton manufacturing industry. Following the slave uprising in Saint Domingue and a major slave conspiracy in Virginia in 1800, security in the slave States was tightened and concessions made to free people of colour in the more idealistic atmosphere of the 1780s were withdrawn. Because the white population grew a little faster than the black, there was still an armed white majority to meet any threat of slave unrest.

The birth of the North American republic had a large impact on the plantation-related trade of the rest of the Americas. United States exports to the French, Spanish, Portuguese and Dutch colonies reached nearly £1 million annually in 1790–92, representing 24 per cent of the total. Provisions and equipment for the plantations loomed large in this trade. The tonnage of US shipping registered as engaged in overseas commerce totalled 346,000 tons, twice that of the tonnage of British shipping involved in the Atlantic trade, in 1770; by 1801 the tonnage of US commercial shipping more than doubled to 718,400. Merchants from New York, Boston and Philadelphia traded with all parts of the Caribbean and Americas in sugar, cotton, coffee, cacao and indigo, much of which was then re-exported to Europe. They offered powerful economic as well as ideological encouragement to creole aspirations to American independence. The total export trade of the United States grew fivefold in the period 1790 to 1807, swelled by its role as entrepôt for the plantation produce of the Americas, to reach over $60 million (over £10 million).[59]

Slavery in Brazil's Golden Age

Portugal's mercantile absolutism received a new infusion of life from the discovery and exploitation of gold in the southern captaincies of Brazil in the late 1690s. In order to defend Portugal's declaration of independence from Spain, and to eject the Dutch from Brazil and Angola, the House of Bragança had been obliged to grant special rights or powers successively to the nobility, the Jesuits, the New Christian merchants, and sections of the colonial elite. The arduous task of negotiating with such discrepant social forces weakened the monarchy. Eventually the best efforts of its more talented, 'modernizing' servants had been frustrated: Father Vieira lost his remaining influence in 1667, and the Count of Ericeira committed suicide in 1690. The arrival of a swelling stream of gold in the first decades of the century strengthened the independence of the monarchy; the Cortes was not called once in the eighteenth century, since royal revenues were sufficient. During the long reign of João V (1706–50) Portugal's new colonial wealth was used mainly to enhance royal power over far-flung dominions and to construct a splendid late baroque Court in Portugal itself. While Portugal's ruling institutions assumed the fixity of a gorgeous tableau, large numbers of Portuguese left a metropolis still afflicted by poverty and backwardness to find their fortune in Brazil.

The productive vigour of Portugal and its Empire had suffered when Vieira's attempt to woo back the New Christians and Ericeira's manufacturing projects had been sabotaged by clerical, commercial and agrarian conservatism. Portugal, a wool-producing country, spent hugely on English woollen goods, re-exporting them to Brazil and Africa. Renewed British help against Spain led to the negotiation of a fateful commercial pact with London, the Methuen Treaty of 1703. Portuguese wines were to be admitted to England at a tariff one-third lower than that applying to French wines, so long as British textile manufactures were accorded a similar preference in the markets of the Portuguese dominions. English exports to Portugal and her colonies rose from about half a million pounds annually, at the time when the Treaty was signed, to £1.1 million annually by 1736–40, out of a total British export trade of £6.1 million. The Methuen Treaty stimulated the wine trade of Oporto and Madeira, a trade largely in the hands of British merchants, but Britain invariably earned a heavy surplus on its commerce with Portugal – the latter was usually paid for by British acquisition of Brazilian gold. Between 1700 and 1760 Britain gained some £25 million in gold bullion from this commerce. This influx of gold made a crucial contribution to the stability of the Bank of England and the City of London. It allowed Britain to finance a deficitary trade with the East; the profitable operations of the East India Company required these infusions, since there was still little demand for European manufactures in India or the Far East. On the other hand, Britain's trade with Portugal and its islands and colonies, above all Brazil, furnished a valuable outlet for wheat, woollen and cotton textiles, and other manufactures.[60]

The uneven commerce between Britain and Portugal claimed the lion's share of the Brazilian gold bonanza. Brazil's annual gold output rose from 4,410 kg annually in 1706–10 to 8,500 kg in 1726–29. From 1730 to 1770, Brazil produced an average of ten thousand kilos – 350,000 ounces

– of gold every year. Gold output peaked in 1760, then declined to 6,285 kg annually in the years 1780–84, and to 4,510 kg in 1790–94. Bullion exports were worth around £750,000 a year in the period of maximum output (1735–65). Although this was certainly an impressive figure – and, because of contraband, may have understated the true amount – it was still not very much greater than the overall value of sugar exports: between £500,000 and £700,000 a year in the early decades of the century.[61] The Methuen Treaty gave no privileges to Brazilian sugar, which had to make its way in European markets without any favours or subsidies. The Portuguese royal officials concentrated much of their attention on making sure that the King received his 'royal fifth' of the gold produced in Brazil, and in so far as they still sought to levy as much as they could on plantation products, this handicapped them in the face of Caribbean competition.

Brazil remained in the front rank of sugar producers for some time after the Peace of Utrecht. Although it did not subsequently match the growth of the Caribbean islands, the volume and value of its sugar output rose rapidly in response to any interruption of Caribbean supplies – most specifically of French supplies, since Brazilian plantations were better able to meet British than French competition. Scattered and incomplete information suggests exports of 15,000 tons in 1710, which must have been difficult to maintain in the 1720s and 1730s. According to Deerr, the 1760 crop reached as much as 28,000 tons; exaggerated as this probably is, Schwartz also cites quite high figures for the captaincies where information is available in the mid 1760s. Finally, Alden has assembled contemporary estimates for all three sugar-producing captaincies – Pernambuco, Bahia and Rio de Janeiro – which come to the modest total of 12,000 tons in 1790, when Brazil's trade would have been squeezed hardest by the sugar industry of Saint Domingue. Seymour Drescher estimates Brazilian sugar exports in 1780 at the rather high figure of 19,150 tons of muscovado sugar, or 6.6 per cent of supplies reaching the North Atlantic markets; at this level, if it was achieved, Brazil was still the third-largest American sugar producer, behind Saint Domingue (29.8 per cent) and Jamaica (17.0 per cent) and just ahead of Martinique (6.5 per cent).[62]

Eighteenth-century Brazil was also an important producer of other plantation crops: tobacco throughout the century and cotton, indigo and rice in the later years. But so long as it lasted – that is to say, down to the end of the 1760s – the gold boom constrained plantation production by placing a strong upward pressure on the price of slaves and of other inputs, such as equipment and provisions; by furnishing a more attractive outlet for available capital; and by pushing up the cost of transport.

Colonial Brazil's primary labour force, whether in the plantations or gold workings, was supplied by enslaved blacks. Semi-servile Indians and free Portuguese immigrants remained of some importance, but did not supply the main labour input for the export sector. The great majority of the roughly 1.8 million Africans brought across the Atlantic by the Luso-Brazilian slave trade remained in Brazil. Since there are no comprehensive census data for Brazil, estimates of its black slave population are highly speculative: in 1700 there could have been 80,000–120,000 black slaves, comprising about a third of the total population; in 1750 there must have been more than half a million black slaves out of a total population of 1.5 million. A census of 1798 recorded the presence of no fewer than 1,582,0000 slaves – some of them, perhaps, Indians – out of a total population of 3,248,000.[63] The greater security, simplicity and cost-efficiency of the South Atlantic branch of the slave traffic meant that, traditionally, prices were lower and slave labour was cheaper for Brazilian planters and miners. A succession of gold rushes pushed prices in the sugar zone up from 80 milreis in 1700 to 120 milreis in 1710 and 140 milreis in 1750. In the gold districts themselves, taxes and transport costs raised the price of a prime male slave to 400 milreis by 1735. The importation of 10,000 slaves annually in 'poor' years, rising to 20,000 slaves annually in the 1730s, was the prodigious colonial response to the opportunities presented by gold mining.[64]

In 1751 the Camara of Salvador estimated that on a sugar estate the cost of slave maintenance ran at 16 per cent of annual expenses, of replacing slaves at 19 per cent, of the salaries of free workers at 23 per cent and of fuel for the mill at between 12 and 21 per cent depending on location. A slave cost one hundred times the price of an *arroba* of sugar, and could produce 40 *arrobas* in one year. In terms of gross revenue the sum spent purchasing a slave would, therefore, be recouped in two years six months. This was twice as long as it took to recoup such an investment in 1700 or earlier. Moreover, in terms of net revenues, deducting all expenses other than slave replacement, it took much longer to recoup the outlay – perhaps six or eight years. The slaves were the most costly factor of production on a sugar estate, accounting for 36 per cent of its value; land was valued at 19 per cent, livestock at 4 per cent, buildings at 18 per cent and machinery at 23 per cent. This breakdown is similar to the Jamaican plantation inventories cited by Sheridan, though the average value of Brazilian sugar estates would have been lower. According to Schwartz, the Bahian sugar mills had an average output of 32 tons a year, those of Pernambuco only 13 tons a year; if earlier achievements are anything to go by, the Rio mills were probably closer to the Bahian average. These quantities compare with sugar output per mill of 124 tons in Saint Domingue in the 1760s and 70 tons per mill in Jamaica in the 1780s. In Brazil, becoming a *senhor de engenho* brought social prestige and conferred some fiscal privileges; *lavradores de cana* sought to enter the ranks of the *senhores de engenho*, and it proved difficult to stop them. The *senhores de engenho* were bidding against the *mineiros* so far as nearly every one of these expenditures was concerned, except for the purchase of the sugar-making equipment itself. However, they did have one resource that was not available to most *mineiros*: access to cheap credit. Charitable brotherhoods such as the Misericordia and the Third Orders of St Francis and St Anthony were willing to make well-secured loans to *senhores de engenho* and *lavradores de cana* at 6.24 per cent per year, a rate fixed by canon and civil law. This facility, together with the inherent versatility of a slave crew that could be switched between different uses and crops, may help to explain some of the resilience of Brazil's sugar mills and estates. While many were to be described as *fogo morto*, or inactive, in the many poor years of this century, several managed to flicker back into life when market conditions improved. The Benedictine estates even managed to combine good results with better conditions for the slaves.[65]

The gold discoveries in the Paulista region to be known as Minas Gerais led to a build-up in its slave population to 33,000 in 1713. Minas Gerais became a captaincy in 1720, and its slave population had grown to over 100,000 by 1738.[66] The large and ill-defined hinterland of São Paulo also contained two other gold-bearing areas, Goias and Mato Grosso, which became separate captaincies in 1744 and 1748 respectively. In a number of districts diamonds as well as gold were discovered. In the early decades of the century some 2,000–3,000 Africans were imported each year by the gold-mining districts, and that figure was greatly exceeded in the middle decades. During the early gold rush, slaveowners from the North East, especially *lavradores de cana* who had no mill investments, were tempted away from sugar cultivation. After the first few lucky strikes, panning for alluvial gold, and washing it in open placer mines, required intense and harsh labour. The royal authorities, and their contractors, would grant concessions to those with the labour to work them. Mining enterprises employing slaves were somewhat easier to invigilate; thus the authorities could be more certain of collecting the royal fifth from them. Companies of Royal Dragoons stationed in the gold fields offered guarantees against both smugglers and recalcitrant slaves.[67]

Royal revenues from the gold fields never quite matched the great expectations invested in them; returns were depleted by corruption or contraband, and considerable sums were absorbed by colonial administration and defence. But if the direct yield to the Crown from the gold fields was disappointing, this was more than compensated for by the royal authorities' success in regulating and taxing colonial commerce as a whole, including imports generated by the gold boom. The build-up of the free and enslaved populations of the interior mining districts created a large demand for equipment and provisions; taxes were payable on all goods entering Minas Gerais, and efforts were made to establish local sources of supply. As late as the 1780s, 4,000 slaves a year were sent to Minas Gerais from Rio, despite the extra taxes that still had to be paid.

According to one estimate, Brazil's trade grew from about £2.5 million in 1710 to reach £4 million by 1750 and as much as £5 million in 1760, when gold output was still high and the colony's sugar industry could take advantage of reduced Caribbean supplies.[68] Tobacco and hides made a significant contribution to colonial commerce and the Royal Exchequer; about 7 million lb of tobacco was exported annually in the first decade of the century, 13 million lb annually in 1756–60 and 23 million in 1774–78. Sweet-cured Brazilian tobacco furnished the Portuguese Crown with its single most important fiscal instrument, and secured specialized markets in Africa, Canada and the Far East. The Crown had a direct stake in the slave trade itself through the Cacheco Company, trading on the Guinea coast. About a third of Brazil's slave imports were paid for directly by the tobacco treated with molasses which West Africans favoured; a trade good which loomed large in the operations of the Cacheco Company. Tobacco was a small planters' crop, but the most onerous processing work – twisting and rolling tobacco leaves steeped in the molasses mixture – was reserved for slaves. Gold also played some part in the Africa trade.[69]

The peculiarly mercantile basis of Portuguese absolutism persisted into the eighteenth century. In 1716 two-thirds of royal revenue still derived from the colonial and mercantile complex: 31.9 per cent from customs duties, 19.2 per cent from the tobacco farm, 5 per cent from the Brazil convoy dues, and 13.7 per cent from the royal mint and gold *quinta*.[70] The gold discoveries boosted this latter item. A convoy system enabled the Crown to keep track of its bullion receipts and colonial trade. For greater security separate fleets were assembled at Recife, Bahia, Belém and Rio de Janeiro. The obligation to use the *frota* raised freight charges, and exposed the planters and merchants to onerous taxation; when the convoy system was discontinued in 1765, it seems to have been followed by an increase in sugar shipments. Merchants as a body were confined within the corporate organization of the economy; the key posts in the Navy, Army and metropolitan administration were still reserved to *fidalgos* and members of the *nobreza militar*. Rich colonials could, however, buy local political office and lucrative contracts supplying the mining districts, the convoys or the slave trade.[71]

The gold workings which supplied the most dynamic element in Brazil's economy in the first half of the century imposed dire mortality rates on those who laboured in them. The slaves worked in groups of six or twelve, with many *mineiros* owning no more slaves than this, though a small number would own as many as thirty or fifty. The work of sifting the gold could be carried on throughout the year; it often required the slaves to spend many hours immersed in cold water, leading to many illnesses and a high death rate. As on the plantations, some skilled or responsible tasks that were assigned to slaves: supervision of the gold teams and prospecting for gold or diamonds were often delegated to trusted slaves by owners who found conditions hard themselves. Minas Gerais attracted many free Paulistas and Portuguese immigrants, but even gold hunger did not lead them to compete for long with slaves in the cruel labour of routine gold-panning. *Mineiros* with a good concession favoured slaves themselves, because their actions were easier to control. The gold worker always had some possibility of cheating the *mineiro* by secreting a small quantity about their person. Black slaves were often forbidden to move from the mine they were working, and heavy sanctions could be attached to those who had commercial dealings with them; free immigrant labourers could not be treated in this way. It was said that the *mineiros* had a preference for slaves arriving from Whydah and Minah, ports whose hinterlands included metalworking regions. Goulart estimates that the number of slaves in the gold fields in mid century totalled approximately 150,000, with slave purchases of 6,000 a year in 1739–59.[72]

The main gold discoveries were the work of seasoned Paulista veterans of the backlands; these men were of partly native extraction, and often spoke Tupi or other Indian languages. If they were successful they gained the rights to exploit a concession, but before long any new mining zone would attract Emboabas, immigrants from Portugal or the coast, who had the resources to import slaves. The royal authorities exploited the antagonism between Paulistas and Emboabas to increase their own leverage. Free blacks, however, were officially discouraged in the mining zone, since they complicated the problem of keeping track of gold; the authorities preferred a situation where any black caught outside the placer mine with gold on his person could be assumed to be a miscreant. However, official attempts to control the mining zone by such regulations were ultimately frustrated. Some *mineiros* found that it made sense to motivate slaves by offering manumission, or payments which could be saved up for this purpose. In the wild conditions prevailing in the mining zone the free black population was swelled by runaways or by the death of intestate owners. The authorities may have encouraged some manumissions by establishing a tax on slaves, set at two oitavos or 7.2 grams of gold.[73]

In the insecure conditions of the mining provinces, free blacks generally needed a powerful protector, so manumission sometimes entailed little besides a formal change. Even those who were formally slaves often worked without supervision and for incentive payments. Masters would arm slaves for their own protection and, on occasion, order them to attack free persons. Some found it more profitable to use their slaves as itinerant pedlars than as miners – female slaves known as *negras de tabuleiro* earned good money for their owners hawking in the streets and taverns. As royal officials themselves complained, slavery in Minas Gerais had a laxity rarely encountered elsewhere in the Americas. In 1719 the Governor wrote:

> Without severe punishment against the blacks it could happen one day that this captaincy shall become a pitiable stage for their evil deeds and that which occurred at Palmares in Pernambuco will be repeated; or even worse for the freedom which the blacks of this captaincy have [is] unlike that in other parts of America, certainly it is not true slavery the manner in which they live today as it more appropriately could be called licentious liberty.[74]

While the special features of the slave order in Gerais helped to boost the size of the free coloured population, a proliferation of militia forces, many recruited from the free people of colour, secured the social order and a flow of revenue. While royal officials wished to ensure slave subordination, they also needed to monitor and repress the slaveowners' gold-smuggling activities. The companies of *pardos e bastardos forros* or *pretos e pardos forros* were deployed by the authorities against any troublemakers or smugglers. The more specific problem of slave run-aways was dealt with by the private bands of the *capitão do mato*, or bush captains.

The royal officials welcomed the gold discoveries – not only because of the revenues they could claim, but also because they boosted the colonial population of the vast interior and drove back the formidable native tribes. The colonial backlands were dominated by the *poderosos do sertão*, men who owned herds of several thousand cattle, claimed hundreds of thousands of hectares of grazing land and could defend their empires by fielding several hundred *agregados*. These men also owned slaves, both Indian and African. They supplied meat to both the mining zones and the plantations; they also sold hides for leathermaking. By 1749 Pernambuco alone had 27 tanneries employing over 300 slaves in an industry that was geared to exports.

During the ministry of the Marquis of Pombal (1750–77), special attempts were made to stimulate and diversify Brazil's plantation economy. Colonial companies chartered in Pará, Maranhão and Pernambuco showed that they could play a part in protecting infant plantations or ailing industries. These companies were allowed to introduce slaves under favourable credit terms. They undertook the large-scale cultivation of rice, cacao, cotton and indigo, with mixed results. These companies enjoyed special privileges and made reasonable profits; the Maranhão Company yielded 8.4 per cent annually to its investors in the years 1768–74, while the Pernambuco Company yielded just under 6 per cent in 1760–79. The merchants and contractors who ran the companies often did better than those who simply invested. Pombal's adherence to mercantilist instruments was not indiscriminate. Since a reform of the convoy system in 1751 failed to make it less cumbersome and expensive, it was abandoned in 1765 as a hindrance to Brazil's trade in plantation produce. Following Pombal's fall, the troubles of other American plantation economies vindicated his investment in diversification. In the 1750s Portugal imported large quantities of rice from South Carolina; by the 1770s all Portugal's rice imports were supplied by Maranhão, free of any tariff. Brazil's cotton output reached 1.6 million lb in 1777, and more than doubled to 3.5 million by 1788. It was reckoned that a cotton estate should produce 20 *arrobas* per slave, while the slave on a sugar estate produced 40 *arrobas*; in 1772, however, the Maranhão company offered twice as much for an *arroba* of cotton as the Pernambuco company paid for sugar.[75]

The collapse of plantation agriculture in Saint Domingue in the 1790s led to the growth of all sectors of Brazilian plantation output. By 1798 cotton production had risen to 7.4 million lb; by 1807 it had reached 17.3 million, and supplied 28 per cent of Portugal's colonial re-exports by value. Sugar output also recovered strongly in these years to reach a recorded output of 24,000 tons, or a little less, in 1807 – by which time it accounted for 57 per cent of Portugal's colonial re-exports by value. Brazil's exports to Portugal in 1798 were worth £3.2 million, and reached just under £4.0 million in 1806. Portugal's textile exports to Brazil during these years – most, but not all, of English or French origin – reached over £1 million annually. Portugal's colonial system was effectively destroyed by Napoleon's invasion of the Peninsula in 1807. In the hectic boom of its last years it was already bursting at the seams, with English and French merchants avidly competing with one another, and impatient of Portuguese attempts to regulate Brazilian supplies and markets. Napoleon undoubtedly hoped to preside over a reorganization of the Iberian empires in the Americas. Instead he handed the British, who transported the Portuguese Royal Family to Rio de Janeiro, all the leverage they could wish to negotiate arrangements with Brazil's plantation economy.[76]

Brazilian sugar plantations, with a capacity to produce from 12,000 to 20,000 tons annually prior to the 1790s, probably had a lower output per worker than those of the Caribbean, and may have required 80,000 slaves to produce this quantity. Replenishing these slave crews could have required the importation of 3,000–4,000 annually, though many more than this in epochs of expansion, such as 1756–62 and the last decade of the century. The growth of the cotton, rice and cacao plantations after about 1760 required the import of perhaps 2,000–3,000 slaves a year. However, even if fairly high estimates are made for the labour needs of the export plantations and gold fields, there still seems to be a gap between these numbers – averaging perhaps 10,000 annually – and records of slave imports, which are a half or a third as high as this.

The problem is, first, accounting for a demographic pattern in which so many slaves disappear; and second, explaining what the surviving slaves were doing. That Brazilian slaves suffered mortality rates as high as those of the Caribbean seems incontestable; the ravages of disease and overwork were probably even greater in the gold fields, possibly a little less in the sugar plantations.[77] Portuguese immigrants to Brazil also experienced high mortality, while the low proportion of women led to a low birth rate. Some 8,000–10,000 Portuguese emigrated every year in the course of the eighteenth century, most of them to Brazil,[78] where the white population grew over the century, but at only half the rate of the white population of

North America. The large scale of free and forced migration into Brazil from two distinct disease zones would probably itself have raised mortality rates.

There is, however, another explanation for the slow advance in the overall size of Brazil's slave population: quite a high manumission rate. Urban slaves, domestic slaves, female slaves, mulatto slaves, trusted slaves in the gold fields, and even runaway slaves all had a greater chance of reaching freedom than the slaves of North America and the Anglo-French Caribbean. As in earlier periods, eighteenth-century Brazilian slaveowners were inclined to offer urban slaves the opportunity to buy their own freedom by pursuing a craft or trade on their own account. Since this practice also gave the slaveowner resources with which to buy new slaves, it would be perfectly consistent with rising slave purchases. Brazilian masters were also quite likely to manumit slave women who had borne them children. If a free man of colour married a slave woman, he would buy her freedom. The adult manumission rate for slave women was twice as high as that for male slaves. In Minas Gerais slaves would be encouraged to declare large finds of precious metal or diamonds by being offered the reward of freedom.

Brazil was notable for its large number of infant foundlings, some of whom would have been the children of slave mothers who did not care to bring them up in slavery. Dauril Alden cites a breakdown of the population of eight of the largest jurisdictions in Brazil at the end of the colonial period which shows whites to have comprised 28 per cent of the population, closely followed by free blacks and mulattoes (27.2 per cent), slaves (38.1 per cent) and Indians (5.7 per cent). Even in the provinces where slaves were most numerous, they did not constitute the majority of the population – 46 per cent of Maranhão's population, 47 per cent of Bahia's and 45.9 per cent of the population of Rio de Janeiro.[79] In consequence, the security of slavery as an institution was somewhat greater than it was on the sugar islands of the Caribbean, so long as the free people of colour were not driven to throw in their lot with the slave masses. The size of the free coloured population reflected the fact that Brazil was the oldest slave colony in the Americas. Nevertheless, it did also testify to a different relationship between slavery and race than had been established in North America. And, of course, a very high proportion of free blacks and mulattoes were creoles – the section of the coloured population with the best chance of reproducing itself.

In Brazil free people of colour were recruited to the militia and the regular army, and could even hold commissions – something that would have been unthinkable in colonial North America. While whites often regarded militia service as an onerous obligation, free blacks and mulattoes welcomed the petty civic privileges it entailed. Free people of colour also supported religious and provident societies of their own, though these 'brotherhoods' had to be registered with the authorities and were required to have a white treasurer or secretary. Mulattoes were considerably more acceptable to colonial society than blacks, and some even received appointments as local magistrates. Marriage between whites and blacks was very rare. White colonists formed their own religious brotherhoods, sometimes refused to work alongside people of colour, and may have inspired decrees which sought to ban free people of colour from wearing the same dress as themselves. Whether they were black or mulatto, free people of colour could – and did – own slaves themselves.[80]

While high rates of manumission and mortality both help to explain the discrepancy between Brazil's huge slave imports and the labour requirements of the export sector, a further element in the explanation is suggested by slave deployment in Minas Gerais in the wake of the gold boom. Once the gold fields were consolidated, a *fazenda* economy developed alongside them, devoted to the cultivation of maize, manioc or beans and to the raising of cattle. Some *mineiros* themselves acquired *fazendas*, on which slaves were put to work, while others would purchase extra supplies for their slave teams from the *fazendeiros*. Slaves whose health had been ruined in the mine workings could still bring some profit to their masters if they were put to work cultivating provisions or tending livestock. In Southern Brazil, as in the North East and Caribbean, slaves could be intensively worked on large ranches, not only tending the cattle but processing the meat to make *charque* and tanning the hides to make leather. Unlike the Caribbean slave colonies, Brazil did not import large quantities of foodstuffs. In the French Antilles the practice of obliging plantation slaves to grow most of their own food was known as the 'Brazilian' system, perhaps in contrast to Barbados, which always relied on massive imports of foodstuffs.

While some general cultivation was undertaken with peasant or free labour in Brazil, this was not as extensive as the incipiently capitalist farming of the North American colonies. The relative cheapness of slave labour in Brazil, and the less intense commercialization of social relations, meant that slaves there were more likely to be engaged in general farming work or even simple subsistence cultivation. Thus an element of slave economy survived the decline of the sugar plantations and the exhaustion of the gold fields in Minas Gerais, with *fazendeiros* working their estates with slaves as well as hired workers and peasants of various sorts. The slave *fazenda* producing for the local market or for subsistence only could survive a poor relation of the slave plantation or mine; if the export sector recovered, *fazenda* slaves or their produce could be sold to it.[81]

*

The success of the English colonies of North America in defeating a far more formidable metropolis than Portugal was bound to find an echo among Brazil's creole elite. Thomas Jefferson, the new Republic's Ambassador to France, when he met a vigorously anti-colonial Brazilian medical student in Nîmes in 1787, explained that the Brazilians should count on their own efforts to free themselves and that, to that end, he and his friends should address themselves to the colonists' economic grievances. But the Brazilian social formation, squeezed by the double weight of Portuguese and British hegemony, lacked the strength and self-confidence of the North Americans. Minas Gerais, where mining had given way to a newly autonomous pattern of cultivation, produced a famous conspiracy, the *Inconfidencia Mineira* (1788–89). This province also had a lively literary and popular culture, with a considerable participation by mulatto writers, artists, sculptors and musicians. The Mineiro conspirators themselves rather vaguely offered freedom to the slaves, but their principal objective was to throw off Portuguese rule and establish an independent Mineiro republic with its own elected authorities, university and citizen militia. The conspirators included a few landowners, officers of the Dragoons, and contractors who owed taxes to the Crown. Before its members could act, however, the Conspiracy was exposed, and the twenty or so main participants were rounded up.[82]

But while the political aspirations of the Mineiros could be stifled, the artistic energy of the province had achieved more tangible form, especially in the sculpture and architecture of Aleijadinho (António Francisco Lisboa), the last and most remarkable exponent of colonial baroque. Aleijadinho helped in the construction and decoration of scores of churches, outstanding among them those of Congonhas do Campo and San Francisco at Ouro Preto. Since he was the illegitimate son of a Portuguese and a black, he could not receive commissions in his own name; in the 1770s, when he was in his forties, he contracted a disease, probably leprosy, which further complicated his existence. While eighteenth-century Portuguese baroque art found expression in exquisitely worked gold and silver objects adorning splendid palaces, with everything carefully regulated by the canons of enlightened good taste, Aleijadinho's sculpture charted new territory, most notably with the statues of the twelve Prophets at Congonhas, with their variety of exotic garments, expansive gestures, pitiful or awesome mien, and such vividly realized companions as Jonas's whale and Daniel's lion. With Aleijadinho, who died in 1816 at the age of eighty-four, the colonial imagination had broken through the last boundary of baroque decorum.[83]

Slavery in Spanish America

Throughout the eighteenth century the Spanish imperial system remained principally orientated towards the extraction of specie. The Spanish colonies, unlike those of France and Britain, were expected to produce a large fiscal surplus, and under the vigorous administration of the new Bourbon dynasty they again began to do so. Spain generally aligned itself with France against what was seen as the more aggressive British. French merchants sold silks, high-quality cottons and wines to the Spanish colonies through the legal Cadiz trade, while British merchants practised a contraband trade. At the Treaty of Utrecht the British had acquired the legal *asiento* for the supply of slaves to Spanish America; they used it to engage in a rather larger contraband trade in manufactures. When the *asiento* was suspended by the Madrid authorities in 1739, the British colonies remained a staging post for the contraband traffic; Spanish gold and silver pieces circulated widely in British America, and were often more important than the official currency. Given the extent of Spanish dominions, some contraband was inevitable. In peacetime conditions the imperial system worked effectively – a fact which no doubt explains British offensives in 1739–40 and 1760–61.

The flow of specie to Spain was still ensured by a heavily regulated pattern of commerce and transportation which discouraged plantation production. Since no other source of silver could compete with the scale of Spanish American output, there was little incentive to improve the efficiency of mining techniques. The flow of silver helped to finance an expensive system of imperial defence in the Caribbean, comprising imposing fortifications and a formidable fleet of *guarda costas*, who not only protected the Spanish fleets but took their toll of British shipping; between 1713 and 1739 they seized 211 British merchantmen. Often British vessels on the West India run paid the price for the contraband activities of their fellow countrymen. Spain's massive expenditures in the Caribbean (incidental to the silver boom) helped to create a wealthy class of creole merchants, contractors, colonial officials and landowners, some of whom purchased sugar estates. Cuba was also important as the source of most of the tobacco purchased by the *factoria* in Seville. Cuba's tobacco farmers owned few or no slaves – indeed, the vigour of tobacco cultivation in this island serves as an example that this crop could be produced advantageously by free labour, helped by the purchasing policies of the state monopoly.[84]

The Spanish and French reverses of the Seven Years War, including British occupation of Havana, led to a streamlining of the apparatus of imperial administration, and some relaxation of commercial restrictions. This did not involve any concession to the British, but did allow more Spanish ports to participate in the colonial trade. The recovery of Mexican silver output was a major success; it was mined by free workers attracted to Guanajato and Zacatecas by quite high wages. The Andean silver mines were still worked by a mixed labour force totalling about 22,000, of whom about 5,000 were supplied by the *mita* system; in the 1780s there were reported to be only 400 blacks employed by the mining economy.[85] The imperial state distributed mining concessions, regulated the flow of goods and labour to the mining zone, took its share of the silver, sought to ensure safe passage of the specie to Spain, and channelled the outward flow of exports to the colonies. Thus Spain's considerable military and civilian establishment in the Americas intertwined itself with the mining economy so that the direct exploiters of mining concessions could not easily dispense with its services. While the creole elite was occasionally restive at imperial tutelage, the threat of popular revolt also helped to encourage their loyalty. In the 1780s Peruvian Vice-Royalty was profoundly shaken by an extensive indigenist revolt covering much of the Andes led by Tupac Amaru II; a rumour that Tupac Amaru had declared emancipation of the slaves alarmed the coastal slaveholders.[86] In Mexico there was quite enough lawlessness and potential for upheaval to ensure that the Andean lesson was not lost on its privileged strata.

A few thousand African slaves were bought by the Spanish American colonists each year for work in gold mines, sugar or cacao plantations, and urban workshops, or for employment as domestics in wealthy households. In small numbers they were to be found throughout Spanish America. As in the previous century the gold mines of New Granada (Colombia), the cacao groves of Venezuela and scattered sugar estates from the Pacific coast to the Caribbean constituted the important enclaves of slave economy in Spanish America. The black slave population of the Choco in New Granada rose from 2,000 in 1724 to 4,231 in 1763, and reached 7,088 in 1782. Most of the slaves worked in *cuadrillas* thirty or forty strong. Every year gold was produced worth some 600,000 pesos, or £120,000. It was sifted by placer mining in rivers; the authorities did not find it easy to keep track of the rate of exploitation, since the *cuadrillas* were constantly moving, and conditions in the jungle-covered region were difficult anyway. Africans were engaged, since they seemed to survive a bit better in the tropical environment and because it was believed that indigenous labourers would be unsuited to the work and difficult to control.

William Sharp estimates that the mine owners received an annual profit rate of 9 to 14 per cent. German Colmenares, taking into account further capital charges, reduces this to 3.9 per cent for one of the Minas de Sesega y el Salto. According to his figures for this mine, the cost of feeding the slaves was a major drain on revenues. Money had to be spent on extra maize, and also to pay Indians to cultivate the provision grounds; evidently this was deemed better than taking slaves away from their work in the *cuadrillas*. It is interesting to note that in this region, where slaves were engaged in financially rewarding employment, the rate of manumission was very low. According to Colmenares, only 472 slaves were manumitted between 1721 and 1800.[87] A trickle of the gold produced was smuggled out of the colony, though whether those mainly responsible were mine concessionaires, slaves, local pedlars and merchants, corrupt officials, or some combination of the foregoing, is not clear. Much of it ended up in the hands of British merchants in exchange for contraband slaves and manufactures; Jamaica's trade accounts reported remittances of about £100,000 worth of gold a year to London, most of which must have been derived from a smuggling trade with Spanish America.[88]

Venezuela – a Captain Generalcy of this name was formed in 1777 – was the only mainland region in Spanish America where slave plantations developed an export trade to Europe on any scale. Cacao cultivation on the Caribbean islands was plagued by plant diseases, leaving the mainland producers in a fairly strong position. A taste for chocolate had developed in both Spain and Spanish America; alternatively, the cacao planters could often sell their product to Dutch traders from Curaçao. Between 1728 and 1784 the Spanish authorities chartered the Caracas Company, with the hope of regulating the already established cacao trade. The Company soon attracted the planters' hostility, but it did organize the sale of slaves to them and exported 58,800 *fanegas* of cacao in 1750, rising to 80,600 *fanegas* in 1780 (a *fanega* was roughly equivalent to a hundredweight or one-twentieth of a ton). The agitation for *comercio libre* eventually persuaded the authorities to wind up the Caracas Company in 1784; by 1789 cacao exports had risen to 103,600 *fanegas* worth about £400,000 at European wholesale prices.

The easing of trade restrictions in Spanish America also led to the rise of indigo cultivation in Venezuela in the 1770s and 1780s. From only 20,000 lb in 1774–78, indigo output reached 718,000 lb in 1789 and 898,000 in 1794, by which time this product accounted for nearly a third of the value of the province's exports. By the end of the eighteenth century there were some 62,000 slaves in Venezuela, most of them engaged in the production of cacao or indigo. Venezuela's chocolate barons, the so-called *grandes cacaos*, did not normally directly supervise the process of production but established sharecropping arrangements with their slaves, some of whom eventually earned enough to buy their freedom. A high rate of manumission is implied by the fact that free people of colour constituted nearly half of the population.[89]

While there is something *sui generis* about the pattern of slave employment in Venezuela, a classic plantation society came into existence in Cuba in the latter half of the eighteenth century. In 1700 slaves may have comprised between a third and half of the island's population of 50,000, with their ownership dispersed among a few sugar or tobacco planters (though most of the latter did not own slaves), urban workshops or households, the royal arsenals and a few large *haciendas* or ranches. By 1774 Cuba's total population reached 175,000, of whom 44,000 were slaves and 31,000 free people of colour.[90]

For much of the eighteenth century tobacco supplied a crucial component of Cuban wealth, with the royal *factoria* buying all that was produced with Mexican silver before reselling it in the Peninsula for a considerable profit. The tobacco *vegueros* owned few or no slaves, but the officials of the *factoria* maintained rich establishments, and some founded slave plantations. In the first half of the century Cuban sugar plantations exported two or three thousand tons per year, mainly to the Peninsula. By 1760 nearly 5,000 tons were produced. But the Cuban plantations were hampered by the high price of slaves and the difficulty of finding markets. During the British occupation of Havana in 1762–63, Cuban planters were able to buy 4,000 slaves from the traders who accompanied the occupying force. Sugar output rose a little. It was not until 1787, however, that Cuban sugar output rose above 10,000 tons – still a fairly modest total for an island with such extensive land suitable for cane.[91]

In the Cuban case, the decisive obstacle holding back its plantation development was undoubtedly the mercantilist restrictions of Spain's colonial system and the fact that Spain had no national slave trade to stock the plantations. As part of a general settlement of frontier disputes between Spain and Portugal, the Treaty of Prado (1778) transferred Fernando Po and Anabon to Spain. Undoubtedly the main value of these islands on the African coast was as bases for the slave trade. By the 1780s Cuba had an aspirant planter class eager to emulate the success of the sugar colonies of the other powers. All it needed was ready access to slaves and to markets.

In 1787 the colonial authorities permitted free entry of slaves for the first time. By the mid 1790s Madrid was no longer able to control its Spanish possessions so tightly, while the main American sugar producer, Saint Domingue, was virtually eliminated. The Cuban sugar planters enjoyed their first 'Dance of the Millions', importing tens of thousands of slaves and propelling their colony into the front rank of sugar producers, with exports of over 40,000 tons in 1802. The royal officials in Cuba gave every assistance to the plantation boom, ignoring metropolitan legislation or instructions where necessary. In 1792 a decree exempted coffee planting from the *alcabala* and *diezmo* taxes; with the help of refugees from Saint Domingue, Cuba became a major producer of coffee. Over a thousand ships called at Havana annually around the turn of the century, many of them North American. Slaves were brought to Cuba by traders of every nationality and none; Cuban merchants and *hacendados* themselves acquired ships, or operated them in partnership with North American sponsors, to buy slaves on the African coast. Before 1789 just under 100,000 slaves had been imported to Cuba; in the years 1790 to 1821 there were registered imports of 240,000, and about 60,000 were probably imported without registration.[92]

The slave society which developed in Cuba combined the traditional Hispanic pattern of diverse slave employment, and a relatively relaxed racial code, with the onset of large-scale sugar cultivation. In the mid eighteenth century many slaves in Cuba were urban artisans; mulatto and *pardo* regiments played an important role in the island's defence. Some exceptional free men of colour even rose to become officers in the militia. In other parts of the Spanish Empire free people of colour also played an important part in sustaining the militia. There were only some 6,000 slaves in Chile at the end of the eighteenth century, and only 10,000 in Mexico, but in both cases black freedmen comprised about a third of the militia. Black officers could claim protection of the *fuero militar*, with its fiscal privileges and right to be tried by military rather than civil courts; they could also purchase exemption from the legal disabilities of their skin colour via the device known as *gracias al sacar*. The colonial authorities looked to the free people of colour as a check on the autonomist proclivities of the colonial elite.[93]

Although they were not producing for the European market, there were also slave plantations in the Audiencia of Quito and on the coast of Peru. The Jesuits maintained eight sugar estates north of Quito until their expulsion in the 1760s. These estates produced sugar for the Mexican and Peruvian markets and, together with a stock farm, most of their own subsistence requirements. Accounts drawn up for the estates after the expulsion of their owners showed that they earned a 5 per cent rate of return on capital invested in them, and were able steadily to increase their slave complement by ploughing back all revenues. In 1768 and 1769 there was slave unrest in the former Jesuit enterprises, protesting against the brusque approach of the new state-appointed administrators. The sugar plantations of Peru were more numerous, engaging about half of the colony's 40,000 slaves in 1791 and producing about 8,000 tons of sugar annually for sale in the local market. There were 13,479 slaves in the city of Lima, where they constituted 25.6 per cent of the population. Those who were not artisans were generally engaged in the retinue of the City's numerous colonial aristocracy.[94]

At the prompting of the 'enlightened' Spanish administration of José de Galvez, a Royal Order was issued suppressing the requirement that every slave entering the Empire should be branded; this measure, adopted to control contraband, was, according to the Royal Order, 'contrary to humanity' [*opuesta a la humanidad*]. In 1789 the Spanish authorities proceeded to issue a 'Real Cedula sobre Educacion, Trato y Ocupaciones de los Esclavos' whose fourteen chapters stipulated that planters must make provision for the religious instruction of their slaves, that they must feed them adequately, and that the crueller punishments or floggings of more than twenty-five blows should be banned. The slaves were to be allowed their 'diversions' on feast days so long as the two sexes were kept separate, the slaves of different plantations did not come together, and these diversions were '*simples y sencillas*'. Observance of the various regulations was to be monitored by the priesthood. This decree caused the utmost consternation, with the last clause possibly stimulating the most alarm. The Intendants of Caracas, Havana, Louisiana and Tocaima (New Granada) urged Madrid that publication of the decree would prejudice the good order of the colonies, and stimulate the pride and expectations of the Negroes. Eventually a resolution of the Council of the Indies was passed on 17 March 1794 suspending the application of the Royal Decree, but reiterating in general terms the need for religious instruction of slaves, humane treatment, slaves' right to marry, and so forth.

In the intervening period the slave rebellion in Saint Domingue in August 1791, and its prodigious consequences, would have helped to inspire caution, notwithstanding the fact that the Spanish authorities of neighbouring Santo Domingo had boldly recruited black rebels to serve the Royalist cause and may well have played a role in the original slave uprising. Spain had long sought to foment slave unrest in the colonies of its enemies, notably the British; it was even more eager to make trouble for the French Republicans. But by the 1790s Spain was, at long last, on the way to developing its own plantation colonies and concerned to protect the promising slave order of its own colonies, especially Cuba. When the Council of the Indies suspended application of its new slave code, it would have been aware that the French National Convention had decreed the ending of slavery in the French colonies in a resolution of 4 February 1794.[95]

The Lesser Producers and the Logic of the Plantation Trade

Eighteenth-century slave economy in the New World was dominated by the British and French West Indies, North America and Brazil. The Caribbean colonies of Denmark and the Netherlands gave them an entrée to the American trade and permitted a modest plantation development. Denmark had acquired the tiny sugar island of St Thomas in the seventeenth century, thanks largely to Dutch sponsorship. In 1733 the Danish Royal Government bought the island of Sainte Croix from France. The transfer provided the opportunity for the slaves to seize a large part of the island; order was eventually restored only with the help of a British warship. The Danish West India Company had access to Northern European sugar markets and organized the importation of a few hundred slaves a year from Africa. In 1755 the Company's monopoly was suspended, and its slave trading activities were transferred to the Baltic–Guinea Company and the Bargum Trading Society.

Sugar output rose to between 4,000 and 8,000 tons annually; by the 1780s there were over 20,000 slaves in Sainte Croix. When warfare interrupted the colonial trade of Britain or France, the Danish merchants and planters often made large profits; the Danish islands were also well placed to conduct a smuggling trade. Such influential families as the Schimmelmans and Reventlows had lucrative investments in West Indian plantations and their own refineries in Copenhagen. However, when peacetime conditions prevailed in the Caribbean the Danish slave trading companies found great difficulty in meeting foreign competition; planters' profits also declined. While the small size of the Danish islands limited their contribution to plantation development, Denmark's naval and military weakness meant that it could never be more than a very minor colonial power in the Americas, tolerated by the larger powers as a useful contraband base for penetrating the colonial systems of their rivals.[96]

While the Dutch Caribbean islands – St Eustatius, St Martin, Saba and Curaçao – were small trading colonies, Surinam, on the 'Wild Coast' or Northern littoral of South America, had considerable plantation potential. Dutch mercantile facilities allowed some of this to be tapped, but the colony's further development continued to be hampered by the poor security of its commerce and plantations. By 1760 Surinam's slave population had reached 60,000, and produced 8,300 tons of sugar annually, as well as significant quantities of coffee, cacao, dyewood and tobacco. By 1775 its annual exports reached £822,900: £347,000 sugar, £350,500 coffee, and £98,000 cotton. This level of development had been achieved by the tolerant and representative regime of the Chartered Society of Surinam, a company half-owned by the new WIC. The planters' assembly, the *Raad*, was allowed a large measure of internal self-government. But the ships which carried Surinam's slave produce to Europe or North America had to endure a long run through the most dangerous Caribbean waters; the Spanish *guarda costas* had good reason to suspect any Dutch ship of engaging in contraband, since this was the main activity of the Dutch islands.

Dutch naval forces no longer commanded respect in American waters. The planters of Surinam also faced a formidable internal threat to their security. From the colony's earliest days no solution had been found to the problem of slave runaways, so that maroon communities came to comprise something like a tenth of the total population. The fact that Surinam was a mainland colony, with a large hinterland behind the coast, certainly assisted the establishment of the maroons. The maroon problem was compounded by the failure of the Surinam Society or the *Raad* to maintain a large military force to police the interior, though admittedly this would have been a costly undertaking. Few Dutch came to live in Surinam, while Dutch capitalists preferred to invest in commerce or at home. Many of Surinam's planters belonged to religious or national minorities – Huguenots, Sephardic Jews, Labadists, Roman Catholics. This pattern was repeated in the other Dutch coastal settlement of Berbice. This entire colony had been seized in a slave revolt led by Coffey in 1763; order was restored only with British help. By the 1780s British planters were playing a leading role in the construction of plantations at the mouth of the Essequibo river.[97]

The development of slave plantations in the eighteenth century required the combined sponsorship of the state and of economic agents, guaranteeing both good security and good commercial conditions. Britain and France had the necessary political and economic resources, but their clashes weakened each another and set the scene for the demise of colonial mercantilism. The slave-related trade, however, itself possessed a dynamic which undermined mercantilism and corporate restriction. In the 1760s all the mercantilist systems had been much weakened by concessions and loopholes. In that decade the Spanish authorities introduced the first steps towards *comercio libre*, the British created 'free ports' in the West Indies, and the French relaxed the provisions of the *exclusif*. In the first instance it was conceded that there was little point in preventing a trade in means of production, such as slaves, even if the commerce in final products remained tightly regulated. But once the principle of a closed colonial system had been breached, it was difficult to resist the freer trading logic of plantation development.

The ambivalent relationship between the slave plantations and the market outlined in Chapter VIII had enabled them to play a key part in sustaining the growth of eighteenth-century Atlantic trade. On the one hand they responded rapidly and appropriately to market opportunities; on the other, when conditions were unfavourable, the slave systems could survive for years cut off from supplies and markets. The impressive growth of the French, British, North American, Cuban or Brazilian plantations in one phase was complemented by their ability to withstand periods of military and commercial hardship. Thus the slave system of Brazil retained great latent strength despite generally adverse conditions in the years 1763 to 1790. The American War of Independence created very difficult conditions for the North American slave system, yet it survived in good shape, with a constantly growing slave population. The resilience and versatility of the New World slave plantation derived from the fact that it walked on two feet: that which stepped forward commercially being able to rely on that which remained fixed to the *terra firma* of natural economy. Planters generally preferred their slaves to be producing commodities for the Atlantic market; but at all times, and especially when the latter were closed, slaves could be directed to produce foodstuffs, manufactures and services – for themselves, for their masters and for the local market.

*

In this chapter and in Chapter X I have explored the many ties between European commerce and the produce of the slave colonies. Evidently the latter were of growing commercial significance in the eighteenth century. By the last days of the Ancien Régime in France its colonies sent it £8.3 million of goods a year; those that were not consumed provided the basis for half of French exports. The tobacco farm supplied the monarchy with income of £1 million annually.[98] In 1790–91 the planters of the French Antilles enjoyed their most extraordinary harvest ever, taking full advantage of upheaval in the metropolis to ignore the restrictions of the *exclusif*. The eruption of the slave revolt in Saint Domingue and the suppression of slavery in the French colonies in 1794 soon eliminated the richest slave colonies in the Caribbean, but as prices rose, so did the output of slave plantations elsewhere in the Americas. By the last years of the century Britain was importing £6 million annually from the British West Indies; the United States exported £3 million of plantation products and recorded re-exports (mainly of plantation produce) of £10 million in 1806; around this same time Brazil's exports to Portugal were worth £4 million.[99]

One way or another slave produce furnished the basis of about a third of European trade. To stock new plantations, between 50,000 and 100,000 slaves were brought across the Atlantic each year. The boom in colonial slavery was, of course, linked to the continuing boom of the European economy, especially the new pattern of British capitalist growth. The British had suffered a momentous defeat in North America, but – at least in economic terms – recovered remarkably quickly. The French had significantly contributed to British defeat at the hands of the rebels. Their system of colonial exchanges was booming even more rapidly than before. Yet French successes proved costly in every way, not least because they boosted the expectations of planters and merchants who made their own remarkable contribution to the crisis of the Ancien Régime.

Notes

1. J.F. Shepherd and G.M. Walton, *Shipping, Maritime Trade and the Economic Development of Colonial North America*, Cambridge 1972, p. 42.

2. Even relatively self-sufficient farmers needed work tools, ammunition, salt, medicines, household utensils, cotton yarn and some clothing; they bought petty luxuries like sugar, tea or coffee, and rum. But see Michael Merrill, 'Cash is Good to Eat': Self-sufficiency and Exchange in the Rural Economy of the United States', *Radical History Review*, 4, Winter 1977, pp. 42–71.

3. Goodman, *Tobacco in History*, p. 145.

4. Allan Kulikoff, *Tobacco and Slaves*, Chapel Hill, NC 1986, pp. 122–4, 141–53, 154.

5. Walsh, 'Slave Life, Slave Society and Tobacco Production', in Ira Berlin and Philip D. Morgan, eds, *Cultivation and Culture*, pp. 184–6.

6. McCusker and Menard, *The Economy of British America*, p. 132.

7. Michael Mullin, *Africa in America: Slave Acculturation and Resistance in the American South and the British Caribbean, 1736–1831*, Urbana and Chicago 1992, pp. 115–25.

8. William Byrd, 'A Progress to the Mines', in Lois B. Wright, ed., *The Prose Works of*

William Byrd of Westover: Narratives of a Colonial Virginian, Cambridge, MA 1966, pp. 339–80 (p. 350).

9. J.P. Greene, ed., *Diary of Landon Carter of Sabine Hall, 1752–1778*, Charlottesville, VA 1965, p. 502.

10. See Lorena Walsh, 'Slave Life, Slave Society, and Tobacco Production', in Berlin and Morgan, *Cultivation and Culture*, for extra work and the sexual division of labour p. 187 and, for gross crop revenues per hand, p. 195. (Compare with the results cited for Jamaica and Saint Dominique in Chapter X, n. 65.)

11. R.C. Nash, 'South Carolina and the Atlantic Economy in the Late Seventeenth and Eighteenth Centuries', *Economic History Review*, vol XLV, no. 4, 1992, pp. 677–702; Joyce Chaplin, *An Anxious Pursuit: Agricultural Innovation and Modernity in the Lower South, 1730–1815*, Chapel Hill, NC 1993, pp. 227–76; Peter Wood, *Black Majority*, New York 1974, pp. 95–130; McCusker and Menard, *The Economy of British America*, p. 174.

12. I give most of the text in Blackburn, *The Overthrow of Colonial Slavery*, p. 46.

13. Chaplin, *An Anxious Pursuit*, pp. 40–41.

14. Julia Floyd Smith, *Slavery and Rice Culture in Low Country Georgia 1750–1860*, Knoxville, TN 1985, pp. 17–22, 141–65; George Fenwisk Jones, *The Georgia Dutch*, Athens, GA 1992, pp. 265–74.

15. Allan Kulikoff, 'A "Prolifick" People: Black Population Growth in the Chesapeake Colonies, 1700–1790', *Southern Studies*, vol. XVI, 1977, pp. 391–428.

16. Kulikoff, *Tobacco and Slaves*, p. 73.

17. For the rhythms of tobacco cultivation see Timothy Breen, *Tobacco Culture: The Mentality of the Great Tidewater Planters on the Eve of Revolution*, Princeton, NJ 1985, pp. 46–55.

18. For the labour regime in Virginia and Jamaica, see Dunn, 'Sugar Production and Slave Women in Jamaica', in Berlin and Morgan, *Cultivation and Culture*, especially pp. 61–3, 68–9, and Richard Dunn, 'A Tale of Two Plantations: Slave Life at Mesopotamia in Jamaica and Mount Airy in Virginia, 1799 to 1828', *William and Mary Quarterly*, 3rd series, vol. 34, 1977, pp. 32–65. For the work expected of slaves in Jamaica, see also B.W. Higman's study, *Slave Populations of the British Caribbean 1807–34*, London 1984, based on a large sample of plantations in the early nineteenth century, p. 188.

19. Herbert Klein, *Slavery in the Americas: A Comparative Study of Cuba and Virginia*, London 1967, pp. 178–80.

20. Watts, *The West Indies*, p. 422. According to Arthur Stinchcombe West Indian slaves engaged in cane-holing would be required to move 40 cubic yards, or six dump truck loads, of earth each day; Stinchcombe, *Sugar Island Slavery in the Age of Enlightenment*, p. 116.

21. Lorena Walsh gives tobacco output per labourer in 'Slave Life, Slave Society and Tobacco Production', in Berlin and Morgan, *Culture and Cultivation*, p. 175. Information on sugar output per slave will be found in Ward, 'The Profitability of Sugar Planting in the West Indies', *Economic History Review*, 1978.

22. Carole Shammas, 'Black Women's Work and the Evolution of Plantation Society in Virginia', *Labor History*, vol. 26, no. 1, Winter 1985, pp. 5–28.

23. Planters and overseers were, of course, guilty of sexually abusing slave women and the written record scarcely permits quantification; but nothing suggests the predatory regime revealed by the Thistlewood diaries for Jamaica. Thus William Byrd's 'secret' diary, written in his own shorthand, shows him to have led an active sexual life in both England and Virginia; in a few instances he imposed himself on slave women, but more often on white maidservants or other white women. See Lois B. Wright and Marion Tinling, *The Secret Diary of William Byrd of Westover*, Richmond, VA 1941; Kenneth Lockridge, *The Diary, and Life, of William Byrd II of Virginia, 1674–1744*, Williamsburg, VA 1987. An English servant in the Carter household paints a fairly decorous picture of the plantation household; though prepared to be shocked by life in a slave society he notes only one possible incident of attempted, and unsuccessful, molestation; H.D. Farish, ed., *The Journals and Letters of Philip Vickers Fithian, 1773–1774*, Williamsburg, VA 1957. See also Kulikoff, *Tobacco and Slaves*, pp. 174–83, 386–7, 395–6, and Jan Lewis, *The Pursuit of Happiness: Family and Values in Jefferson's Virginia*, Cambridge 1983, pp. 1–39, 169–208. The relatively small proportion of mulattoes in the African–American population of North America – only 7.7 per cent prior to 1850 – is discussed by Robert Fogel and Stanley Engerman in *Time on the Cross*, New York 1989, pp. 130–32.

24. Quoted in Littlefield, *Rice and Slaves*, pp. 62, 65; and Joyce Chaplin, 'Slavery and the Principle of Humanity: A Modern Idea in the Early Lower South', *Journal of Social History*,

Winter 1990, pp. 299–315. I would like to thank Emory Evans for sending me the letter used in the epigraph; the slave Aron, to whom it is addressed, had spent some time in England with his master.

25. The demography and life experience of enslaved blacks in eighteenth-century North America are surveyed in John B. Boles, *Black Southerners, 1619–1869*, Lexington, VA 1983, pp. 32–48, and references pp. 220–22.

26. Higman, 'Household Structure and Fertility on Jamaican Plantations', in Beckles and Shepherd, *Caribbean Slave Society and Economy*, p. 257; Herbert G. Gutman, *The Black Family in Slavery and Freedom, 1750–1925*, Oxford 1976; for South Carolina slave families see Philip Morgan, 'Black Society in the Low Country', in Ira Berlin and Ronald Hoffman, eds, *Slavery and Freedom in the Age of the American Revolution*, Charlottesville, VA 1983, pp. 83–142 (p. 128).

27. Kulikoff, *Tobacco and Slaves*, pp. 358–72.

28. The ingenious suggestion that lower interest rates may have encouraged slave owners to make more provision for slave reproduction is made by Dave Denslow, 'Economic Considerations in the Treatment of Slaves in Brazil and Cuba', University of Florida n.d. (1982?), pp. 16–18. However, it is not clear (1) whether interest rates available to Virginian planters really were lower than those available to Jamaican planters or (2) whether the policies of slaveowners were a critical factor in slave reproduction rates.

29. The higher birth rate on Caribbean plantations where slaves received larger rations and were less reliant on their own provision grounds is identified by Higman, 'Household Structure and Fertility on Jamaican Slave Plantations: A Nineteenth Century Example', in Beckles and Shepherd, eds, *Caribbean Slave Society and Economy*, pp. 250–72 (p. 270). For corn-shucking see Eugene Genovese, *Roll, Jordan, Roll: The World the Slaves Made*, London 1978, pp. 315–19.

30. Bennett, *Bondsmen and Bishops*, p. 27. Debien notes that branding of slaves in the French Antilles could reduce their value: *Études antillaises*, p. 107.

31. Quoted in Mechal Sobel, ' "All Americans are Part African": Slave Influence on "White" Values', in Leonie Archer, ed., *Slavery and Other Forms of Unfree Labour*, London 1987, pp. 176–87 (p. 179). For this general theme see Mechal Sobel, *The World They Made Together: Black and White Values in Eighteenth Century Virginia*, Princeton, NJ 1987 and Kulikoff, *Tobacco and Slaves*, chapter 8.

32. Quoted in Sobel, ' "All Americans are Part African" ', in Archer, *Slavery and Other Forms of Unfree Labour*, p. 183. Rhett Jones has cautioned against portraying the slave condition in colonial America in terms which ignore the ferocious oppression of slaveholding. Against those who claim too much autonomy and integrity for the 'slave community' he argues: 'Black folks were not the victors, but the vanquished.' But such strictures do not really apply to Sobel's argument. See Rhett Jones, 'In the Absence of Ideology: Blacks in Colonial America and the Modern Experience', *Western Journal of Black Studies*, Spring 1988, vol. 12, no. 1, pp. 30–39 (p. 35).

33. Thomas Ingersoll, ' "Releese us out of this Cruell Bondegg": An Appeal from Virginia in 1723', *William and Mary Quarterly*, 3rd series, LI, no. 4, October 1994, pp. 777–82 (pp. 781–2).

34. Parke Rouse, *James Blair of Virginia*, pp. 223, 244.

35. Letter of 12 July 1736, quoted in Pierre Marambaud, *William Byrd of Westover, 1674–1744*, Charlottesville, VA 1971, p. 172. Byrd concludes this passage with the reflection: 'It were therefore worth the consideration of a British Parliament, my Lord, to put an end to this unchristian traffic of making merchandise of our fellow creatures.'

36. James Oglethorpe, 'An Account of the Negro Insurrection in South Carolina' (1740), in *The Publications of James Edward Oglethorpe*, Rodney Blaine, ed., Athens, GA 1994, pp. 253–5.

37. Peter Wood, *Black Majority*, chapters 11 and 12: Berlin, 'From Creole to African', *William and Mary Quarterly*, April 1996, pp. 251–88 (pp. 280–81).

38. Michael Mullin, *Africa in America*, pp. 188–9.

39. Alan Gally, 'Planters and Slaves in the Great Awakening', in John B. Boles, ed., *Masters and Slaves in the House of the Lord*, Lexington, VA 1988, pp. 19–36 (p. 31); other quotes are from Frank Lambert, ' "I Saw the Book Talk": Slave Readings of the First Great Awakening', *The Journal of Negro History*, LXXVII, no. 4, Fall 1992, pp. 185–99.

40. A theme explored by Edmund Morgan, *American Freedom, American Slavery*, New York 1975, pp. 293–362.

41. G.M. Walton and J.F. Shepherd, *The Economic Rise of Early America*, Cambridge 1979, p. 45.

42. The quote is from a most informative and insightful essay by Ira Berlin, 'Time, Space, and the Evolution of Afro-American Society in British Mainland North America', *The American Historical Review*, vol. 85, no. 1, February 1980, pp. 44–86 (p. 45). In another helpful survey Duncan Macleod relates growing reliance on slaves in the South, and declining reliance in the North, to the numbers and influence of white immigrants in the respective colonies: see 'Toward Caste', in Berlin and Hoffman, *Slavery and Freedom*, pp. 217–36. For the number of frost-free days see Paul A. David and Peter Temin, 'Slavery: The Progressive Institution?', in Paul A. David et al., *Reckoning with Slavery*, New York 1976, pp. 165–230 (p. 209).

43. Thomas J. Davis, *The New York Slave Conspiracy*, Boston, MA 1971; Gary Nash and Jean R. Soderland, *Freedom by Degrees*, p. 7; Peter Linebaugh and Marcus Rediker, *The Many-headed Hydra*, Boston, MA forthcoming. The linking of urban slaves to arson also arose, as noted in the previous chapter, in Port au Prince in 1787 and was frequently alleged in the Dutch eighteenth-century Cape colony in South Africa (see Robert Shell, *Children of Bondage*, pp. 248, 264–5, 272, 279).

44. Rostow, *How It All Began*, p. 128.

45. Walton and Shepherd, *The Economic Rise of Early America*, p. 117.

46. Breen, *Tobacco Culture*.

47. John Syme to Farrell and Jones, 2 June 1760, quoted in Breen, *Tobacco Culture*, p. 157.

48. Archibald Cary to the agent of Virginia, 17 April 1766, quoted in Breen, *Tobacco Culture*, p. 140.

49. Jacob Price, *Capital and Credit in British Overseas Trade: The View from the Chesapeake*, Cambridge, MA 1980, p. 128.

50. R.P. Thomas and D.N. McCloskey, 'Overseas Trade and Empire', in Roderick Floud and Donald McCloskey, eds, *The Economic History of Britain Since 1700*, vol. I, *1700–1800*, London 1981, pp. 87–102 (p. 96).

51. McCusker and Menard, *The Economy of British America*, pp. 290–93, 319–21, 326.

52. Walton and Shepherd, *The Economic Rise of Early America*, p. 101.

53. Alice Hanson Jones, *Wealth of a Nation to Be*, New York 1980, p. 118.

54. Ibid., pp. 102–4, 118–19, 228.

55. Stanley Engerman and Kenneth Sokoloff, *Factor Endowments, Institutions and Differential Paths of Growth Among New World Economies*, Historical Paper no. 66, National Bureau of Economic Research, 1994.

56. Sylvia Frey, *Water from the Rock: Black Resistance in a Revolutionary Age*, Princeton, NJ 1991. I explore the wider significance of these events in Blackburn, *The Overthrow of Colonial Slavery*, especially chapters 3 and 4.

57. Richard Dunn, 'Black Society in the Chesapeake', in Ira Berlin and Ronald Hoffman, eds, *Slavery and Freedom in the Age of the American Revolution*, pp. 49–82.

58. Boles, *Black Southerners*, p. 55.

59. For commercial performance of the USA in 1790–92 see J.F. Shepherd and G.M. Walton, 'Economic Change after the American Revolution', *Explorations in Economic History*, 13, 1976, pp. 397–422. For the 1790–1817 entrepôt boom see Douglass North, *The Economic Growth of the United States, 1790–1860*, Englewood Cliffs, NJ 1961, pp. 26, 28.

60. H.E.S. Fisher, *The Portugal Trade: A study of Anglo-Portuguese Commerce 1700–1770*, London 1971, pp. 126, 128–39; for figures implying a higher total for Brazilian gold exports see Virgilio Noya Pinto, *O ouro brasileiro e o comércio anglo-português*, São Paulo 1979, p. 114.

61. Vilar, *A History of Gold and Money*, pp. 222–31; Simonsen, *História econômica do Brasil*, II, p. 222 and facing page. I have scaled down Simonsen's estimate of the value of the sugar crop to take account of the somewhat lower, but incomplete, figures given by Stuart Schwartz, 'Plantations and Peripheries', in Leslie Bethell, ed., *Colonial Brazil*, Cambridge 1987, pp. 67–144, especially p. 76, and Dauril Alden, 'Late Colonial Brazil', in Bethell, *Colonial Brazil*, pp. 284–343, especially pp. 312–14.

62. Deerr and Drescher are well-informed about European markets and look at the Americas as a whole. Schwartz and Alden, basing their partial series on Brazilian documentation, imply somewhat lower figures. Simonsen's less cautious and unexplained estimates must

be treated with reserve. See Deerr, *The History of Sugar*, I, p. 112 and II, p. 530; Schwartz, 'Plantations and Peripheries', in Bethell, *Colonial Brazil*, p. 76; Dauril Alden, 'Late Colonial Brazil', in Bethell, *Colonial Brazil*, pp. 312–14; and Drescher, *Econocide*, p. 48. Simonsen, *História Econômica do Brasil*, II, p. 222 and facing page.

63. For a discussion of the problems with this census, which probably overstated slave numbers, see Dauril Alden, 'The Population of Brazil in the Late Eighteenth Century', *Hispanic American Historical Review*, vol. 43, 1963, pp. 173–205.

64. Lang, *Portuguese Brazil*, p. 144; Schwartz, 'Plantations and Peripheries', in Bethell, *Colonial Brazil*, p. 83, and A.J. Russell-Wood, 'The Gold Cycle', in Bethell, *Colonial Brazil*, pp. 190–243 (p. 218).

65. Schwartz, 'Plantations and Peripheries', in Bethell, *Colonial Brazil*, pp. 76, 83, 93–4. The output figures for Jamaica and Saint Domingue are cited from the previous chapter, but see also the very similar comparisons made in Sergio Buarque de Holanda, *História Geral da Civilizacão Brasileira*, vol. 1, *A Epoca Colonial*, vol. 2, 2nd edn, São Paulo 1968, p. 210. For the Benedictine estates see Schwartz, *Sugar Plantations in the Formation of Brazilian Society*, pp. 222–3, 234–7. According to this account the Benedictines achieved almost a 'North American' pattern of slavery by feeding their slaves better, promoting slave artisans and favouring higher reproduction rates.

66. Goulart, *Escravidão Africana no Brasil*, pp. 141–4.

67. C.R. Boxer, *The Golden Age in Brazil: 1695–1750*, London 1962, pp. 82–5, 160–61, 175, 182–4; Gorender, *O Escravismo Colonial*, pp. 427–50; A.J.R. Russell-Wood, 'Colonial Brazil: The Gold Cycle, c. 1690–1750, in Bethell, ed., *Cambridge History of Latin America*, pp. 547–600.

68. Lang, *Portuguese Brazil*, p. 151, quoting Antonio de Sousa Pedroso, Visconde de Carnaxide, *O Brasil no administracão Pombalina*, p. 81.

69. For tobacco Sergio Buarque de Holanda, *A Epoca Colonial*, vol. 2, pp. 211–13 and Lang, *Portuguese Brazil*, pp. 141–3, 167.

70. V. Magalhães Godinho, 'Portugal and Her Empire, 1680–1720', in J.S. Bromley, ed., *The New Cambridge Modern History*, IV, Cambridge 1970, pp. 509–40 (p. 536). See also Hanson, *Economy and Society in Baroque Portugal*, pp. 260–76.

71. Lang, *Portuguese Brazil*, pp. 107, 147; Boxer, *The Portuguese Seaborne Empire*, p. 217; cf. also the observations of Carl Hanson, *Economy and Society in Baroque Portugal*, p. 271.

72. Goulart, *Escravidão Africana no Brasil*, p. 171.

73. Russell-Wood, 'The Gold Cycle', in Bethell, *Colonial Brazil*, pp. 217–18.

74. Quoted in Kathleen J. Higgins, 'Masters and Slaves in a Mining Society: A Study of Eighteenth Century Sabara, Minas Gerais', *Slavery and Abolition*, vol. II, no. 1, May 1990, pp. 58–73 (p. 59).

75. Buarque de Holanda, *A Epoca Colonial*, vol. 2, pp. 318–26; Alden, 'Late Colonial Brazil', in Bethell, *Colonial Brazil*, p. 321; Kenneth Maxwell, *Pombal: Paradox of the Enlightenment*, Cambridge 1995, pp. 119–28, 134–48.

76. Alden, 'Late Colonial Brazil', *Cambridge History of Latin America*, II, for cotton pp. 635–9, rice, pp. 639–42, tobacco, pp. 631–5, colonial company profits, pp. 622–4, turn-of-the-century trade boom, pp. 650–51. For this latter topic see also Fernando A. Novais, *Portugal e Brasil na crise do Antigo Sistema Colonial (1777–1808)*, São Paulo 1983, with data pp. 306–86. For the growing British presence from 1808 see Sergio Buarque de Holanda, *História Geral da Civilizacão Brasileira*, vol. 2, *O Brasil Monarquico*, vol. 1, 2nd edn, São Paulo 1965, pp. 64–99.

77. Goulart, *Escravidão Africana no Brasil*, pp. 154–7.

78. Magalhães Godinho, *A Estrutura na Antiga Sociedade Portuguesa*, p. 43.

79. Alden, 'Late Colonial Brazil', in Bethell, *Colonial Brazil*, p. 290.

80. Russell-Wood, *The Black Man in Slavery and Freedom in Colonial Brazil*, pp. 128–60.

81. Caio Prado Jnr, *The Colonial Background of Modern Brazil*, Berkeley, CA 1967, pp. 174–5, 186–7, 227–31, 272–3.

82. Kenneth Maxwell, *Conflicts and Conspiracies: Brazil and Portugal 1750–1808*, Cambridge 1973.

83. Frédéric Mauro, *Le Brésil*, Paris 1977, pp. 220–21; G. Bazin, *Aleijadinho*, Paris 1963.

84. Richard Pares, *War and Trade in the West Indies*. The tobacco monopoly played a double role, guaranteeing outlets to the tobacco farmers but also repressing their aspiration to

508   *Slavery and Accumulation*

commercial independence and skimming a sizeable surplus from their output. C.f. José Luciano Franco, *Ensayos Históricos*, Havana 1974, pp. 17–19.

85. D.A. Brading, *Miners and Merchants in Bourbon Mexico, 1763–1810*, Cambridge 1971, pp. 146–9; Enrique Tandeter, 'Free and Forced Labour in the Mines of Potosi', *Hispanic American Historical Review*, 1982.

86. Alberto Flores Galindo, *Aristocracia y Plebe: Lima, 1760–1830*, Lima 1984, p. 96.

87. William F. Sharp, *Slavery on the Spanish Frontier*, Norman, Oklahoma, OK 1976, pp. 22, 73, 181; German Colmenares, *História Econômica y Social de Colombia*, Tomo II, *Popayán: una sociedad esclavista 1680–1800*, Bogota 1986, pp. 99, 158–61.

88. Jamaica's bullion exports are given in Sheridan, *Sugar and Slavery*, p. 506.

89. Gastón Carvallo, 'Notas Para el Estudio del Binomio Plantación-Conuco en la Hacienda Agricola Venezolana', CENDES, Caracas 1979; Miguel Acosta Saignes, *Vida de los Negros en Venezuela*, Havana 1978, pp. 211–38; R.D. Hussey, *The Caracas Company, 1728–84*, London 1934.

90. Fernando Ortiz, *Los Negros Esclavos*, Havana 1916, pp. 22–3.

91. Heinrich Friedlander, *Historia Económica de Cuba*, I, Havana 1976, p. 92; Manuel Moreno Fraginals, *El Ingenio*, III, Havana 1977, p. 43.

92. Moreno Fraginals, *El Ingenio*, I, Havana 1977, pp. 95–102; David Murray, *Odious Commerce*, Cambridge 1981.

93. Jorge Dominguez, *Insurrection or Loyalty: The Breakdown of the Spanish American Empire*, London 1980, pp. 37–9, 79; for the diverse pattern of slave employment in Spanish America see also Klein, *Slavery in the Americas*.

94. Rosario Coronel Feijoo, *El Valle Sangriento*, Quito 1991, pp. 115–17; Alberto Flores Galindo, *Aristocracia y Plebe: Lima, 1760–1830*, Lima 1984, pp. 30, 101.

95. Manuel Lucena Salmoral, *Sangre Sobre Piel Negro: la esclavitud quiteña en el contexto del reformismo borbónico*, Quito 1994, pp. 39–52. The text of the 1789 Royal Order and the circular withdrawing of it are given on pp. 197–221. For the atmosphere of royalist plots and Bourbon conspiracies in Saint Domingue in 1791 see David Geggus, *Slavery, War and Revolution: The British Occupation of Saint Domingue*, Oxford 1982, p. 40 and José L. Franco, *Historia de la Revolución de Haití*, Havana 1966.

96. Svend E. Green Pedersen, 'The Scope and Structure of the Danish Negro Slave Trade', *Scandinavian Economic History Review*, vol. 19, 1971, pp. 149–97.

97. Goslinga, *A Short History of the Netherlands Antilles*, p. 100; Sheridan, *An Era of West Indian Prosperity, 1750–75*, pp. 91–2. According to Alex Van Stipriaan the sugar industry in Surinam, following a speculative crash in 1770, produced only a little over 6,000 tons of sugar from 111 plantations in 1775; however the coffee sector grew between 1755, when there were 235 estates with an average complement of 41 field slaves each, to 295 estates in 1775, with an average of 68 field slaves each. Alex Van Stipriaan, 'Surinam and the Abolition of Slavery', in Gert Oostindie, ed., *Fifty Years Later: Anti-Slavery, Capitalism and Modernity in the Dutch Orbit*, Pittsburg, PA 1996, pp. 117–142 (120,123).

98. Henry Brougham, *The Colonial Policy of the European Powers*, vol. I, Edinburgh 1803, pp. 538–9; Jacob Price, *France and the Chesapeake. A History of the French Tobacco Monopoly, 1674–1791*, Ann Arbor, MI 1973, 2 vols, I, p. 541.

99. Drescher, *Econocide*, p. xx; North, *American Economy*, p. xx; Novais, *Portugal e Brasil na crise do Antigo Sistema Colonial*, pp. 370–86.

XII

New World Slavery, Primitive Accumulation and British Industrialization

Table XII.0

Volume and Profitability of the British Slave Trade 1761–1807

	1	2	3	4	5	6	7	8	9	10	11	12	13	14
	Voyages	Tons	Slaves landed	Slaves landed per ton	Average gross sale price £	Gross receipts on slaves £	Net receipts (82%) £	Net receipts after discounting £	Residual value less 5% for produce £	Total Credit £ (cols. 8+9)	Outset less 5% for produce≠	Profit £	% profit	Resource increment £ (cols. 7+9– col. 11)
1761–70	1368	153,006	284,834	1.86	29	8,260,186	6,773,353	6,421,139	784,921	7,206,060	6,657,291	548,769	8.2	900,983
1771–80	1080	120,652	233,042	1.93	35	8,156,470	6,688,305	5,952,591	687,716	6,640,307	5,925,823	714,484	12.1	1,450,198
1781–90	998	159,757	294,865	1.85	36	10,615,140	8,704,415	7,799,156	971,323	8,770,479	7,922,350	848,129	10.7	1,753,388
1791–1800	1341	278,537	393,404	1.43	50	19,920,200	16,334,564	14,439,755	2,011,037	16,450,792	14,553,558	1,897,234	13.0	3,792,043
1801–07	906	218,690	217,556	0.99	60	13,053,360	10,703,755	9,483,527	1,973,677	11,457,204	11,094,144	363,060	3.3	1,583,288
Aggregates	5693	930,642	1,428,701	1.54	42	60,005,356	49,204,392	44,096,168	6,428,674	50,524,842	46,153,166	4,371,676	9.5	9,479,900

Source: Roger Anstey, The Atlantic Slave Trade and British Abolition, London 1975, p. 47.

The ability of the British to maintain and extend their advantageous relationship to the Atlantic boom was powerfully assisted by the increasing competitiveness of their manufactures. Even when they lost their North American colonies, they did not lose the North American trade, since American farmers and planters still found that they preferred many British products. The growth of Brazil and Cuba, and the renewed prosperity of the British West Indies, also boosted British exports. Right down to 1815 the governments of France never acquiesced in British hegemony in the Atlantic zone. Confronting a British government which, with the active connivance of the French planters, was occupying one of its sugar islands after another, the Revolutionary Convention, in February 1794, went so far as to declare war on slavery in the Americas. Despite some success, this strategy was abandoned by Napoleon, who preferred to challenge British Atlantic pre-eminence by means of an accommodation with Jefferson's United States (the Louisiana Purchase), alliance with Spain, a continental boycott of British goods (including colonial produce), and an invasion of the Peninsula.

The outbreak of war between Britain and the United States in 1812, and the complicated situation in Spanish and Portuguese America, meant that French hopes of disputing British hegemony were not finally dashed until Waterloo. The success of the black armies of Haiti in 1804, the Battle of Trafalgar in 1805 and a host of other momentous political and military developments helped to frustrate Napoleon. But Britain's surging economic strength was also an essential part of the story. It enabled Britain to absorb the loss of the American colonies, to finance the wars against France, and to adjust to its own defeat at the hands of the rebels of Saint Domingue in 1798. During the eighteenth century Britain had constructed an Atlantic system which had nourished its economic strength and helped it to withstand the test of war. Previous chapters have examined colonial slavery primarily in its New World context. We must now address the question of what role slavery-based Atlantic exchanges played in the momentous development of British industry in the years 1760 to 1820.

Were the slave plantations mighty little tugboats, their engines racing, towing the ocean liner of the British economy out into the open seas of industrial accumulation? Or, alternatively, were they nothing more than jolly boats, tied to the stern of the new steamship and bobbing up and down in its wake? The bare fact that the commerce of the slave systems grew more rapidly than that of the metropolis does not decide the matter, since any advance in prosperity was bound to produce a more than proportionate rise in the demand for luxuries as the margin above necessity widened for different strata of the population. The plantation revolution whose course we have traced evidently did help to form new patterns of consumption. Did it also help to foster the transition to new forms of production in the metropolis? In addressing this question it will be helpful to examine whether the slave systems (1) generated markets and a surplus which could help to kick-start the motor of industrial accumulation; (2) supplied key inputs to the industrial processes.

The classic problem of a 'previous' or 'primitive' accumulation is posed by these questions. Adam Smith asserted that a more advanced division of labour could arise only where there had been a prior accumulation on some more primitive basis: 'As the accumulation of stock must, in the nature of things, be previous to the division of labour, so labour can be more and more subdivided in proportion only as stock is previously more and more accumulated.'[1] Smith also stressed the necessity for a widening of the extent of the market if a complex division of labour was to be achieved.

Karl Marx, while he scorned the notion that this 'primitive accumulation' should be allotted 'approximately the same role in political economy as original sin . . . in theology', insisted that there was nevertheless a real problem of accounting for the emergence and consolidation of capitalist accumulation out of an essentially *non-capitalist* context:

> the accumulation of capital presupposes surplus value; surplus value presupposes capitalist production; capitalist production presupposes the availability of considerable masses of capital and labour power in the hands of commodity producers. The whole movement therefore seems to turn around in a never ending circle, which we can only get out of by assuming a primitive accumulation (the 'previous' accumulation of Adam Smith) which precedes capitalist accumulation; an accumulation which is not the result of the capitalist mode of production but its point of departure.'[2]

Marx saw the transition to capitalist accumulation arising in the first place from the expropriation of a layer of the agricultural population, separating some of the direct producers from direct access to the means of production and consequently permitting the emergence of a class of rural wage labourers and capitalist farmers; in the English case, and in some other parts of North West Europe, these were tenant farmers who needed cash to pay rent to the landlords and to pay labourers, and whose leases allowed them to gain from agricultural improvements. The fact that such farmers controlled the process of production, were in competition with one another, could employ wage labourers and enjoyed some property rights encouraged them to invest part of their revenue in better equipment, farm buildings, drainage, fencing and other improvements. Landlords could use their rent rolls to finance enclosure of common lands, which would in turn be let to old or new tenants. Alternatively, some prosperous tenants would buy land and farm it with the help of wage labour.

Once they were consolidated, these developments created wider demand in which the extension of the internal market allowed some merchants and manufacturers gradually to escape the restraints of regulation. The farmer with access to wage labour could raise output and control methods of cultivation. Those paid a wage or salary by the capitalist farmer reproduced themselves and their families increasingly by buying subsistence and production goods on the market. To the extent that farmers engaged wage labour, they could treat it as a variable cost of production; in the context of a competitive market, this was more likely to be associated with a willingness to invest in improvements and adopt innovations.

Here was a vital element of capitalism in contrast to peasant communities meeting their own subsistence needs and employing family labour which would lack the motive and the means to undertake the sort of improvements that boosted a marketable surplus. However, the emergence of these new social relations was patchy, localized and contested. Labourers who could acquire a subsistence by working common lands, or garden plots, were to that extent less dependent on selling their labour-power. Capitalist farmers also engaged in subsistence cultivation and relied on family labour. The logic of capitalist accumulation was cramped by the narrow horizons of the rural world; wherever there were the makings of a broader prosperity, tapping into wider markets, it would be vulnerable to the predatory attentions of feudal monarchs and merchant monopolists who would impede or destroy the mechanisms of free competition and spontaneous accumulation.

The appearance of capitalist social relations in the English countryside in the early modern period added a new dimension to prevailing forms of mercantile and manufacturing capital, and was nourished by a dynamic woollen industry. But the consolidation of capitalist relations also required the protection and patronage of a concentrated social power, the state, with its Acts of enclosure, its labour statutes and Poor Laws, armed bodies of men, contracts for supply, commercial agreements and treaties, guarantees of markets, property, means of exchange and credit. Only with the sponsorship of the state could incipiently capitalist social forces find the scale and stability they needed to make the transition to industrial accumulation proper, since the latter needed extensive markets and a protected space within which commodity production and exchange could be carried out.

But if capitalist social relations needed a degree of state sponsorship, they could also be constrained and frustrated by corporate restriction and regulation, imposed with the aim of raising revenue or bestowing privilege. The early absolutist states furnished some of the necessary protections, but at a high price. The commercial republics tended to succumb to conservative corporate oligarchies, especially when their expansion was checked by military weakness. Severally and in combination the early modern states allowed European capitalism to install itself at the heart of a world market, finding there resources which would help to promote the accumulation process in Europe itself.

Marx summarized his conception of these developments in a famous passage:

> The discovery of gold and silver in America, the extirpation, enslavement and entombment in mines of the indigenous population of that continent, the beginnings of the conquest and plunder of India, and the conversion of Africa into a preserve for the commercial hunting of blackskins, are all things which characterise the dawn of the era of capitalist production. These idyllic proceedings are the chief moments of primitive accumulation. Hard on their heels follows the commercial war of the European nations which has the world as its battlefield. .... The different moments of primitive accumulation can be assigned in particular to Spain, Portugal, Holland, France and England, in more or less chronological order. These different moments are systematically combined together at the end of the seventeenth century in England; the combination embraces the colonies, the national debt, the modern tax system, and the system of protection. These methods depend in part on brute force, for instance the colonial system. But they all employ the power of the state, the concentrated and organized force of society, to hasten, as in a hothouse, the process of transformation of the feudal mode of production into the capitalist mode, and to shorten the transition.[3]

From the standpoint of Marx's own notion of primitive accumulation, however, some of these forms of depredation did not promote truly capitalist accumulation because their profits were seized by rulers who spent them on their own aggrandizement, or adventurers who aspired to become landed aristocrats. Both mercantile city-states and early absolutisms could be greedy, or could impose conservative and burdensome systems of mercantile regulation, often at the behest of vested interests. Their privileged classes generally saw no interest in a broader social development.

These states could also fail militarily, with damaging consequences for accumulation. Spanish absolutism plundered the Americas, as we have seen, but did not provide a stable financial environment or encourage the development of an independent mercantile class. The Dutch ultimately lacked the resources and people needed to consolidate a transatlantic empire, suffering costly reverses and ultimately succumbing to a conservative involution. The French state succeeded in sponsoring a plantation agriculture, but lacked the commercial integration and fiscal stability achieved by the British Atlantic Empire. The reconstruction of the English state in the course of the seventeenth-century revolutions had witnessed the emergence of a state that promoted mercantile and manufacturing interests without imposing upon them a straitjacket of control.[4]

The new British state could command the confidence of the financial markets. It maintained a relatively stable currency and low real interest rates. The achievement of this modern financial system, with the founding of the Bank of England and parliamentary control of the budget, was nevertheless buttressed, as Marx claimed, by the ability of Britain's

merchants, with state backing, to dominate exchanges with the plantations. This was 'primitive accumulation' conceived of not as an episode but
as an on-going aspect of the metropolitan accumulation process – what
might be termed 'extended primitive accumulation'. It did not invent
capitalism but, rather, assured the further development of an already-
existing agrarian and mercantile–manufacturing capitalist complex, through
exchanges with the plantation zone. It was orchestrated by an inverted
mercantilism – that is to say, not by financiers and merchants serving
raison d'état but by the state serving capitalist purposes. The whole point
was that the state created a zone of imperial 'free trade' for its merchants
and manufacturers, offered them protection, and gained favourable terms
for their entry to other markets. The colonial and Atlantic regime of
extended primitive accumulation allowed metropolitan accumulation to
break out of its agrarian and national limits and discover an industrial and
global destiny.

The early capitalism of the Netherlands or England led to a boom in the
New World slave systems long before it inaugurated any generalized
industrial transformation. The plantation revolution preceded industrialization by at least a century. Whether or not some other path might have
been possible or desirable, the actual transition to capitalist industrialization was to pass through extensive exchanges with the slave plantations. It
is that sequence which this chapter will seek to illuminate. The slave
economies count as a form of 'primitive' accumulation because their
productive organization was based on non-economic coercion; the direct
producers were obliged by brute force to produce a surplus and a
marketable commodity. Both the formal colonial systems, and Britain's
'informal empire' of advantageous commercial agreements, themselves
rested on economic and military, especially naval, strength. If Britain had
already combined the chief moments of primitive accumulation in 1700, it
needed to defend and extend that strategic emplacement over the next
century or more: down to and after the consolidation of a Pax Britannica
in 1815.

Marx, writing at the Victorian meridian of the Pax Britannica, wanted
to draw attention to capitalism's bloody birth and to the ways in which it
had been, and continued to be, nourished by forced labour and forced
exchange. But he never described this as the optimum path of development
– merely the one that had actually been taken. In his view the 'really
revolutionary' path to accumulation proceeded through the activities of
small producers, including farmers and manufacturers, willing to adopt
innovations and raise the productivity of labour. But such producers did
not live in a world of their own making.[5]

Adam Smith, writing in the 1770s at a time when war, taxation and
protection appeared to menace continuation of the Atlantic boom, offered

an apparently quite different conclusion. For him the success of the English colonies in the Americas was rooted in the fact that the colonial state generally allowed a free rein to their internal development, abstained from onerous taxation or regulation, and guaranteed free trade within the Empire and reasonable access to wider markets. All this permitted colonial producers to retain and reinvest a larger proportion of their income compared with British proprietors, let alone with the cowed and priest-ridden subjects of the Spanish Crown. Smith was happy to note the prosperity accruing to independent planters, farmers and labourers under a system which allowed them to organize their own affairs in their own way. He deplored the violent dispossession of indigenous inhabitants and bloody wars between rival powers associated with European colonial expansion – he did not commend slavery, but chose to stress what had been achieved by free and independent labour.[6] The analytic gap between Marx and Smith was thus less substantial than it appears. Both saw independent production, linked to wage labour, as the positive pole of the new capitalist system. I believe that Marx was sharper and more candid in assessing the actual costs and transitional forms of capitalist development. Smith's political economy invited a selective and complacent view of the workings of capitalist accumulation; in Marx's case the risk was different: his account of 'primitive accumulation' could be read as some sort of recipe for development by those, like Stalin, who did not share his evident revulsion at its ferocity.

Marx pointed to Britain's special position, and was right to do so. In previous chapters we have seen that both Britain and France built flourishing slave systems in the New World in the course of the eighteenth century. France's colonial products helped to supply raw material for impressive commercial and manufacturing advance in high-quality textiles and other luxury goods – but colonial markets as such accounted for only about a fifth of exports: no more than 19 per cent in 1789. Britain's colonial markets absorbed 38 per cent of her exports in 1770; the War with the thirteen North American colonies caused serious dislocation while it lasted, but British commerce, including that with the United States, soon bounced back. By 1796–98 New World markets accounted for two-thirds of all British exports.[7] In about 1770 the New World slave colonies were supplying commercial profits and manufacturing outlets to merchants and manufacturers in Portugal and Spain as well as France and Britain, even if the latter already had an edge. The Revolution in Saint Domingue in the 1790s and the proclamation of Haiti in 1804 removed France as a leading American power. By 1816 Britain could exploit a far-reaching commercial and industrial ascendancy in the New World. It will, therefore, be appropriate to concentrate attention on the British case as the leading beneficiary of New World commerce.

*

A tradition of British Marxist historiography – culminating in Eric Hobs-bawm's *Industry and Empire* (1964) and Christopher Hill's *From Reformation to Industrial Revolution* (1968) – has argued that British colonial expansion did indeed furnish crucial economic space for British capitalist development. Writers in this tradition had no difficulty finding seventeenth- and eighteenth-century statesmen and political economists who urged colonial development on the grounds that it would boost the national economy. The evidence of official statistics seemed to confirm the picture, but a traditional view of this sort was bound to furnish the target for a wave of revisionism. Approaches inspired by a variety of economic models – classical, neoclassical and Marxist – came to reject the thesis that there was a 'primitive' contribution to Britain's industrialization; in some quarters the problematic of a 'primitive' accumulation was itself deemed primitive in conception. After all, Britain's internal market had grown rapidly in the seventeenth century, and was probably growing as fast as foreign trade in the eighteenth.

Historians as different in their approach as Charles Kindleberger, a neoclassical economic historian, Paul Bairoch, a neo-Physiocrat member of the *Annales* school, and Robert Brenner, a Marxist, all challenged the view that colonies or commerce made any decisive contribution to Britain's capitalist industrialization. The arguments they advanced appeared so cogent that for much of the 1970s and 1980s they enjoyed a certain hegemony.[8] Bairoch contended, against Hobsbawm, that colonial markets and profits made a very modest contribution to capital formation in Britain during the Industrial Revolution, and that it was, rather, the 'agricultural revolution' of roughly 1660–1800 which opened up the space for economic growth. Brenner, as a Marxist, argued that the decisive moments of capitalist development were those which transformed social relations in the West European countryside, and that no essential contribution was made by colonial markets or by surplus extracted on the slave plantations; in Brenner's case it was the capitalist world-system approach of Immanuel Wallerstein that furnished the object of his critique.

Historians of the slave systems in the Americas have had their own version of the controversy over 'primitive accumulation' and the importance of trade to capitalist development. The classic reference here is, of course, Eric Williams's *Capitalism and Slavery*, first published in 1944 and seldom out of print since. Its argument was placed within a broader framework by the same author's history of the Caribbean, *From Columbus to Castro*, published in 1962. In the ensuing decades – and most particularly in the 1960s and 1970s – many challenges were mounted to Williams's contention that the profits of Britain's 'triangular trade' with Africa and the West Indies lent a major impulse to the Industrial Revolution. The so-called 'Williams thesis' became the target of repeated attempts to show that neither the Atlantic slave trade nor the plantation trades had made any large or decisive contribution to British economic growth. In 1973 Roger

Anstey published a major investigation of Britain's involvement in the Atlantic slave trade, conceived as a comprehensive refutation of Williams's arguments.[9]

The putative contribution of colonial profits was challenged in a different way by those who questioned whether an 'industrial revolution' had even taken place in Britain in the eighteenth or early nineteenth centuries. New calculations of British economic growth during this period suggested that it was modest compared with modern, especially post-World War II, rates of growth, and that it may have been similar to the rate of growth already achieved in England in the seventeenth century. It could also be shown that the growth of agriculture had made a large contribution to the advance of overall output, for some time overshadowing the relatively small manufacturing sector. But in fact the new models and new evidence did not give good grounds for abandoning the idea of an 'industrial revolution', while the new findings on trade, growth and capital formation actually increase the significance of the colonial contribution, as we will see. Britain was the first country to undergo an industrial transformation such that the agricultural workforce was overtaken by urban or manufacturing employment. The share of the male labour force in industry grew steadily: 18.5 per cent in 1688, 23.8 per cent in 1759, 29.5 per cent in 1801 and 47.3 per cent in 1847.[10] Agriculture grew in absolute terms, but accounted for a declining share of national income: 45 per cent in 1770, 33 per cent in 1801 and 20 per cent in 1851.[11]

Such developments proved to be a watershed in human history, inaugurating a new pattern of society. While agricultural advance helped to create the space for structural change, industrialism and urbanism provided a livelihood and a new pattern of life for the majority. Of course, the Industrial Revolution itself took place against the highly unusual and propitious background of a prior capitalist development and dramatic advances in several sectors, many linked to the slave-based economy of the Atlantic. This is, in fact, to be the theme of this chapter as it assesses the colonial contribution as it affected markets, investment, institutions, supplies, government and war. Fortunately, these dimensions of British growth have attracted considerable research from historians of the metropolis as well as the colonies.[12]

Markets in Africa and the New World

Let us first consider the significance of colonial markets. In a still largely non-capitalist world, a critical problem confronting the entrepreneur considering the adoption of new industrial methods was the size of the available market. Mercantilist policies of exclusion of foreign products and sponsorship of national manufacture exacerbated this problem. To what extent did the New World slave plantations constitute a vital market for early industrial products? Were they a stepping stone to the global markets reached by British exports in the mid nineteenth century? In a first approximation to answering this question, Britain's own direct trade in manufactures with its American colonies and with Africa will be considered. Of course, these colonial markets were not fully coextensive with markets directly generated by plantation demand, both because Britain exported manufactures to foreign slave colonies and because slavery was marginal in New England and the Middle colonies of North America. But it was the commerce of the slave zone that sustained the purchasing power of the entire North American economy; this makes the scope of Britain's exports to all its American colonies a useful starting point.

In considering the evidence I will draw both on new, recalculated data for trade and output, and on the pioneer attempts to quantify the British economy by historians such as Elizabeth Schumpeter, Phyllis Deane and W.A. Cole.[13] In 1979 Ralph Davis published new estimates of British overseas trade, correcting for the tendency of official values to depart from market values. In 1985 N.F.R. Crafts published an ambitious model of the British economy as a whole in the eighteenth and early nineteenth century which, by revising downwards previous estimates of industrial output and growth, put into even stronger relief the contributions of overseas markets.[14] Unsurprisingly, some of Crafts's conclusions have been challenged, though even critics are inclined to see merit in his lower industrial output estimates.[15] I will cite evidence based on both old and new calculations, since the former still have value for some purposes, and because doing so furnishes a strong test of my argument.

Table XII.1 gives a broad picture of the eighteenth-century rise of British manufacturing exports to the new colonial markets, making up for relatively stagnant exports to Europe, where each government sought to foster national production.

Table XII.1   Exports of Manufactures from England – £000

Ann. Av.	Cont. Europe	Ireland	America/Africa	Asia
1699–1701	3,201	86	475	111
1772–74	3,617	499	3,681	690

Source: Ralph Davis, 'English Foreign Trade 1700–1774', *Economic History Review*, Second Series, 15, 1962, pp. 302–3.

Ralph Davis concluded that exports provided the outlet for approximately a third of all British manufacturing production in both 1700 and 1774. Colonial demand enabled English exports to double within this period, and to make up for the stagnation in European markets. Subsequent refinement of both trade and output figures accentuate rather than weaken this broad assessment of the importance of colonial commerce.

The colonies imported every type of manufacture, but they were a particularly good market for the products of the newer industries, or those undergoing technical transformation. Examining the pattern behind the broad totals, Walter Minchinton, in a survey of overseas trade in the eighteenth century, concluded:

> With the expansion of the slave trade and plantation agriculture, which required a specialized product, the demand for printed cottons and linens abroad grew. There was a sharp rise after mid-century: exports of linens were half as much again, and those of checked cotton about two and a half times as much, in 1770 as they had been in 1756.... The second main group of industries involved in overseas trade in this period were the metal industries for whose products demand grew abroad, and particularly in the American colonies, in the course of the eighteenth century. Nails, pots and pans, axes and ploughshares, kitchen and dairy utensils, buttons and buckles, anchors and other ships' wares were among the articles sent overseas.[16]

When Phyllis Deane produced her own account, she argued that foreign trade was the leading sector in Britain's economy in this period:

> Undoubtedly domestic exports grew faster than population in the second half of the eighteenth century.... More significant ... than the change in the volume of exports was the change in its composition – the shift from primary products to manufactured goods and from the products of the old domestic type of industry to the products of the new capitalistic factory industry.[17]

Specific information concerning key export items bore out these contentions. Table XII.2 gives the proportion of all English exports of nails and wrought iron going to the West Indies, the North American colonies (after 1776 the United States), Africa and the East Indies (exports to the latter two zones are not distinguished; the East Indian share would probably have been much the smaller).

Table XII.2   Colonial and African Trade as a Proportion of the Exports of Each Commodity

%	Nails	Wrought Iron
1700	73.5	70.0
1750	95.5	61.8
1760	95.5	79.2
1770	96.3	70.5
1780	77.3	55.8
1790	82.6	67.1
1800	87.5	62.0

Source: Calculated from Elizabeth Schumpeter, *English Overseas Trade, 1697–1808*, Oxford 1960, pp. 64–6.

In most years the British West Indies imported more wrought iron than either Africa/Asia combined or the Northern colonies; in the decade or so before 1775 Virginia, Maryland and Carolina were usually responsible for a half or more of the total wrought-iron imports of the Northern colonies as a whole.[18]

Deane and Cole pointed out that Britain's metal industries went through a difficult time in the years 1725–45, and suggested that 'almost the whole of the increase in the output of wrought iron was sent abroad in this period'. They added: 'while the home consumption of copper and brass seems actually to have fallen from 1725 to 1745, exports were booming'.[19] During these years of stagnant home demand, exports encouraged metal producers. In the early years of the century the English metal industry, hampered by the poor quality of available charcoal, could not even supply the whole of the home market. Between 1707, when Abraham Darby took out a patent for smelting iron ore using coke, and 1780, when Henry Cort perfected the process of puddling and rolling wrought iron, there was a steady accretion of technical improvements which transformed the English iron industry into the most advanced in Europe. Even at the end of the century much of metalworking was conducted on a local scale for local markets, but the export trade required larger producers and a more standardized product.

Paul Bairoch has been generally sceptical of the contribution made by foreign markets to sustaining industrial advance. Nevertheless, he conceded that in the case of iron exports the 'incremental ratio', or contribution made by the rise in export volume to the increase in overall output, was quite significant in this case, as Table XII.3 reveals:

Table XII.3 British Exports of Iron Manufactures and Domestic Iron Consumption

Annual average for	Exports 000 tons	As % Consumption
1700–09	1.5	3.8–5.0
1710–19	2.1	5.1–6.4
1720–29	2.8	6.1–7.4
1730–39	4.1	7.6–8.7
1740–49	6.8	13.1–15.1
1750–59	9.3	15.2–16.9
1760–69	13.3	17.7–19.0
1770–79	14.5	16.4–17.2
1780–89	14.3	14.8–15.5
1790–99	27.8	15.9–16.9

Source: Paul Bairoch, 'Commerce international et genèse de la révolution industrielle anglaise', *Annales*, XXVII, 1973, p. 561.

According to Bairoch's calculations, 30 per cent of the increase in demand for iron in the 1750s was generated by exports, rising to 40 per cent in the

1760s. The author of a later study of the iron industry confirms this view: 'the middle of the eighteenth century was a turning point of fundamental importance in the history of the industry.... If one seeks to choose a particular point at which the industry indisputably "took off" into rapid and sustained growth then it must be around 1750.'[20]

Important though it was, the metalworking industry did not witness such a dramatic technical breakthrough as occurred in cotton textiles. On the demand side the trade with Africa and America played a very important role in the birth of the new cotton industry in the 1760s, and at certain subsequent periods (e.g. 1784–1804), but the home market absorbed large quantities of the new textiles when access to overseas markets was interrupted. When Ralph Davis published the results of his recalculation of the values of British trade in 1982, he presented the value of cotton exports set against the estimated production figures elaborated by Deane and Cole (see Table XII.4).

Table XII.4   Exports of Cotton Goods as % of Total Production

£ million	Production	Exports	%
1760	0.6	0.3	50
1772–74	0.9	0.3	33
1784–86	5.4	0.8	15
1794–96	10.0	3.4	34

Source: Production figures adapted from Deane and Cole, *British Economic Growth*, p. 185; exports from Davis, *The Industrial Revolution and British Overseas Trade*, p. 66.

The earliest exports of the cotton industry went almost exclusively to African and West Indian markets. During this phase the industrial method was in a largely experimental mode, and the products themselves were of uncertain quality. The trend to supplying home consumption was greatly accentuated by the disruption of colonial trade during the American War of Independence. After the War British cotton exports not only regained much of the North American market but, in the wake of the wars and revolutions of the epoch, captured important new markets in the Americas. François Crouzet, basing his conclusions on newly calculated trade data, describes the surge in cotton exports that began in 1784–94:

> Though the spectacular rise in cotton exports was a crucial and novel development [in the 1780s], there was still an advance on a broad front like that earlier in the century. It was only during the 1790s and 1800s that the position changed rather drastically. The growth of the volume of cotton product exports accelerated and, from 1792 to 1802, reached the amazing and record rate of 17.3% a year; it was to go on during the next decade at a slower but still impressive rate.[21]

In the period following the Napoleonic Wars Britain maintained a high volume of cotton exports to the New World – notably to territories like

Brazil and Cuba, where the slave economy was expanding rapidly – but did not sustain the phenomenally high growth rates achieved in 1794–1804. Later in the nineteenth century, India became the main export market for British cottons; this happened only as the extension of British rule in the subcontinent paved the way for the destruction of the traditionally strong indigenous textile industry.

Crouzet adopts a similar procedure to that used by Bairoch to establish the proportion of the expansion of output attributable to the growth of cotton exports in the periods 1760–1869/71. Table XII.5 brings out the continuing oscillation between home and overseas demand.

Table XII.5   Demand for British Cottons

Export Growth as Proportion of Output Growth	
1760 to 1784/6	13%
1784/6 to 1805/7	87%
1805/7 to 1839/41	42%
1839/41 to 1869/71	79%

Source: François Crouzet, 'Toward an Export Economy: British Exports during the Industrial Revolution', *Explorations in Economic History*, vol. 17, 1980, pp. 48–93 (p. 90).

Although data are available only for arbitrarily selected years, the remarkable spurt in the last two decades of the eighteenth century coincided with the transition to large-scale industrial methods, and the adoption of steam power, in the most advanced sectors of the industry. During the Napoleonic Wars British textile manufactures achieved a virtual monopoly in American markets. From 1815 to 1840 about a third of British cotton exports went to American markets, after which the proportion steadily declined. Down to the last days of the Atlantic slave trade in the mid nineteenth century, however, British cotton goods, bought on favourable terms by Cuban or Brazilian merchants, were still exchanged for slaves on the African coast.

The expansion of cotton production and exports from 1780 onwards was so considerable that it began to have an impact on the overall relationship between trade and national output, while it displayed some of the same alternating pattern noted above for cotton markets:

> During the decisive stage of the Industrial Revolution, in the twenty years which followed the peace of 1783, the incremental ratio of exports to national product seems to have been as high as 40%; but from the early 1800s up to the 1830s and even circa. 1841, it was quite low . . . it rose sharply in the 1840s and from 1841 to 1871 it was about 37%.[22]

Within this wider pattern Crouzet advances a conclusion which has a special relevance for the present discussion:

> the twenty years from 1782 to 1802 have a marked originality, owing to their very high rate of growth of exports, to the 'leading sector' part which cottons

played in export expansion, to the predominant role of American markets, and to the undoubtedly strong impact of foreign demand on Britain's economic growth (and though export expansion came after the technological break-throughs it certainly accelerated their diffusion).[23]

In his reconstruction of the values of trade and manufacture within national output, Nicholas Crafts has estimated that exports never reached a fifth of total British GNP (Gross National Product) in the eighteenth century. The new cotton manufacture was still of modest dimensions, supplying only 2.6 per cent of value added in British industry in 1770, but rising to 17.0 per cent by 1800. Crafts's figures also show that the rise in exports absorbed 30.4 per cent of the rise of total GNP between 1700 and 1760, 5.1 per cent of the increase between 1760 and 1780, and 21.0 per cent of the increase between 1780 and 1800. If the contribution of the rise in exports to industrial (rather than gross) output is considered, the proportion is 56.3 per cent between 1700 and 1760, only 2.5 per cent between 1760 and 1780, and 46.2 per cent between 1780 and 1800. Crafts also argues that the rise in exports generally explains far more of the increase in output than the increase in 'workers' consumption', or even 'capitalists' consumption', though home demand as a whole, including investment and 'agriculturalists' uses', was more important than foreign trade.[24] It should be stressed that these calculations present snapshots of the British economy at widely separated intervals; the benchmarks chosen are not necessarily turning points so far as Atlantic trade flows are concerned, and it would be wrong simply to draw a straight trend line between them. The disruption caused to British trade by the American War of Independence is certainly evident in the figure for 1780. David Richardson has pointed out that exports to the British Caribbean and North America continued to rise strongly for over a decade after 1760, probably bringing into play resources that would otherwise have been unemployed.[25]

The global category of 'foreign trade' has been used without indicating the special contribution of 'Atlantic' markets (i.e. Africa, the United States, the West Indies and Latin America). The latter's special importance in the period 1784–1816 is brought out in Table XII.6.

Table XII.6   Britain's Exports of Manufactures by Area in %

	Europe	Asia	Atlantic	Africa	US	Carib	Latin America
1784–86	36	17	43	5	26	12	–
1794–96	22	17	59	2	36	21	–
1804–06	33	7	57	3	30	21	3
1814–16	44	6	42	1	19	16	6
1824–26	38	10	44	1	17	11	15

Source: Calculated from Davis, *The Industrial Revolution and British Overseas Trade*, p. 88.

The rise in the share of exports taken by the plantation-related Atlantic markets – from 43 per cent to 57–59 per cent over the period 1784 to 1806 – is the more remarkable in that total exports of manufactures doubled and trebled over this period: from £10.7 million in 1784–86 to £19.0 million in 1794–96, reaching £33.8 million in 1804–06. Within the overall pattern of British manufacturing exports the share of cotton manufactures going to the Atlantic markets was particularly high: 57 per cent in 1784–86, 74 per cent in 1794–96 and 55 per cent in 1804–06; in absolute terms this was an increase from £0.4 million in 1784–86, to 2.5 million in 1794–96, to 7.7 million in 1804–06.[26]

Britain's export trade in the whole period 1760 to 1820 was both shaped and distorted by the fortunes of war. Trade with North America was hit by political conflict in the years 1776–83 and 1808–15, but trade with the West Indies remained at a high level throughout. During this crucial phase of Britain's industrialization the Atlantic trades were alternatively a vaulting poll or a crutch – the latter in those years when Napoleon's Continental System excluded British goods from many parts of Europe. By keeping Atlantic markets open for by far the greater part of this period, British naval supremacy made a crucial contribution.

The evidence advanced in this section does not prove that Britain could not have industrialized at all without Atlantic markets. During the two conflicts with North America the British home market showed that it was ample enough to prevent industrial collapse – though industrialists did face grave problems during these times, and many went to the wall. The markets supplied by Britain's formal and informal commercial empire helped to extend and hasten an industrial advance in a few key industries that would no doubt have proceeded, but much more slowly, in their absence.

There is some difficulty in ascribing precise causal links between metropolitan growth and the rise of exports. Deane and Cole themselves argued in 1969 that the surge in British eighteenth-century exports was not an exogenous trigger of industrial advance, since it reflected a rise in colonial purchasing power generated largely by trade with Britain. In their view, Britain's Atlantic exchanges were conducted largely within the 'closed economy' of the colonial system, so that plantation-related demand would be a lagged reflection of British demand for plantation products. Ralph Davis also stressed an initial independent impulse from the home market, with foreign trade playing a larger role only as industrialization got into its stride. The relatively high degree of complementarity between home demand for plantation products and plantation demand for metropolitan products was, of course, an asset to the British accumulation process. Crouzet's essay quoted above, using Davis's recalculated trade data, does suggest that from about 1784 Britain was breaking out of the limits of a closed economy, and tapping demand throughout the Atlantic zone.[27]

The subsequent calculations of British GNP by Crafts also allow, as we have seen, for an even stronger export contribution to growth; a lower rate of growth for British industry boosts the relative importance of exports as a factor generating demand in this sector. Moreover, in Crafts's model foreign trade is not itself used, as it was by Deane and Cole, as a proxy for industrial growth – a procedure that made it more difficult to establish the relations between the two.

Writing before the publication of Crafts's new calculations, Joel Mokyr argued that there was little evidence of an overall shortfall in demand in eighteenth-century Britain, and that in consequence any stimulus furnished by exports was redundant.[28] Mokyr argued that exported production was lost production from the standpoint of the British consumer; and if the export markets had not been available, fewer cottons, for example, would have been sold, but those sold in Britain would have been cheaper. But this line of thought is not well founded. Colonial demand was not an abstract homogeneous entity but highly concentrated, as we have seen, in the modernizing sectors. If the latter had been deprived of export outlets, they would have had many fewer resources, and much less incentive to experiment with new or modified industrial methods. Export markets were, in general, more receptive to the industrial product, whereas the home market still favoured more fashion-conscious, less standardized items. Moreover, as Mokyr concedes, well-informed contemporaries such as William Petty, James Steuart and George Berkeley certainly thought that there was a problem of deficient demand.[29] When colonial demand was briefly cut off during the American War of Independence, there was some sign of reduced growth despite increasing military expenditure.

Export markets have played a key role in the industrial development of many countries – Germany, Japan, South Korea, Taiwan and China, to name but a few – allowing them to achieve economies of scale and to reap the rewards of temporary monopolies or productivity advantages. In the early eighteenth century Britain still had a largely pre-modern economy. There was much concealed unemployment and underemployment, if the norms of an industrial economy are used as the standard of comparison. McCloskey, another sceptic concerning demand deficiency in eighteenth-century Britain, concedes that demand arising from new quarters was likely to have changed the composition of output.[30] In the case we are considering here, the effect was to skew demand somewhat towards the new mass-production industries. If these outlets had not been available, then – even assuming the argument that domestic demand would have taken up the slack – the probable composition of that demand would have been close to the overall pattern, in which new products were much less prominent than they were in the colonial trades. Likewise, if British consumers had been unable to buy the plantation staples, it is unlikely that they would have spent the money saved in such a way as to make up for the lost colonial markets.

Anticipating a little an argument developed below, it should also be made clear that colonial imports very probably had a capacity to expand both demand and production since, at the margin, eighteenth-century consumers would work a bit harder, and spend a bit more, to acquire tobacco, sugar, cotton goods, and so forth. Moreover, British spending on colonial goods also manifestly elicited a more intense use of factors of production as well as generating demand for British products. In sum, the peculiarity of the Atlantic system was that it really did expand overall output, albeit in ways that benefited some and harmed others.

Even if it is granted that colonial demand was important, and that much of it was for goods produced by those sectors which were adopting innovations and industrial methods, the connection could simply be coincidence. There were many small firms, so – it could be argued – the structure of British manufacturing at this time was competitive. Even if demand had been contracting, firms would still have had an incentive to innovate in order to claim a larger share of what remained, and to improve their own costs. Some innovations may have been first adopted in times of difficulty, such as those precipitated by the American War. Others were encouraged by buoyant prices and good sales prospects in expanding markets. As Jacob Price points out:

> with domestic demand more than fully utilizing available local supplies of iron and linen, and cotton yarn, the extra or marginal demand coming from overseas, particularly the colonies, should have seen a marked upward pressure on prices and thus significantly increased the incentives to experiment with new cost-reducing technologies. In this sense colonial demand *was* particularly strategic.[31]

Manufacturers who did innovate sometimes did acquire temporary monopolies, since the combination of new product and new price could give them the lion's share of the market. Anything which broadened demand, as trade did, was conducive to a more expansive and optimistic approach by manufacturers; it also was likely to increase their number, and thus the statistical chance that there would be an innovator among them. Finally, even if the initial innovation was entirely independent of the size of the market, as it may sometimes have been, the wider the market, the greater scope there would be for adopting the innovation, and thus the greater the contribution towards overall productive performance.

The evidence of trade flows and their implications will no doubt remain open to further refinement and reconceptualization. But so far the direction of these revisions has helped to convince even former sceptics, such as P.K. O'Brien and Stanley Engerman, that a stimulant role in the industrializing process was played by overseas trade in general and colonial demand in particular.[32] Furthermore, the vital 'slave contribution' to economic advance can be registered along other dimensions, such as resources for investment, and raw materials needed.

Profits and Investment

The simple amassing of wealth is a secondary aspect of 'primitive accumulation', since capitalist industrialization required an appropriate framework of institutions and production relations capable of converting wealth into capital. The history of the New World itself shows that development required not only resources and markets but also a supply of labour. But once such points have been made, it remains to be established whether the potential investment fund derived from colonial and slavery profits was large enough to be significant in terms of metropolitan accumulation as a whole, and whether there are any indications that such profits were a source of investment or credit.

In the article cited above, Paul Bairoch argued that the profits of English overseas trade as a whole played a minuscule role in financing investment in the first stages of the Industrial Revolution. In the years 1700 to 1779, he estimated, the most probable contribution of commercial profits to gross capital formation was in the range 6–8 per cent, rising to perhaps 7–9 per cent in the years 1760–80.[33] During the first eight decades of the eighteenth century, according to Bairoch's calculations, the rate of growth of Gross Domestic Product (GDP) was in the range 0.8–1.2 per cent a year, while the rate of export growth was 1.0–1.2 per cent a year. Bairoch's calculations were based on estimates of the size of the home market by well-informed contemporaries. The two crucial estimates of national income are those made by Gregory King in 1688 and Arthur Young in the 1770s. King's estimate of the size of the home market is widely regarded as too small; if this is indeed the case, then any eighteenth-century rise in the significance of foreign trade, and hence of commercial profits, would tend to be understated by Bairoch's calculations. Crafts's recalculations have attempted to remedy this source of distortion.[34]

This and similar objections to the detail of Bairoch's figures do not, however, affect the kernel of his argument, which depends on certain crude magnitudes which are not open to doubt. In the decades preceding the industrial watershed in England, foreign trade constituted around 10 per cent of GNP. Even assuming that profits on foreign trade were somewhat higher than those in agriculture, manufacturing and internal trade, they would still not have accounted for much more than, say, 12 per cent of gross capital formation. Moreover, it is not clear that merchants had a much higher propensity to reinvest profits than manufacturers, landlords or farmers, or that such reinvestment would have stimulated industry. Bairoch's own view is that the agricultural surplus yielded by the 'agricultural revolution' played the decisive part in opening the way to the Industrial Revolution. First, the continuing increase in agricultural output in England after 1660 allowed a larger proportion of the population to live in towns. Many of the new agricultural techniques employed implements with a high metal content compared with those they replaced, as in the switch from wooden to iron ploughs. Increased productivity boosted rural demand for both producer and consumer goods, and helped to furnish the strong and expanding home market which sustained early industrial advance.

There is much common ground between a Marxist approach and the emphasis to be found in Bairoch's studies, with their explicit invocation of the Physiocratic doctrine of the primacy of agricultural surplus. As noted above, Marx himself specifically invoked an agricultural revolution, conceived as a transformation of both social and productive relations in the countryside, as the indispensable preliminary to capitalist industrialization. Ernest Mandel opens his textbook discussion of 'The Development of Capital' with the peremptory observation:

> Agricultural surplus product is the basis of all surplus product and thereby of all civilization. If society were to devote all its working time to producing the means of subsistence, no other specialized activity, whether craft, industrial, scientific or artistic, would be possible.[35]

Christopher Hill, surveying Britain's economy and society between 1530 and 1780, saw agricultural revolution, the growth of the home market and domestic sources of industrial investment as supplying the essential framework of industrial advance. He writes of the agricultural revolution that it made possible 'the great expansion of the urban population which provided both the home market and the labour force for the industrial revolution'. After enumerating the various foreign sources of investment capital, he comments:

> But in the early stages of England's industrial development we should probably attach even more significance to family and group savings of small producers who ploughed back their profits into industry or agriculture. Gregory King thought in 1688 the largest total contribution to savings came from freeholders and farmers who would often themselves be industrialists.

In a later passage Hill declares:

> Of the significance, and the rising significance, of domestic demand there can be no doubt.... All roads thus led to the expansion of the home market. Commercialization of farming, enclosure and eviction, and the undermining of small, self-sufficient craftsmen's households, created a market for products of large scale manufacture. Those at the bottom of the ladder had to buy more, the more fortunate both bought and consumed more.[36]

Finally, Hobsbawm, in *Industry and Empire* – a book whose discussion of the foreign trade impetus was the starting point of Bairoch's critique – emphasized the importance of rural manufactures and the spread of capitalist social relations in the countryside. In an earlier work Hobsbawm wrote that on the eve of the Industrial Revolution:

> Agriculture was already prepared to carry out its three fundamental functions in an era of industrialization: to increase production and productivity, so as to feed a rapidly rising non-agricultural population; to produce a large and rising surplus of potential recruits for the towns and industries; and to provide a mechanism for the accumulation of capital to be used in the more modern sectors of the economy.[37]

These passages help to put trade flows into perspective, and are a useful reminder that the most decisive transformations of a social formation are usually those which tap resources internal to it: in this case, the victory of capitalist agriculture in England. The new model of British advance proposed by Crafts also allots greater weight to agricultural growth, though Patrick O'Brien remains sceptical of the impact of agricultural demand on industry at this time.[38] Once all necessary allowance has been made for the role of capital accumulation in the countryside, both 'primitive' and otherwise, what remains to be said of the contribution of colonial slavery and the Atlantic trades to financing industrial investment?

Without concomitant industrial development, agricultural improvements would have created more unemployment, and might have damped agricultural advance itself by denying it a flow of implements and a ready market. There is also evidence that the agricultural revolution itself was stimulated by the linked processes of urbanization and commercial expansion, since these provided agricultural producers with the markets which facilitated and justified technical advance. George Grantham points to the significant fact that agricultural advance took place 'around Europe's cities, in a common process that began in the Low Countries, passed to south eastern England and north eastern France, and finally in the early nineteenth century spread across the entire face of Northern Europe'.[39]

The view that profits from the Atlantic or 'triangular' trade made a vital contribution to British industrialization is above all associated with Eric Williams, who claimed in *Capitalism and Slavery* that the profits of slavery were such as to fertilize every branch of national production and set British capitalism off to a flying start.[40] Unlike the Marxists, he was not concerned with investigating the relations of production that made industrial capitalism a possibility in the first place. The main force of his book – which is considerable – derives from its vivid illustration of the intimacy between early industrial capitalism and the slave systems. The book attempted no quantitative demonstration of its thesis, and dwelt more on the British slave trade than on the entire commerce sustained by New World slavery. After this interval, as Barbara Solow and Stanley Engerman have pointed out, it is possible not only to reformulate some of the questions raised by Williams but also to draw upon more detailed research than was available to him – some of it specifically aimed at refuting the 'Williams thesis'.[41]

Capitalism and Slavery used the term 'triangular trade' as a shorthand expression to refer to every branch of the Atlantic plantation commerce, though it should be borne in mind that most plantation produce was brought to Europe by ships which specialized in this commerce, and did not visit Africa. Williams's illustrations were taken from the Africa and West India trades, and thus did not fully take the measure of Britain's Atlantic commercial system. Some critics, such as Roger Anstey in *The Atlantic Slave Trade and British Abolition*, assumed that Williams was arguing that slave trade profits alone had sponsored the industrialization process. In what follows an attempt will be made to summarize the overall contribution of the different branches of the plantation-related trades, and to measure this against the demands of the metropolitan industrializing process itself. In this context the questions raised by Bairoch, Brenner and others concerning the possible contribution of overseas trade to the accumulation process supply a helpful initial framework.

Do the figures adduced by Bairoch, and other similar exercises, show that there was a theoretical possibility that the British economy could have industrialized according to a purely internal and, as it were, organic growth, once capitalist social relations dominated the countryside? Could a virtuous circle of rising agricultural productivity, an expanding home market, larger urban populations and steady improvements to manufacture have carried the British economy inexorably in the direction of industrialization, without the need for the erratic stimulus of foreign trade – or the flashy but insubstantial profits of slave trading and slave plantations? Bairoch himself claims that if his demonstration is sound, the colonial contribution to industrial investment must have been negligible. Robert Brenner, addressing himself to the entire transition to capitalism, suggests a similar perspective:

> Those Marxists who, like Wallerstein, stress the significance of an original massing of wealth in either money or natural form often tend to beg the fundamental questions. In the first place, they do not say why such a build-up of wealth 'from the outside' – from the periphery to the core – was necessary for further economic advance at the time of the origins of capitalism. Were there, for example, technological blocks requiring an immense concentration of capital to be overcome: blockages which demanded even more resources than could be brought together from within the core? Even more importantly, what allowed for, and ensured that wealth brought into the core from the periphery would be used for productive rather than non-productive purposes?[42]

Brenner's remarks partly concern the early phase of capitalist 'origins', but they also claim a more general reference. Thus he explains in a footnote: 'It is, for example, today widely accepted that fixed capital requirements in manufacturing, even through the first stages of the industrial revolution, were relatively small.'[43] The critics of the 'Williams thesis' also insisted that the fixed capital demands of the industrializing manufacturers were so modest that external finance was unnecessary. This may have some validity so far as the fixed capital requirements of the individual enterprise were concerned, but it neglects two facts. First, over the economy as a whole large-scale investments were made in canals, roads, harbours, docks, shipping, mines, agricultural drainage, and so forth. In fact British economic advance in the eighteenth century and beyond entailed huge expenditures on infrastructure, many intimately connected with overseas trade; the advance of the individual enterprise was often premised on the facilities provided by such investments. Secondly, if we scrutinize the capital needed by the individual enterprise we find that outside heavy industry, the main need was not for *fixed capital* but for *working capital* or commercial credit. In the early industrial era the turnaround time of circulating capital was quite sluggish, since goods took a long time to reach their market. In fact, research into the origins of early industrialists shows that they needed to command considerable resources, and that few who were not from a quite wealthy background became cotton masters.[44] The early cotton factory itself could, perhaps, be set up for less than a thousand pounds, since buildings could be rented rather than purchased. But the early cotton manufacturer would need to be backed by several times this amount of working capital or commercial credit if he was to purchase raw materials and pay wages until he could count on a steady stream of returns from sales. Access to several thousand pounds of ready cash or credit implied considerable wealth in the mid or late eighteenth century. It implied, in fact, prior wealth or business success, or wealthy relatives or partners. Once he was in business, the cotton or metal manufacturer had a fairly constant need for credit. Foreign merchants were undoubtedly major suppliers of this credit in the innovating sectors.[45]

If profits from the slave trade and the American plantations made any contribution to British industrialization, it would have to be either (1) because these profits were large enough to affect the prosperity of the economy as a whole; or (2) because they eased the financial or credit problems of the technically progressive sectors in particular. As we shall see, there is reason to believe that the slave trading and planting complex contributed in both these ways. The potential for a 'macro' and 'micro' contribution will be considered in turn.

R.B. Sheridan, basing himself on estimates of Jamaican planting profits made by the planter Edward Long, has computed the annual net revenue drawn by British interests from Jamaica in 1770 (see Table XII.7):

Table XII.7   Profits from Jamaican Plantations and Trade in 1770

	£000
Profits on Plantation Production	
retained profit	250
remittances to Britain	200
Profits on Trade, Credit, and Manufacture	
freight	419
insurance	20
commission and brokerage	260
indirect remittances	60
interest on loans	35
slave trade profits	125
profit of manufactures	130
Total	1,499

Source: Sheridan, 'The Wealth of Jamaica', *Economic History Review*, 18, 1965, pp. 292–311.

Sheridan's calculations concern total revenue arising to British private interests from Jamaican plantations and trade, not simply commercial profit from trade alone. He argues that if similar returns were made from Britain's other West Indian slave colonies, total profits from this source would have been £2,300,000 in 1770. He explains that the conceptual framework for his estimates is supplied by the 'staple theory of economic growth'. This theory, which differs from the econometric models used by some quantitative economic historians to analyse sectoral contributions, seeks to establish:

> backward linkages, or the inducement to invest in the production of such plantation inputs and transportation equipment as ships, textiles, hardware, and foodstuffs; forward linkages, or the inducement to invest in sugar refineries and textile mills which used the output of the export industry; and final demand linkages, or the inducement to invest in metropolitan industries which produced consumer goods for factors in the plantation supply and processing sectors.[46]

This approach carries the danger of double-counting or the misattribution of profits between sectors. In the summary just quoted, it is not entirely clear whether comprehensive itemization has not led to the snake swallowing its own tail, with some 'final demand' linkages ('plantation supply') having already been entered as 'backward linkages' ('plantation inputs'). If these practices are not avoided, the 'staple' theory can be a particularly unfair weapon to use against proponents of the primacy of domestic agriculture: whereas it gives scope for multiplying the impact of a branch accounting for, say, 5 per cent or 10 per cent of GNP, it can scarcely perform the same feat for a sector which already accounts for 70 or 80 per cent of GNP in a pre-industrial economy. In this instance there are two pitfalls which must be avoided in the use of Sheridan's data. First, his figures include operating costs for the services required by the plantation trade. Second, he includes as 'profits on trade' the profits made by British manufacturers selling to the West Indies; likewise, he includes the profits made by those shipping plantation products. From the standpoint of Marxist political economy such profits did not represent the surplus-value extracted from the slaves but, in the first instance, the surplus-value extracted from factory workers and sailors. However, it is a perfectly valid exercise to include such profits under the heading of surplus-value *realized* as a consequence of plantation demand, especially in view of the difficulty of finding other outlets for these goods and services. As shown in the previous section, the 'realization effect' of plantation demand was a major stimulus to British capital accumulation, and there is every reason to attempt to quantify it.[47]

Sheridan's estimates were criticized from two standpoints: R.P. Thomas has argued that they do not adequately reflect costs, while J.R. Ward's research into planting profits – cited in Chapter X – indicates that Sheridan understated the West Indian profit rate. Thomas argued for a reduction of Sheridan's figures on three counts. First, he argued that the cost of supplying services to the colonial trade is not properly deducted from the figures for outlays on freight, commission and brokerage; and that figures for profits on the slave trade and on manufactures represent gross rather than net profits. Thomas's alternative figures supply an interesting corrective, though from the standpoint of Marxist political economy they somewhat understate realized surplus-value, since they exclude that portion of profit reinvested in facilities for production or transportation. Commission and brokerage is an awkward item but should probably be included *in toto*, without attempting to estimate its *faux frais*, in the surplus-value generated by slave labour.

Thomas's two other criticisms of the Sheridan figures are not relevant to the present discussion. He deducts from planting profits the British Government's outlays for the defence of the Sugar Islands, while he does not offset them against the yield of the sugar duties. Since defence expenditures did not directly subtract from private profits, which concern us here, consideration of this point will be postponed to a later section. Thomas's third deduction obliges us to spell out in what sense slaves produced a surplus. He argues that the system of colonial protection obliged British consumers to pay more for their sugar than if they had access to the sugar of the French islands: he therefore deducts no less than £383,000 from the total annual revenue figure on the grounds that this was a concealed 'sugar subsidy' to the British planters extracted from the British consumer, and therefore not a profit to the Empire as a whole.[48]

Protection of the British sugar plantations did entail a notional cost to British consumers, but led to real profits in the hands of the planters and those doing business with them. The somewhat lower price of French sugars resulted from, among other things, the more effective super-exploitation of slaves in the French plantations, and should not be regarded as some sort of norm with which to deflate the super-exploitation of the slaves in the British colonies. The slaves, of course, were not obtaining the market value of their labour. But the price of sugar to the consumer also reflected the sugar duties, other taxes and the super-profits accruing to merchants and planters who often enjoyed monopolistic leverage, so that sugar produced by free workers might not have been dearer. The slaves' prodigious surplus labour and surplus product – amounting to the fruits of roughly five-sevenths of their weekly labour – became realized as 'surplus-value' only because of the englobing context of the capitalist market and the scope for capitalist accumulation in the metropolis. From this standpoint the British planters' ability to charge higher prices because of the tariff favouring colonial sugar was a device enabling them to garner more of this surplus-value.

If Thomas's deductions for defence and for the 'sugar subsidy' are set aside, Sheridan's estimates can be rearranged as in Table XII.8:

Table XII.8   Jamaican Trade Profits c. 1770

	£000
Freight	168
Insurance	20
Interest on loans	5
Commission and brokerage	94
Profits on manufacturing	104
Slave trade	30
Subtotal	420
Planting profits (Thomas)	450
Total	870

Source: adapted from R.P. Thomas, 'The Sugar Colonies of the Old Empire', *Economic History Review*, XXI, 1968, p. 36.

Sheridan and Thomas differed over methods of computing profit, but both worked from the basic revenue estimates taken from Edward Long. Sheridan's approach brings out the full contribution of the plantation trade to maintaining the commercial, financial and transportation infrastructure controlled by metropolitan interests; Thomas's figures give the net profits arising from the trade available for investment or capitalists' consumption.

J.R. Ward's investigations into the accounts of a sample of Jamaican and West Indian sugar plantations led him to conclude that Edward Long understated their true profit rates, and that instead of profits of £450,000 per year, the real figure was nearly twice as high: 'The sample estimates suggest instead an annual profit on sugar production of £800,000 in Jamaica and £1,700,000 in the British West Indies as a whole, or about £1,200,000 and £2,500,000 respectively if profits from other staples were included.'[49] If the Ward figures for Jamaican profits are aggregated with the Sheridan and Ward figures for the profits on trade, the results shown in Table XII.9 are obtained:

Table XII.9   Jamaican Profits c. 1770

£000	Ward/Sheridan	Ward/Thomas
Profits on production	800	800
Profits on trade	1,499	870
Total	2,299	1,670

Ward's figures for plantation profits throughout the British West Indies are not based on simple extrapolation of Jamaican data, since his research included sample plantations from other islands. As noted in Chapter X,

David Hancock finds considerably higher planting and commercial profits for his London merchants during this period than Ward's average; their individual fortunes from Atlantic trade ranged from £50,000 to £500,000 (the total value of capital invested in the cotton industry in 1788, buildings as well as machinery, was only £1,856,000).[50] Ward's figures now seem conservative. If his estimate for overall British West Indian plantation profits is combined with the Sheridan and Thomas estimates of overall commercial profits, we obtain the results shown in Table XII.10:

Table XII.10   British West Indian Profits c. 1770

£000 Annual Rate	Ward/Sheridan	Ward/Thomas
Profits on production	2,500	2,500
Profits on trade	2,600	1,271
Total	5,100	3,771

How much plantation profit, thus estimated, was likely to be retained, and how much remitted? Long's original figures for plantation expenditure are more likely to have been accurate than his figures for profits; they do seem compatible with the value of colonial commerce. Since a large number of plantation owners were absentees, they were inclined to remit profits to Britain with some adjustment according to their estimate of commercial prospects. As noted in Chapter X, 'Island Expenses' were paid for largely from the sales of secondary crops and by-products. The main crop was sold by the planter in Britain; the lion's share of the proceeds were thus available for expenditure or investment in the metropolis. However, since we are arguing here that plantation profits *were* important to domestic capital formation in Britain, the best procedure to adopt is that of selecting a reasonable assumption that errs, if at all, on the side of understating plantation profits. Accordingly, it will be assumed that the proportion of profits retained in the Long estimates applies, rather than the absolute amount he indicated. If this is done, then £1.1 million was remitted, and the scaled-down net profit figure for the West Indies as a whole would be:

Sheridan/Ward   £3,711,000
Thomas/Ward   £2,382,000

These total profits arising from the colonial system in the West Indies can be subdivided, as we saw above, into those *extracted* through exploitation of the slaves, and profits made from the sweated labour of British factory operatives and transport workers *realized* through exchanges with the West Indian slave system. Profits arising directly from the slaves and remitted back to Britain would be £1,307,000, with a further 'realization effect' of

£1,075,000 on British profits. According to the Thomas/Ward composite figure, direct profits on slave labour would be £1,307,000, with a further 'realization effect' of £1,075,000 on British profits. This, however, represents the results of a rough-and-ready division carried out on the basis of figures that are not well adapted to the purpose. And while slave plantation profits are 'primitive accumulation' in the strict sense, the profits realized from English wage labourers are not, despite the atrocious conditions prevailing in the new industrial regions, and must instead be classed as capitalist accumulation proper.

In order to arrive at a global figure for British profits arising from the 'triangular trade' as a whole, the best available estimates for the earnings of the British slave trade should also be taken into account. Both the Sheridan and the Thomas estimates contain an entry for slave trading profits, but – following research into this commerce by Roger Anstey – it is possible to obtain a more accurate global figure. Table XII.0 (p. 510) gives the overall results of Anstey's researches and calculations for the period 1761 to 1807. His figure deducts 5 per cent of total outset costs and 5 per cent of net receipts in order to eliminate profit on commodities other than slaves purchased on the African coasts (columns 9 and 11). He also deducted from gross receipts (column 6) an estimated 18 per cent to account for commissions paid on slave sales to the ships' captains, surgeons and other officers, and bonus payments to the crew over and above their wages, to obtain a figure for 'net receipts' accruing to the ships' owners (column 7). Finally, Anstey also deducted from these net receipts the cost of discounting the West Indian planters' bills of exchange over a two-year period. After all these deductions have been made, Anstey calculates the net profit (column 13) and the 'resource increment' to the British economy (column 14), which adds the slave traders' profit to the discounting commission.

For present purposes, it is the 'resource increment' which is most relevant. Indeed, there would be a case for including profits on the non-slave African commodity trade and at least a part of the payments made to the officers of the slave trading vessels, some of whose funds would have been invested. Anstey was at pains to point out that his calculations related narrowly to profits from the trade in slaves; they were not concerned to establish the surplus generated by the triangular trade overall.[51] Joseph Inikori and others have urged that profits were, in fact, considerably greater than Anstey allowed.[52] However, on the general principle of adopting the more conservative estimates of British gains from the colonial system, we will agree the Anstey figures from column 14 and accept that the British slave trading surplus in 1770 was somewhere between £90,000 and £145,000, the averages for the preceding and succeeding decades – say £115,000. This figure would refer exclusively to commercial and financial profits, and would not take account of the realization of manufacturers' profits on the trade goods supplied to the slave traders, or the profit on the outfitting of the slave trading vessel. Anstey's estimate for total outset costs less 5 per cent (column 11) takes into account both the cost of acquiring trade goods and the cost of outfitting the slave ship, less its written-down value at the end of the voyage. If manufacturers' and outfitters' profits ran at 5 per cent of outlays, they would have realized £300,000 a year in the decades 1760–80, as a consequence of the slave trade. The cargo accounted for 65 per cent of outset costs, while the written-down value of the slave trading vessels was in the region 12–18 per cent of outset costs. The manufacturers' share of realized profits would have been in the range £200,000 to £240,000.

In considering these estimates for profits made in the West Indian and African trade, it is relevant that the year 1770 by no means represented a peak, but something close to an average for the peacetime years between 1763 and 1776. According to Ward's calculations, plantation profits were somewhat lower during this period than they had been between 1714 and 1762. Between 1776 and 1783 there was an appreciable decline, followed by recovery (1783–91) leading on to a sustained boom lasting for nearly a quarter of a century (1792–1816). According to Ward, the plantation profit rate ran at 12.6 per cent in the years 1792–98 and 9.6 per cent in 1799–1819, compared with 9.2 per cent in 1763–75. It should be borne in mind that the number and value of British West Indian sugar estates grew over this period: their total value was estimated to have grown by 20 per cent between 1775 and 1790, and to have doubled between 1789 and 1814, partly because of wartime acquisitions. The mass of planting profits grew threefold between 1770–75 and 1806–14, reaching £13.9 million if the value set on British plantations by Coloquhoun's *British Empire* is multiplied by Ward's 9.6 per cent profit rate; over the same period Britain's national income also roughly trebled.[53]

So far as the slave trade is concerned, it will be seen from Anstey's calculations that both the volume and the profitability of the trade had more than doubled by the last decades of the century compared with 1761–80. So far as Britain's industrial growth is concerned the period 1783–1808, when planting and trading profits were at their height, is just as significant as the earlier period around 1770; many recent accounts of British economic growth stress the importance of the breakthroughs achieved in the later period. However, it will be convenient to stay with the estimates for 1770, as elaborated above, since this year does lie towards the beginning of the era of industrial transformations, and provides a test of the contribution of 'triangular' profits in an average rather than a good year.

Only profits arising from the African and British West Indian trades have been considered hitherto. There was some British investment in slave plantations in North America and in the Dutch and Danish colonies, but its size would not have been such as to alter materially the orders of magnitude outlined above. Profits on British peacetime exports to North America were very considerable. In the preceding section and in Chapter

IX we have given data for the North American trade as a whole. About 44 per cent of British exports to the North American colonies in the years 1768–72 went to the Southern colonies, where slave labour sustained the export sector.[54] For the purposes of this exercise it will be appropriate to exclude the profits made on exports to the Northern zone, where slavery was marginal, even though Northern purchasing power did largely derive from the plantation carrying trade.

The value of British exports to the Southern plantation zone in 1768–72 averaged about £1,750,000 annually – representing, perhaps, £150,000 annually of profit to British merchants and manufacturers. This profit, however, was to be cut short in 1775–85. Moreover, at the outbreak of hostilities British traders claimed that they were owed as much as £2.5 million by Americans in the plantation zone; these claims may have been much exaggerated, and referred in the main to advances made to planters in earlier periods (the claims were mostly settled in the 1780s). As we will see later, the interruption of this branch of trade directly pushed some British – especially Scottish – manufacturers and merchants to turn to industrial investments. The later revival of the North America trade certainly boosted mercantile and manufacturing profits; indeed, even earlier debts were recovered. But for the purposes of macro-economic calculation centred in the 1770s, it seems best to reserve consideration of profits from this source to an 'upper bound' estimate, and to exclude it from the basic assessment of triangular trade profits.

Finally, a full inventory of the profits made by those involved in Britain's slave-related Atlantic commerce would have to include profits on exports to Brazil, Saint Domingue and the American colonies of other European powers. Britain's annual trade with Portugal ran at around £1 million in the 1750s, with wheat and woollen manufactures looming large. Pombal went so far as to declare: 'Gold and silver are fictitious riches; the negroes that work in the mines of Brazil must be clothed by England, by which the value of their produce becomes relative to the price of cloth.'[55] He might have added that English cloth became an important trade good, thus making it an even more direct measure of slave value. Pombal's programme of national and colonial development included encouragement for a Portuguese textile industry which, in combination with recession in Brazil after 1760, cut into British exports. By 1770 British exports to Portugal ran at around £700,000 annually, of which roughly a half was destined for the Brazilian or African market. The slave-related portion of the Portuguese trade might have realized mercantile and manufacturing profits of around £35,000 annually. Likewise, Ireland's ability to buy English manufactures partly reflected the strength of Irish exports to the plantations.[56] Much of Britain's trade with the colonies of other powers was contraband, and cannot be accurately calculated. Again, the best procedure will be to separate out consideration of profits arising from this wider Atlantic trade, and to identify the core West Indian and African slave-related earnings.

How do such profits compare with Britain's wealth, income and investment in 1770?

In a contribution of 1975 which tended to reject the 'Williams thesis', Stanley Engerman wrote: 'the contribution of the profits of the slave trade plus those estimated by Sheridan from the West Indian plantations was below 5 per cent of British income in the early years of the Industrial Revolution'.[57] At this time Engerman regarded this proportion of externally produced or induced profits as rather low. Yet if it was sustained, a proportion of this sort would certainly have been making a respectable contribution, at the margin, to British prosperity. And such a percentage takes no account of the slave trade's 'realization effect' on domestic profits – a point that could also be made about Anstey's attempt to draw conclusions from his own figures. Anstey, unlike Engerman, did not compare slave trading profits only with national income but also with gross capital formation. For the present discussion the key relationship is between the portion of 'triangular trade' profits invested in the British economy and gross capital formation.

C.H. Feinstein's investigations of capital formation in Britain revised downwards the previously accepted estimates for the late eighteenth century, but with a pronounced rising tendency around the turn of the century. While they replaced somewhat higher estimates by Sidney Pollard for the eighteenth century, Crafts's calculations come out somewhat lower. Since Feinstein's estimates occupy the mid-range and are based on research rather than model-building, it will be appropriate to use them here (see Table XII.11).

Table XII.11   Gross Fixed Capital Formation: Great Britain 1770–1815

£ million at current prices

c.1770	c.1790–93	c.1815	c.1830–35
4.0	11.4	26.5	28.2

Source: C.H. Feinstein, 'Capital Expenditure in Great Britain', in *Cambridge Economic History of Europe*, Cambridge 1978, p. 74.

These estimates do not include the manufacturers' and merchants' investment in stock, which amounted to some £1.5 million in 1770 compared with £0.8 million for investments in machinery; they do, however, include £1.3 million for transport, including ships, in 1770.[58]

These figures for gross fixed capital formation in 1770 may be compared with triangular trade profits, as specified above. Table XII.12 includes both a 'basic' estimate, made on the most conservative basis, and an 'upper bound' estimate using Sheridan's figures and including all branches of the trade.

Table XII.12   The Triangular Trade 1770: Direct and Indirect Profits

	£	
Basic Estimates		
Direct Profits/Surplus		
Thomas/Ward plantation profits	1,307,000	
Anstey slave trade profits	115,000	
Subtotal	1,422,000	
Indirect Profits/Surplus Realization		
West Indian trade	1,075,000	
African trade	300,000	
Subtotal	1,375,000	
Grand Total		2,797,000
Upper Bound Estimates		
Direct Profits/Surplus		
Sheridan/Ward	1,796,000	
Anstey	115,000	
Subtotal	1,911,000	
Indirect Profits/Surplus Realization		
West Indian trade	1,915,000	
African trade	300,000	
North American plantation trade	150,000	
Brazil/Portugal trade	60,000	
Subtotal	2,425,000	
Grand Total		4,336,000

It will be seen that the Basic Estimate is equivalent to about half of total capital formation, including merchants' stock, while the Upper Bound Estimate reaches some four-fifths of the same total. It is unrealistic, of course, to suppose that all profits were reinvested. In the case of merchants and manufacturers there is some reason to believe that the ratio of reinvestment in trade or industry was quite high. But the absentee planters, and some of the West India merchants, were famous for their extravagant lifestyle. As Richard Pares put it, they 'built more Fonthills than factories'.[59] But even the absentee who expended plantation profits upon a Palladian mansion, set in a landscaped park in the English or Welsh countryside, was likely also to be making some agricultural investments, if only in enclosure or drainage. Alternatively, the recipients of plantation profits might keep them in an account with their factor, merchant house or banker, thus assisting the latter to make investments.

Triangular trade profits went to the wealthier classes who probably saved a greater than average proportion of their incomes. Pending more detailed information relating to this question, it seems not unreasonable to suppose that between 30 per cent and 50 per cent of triangular trade profits were reinvested. Of course, such a figure would itself have been a tribute to the spirit of accumulation which had already asserted itself within the British social formation. If the reinvestment rate was at the lower end of the range proposed (i.e. 30 per cent) then, according to the 'basic' estimates, triangular trade profits could have supplied 20.9 per cent of Britain's gross fixed capital formation. On the other hand, if 50 per cent of 'basic' profits were reinvested, then the proportion would rise to 28.7 per cent. If we take the 'upper bound' estimate, then between £2.2 million and £1.4 million could have been reinvested from triangular trade profits, ranging between 35 and 55 per cent of Feinstein's estimate.[60]

At their extreme, the estimates proposed here suggest that profits derived from the triangular trade could have furnished anything from 20.9 per cent to 55 per cent of Britain's gross fixed capital formation in 1770. This range could be narrowed down to between 20.9 per cent and 35.0 per cent if we match the 'basic estimate' of triangular trade profits against Feinstein's findings concerning Britain's capital formation in those years. Macro-economic calculations of this sort certainly have limitations, but even in the lower range they are consistent with the strong version of the 'Williams thesis', according to which the profits generated by the 'triangular trade' 'fertilized the entire productive system of the country'.[61] Such a conclusion is, of course, very general, and tells us nothing of the particular channels which might have linked triangular profits to specifically capitalist or philo-industrial forms of investment in the metropolitan economy. Before proceeding to a consideration of what these links might have been, two further general observations are in order.

First, it seems probable that triangular trade profits as a whole grew at least as fast in the late eighteenth century as did Britain's metropolitan economy. It has already been pointed out that the mass of planting profits in the British West Indies multiplied three times over between the early 1770s and the turn of the century. Likewise, the data cited above from Anstey show that the 'resource increment' earned by the slave trade rose from about £115,000 annually around 1770 to £379,200 annually during the 1790s. The halting of the slave trade in 1807–08 brought this to an end, but did not damage – indeed, rather enhanced – the profitability of the British plantations and the trade they generated. To this must be added the fact that British exports to the United States, Brazil and Spanish America were rising rapidly in the last decade or more of the eighteenth century. While British national income nearly trebled in three decades (1770 to 1800), British exports to the plantation zone trebled in two (1784–86 to 1804–06). Feinstein's data suggest that capital formation rose as a proportion of national income from 7 per cent in 1760 to 11 per cent in the 1790s.[62] If 'triangular profits' helped to make economic space for investment in 1770, it seems likely that this role was maintained, or even enhanced, in the last two decades of the century.

A second observation should be made concerning triangular trade profits. In the late eighteenth century Britain was awash with the profits of empire. Despite loss of the American colonies the flow of colonial tribute in one form or another continued, and even increased. The profits of the plantations and of the slave-based trades probably constituted the largest single source of imperial gains, but Ireland and India greatly swelled the revenues available to Britain's ruling class. Around mid century the Irish rents remitted to absentee landlords in Britain amounted to some £750,000 a year.[63] By the 1770s the East India Company was converting itself from a fairly profitable commercial enterprise into a government, directly extracting a gigantic surplus from Bengal and other parts of the subcontinent over which it exercised its sway. Between 1756 and 1770 the Company and its officials directly remitted £2.7 million from India to Britain: these direct remittances rose to £5.4 million between 1770 and 1784, or at a rate of some £386,000 annually.[64] The export trade to the East remained modest until the second and third decades of the nineteenth century, so it did not generate the considerable 'realization effect' which we have identified in the case of the Atlantic trades.

Colonial tribute on this scale can scarcely have been without effect on the path of metropolitan accumulation. In some earlier decades of the eighteenth century it is possible that the scope for colonial super-profits even diverted investable resources away from less attractive employments in the metropolis. But for much of the century, and especially towards its close, there was as much emphasis on profit-taking as on profit-making. On the one hand, the proto-capitalist development of agriculture and manufacture in the metropolis furnished a rewarding field for investment; on the other, the scope for new investment in colonial enterprises was limited. Some British planters did expand their operations – for example, into newly acquired territories such as Grenada and, later, Guyana – but this only required a modest slice of the huge profits being made during the British West Indian 'dance of the millions' in 1792–1816. Planters knew well enough that this bonanza was linked to high wartime prices, so they were discouraged from financing long-term investment projects in the West Indies out of the profits they were making. The passage of the Act abolishing the British slave trade in 1807 eliminated the possibility of new investments in African slaves; thus it probably encouraged further siphoning-off of profits which continued at a high level. From the 1790s, if not before, the plantations were not so much a 'leading sector' as a 'milch-cow sector'.

In the late eighteenth and early nineteenth centuries Britain undertook a major series of investment programmes: in the merchant marine, in harbours and docks, in canals, in agricultural improvements and in developing the new industrial machinery. Moreover, these vast expenditures were undertaken at a time when population was rising, and during a period of unprecedented military outlays. The profits of empire and slavery helped to make this possible, enlarging the resources at the command of public authorities, improving landlords, enterprising merchants and innovating manufacturers. Because of the prior transformation in agriculture, and in British society as a whole, colonial and mercantile wealth could be transmuted into capital employing wage labour. Compared to the transformative processes of a modern capitalist economy, the mechanisms at work here were inefficient and wasteful, and wealth hoarded in one sector by no means automatically released resources for investment in another.

While John Cartright was struggling to find funds for his 'Revolution' mill, founded to commemorate the centenary of 1688, the stock jobbers of the City and the protégés of Henry Dundas were gorging themselves on the flesh of Bengal. Colonial tribute facilitated the advance to industrialism, but it also left its curse on British bourgeois institutions – preserving and strengthening an entrenched mercantile–financial complex which preferred the lush pastures of public and imperial finance, and the easy pickings of commercial speculation, to the rigours of industrial investment. Some of the larger projects for improving public communications did attract the support of the major institutions, but at the micro level provincial banks and merchant houses played a more important part in financing industrialization than the banks and merchant houses of the City of London.

David Hancock's twenty-three London merchant associates give us some idea of the variety of ways in which mercantile profits were ploughed back into the domestic economy. They made a large number of loans to acquaintances and family members, they held money with banks, they purchased and improved landed estates, they invested in the Funds and dabbled in manufacturing ventures. Simply by outfitting new voyages to Africa or the Americas, they stimulated investment in British manufactures. Oswald put money into a Pittenweem carpet venture, the Forth Clyde Canal and a Kilmarnock woollen factory. But as they grew wealthier, the balance of the mercantile associates' estates tilted towards land. This might seem simply to confirm the cliché of the rich merchant doing his best to turn himself into a useless aristocrat, but Hancock's study paints a significantly different picture. In order to be accepted as gentlemen, his merchants strove to prove themselves enlightened 'improvers', patrons of the arts and sciences, investors in educational schemes and projects for better systems of transport and communication. Hancock writes:

> The associates played their part in building roads and bridges, and to a lesser extent, canals and lighthouses. They used their business and social networks to obtain expert assistance with their projects: they drew upon their management experience to bring together laborers and supplies in construction projects.... The associates also participated in local industrial ventures.... Even an incomplete reconstruction of the associates' industrial portfolios suggests a wider range of commitment than is generally realized. They invested in maritime undertak-

ings, especially whaling; the making of cloth, mainly wool; mining, particularly salt, coal and lime; and the production of building materials, such as lumber, rope, iron and glass.[65]

The arriviste who neglected to busy himself with projects for improving local infrastructure or investments in national industries would seem narrow-minded and boorish by comparison with these expansive entrepreneurs. Nevertheless such 'gentlemanly capitalists' did not turn themselves into industrial magnates; their scatter of productive investments reflected rather than created an economic pattern. Now that we have noted this general point, it will be appropriate to look at the different sectors which could have benefited.

Sectors of Investment and New Financial Instruments

Between 1760 and 1800 the share of agriculture in the composition of national wealth in Britain dropped from 77 per cent to 68 per cent, while that of commerce and industry rose from 5 per cent to 10.[66] As agriculture constituted the largest single sector it required heavy investments, many of which are difficult to estimate, since they involved the maintenance and replenishment of stocks of animals, pastures and orchards, of drainage systems and fences. Annual investment in horses – or 'gross horse formation', as some economic historians call it – may have absorbed as much as £1 million a year in the late eighteenth century.

A great deal of the reproduction and expansion of agricultural resources bore no direct relationship to the surplus generated in other sectors. However, the increase in output and productivity achieved in the period 1750 to 1825 did bear witness to a quickening agricultural revolution. Metal implements replaced wooden tools, and more scientific farming practices spread. Landlords with sufficient resources and political influence were able greatly to extend the enclosure of common and waste lands, bringing vast tracts in the Midlands within a more capitalist farming structure. Those seeking to promote an enclosure needed ready cash to obtain the consent of freeholders and copyholders, and to finance the passage of an Act of Parliament. Eric Williams cites a number of examples of well-known improving landlords, like the Penryns, who derived wealth from West Indian plantations. More generally, G.E. Mingay refers to West Indian fortunes as one source of agricultural finance in eighteenth-century England.[67] But neither these observations nor more localized monographs permit any precise quantitative assessment. The contribution of triangular profits to agricultural improvement was most probably modest. At the margin it may have boosted agricultural investment by helping to finance enclosure, and thus have promoted, at least indirectly, an agrarian structure more suited to capitalist agriculture.

Investments in canals absorbed very large sums in this period, and made an important contribution to overall growth. Between 1755 and 1815 a total of about £17 million was spent on inland navigational investments, creating a network of canals and rivers which helped to integrate the home market, and connect manufacturing and mining centres with one another and with the wider world. J.T. Ward has studied the pattern of shareholding in canal companies responsible for about £5 million of this investment. His analysis of the occupation or status of these shareholdings reveals the distribution in Table XII.13:

Table XII.13   Finance of Canal Building in Eighteenth-Century England: Percentage Contributions

I	Peers	5.4	VI	Tradesmen	17.6
II	Landed gentry	17.3	VII	Professionals	10.0
III	Farmers	1.6	VIII	Clergymen	5.5
IV	Capitalists	21.4	IX	Women	6.5
X	Manufacturers	14.7			

Source: J.T. Ward, *The Finance of Canal Building in Eighteenth Century England*, p. 74.

The two categories here most linked to overseas and colonial trade would be 'capitalists' – that is, merchants and bankers – and 'manufacturers'. Together they contributed 36.1 per cent of the funds employed. However, as Ward points out: 'The close intermingling of commercial and landed wealth in eighteenth century England is a commonplace: the fortune of a "landowner" might have originated in the East or West Indies or in some trade nearer home.'[68] Equally, the money invested by women, or professionals, might derive from the colonial and overseas trading complex. Ward points out that 'the investments of the principal occupational classes were roughly proportional to their share of the nation's larger incomes'.[69] Thus the contribution by tenant farmers and smallholders was very small: no doubt their surplus was largely absorbed by the demands of agricultural investment. There is some reason to suppose that it was the 'capitalists' and manufacturers most closely linked to overseas trade who figured largest in subscriptions to canal companies. Thus Ward writes of the 'importance of commercial capital from London and Bristol' in the financing of canals throughout Southern England. He adds:

> it appears that the share of manufacturers in the finance of canals rather exceeded their share of the nation's large incomes; the investments of some of the most ambitious industrialists, of Lancashire's cotton spinners, for example, were very substantial indeed. Furthermore there is no evidence that as a class manufacturers found it particularly difficult to produce the sums for which they subscribed.[70]

According to Ward, Liverpool merchants also figured prominently in the subscribers' lists.

Although the evidence cited is no more than suggestive, it does seem probable that manufacturers and merchants who wished to reach out to overseas markets had an extra motive for investing in canals. By the same token, they undertook the major proportion of investment in the merchant marine; though the success of Britain's overseas trade also attracted capital into the mercantile–manufacturing regions from other parts of the country and from abroad.

If we turn to the capital needs of industry, the logical connection with Atlantic trade profits seems even stronger. As noted above, the early industrial concerns had great need of commercial credit and working capital. Crouzet writes: 'Merchant firms, which supplied industry with a large part of its circulating capital, thus played a dominant and decisive part in the industrial revolution, and the financing of stocks by mercantile capital was much more important than industry's self-finance, at least up to 1814.'[71]

In the special case of the cotton industry, there were especially close links between the early industrialists and the merchants engaged in one or another branch of the triangular trade. Research into the links between the ports engaged in the African and American trades and the growth of the cotton industry in the hinterland is not conclusive, but it does all point in the same direction. The classic study of the early cotton industry, *The Cotton Trade and Industrial Lancashire*, by A.P. Wadworth and J. de L. Mann, published in 1931, identified a strong connection between overseas trade and the initial growth of cotton manufacturing. More recently, Douglas Farnie's study *The English Cotton Industry and the World Market* stresses the isolation of the cotton districts from the wider national economy, and their integration within an Atlantic-facing mercantile complex based on Liverpool and Manchester.[72]

Those who have studied the activities of particular slave traders reveal an extended and reciprocal network of relations with producers of cotton goods, metal goods and other manufactures. The industrially produced cotton goods and fustians were cheap so long as large runs were undertaken. The slave trading business was in the hands of quite a small number of merchants who acted as agents for a much larger number of investors. David Richardson has identified twenty merchants who were responsible for 70 per cent of the total number of slave trading voyages to leave Liverpool in the years 1766 to 1774.[73] These men acted as agents for those who wished to invest in the trade, their own stake in any one voyage being quite small. In a study of the accounts of a Liverpool slave merchant, B.L. Anderson discovered entries for a large number of manufacturers from such towns as Manchester, Rochdale, Stockport and Preston, and concludes: 'for a short but crucial period, the slave trade was an important route along which British, and especially Lancashire, manufactures tested their competitive strength in the expanding markets served by the colonial trade'.[74]

S.D. Chapman, investigating the financial ramifications of the cotton industry in the 1780s and 1790s, confirmed that there was a 'web of credit' that 'included Manchester merchants and cotton dealers, Liverpool merchants and cotton brokers, leading calicoe printers and fustian manufacturers, and local bankers with their London connections'.[75] He points out that the Manchester section of the *Universal British Directory* listed sixty firms which combined manufacturing and mercantile functions. B.K. Drake writes in a study of Liverpool traders: 'Financing voyages from within the port was facilitated by the availability of long term credits, of up to eighteen months, particularly from the Manchester manufacturers.' The same author points out that 'the nature of the "general trading" often allowed a slave trader to include commodities for export to Africa which were acquired through an extension of his other interests, at primary or wholesale cost'.[76]

In a survey of the role of merchants, Jacob Price reports that the British trade in 'sugar, tobacco and slaves' showed a pronounced eighteenth-century tendency for the concentration of business in a few hands. He adds:

> Since they focused on problems related to credit and liquidity, the great port merchants turned naturally to a variety of new commercial and financial departures. . . . The early partners of the numerous private banks founded in London and the principal outports came overwhelmingly from the same merchant-wholesaler background. Though few became industrialists, a significant number took shares in early manufacturing ventures.[77]

Price also stresses that the export trades made a large contribution to developing a sophisticated infrastructure of commercial institutions and means of communication.

These various studies, working from the accounts of merchants and manufacturers, build up a picture of a circuit of mercantile and industrial capital linking many manufacturers with the profits of the triangular trades. Indeed, so close was the connection that some early manufacturers must have lost money or stock through unwise or unlucky speculations, while all such investors will have seen their returns reduced by the slow turnaround of the overseas trade. More generally, manufacturers were net receivers of credit, as Pat Hudson has established, allowing merchant suppliers to take some risk off their shoulders.[78] In principle overseas outlets may have been a 'second best' – a method of moving stock which could not be sold in sufficient quantity on the home market. So far as the individual investment was concerned, the Africa trade was a bit like a lottery, in that some would profit greatly while others lost out, with the pleasing difference that the odds were stacked in favour of the punter. Manufacturing participation in the slave trade would have had the tendency to concentrate capitals, since large investors would obtain the high average rates of return, while lucky investors would become large. Both the American and African trades would have had a tendency to favour manufacturers who could afford long runs and slow returns, offering premium profits to those with sufficient scale and resources. Intuitively, such features of the Atlantic trade would fit well with the transition to factory methods and steam power.

It was once supposed that the early cotton-spinners were men of modest means. Katrina Honeyman's research has shown that this view is erroneous. She finds that the early factories were built up neither by rising artisans nor by London bankers but, rather, by local businessmen who had accumulated resources through trade or pre-industrial textiles:

> As early as 1787 the cotton industry was concentrated in Lancashire, where forty-three Arkwright-type mills were in production. The capital for the new industry was recruited almost entirely from local sources; and the background of all the early Lancashire cotton spinners included in the survey involved some contact, direct or indirect, with the textile trade. Local directories for 1772 and 1781 indicate a predominance of former fustian manufacturers.... Each of these cases indicated a moderate degree of upward mobility in the progression to cotton spinning, and each illustrated the role of either inherited wealth, or, more important, capital accumulated in previous textile enterprises.[79]

Honeyman argues that the working capital needed to survive as a cotton-spinner was such as to privilege those who already possessed resources or credit. On the financing of the transition to the factory system, she writes: 'The evidence of our study indicates a predominance of merchant capital, if not mercantile activity, and a large scale migration of capital from other spheres of the textile industry.'[80] Given the salience of exports for the textile industry, it can be assumed that much of this merchant capital was engaged in overseas trade.

Peter Mathias describes the passing on of credit between merchants, spinners and manufacturers:

> The traditional 3–6 month credit period in raw-material purchasing in cotton, for example, often allowed spinners to get cash for their sales of yarn (by discounting the bills of exchange) before they had put down cash for the raw cotton purchases that went into these sales. Dealers and yarn merchants could often give credit, or short-term accommodation, to allow manufacturers a cushion of credit on the selling side of the business.[81]

Of course the willingness of suppliers, merchants or banks to give credit to manufacturers will have reflected their estimate of the latter's commercial viability – it was a judgement of the cotton manufacturer's own probable success as a capitalist entrepreneur exploiting wage labour. The sphere of credit thus brings together different worlds of production, with the possibility that circuits of capital could go in both directions. Cotton manufacturers often extended credit to merchants, merchants to planters, but such a chain of credit was usually justified by eventual payment with interest. On the African coast credit was not unknown, but all parties tried to avoid giving it.

Investment in the plantations or triangular trades might have slowed down investment in the factory system *either* if it had yielded a low or negative rate of return *or* if it had yielded such a high rate of return that alternatives seemed unattractive. But average profits for the slave trade at the level calculated by Anstey – around 9 per cent – involved neither losses nor gains likely to eclipse investment in cotton-spinning, especially since there was an evident complementarity between the two types of investment. Indeed, the connections between the triangular trades and textiles were so close that in some periods (e.g. 1770 or 1790) an investment in the one was tantamount to an investment in the other. It is, perhaps, significant that when the slave trade became a centre of controversy in British politics, leading textile manufacturers were willing to defend it on the grounds that it was a valuable component of national trade. Thus the fustian manufacturers of Manchester rallied to the unpopular cause of slave-trafficking in 1791, while as late as 1806 the leading concerns of both Robert Peel and William Clegg subscribed to a petition in its defence.[82] Fustians and cheap cottons were standard issue on the plantations, while calicoes and muslins were very acceptable on the African coast.

Mercantile investment in plantations invariably took the form of allowing credit on supplies, so it also benefited metropolitan manufacturers supplying plantation equipment or cloth. Nevertheless, much of the quite extensive investment in the whole maritime/colonial complex in the years 1660–1750 might, if denied this outlet, have been invested in the domestic economy. In the absence of colonial markets, however, it would have been less concentrated on metal manufactures, or subsequently textiles, where industrial breakthroughs were technically easier to make. Moreover, once the pattern revealed in the 1770 figures was established, the plantations were sufficiently profitable to finance both their own expansion and large remittances to the metropolis. Seymour Drescher has pointed out that the evidence of planter indebtedness and bankruptcy cited by Lowell Ragatz was heavily weighted by the very difficult years 1777–85, when war and hurricanes drove many planters to the wall (though others still made a profit). In the earlier 'golden age' of 1762–76 profits had been good, and for those who survived the difficult years they were to be even better in 1785–1815.[83]

For obvious reasons, sugar refining and tobacco manufacture were also branches of industry with particularly close ties to the plantation trades. The hinterland of the main Atlantic ports – not only Liverpool, but Bristol and Glasgow as well – witnessed the pioneering use of industrial methods. One of the early propagandists for such methods was John Cary:

> The works of John Cary, the late seventeenth century Bristol sugar merchant, were reprinted in 1715 and 1745. Against the general tenor of opinion in favour of lower wages and schemes for employing the poor, Cary presented very detailed work on wages and productivity, new manufactures and technical change. He pointed out the extent to which technical change had succeeded in

reducing costs in a whole series of industries including sugar refining, distilling, tobacco manufacture, woodworking and lead smelting.[84]

A study of the 'Tobacco Lords' of Glasgow concludes: 'there would appear to be a fairly close connection between the rise of the tobacco commerce and the foundation of manufactures'.[85] The factors employed by the tobacco merchants were often the conduit through which planters made their orders in the metropolis; placing large orders for bulk supplies involved these merchants in sponsoring early factories, and suggested to them an alternative outlet for their resources in 1776, when the American revolt interrupted their tobacco business.

Perhaps the most famous case of a link between the triangular trade and the onset of industrialization is provided by the firm of Watt & Boulton. As John Lord points out: 'it was with money gained from the West India trade that capital was eventually found to finance Watt'.[86] The metal trades of the Midlands generally found useful markets in Africa and America; some factories specialized in producing nails or guns for these destinations. Arthur Young reported in 1776 that the road from the Soho works was one long village of nailers complaining at the disruption of the American trades.[87] If Atlantic demand stimulated some new industries, it also provided an outlet for more traditional manufactures and artisanal products. Thus the vicissitudes of the Essex textile industry owed much to fluctuating exports of says and bays to Portugal; similarly, Birmingham's metal manufactures were often produced by traditional methods.[88]

A useful summary statement, with evident implications for colonial profits, is supplied by Phyllis Deane:

> It would have been surprising if a proportion of the cumulating surplus generated by three decades [i.e. 1740–70] of trading prosperity had not found its way into the manufacturing industries whose products were the merchants' main stock in trade. With markets expanding, interest rates low, and wage rates tending to rise, there was a positive incentive to search for and to adopt innovations which saved labour – particularly skilled labour.[89]

There is also good reason to suppose that the profits of the Atlantic trades could be drawn upon by industries with little or no direct connection to overseas commerce. Thus both brewing and baking turned into big business in the course of the eighteenth century, catering for the needs of a new urban population. Accidents of geography and kinship meant that a commercial surplus earned in the West Indian trade could help to meet the heavy credit requirements of those brewers and bakers who made the breakthrough to large-scale production methods. Naturally, both brewers and bakers looked in the first instance to domestic sources for savings, investment and credit, but given the close connection between these new industries and the agricultural sector, the bad years which overstretched their credit frequently coincided with the years when farmers found it more difficult to make advances to them. At crucial points the 'power loom brewers' found it necessary to turn for credit to friends or relatives in the mercantile and banking sector connected with the export trade. In this way such merchants and bankers as the Barclays, Bevans, Gurneys, Hoares and Hanburys extended their interests to brewing.[90] Family ties and religious connections facilitated these transfusions, but so did more impersonal mechanisms.

Britain's eighteenth-century economy offered few institutional sources of credit, and suffered from a shortage of currency; bills drawn upon plantation produce often circulated as a species of quasi-money. Peter Mathias explains:

> The expansion of financial facilities, more particularly in London, which made sugar bills and tobacco bills as freely negotiable at equivalently fine margins as governmental securities meant that short term credit became the most efficient and the most mobile factor of production in the eighteenth century. During the first half of the century London dominated these flows, supported by satellite centres at the older provincial bases of foreign trade, such as Bristol. During the second half of the century the London money market maintained its dominance, but increasingly on the basis of the great creation and mobilisation of provincial wealth.... Rising provincial wealth came partly from the diversification of foreign trade, with West coast ports such as Glasgow, Whitehaven, Liverpool and Bristol becoming main centres of long distance trade; and partly from the great development of agricultural wealth, industry and commerce in provincial England. Banking specialized out primarily to serve foreign trade in Bristol and Glasgow after 1750, in Liverpool after 1770.[91]

It would seem that sugar and tobacco bills as a monetary facility were no less the fruit of slave labour than the gold sovereigns which they rivalled as a circulating medium. On the other hand, such financial instruments were far more likely to be drawn to the modernizing sectors of the economy. Barbara Solow and Pat Hudson have urged that the slave-based trades offered multiple facilities to economic change and growth throughout the period of industrialization.[92] And while Atlantic profits were large enough to have an impact on the economy as a whole, it is even clearer that they had a concentrated effect in the industrializing branches – even the 'basic estimate' for such profits in 1770 is considerably larger than total investment in that year in manufacturers' equipment and stock.

A remaining problem for analysis is that of separating out the slave sector from that of the metropolitan economy, with which it was so closely enmeshed. With reference to Britain's slave trading profits, Stanley Engerman wrote in 1975:

> rather than looking at the slave trade as an exogenous, independent initiator of growth, an argument made suspicious by the failure of the Portuguese, French and Dutch, among others, to industrialize, it is the process of growth which can help to explain the differences in the rates of profits among slave trading nations

(and the differential economic impact of the slave economies). Thus the entire slave economy plays a role in economic growth no different from other sectors, and, while a particularly immoral part of the process, one whose success and impact are largely dependent upon a variety of other social and economic forces.[93]

This judgement does capture something of the integration of slavery and capitalism, but it does not take full measure of the substantial contribution of the former to the latter. The slave-based enterprises of the Americas furnished the rather different proto-capitalist transitional economy of the metropolis with a crucial complement. With a good following wind, the early steam ships used in the mid-nineteenth-century Atlantic slave trade would find that sail drove them more swiftly and cheaply than the engine. The hybrid of slave economy and capitalist industrialization may be better captured by such an image than the alternative of tugboat or jolly boat offered at the beginning of this chapter.

Engerman is right to argue that slave trading by itself furnished no adequate basis for industrialization, and to point out that British economic 'efficiency' contributed to a more profitable slave trade. But his references to the supposed counter-example represented by the other colonial powers does not take due account of the British success. The British slave-based commercial empire was larger than that of its rivals, and far better integrated, so that colonial demand and profits fed back to the metropolis more reliably. Moreover, a combination of naval, commercial and industrial power enabled British merchants to penetrate the commercial systems of these other colonial empires. Britain's naval and manufacturing lead was not, in fact, replicated in all other sectors; as noted in Chapter XI, French sugar planting was the more productive. Engerman would seem to be alluding to a sort of generalized efficiency of enterprises within the British Empire that is similar to 'total factor productivity'. While the British economy almost certainly did enjoy an edge of this sort over its rivals, it is worth noting that Crafts's calculations have claimed that the amount of growth before 1831 which cannot be explained as due to extra capital, labour and land was still comparatively modest.

Crafts believes that in the period 1760 to 1800 the average annual growth of the British economy ran at 1 per cent, and that 0.35 of this was due to increasing amounts of capital, 0.4 due to additional labour inputs and only 0.2 as the contribution of 'total factor productivity' (TFP). As the industrial sector grew, so did the contribution of TFP, but that of capital growth remained important – annual growth in 1801–31, in his view, rose to 2 per cent, with the increase due to capital 0.5 and to TFP 0.7. Thus Crafts's calculations highlight the contribution of capital inputs to British growth, a conclusion which throws into even greater prominence the role of colonial slavery profits in capital formation.[94] Crafts himself has urged that British economic advance derived impetus from 'macro-inventions', in the form of clusters of new methods, operating together and linked by infrastructural investment, all of which required finance. The traditional notion of an industrial revolution thus comes to embrace the impact of a 'technological shock', which in turn required what we might call a 'capital shock'.[95]

Raw Materials

The link between New World slavery and British industrialization has so far been considered from the standpoint of markets and sources of investment. Macro-economic calculations have been advanced showing that plantation-related demand and profits were large enough to have played an important role in the onset of industrial accumulation. Some plausible and specific micro-economic or sectoral links have been proposed. But the very rise of a linked industrial and commercial complex, with its decisive turning point in the 1780s, has made it more difficult to delimit the differential contribution of the slave systems. If we turn to raw material supplies, the evidence for a differential and systematic contribution is strong and direct. The slave plantation became the principal supplier of the crucial industrial input: raw cotton. In this area, 'primitive accumulation' can be seen for what it is – not an episode or a moment, not a fateful biting of the apple located in an antediluvian past, but a continuing and relentless process whereby capitalist accumulation battens on pre-capitalist modes of exploitation, greatly extending their scope, until it has exhausted or transformed them. Capital's thirst for surplus-value and the necessarily uneven advance of mechanization has, indeed, repeatedly produced regimes of *extended primitive accumulation*, in which forced or sweated labour is driven to match the pace of machine industry, and expected to rely on 'natural economy' or communal resources for their reproduction. New World slavery was the first and least-camouflaged expression of this capitalist logic.

The early Industrial Revolution was heavily concentrated in the textile sector. Textiles accounted for 75 per cent of industrial employment in England in 1840, and cotton textiles accounted for a half of this total. Paul Bairoch, in a study of 'Agriculture and the Industrial Revolution', has pointed out that cotton was far more suited to the use of industrial methods than European-produced fibres. As he observes:

> cotton played an important qualitative role. For its fibres particularly lend themselves to mechanical treatment and this was the impulse for mechanization of the textile industry. When we consider the difficulties of adapting cotton spinning machines (which their inventors did not think of as solely for cotton) to wool, or even more to flax, we soon realize that the mechanization of textile work, which marked and profoundly influenced the start of the industrial revolution, would probably never have come about but for this particular fibre, so uniquely suited to mechanical treatment.[96]

From the supply side, an extraordinary feature of the cotton industry was its seemingly unlimited access to raw material. Most early industries, whether dependent on agriculture or mining for their raw materials, soon encountered supply bottlenecks and steeply rising costs, if they expanded rapidly. The early cotton industries found, on the contrary, that prices began to fall as demand increased. This simplification of the problems confronting the cotton manufacturers allowed them to explore the advantages of new power sources and new methods, even if this later took its toll: 'The fact that the cotton industry was singularly free from raw material supply problems marked it out from many others, at once facilitating expansion at an early date and isolating it from a range of problems faced and solved by many other industries.'[97] Douglas Farnie's judgement is very similar:

> The greatest single advantage enjoyed by the industry after 1801 undoubtedly lay in its access to an ample supply of cheap raw material. . . . Cheap cotton gave the industry an incomparable advantage over all other textiles. . . . The productivity of American agriculture proved of unprecedented and unparalleled importance in reducing the costs of British industry.[98]

Plantation cotton supplied British manufacturers with the means to overcome formidable Indian competition. In the mid eighteenth century Indian cotton textiles still enjoyed the leading position in world markets. Indian manufacturers commanded a highly skilled and relatively cheap labour force, with plentiful and direct supplies of cotton. English producers could not have competed with the Indian producers unless they had possessed *both* an efficient, labour-saving method of production *and* cheap, reliable sources of cotton.[99]

It was the combination of cheapness with reasonable quality which enabled English cotton goods to capture world markets in the late eighteenth and early nineteenth centuries. In 1784 raw cotton cost the English manufacturer 2*s.* a lb, in 1812 1*s.* 6*d.*, in 1832 7½*d.* a lb, a drop of approximately two-thirds over the period as a whole.[100] The contribution of slave-grown cotton to the cost structure of the English cotton industry enabled the price of English cotton goods in the period 1815–50 to drop roughly twice as fast as it would have done if the raw cotton price had been constant. Beyond conjunctural fluctuations, the circumstance that permitted a drop in the price of raw cotton was the adoption of Eli Whitney's cotton gin and the extension of cotton planting to the inland states of the US South. The biggest drop in price came between 1817, when raw cotton was selling for 26.5 cents a lb, and 1826, when it sold for 12.2 cents a lb, reflecting the planters' response to the favourable postwar conjuncture.[101]

Even before the rise of the cotton plantations of the US South, the slave plantations of the New World were supplying nearly three-quarters of Britain's imports of raw cotton. Imports from the British West Indies rose from 3.3 million lb annually in 1761–65 to 6.1 million lb in 1781–85, to

11.6 million in 1791–95, and reached 16.0 million annually in 1801–05.[102] The British West Indies did not enjoy either natural advantages or tariff protection so far as cotton cultivation was concerned; they could supply only a quarter or less of Britain's raw cotton requirements. The sources of Britain's raw cotton supplies towards the end of the eighteenth century are set out in Table XII.14:

Table XII.14   Sources of British Cotton 1786/87 and 1796–1805

000 lb and %	1786/87	1796–1805
British West Indies	5,050 (25.4%)	8,114 (17%)
British-occupied W.I.	–	7,853 (16.5%)
Foreign W.I.	6,214 (31.3%)	944 (2.0%)
Brazil	2,500 (12.6%)	7,971 (16.7%)
Louisiana	–	1,453 (3.0%)
USA (incl. re-ex)	–	14,978 (31.4%)
New World Total	13,764 (69.3%)	41,797 (87.8%)
Turkey (Smyrna)	6,000 (30.2%)	969 (2.0%)
East Indies	90 (0.5%)	5,171 (8.9%)
Grand Total	*19,854*	*47,631*

Source: Drescher, *Econocide*, pp. 57, 84–5.

As British demand for cotton grew, so did the proportion of that cotton supplied by American slave plantations. When embargo and war interrupted North American supplies, their place was taken by an expansion in Caribbean and Brazilian output. With the restoration of peace, the US plantations immediately came to supply half of Britain's raw cotton supplies, rising to three-quarters in the 1820s.[103]

Neither the Levant nor the East could match the performance of the American plantations. The latter certainly enjoyed some natural advantages, but it was slave labour which enabled these to be exploited. The labouring population dominated by the planters was no larger than that subject to the Zamindars of India, or the Beys and Pashas of Egypt or Anatolia, but the American slave planters were at once more adaptable and more attuned to the emerging world market. The exploiting classes of the East had no necessity, and little incentive, to cater to European demand; moreover, the peasants they exploited could not be mobilized at will, nor their cultivating and processing methods prescribed. In Asia the extraction of a surplus from the direct producers was likely to be defined by customary quantities and customary crops. In what was still an essentially pre-colonial epoch in Asia, there were many baffles and barriers to market pressure emanating from the West. The American slaveowners, by contrast, were active and innovative players in the Atlantic marketplace.

However much Brazilian or North American planters prided themselves on the patriarchal and paternalistic character of their relationship with their slaves, they remained subject to market pressures and incentives. A slave crew that was not producing commodities was a dead weight in the planter's ledger. The planter needed cash to meet the needs of his own household, to pay wages to an overseer, to cover the material costs of keeping his estate in good repair. Some minimal outlays would even be needed to maintain the slave crew itself. In Chapter XI we saw that planters could withdraw their plantations within the shell of natural economy; nevertheless, their operations still remained partially exposed to market pressure; at the limit, slaves would be sold to those who could make better use of them – usually this meant making more money out of their labour. Thus Virginian slaveholders could never completely avoid pressure to earn money from their estates, since there were constant outgoings:

> The cold Chesapeake winters, in part, necessitated the purchase of large amounts of clothing but the planters apparently accepted large expenditures for their slaves as a year-round responsibility. In addition to providing clothing, the planter had to pay taxes, give an overseer one tenth to one seventh of the crop, and purchase rum and beer at harvest time.[104]

American planters and political authorities became aware at an early stage of the huge gains to be made by meeting the growing demand for cotton. The State of Georgia in the US South appointed a commission to investigate the possibility of a gin that could clean the fibres of the short-staple variety of cotton which could be grown in inland areas. Public attention was thus already focused on this problem when the New England teacher Eli Whitney visited Georgia in 1793. The invention of the gin emerged from economic pressures, and a technically minded culture, not so different from that which saw the invention of the spinning jenny and the steam engine; Whitney's gin was itself to be so adapted and improved by planters that he had difficulty defending his patent. Pressed ahead by planters alert to a lucrative new opportunity, cotton cultivation spread rapidly to the inland states; parcels of slaves or entire crews were transferred from declining or stagnant sectors of the slave economy to the new cotton belt. In some cases planters would emigrate with their slaves; in others an internal slave trade effected the transfer.

The North American slave system had found a new and profitable use for slave labour. Gavin Wright writes: 'The prime mover in the rise of the Cotton Kingdom was ... the Industrial Revolution itself, and from this date forward the fortunes of the Southern economy were closely tied to the progress of the British textile industry.'[105] American slavery had been yoked to the juggernaut of industrial capital almost as securely as the cotton districts of Lancashire. But in both cases we should be careful that an account of structural forces does not discount the role of the different types of entrepreneur involved: the master-manufacturer in one case and the slaveowning planter in another. Joyce Caplin writes of the slaveowners' pattern of 'inventive adaption' and 'selective modernization': 'Any claim that something like the cotton gin or the British market created the Cotton South ignores how the real consequences of commercial cultivation in the upcountry, western expansion of slavery, was the conscious handiwork of intelligent and articulate people – a much uglier reality.'[106]

The early cotton manufacturers purchased raw materials and sold their products in a competitive market environment. During war years prices might be abnormally high or low, but on average the price of plantation produce was bound to reflect the comparatively modest costs of reproducing the slave plantation. The slaves, as we have seen, covered the larger part of their own reproduction costs through their own direct efforts. Since planters were competing quite keenly with one another, their path to a larger mass of profit was to increase their output to the maximum. This exercised a downward pressure on prices – albeit somewhat counterbalanced by rising demand. The hybrid character of the slave plantation thus made it a powerful engine of primitive accumulation, returning reasonable profits to its owner but also cheapening the supply of means of production or reproduction to the metropolitan regions.

Slave-produced cotton or indigo as a raw material fits easily into a schema of extended primitive accumulation; though in the long run the costs which would have resulted from employing wage labourers to clear and cultivate the American plantations would not necessarily have been greater. Less directly, sugar and other plantation products, by encouraging and cheapening the reproduction of labour-power as a commodity, also contributed to the metropolitan accumulation process. It is important to understand the impact of the plantation products in terms not only of political economy but also of the birth of a new subjectivity, subjacent to market relations but also influencing their direction and specific content.

Plantation Products and the New World of Consumption

In exploring the links between the slave systems and the dynamic of the British economy markets, we have considered profits and raw materials but not the new mode of consumption with which plantation products were peculiarly associated. Because they came from foreign climes, the plantation products had the allure of an exotic luxury; because they were produced by expanding slave populations, they could be supplied on a larger scale than traditional luxuries. They could thus make a special contribution to drawing metropolitan populations into the sphere of generalized commodity exchange. The new salaried personnel and wage labourers sustained themselves through recourse to the market, with household and subsistence economy relegated to a minor position. John Kennedy, a cotton manufacturer, was to declare: 'Among the lower orders it may, I think, be safely affirmed, that industry may only be found, where artificial wants have crept in, and have acquired the character of necessities.'[107]

Cotton textiles themselves, offering superior comfort, hygiene and economy, were rapidly adopted by the new urban populations and the rural middle classes. Sugar and exotic beverages also became, to differing degrees, characteristic compensations of the new bourgeois and proletarian existence, and an incentive for small producers to earn cash. Tea, coffee, chocolate and sugar were much easier to store and transport than many other food items. The new beverages were mostly sweetened with sugar, and had the health advantage that the water with which they were prepared had to be boiled. Those who found themselves dependent on salaries or wages for their reproduction often had little choice in accepting their condition; migration from the land might well be the result of a sheer inability to continue living there. But the more 'artificial' existence of the urban dweller or propertyless wage worker was a little alleviated by cheap luxuries which helped to construct a new subjectivity and afforded a modest but significant space within which new choices could be made. We have already traced the emergence of tobacco as a popular pleasure in the seventeenth century; sugar and cotton were likewise linked to new popular tastes which must be accorded a certain autonomy. The role played by exotic products in breaking down the self-sufficiency and autarkic inclinations of independent small producers was also important – especially if we bear in mind how widespread small production was in the Atlantic world of the eighteenth century.[108]

The rise of the grocery shop was closely linked to the retailing of exotic foodstuffs. Dorothy Davis writes:

> retail grocers, while still stocking miscellaneous household materials like firewood, paper, paints, wax, canvas, arsenic, tar, and so forth, were beginning to lose their former marine store character and to concentrate on the non-perishable food items available in ever increasing quantities from the Mediterranean, the Far East and the New World. One of the most important of these was sugar.

She also notes: 'In 1722 the English were buying tea at an average rate of an ounce a head per month and over the next hundred years this increased steadily to an ounce a head per week, while over the same period the drinking of beer was almost exactly halved.'[109] Tea was not as bulky a product as the sugar with which it was consumed, and could thus bear the cost of transportation from the Far East. Besides being stirred into tea, sugar entered into the making of the shop-bought pastries and confectionery that also became a common addition to the urban diet: 'pastry cook shops went from strength to strength. . . . Sugar and dried fruits, once the luxuries of the rich, lent to ready made cakes a wide appeal.'[110]

Hoh-cheung and Lorna Mui have drawn attention to the large and growing number of shopkeepers in eighteenth-century Britain. By 1801, 62,000 shopkeepers were licensed tea dealers, and the total number of retail shops was around 177,000; these proper shops had to compete with large numbers of market traders, hawkers, and backstreet stores. The key 'incentive goods' like sugar, and the various beverages and confections it sweetened, were a vital stock in trade, as were cotton goods. The arrival of a mill at Wilmslow transforms the Cheshire village, as the number of shopkeepers had 'increased amazingly, some of whom dealt in a great variety of articles . . . tea, coffee, loafe sugar, spices, printed cottons . . .'.[111]

Between 1715–24 and 1785–1800, retained imports of sugar to England and Wales suggest that per capita consumption doubled from about 12 lb to about 24 lb annually. An estimate for the weekly expenditure of a saddler, his wife and three children in 1775 allows 1s. 5d. on sugar and 11¼d. on tea, out of a total of £1 0s. 6½d. – these being the only 'luxuries' permitted in the family budget.[112] A sweetened brew made from used tea leaves often helped the tenement dweller or rural day labourer to bear the rigours of a harsh existence. While the bulk of consumption was still accounted for by those of middling income, the relative cheapness of sugar now made it attractive to working-class consumers. Because of tariff protection, sugar was more expensive in London than it was in Amsterdam, but this did not stop English consumption rising. Indeed, widespread sugar consumption was seen – somewhat complacently – as an index of English prosperity, as in the following observation of 1763:

> if the wealth of *France* was as great or as greatly diffused, that is, if the mass of their people were as thoroughly employed, and thereby as easy in their circumstances, as the bulk of the *British* nation actually are, then they would of course consume much more [sugar] and export far less.[113]

One of the most cited contemporary estimates of Britain's social and occupational structure in the eighteenth century is an exercise in 'political arithmetic' by Joseph Massie which ranks the various strata by reference to their annual sugar consumption; his purpose was to show how widespread an interest there was in opposing the West India lobby and lowering the price of sugar.[114]

In a provocative essay, Jan de Vries has argued that seventeenth- and eighteenth-century Europe witnessed an 'industrious revolution' driven by the popular appetite for a more varied and cost-effective basket of consumption goods. Dutch and British labourers were drawn to more extensive participation in the market – partly by such imposed constraints as taxation, but also by the lure of cheaper exotic goods or manufactures. Men worked for more days each year; women and children entered the labour force. The quickening of economic activity which preceded and accompanied the Industrial Revolution, and helped to make it possible, required a labour force motivated to greater participation in market structures. Whether one views the substitution of sweetened tea for beer, or cotton for linen textiles, or the smoking of tobacco, as gains for the quality of life is not really the point. The availability of a wider choice of popular necessities and luxuries was some compensation for dependence on a wage – and dependence on a wage could seem greatly preferable to dependence on a master or mistress.[115] Yet De Vries is careful to make it clear that the world of wage dependency and accelerated industriousness imposed new rigours and uncertainties. Evidence that the average height of recruits to the British Army actually fell over most of the period 1780 to 1850 would appear to bear this out.[116]

Carole Shammas finds that the new urban populations compensated for diminished access to fresh milk and vegetables by increasing use of colonial groceries. For poorer consumers, the extra calories obtained from sugar became important:

> low levels of calories seem to have been the norm for many English workers during the later eighteenth century and for a number of decades in the nineteenth century as well. If there is a dietary change that can be documented as occurring in the eighteenth and nineteenth centuries, it is the increasing reliance on appetite appeasers such as tobacco, caffeine drinks, and sugar. . . . The picture one comes away with from looking at a wide variety of sources on diet in early modern England and America is not of starvation among large numbers of the working class, so much as a continual longing for greater quantities of the new commodities and for more – and better quality – bread, meat and milk. It is hard to believe that food was not constantly on the mind of a large percentage of the working people. . . . In other words the English population was already having problems with its traditional diet, and the calorific content of that diet for the poorer elements in society was apparently very low: insufficient, it seems, for completing a full day's manual work. Under these conditions the appetite-abating and energizing properties of tobacco and caffeine drinks might well have been especially attractive. Tobacco and the hot tea, coffee and chocolate beverages stimulated the consumption of clay pipes and pottery dishes.[117]

Boiling water for sweetened beverages probably helped to check contamination, but the dawn of the age of industrial living and junk food was not otherwise good for the health. The hours of toil in the new industrial plants were often as long as those in the West Indian plantations. Hunger rather than the whip was the goad to labour. Young children and pregnant or nursing mothers had to work long hours to keep body and soul together. The numbers of infants dying in the first year of life ran between 150 and 250 per thousand in the British West Indies in the early years of the nineteenth century compared with 171 for London, 239 for Leeds and 144 for Essex.[118] Thus, in prevailing conditions, the 'free market' exploitation of wage labour – yielding a 'normal' capitalist surplus – could be as deadly, or almost as deadly, as the super-exploitation of slave labour.

War, Colonies and Industrialization

The examination of the triangular trade's contribution to Britain's industrial advance has so far not addressed warfare, taxation and government expenditure. Yet the eighteenth-century colonial systems generated wars just as surely as they generated plantation profits. In fact, a significant part of the expenses of war must be deducted from any calculation of the colonial surplus, and the value of colonial markets and sources of supply. When R.P. Thomas objected to Sheridan's estimate of the profits of Empire, one of the debits he proposed related to expenditure on the West Indian squadron and garrison. In around 1770 expenditure on the Jamaican squadron ran at £319,000, and on the garrison at £115,000, annually.[119] Although these debits reduced the estimate for Jamaican profits, they still allowed for a handsome rate of return. And as Sheridan points out, the London Government could offset such expenditures against the revenue yielded by the Sugar Duty: this brought in £700,000 in 1770, and rose steadily in subsequent decades.[120] The Sugar Duty has been regarded as a tax on consumers – though this result could not have been achieved without the prior appropriation of surplus produced by the slaves, and a tax on popular consumption of this sort should, perhaps, best be seen as a social surplus appropriated by the state from its supervision of the relations established between producers in both metropolis and plantations. But whichever approach is adopted, factoring in the receipts of the Sugar Duty, the Tobacco Duty, and so forth does not dispose of the problem of accounting for military expenditure in any estimate of the colonial contribution to metropolitan growth, since in wartime such expenditure grew to gigantic proportions.

I have shown that the triangular trades were profitable, or advantageous, to a series of specific interests and industries. But such macro-economic calculations could be swamped if full account is taken of the cost of warfare and colonial monopoly, not to speak of the human costs of the triangular trades and of the industrialization process itself. R.P. Thomas and D.N. McCloskey have roundly declared: 'what was in the interest of the Manchester textile manufacturer or the Bristol slave trader or the West Indian planter was usually not in the interest of the British economy as a whole'.[121] There is much to be said for this judgement, so long as it does not lead us to suppose that there was a harmonious and homogeneous entity, the 'British economy', which can be counterposed to the various antagonistic interests and classes which actually composed the social formation. Both severally and collectively the traders, manufacturers and planters were influential and weighty members of the economic community; over and against these appropriators were large numbers of wealth-creators – labourers, artisans, small producers, suppliers of needed services, and – overseas, but within the economic system – the slaves. Given prevailing social relations, exchanges with the plantations helped the exploiting classes to propel 'the economy' forward, mobilizing slave-produced surplus and realizing profits in the new branches of production. They also helped to defray state expenses that did not arise simply on account of the colonies.

In 1770 Britain's total military expenses ran at £3.9 million, or somewhere in the middle of the range of estimates of triangular trade profits in that year. But this, of course, was a peacetime year. In 1760, at the height of Pitt the Elder's war of colonial acquisition, Britain's military expenditures totalled £13.5 million. In 1780, in the midst of the desperate attempt to crush the colonial revolt in North America, they reached £14.9 million. These peaks were to be greatly exceeded during the French Revolutionary and Napoleonic Wars: £26.3 million went to the military, much of it for operations in the Caribbean, in 1795. Even in peacetime, military expenditure was two or three times as large as civil expenditure. The other major component of state expenditure was interest on the national debt, accumulated through previous wars. Wartime expenses could never be met from current revenue, so they were financed by enlargement of the national debt: in peacetime years, servicing the debt was the largest single budget item, exceeding military outlays.[122] Despite attempts to establish a 'sinking fund', the size of the debt, and of interest payments on it, grew constantly. Public bonds mobilized wealth for military purposes, and gave that crucial layer of wealth-holders who owned them a special stake in the political regime and its fiscal system. They financed public expenditure which, in its turn, allowed for generous levels of profit, thus concentrating capital. David Hancock's twenty-three mercantile associates achieved higher rates of profit when they were engaged as military contractors than in any other activity.[123]

There are several reasons why it would be wrong to set military outlays against the profits of Empire. Britain's ruling class did not fight wars only to acquire colonies. The European state system threatened war for a great variety of reasons; states without colonies or a slave trade did not thereby avoid war. Among other objectives important to Britain's rulers at this time were keeping the Scheldt closed, preventing France from upsetting the 'balance of power' in Europe and defending Hanover – this was the price of the Protestant succession.[124] In both the short and the long run the colonial and naval theatres of war were more likely to bring direct economic rewards than such classic goals of Britain's European policy.

Eighteenth-century military outlays were huge, but they did not constitute a simple deduction from accumulation. If we examine the sources of state revenue, we discover 'an overwhelming conclusion': 'the absence of the levies falling upon wealth and accumulated capital'.[125] The Land Tax was of declining importance: between 1770 and 1790 direct taxes contributed only 17–18 per cent of total revenues. Mercantile and manufacturing accumulation was almost entirely untaxed, while the atrophy of the Land

Tax valuations benefited those carrying out improvements. After 1706 receipts from the Land Tax were always less than payments of interest on the national debt, so that wealth-holders made no net contribution whatsoever to state revenues. The great bulk of revenues was raised by Customs and Excise: together these never accounted for less than a half of all revenues, and in peacetime usually over 70 per cent.

Customs and Excise were raised principally on items of popular consumption, such as ale and beer, salt, leather, candles, sugar and tobacco. The spread of salaried and waged labour, and of monetized social relations generally, allowed the state great scope for raising resources in this way. Consumption taxes were also a convenient source of revenue in an economy with much independent small production in agriculture, manufacturing and services, though it was no less resented for this reason. Peter Mathias concludes: 'Of the general social regressiveness of the customs and excise revenues there is no doubt, in my view.'[126] By the end of the eighteenth century Stamp Duty accounted for nearly 8 per cent of total receipts, their incidence falling chiefly on the middle classes, but this was one of the few taxes which did not bear down on the mass of the population. Joseph Massie's calculations imply that only the very poorest escaped paying the Sugar Duty; the great mass of this tax was paid by the poor and middling sections of the population, and only 28 per cent of it by the combined ranks of the Landed and Financial Aristocracy, Gentry, Merchants, Leading Tradesmen, Master Manufacturers, Military Officers, Clergy, Professions and the Civil Officers.[127]

There is no evidence that wages were able to compensate for fluctuations in the rate of taxation. The reduction of popular purchasing power might itself have restricted the scope of manufacturing and mercantile accumulation, but for the fact that military outlays offered rich pickings to those who supplied guns, uniforms, metal utensils, provisions, ships, and so forth – a list which, as we will see, overlapped with the type of demand generated by the plantation and slave trades. The proportion of Britain's national income taken by taxes rose from 9.1 per cent in 1700 to 12.9 per cent in 1750 and reached 20.3 per cent in 1803.[128] And of course, where military expenditure led to naval supremacy and the opening of markets, it could also be seen as investment in the export trade. The success of Britain's rulers in mobilizing economic resources for the wars they needed to win was itself a – perhaps the – major ingredient in victory.

All this suggests that the Hanoverian state became a highly effective instrument for the extraction of surplus, but one with an especially light impact on the areas of greatest economic potential: manufacture and improved agriculture. If the taxation of items of popular consumption exercised some upward pressure on wage rates, this was an incentive to adopt methods which boosted productivity and reduced average labour costs. The wages paid to industrial workers in Britain were quite modest, but they were likely to be higher than those earned by rural day labourers;

most travellers were agreed that popular living standards were higher in Britain than they were in France. Taxation per capita was also higher in Britain than it was in any other European country. Evidently the determining factor here, underlying and lending coherence to these phenomena, was the development of monetized and proto-capitalist relations of production. The innovation represented by the new industries in the sphere of social relations was as important as the technological breakthroughs which accompanied them. Thus woollen textiles, Britain's premier traditional manufacture, had never entirely shaken free of the seasonal rhythms of agriculture, both because of the periodicity of shearing and because of the overlap between agricultural and manufacturing employment. Cotton manufacturers achieved the breakthrough to a more permanent workforce because of the constant availability of cotton, and because they learnt how to harness constant sources of energy: water and steam.

The cotton industries notoriously involved an integration of wage labour with household and family economy, but the link with agriculture was much reduced. The employment of women and children in the cotton mills permitted family income to rise to the point where it could support outlays for bread, clothing, and other necessary items of popular consumption. By gathering the workers under one roof, and subordinating them to one discipline, the new industrial employers were able to garner the profits of industrial co-operation and invigilation – as it were adapting the plantation model (which is why people came to speak of steel 'plants'). In domestic agriculture such trends were less complete, but the new methods ironed out fluctuations in labour requirements, as tenant farmers were encouraged to substitute machinery for labour at planting and harvesting time. So far as the landlord was concerned, outright ownership of the land gave a clear interest in improvements.

I have sought to show that, in general, state expenditure in Hanoverian Britain constituted no direct deduction from capitalist accumulation, and that taxation was harnessed to the dynamic of an increasingly monetized social formation. But at between 10 and 20 per cent of national income, state expenditures were quite large enough drastically to reshape the pattern of demand, sometimes in ways that inhibited the advance of the economy.[129] The overall impact of state policies preserved or expanded the resources commanded by the rich, while it restricted those of the rest. In so far as the former preferred luxury consumption to investment, and the reduced purchasing power of the latter restricted the size of the internal market, the economic operations of the state did constitute a drag on the accumulation process. In fact rates of economic growth, averaging less than 2 per cent a year, were scarcely spectacular, though sufficient to generate qualitative as well as quantitative advance. War contracts had some spin-off effect on the industrializing process, leading to the use of large-scale production methods and helping to underwrite the cost of some investments in infrastructure. But the real problem of war for eighteenth-century Britain was that it exposed overseas trade to risks: for this reason – and because of the linkages we have established in earlier sections – war was bad for the economy as a whole. Britain's rate of growth slowed down during the major eighteenth-century wars, only to reach an even higher level than before in the following five years of peace.[130] Britain needed to win its wars against France, Spain and Holland but, as it turned out, not the war against the North Americans.[131]

On several occasions the burden of financing war expenditures led to an increase in the rate of interest, making plausible the idea that productive investment was being 'crowded out' and manufacturers were being starved of funds. While such an effect is plausible, it could be offset to some extent by the general buoyancy of mercantile capital. During much of the eighteenth century Dutch funds, themselves derived in part from Atlantic commerce, entered the London market, and were more likely to do so when interest rates were high and conditions on the Continent unsettled. But during the Wars against the French Revolution and Napoleon, when the pressure of military expenditure was greatest, Dutch capital was unable to play the same role. As we have seen, the years 1793 to 1815 witnessed a strong boom in plantation profits, with a high rate of remission to the metropolis. These profits must have helped greatly to reduce the pressure for further increases in the rate of interest.[132]

It would be possible to construct a hypothetical model of capitalist advance in Britain in the seventeenth and eighteenth centuries based on internal exchanges and on those avenues of foreign trade which would have remained open with little or no military expenditures. The Dutch republic found itself obliged to follow such a path out of military weakness and vulnerability during much of the eighteenth century. Dutch commerce and banking remained quite prosperous; Dutch capitalists invested much of their funds in the London market. Dutch living standards were high, while sugar could be bought more cheaply than in Britain. But then no breakthrough to a new type of industrial economy was made in the eighteenth-century Netherlands; its manufactures were hemmed in by the small size of the home market, and the characteristic limitations on the trade with Central and Eastern Europe. That the rulers of the Dutch state found this a second-best option may be inferred from the fact that they adopted it only after receiving a battering from England and France.

Britain's island position and its somewhat larger home market might be thought to have rendered such a pacific strategy both more viable in military terms and more conducive to economic advance. It might be asked whether the larger home market, with a more egalitarian social structure, could have compensated for exclusion from many overseas markets. There have been periods in the history of Switzerland and Sweden when capitalist advance was secured without recourse to warfare or colonial acquisitions. In such cases small producers have invariably enjoyed considerable social weight. The path of industrialization and the factory system was a quite different one which marginalized the small producer. After 1815 British governments themselves fostered an imperial Pax Britannica that proved perfectly consistent with capitalist consolidation and industrial advance. Yet this was on the basis of an already-acquired position of strength reached after extraordinary military exertions, from the Anglo-Dutch to the Napoleonic wars.

By the end of this epoch more voices were raised in favour of a pacific model of development than had been heard in earlier periods but they remained marginal. Cromwell's war against the Dutch had received strong support even from many Puritans, such as the radical Fifth Monarchy men; Commonwealth conquests of Ireland evoked protests, but those in the Caribbean none. The fact that Quakers subsequently became pacifists was significant, though their pacifism was often advocated as a private commitment rather than public policy. Walpole supported a relatively pacific policy, but only on the basis secured by the Treaty of Utrecht. The Tory opposition often opposed warmaking – but in power they devised wars of their own. The British state was itself the product of an internal process of conquest and colonization, tending to unify the British Isles, and it had learnt to survive keen competition from the militarily formidable Absolutist regimes. The seventeenth-century revolutions constructed a state machine highly adapted to waging wars of naval aggression and colonial expansion. The more belligerent factions of the ruling class – often those associated with overseas commerce – thereafter usually made the running in the determination of public policy. Safeguarding the Protestant succession itself required a readiness to resist those powers who backed the Jacobite Pretenders.

The European state system of the epoch was built around the semi-permanent prospect of war; the new economic forces orientated towards the slave plantations of the New World further compounded this propensity to warmaking. The value of each plantation colony's exports was between a third and two-thirds as great as that of its imports: states seeking a balanced trade or commercial surplus therefore needed access to the markets not only of their own colonies but of the colonies of other powers as well. For this reason – among others – Hobsbawm was probably right to argue that there was space for only one pioneering capitalist industrialization in the Atlantic world of the seventeenth and eighteenth centuries. Here, of course, we are entirely within that sphere of primitive accumulation about which Marx wrote in the 26th chapter of *Capital* Volume One: commercial wars, slavery, national debts, force as an economic power. To postulate an alternative vision in which the feudal lion and the capitalist tiger would have lain down together, and both agreed to stop molesting the colonial lambs, would be not merely 'counterfactual' but deeply at odds with the nature of the power-holding classes and states competing for dominance in Europe and the New World from 1640 to 1815. The Atlantic boom nourished the social forces associated with an Atlantic-wide democratic revolution, and here there were indeed intimations of possible alternative paths of development. But it also fed the warmaking proclivities of the leading Atlantic states, and gave new powers and initiative to merchant oligarchs who controlled capital.[133]

The Anglo-French Wars of 1793–1815: A Test

The wars between Britain and France (1793–1815) provided a rough-and-ready test of the value of Atlantic commerce to the transitional economies of Western Europe. The outbreak of hostilities between Britain and France in 1793 ended the period of freer trade between the two countries initiated by the Anglo-French Trade Treaty of 1787. With the exception of brief interludes such as that afforded by the Peace of Amiens (1801–03), British traders found themselves progressively excluded from European markets. The British capture of French and Dutch territories in the Caribbean provided some compensation, as did the rise of the London entrepôt trade in plantation produce. But French merchants, with some help from their government, sought to secure supplies of plantation produce by expanding trade with Brazil, Spanish America and the United States. The Directory negotiated a formal alliance with Madrid in 1795 and an informal alliance with the US in 1798; such agreements facilitated the exchange of plantation produce for manufactures. France's land conquests in Europe, coupled with a somewhat more egalitarian social order, gave a fillip to French industry and stimulated its demand for raw materials. Combining trade and destruction was always the difficult part of commercial war. The privateering licensed by the Directory in the Caribbean brought in an irregular harvest of plantation booty, but alienated the North Americans.

Napoleon found it easier to strike at British trade than to promote new branches of overseas commerce. The victory of the British fleet at Trafalgar made London the arbiter of Atlantic commerce, and drew Napoleon into attempting a European defiance of the crucial role of New World trade. He sought to strengthen the barriers against British exports and re-exports with the Berlin decrees of 1806 and the subsequent extension of the Continental System to all the major European powers. Napoleon's blockade caused great losses to British manufacturers and traders, but it was also costly to the Empire and never entirely effective. Those who sought to breach the system were assisted by the fact that they brought with them not only cotton fabrics but also the coveted delicacies of the colonial trade.

If the Grande Armée was thrown back from the East with the help of Generals October, November and December, the integrity of the Continental System in the West suffered from the encroachments of Generals Sugar,

Chocolate and Coffee. The British exporters could also make up for their remaining European losses by entry to new markets in Southern and Central America. Following Napoleon's invasion of the Peninsula, Britain was able to capture the lion's share of the colonial trade of Portugal and Spain. The London Government's 'Orders in Council' of 1805 and 1806 ruthlessly deployed British naval strength against 'neutral' as well as enemy shipping, to the special detriment of US shipping and sailors. The fortunes of war thus separated a British-supervised 'Atlantic System' from a French-dominated 'Continental System'. In this species of geopolitical laboratory test, the former gained a narrow edge over the latter.

British commercial access to the Atlantic grew steadily throughout the period 1787 to 1808, and was only partially and temporarily checked by the subsequent conflict with the United States. Despite the difficulties caused by the interruption of the North American trade, Britain's Atlantic supremacy throughout the period as a whole helped to sustain an extra-ordinary export boom, as we have seen. The experience of the French economy during the same period illustrates the difficulties of industrializing on the exclusive basis of a large home market. With the troubles in Saint Domingue, France's trade with its colonies dropped sharply from 1792; one of the few points on which the white *colons* and the black revolution-aries could agree was the inconvenience of respecting the exclusive commer-cial claims of the metropolis. Toussaint L'Ouverture expelled the British in 1798, but also concluded a commercial agreement with them. British forces occupied Martinique with the compliance of local planters in 1794 and held it, apart from a brief interlude during 1802–03, until 1814. Napo-leon's attempt to reconquer Saint Domingue in 1802–03, and to restore slavery throughout the French colonies, showed a recognition of the strategic significance of New World resources – but the attempt was to fail miserably with the defeat of Leclerc's expedition and the establishment of Haiti. The British successively captured the plantation colonies of France and its allies: Demerara, Essequibo, Trinidad, Tobago, St Lucia, Guade-loupe, Îsle de France, Réunion. Napoleon's decision to sell Louisiana to the United States might be thought to reflect a failure to grasp the significance of the plantation trades. This, however, is not the case, since this sale was intended to cement the alliance with the United States, fast becoming Britain's chief rival as Europe's main supplier of plantation products. The advantages of this liaison were greatly reduced by defeat in the Caribbean and at Trafalgar.

Both the Directory and the Empire worked to promote the interests of French manufacturing. French victories opened up continental markets, and were followed by decrees privileging the Francophone metropolis over the conquered periphery. Some industrial development did ensue, but the progressive loss of Atlantic trade proved a crippling blow. Bergeron observes: 'The internal market, ample in demographic terms, was undoubt-edly incapable of absorbing large quantities of those goods produced by the mechanized textile industry.'[134] This was partly because urban, mercantile and manufacturing incomes were depressed, especially along the Atlantic seaboard:

> Still other factors entered into the balance to impede industrial progress. Raw cotton was expensive because of supply difficulties. Rural spinners – spinning was neither concentrated nor mechanized – demanded equally high prices. The products of 'mechanical' industry undoubtedly had difficulty in imposing themselves on rural consumers in preference to artisanal products.[135]

Despite such problems, French textile manufacturers secured some raw cotton supplies from the Levant, and from those who broke the British naval blockade. Between 1790 and 1810 French cotton textile output rose threefold; during the same period, however, Britain's cotton industry, starting from a higher base, quadrupled its output.[136]

The colonial trade of the *ancien régime* had been highly concentrated on entrepôt exchanges, and its vigour had not been fully communicated to wide sectors of the French economy. Nevertheless, French industrial and manufacturing development in 1790 was quite impressive, even if it was less committed to the new industrial methods that were making their appearance in Britain.

France's colonial trades had encouraged manufacturing industries and naval construction in the hinterland of the Atlantic ports, and sometimes even further afield: in the Dauphinée, for example, as well as Brittany. The decimation of the Empire's Atlantic trade had a devastating effect on many branches of manufacture. Crouzet sums up the consequences:

> The great sea-ports of the Continent, which had been the hubs of economic life in the eighteenth century, were completely crippled from 1807 onwards. Harbours were deserted, grass was growing in the streets, and in large towns like Amsterdam, Bordeaux and Marseilles, population did actually decrease ... the collapse of industrial production has not been much noticed. It resulted from the loss of overseas markets and to a lesser degree from the difficulty of obtaining raw materials. In Marseilles, the value of industrial output fell from 50 million francs in 1789 to 12 million francs in 1813. Among the victims were, of course, shipbuilding and its ancillary industries, such as sail and rope-making. ... Other industries to suffer were those processing imported colonial produce – especially sugar refining (Amsterdam had 80 refineries in 1796, 3 in 1813; Bordeaux 40 before the Revolution, 8 in 1809), also tobacco factories, and tanneries, because of the shortage of hides which had been imported from South America. Also affected were industries which had been preparing foodstuffs for overseas markets or for provisioning ships. ... In Nantes and Hamburg cotton printing was almost entirely wiped out. ... The most important casualty was the linen industry. ... It was an export industry ... with its main markets overseas, in the West Indies and Spanish America.[137]

Crouzet's litany of the woes of the European economy when it was cut off from the New World provides a negative illustration of some of the positive linkages explored in the preceding discussion of the role of trade in Britain's path to industrialization. It is true that the period involved was short, and that the disturbances and exactions of war were taking a toll on the internal market. War contracts could only partially compensate for this. Experiments with the extraction of sugar from beet were of momentous significance, but did not yield fully satisfactory results until the 1840s and after.

The economy of continental Europe was not nearly so implicated in overseas trade as that of Britain. Nevertheless, the record of the Imperial economy was not much of an advertisement for the tonic effects of withdrawal from the Atlantic system of exchanges. Napoleon himself was intermittently aware of the dangers of asphyxiation for French industry should it be cut off from valuable markets and sources of supply. His expedition to Egypt, his friendly relations with Jefferson, the attempt to reconquer Saint Domingue, the invasion of Spain and Portugal, can all be viewed as desperate attempts to find a complementary pole to the development of a more advanced French capitalism. His military adventures were by no means exclusively economic in motivation, but it would be just as wrong to see them purely in terms of the pursuit of glory and conquest for its own sake.

From the days of his marriage to Joséphine Beauharnais, the future Emperor had been an intimate of the colonial milieu of speculators, planters and merchants. At their behest he had sought to re-establish slavery in the French colonies as well as to regain Saint Domingue. More generally, he made it his business to be attentive to the needs of commerce and industry. He knew that the European economy needed raw cotton and exotic foodstuffs, either from the New World or from the Near East. Bergeron writes:

> Napoleon was certainly not insensible to the idea of a dramatic re-assertion of France's Oceanic position, sustained by the enthusiasm of capitalists some of whom were close to him, through strengthening the naval capability of France and Spain and re-establishing the colonial empire. Undoubtedly he never abandoned this idea completely – some French efforts to intervene in the First Latin American attempts at Independence confirm this.[138]

However, Napoleon was to give priority not to this 'Western Design' but to 'the economic domination of a closely defended continental sphere'. The limited but real industrial advances associated with the latter barely compensated for the lost 'Atlantic dimension'. Crouzet speaks of a 'de-industrialization' and 'pastoralization' of previously flourishing regions: 'The "Atlantic" sector of the European economy was not to recover when peace was restored in 1815.'[139]

Following the peace, French manufacturing suffered from a withering blast of competition from Britain's new industries. Indeed, it is to this era of postwar troubles, and to its perceived roots in the undercutting of French manufactures by British, that we owe the French invention of the term 'industrial revolution' itself. The economists J.-B. Say, Charles Comte and

J. Sismondi not only debated the revolutionary impact of industrial transformations – seen as portending far more than the simple arrival of new processing methods – but also began to raise questions about what they saw as distortions of *laissez-faire* principles involved in the recourse to unfree labour. British cotton textiles furnished them with a prime example of an accumulation process assisted by cheap raw materials. The arguments of these men helped to lend a new depth to anti-slavery sentiment in the 1820s and 1830s, as it came to stress that forms of production based on unfree labour – 'extended primitive accumulation' – would nourish political regression and illiberal forms of the state.

French experience and French debates were destined to acquire relevance to other countries. The disasters which befell the industries of Catalonia or Northern Portugal after the independence of Spanish America and Brazil could only emphasize the value of colonial markets. On the other hand, it could be objected that if the United States were chosen for comparison with Britain, its experience during the Anglo-French wars would not bear out the points made above. Although the US economy encountered some problems during its period of commercial isolation after 1807–08, there were also signs of continuing economic strength and the beginnings of industrial advance. US commercial exchanges with other parts of the Americas and with Europe were greatly impeded, but the social formation of the United States itself contained a strong slave plantation sector which helped to underwrite the resilience and manufacturing advance of the years 1808–15. The strong US internal market was itself a microcosm of exchanges between farmers, manufacturers, artisans and planters, and demonstrated its transitional dynamic.[140]

We have seen that the pace of capitalist industrialization in Britain was decisively advanced by its success in creating a regime of extended primitive accumulation and battening upon the super-exploitation of slaves in the Americas. Such a conclusion certainly does not imply that Britain followed some optimum path of accumulation in this period, or that this aspect of economic advance gave unambiguous benefits outside a privileged minority in the metropolis. Nor does our survey lead to the conclusion that New World slavery produced capitalism. What it does show is that exchanges with the slave plantations helped British capitalism to make a breakthrough to industrialism and global hegemony ahead of its rivals. It also shows that industrial capitalism boosted slavery. The advances of capitalism and industrialism nourished, in fateful combination, the demand for exotic produce and the capacity to meet this large-scale demand through the deployment of slave labour. The slave systems of the late-eighteenth- and early-nineteenth-century New World had far outstripped those of the earlier mercantilist epoch. Although New World slavery now confronted mortal antagonists, it had yet to reach its apogee.

*

In this chapter and its predecessor the focus has been on the economic advance of the plantations and the slave trade, largely abstracting from social and political development internal to the social formations of the Atlantic states. The political, social – and, indeed, cultural and ideological – implications and reverberations of Atlantic development were immense in the latter half of the eighteenth century and beyond. But developments within the economic system do seem prior, both in the sense that they could scarcely have been arrested and in the sense that they created the socio-economic forces and contradictions whose clash led to many of the decisive confrontations of the 'Age of Revolution'.

The formula of the Atlantic economy, and the juggernaut of capitalist accumulation, had sufficient vigour not to be deflected for long even by adverse developments; but at the same time, it certainly threw up many profound questions concerning the shape and direction of political and social progress. A new 'mode of production' was being born, but as yet the wider implications of this for the state, for the family, for the organization of civil society, had not been confronted or settled. The British path to industrialization had been smoothed by the aggressive and relentless application of force. By the end of the eighteenth century the growth of capitalist industrialism had given employers new leverage with wage workers and Britain's rulers new weapons with which to impose a global pre-eminence. But it also confronted them with new problems and new social antagonists, both at home and overseas.

Notes

1. Adam Smith, *An Inquiry into the Nature and Causes of the Wealth of Nations*, vol. 1, Oxford 1976, p. 277.

2. Karl Marx, *Capital*, vol. 1, Part Eight, Chapter 26, London 1976, p. 874.

3. Ibid., ch. 31, p. 915.

4. This momentous development is clearly traced in Robert Brenner, *Merchants and Revolution*, Princeton, NJ 1993; and John Brewer, *Sinews of Power*, New York 1990.

5. Maurice Dobb developed this approach in *Studies in the Development of Capitalism*, London 1954, pp. 123–76.

6. Smith, *An Inquiry into the Nature and Causes of the Wealth of Nations*, vol. 2, Oxford 1976, pp. 556–90.

7. Chaptal, *De l'industrie française*, Paris 1819, pp. 134–5; Deane and Cole, *British Economic Growth*, p. 89.

8. Paul Bairoch, 'Commerce international et genèse de la révolution industrielle anglaise', *Annales*, vol. 28, 1973, pp. 541–71; Charles Kindleberger, 'Commercial Expansion and the Industrial Revolution', *Journal of European Economic History*, vol. 4, no. 3, Winter 1975, pp. 613–54; Robert Brenner, 'The Origins of Capitalism', *New Left Review*, 104, July–August 1977, pp. 25–93. For discounting of the colonial contribution to British eighteenth-century growth see the contributions by McCloskey and Thomas in Roderick Floud and D.N. McCloskey, eds, *The Economic History of Britain since 1700*, Cambridge 1981.

9. Eric Williams, *Capitalism and Slavery*, 1st edn, Chapel Hill, NC 1944, reprinted on several occasions including London 1964, and *From Columbus to Castro*, London 1962, 1970. For Roger Anstey's criticism of Williams's work see *The Atlantic Slave Trade and British Abolition, 1760–1810*, London 1975. A generally critical approach to Williams was

also to be found in a special issue of the *Revue française d'histoire d'outre mer*, 1975, which brought together much new work in English and French on the Atlantic slave trade. Full references to the controversies sparked off by Williams's work will be found in Barbara L. Solow and Stanley L. Engerman, *British Capitalism and Caribbean Slavery*, Cambridge 1987; see particularly the contribution by Richard Sheridan. The economic essays in this work by its editors, Joseph Inikori and David Richardson, began a re-evaluation and reformulation that was more supportive of the Williams thesis.

10. P.H. Lindert, 'English Occupations, 1688–1811', *Journal of Economic History*, 40, 1980, pp. 685–712.

11. Peter Mathias, 'The Industrial Revolution: Concept and Reality', in Peter Mathias and John A. Davis, eds, *The First Industrial Revolution*, Oxford 1989, p. 18. For a defence of the concept of industrial revolution see also Patrick O'Brien's Introduction to Patrick O'Brien and Roland Quinault, eds, *The Industrial Revolution and British Society*, Cambridge 1993, pp. 1–30.

12. The most notable examples being P.K. O'Brien and Stanley Engerman, 'Exports and the Growth of the British Economy from the Glorious Revolution to the Peace of Amiens', in Barbara Solow, ed., *Slavery and the Rise of the Atlantic System*, London 1991 and the discussion in Pat Hudson, *The Industrial Revolution*, London 1992, pp. 192–9.

13. Phyllis Deane and W.A. Cole, *British Economic Growth, 1688–1959*, Cambridge 1962; Elizabeth Schumpeter, *English Overseas Trade, 1697–1808*, Oxford 1960.

14. Ralph Davis, *The Industrial Revolution and British Overseas Trade*, Leicester 1979; N.F.R. Crafts, *British Economic Growth during the Industrial Revolution*, Oxford 1985.

15. E.g. R.V. Jackson, 'What was the Rate of Growth during the Industrial Revolution?', in G.D. Snooks, *Was the Industrial Revolution Really Necessary?*, London 1994, pp. 79–95 and Pat Hudson, *The Industrial Revolution*, pp. 37–45. Crafts's own view is given in 'The New Economic History and the Industrial Revolution', in Peter Mathias and John A. Davis, eds, *The First Industrial Revolution*, pp. 25–43.

16. Walter Minchinton, Introduction to W. Minchinton, ed., *The Growth of English Overseas Trade in the Seventeenth and Eighteenth Centuries*, London 1969, pp. 41–2.

17. Phyllis Deane, *The First Industrial Revolution*, London 1965, p. 63.

18. US Bureau of Census, *Historical Statistics*, Washington, DC 1970.

19. Deane and Cole, *British Economic Growth*, p. 58.

20. Philip Riden, 'The Output of the British Iron Industry before 1870', *Economic History Review*, 2nd series, vol. 30, no. 3, 1977, p. 456.

21. François Crouzet, 'Toward an Export Economy: British Exports during the Industrial Revolution', *Explorations in Economic History*, vol. 17, 1980, pp. 48–93 (p. 63). Crouzet's article is in part a critical elaboration and qualification to the previously cited article by Bairoch (see note 8 above). Crouzet uses as his statistical base the data recalculated by Ralph Davis in *The Industrial Revolution and British Overseas Trade*, London 1978; the advantage of Davis's recalculations is that they overcome some of the stereotyped distortions of trade data that were entered at 'official values' increasingly at variance with traded values.

22. Crouzet, 'Toward an Export Economy', p. 82.

23. Ibid., p. 92.

24. N.F.R. Crafts, *British Economic Growth during the Industrial Revolution*, Oxford 1985, pp. 22, 131–2. Crafts disputes Crouzet's ratios (pp. 130–31) on the grounds that they overstate GNP in 1780, but finds exports to be the largest of the three aggregate categories of expenditure and sees evidence to believe that they were an exogenous factor (p. 134).

25. David Richardson, 'The Slave Trade, Sugar, and British Economic Growth', in Solow and Engerman, *British Capitalism and Caribbean Slavery*, pp. 103–33.

26. Davis, *The Industrial Revolution and British Overseas Trade*, p. 88.

27. Deane and Cole, *British Economic Growth*, pp. 85, 86–8. However, W.A. Cole subsequently qualified his argument: see 'Eighteenth Century Growth Revisited', *Explorations in Economic History*, vol. 10, no. 4, 1973, pp. 327–49 and 'Factors in Demand', in Roderick Floud and Donald McCloskey, eds, *The Economic History of Britain since 1700*, vol. I, London 1981, pp. 327–48. The most elaborate statistical tests have yet to establish whether foreign trade was an independent generator of growth but they do suggest increasing autonomy from about 1780: see, T.J. Hatton, J.S. Lyons and S.E. Satchell, 'Eighteenth Century British Trade: Homespun or Empire Made?', *Explorations in Economic History*, vol. 20, 1983, pp. 163–82. The watershed of the 1780s for general economic advance is suggested by J.G. Williamson, 'Reinterpreting Britain's Social Tables, 1688–1913', *Explorations in Economic*

History, vol. 20, 1983, pp. 94–109. That colonial demand furnished a useful complement to the rise of industry in Britain is also argued by Barbara Solow and Stanley Engerman in their introduction to *British Capitalism and Caribbean Slavery* pp. 1–24. O'Brien and Engerman find the evidence from exports persuasive in their contribution to Solow, *Slavery and the Rise of Atlantic Economy*.

28. See Joel Mokyr, Introduction, to the volume he edits entitled *The Economics of the Industrial Revolution*, Totowa, NJ 1985, pp. 1–52.

29. Mokyr, 'Demand vs Supply', in Mokyr, ed., *The Economics of the Industrial Revolution*, pp. 97–118.

30. D.N. McCloskey, 'The Industrial Revolution 1780–1860: A Survey' in R. Floud, ed., *The Economic History of Britain*, Cambridge 1981, p. 180.

31. Jacob Price, 'Colonial Trade and British Economic Development, 1660–1775', *Lex et Scientia*, XIV, 1974, pp. 101–26, 122–3.

32. See P.K. O'Brien and Stanley Engerman, 'Exports and the Growth of the British Economy', in Barbara Solow, ed., *Slavery and the Rise of the Atlantic System*, Cambridge 1991, pp. 177–209. For O'Brien's former scepticism see Patrick K. O'Brien, 'European Economic Development: The Contribution of the Periphery', *Economic History Review*, 2nd series, vol. 35, 1982, pp. 1–18. For his part Stanley Engerman contributed an essay fairly critical of Williams to the special issue of *Revue française d'histoire d'outre mer*, 1975. The publication of Crafts's work was one factor leading these authors to a new emphasis.

33. Bairoch, 'Commerce international et genèse de la révolution industrielle anglaise', pp. 545–7.

34. Thus Ralph Davis refers to King's estimate of national income in 1688 as 'demonstrably too low'. Davis, *The Industrial Revolution and Overseas Trade*, p. 13.

35. Ernest Mandel, *Marxist Economic Theory*, London 1968, p. 95.

36. Christopher Hill, *Reformation to Industrial Revolution*, pp. 121, 203.

37. E.J. Hobsbawm, *Industry and Empire*, Harmondsworth 1970, pp. 29–31, see also p. 97; E.J. Hobsbawm, *The Age of Revolution*, p. 31. The three authors cited, while acknowledging the importance of domestic agriculture and the home market, nevertheless do accord importance to external 'primitive accumulation', such as that promoted by the slave and plantation trades. However, the Marxist understanding of the rise of capitalism certainly tends to ascribe primacy to internal as against external forms of 'primitive accumulation', and some Marxist authors, such as Brenner, have even been inclined to deny any necessary significance to the overseas forms, as we will see below.

38. Patrick O'Brien, 'Agriculture and the Home Market for English Industry, 1660–1820', *Economic History Review*, CCCXCIV, 1985.

39. George Grantham, 'Agricultural Supply during the Industrial Revolution', *Journal of Economic History*, vol. 49, no. 1, March 1989, pp. 43–72 (p. 70).

40. Williams, *Capitalism and Slavery*, p. 105.

41. Solow and Engerman, eds, *British Capitalism and Caribbean Slavery*, p. 11.

42. Brenner, 'The Origins of Capitalism', p. 67.

43. Ibid.

44. Katrina Honeyman, *Origins of Enterprise: Business Leadership in the Industrial Revolution*, Manchester 1982, pp. 162–3.

45. J.M. Price, 'What Did Merchants Do?', *Journal of Economic History*, XLIX, 1989, pp. 267–84.

46. Melville H. Watkins, 'A Staple Theory of Economic Growth', *Canadian Journal of Economic and Political Science*, 1940, pp. 141–54; Sheridan, 'The Wealth of Jamaica: A Rejoinder', *Economic History Review*, 21, 1968, pp. 46–61 (p. 59).

47. We will treat profits of the slave trade as the discounted future value of exploiting slave labour. The profits of the West Indian carrying trade are treated as profits 'realized' by slave-related trade. There is something arbitrary about both allocations. For problems of analysing surplus-value arising from circulation of commodities, and that arising from commodity production, see Ernest Mandel, *Marxist Economic Theory*, I, pp. 85–91, 95–132, 182–210; a discussion of the distinction between the production and the realization of surplus-value is found on pp. 184–6. The essential point is as follows: 'When the production of commodities is completed, the industrial capitalist already possesses the surplus value produced by his workers. But this surplus value exists in a particular form; it is still crystallised in commodities, just as the capital advanced by the industrialist is too. The capitalist can neither reconstitute this capital nor appropriate the surplus value so long as they retain this form of existence. . . .

To realise the surplus value he must sell the surplus value produced' (p. 185). It could, of course, be argued that if the manufacturer's profits had not been realized by sales to the plantations, or exchanges on the coast of Africa, then they could have been realized either by selling the goods in another market, or by investing the initial capital in some other field. In the case of the British manufactures under consideration here it is most unlikely that other markets could have been found for these goods; long-distance trade, with its lengthy turn-around times, was, in principle, a market of last resort. Of course the initial capital of those who invested in the 'triangular trade' could have been otherwise deployed, but, presumably, (1) profits would have been somewhat lower, since they were scarcely invested in the slave trade for non-pecuniary motives, such as philanthropy or prestige; (2) the other likely investments (e.g. in the funds, land, etc.) would not have promoted industrial development. All these considerations tend to make a consideration of the 'realization effect' a valid and worthwhile undertaking. For further discussion of the problems of realization see Michael De Vroey's contribution in I. Steedman *et al.*, *The Value Controversy*, London 1981.

48. R.P. Thomas, 'The Sugar Colonies of the Old Empire: Profit or Loss for Great Britain?', *Economic History Review*, vol. 21, 1968, pp. 30–45.

49. J.R. Ward, 'The Profitability of Sugar Planting in the British West Indies: 1650–1834', *Economic History Review*, 2nd series, vol. 21, no. 2, May 1978, pp. 197–213.

50. Hancock, *Citizens of the World*, pp. 383–98,409–24; S. Chapman and J. Butt, 'The Cotton Industry, 1775–1856', in C.H. Feinstein and S. Pollard, eds, *Studies in Capital Formation in the United Kingdom 1750–1920*, Oxford 1988, pp. 103–25 (p. 109).

51. Anstey, *The Atlantic Slave Trade and British Abolition*, p. 47.

52. Inikori, 'Market Structure and the Profits of the British African Trade in the Late Eighteenth Century', *Journal of Economic History*, vol. XXXIV, 1974, pp. 885–914.

53. In a discussion of contemporary estimates of the value of British West Indian properties Drescher points out that whether the planters' figures are taken or those of their opponents overall value rises by about a fifth over the years 1775–90 and doubles in the years 1790–1814 (*Econocide*, pp. 22–3). Patrick Coloquhoun's *Treatise on the Wealth, Power and Resources of the British Empire* was published in London in 1815; for his estimate of colonial income and property see p. 59. The accounts for Worthy Park show that the rise in profitability during the French wars boosted the value of the plantation; during this period average annual profits were around £13,000 (Craton, *In Search of the Invisible Man*, p. 138). Worthy Park was a large plantation. If the global West Indian profit figure given in the text is accurate (£13.9 million) then there would have had to be the equivalent of just over 1,000 Worthy Parks in the British-controlled West Indies in the years 1793–1814. This seems entirely possible. According to Bryan Edwards there were 767 sugar estates in Jamaica alone, about 100 of them similar in size to Worthy Park; Jamaica accounted for roughly one half of British West Indian sugar output. In addition to sugar estates there were 607 coffee estates in Jamaica in 1793, 1,047 grazing pens, several hundred cotton or pimento estates and dozens of indigo works. (Craton, *Searching for the Invisible Man*, pp. 404–5, notes 32 and 35; Bryan Edwards, *The History . . . of the British West Indies*, London 1793, vol. 1, pp. 311–15.) As for British national income, Peter Mathias estimated that this grew from £80 million in 1770 to £232 million, in *The Transformation of England*, London 1979, p. 118, though the new calculations of the 1980s led to a widespread view that growth has been slower. Given the unavoidably rough-and-ready character of these estimates of national and colonial wealth, it is not possible to be sure which grew fastest; for what it is worth the data cited in this note suggest a slightly faster rate of growth for colonial wealth during the French wars, after which it stagnated and then, from about 1819, declined sharply.

54. Shepherd and Walton, *Shipping, Maritime Trade and the Economic Development of Colonial North America*, pp. 107–8.

55. Pombal is quoted by Lang, *Portuguese Brazil*, p. 155. For trade figures see H.E.S. Fisher, *The Portugal Trade*, London 1971, p. 26 and Armando Castro, *A dominacão inglesa em Portugal*, Porto 1972, pp. 18–23.

56. See Thomas M. Truxes, *Irish–American Trade, 1660–1783*, Cambridge 1988. Truxes's study stresses how important the American plantations were to the structure of Irish trade.

57. Stanley Engerman, 'Richardson, Boulle and the "Williams theses"', in 'The Atlantic Slave Trade: New Approaches', *Revue française d'histoire d'outre mer*, 1975, p. 333.

58. C.H. Feinstein, 'Capital Expenditure in Great Britain', *Cambridge Economic History of Europe*, vol. 7, London 1978, p. 74. See also François Crouzet, Editor's Introduction, *Capital Formation in the Industrial Revolution*, London 1972, pp. 25–6. Since Crouzet's later

work has been drawn on above it is, perhaps, necessary to point out that in this text he is sceptical concerning the contribution of colonial profits to British capital formation. While he cites a number of examples of colonial profits contributing to investment projects he doubts their overall significance on the following grounds: 'the Industrial Revolution gathered momentum after 1783, by which time Britain had lost the thirteen colonies and the sugar islands were on the wane' (p. 177). Dating the decline of the British West Indies from as early as 1783 is a myth that has been demolished by Seymour Drescher, J.R. Ward and Michael Craton in the works cited above. Crouzet's judgement here also predates Anstey's findings concerning the slave trade and Crouzet's own reconstruction of the surge of British exports to the Americas after 1783, including North America. Nevertheless Crouzet's essay helps to establish the overall context; see also his essay 'England and France in the Eighteenth Century', in R.M. Hartwell, ed., *Causes of the Industrial Revolution*, London 1966.

59. Pares, *Merchants and Planters*, p. 50. Fonthill was a gothic 'folly' constructed for the fabulously wealthy heir to a West Indian fortune, William Beckford the Second; it collapsed ten years after it was built.

60. Feinstein, 'Capital Formation in Great Britain', *Cambridge Economic History of Europe*, vol. 7, p. 78.

61. Williams, *Capitalism and Slavery*, p. 105.

62. Feinstein, 'Capital Formation in Great Britain', *Cambridge Economic History of Europe*, vol. 7, pp. 90–91. The halting of the slave trade stopped the process whereby English traders built up the labour force of the 'foreign' colonies, or newly acquired territories, at the expense of Britain's old colonies and for this reason afforded the latter some protection; though this was a consideration in British acceptance of Abolition it was, in my view, a secondary one (see Blackburn, *The Overthrow of Colonial Slavery*).

63. Hill, *Reformation to Industrial Revolution*, p. 164.

64. P.J. Marshall, *East India Fortunes: The British in Bengal in the Eighteenth Century*, Oxford 1976, p. 241. In addition to the direct remittance of £2.7 million in 1756–70 Marshall estimates that a further £2 million was remitted indirectly or in kind (p. 243). In 1770 Bengal was afflicted by a terrible famine in which ten million of the province's inhabitants perished. The Company's reckless pillage certainly bore a measure of responsibility for the disaster – in its aftermath there were attempts to reorganize Company rule along more rationally exploitative lines. By the latter part of the century Bengal alone yielded £500,000 net annually; Marshall estimates total British profits from India in the eighteenth century at £18 million. He adds: 'fortunes were generally made by men whose families were already of some social standing and valued land as the supremely desirable possession. Money acquired in India was used to acquire more land, to build on it or to lend to the government in return for an income with which to support life in the country' (p. 256).

65. Hancock, *Citizens of the World*, pp. 259, 301–2, 305–6.

66. Feinstein, 'Capital Formation in Great Britain', *Cambridge Economic History of Europe*, vol. 7, pp. 88–9.

67. G.E. Mingay, *English Landed Society in the Eighteenth Century*, London 1963, pp. 73, 104–5, 166; Williams, *Capitalism and Slavery*, pp. 102–3. Sheridan cites Arthur Young, Henry Brougham and Lord Shelburne to the effect that West Indian profits helped to finance agricultural enclosure and improvements, *Sugar and Slavery*, pp. 473–4. Though it could be pure coincidence the number of Enclosure Bills presented to Parliament closely follows Ward's findings for plantation profitability, with a drop from 1776 to 1784, followed by a boom during the French wars. (For Enclosure Bills, which were quite expensive to finance, see J.D. Chambers and G.E. Mingay, *The Agricultural Revolution*, London 1966, p. 83.) See also Mark Overton, *The Agricultural Revolution in England*, Cambridge 1996, pp. 132–5.

68. J.T. Ward, *The Finance of Canal Building in Eighteenth Century England*, Oxford 1974, p. 23.

69. Ibid., p. 77.

70. Ibid., pp. 76–7.

71. Editor's Introduction, Grouzet, ed., *Capital Formation in the Industrial Revolution*, p. 45. According to Honeyman, the cotton masters found that credit, though vitally important, was 'virtually impossible to obtain through institutional mechanisms because of the unstable and unpredictable nature of the industry . . .', Honeyman, *Origins of Enterprise*, p. 163.

72. Douglas Farnie, *The English Cotton Industry and the World Market, 1815–1896*, Oxford 1979, especially pp. 56–61. The regional dynamics of industrialization have been

stressed by Sidney Pollard, *Peaceful Conquest: The Industrialization of Europe 1760–1970*, Oxford 1981; see, for Lancashire, pp. 16–17, 37–8.

73. David Richardson, 'Profits in the Liverpool Slave Trade', in R. Anstey and P.E.H. Hair, eds, *Liverpool, the African Slave Trade and Abolition*, p. 68.

74. B.L. Anderson, 'The Lancashire Bill System and its Liverpool Practitioners: The Case of a Slave Merchant', in W.H. Chaloner and Barrie Ratcliffe, eds, *Trade and Transport*, Manchester 1977, pp. 62, 64–5.

75. S.D. Chapman, 'Financial Restraints on the Growth of Firms in the Cotton Industry, 1790–1850', *Economic History Review*, 2nd series, vol. 32, no. 1, February 1979, pp. 50–69 (p. 53).

76. B.K. Drake, 'The Liverpool African Voyage c. 1790–1807: Commercial Problems', in Anstey and Hair, *Liverpool, the African Slave trade, and Abolition*, pp. 128–9.

77. Jacob Price, 'What Did Merchants Do?', pp. 281–2.

78. Pat Hudson, *The Genesis of Industrial Capital*, Cambridge 1986, chapters 5–8. This is not, of course, the same as claiming that manufacturers were themselves merchants by origin. According to Crouzet only about a fifth of manufacturers started out as merchants or traders. François Crouzet, *The First Industrialists*, Cambridge 1985, pp. 147, 151.

79. Honeyman, *Origins of Enterprise*, pp. 61–2.

80. Ibid., pp. 108–9, 163–4.

81. Peter Mathias, 'Financing the Industrial Revolution', in Mathias and Davis, eds, *The First Industrial Revolution*, pp. 69–85 (p. 77).

82. 'Petitions presented on 7th May and 13th May, 1806, from merchants and manufacturers interested in the African and colonial trades', House of Lords Record Office. The petitions attracted, respectively, 82 and 113 signatories.

83. Drescher, *Econocide*, pp. 42–4.

84. Berg, *The Age of Manufactures*, p. 51.

85. T.M. Devine, *The Tobacco Lords*, Edinburgh 1975, pp. 34–5, 113. Jacob Price and Paul Clemens have shown that the size and sophistication of the British enterprises trading with the American plantations grew rapidly in the eighteenth century; see 'A Revolution of Scale in Overseas Trade: British Firms in the Chesapeake Trade, 1675–1775', *The Journal of Economic History*, vol. 47, March 1987, no. 1, pp. 1–44.

86. John Lord, *Capital and Steam Power, 1750–1850*, London 1923, p. 113.

87. Berg, *The Age of Manufactures*, pp. 290, 294–5.

88. Ibid., p. 117. That the plantations trades had long been connected with 'proto-industrial' development in several parts of Western Europe is explained by Peter Kriedte, 'The Origins, the Agrarian Context and Conditions in the World Market', in P. Kriedte, Hans Medick and Jürgen Schumbohm, *Industrialization Before Industrialization*, Cambridge 1981, pp. 12–37, especially pp. 33–7.

89. Phyllis Deane, 'Great Britain', in C.M. Cipolla, ed., *The Fontana Economic History of Europe*, 4, *The Emergence of Industrial Societies*, vol. 1, London 1973, p. 178.

90. Peter Mathias, *The Transformation of England*, pp. 210–12, 238–9; David Brion Davis, *The Problem of Slavery in the Age of Revolution*, New York 1975, pp. 233–9.

91. Mathias, *The Transformation of England*, pp. 97–8. Cf. also P.G.M. Dickinson, *The Financial Revolution*, London 1967, p. 8.

92. Barbara Solow, Introduction, to Solow, *Slavery and the Rise of the Atlantic Economy*; Pat Hudson, *Industrial Revolution*, pp. 196–200.

93. Stanley Engerman, 'Richardson, Boulle and the "Williams thesis"', p. 333.

94. Crafts, *British Economic Growth during the Industrial Revolution*, p. 81.

95. N.F.R. Crafts, 'Exogenous or Endogenous Growth? The Industrial Revolution Reconsidered', *Journal of Economic History*, vol. 55, no. 4, December 1995, pp. 745–72; for the new stress on 'technological shock' see Joel Mokyr, 'Introduction: The New Economic History and the Industrial Revolution', in Mokyr, ed., *The British Industrial Revolution: An Economic Perspective*, Oxford 1993, pp. 1–131.

96. Paul Bairoch, 'Agriculture and the Industrial Revolution: 1700–1914', in Cipolla, *The Fontana Economic History of Europe*, vol. 3, *The Industrial Revolution*, pp. 486–7.

97. E.A. Wrigley, 'The Supply of Raw Materials in the Industrial Revolution', in R.M. Hartwell, ed., *The Causes of the Industrial Revolution*, London 1967, p. 116.

98. Farnie, *The English Cotton Industry and the World Market*, pp. 82–3.

99. The assumption here is that even without the cruel and destructive actions of the East

India Company, textile production in the subcontinent would have found it difficult to compete with Lancashire textiles.

100. Hobsbawm, *Industry and Empire*, p. 76.

101. A.H. Imlah, *Economic Aspects of the Pax Britannica*, Cambridge, MA 1958, p. 108.

102. Drescher, *Econocide*, p. 57.

103. J. Potter, 'Atlantic Economy, 1815–60: The USA and the Industrial Revolution in Britain', in L.S. Pressnel, ed., *Studies in the Industrial Revolution*, London 1960, p. 247.

104. Paul G.E. Clemens, 'The Operation of an Eighteenth Century Chesapeake Tobacco Plantation', *Agricultural History*, vol. 49, no. 3, July 1975, pp. 517–32 (p. 525). Planters probably felt that keeping their slaves fully occupied was good for security, on the general grounds that idle hands got up to mischief. Plantation revolts and conspiracies often came in the slack season rather than during the harvest. See Gorender's remarks on the advantages and dangers for the planter of withdrawing into the shell of natural economy, *O escravismo colonial*, p. 242. So far as the purely economic pressure of US slaveowners is concerned, note this was peculiarly intense in Georgia in the 1790s where per capita exports had declined from £3.17 in 1768–72 to only £1.17 in 1791–92 (constant prices); in the Upper South the decline in per capita exports was less severe, from £1.79 in 1768–72 to £1.09 in 1791–92. Cf. Walton and Shepherd, *The Economic Rise of Early America*, pp. 192, 196.

105. Gavin Wright, *The Political Economy of the Slave South*, New York 1978, p. 14. For an account the context of Whitney's discovery which suggests that it could not have been long delayed, see Jeanette Mirsky and Allan Nevins, *The World of Eli Whitney*, New York 1952, p. 81.

106. Chaplin, *An Anxious Pursuit: Agricultural Innovation and Modernity in the Lower South*, pp. 328, 329.

107. Quoted in Sheridan, *Sugar and Slavery*, p. 35.

108. There has been a tendency in Marxist writings to ignore the relative autonomy of consumption needs, though Marx himself did sometimes refer to the important cultural dimension of wage workers' consumption choices; see, for example, Karl Marx, Draft for the Sixth Chapter, *Capital*, vol. 1, London 1976, pp. 1034–5. The traditional Marxist view is found in Edmond Preteceille and Jean-Pierre Terrail, *Capitalism, Consumption and Human Needs*, Oxford 1985, especially pp. 37–82. For a corrective to the idealist assumptions of this work see Sebastiano Timpanaro, *Considerations on Materialism*, London 1976. The work of Raymond Williams, especially *Materialism and Culture*, London 1979, outlines a theory of cultural materialism which has much to contribute to understanding 'consumption' as other than a purely passive affair. For a marvellous evocation of the impact of sugar on the mode of consumption see Sidney Mintz, *Sweetness and Power*. For an impressionistic but still informative exploration of the new modes of consumption developing in Hanoverian Britain see Neil McKendrick, John Brewer and J.H. Plumb, *The Birth of a Consumer Society*, London 1983. However, it should be stressed that recognition of the element of autonomy in consumption does not require a particularly 'optimistic' reading of the condition of the new wage- and salary-dependent classes. The new world of consumption carried with it dangers of several sorts, and even its supposed benefits were very unevenly distributed.

109. Dorothy Davis, *A History of Shopping*, London 1966, p. 73.

110. Ibid., p. 194.

111. A contemporary comment quoted in Hoh-cheung and Lorna H. Mui, *Shops and Shopkeeping in Eighteenth Century England*, London 1989, p. 196. See also the observations of Brewer, *Sinews of Power*, pp. 183–5.

112. Sugar consumption calculated from Schumpeter, *English Overseas Trade Statistics*, Table XVIII. The saddler's budget is given by Davis, *A History of Shopping*, p. 213. In this instance sugar purchases comprise 7 per cent of the total family budget, which seems high even for an urban worker.

113. John Campbell, *The Nature of the Sugar Trade*, London 1774, p. 31.

114. Cf. Mathias, 'The Social Structure of the Eighteenth Century: A Calculation', *The Transformation of England*, pp. 171–89.

115. Jan de Vries, 'Between Purchasing Power and the World of Goods: Understanding the Household Economy in Early Modern Europe', in John Brewer and Roy Porter, eds, *Consumption and the World of Goods*, London 1993, pp. 85–132.

116. Cormac O Grada, *Ireland: A New Economic History, 1780–1939*, Oxford 1994, p. 105. See also John Komlos, 'The Secular Trend in the Biological Standard of Living in the UK, 1730–1860', *Economic History Review*, vol. 26 no. 1, 1993 and Joel Mokyr, 'Is There

Still Life in the Pessimist Case? Consumption during the Industrial Revolution', *Journal of Economic History*, 48, 1988, pp. 69–92.

117. Shammas, *The Preindustrial Consumer*, pp. 147–8, 297. Shammas also observes: 'Our understanding of how calories were distributed between and within households is, of course, very limited. Who sacrificed – the labouring poor in general? Women? Children? The old? The disabled?' (p. 297).

118. Craton, *Searching for the Invisible Man*, p. 116.

119. R.P. Thomas, 'The Sugar Colonies of the Old Empire', *Economic History Review*, 2nd series, vol. 21, no. 9, 1968, pp. 30–45.

120. R.B. Sheridan, *Sugar and Slavery*, pp. 471–3.

121. R.P. Thomas and D.N. McCloskey, 'Overseas Trade and Empire: 1700–1860', in Roderick Floud and D.N. McCloskey, eds, *The Economic History of Britain since 1700*, vol. 1, *1700–1860*, London 1981, pp. 87–102 (p. 99).

122. For military outlays see Michael Mann, 'State and Society, 1130–1815: An Analysis of English State Finances', in Maurice Zeitlin, ed., *Political Power and Social Theory*, vol. 1, 1980, pp. 165–208 (p. 193).

123. Hancock, *Citizens of the World*, pp. 237–9.

124. Jones, *Britain and the World*, pp. 115–94.

125. Mathias, *The Transformation of England*, p. 125.

126. Ibid., p. 127.

127. Joseph Massie, *A Computation of the Money that hath been exorbitantly raised upon the People of Great Britain by the Sugar Planters*, London 1760.

128. Mathias, *The Transformation of England*, pp. 118–19. For the reasons why the British economy could bear heavier taxes see Peter Mathias and Patrick O'Brien, 'Taxation in Britain and France, 1715–1810', *Journal of European Economic History*, vol. 5, no. 3, Winter 1976, pp. 601–50 (p. 605).

129. Mathias, *The Transformation of England*, pp. 118–19.

130. Rostow, *How It All Began*, p. 43. However, T.S.Ashton has shown that if Britain had been able entirely to avoid these wars its growth might have been more rapid: Ashton, *Economic Fluctuations in England, 1700–1800*, Oxford 1959, pp. 83, 183–4, 188.

131. Patrick O'Brien has many pertinent reflections on these issues in 'Political Preconditions for the Industrial Revolution', in O'Brien, ed., *The Industrial Revolution and British Society*, pp. 124–55.

132. For 'crowding out' see R.A. Black and C.G. Gilmore, 'Crowding Out During Britain's Industrial Revolution', *The Journal of Economic History*, vol. 50, no. 1, March 1990, pp. 109–32.

133. E.J. Hobsbawm, 'The Seventeenth Century in the Development of Capitalism', *Science and Society*, vol. 24, no. 2, Spring 1960, pp. 97–112. Hobsbawm's theses concerning Britain's role elaborate Marx's observations in chapter 31 of *Capital*, vol. I. Of course, recognition of the pivotal role of Atlantic trade, of colonial and commercial wars, of the creation of the national debt, and so forth, is not confined to Marxist authors. See Charles Wilson, *England's Apprenticeship 1603–1763*, London 1965, pp. 160–85, 263–88, 313–36. Wilson observes: 'The rise of the British economy was based, historically, on the conscious and successful application of strength; just as the decline of the Dutch economy was based on the inability of a small and weak state to maintain its position against stronger states' (p. 287). More on this aspect of the mobilization of the British state has been documented by John Brewer, *The Sinews of Power*, Cambridge, MA 1990.

134. Louis Bergeron, *L'Épisode napoléonien, Aspects intérieurs, 1799–1815*, Paris 1972, p. 196.

135. Ibid.

136. F. Crouzet, 'Wars, Blockade, and Economic Change in Europe, 1792–1815', *Journal of Economic History*, 1964, pp. 567–88 (p. 578).

137. Ibid., p. 571.

138. Bergeron, *L'Épisode napoléonien*, pp. 189–90.

139. Crouzet, 'Wars, Blockade, and Economic Change in Europe', p. 572.

140. Claudia D. Goldin and Frank Lewis, 'The Role of Exports in American Economic Growth during the Napoleonic Wars, 1793–1807', *Explorations in Economic History*, vol. 17, 1980, pp. 6–25.

Epilogue

The technicalities of the previous chapter can, if we wish, be simplified. By 1800 there were 600,000 slaves in the British West Indies, another 150,000 slaves in colonies occupied by Britain, 857,000 slaves in the United States, about one and a half million in Brazil and around 250,000 in Spanish America. Given Britain's prominence in Atlantic trade, and bearing in mind that the slave population comprised a high proportion of field or craft workers, it could be said that Britain acquired the produce of around one million slaves, each working for an average of 2,500 to 3,000 hours in the year and producing crops worth around £18. About half of these slaves worked on British-owned plantations. The slaves worked under compulsion, their only incentive being the receipt of some bare necessities and/or the chance to feed themselves by working extra time on top of an already very lengthy work week. The greater part of the money paid for the plantation crops returned to the metropolis as mercantile profit, planters' profit, customs' duties, outlay on provisions, textiles, new equipment and the like; a smaller proportion would comprise wages and salaries paid to free workers on plantations, docks and ships. Thus sugar, tobacco and cotton which had cost the slaves 2,500,000,000 hours of toil was sold by metropolitan merchants or manufacturers to consumers who, in order to afford these purchases, themselves had to labour for hundreds or thousands of millions of hours for their employers. At retail prices these consumers had to pay a gross sum that could not have been much less than £35,000,000 around the turn of the century.

Earning the necessities of life, and acquiring the little luxuries that helped to make a hard existence supportable, required lengthy stints in the new factories. The industrial workers were induced voluntarily to accept disciplines nearly as severe as those which slavery imposed by use of the lash. Hours of work and life expectancy among the early industrial operatives and in the new conurbations where they lived were, as pointed out in Chapter X, often little better than those on the plantations. Sir Alexander Grant and his associates were not only super-exploiting the slaves, and skimming an impressive surplus from exchanges made possible by seamen, dockers and factory operatives, but also determining by their activities the path of accumulation. Indeed British capitalism became 'path dependent' in the sense that a mercantile and financial complex reproduced itself by balancing colonial, manufacturing and real estate investments, in what some have termed the pattern of 'gentlemanly capitalism'.[1]

While the above orders of magnitude bear out the importance of the plantations it might seem that they also belie the claim made in Chapter VIII that a benign, or at least much less destructive, path of economic growth, eschewing slavery, could have been pursued. How on earth could all those hours of toil have been exacted except through forced labour? This is a sobering thought but not, as it turns out, a decisive objection. In prevailing conditions the material situation of 'free' wage workers would have been only modestly preferable to outright slavery, since they were constrained to work long hours in often atrocious conditions simply in order to feed themselves. There is one small but not insignificant contrast which bears on this possibility. On the one hand, during the period 1780–1850 the height of recruits to the British army dropped, reflecting the impact of industrialization and urbanization. On the other, American-born slaves tended to be an average of 1 to 2 inches taller than African-born slaves, whether in the Caribbean or North America, just as whites born in the United States were taller than English artisans, or Italian peasants. The relative abundance of food in the New World helps to explain this contrast. The slaveowner was able to reap most of the benefit of any improvement encountered by the slave but that would not have been the case for free immigrants.[2]

All in all New World fertility could have allowed an advantageous deal to be struck between immigrants, natives and public authorities. Instead the black labourers of the New World were yoked to an implacable treadmill which paced both their toil and that of the new industrial proletariat in the Old. The fact that the wage workers had freedom of movement eventually gave them a leverage over their employers which allowed them to improve their situation. It was the tied character of slave labour which attracted the planter. An alternative labour regime for the plantations would have had to be able to offer reasonable wages if it was to attract and keep enough labourers – but if the burden of customs duty and profit had been lighter then such wages could have been paid. Recruiting wage workers to work in sugar mills need not have been so different, in principle, from recruiting them to work in cotton mills so long as land was not freely available. The manageable size of the sugar islands would have enabled the colonial authorities, if they so wished, to control access to it on terms which encouraged the production of both cane and foodstuffs for sale. However a critical issue would have been avoidance of the negative reproduction rates which characterized the slave populations of the West Indies and Brazil. I have argued that the contrasting North American pattern of natural growth in the size of the slave population was owed partly to differences in the work regime and climate but principally to the fact that individual slaves, and notably slave mothers and their children, were not left to feed themselves by relying mainly on their own efforts but could count on receiving a share of the collectively cultivated food crops. These arrangements, I have argued, encouraged slave women to have more children – a decisive consideration since one way or another these women did have a real degree of control over their fertility.

The contrast in the demographic pattern between North America and the Caribbean had large consequences for the size of the resulting population. While the import of some 660,000 slaves produced a slave population of over a million in North America in 1810, the British Caribbean slave population was only 600,000, despite the fact that the islands had received over a million and a half slaves. If an alternative to slavery had been able to ensure rising population levels then wage labour would have been forthcoming. Immigrants from either Europe or Africa could have been offered land subject to payment of rent or taxes that would have obliged them to cultivate a cash crop. The British government was in fact to pursue two initially divergent methods for the colonization of the Antipodes showing that alternative solutions did exist. In Australia the colonization effort was initially based on convict labour and the dispossession of the natives. In New Zealand a colonial chartered company influenced by Abolitionism based its project exclusively on free and independent labour, and even aspired to better relations with the natives. In the event the Treaty made with the Maori peoples was not honoured; many settlers proved rapacious and were not restrained either by the humanitarian sponsors or by the colonial power. Nevertheless the early New Zealand experience, despite its chicanery and bloodshed, did at least avoid penal labour and established a signal reference point for the Maori struggle for their rights.[3]

This book has charted the rise of the slave systems of the New World and examined their decisive impact on the breakthrough to industrial accumulation. The first part focused on the construction of the new identities and structures of colonial slavery, and on the competitive selection of the slave plantation and racial slavery as instruments of mercantile accumulation and interstate rivalry. The second part, taking social identities as largely given, though not free from conflict, has focused mainly on the rhythms of economic accumulation, on political and demographic constraints, and on the insertion of plantation slavery in the larger accumulation process. But identity and political economy were not sealed in water-tight compartments. They conditioned one another in asymmetric ways, with economic pressure hardening racial boundaries in the early colonial phase, while a more complex economic development pressed against colonial limitations and officially sanctioned identities by the latter half of the eighteenth century.

In the making of the New World slave systems there was an element of conscious construction, but also much improvisation and accident, whose results then had to be accommodated by reworked social identities. The baroque moment had reflected a striving to keep the multiple dimensions of European expansion (the internal development of social powers as well as the overseas exploits of merchants and colonists) within the bounds of a conscious project, its unifying aesthetic symbolizing accountability to religious and royal authority. Here there was a place allotted to everyone, however lowly. The colonist had been recognized as faithful servant of the Church and monarch, the slave as faithful servant of the colonist, and the native protégés, under their caciques, as new vassals. This model, though thoroughly ideological, came closest to realization in Spanish America. The moment of capitalist modernity associated with the takeoff of the plantations was different. Here there was a more narrowly focused project; slaves were needed as a means and their great advantage was that they had no being or identity of their own. In Orlando Patterson's chilling but accurate phrase the slave was socially dead.[4]

Etymologically the word capital derives from the Latin word for head, as in head of cattle. Slaves, usually all too literally, were regarded as human cattle – but they were also feared as potentially murderous wild beasts. They were known as 'chattel' slaves, another word stemming from the same Latin root as the words 'cattle' and 'capital'. The practical ideology of the New World slave systems thus postulated that the captives were sub-human; yet at the same time slaveholder strategies for security, or work motivation or reproduction, had to find some way of taking account of the slaves' very human capacities.

Evidently moral teaching lagged badly behind the new social powers being developed by the merchants and planters. Traditional restraints on slavery such as those embodied in the *Siete Partidas* had no purchase on the new realities of the slave trade and plantations. I have noted instances of unease at the workings of the slave trade or slavery and some attempts to justify them. European religion and literature did contain warnings against greed and avarice. But slaveholders and slave traders who lived sober, charitable and respectable lives could avoid reproach on this score. Since the Christian churches of colonial America claimed to be the arbiters of social and private morality, and since their claims were upheld by the colonial authorities and widely accepted by colonists, the Christian teaching on the legitimacy of slavery, including the enslavement of whole descent groups, posed no ideological challenge to the slave systems. Had they opposed slavery it would undoubtedly have made the construction of the slave systems a highly problematic, even impossible, undertaking. When a few independent churches eventually and cautiously withdrew their approbation of slave trading and slave holding in the third quarter of the eighteenth century this began to open a significant fissure in the slave systems.

In the early phase colonial entrepreneurs, new merchants, sea captains and planters used tied labour to develop new sources of economic power and colonial states discovered the advantage to be derived from controlling the plantation trade. Europe's craving for exotic products and the increasingly monetized social relations of an emergent capitalist order played the key part in this development. The seventeenth-century Dutch and English, with their commercial mentalities, saw no reason not to avail themselves of captive labour: the human costs of doing so did not show up in the account books. Not for the last time freer markets exposed those most vulnerable to heightened exploitation and competitive pressures encouraged callous disregard.[5]

'Economic' considerations did not have naked priority however, since for a partner or agent to disregard an opportunity for gain, or lack zeal in exploiting it, would be a breach of trust. Religious, national and racial exclusions also helped to harden the heart of the slave trader and planter. White European indentured servants could be treated fairly badly, especially if of another confession, but black African captives were treated worse. Many of the new merchants or planters were law-abiding and godly men devoted to the Puritan work ethic. Pressed for justification they might declare that the African captive had been reduced to slavery by local laws and practices, or they might refer to the threadbare claim that the captive was being introduced to Christianity or to the fanciful story of Noah's curse. Sadly, the diffuse popular prejudice against slavery, self-interested as it might be, received no authoritative backing from political, legal or religious leaders. In the plantation zone it was stifled by fear and privilege. In European ports, and in colonies where free or independent labour predominated, popular sentiment hostile to slavery became a force which had to be taken into account even by gentlemanly and mercantile elites who themselves had a stake in the slavery-based Atlantic economy.

That slaves were sold in Africa or bought by merchants was not new. The novelty of New World slavery resided in the scale and intensity of the slave traffic and the plantation trades. Earlier forms of slavery had been geared to household service, or the strengthening of a lineage, or the construction of a military apparatus, or to relatively modest enclaves of estate or mine labour. The New World slave plantations, by contrast, had established permanent and hereditary slavery of the most onerous sort, breaking with any geographical constraint and displaying an unquenchable thirst for slave labour and slave lives. Traditional defences of slavery, and established racial notions, were inadequate to the task of explaining this Great Captivity. Even if Africans had committed some crime, why should their children pay for it? If they inherited some ancestral curse this could not justify, as Sandoval, Vieira and Godwyn pointed out, the abuse and neglect to which they were subject. The failure to attend to the religious needs of the slaves was manifest in every plantation colony. New World slavery thus brought about a degradation of the slave condition, and of the ideologies which justified or explained it.

The slave status in the Americas was defined by two core features – namely that slaves were private property and that, after a while, only those of African descent were enslaved. The most important feature fixing slave identity in the Americas was the property regime and appropriate title deeds. The Roman *jus gentium* and its acceptance of private property in persons furnished elements of a model in all the slave colonies. But running it a close second was dark skin pigmentation; the terms black, *nègre* or Negro were used interchangeably with that of slave. The presence of some free people of colour could still allow for an assumption that blacks were slaves, a circumstance which affected the outlook of even coloured slaveholders.

The definitions of property and race at first helped to stabilize one another. Property that could run away, make up stories and resist recapture was made the more readily identifiable by colour coding. Likewise property law and title deeds could arbitrate delicate questions of where the borderline between free and slave should be drawn. In all the plantation societies mulattoes could be and were held as slaves, despite the likelihood of white paternity. At the limit the 'racial' definition via skin colour could cause problems for the property system since there were inevitably a few very light-skinned slaves, some with a disturbing resemblance to powerful whites. They could be sold, manumitted or assigned lighter duties but the tension was there all the same. St-Méry claimed that 15 per cent of the free mulattoes in Saint Domingue were indistinguishable from whites just as 10 per cent of the whites were in fact *sangs melés*.

The racial regime in the different colonies varied according to the proportion of slaves in the total population and according to religious and national traditions. Where blacks and coloureds together were an absolute majority both the authorities and the planters had an interest in securing the support of a layer of the coloured population; but this was as likely to lead to promotion of a slave elite as to recognition of the rights of free coloureds. The eventual emergence of an influential body of free people of colour in Saint Domingue in the latter half of the eighteenth century – or in Jamaica in the early nineteenth – was not a development planned by the colonial authorities, though they certainly sought to extract advantage from it once it had occurred, using the free people of colour as a counterweight to both wayward white colonists and slaves. The presence of a relatively numerous free coloured population in Brazil and Spanish America and their enjoyment of some collective rights reflected Iberian social and cultural traditions and institutions. The baroque monarchies sought to promote an elaborate hierarchy of different estates and castes; in their plantation colonies modest corporate privileges accorded to free people of colour helped to buttress the slave regime. The English colonies of North America promoted subordination by means of a racial exclusion that privileged non-slaveholding whites, a system that proved less effective outside the plantation zone.

Racial definitions were inherently more slippery and subjective than title deeds. The Catholic Church claimed to regulate genealogy via legitimate marriage, monogamy and succession, and was uncomfortable with any precept which took such matters out of its hands. The use of skin colour to indicate slave status, or vulnerability to enslavement, opened up a breach in clerical authority, even if some religious justification for the practice was offered. When planters denied the clergy access to their slaves this would affront the more conscientious: such a reaction was occasionally found among Anglican clergy as well.

Those churches and religious bodies which endorsed slavery – the great majority – were gradually to align themselves with policies of 'amelioration', policies which hoped to raise the rate of reproduction by encouraging family life, maternity and a degree of religious recognition. This reformist response to the challenge represented by nakedly commercial slavery was sometimes exhibited by the Benedictines and Jesuits in South America and it was also to be experimented with by some British slaveowners, for humanitarian or religious reasons. Where successful it led to a model of slavery closer to that prevailing in North America, and could yield some improvement in the material situation of potential slave mothers. The closing of the slave trade to the British islands in 1807 encouraged the adoption of natalist policies of this sort. On the other hand it led to no alleviation in the regime of punishing toil for the majority of slaves; indeed the absence of newcomers to replenish the ranks of the slave gangs limited the previous possibilities of social promotion for older slaves and creole slaves since they were still needed in the fields.[6]

This disruption of expectations was to be a source of slave unrest, as was heightened mobilization for toil. At the limit some idealistic planters, like 'Monk' Lewis, were prepared to dismantle the apparatus of coercion. But in this case the result could be a dissolution of the plantation regime. Lewis banned the whip during a visit in 1816 and then noted: 'The negroes certainly are perverse beings. They had been praying for the sight of their master year after year; they were in raptures at my arrival; I have suffered no-one to be punished, and shown them every possible indulgence during my residence among them; and one and all they declare themselves perfectly happy and well-treated. Yet previous to my arrival they made thirty-three hogsheads a week; in a fortnight after my landing, their product dwindled to twenty-three; during this last week they have managed to make but thirteen. Still they are not ungrateful, only selfish; they love me very well but they love themselves a great deal better.'[7]

The secular thought of the Enlightenment was important for anti-slavery because it explored alternative ways of motivating labourers. It established the argument that modern conditions did not require tied labour. Political economists argued that labourers who needed to earn to feed themselves and their families would be willing to work; and to the extent that their self-interest was engaged they would work far more effectively than forced labourers. Likewise smallholders or tenants could be motivated to engage in commercial cultivation in order to meet rent and tax demands, or to acquire better tools or simply to enjoy a more attractive standard of consumption. Some of these processes – the separation of direct producers from means of production – constitute the primary meaning of the classical notion of 'primitive accumulation' and required non-economic coercion. But in the Revolutionary epoch and its aftermath many North American farmers began to embrace a less autarkic model of economic activity, not because they had been deprived of their farms or forced to pay heavy taxes but because they wished to diversify the basket of consumer goods available to themselves and their families.[8] This phenomenon showed that producers could be motivated mainly by positive incentives; on the other hand, in line with the theme of Part Two of this study, it remained the case that the products the farmers wished to acquire included cotton goods, sugar, rum, coffee and the like. By the last decades of the eighteenth century the writings of the Scottish political economists and of some of the French *philosophes* – above all Condorcet – began to postulate free labour as the alternative to slavery and to explore the institutional guarantees that a free labour regime required. Condorcet's booklet on slavery, published in 1781 and reprinted in 1788 by the *Amis des Noirs*, actually anticipated features of the post-slavery regimes that would be developed after emancipation, with the development of satellite farms supplying a central sugar mill with cane.[9] By the time Condorcet wrote those who took an interest in the colonies knew that the slaves grew much of the food consumed in the islands and that they were discouraged from growing sugar cane by harsh penalties.

The contribution of New World slavery to the evolution of industrial discipline and principles of capitalist rationalization has been neglected. Referring to two influential traditions of social analysis Bryan Turner writes: 'Both Foucault and Weber see modern rational practices emerging from the monastery and the army and spreading outwards towards the factory, the hospital and the home.'[10] Marxist writers have instead stressed capitalist agriculture and the social relations which facilitated it. This book has argued that slave plantations, and the maritime entrepreneurs who sponsored and serviced them, furnished an important intermediary form of economic rationality – notwithstanding their many destructive and inhumane features. Indeed so far as plantation slavery was concerned the point would be that, firstly, it embodied some principles of productive rational organization and that, secondly, it did so in such a partial, or even contradictory, manner that it provoked critical reflection, resistance and innovation. Anti-slavery was to explore the preconditions of human sustainability and motivation in ways which helped to invent many of the characteristic institutions of a modern social order. Not by chance were prominent Abolitionists in the forefront of prison reform, factory legislation and the promotion of public education. In each area progress was to be potentially double-edged, entwining empowerment and discipline.

The Jesuits and monastic orders helped establish some early Portuguese and Spanish plantations; their notions of control, of physical mortification and of corporate organization contributed something to the early plantation formula. But the plantation revolution traced in this book was the work of Dutch and English traders and captains who knew little of the monastic model. Indirectly the military revolution contributed to the plantation formula but the decisive input was unrestrained commercial calculation. The explosive force of bourgeois revolution in the Netherlands and England battered down Iberian monopoly and constructed new and more expansive commercial exchanges. Since they were still incomplete capitalist societies the plantation colonies, with their slave 'hands', supplied them with the social equivalent of an artificial limb. French success did not contradict this logic. The French colonial system could copy and improve upon the colonial feats of the bourgeois powers because it too could avail itself of the plasticity of the social relations of slavery. Jean Baudrillard has observed that the spirit of the baroque was simulation and that stucco, with its ability to assume almost any shape, was for this reason the characteristic medium of baroque construction.[11] Slavery was a sort of social stucco and the French colonial system was to be a brilliant imitation of the English. Yet although the imitation improved on the original so far as productive organization was concerned, it failed to match its commercial coherence – ultimately the continuing strength of non-capitalist social relations in Absolutist France limited the benefit which it could extract from its achievement in the Caribbean.

The colonial identities forged in the seventeenth century were soon required to accommodate a vastly more commercialized and extensive system of slavery than had ever been witnessed before. Traditional stereotypes of the Other had been given a virulent twist in the direction of modern racism. As the logic of a freer trade was allowed to assert itself millions of Africans were taken from their native continent and plunged into a world of toil which neither they nor their captors had conceived possible. Once the genie of capitalist accumulation was loose it penetrated and reshaped even the most traditional social forms. And if economic imperatives surfaced in and through the formation of colonial slave identities so the eighteenth-century boom in plantation output set the scene for the emergence of new social subjects – Patriot planters, rebellious creoles, coloured slaveholders, Black Jacobins, African Methodist preachers, and many more – who were difficult to reconcile to the official protocols of colonial slavery. The initial chain of equivalences – on the one hand European, Christian, white, civilized, slave-owning; on the other alien, heathen, coloured, barbaric, enslaved – was broken.

Colonial slavery was disturbed by the uneven advance of creolization. On the mainland the planters were far more likely to be American-born than in the Caribbean, and hence more likely to discover a patriot cause of their own. So long as their slaves still included a large contingent of

Africans there was a tendency for the planters to be culturally more homogeneous than the slaves. In the Caribbean many planters were not only foreign-born but also absentee. The slave population developed over time a larger creole component while the free people of colour were almost wholly American-born and thus distinctive contributors to creole culture. These developments favoured planter hegemony on the mainland but undermined it in the Caribbean. When Jefferson and Madison proudly described themselves as Americans they were asserting a species of creole identity in much the same fashion as Bolívar or Santander were to do; and those black generals who chose the (Amerindian) name Haiti for their new state were also acknowledging an American or creole identity.

The seventeenth and eighteenth centuries had nourished and tempered systems of New World slavery that could outlast colonialism. New World planters and Atlantic merchants were still in the vanguard of progress. It was not only Virginia, Maryland and South Carolina which produced slaveowning revolutionaries and enlightened planter statesmen as the epoch of colonial slavery drew to a close; Moreau de St-Méry or Alexandre Beauharnais, Simon Bolívar or Bernardo O'Higgins were Latin creole cousins of Jefferson, Washington, or Madison. The Girondins of Bordeaux and the Jacobins of Nantes – the two clubs were based on networks that stemmed from these ports – organized within a National Assembly, one tenth of whose members owned colonial property. Venezuela with its cacao groves, and coastal Peru with its sugar estates, were to be cradles of the South American Revolution. Brazil's defiance of Portugal was to be solidly backed by its planter class.[12]

The Enlightenment was not so antagonistic to slavery as was once thought. Voltaire was capable of racial slurs as well as deprecations of slavery. As religious justifications of slavery came to seem hollow and absurd the pseudo-science of racial anthropology was encouraged by the speculations of Linnaeus and such enlightened dabblers as the Scottish lords Kames and Monboddo. Even such distinguished intellects as David Hume, Immanuel Kant and Georg Hegel casually employed racial stereotypes derogatory to Africans. Meanwhile the technological fruits of industrial advance gave a strong fillip to plantation agriculture, as steam power was harnessed to sugar mills and cotton balers, and as railways and steamboats opened up vast new territories in the interior of the Americas. The productivity of sugar plantations, as measured by output-per-slave, began to rise once again after about a century of stagnation. The defeats inflicted upon colonial mercantilism boosted the Atlantic traffic in slave produce. The overthrow of the French slave system in the 1790s and the beginnings of the decline of the British after 1815, allowed others to serve their markets. The momentum of the slave economies was to carry through well into the nineteenth century. The spread of philosophical enlightenment, the advent of industrialization and the eruption of revolution was, for a time, compatible with a continuing growth of slave populations and a mounting total of slave produce.

The year 1776 was to witness upheavals which bore directly on the processes examined in this book. The year of the opening of the War of American Independence was also the year of the partition of Poland. The vigour and confidence of the Virginian planters contrasted with the defeat of the serflords of Eastern Europe, confirming that the two social categories should not be equated. While Atlantic trade boomed, Baltic trade faltered. But the Atlantic boom was fed by the Atlantic slave trade and the ravages of the traffic in Africa also produced the revolution in Fuuta-Tooro in 1776 which aimed to stem the human haemorrhage from West Africa. In fact the coming Age of Revolution was to witness both the apogee of the slave traffic and also the beginning of the end of the slave systems, as colonial and planter revolts furnished opportunities to slave rebels and anti-slavery democrats.

The *anciens régimes* unloosed some parting shots against the planter patriots. The colonial powers met settler insubordination with what Spanish officials termed *insurreción de otra especie* – Lord Dunmore's appeal of 1775, the royalist intrigues in Saint Domingue in the 1790s, the Spanish appeal to downtrodden blacks and excluded vaqueros in 1812–15. British anti-slavery itself derived some inspiration from those who, like Samuel Johnson, distrusted slaveowners who yelped about liberty and from Tories, like Wilberforce, who were culturally reactionary and authoritarian. But anti-slavery could not make substantial advances until the sacred rights of private property were challenged, and the desirability of public invigilation of commerce recognized, as they were to be in Philadelphia in 1780 or Paris in 1794.

Struggles against the old order widened the bounds of political participation, albeit that the protagonists of 'bourgeois revolution', who might be country gentlemen or colonial speculators, privateers and slave traders, sought to set their own limits on the scope of citizenship. The growth of a diverse maritime commerce brought new working populations into contact with one another. The freedom suits fought by slaves on both sides of the Atlantic were often to receive the support of free dockers and seafarers. While every free black knew that he could be cheated, even kidnapped, by unscrupulous whites, the nexus of fear between black and white characteristic of the slave zone was dissipated – and poor whites also had reason to fear kidnapping in the shape of the press gang. The development of baroque music had incorporated African motifs and instruments, such as the kettle drum. Not surprisingly it gave some employment to African musicians. The pioneer of anti-slavery campaigning, Granville Sharp, first encountered the problems of London's Africans in the 1760s through the connections of his musical family's private orchestra; and it is likely that the veteran French Abolitionist Victor Schoelcher, a passionate Handelian, had similar contacts in Paris in the 1820s and 1830s.

The life and journal of Olaudah Equiano, who also sometimes worked as a musician, furnishes us with a vivid account of the conflict and camaraderie that could ensue at the junction of black and white, slave and free, English and Portuguese, Indian and Spanish. Equiano's journal maps a narrative of enslavement and emancipation on to the story of a sinner finding his way to Christ. But at the same time he writes of the fellowship he sometimes found on board ship among profane mariners or on shore at the dances of his people in the Caribbean. Equiano became involved in anti-slavery when he learnt that an English slave-trade captain, the master of the *Zong*, had thrown 131 sick slaves over-board in the hope of recovering insurance in 1781; Equiano told Sharp of these mercenary homicides and together they brought the scandal to a wider public. Equiano was commonly called Gustavus Vasa, the name given him by his first master; but he was happy to sign his book Olaudah Equiano, 'the African'. The concept of Africa was derived from the Ancient world and seemed entirely honourable; Equiano further argued that the customs of his people were close to those of the Jews, to whom they were probably related. A born-again Christian who had heard Whitefield preach, Equiano was to become both an early member of the London Corresponding Society and an author who successfully published and distributed his own writings, leaving property worth over £900 (nearly £100,000 in 1996 values) at his death.[13]

In the plantation zone itself the advance of revolution furnished some openings to slave rebels and insurgents, from the tens of thousands who made good their escape during the American Revolution to the Black Jacobins of Saint Domingue and the black Patriots of South America. The slogan 'Liberty, Equality, Fraternity' was translated into the American languages, most particularly Kréyole. And when the white Jacobins were put to the test some – Sonthonax, Laveaux, Danton, Robespierre – were to side, perhaps decisively, with black liberation. Given intense factional and national struggles the motives of the Revolutionary statesmen were mixed, but nevertheless they found in themselves principles which went beyond the tactical insurrectionism of the royalist provocateurs. The irony of Montesquieu, the scientific restraint of Blumenbach and the historical critique of Condorcet meant that the Enlightenment did not always betray its own best ambitions. It forged concepts that could be appropriated – and radicalized – in the complex, stormy class struggles of the Atlantic world.[14]

Notes

1. See P.J. Cain and A.G. Hopkins, *British Imperialism: Innovation and Expansion, 1688–1914*, London 1993, pp. 53–103; and Anderson, 'The Figures of Descent', *English Questions*, pp. 121–92.

2. Robert Fogel, *Without Consent or Contract: The Rise and Fall of American Slavery*, New York 1988, p. 141. The studies Fogel cites relate to the nineteenth century, including

early-nineteenth-century Trinidad, Jamaica, Cuba and the United States, in each case showing some height discrepancy between African and creole slaves. He also cites data showing a difference in average height between English artisans and US Northerners and between literate and illiterate Frenchmen. For the height of British army recruits see Cormac O'Grada, *Ireland*, p. 105, and for mortality rates in English industrial cities see Craton, *Searching for the Invisible Man*, p. 116.

3. See Robert Miles, *Capitalism and Unfree Labour*, pp. 94–117; Robert Hughes, *The Fatal Shore: A History of the Transportation of Convicts to Australia, 1797–1868*, London 1987; William Pember Reeves, *The Long White Cloud*, London 1898; Keith Sinclair, *The Origins of the Maori Wars*, Wellington, NZ 1957; Paul McHugh, *The Maori Magna Carta*, Oxford 1991.

4. Orlando Patterson, *Slavery and Social Death: A Comparative Study*, Cambridge, MA 1982.

5. According to an ILO report there were many millions of child labourers in 1995, with a rising incidence of the worst abuses – debt bondage or thinly veiled slavery condemning many to long hours, dangerous conditions, prostitution and early death. Promoting such treatment are negligent public authorities, rapacious commercial interests, de-regulation, poverty, famine and technologies which favour nimbleness rather than strength. Age is a more important factor than race in this case. See International Labour Organization, *Child Labour: Targetting the Intolerable*, Geneva 1996. True chattel slavery is rare but there are said to be 100,000 slaves in Mauritania: Simon Sebag Montefiore, 'Black Market', *Sunday Times Magazine*, 17 November 1996. Interestingly the prices of adult slaves quoted in this report – £15,000–£20,000 each – are similar in magnitude, after adjustment for inflation, to those prevailing in the late eighteenth century (see chapter IX above).

6. See B.W. Higman, *Slave Population and Economy in Jamaica, 1807–34*, Cambridge 1976.

7. M.G. Lewis, *Journal of a West India Proprietor, 1815–17*, London 1929, p. 186.

8. Gordon Wood, *The Radicalism of the American Revolution*, New York 1992. Wood's work links up in unexpected ways with the thesis of 'bourgeois revolution': see, for example, Anderson, *English Questions*, pp. 105–18 and Alex Callinicos, 'England's Transition to Capitalism: Robert Brenner's *Merchants and Revolution*', *New Left Review*, no. 207, September–October 1994, pp. 124–33.

9. Antoine-Nicolas de Condorcet, 'Reflexions sur l'esclavage des negres, 1781', in A. Condorcet O'Connor and M.F. Arago, *Oeuvres de Condorcet*, VII, Paris 1847, pp. 61–140. That history might have taken a course more favourable to small producers is a theme to be found in Roberto Mangabeira Unger's *False Necessity*, Cambridge 1987.

10. Bryan Turner, 'The Rationalisation of the Body', in Scott Lash and Sam Whimster, eds, *Max Weber, Rationality and Modernity*, London 1987, pp. 222–41 (p. 232).

11. In a suggestive passage Baudrillard sees the Jesuits and the baroque as having pioneered productivist rationality: see epigraph, p. 1. this volume, from Jean Baudrillard, *Simulations*, New York 1983, pp. 87–9. Evidently colonial slavery can be seen as another anticipatory social form, itself borrowing and blending elements of the baroque and the mercantile. For illuminating accounts of the political economy of colonial slavery which help to explain this cultural formation see, for Brazil, João Fragoso and Manolo Florentino, *O Arcaísmo como projeto*, Rio de Janeiro 1993; and, for the French colonies, Olivier Pétré-Grenouilleau, *L'argent de la traite*, Paris 1996.

12. Blackburn, *The Overthrow of Colonial Slavery*, chapters V, XIX and X.

13. Equiano, *The Interesting Narrative and Other Writings*. For the Zong affair see J. Walvin, *Black Ivory*, pp. 16–21.

14. See Blackburn, *The Overthrow of Colonial Slavery*, especially pp. 33–66; Hannaford, *Race*, pp. 205–8; M. Duchet, *L'anthropologie et l'histoire au siècle des lumières*, Paris 1971; Dorinda Outram, *The Enlightenment*, Cambridge 1995, pp. 63–79; and Kenan Malik, *The Meaning of Race*, London 1996. While Enlightenment thinkers sometimes endorsed racially tinged ideas they rarely backed slavery. Defences of racial slavery were still often couched in religious terms: see, for example, J. Bellon de Saint Quentin, *Dissertation sur le traite et le commerce des négres* [sic], Paris 1764. On the other hand legal challenges to slavery in France itself received significant support from jurists influenced by Gallican and Jansenist doctrines. See Peabody, '*There Are No Slaves in France*', pp. 20–22.

Index